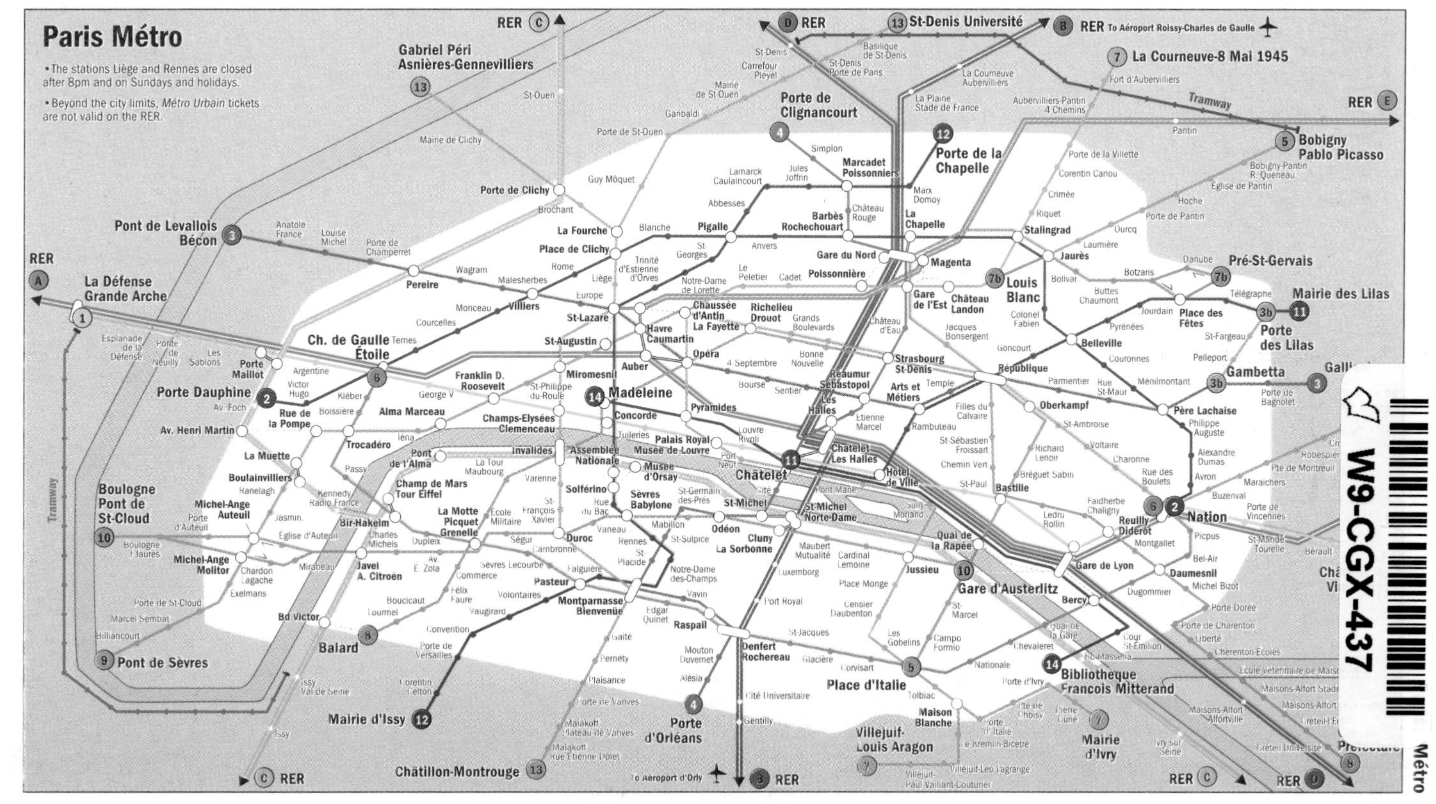
Paris Métro
• The stations Liège and Rennes are closed after 8pm and on Sundays and holidays.
• Beyond the city limits, Métro Urbain tickets are not valid on the RER.
Gabriel Péri Asnières-Gennevilliers
St-Denis Université
RER To Aéroport Roissy-Charles de Gaulle
La Courneuve-8 Mai 1945
Porte de Clignancourt
Porte de la Chapelle
Bobigny Pablo Picasso
Pont de Levallois Bécon
La Défense Grande Arche
Porte de Clichy
Pré-St-Gervais
Mairie des Lilas
Porte des Lilas
Gambetta
Louis Blanc
Ch. de Gaulle Étoile
Porte Dauphine
Madeleine
Châtelet
Nation
Gare de Lyon
Gare d'Austerlitz
Boulogne Pont de St-Cloud
Pont de Sèvres
Balard
Mairie d'Issy
Châtillon-Montrouge
Porte d'Orléans
To Aéroport d'Orly
Place d'Italie
Villejuif-Louis Aragon
Bibliothèque François Mitterand
Mairie d'Ivry
Tramway
RER

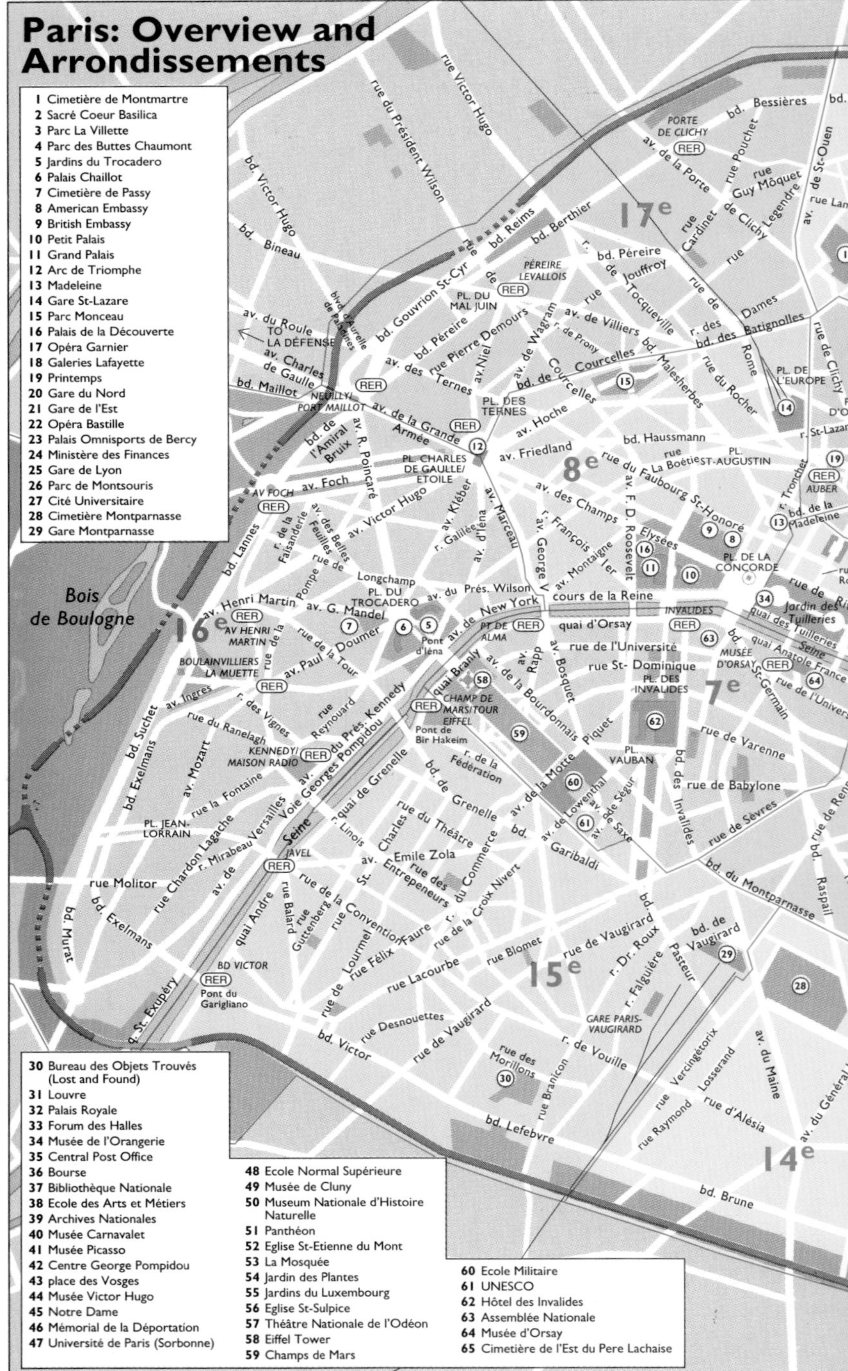
Paris: Overview and Arrondissements
1 Cimetière de Montmartre
2 Sacré Coeur Basilica
3 Parc La Villette
4 Parc des Buttes Chaumont
5 Jardins du Trocadero
6 Palais Chaillot
7 Cimetière de Passy
8 American Embassy
9 British Embassy
10 Petit Palais
11 Grand Palais
12 Arc de Triomphe
13 Madeleine
14 Gare St-Lazare
15 Parc Monceau
16 Palais de la Découverte
17 Opéra Garnier
18 Galeries Lafayette
19 Printemps
20 Gare du Nord
21 Gare de l'Est
22 Opéra Bastille
23 Palais Omnisports de Bercy
24 Ministère des Finances
25 Gare de Lyon
26 Parc de Montsouris
27 Cité Universitaire
28 Cimetière Montparnasse
29 Gare Montparnasse
30 Bureau des Objets Trouvés (Lost and Found)
31 Louvre
32 Palais Royale
33 Forum des Halles
34 Musée de l'Orangerie
35 Central Post Office
36 Bourse
37 Bibliothèque Nationale
38 Ecole des Arts et Métiers
39 Archives Nationales
40 Musée Carnavalet
41 Musée Picasso
42 Centre George Pompidou
43 place des Vosges
44 Musée Victor Hugo
45 Notre Dame
46 Mémorial de la Déportation
47 Université de Paris (Sorbonne)
48 Ecole Normal Supérieure
49 Musée de Cluny
50 Museum Nationale d'Histoire Naturelle
51 Panthéon
52 Eglise St-Etienne du Mont
53 La Mosquée
54 Jardin des Plantes
55 Jardins du Luxembourg
56 Eglise St-Sulpice
57 Théâtre Nationale de l'Odéon
58 Eiffel Tower
59 Champs de Mars
60 Ecole Militaire
61 UNESCO
62 Hôtel des Invalides
63 Assemblée Nationale
64 Musée d'Orsay
65 Cimetière de l'Est du Pere Lachaise
Bois de Boulogne
Seine
TO LA DÉFENSE
7e
8e
14e
15e
16e
17e

Paris: 1er and 2e

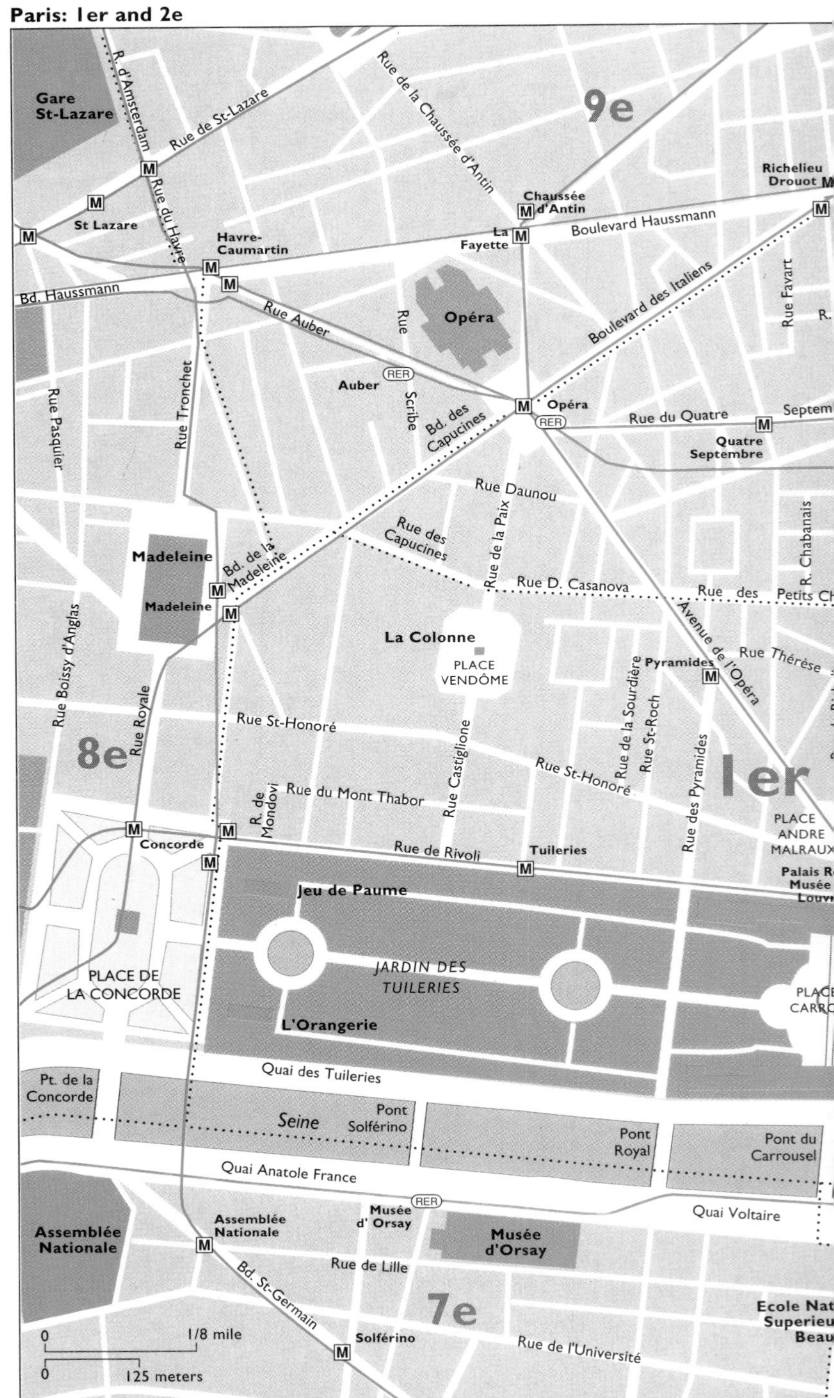

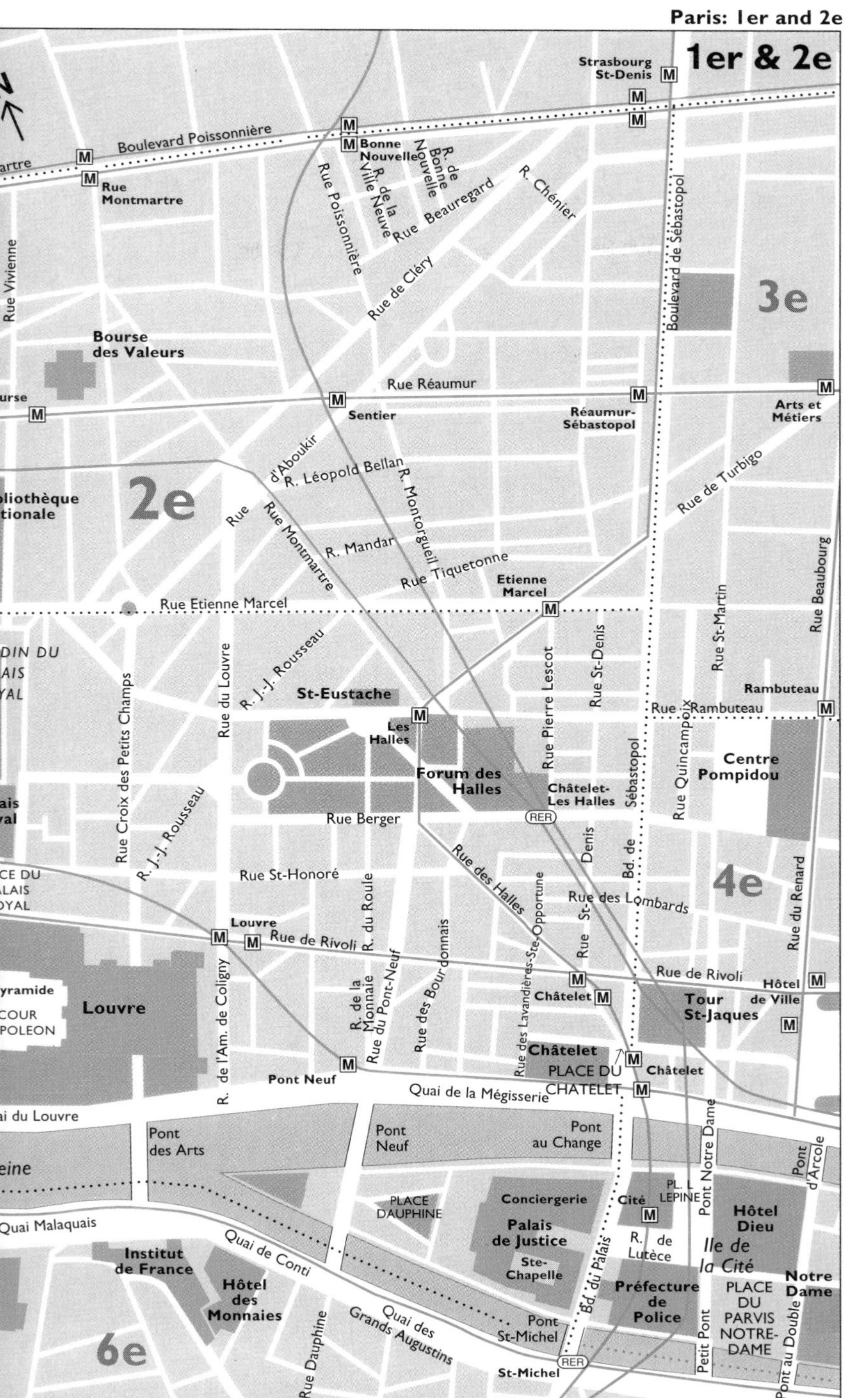
1er & 2e
2e
3e
4e
6e
Strasbourg St-Denis
Boulevard Poissonnière
Bonne Nouvelle
Rue Montmartre
R. de Bonne Nouvelle
R. de la Ville Neuve
Rue Beauregard
R. Chénier
Rue Poissonnière
Rue de Cléry
Boulevard de Sébastopol
Rue Vivienne
Bourse des Valeurs
Rue Réaumur
Sentier
Réaumur-Sébastopol
Arts et Métiers
Rue d'Aboukir
R. Léopold Bellan
R. Montorgueil
Rue de Turbigo
R. Mandar
Rue Montmartre
Rue Tiquetonne
Etienne Marcel
Rue Etienne Marcel
R. J.-J. Rousseau
Rue du Louvre
Rue Croix des Petits Champs
St-Eustache
Les Halles
Forum des Halles
Rue Pierre Lescot
Rue St-Denis
Rue St-Martin
Rue Beaubourg
Rambuteau
Rue Rambuteau
Rue Quincampoix
Centre Pompidou
Châtelet-Les Halles
RER
Rue Berger
Rue St-Honoré
Rue des Halles
Rue des Lavandières-Ste-Opportune
Rue des Lombards
Bd. de Sébastopol
Rue du Renard
Louvre
Rue de Rivoli
R. du Roule
Rue des Bourdonnais
R. de la Monnaie
Rue du Pont-Neuf
R. de l'Am. de Coligny
Châtelet
Hôtel de Ville
Tour St-Jaques
Pyramide
COUR NAPOLEON
Louvre
Pont Neuf
Quai de la Mégisserie
PLACE DU CHATELET
Quai du Louvre
Pont des Arts
Pont Neuf
Pont au Change
Pont Notre Dame
Pont d'Arcole
Seine
Quai Malaquais
Quai de Conti
PLACE DAUPHINE
Conciergerie
Palais de Justice
Ste-Chapelle
Cité
PL. L LEPINE
R. de Lutèce
Ile de la Cité
Hôtel Dieu
Institut de France
Hôtel des Monnaies
Quai des Grands Augustins
Pont St-Michel
Bd. du Palais
Préfecture de Police
PLACE DU PARVIS NOTRE-DAME
Notre Dame
Petit Pont
Pont au Double
Rue Dauphine
St-Michel

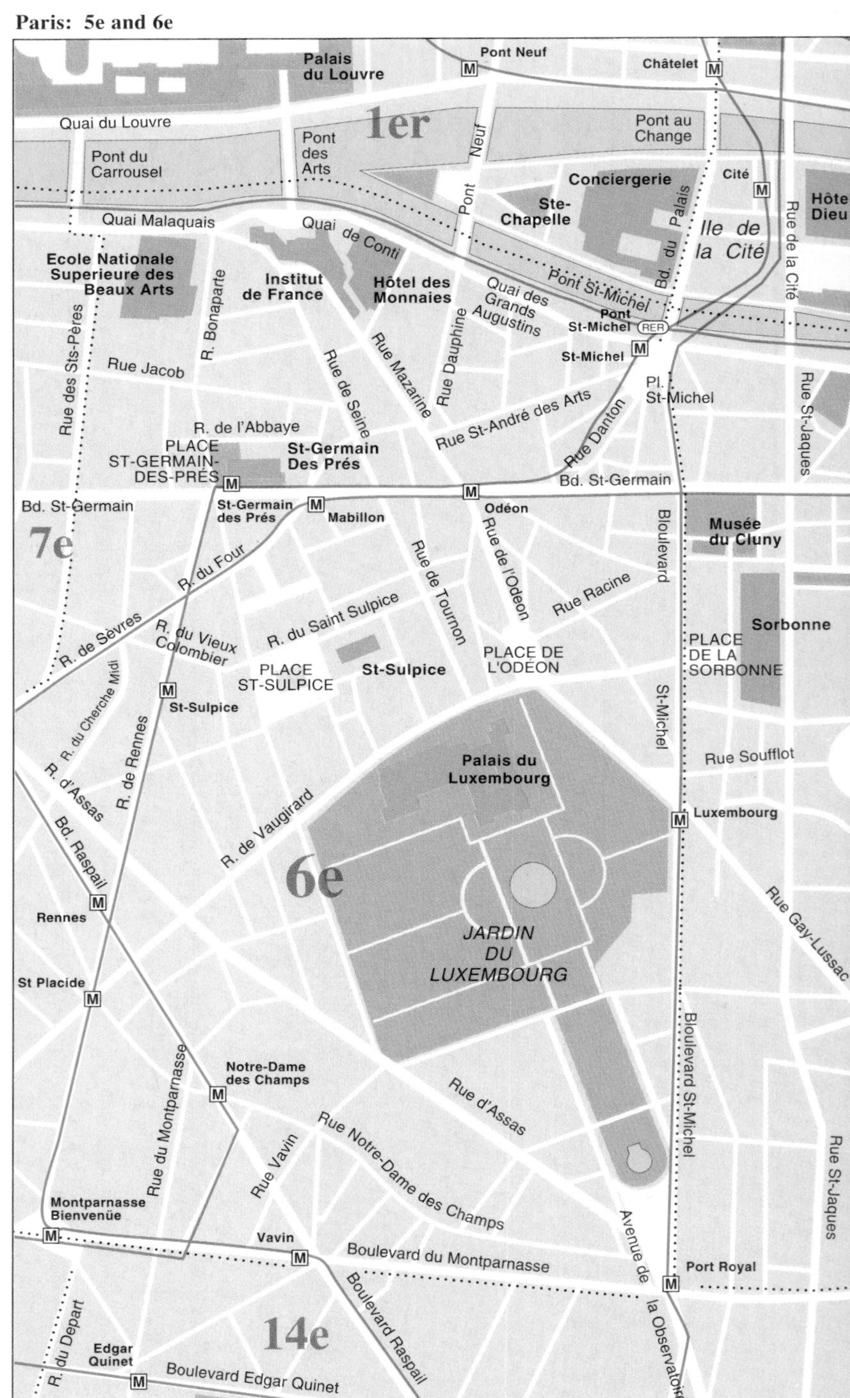
Palais du Louvre
Pont Neuf
Châtelet
1er
Quai du Louvre
Pont du Carrousel
Pont des Arts
Pont Neuf
Pont au Change
Conciergerie
Cité
Hôtel Dieu
Ste-Chapelle
Bd. du Palais
Ile de la Cité
Rue de la Cité
Quai Malaquais
Quai de Conti
Ecole Nationale Superieure des Beaux Arts
Institut de France
Hôtel des Monnaies
Quai des Grands Augustins
Pont St-Michel
Pont St-Michel
RER
St-Michel
R. Bonaparte
Rue des Sts-Pères
Rue Jacob
Rue de Seine
Rue Mazarine
Rue Dauphine
Pl. St-Michel
Rue St-Jacques
Rue St-André des Arts
Rue Danton
R. de l'Abbaye
PLACE ST-GERMAIN-DES-PRES
St-Germain Des Prés
Bd. St-Germain
Bd. St-Germain
St-Germain des Prés
Mabillon
Odéon
Boulevard St-Michel
Musée du Cluny
7e
Rue de Tournon
Rue de l'Odeon
R. du Four
Rue Racine
Sorbonne
R. du Saint Sulpice
R. de Sèvres
R. du Vieux Colombier
PLACE DE L'ODEON
PLACE DE LA SORBONNE
PLACE ST-SULPICE
St-Sulpice
St-Sulpice
R. du Cherche Midi
R. de Rennes
Palais du Luxembourg
Rue Soufflot
R. d'Assas
R. de Vaugirard
Luxembourg
Bd. Raspail
6e
Rue Gay-Lussac
Rennes
JARDIN DU LUXEMBOURG
St Placide
Boulevard St-Michel
Notre-Dame des Champs
Rue du Montparnasse
Rue d'Assas
Rue Notre-Dame des Champs
Rue Vavin
Rue St-Jacques
Montparnasse Bienvenüe
Vavin
Boulevard du Montparnasse
Avenue de la Observatoire
Port Royal
Boulevard Raspail
14e
R. du Depart
Edgar Quinet
Boulevard Edgar Quinet

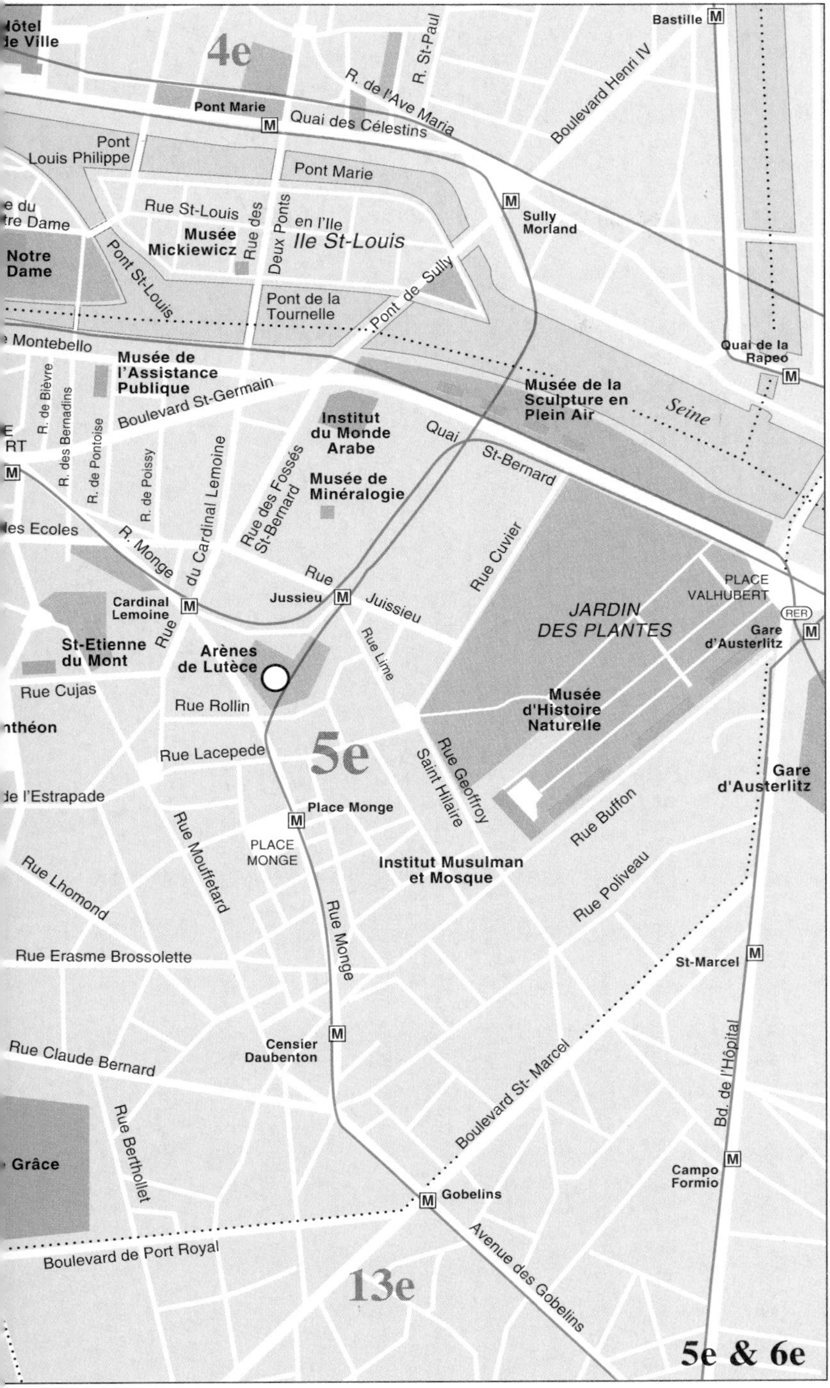

4e
Hôtel de Ville
Pont Marie
Quai des Célestins
R. de l'Ave Maria
R. St-Paul
Bastille
Boulevard Henri IV
Pont Louis Philippe
Pont Marie
Sully Morland
Rue St-Louis en l'Ile
Rue des Deux Ponts
Musée Mickiewicz
Ile St-Louis
Notre Dame
Pont St-Louis
Pont de la Tournelle
Pont de Sully
Quai de la Rapeo
Montebello
Musée de l'Assistance Publique
Boulevard St-Germain
Institut du Monde Arabe
Musée de la Sculpture en Plein Air
Seine
Quai St-Bernard
R. de Bièvre
R. des Bernadins
R. de Pontoise
R. de Poissy
Rue du Cardinal Lemoine
Rue des Fossés St-Bernard
Musée de Minéralogie
des Ecoles
R. Monge
Rue Jussieu
Rue Cuvier
Jussieu
Cardinal Lemoine
PLACE VALHUBERT
JARDIN DES PLANTES
RER
Gare d'Austerlitz
St-Etienne du Mont
Arènes de Lutèce
Rue Lime
Rue Cujas
Rue Rollin
Musée d'Histoire Naturelle
Panthéon
Rue Lacepede
5e
Rue Geoffroy Saint Hilaire
Gare d'Austerlitz
de l'Estrapade
Place Monge
PLACE MONGE
Rue Mouffetard
Rue Buffon
Rue Lhomond
Institut Musulman et Mosque
Rue Poliveau
Rue Monge
Rue Erasme Brossolette
St-Marcel
Censier Daubenton
Rue Claude Bernard
Boulevard St-Marcel
Bd. de l'Hôpital
Rue Berthollet
Grâce
Campo Formio
Gobelins
Avenue des Gobelins
Boulevard de Port Royal
13e

5e & 6e

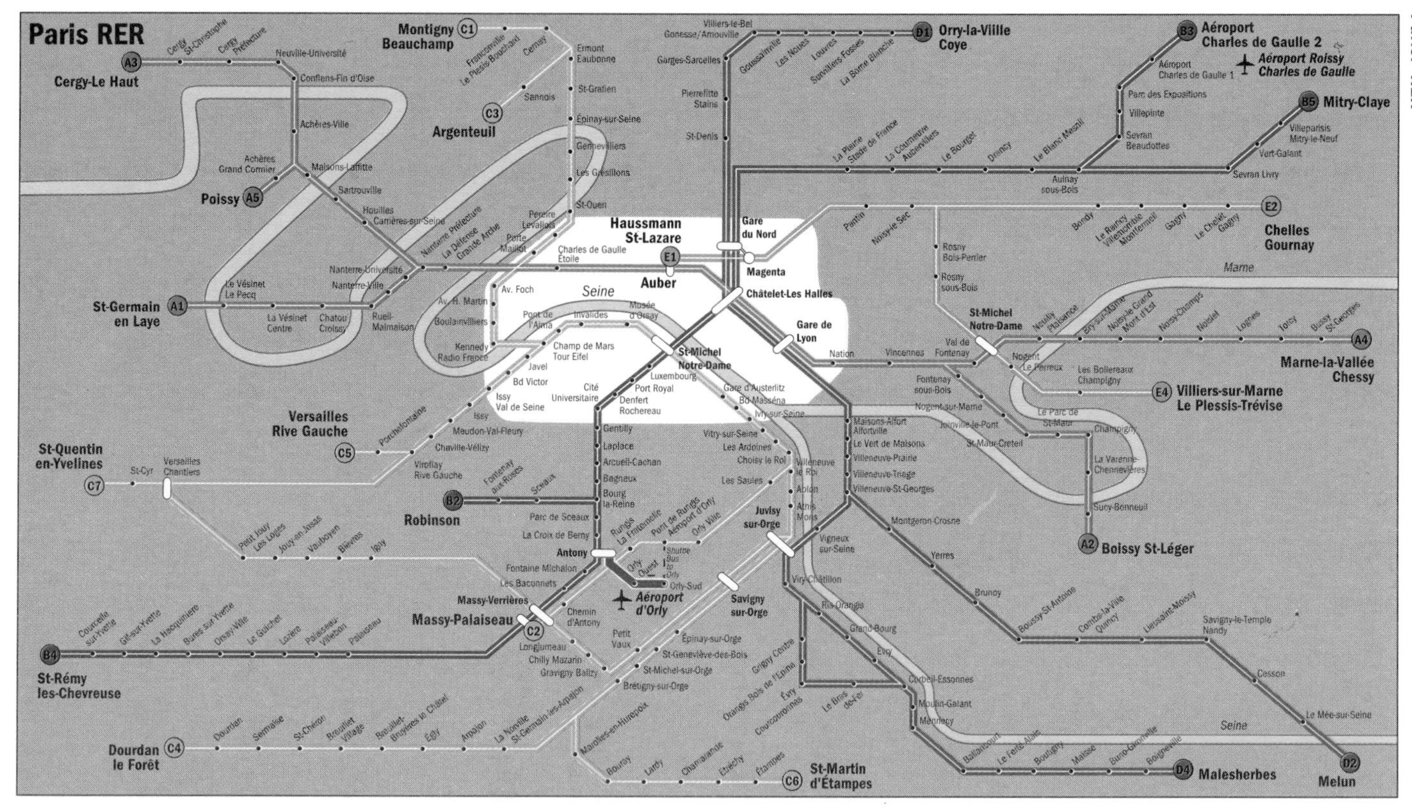

Paris RER
A3 Cergy-Le Haut
Cergy St-Christophe
Cergy Préfecture
Neuville-Université
Conflans-Fin d'Oise
Achères-Ville
Maisons-Laffitte
Sartrouville
Houilles Carrières-sur-Seine
Nanterre-Préfecture
La Défense Grande Arche
Nanterre-Université
Nanterre-Ville
Rueil-Malmaison
Chatou Croissy
Le Vésinet Centre
Le Vésinet Le Pecq
A1 St-Germain en Laye
A5 Poissy
Achères Grand Cormier
C1 Montigny Beauchamp
Franconville Le Plessis-Bouchard
Cernay
Ermont Eaubonne
St-Gratien
Sannois
C3 Argenteuil
Épinay-sur-Seine
Gennevilliers
Les Grésillons
St-Ouen
Pereire Levallois
Porte Maillot
Av. Foch
Av. H. Martin
Boulainvilliers
Kennedy Radio France
Charles de Gaulle Étoile
Haussmann St-Lazare
E1
Auber
Seine
Pont de l'Alma
Invalides
Musée d'Orsay
Champ de Mars Tour Eiffel
Javel
Bd Victor
Issy Val de Seine
Issy
Meudon-Val-Fleury
Chaville-Vélizy
Viroflay Rive Gauche
Porchefontaine
C5 Versailles Rive Gauche
Versailles Chantiers
St-Cyr
C7 St-Quentin en-Yvelines
Cité Universitaire
Denfert Rochereau
Port Royal
Luxembourg
St-Michel Notre-Dame
Gare d'Austerlitz
Bd Masséna
Ivry-sur-Seine
Vitry-sur-Seine
Les Ardoines
Choisy le Roi
Les Saules
Gentilly
Laplace
Arcueil-Cachan
Bagneux
Bourg la-Reine
Sceaux
Fontenay aux-Roses
B2 Robinson
Parc de Sceaux
La Croix de Berny
Antony
Fontaine Michalon
Les Baconnets
Massy-Verrières
Massy-Palaiseau
C2
Palaiseau
Palaiseau Villebon
Lozère
Le Guichet
Orsay-Ville
Bures-sur-Yvette
La Hacquinière
Gif-sur-Yvette
Courcelle sur-Yvette
B4 St-Rémy lès-Chevreuse
Igny
Bièvres
Vauboyen
Jouy-en-Josas
Les Loges
Petit Jouy
Rungis La Fraternité
Pont de Rungis Aéroport d'Orly
Orly Ville
Shuttle Bus to Orly
Orly Ouest
Orly-Sud
Aéroport d'Orly
Chemin d'Antony
Petit Vaux
Longjumeau
Chilly Mazarin
Gravigny Balizy
Épinay-sur-Orge
Ste-Geneviève-des-Bois
St-Michel-sur-Orge
Brétigny-sur-Orge
Marolles-en-Hurepoix
Bouray
Lardy
Chamarande
Étréchy
Étampes
C6 St-Martin d'Étampes
La Norville St-Germain-lès-Arpajon
Arpajon
Egly
Breuillet Bruyères le Châtel
Breuillet Village
St-Chéron
Sermaise
Dourdan
C4 Dourdan le Forêt
Savigny sur-Orge
Juvisy sur-Orge
Athis Mons
Ablon
Villeneuve le Roi
Vigneux sur-Seine
Viry-Châtillon
Ris-Orangis
Grand-Bourg
Évry
Grigny Centre
Orangis Bois de l'Epine
Évry Courcouronnes
Le Bras de Fer
Corbeil-Essonnes
Moulin-Galant
Mennecy
Ballancourt
La Ferté-Alais
Boutigny
Maisse
Buno-Gironville
Boigneville
D4 Malesherbes
Seine
Villeneuve-St-Georges
Villeneuve-Triage
Villeneuve-Prairie
Le Vert de Maisons
Maisons-Alfort Alfortville
Montgeron-Crosne
Yerres
Brunoy
Boussy-St-Antoine
Combs-la-Ville Quincy
Lieusaint-Moissy
Savigny-le-Temple Nandy
Cesson
Le Mée-sur-Seine
D2 Melun
Gare de Lyon
Châtelet-Les Halles
Nation
Vincennes
Fontenay sous-Bois
Nogent-sur-Marne
Joinville-le-Pont
St-Maur-Créteil
Le Parc de St-Maur
Champigny
La Varenne-Chennevières
Sucy-Bonneuil
A2 Boissy St-Léger
Val de Fontenay
Neuilly Plaisance
Bry-sur-Marne
Noisy-le-Grand Mont d'Est
Noisy-Champs
Noisiel
Lognes
Torcy
Bussy St-Georges
A4 Marne-la-Vallée Chessy
Marne
Nogent Le Perreux
Les Boullereaux Champigny
E4 Villiers-sur-Marne Le Plessis-Trévise
St-Michel Notre-Dame
Rosny Bois-Perrier
Rosny sous-Bois
Magenta
Gare du Nord
Pantin
Noisy-le-Sec
Bondy
Le Raincy Villemomble Montfermeil
Gagny
Le Chénay Gagny
E2 Chelles Gournay
St-Denis
Pierrefitte Stains
Garges-Sarcelles
Villiers-le-Bel Gonesse/Arnouville
Goussainville
Les Noues
Louvres
Survilliers-Fosses
La Borne Blanche
D1 Orry-la-Ville Coye
La Plaine Stade de France
La Courneuve Aubervilliers
Le Bourget
Drancy
Le Blanc-Mesnil
Aulnay sous-Bois
Sevran Beaudottes
Villepinte
Parc des Expositions
Aéroport Charles de Gaulle 1
B3 Aéroport Charles de Gaulle 2
Aéroport Roissy Charles de Gaulle
Sevran Livry
Vert-Galant
Villeparisis Mitry-le-Neuf
B5 Mitry-Claye

Let's Go writers travel on your budget.

"Guides that penetrate the veneer of the holiday brochures and mine the grit of real life."

—The Economist

"The writers seem to have experienced every rooster-packed bus and lunar-surfaced mattress about which they write."

—The New York Times

"All the dirt, dirt cheap."

—People

Great for independent travelers.

"The guides are aimed not only at young budget travelers but at the independent traveler; a sort of streetwise cookbook for traveling alone."

—The New York Times

"Flush with candor and irreverence, chock full of budget travel advice."

—The Des Moines Register

"An indispensible resource, *Let's Go*'s practical information can be used by every traveler."

—The Chattanooga Free Press

Let's Go is completely revised each year.

"Only *Let's Go* has the zeal to annually update every title on its list."

—The Boston Globe

"Unbeatable: good sightseeing advice; up-to-date info on restaurants, hotels, and inns; a commitment to money-saving travel; and a wry style that brightens nearly every page."

—The Washington Post

All the important information you need.

"*Let's Go* authors provide a comedic element while still providing concise information and thorough coverage of the country. Anything you need to know about budget traveling is detailed in this book."

—The Chicago Sun-Times

"Value-packed, unbeatable, accurate, and comprehensive."

—Los Angeles Times

Let's Go Publications

Let's Go: Alaska & the Pacific Northwest 2001
Let's Go: Australia 2001
Let's Go: Austria & Switzerland 2001
Let's Go: Boston 2001 **New Title!**
Let's Go: Britain & Ireland 2001
Let's Go: California 2001
Let's Go: Central America 2001
Let's Go: China 2001
Let's Go: Eastern Europe 2001
Let's Go: Europe 2001
Let's Go: France 2001
Let's Go: Germany 2001
Let's Go: Greece 2001
Let's Go: India & Nepal 2001
Let's Go: Ireland 2001
Let's Go: Israel 2001
Let's Go: Italy 2001
Let's Go: London 2001
Let's Go: Mexico 2001
Let's Go: Middle East 2001
Let's Go: New York City 2001
Let's Go: New Zealand 2001
Let's Go: Paris 2001
Let's Go: Peru, Bolivia & Ecuador 2001 **New Title!**
Let's Go: Rome 2001
Let's Go: San Francisco 2001 **New Title!**
Let's Go: South Africa 2001
Let's Go: Southeast Asia 2001
Let's Go: Spain & Portugal 2001
Let's Go: Turkey 2001
Let's Go: USA 2001
Let's Go: Washington, D.C. 2001
Let's Go: Western Europe 2001 **New Title!**

Let's Go *Map Guides*

Amsterdam
Berlin
Boston
Chicago
Florence
Hong Kong
London
Los Angeles
Madrid
New Orleans
New York City
Paris
Prague
Rome
San Francisco
Seattle
Sydney
Washington, D.C.

Coming Soon: *Dublin* and *Venice*

Paris

2001

Lucy Ives editor

researcher-writers
Alexander Reed Clark
Anna Kate Fishko
Alexandra Haggiag

Mike Durcak map editor
Luke Marion photographer

St. Martin's Press New York

HELPING LET'S GO

If you want to share your discoveries, suggestions, or corrections, please drop us a line. We read every piece of correspondence, whether a postcard, a 10-page email, or a coconut. Please note that mail received after May 2001 may be too late for the 2002 book, but will be kept for future editions. **Address mail to:**

Let's Go: Paris
67 Mount Auburn Street
Cambridge, MA 02138
USA

Visit Let's Go at **http://www.letsgo.com,** or send email to:

feedback@letsgo.com
Subject: "Let's Go: Paris"

In addition to the invaluable travel advice our readers share with us, many are kind enough to offer their services as researchers or editors. Unfortunately, our charter enables us to employ only currently enrolled Harvard students.

Distributed outside the USA and Canada by Macmillan.

ISBN: 0-312-24686-2

First edition
10 9 8 7 6 5 4 3 2 1

Let's Go: Paris is written by Let's Go Publications, 67 Mount Auburn Street, Cambridge, MA 02138, USA.

ADVERTISING DISCLAIMER

All advertisements appearing in Let's Go publications are sold by an independent agency not affiliated with the editorial production of the guides. Advertisers are never given preferential treatment, and the guides are researched, written, and published independent of advertising. Advertisements do not imply endorsement of products or services by Let's Go, and Let's Go does not vouch for the accuracy of information provided in advertisements.

If you are interested in purchasing advertising space in a Let's Go publication, contact: Let's Go Advertising Sales, 67 Mount Auburn St., Cambridge, MA 02138, USA.

HOW TO USE THIS BOOK

Do you want to use this book? No, no, come closer. Take the yellow spine in hand and listen to what Lili Marlene has to say [lights cigarette, tips wine bottle]. *Mon enfant*, this is a **brand-new, redesigned** guide. It is lined with the **photographs** of Paris, with **new chapters.** It is simply too irresistible to put down. It was made for one such as yourself, one who would scale the heights and crawl the depths of Paris.

Discover the city. Or if you are afraid, open to p. 1, and read how to get Paris to open her arms to you. Like all jealous young lovers, you must know who she has been with in the past. Scour **Life and Times** (p. 25)—you will be rewarded with knowledge of her innermost being. But how will you arrive? Do you know where Paris is? Consult **Planning your Trip** (p. 217). And will you stay forever, perhaps a year and a day? Then you must take advantage of **Once in Paris** (p. 11) and **Living in the Paris** (p. 265). Learn where to work, where to study, where to live, and how to ride around in a French subway [empties wineglass].

Most of all, you probably want to know where you can find a cheap bed for a few nights. No, don't look at me that way—we all need **Accommodations** (p. 245). We are thankful for their honest reviews, and for the mark of the thumbpick. Look: . Under the thumb, you sleep safe, warm, and dry. The thumb, here as elsewhere in the book, is a mark of excellence.

Ah, **Sights** [belches discreetly]. Here is all of Paris laid out before you, elegantly enclosed in nice fonts. And what is this? You have been provided with walking tours (p. 49), with well-made **Oh for a Day** sidebars, punctuated as if someone had been excited by the dark box. Here is something better, more blasphemous [thoughtfully strums miniature ukelele].

Crowning the succulent **Food and Drink** section (p. 155), is a **Menu Reader,** that you may decipher the Gallic tongue and enjoy your own palate more. **Museums** (p. 115) provides more feasts for your eyes, elegantly arranged, with new **Gallery** listings.

What is more, *cheri,* and do not be afraid, there are times when we must leave Paris behind. **Daytripping** (p. 199), in a shiny automobile or a fast train, is one of the most liberating of weekend pasttimes. Or we remain in the city, to drown our curiosity in wine and music. Turn to **Nightlife** (p. 183) and **Entertainment** (p. 149). Turn away from the everyday.

Or turn to the back of the book [draws shawl around shoulders]. Here you will find the **Service Directory** (p. 273), that most banal and embarassingly useful piece of text. Here are tourist offices, here are emergency phonenumbers.

There, that is all. I am so proud of you. So filled with hope. Perhaps you will leave this little yellow book behind one day and set out on your own. It has been made to aid you, but too frequently consulted, it will hold you back.

For now, be quiet. Here, finish this glass of wine. Your journey is about to begin. Listen, my dear, listen to the soft night who's walking.

A NOTE TO OUR READERS The information for this book was gathered by *Let's Go* researchers from May through August of 2000. Each listing is based on one researcher's opinion, formed during his or her visit at a particular time. Those traveling at other times may have different experiences since prices, dates, hours, and conditions are always subject to change. You are urged to check the facts presented in this book beforehand to avoid inconvenience and surprises.

Contents

ACKNOWLEDGMENTS

Anna and Alex thank Rashed Butt; the guys at Guzel Yurt; Yannik; Gummy Tooth; everyone's mom and dad and family; Alexi; Max Fishko; and most of all Ashley; *Sexe Attitudes* is a great film!

Lucy thanks the lord above for such damn, damn, damn (they were good) researchers; Diane for the last-minute purple claw, bumming, and fine advice; Jeff for the reminder that there is a world still—out there; !C!hris for himself and his cannon-fire manifesto; Rev. Rob Denis for preventing Mass Ave suicide with patience and all-around miraculousness (see p. 178); Max for introducing her to Berlin; Nora for a slurpee and good company; Café de la Cité, Wesley Willis, and the pod de la Cité for succumbing to her colonial rule and then not stabbing her in the ass; Mike for all those maps, but also b/c he made her dance; Melissa for being laidback and setting a good example; Alexi for writing emails just as crazy (see p. 109); Will for meeting her again; Mom&Dad for keeping it together, plus meals, plus lodging, plus lending her the car even though she had no right!; Nate for giving her dinner and having an eco-mole deep inside; Frank Stanford, Anne Carson, Linda Gregg, Fanny Howe, and Raymond Carver for keeping it real; Filip for his coffee can, his hospitality, for the metaphysics of cattle

RESEARCHER-WRITERS

Alexander Reed Clark (*3ème, 4ème, 12ème, 14ème, 17ème, 19ème, 20ème*)

Alex "Marais Man" Clark was all that, on a moped. His blonde grin, his fierce respect for all things *branché*—their capitulation before his nimble pencil. It was he who brought you the beer breakdown; he who made the most of every club and any sight. Bionic map revisions were soon to come. The Marais Man coaxed like a mamma and accomplished like a demon, whether he was recording near-lost legends of Père Lachaise, wooing *hôtelières* in tube-tops, or writing the copy that tore down the Bastille.

Anna Kate Fishko (Île St-Louis, *1er, 5ème, 6ème, 9ème, 10ème, 16ème, 18ème*)

Mastermind Anna "L'Art de Faire" Fishko has respect for the city, and then again, she brings it to its knees. Her selective eye sends us the latest gallery array. Her palate holds the restaurant section to a new standard. Not detered by *draguers*, she pounded the pavement and scoured the Latin Quarter for bargains *sans sketch*. A skeptic and a lover, Lady L'Art took the Louvre, she took Versailles, and when they showed her what they had, she threw back her head, laughed, and said, "What? No walking tour?"

Alexandra Haggiag (Île de la Cité, *2ème, 7ème, 8ème, 11ème, 13ème, 15ème*)

Alex "Bijou" Haggiag arrived in Paris with glamour to spare. And then she went shopping. Her prose was first elegant, and as it learned the nightlife ropes and went further afield to Auvers and irony, it brought back stranger turns of phrase. What were these well-made lines, in praise of sirop and Morisot? Never before had such precise knowledge of Parisian history been combined with so a deft touch on the laptop. Wherever this Brit cast her net, pearls appeared.

ABOUT LET'S GO

FORTY YEARS OF WISDOM

As a new millennium arrives, *Let's Go: Europe*, now in its 41st edition and translated into seven languages, reigns as the world's bestselling international travel guide. For over four decades, travelers criss-crossing the Continent have relied on *Let's Go* for inside information on the hippest backstreet cafes, the most pristine secluded beaches, and the best routes from border to border. In the last 20 years, our rugged researchers have stretched the frontiers of backpacking and expanded our coverage into Asia, Africa, Australia, and the Americas. This year, we've introduced a new city guide series with titles to San Francisco and our hometown, Boston. Now, our seven city guides feature sharp photos, more maps, and an overall more user-friendly design. We've also returned to our roots with the inaugural edition of *Let's Go: Western Europe*.

It all started in 1960 when a handful of well-traveled students at Harvard University handed out a 20-page mimeographed pamphlet offering a collection of their tips on budget travel to passengers on student charter flights to Europe. The following year, in response to the instant popularity of the first volume, students traveling to Europe researched the first full-fledged edition of *Let's Go: Europe*, a pocket-sized book featuring honest, practical advice, witty writing, and a decidedly youthful slant on the world. Throughout the 60s and 70s, our guides reflected the times. In 1969 we taught travelers how to get from Paris to Prague on "no dollars a day" by singing in the street. In the 80s and 90s, we looked beyond Europe and North America and set off to all corners of the earth. Meanwhile, we focused in on the world's most exciting urban areas to produce in-depth, fold-out map guides. Our new guides bring the total number of titles to 51, each infused with the spirit of adventure and voice of opinion that travelers around the world have come to count on. But some things never change: our guides are still researched, written, and produced entirely by students who know first-hand how to see the world on the cheap.

HOW WE DO IT

Each guide is completely revised and thoroughly updated every year by a well-traveled set of nearly 300 students. Every spring, we recruit over 200 researchers and 90 editors to overhaul every book. After several months of training, researcher-writers hit the road for seven weeks of exploration, from Anchorage to Adelaide, Estonia to El Salvador, Iceland to Indonesia. Hired for their rare combination of budget travel sense, writing ability, stamina, and courage, these adventurous travelers know that train strikes, stolen luggage, food poisoning, and marriage proposals are all part of a day's work. Back at our offices, editors work from spring to fall, massaging copy written on Himalayan bus rides into witty, informative prose. A student staff of typesetters, cartographers, publicists, and managers keeps our lively team together. In September, the collected efforts of the summer are delivered to our printer, who turns them into books in record time, so that you have the most up-to-date information available for your vacation. Even as you read this, work on next year's editions is well underway.

WHY WE DO IT

We don't think of budget travel as the last recourse of the destitute; we believe that it's the only way to travel. Living cheaply and simply brings you closer to the people and places you've been saving up to visit. Our books will ease your anxieties and answer your questions about the basics—so you can get off the beaten track and explore. Once you learn the ropes, we encourage you to put *Let's Go* down now and then to strike out on your own. You know as well as we that the best discoveries are often those you make yourself. When you find something worth sharing, please drop us a line. We're Let's Go Publications, 67 Mount Auburn St., Cambridge, MA 02138, USA (email: feedback@letsgo.com). For more info, visit our website, www.letsgo.com.

INSIDE

Discover Paris

City of light, site of majestic panoramas and showy store windows, unsightly city, invisible city—Paris is as much the iron finger of the Eiffel Tower bronzing in the midday sun as it is the miles of electrical wiring that course beneath the Champs de Mars to feed the tower's millennial light system. Paris is an ancient, infamous, and lovely tourist trap of catacombs, palaces, cemeteries, museums, and cabarets. It is a living city full of beautiful people, art, and excellent clothes. It is open air markets; it is manicured parks; and, most of all, it is sitting for hours outside at a café.

From alleys that shelter the world's best bistros to broad avenues flaunting the highest of *haute couture*, from the old stone of Notre-Dame to the futuristic motions of the Parc de la Villette, from street performers to the *Comédie Française*, from the relics of the first millennium to the celebration of the second, Paris presents itself as both a harbor of tradition on the Seine and a place of impulse. You can't conquer Paris, old or new, in one week or in thirty years, but here are some ways for the traveler to get acquainted:

FOOD AND FILM NOIR. Follow the mist from the Seine that drifts into the city just before dawn, clinging to bridges and lampposts, capture Paris at its famed black-and-white best, and then get on to the good stuff: the bakeries and pastry shops (see **Specialty Shops,** p. 179) that spin out warm, flaky treats each morning. You can enjoy these tarty delicacies all day, or lunch on a sandwich of apples, brie, and sweet walnuts at the zoo in the Jardin des Plantes (see **Sights,** p. 75). Perhaps if you discretely hide your belly behind a palm, you can still successfully seduce your own Boggart. Or spend a rainy afternoon sipping tea in a *salon de thé* (see p. 177) with a view of an old metro entrance. Watch men outside adjust their raincoats, then move on to a piano bar (see **Nightlife,** p. 186) for a whiskey and Piaf impersonators under the full moon. And although it's better in color, the Parisian bistro will not disappoint—beautiful with brass, even lovelier with well-sauced *plats*, and best if enjoyed with a fine red wine (see **Restaurants,** p. 160). And for those who

FACTS AND FIGURES

Population:
10,788,318

Surface Area:
roughly 40 sq. mi

Length Of The Seine In Paris:
13km

Total Length Of Tunnels Under Paris:
300 km

Total Number Of Steps On The Eiffel Tower:
1792

Most Expensive Cup Of Coffee:
US$12

Estimated Number Of "Romantic Encounters" Per Day:
4,959,476

Estimated Pounds Of Lingerie Purchased Per Day:
238

Revolutions To Date:
4

Revolutions To Come?
C'est la vie.

tire of feeding their faces, Paris is of course a feast for the eyes. Paris has more movie theaters and film festivals than any other city on earth (see **Entertainment,** p. 151). See it in the movies if you can't be it.

LOVE, GILT, AND REVOLUTION. The soul of Paris is rooted in a 2000-year history filled with controversy, revolution, passion, and another revolution (see **Life and Times,** p. 25). You could choose just one Parisien(ne) to love, or rebel against such monogamous notions, in keeping with Paris's multiple revolutions (see **Sights of the Revolution,** p. 49). Perhaps it's time to hit the hall of mirrors at Versailles if there's not enough of you to go around (see **Daytripping,** p. 199). Will you side with the aristocrats, the people, or the *Communards*, those crazy communists who tried (and failed) to turn Paris from its destiny as shopping Mecca (see **Shopping,** p. 141)? For those who must repent their capitalist cravings, Paris is full of churches and cathedrals where you can do penance (see **Sights,** p. 55)—but perhaps the best cure for one too many hours at Galleries Lafayettes is an afternoon in the green of one of the city's many parks. Here you can relinquish your yearning for the material, and perhaps pick up a little passion to start it all over again.

ART. The Louvre, the Centre Georges Pompidou, and the Musée d'Orsay display some of the most inspiring and well-known artwork in the world (see **Museums,** p. 115)—but depending on your mood, happiness could just as well be lingering in an independent gallery (see **Galleries,** p. 137), an air-conditioned movie theatre on the Champs-Elysées (see **Cinema,** p. 151), or in the makeup-covered hands of a mime. No matter where you stroll, dance, or groove to the beat, you will be following in the footsteps of someone who came to Paris in search of inspiration. A generation of hungry intellectuals was lured to Paris by the call of academic and artistic freedom (not to mention warm *croissants*) during and after World War II (see **Expatriate Literature,** p. 37). Under the influence of very potent espresso, they set the dramatic tone for the artistic community that prevails in Parisian cafés today (see **Restaurants and Cafés,** p. 160).

TRIP TO THE FUTURE. An afternoon among the high-rises of La Défense (see p. 112) or high noon at the Centre Pompidou's famous fountain (see **Museums,** p. 122) are both ways to get there: people often use architecture to describe Paris's forward-looking tendencies. Parc de la Villette is a postmodern express train to the year 2500 (and a park, too; see p. 126). Other revamped institutions like the Opéra Bastille (see **Sights,** p. 94) and the Institut du Monde Arabe de Paris (see **Sights,** p. 76) prove that Paris has her eye on the cultural horizon. But you should not have to look far to behold the new—even the city's break-neck *circulation* (traffic; see **Once in Paris,** p. 21) and beautiful bodies gyrating in the *discothèque* (see **Nightlife,** p. 186) scream that Paris is the fastest city this side of the channel.

TOP 25 PARISIAN SIGHTS

25. Passages of the 2*ème* arrondissement. Shopping, old school. Here you can behold glorious stained glass and well-tiled boutiques. See p. 49.
24. Canal St-Martin. The smaller sister of the river Seine, this canal can give you a boat tour (see p. 278) or just grounds for strolling. See p. 92.
23. Institut du Monde Arabe. This modern, left-bank beauty addresses the Seine with art from the Near and Middle East, film festivals, and a lux rooftop terrace. The nearby **Mosquée de Paris** has soothing fountains and lush cloisters. See p. 76.
22. La Défense. Where Paris does business and where you wander among corporate towers or lounge beneath the giant arch. An alternate universe. See p. 112.
21. Panthéon. This big dome in the Latin Quarter contains the world's favorite physics experiment, **Foucault's Pendulum.** See p. 74.
20. Centre Pompidou. Plumbing on the outside, contemporary art on the inside, and a squiggly fountain. Not your average museum. See p. 122.
19. Les Invalides. Four nationalist museums and Napoleon's tomb, all in the same golden complex. Little Bonaparte now rests in the grand body he always wanted. See p. 124.
18. Catacombs. Because, like Jacques Cousteau, we like to dive low. And see tunnels and tunnels of subterranean skulls. See p. 97.
17. Les Puces de St-Ouen. The largest flea market in France. Clothing, antiques, housewares, car parts, and the kitchen sink. See p. 146.
16. The Marais. Because never before have so many lovely bars, bistros, cafés, boutiques and boys come together in one neighborhood. See p. 68.
15. Jardin des Plantes. With a steamy greenhouse, beastly kids' zoo, rose arbors, and four natural history museums, this *jardin* has enough for many a pleasant afternoon. See p. 75.
14. Arc de Triomphe. Don't try to fight the traffic in the *Etoile*—go underground to arrive at the tomb of the unknown soldier, an "eternal" flame, and a great view from the roof. It's the big, yellow arch in the middle of all those speeding cars. See p. 84.
13. Picasso Museum. The building itself is no masterpiece, but the sparely decorated rooms have a whole lot of ladies with their faces in lovely disarray. See p. 125.
12. Opéra Garnier. The Phantom of the Opera allegedly swept through the basement of this decadent red and gilt opera hall. Venture into the boxes and imagine the social lives of 19th-century Parisians who went to see and be seen. See p. 89.
11. St-Germain-des-Prés. This neighborhood in the student-centric *quartier latin* means serious galleries, cafés, and pleasant walking. See p. 78.
10. Champs-Elysées. No trip is complete without a stroll down this flashing avenue. See p. 86.
9. The Seine. At night by boat or for a daytime stroll with wine and baguette in tow, this is *l'amour.* Swimming for locals with years of immunity only—visitors must settle for the *quais* and bridges. See p. 55.
8. Musée d'Orsay. A former train station shelters the masterpieces of Impressionism and more. See p. 119.
7. Jardin des Tuileries. The Sun King's pleasure garden runs from the courtyards of the Louvre—manicured lawns, manicured statues, and a ferris wheel. See p. 61.
6. Père Lachaise Cemetery. Practically a city is its own right, immense Père Lachaise is riddled with famous dead folk, including Jim Morrison, Oscar Wilde, and Edith Piaf. Your mausoleum should look so good. See p. 105.
5. Montmartre. A former artists' quarter and now perhaps a tourist trap. The holy whiteness of **Basilique Sacré-Coeur** and heavenly view are your reason for scaling the heights of Montmartre's well-café-ed hill. See p. 101.
4. Parc de la Villette. Did you ever dream of a beautiful park of the future? Well scratch that, and take the manifestations of your unconscious and spread them across a lawn. Kooky and gorgeous la Villette has sculpture gardens, science museums, jazz, and film festivals; but, basically, you just have to see it to believe it. See p. 126.
3. Musée du Louvre. Once a palace of kings, and now the home of Mona Lisa, Victory of Samothrace, Venus de Milo, and legions of appreciators. See p. 115.
2. Notre-Dame Cathedral. The home of the hunchback and so many gargoyles merits your attention: if not for the legends, then for stained glass and towering flying buttresses. See p. 55.

1. The Eiffel Tower. No matter how many desk-sized reproductions you may have seen, nothing can prepare you for the sheer height and grace of this iron lady. A romp on the **Champ de Mars,** the lawn stretching from her feet, is good for your sense of proportion. Go and see what "big and beautiful" is really about. See p. 81.

Place Vendôme

PARIS IN ONE WEEK (OR LESS)

Here are some suggested itineraries for travelers who want to see it all without the *oh là là* (French expression of exasperation). For itineraries within specific *arrondissements* (neighborhoods), see **Oh for a Day!** sidebars in **Sights**.

THREE DAYS

DAY ONE: CENTRAL SIGHTS. Begin on the **Île de la Cité** with **Notre-Dame** (p. 55), then move inland over the **Pont Neuf** to the **Louvre** (p. 115). If you're not too jetlagged, either the **Marais** (p. 67) or **Montmartre** (p. 101) will be good afternoon options—both have plenty of cafés for cooling your heels and lowkey sights. The *3ème*'s **Musée Picasso** (p. 125) and **Musée Carnavalet** (p. 130) are both fascinating; the **Basilique Sacré Coeur** (p. 101), at the height of Montmartre's hill, holds a different type of fascination.

Notre-Dame

DAY TWO: THE TOWER, ORSAY, AND RODIN. Step out of the métro under the **Eiffel Tower**'s legs (p. 81) and then scale her if you dare. You can bop along the Seine to the **Musée d'Orsay** (p. 119) and then if you can stomach any more art, lounge in the delicious gardens of the **Musée Rodin** (p. 123) for the remains of the day. Try some of Paris's Champs-Elysée **nightlife** (p. 186) when the sun goes down.

DAY THREE: THE LATIN QUARTER. The Left Bank is full of romantic students and fancy-pants intellectuals. Visit the **Sorbonne** (p. 73) to catch them where they live, or stroll the **Mouff'** (rue Mouffetard; p. 75) to view the places they shop. The **Musée de Cluny** (p. 126) has classy medieval art. The **Jardin des Plantes** (p. 75) holds gorgeous vegetation. The **Mosquée** (p. 76) presents a lovely facade and an even lovelier tea room; its sister, the **Institute du Monde Arabe du Paris** (p. 76) exhibits art from the Arab world. Try the jazz at central **Au Duc des Lombards** (p. 196) on your last night out.

FIVE DAYS

Take **Three Days,** and add two more, because you just can't get enough.

DAY FOUR: LA VILLETTE, PÈRE LACHAISE. Once you've explored central Paris, you may want to get away from it all. Not too far off by métro are **Parc de la Villette** (p. 104), a carpet of green with science museums and sculpture gardens. Neighboring it in the periphery you'll find **Père Lachaise Cemetery,** full of mausoleums and the famous dead of Paris's past (p. 105).

Musée Rodin

DAY FIVE: OPÉRA AND SHOPPING. Because no trip to Paris would be complete without a little self-indulgence on the **Champs-Elysées** (p. 84). Begin at the **Arc de Triomphe** (p. 84) and end at **pl. de la Concord** (p. 87). Follow this up with some Empire pomp at the grand old **Opéra Garnier** (p. 89), and perhaps purchase yourself tickets for later that evening. And if you haven't spent enough money, there's always the *grands magasins* (department stores) next door: **Galeries Lafayette** and **Au Printemps** (p. 142).

SEVEN DAYS

Five Days came and went. You're still in the City of Light. Whatcha' doing?

DAY SIX: THE MUSEUMS OF THE 16ÈME AND LA DÉFENSE. Begin at M: Iéna and visit the **Palais de Tokyo** (p. 99), the **Musée d'Art Moderne** (p. 134), the **Musée de Mode et Costume** (Museum of Fashion and Clothing; p. 136), and the **Musée National des Arts Asiatiques** (p. 135) in one fell swoop. Hop to M: Muette to visit the **Musée Marmottan** (p. 134), and then ride the RER out to **La Défense** (p. 112). In Paris's surprisingly lovely business center, you can gawk at gracious sky-scrapers or recline beneath the **Arc de la Défense** (p. 112).

DAY SEVEN: VERSAILLES. Go out with a bang. Jump a train early in the morning and head out on Paris's most Baroque daytrip to see the **Hall of Mirrors,** Marie Antoinette's **Hameau,** and some intensely landscaped **gardens** bursting with fountains and statuary (p. 199).

PARIS BY SEASON

Paris is a city where nearly every art form, historical moment, or celebrity has a corresponding festival or cultural event, offering year-round opportunities to celebrate with various degrees of pomp and libation. While the city-wide **Fête de la Musique** and **Bastille Day** are difficult to miss—even if you want to—some of the smaller festivities require explanation. The Office de Tourisme (see p. 277) has a home page (www.paris-touristoffice.com) and a pricey info line (☎08 36 68 31 12; 2.23F/min.). Another good source of information, closer to the date of the event, is *Pariscope,* and its English-language insert, *Time Out,* which come out on Wednesdays. You can also get a listing of festivals before you leave home by writing the French Government Tourist Office. *Let's Go* lists its favorite **Festivals** (see below)—this ain't all of them, just the good ones.

NATIONAL HOLIDAYS

When a holiday falls on a Tuesday or Thursday, the French often take off Monday or Friday, a practice known as *faire le pont* (to make a bridge). Banks and public offices close at noon on the nearest working day before a public holiday.

FESTIVALS

DATE	FESTIVAL	ENGLISH
January 1	Le Jour de l'An	New Year's Day
April 15	Le Lundi de Pâques	Easter Monday
May 1	La Fête du Travail	Labor Day
May 8	L'Anniversaire de la Libération	Anniversary of the Liberation of Europe
May 24	L'Ascension	Ascension Day
June 3	Le Lundi de Pentecôte	Whit Monday
July 14	La Fête Nationale	Bastille Day
August 15	L'Assomption	Feast of the Assumption
November 1	La Toussaint	All Saints' Day
November 11	L'Armistice 1918	Armistice Day
December 25	Le Noël	Christmas

SPRING

Foire du Trône, late Mar. to early June (☎46 27 52 29). M: Porte Dorée. On Reuilly Lawn, Bois de Vincennes, 12*ème.* A European fun fair replete with carnival rides (10-20F), *barbe à papa* (cotton candy), and a freak show. Open Su-Th 2pm-midnight, F-Sa and holidays 2pm-1am.

Ateliers d'Artistes-Portes Ouverts, May-June. Call tourist office for details. For selected days during the year, each *quartier's* resident artists open their workshops to the public for show-and-tell.

SUMMER

Festivals du Parc Floral de Paris, May-Sept. (☎43 43 92 95; www.quartierd'ete.com). Three separate festivals held at the Kiosque Géand de la Vallée des Fleurs (Route de la Pyramide, Bois de Vincennes). *Festival Jeune Public* offers kids a different show every W at 2:30pm. The *Festival* *à Fleur de Jazz* offers jazz concerts Sa at 4pm. And the *Festival Classique au Vert* offers classical concerts Su at 4:30pm. All shows free with 10F park entrance. Pick up a schedule at the tourist office or see *Pariscope,* as the schedule will not be released over the phone.

Grandes Eaux Musicales de Versailles, early May to mid-Oct. (☎39 50 36 22). Weekly outdoor concerts and fountain displays every Su at Parc du Château de Versailles, RER C7. A magical event where you will see the splendors of Versailles's gardens in all their excess and glory. Let them spray water! Tickets 25F, reduced 15F.

Sacré Coeur

Gay Pride (Fierté), last Sa in June. Gay Paree celebrates with parties, special events, film festivals, demonstrations, art exhibits, concerts, and a huge Pride Parade through the Marais. For specific dates and events, call the Centre Gai et Lesbien (☎43 57 21 47) or Les Mots à la Bouche bookstore (☎42 78 88 30). Or check Marais bars and cafés for posters.

Course des Serveuses et Garçons de Café, mid-June (☎42 96 60 75). If you thought service was slow by necessity, let this race change your mind. Over five-hundred tuxedoed waiters and waitresses sprint through the streets on an 8km course carrying a full bottle and glass on a tray. Starts and finishes at Hôtel de Ville, 4*ème.* If you're in town, do not miss it. Look for posters.

Festival Chopin, mid-June to mid-July (☎45 00 22 19). Route de la Reine Marguerite. From M: Porte Maillot, take bus #244 to Pré Catelan, stop #12. Concerts and recitals held at the Orangerie du Parc de Bagatelle in the Bois de Boulogne. Not all Chopin, but all piano, arranged each year around a different aspect of the Polish francophile's *oeuvre.* Prices vary (usually 80-150F).

Jardin des Plantes

La Villette Jazz Festival, late June to early July (☎40 03 75 75 or 01 44 84 44 84; www.la-villette.com). M: Porte de Pantin. At Parc de la Villette. A week-long celebration of jazz from big bands to new international talents, as well as seminars, films, and sculptural exhibits. Past performers have included Herbie Hancock, Ravi Coltrane, Taj Mahal, and B.B. King. Marching bands parade every day and an enormous picnic closes the festival. Some concerts are free; call for info and ticket prices. A *forfait-soirée* gives access to a number of events for one night of the festival for 170F; students, under 26, and seniors, 145F.

Fête des Tuileries, late June to late Aug. (☎46 27 52 29). M: Tuileries. A big fair held on the terrace of the Jardin des Tuileries. Huge ferris wheel with views of nighttime Paris, and proof positive that the carnival ethos is the same the world over. Open M-Th 11am-midnight, F-Sa 11am-1am. Free entrance, ferris wheel 25F.

Fête de la Musique, June 21 (☎40 03 94 70). Also called "faîtes de la musique" ("make music"), this summer solstice celebration gives everyone in the city the chance to make as much racket as possible; noise laws don't apply on this day. Closet musicians fill the streets, strumming everything from banjos and ukuleles to Russian *balalaikas.* Major concerts at La Villette, pl. de la Bastille, pl. de la République, and the Latin Quarter. This festival is one of Paris's best, and everyone comes out for the music and the camaraderie. If you're not humming by noon, you need to reprioritize. Partying in all open spaces. Before you join that samba or hari krishna parade, put your wallet in a safe place. Avoid the métro. Free.

Jardin des Tuileries

Feux de la St-Jean Baptiste (Fête Nationale du Québec), June 24 (☎45 08 55 61 or 45 08 55 25). Magnificent fireworks at 11pm in the Jardin de Tino Rossi at quai St-Bernard, 5*ème,* honoring the Feast of St. John the Baptist. For a bird's-eye view of the spectacle, stand in front of Sacré-Coeur. There is also an elaborate display at the Canal de l'Ourcq in the Parc de la Villette. In addition, Quebec's National Holiday is celebrated by Paris's Québecois community with dancing, *drapeaux fleurs-de-lys,* and music at the Librairie Québecoise, 5*ème* (see **Books,** p. 145); the Délégation Générale du Québec, 66, r. Pergolèse, 16*ème* (☎40 67 85 00); the Association Paris-Québec, 5, r. de la Boule Rouge, 9*ème*; and the Centre Culturel Québecois, 5, r. de Constantine, 7*ème* (M: Invalides). As Charles de Gaulle said, *Vive le Québec Libre!*

Fête du Cinéma, around June 28. A Parisian institution, this festival is one of the city's best—don't miss it. Purchase 1 ticket at full price and receive a passport that admits you to an unlimited number of movies for the duration of the 3-day festival for 10F each. Choose your first film carefully; full-price tickets vary considerably from cinema to cinema. Expect long lines and get there at least 30min. early for popular movies. Hundreds of films are shown during the festival, from major blockbusters to classics and experimental flicks. If any of the films mentioned in our Film section entice you (see **Film,** p. 45), it will probably be shown in one of Paris's hundreds of cinemas during the festival. Look for posters in the métro or ask at cinemas for the specific dates.

Paris, Quartier d'Eté, mid-July to mid-Aug. (☎44 94 98 00; www.quartierdete.com). This city-wide, multifaceted festival features dance, music of the world, a giant parade, promenade concerts, and jazz. Locations vary, but many events are usually held in the Jardin des Tuileries, Jardin du Luxembourg, and Parc de la Villette. This festival is one of Paris's largest and includes both world-class (i.e. international ballet companies and top-10 rock bands) and local artists, musicians, and performers. Prices vary, but much is free. Pick up a brochure at the tourist office.

Bastille Day (Fête Nationale), July 14. Festivities begin the night before France's independence day, with traditional street dances at the tip of Île St-Louis. The *Bals Pompiers* (Firemen's Balls) take place inside every Parisian fire station the night of the 13th, with DJs, bands, and cheap alcohol. Free of charge, these balls are the best of Paris's Bastille Day celebrations. The fire stations on rue Blanche, bd. du Port-Royal, rue des Vieux-Colombiers, and the Gay Ball near quai de la Tournelle in the 5*ème* are probably your best bets. There is dancing at Place de la Bastille with a concert, but be careful as young kids sometimes throw fireworks into the crowd. July 14 begins with the army parading down the Champs-Elysées at 10:30am and ends with fireworks at 10:30pm. The fireworks can be seen from any bridge on the Seine or from the Champs de Mars. Be aware that for the parade and fireworks the métro stations along the Champs and at the Trocadéro are closed. Groups also gather in the 19*ème* and 20*ème* (especially in the Parc de Belleville) where the hilly topography allows a long-distance view to the Trocadéro. Unfortunately, the entire city also becomes a nightmarish combat zone with firecrackers underfoot; avoid the métro and deserted areas if possible. *Vive la France!*

Tour de France, 4th Su in July (☎41 33 15 00; www.letour.fr). The Tour de France, the world's premier long-distance bicycling event, ends in Paris and thousands turn out at the finish line to see who will win the *chemise d'or.* Expect huge crowds at pl. de la Concorde as well as along the av. des Champs-Elysées. You may never see calves this strong again in your life.

FALL

Fête de l'Humanité, 2nd weekend of Sept. (☎49 22 72 72 or 01 49 22 73 86). At the Parc de la Courneuve. Take the métro to Porte de la Villette and then bus #177 or one of the special buses. The annual fair of the French Communist Party. Charles Mingus, Marcel Marceau, the Bolshoi Ballet, and radical theater troupes have appeared in recent years. Three-day pass 60F.

Festival d'Automne, mid-Sept. to late Dec. (☎53 45 17 17; www.festival-automme.com). Notoriously highbrow and *avant* drama, ballet, and music arranged around a different theme each year. Many events held at the Théâtre du Châtelet, 1*er;* the Théâtre de la Ville, 4*ème;* and the Cité de la Musique, 19*ème.* Ticket prices vary according to venue.

Journées du Patrimoine, 3rd weekend of Sept. (☎44 61 21 00). The few days each year when national palaces, ministries, monuments, and some townhouses are opened to the public. The Hôtel de Ville should be on your list, as well as Jaques Chirac's bathroom in the Palais de l'Elysée. Free.

Fête des Vendanges à Montmartre, first weekend in Oct. R. des Saules, 18*ème* (☎53 41 18 18). M: Lamarck-Caulaincourt. A celebration of the harvest from Montmartre's vineyards. Folksongs, wine tasting, and the picking and stomping of grapes. Much wine is consumed. *Santé!*

WINTER

Christmas (Noël), Dec. 24-25. At midnight on Christmas eve, Nôtre-Dame becomes what it only claims to be the rest of the year: the cathedral of the city of Paris. Midnight mass is celebrated with pomp and incense. Get there early to get a seat. Christmas Eve is more important than Christmas Day in France.

Families gather to exchange gifts and eat Christmas food, including *bûche de Noël* (Christmas Yule Log), a rich chocolate cake. During the season leading up to Dec. 24, the city illuminates the major *boulevards,* including the Champs-Elysées, in holiday lights and decorations. A huge *crèche* (nativity scene) is displayed on pl. Hôtel de Ville. Restaurants offer Christmas specialties and special *menus.*

New Year's Eve and Day, Dec. 31-Jan. 1. Young punks and tons of tourists throng the Champs-Elysées to set off fireworks, while restaurants host pricey evenings of *foie gras* and champagne galore. On New Year's Day there is a parade with floats and dolled up dames from pl. Pigalle to pl. Jules-Joffrin.

LET'S GO PICKS

Let's face it: this entire city is fabulous, and you know it. But sometimes there is just a little more fabulous than the rest.

BEST FAKE CLIFFS

It's a bit of a trek out to the 19*ème*'s **Parc au Buttes-Chaumont** (**p. 104**), but once you survey the city from one of its falsie mountains, you will gain a certain appreciation for cosmetic surgery.

MOST WELL-ENDOWED TOMBSTONE

After a deadly showdown with Oscar Wilde's strutting Egyptian, **Victor Noir's bronze body cast** wins with the shiniest masculinity of all. Judge for yourself at Père Lachaise (p. 105). Just don't touch. Or do.

MOST UNFORTUNATELY NAMED RESTAURANT

L'As du Falafel (p. 176). But Lenny Kravitz says it's really tasty. Also, it's dag cheap. Jelly or syrup on that salad? *Let's Go* prefers syrup.

BEST MUSEUM

No, it's not the Louvre or the Orsay. We'll let the big boys duke it out elsewhere. Here in the land of *Let's Go,* the Jardin des Plantes's **Grand Galerie d'Evolution** (p. 131) is king—with the glossy stuffed birds, blubbery mummified fish, special effects, and mood music to prove it.

BEST PEDESTRIAN QUARTER

Quartier Montorgueil can't help but please: it's full of fresh fruits and vegetables, scrumptious strolling Parisians. Plus, red-light row, r. St-Denis, is just a stone's throw away!

BEST, QUICKEST, NON-EIFFEL VIEW OF THE CITY

The observation deck atop **La Samaritaine** department store (p. 143).

BEST FRENCHIE CIGARETTES

At 27 or so francs a pop (about $4), you can't beat the value (or the flavor) of a 30-pack of **Gauloises** (also available in 20's and 10's).

MOST LIBERATING PLACE TO SMOKE YOUR FRENCHIE CIGARETTES

Charles de Gaulle airport (p. 15), fresh off the plane. What better cure for jetlag?

BEST GAY RENDEZ-VOUS FOR TOURISTS

Open Café (**p. 188**). Open late. Very late.

BEST STRAIGHT RENDEZ-VOUS FOR TOURISTS

Flann O'Brien's (**p. 186**). Irish to the max.

BEST WAY TO END UP WITH A PARIS POOCH ALL YOUR OWN

Check out the pet shops along the **quai de la Megisserie.** You'll see what we mean.

BEST TASTE-OF-PARIS EVENING SPLURGE

4 courses for 120F at **Jules** (p. 161) followed by people- and even show-watching at the **Palais Garnier** (tickets as low as 60F; p. 153).

EASIEST, CHEAPEST WAY TO GET DRUNK

"Une pression, s'il vous plaît." Rinse, repeat.

INSIDE

Once in Paris

ORIENTATION

Flowing from east to west, the **Seine River** crosses the heart of Paris. The **Île de la Cité** and neighboring **Île St-Louis** sit at the geographical center of the city, while the Seine splits Paris into two large expanses—the Rive Gauche (Left Bank) to its south and the Rive Droite (Right Bank) to its north. In the time of Louis XIV, the city had grown to 20 *quartiers*. Modern Paris is divided into 20 *arrondissements* (districts) that spiral clockwise around the Louvre.

SEINE ISLANDS

ÎLE DE LA CITÉ. If any place could be called the heart of Paris, it is this slip in the river. Île de la Cité sits in the very center of the city and at the center of the **Île de France,** the geographical region surrounding Paris and bordered by the Seine, the Marne, and the Oise Rivers (see the map for **Daytripping,** p. 199). All distance points in France are measured from **kilomètre zéro**, a circular sundial in front of Notre-Dame (see **Sights,** p. 55).

ÎLE ST-LOUIS. Floating somewhere between a small village and an exclusive neighborhood, this island retains a certain remoteness from the rest of Paris. Older residents say "Je vais à Paris" ("I'm going to Paris") when leaving by one of the four bridges linking Île St-Louis and the mainland. Inhabitants even declared the island an independent republic in the 1930s.

ÈME?

The French equivalent of "th" (e.g. fourth or fifth) is *ème*. When you *see* an arrondissement referrred to as 16*ème*, the proper pronunciation is to add "iemme" to the French number. So 16*ème* is *seizième* (SEZ-yem), not sixteenthieme. The exception is 1st. The French abbreviation is 1*er (premier,* PREM-yay*)*.

RIVE GAUCHE (LEFT BANK)

The *"gauche"* in Rive Gauche once signified a secondary, lower-class lifestyle, the kind flaunted by the perennially impoverished students who stayed there. Today, the Left Bank is the traveler's first choice for accommodations because of its alternative crowd and the allure of its inexpensive cafés and bars.

LATIN QUARTER: 5ÈME AND 6ÈME ARRONDISSEMENTS. The **Latin Quarter,** which has a serious intellectual reputation, contains the **Sorbonne** and encompasses the **5ème arrondissement** and parts of the **6ème.** The boundary between the 5*ème* and the 6*ème*, **bd. St-Michel,** overflows with cafés, cinemas, boutiques, and bookstores. As you head southeast, hotel prices fall. Farther east, the neighborhood around **pl. de la Contrescarpe,** at the center of the 5*ème*, is more intimate and even cheaper. A cornucopia of ethnic restaurants graces **r. Mouffetard,** the indisputable culinary heart of the 5*ème*. Crossing bd. St-Michel and running east-west, **bd. St-Germain** in the 6*ème arrondissement* lends its name to the neighborhood **St-Germain-des-Prés,** which has turned the sidewalk café into an art form and amused everyone from Rimbaud to Sartre. Tiny restaurants with cheap *menus*, however, are around r. de Buci, r. Dauphine, r. du Seine, as do street markets with fresh produce.

7ÈME ARRONDISSEMENT. Don't stay in the **7ème** for the view or for the party atmosphere. A haven for civil servants, filled with traveling businesspeople, the 7*ème* proffers pricey, small rooms that promise (but don't necessarily provide) views of the Eiffel Tower. The military and ministerial 7*ème* houses "serious date" restaurants but little in the way of affordable food.

MONTPARNASSE: 13ÈME AND 14ÈME ARRONDISSEMENTS. With the central arrondissements losing artistic momentum because of high prices and gentrification, the periphery has established itself as the seat of French intellectual and cultural life. The heart of Paris now rests in its lower right corner. A vast urban sprawl in the midst of an architectural face-lift, the **13ème** is in the fetal stages of a hip rebirth. **Montparnasse,** where the chic 6*ème* meets the commercial **14ème** just south of the Latin Quarter, attracted expatriates in the 1920s. Picasso, Hemingway, and Stein kicked up their heels in the cafés and *crêperies* here. Today, areas near the fashionable **bd. du Montparnasse** maintain their glamor, while adjoining blocks are more residential. Sex shops and sleazy nightlife dominate the northern end of av. du Maine. East of the 14*ème*, Paris's "Chinatown" overflows with Vietnamese, Lao, Thai, and Cambodian cuisine.

15ÈME ARRONDISSEMENT. The most populous *arrondissement*, middling in incomes and politics, the **15ème** is the picture of middle-class Parisian life. The expansive **Parc des Expositions** attracts execs in winter. In summer, hotels scramble for guests, and tourists can sometimes bargain for rates. Locals have their favorites among the grocers on r. du Commerce, the cafés at the corner of r. de la Convention and r. de Vaugirard, and the specialty shops along av. Emile Zola.

Metro

RIVE DROITE (RIGHT BANK)

The first four *arrondissements* comprise what has historically been central Paris and contain the oldest streets and residences in the city. Still, because of the Left Bank's appeal, hotels here may have unexpected vacancies. In general, hotel prices rise with proximity to the Louvre and the Opéra, and supermarkets and inexpensive restaurants are rare.

1ER ARRONDISSEMENT. Paris's royal past is conspicuous in much of the **1er,** home to the Louvre. Chanel and the Ritz hotel set the scene; the few budget hotels here are rarely accompanied by budget accoutrements (laundromats, grocery stores, etc.). Although above ground the 1*er* is one of the safest areas in Paris, the métro stops are best avoided at night, when M: Châtelet and Les Halles are claimed by drug dealers.

View from L'Arc de Triomphe

2ÈME ARRONDISSEMENT. Devoid of its own sights, the **2ème** is within easy walking distance of the Marais, the Centre Pompidou, the Louvre, the Palais-Royal, Notre-Dame, and more. Many cheap little restaurants and hotels populate this mostly working-class area and make it an excellent place to stay. Although the eastern end of r. St-Denis is a center of prostitution and pornography, its seediness does not spill far.

MARAIS: 3ÈME AND 4ÈME ARRONDISSEMENTS. Absolutely *the* place to live in the 17th century, the **Marais,** in the **3ème** and **4ème,** has regained its swish, thanks to 30 years of extensive renovations. Once-palatial mansions have become exquisite museums, and the tiny twisting streets have been adopted by fashionable boutiques and galleries. The area shelters some terrific accommodations at reasonable rates. Prices drop as you head north through the *4ème* into the *3ème.* **R. des Rosiers,** in the heart of the *4ème*, is the focal point of the city's Jewish population. Superb kosher delicatessens neighbor Middle Eastern and Eastern European restaurants. The area is lively on Sundays, when other districts shut down. The Marais has also recently become the center of gay Paris.

Rue de Temple

8ÈME ARRONDISSEMENT. Full of expansive mansions, expensive shops and restaurants, grand boulevards, and grandiose monuments, the *8ème* is probably Paris's most glamorous arrondissement. Obscenely upscale *haute couture* boutiques (Hermès, Louis Vuitton, and Chanel) line the Champs-Elysées, the Madeleine, and the eternally fashionable r. du Faubourg St-Honoré. As it is also the beating heart of Parisian national pride, euphoric mobs rush to the *8ème* when France succeeds—most recently whipping out the bands of red, white, and blue for the World Cup final, the end of the Tour de France, and boisterous Bastille Day celebrations. But

TALE OF TWO CITIES

Springtime in Paris. Autumn in New York. But there's a transantlantic connection between N.Y.C. and Paris in addition to the jazz standards and the Statue of Liberty: neighborhoods. When it comes to places to live, the Marais, the *3ème* and *4ème* arrondissements, is sort of like Greenwich Village or Soho (even aside from the gay thing) in as much as it's trendy, but has seen trendier days. The *13ème* strikes as a newer "it" spot, much like yuppified Brooklyn. The *16ème* is the upper East side. The *20ème* is Jersey.

don't expect inexpensive eateries amid embassies and *haute couture* salons. For the most part, budget travelers should visit the *8ème*'s *grands boulevards* and then dine elsewhere.

9ÈME ARRONDISSEMENT. The **9ème arrondissement** links some of Paris's most affluent and touristed quarters with less popular and affluent ones. There are plenty of hotels, but many to the north are used for the local flesh trade. Nicer but not-so-cheap hotels are available near the respectable and central bd. des Italiens and bd. Montmartre.

10ÈME ARRONDISSEMENT. For most visitors, the **10ème arrondissement** means little more than Gare de l'Est and Gare du Nord. A flock of inexpensive hotels roosts near the stations, but the area is far from sights and nightlife and is somewhat unsafe. Use special caution west of pl. de la République along r. du Château d'Eau. Don't write the *10ème* off, though. Good, cheap ethnic restaurants abound, and some areas make for pleasant wandering.

11ÈME ARRONDISSEMENT. Five métro lines converge at M: République and three at M: Bastille, making the **11ème** a transportation hub and mammoth center of action, the hangout of the young and electric. Here contemporary galleries, boutiques, ethnic restaurants, and a very lively bar scene have replaced the old dance halls of **Oberkampf** and **Bastille.** Budget accommodations line these streets and are likely to have space. The Bastille area hums with nightlife; it's rough, but mostly safe. At night, be wary in the pickpocket-strewn pl. de la République.

12ÈME ARRONDISSEMENT. The **12ème arrondissement** is generally safe (although be careful around Gare de Lyon); the streets around the Bois de Vincennes offer some of the city's most pleasant places to stay, but are removed from the city center.

16ÈME ARRONDISSEMENT. Wealthy and residential, the museum-spattered **16ème** is a short walk from the Eiffel Tower but a 20-minute métro ride to the center. Here *hôtels particuliers* (mansions and gardened townhouses) retire graciously along quiet avenues, and businesses, storefronts, and tackiness are at a minimum. This quarter has over 60 embassies, about half of Paris's museums, the Trocadéro, and the rambling Bois de Boulogne (see **Bois de Boulogne,** p. 112). Métro stops are few and far between, as are inexpensive restaurants. Hotels here are relatively luxurious and apt to have vacancies.

17ÈME ARRONDISSEMENT. Hugging the northwestern edge of the city and sandwiched in between more luxurious and famous arrondissements, the **17ème** suffers from a bit of multiple personality disorder. Like its aristocrat neighbors in the *8ème*, *16ème*, and Neuilly, the *arrondissement*'s southern border looks like old money. Like its more tawdry eastern neighbors, Pigalle and the *18ème*, the arrondissement's eastern border can be seedy, especially around pl. de Clichy. In between these two extremes, the *17ème* is a working-class residential neighborhood. Some of its hotels cater to prostitutes, others to visiting businesspeople. Safety is an issue where it borders the *18ème*—be careful near pl. de Clichy.

MONTMARTRE: 18ÈME ARRONDISSEMENT. The area known as **Montmartre** (the *18ème*) owes its reputation to the fame of artists who lived there. Hotel rates rise as you climb the hill to the Basilique Sacré-Coeur. Food near the church and pl. du Tertre is pricey. Downhill and south at seedy pl. Pigalle, hotels tend to rent by the hour. At night avoid M: Anvers, M: Pigalle, and M: Barbès-Rochechouart; use M: Abbesses instead.

19ÈME AND 20ÈME ARRONDISSEMENTS. The **19ème** and **20ème arrondissements** are by no means central; apart from the Parc de la Villette in the *19ème* and Père-Lachaise in the *20ème*, expect at least a half-hour métro ride to the city's sights. The *19ème's* Parc des Buttes-Chaumont is great for picnics and jogs. Although cheap high-rises dot the hillsides, a few charming streets preserve an old-Paris feel. Two-star hotels here are a good bet if you're stuck without a bed. r. de Belleville can be dangerous at night.

THE BANLIEUE

The *banlieue* are the suburbs of Paris. They have recently gained international attention in the film *La Haine* as sites of poverty and racism, although they in fact range in socioeconomic status—from extremely wealthy to extremely depressed. The nearest, *proche-banlieue*, are accessible by the métro and bus lines from the city. These include the Vallé de Chevreuse towns to the south; St-Cloud, Neuilly, and Boulogne to the west past the Bois de Boulogne (see **Sights**, p. 107); St-Mandé and Vincennes to the east past the Bois de Vincennes (see **Sights**, p. 110); and to the north, the towns of housing projects known as *zones* or *cités*, Pantin, Aubervilliers, and la Courneuve, which have recently experienced high levels of crime and drug traffic. Apparently, the Paris *Commune* of 1871 (see **History**, p. 30) was not completely in vain, since the *banlieue rouges* (red suburbs), Montreuil, Bagnolet, Bobigny, and Kremlin-Bicêtre, flourish with communist governments. These areas often have cheaper housing because of government regulations, and are home to artists' communities. The *grandes banlieue*, farther afield, Versailles, Chantilly, and St-Germain-en-Laye, can be reached by RER or commuter train. The *banlieue* also bring you the Banlieue Jazz and the Banlieue Blues festivals every summer.

GETTING INTO PARIS

TO AND FROM THE AIRPORTS

ROISSY-CHARLES DE GAULLE

Most transatlantic flights land at **Aéroport Roissy-Charles de Gaulle,** 23km northeast of Paris. For info call the 24-hour English-speaking information center (☎48 62 22 80) or look it up on the web at **www.parisairports.com.** The two cheapest and fastest ways to get into the city from de Gaulle are by RER or bus.

RER. To take the RER train from de Gaulle to Paris, first take the free shuttle bus from Terminal 1, 2A, 2B, or 2D to the Roissy train station (departures every 10-15min.). From there, the RER B3 (one of the Parisian commuter rail lines) will transport you to central Paris. To transfer to the métro, get off at Gare du Nord, Châtelet-Les-Halles, or St-Michel, all of which are RER and métro stops. To go to de Gaulle from Paris, take the RER B3, any train with a name starting with the letter "E," to "Roissy," which is the end of the line. Then change to the free shuttle bus (RER departs every 20min., 5am-12:30am, duration 30-35min.; bus 10min.; 49F).

SHUTTLE BUS. Taking a shuttle bus the whole distance is somewhat simpler than the RER, and takes about the same time. The Roissybus (☎48 04 18 24) leaves from in front of the American Express office on r. Scribe, near M: Opéra, and stops at Terminals 2A, 2C, 2F, 2D, 2B, T9, and 1. From de Gaulle, the bus leaves from gate A10 of terminals 2A and 2C, gate D11 of terminals 2B and 2D, gate H (arrivals level) of terminal 2F, terminal T9, and gate 30 (arrivals level) of terminal 1. Tickets can be bought on the bus (departures to airport every 15min., 5:45am-11pm, from airport 6am-11pm; 45min.; 48F).

The **Daily Air France Buses** (☎41 56 89 00) run to two areas of the city. Line 2 runs to and from the Arc de Triomphe (M: Charles de Gaulle-Etoile) at 1, av. Carnot (every 12min., 5:50am-11pm; 35min.; one-way 60F, round-trip 105F), and to and from the pl. de la Porte de Maillot/Palais des Congrès (M: Porte de Maillot) on bd. Gouvion St-Cyr (same schedule and prices). Line 4 runs to and from r. du Commandant Mouchette in front of the Méridien Hotel (M: Montparnasse-Bienvenue; to the airport every 30min. from 7am-9pm; one-way 70F, round-trip 120F); and to and from Gare de Lyon (M: Gare de Lyon), at 20, bd. Diderot (same schedule and prices). The shuttle stops at or between terminals 2A-2F, and at terminal 1 on the arrivals level, outside exit 34. Tickets can be purchased on the bus itself. Call 41 56 89 00 for recorded information, available in English, on all Air France airport shuttles.

DOOR-TO-DOOR SERVICE. While the RER B and shuttle buses are the cheapest means of transportation, it can be a somewhat harrowing experience to navigate the train and métro stations if you are loaded down with heavy baggage. As **taxis** are exorbitantly expensive (250-300F to the center of Paris), shuttle vans are the best option for door-to-door service. **Airport Shuttle** (☎45 38 55 72) charges 120F for one person, 89F per passenger for two or more people for Roissy-CDG or Orly. **Paris Shuttle** (☎43 90 91 91) charges 85F per passenger for two or more to Roissy-CDG or Orly. **Paris Airports Service** (☎49 62 78 78) charges 120F for one and 140F for two passengers to Orly; to Roissy-CDG the charge is 150F for one, 185F for two. The shuttle van ride takes between one hour and 90 minutes from the center of Paris.

ORLY

Aéroport d'Orly (☎49 75 15 15 for info, in English, 6am-11:45pm), 18km south of the city, is used by charters and many continental flights.

RER. From Orly Sud gate H or gate I, platform 1, or Orly Ouest arrival level gate F, take the **Orly-Rail** shuttle bus (every 15min., 5:40am-11:15pm) to the **Pont de Rungis/Aéroport d'Orly** train stop, where you can board the **RER C2** for a number of destinations in Paris (call RATP at 08 36 68 77 14 (French) or 08 36 68 41 14 (English) for info; every 15min., 6am-11pm; 25min.; 35F). The **Jetbus** (every 12min.; 5:45am-11:30pm; 22F), provides a quick connection between Orly Sud, gate H, platform 2, or Orly Ouest arrival level gate C and M: Villejuif-Louis Aragon on line 7 of the métro.

BUS. Another option is the RATP **Orlybus,** which runs to and from métro and RER stop Denfert-Rochereau, 14*ème*. Board at Orly Sud, gate H, platform 4 or Orly Ouest level 0, gate J (every 16-20min., 6am-11pm; takes 30min.; 35F). **Air France buses** run between Orly and **Gare Montparnasse,** 36, r. du Commandant Mouchotte, 6*ème* (M: Montparnasse-Bienvenüe), and the Invalides Air France agency, pl. des Invalides (every 12min., 6am-11pm; 30min.; 45F one-way, 75F round-trip). Air France shuttles stop at Orly Sud, gate J and Orly Ouest, gate E, (arrivals level).

ORLYVAL. RATP also runs **Orlyval** (☎08 36 68 41 14), a combination of métro, RER, and VAL rail shuttle. To get to Orly, buy an Orlyval ticket (57F), take the métro to Gare du Nord, Châtelet-Les-Halles, or St-Michel and change to the RER B. Make sure that the station Antony-Orly is lit up on the changing schedule panel next to the track (see **Getting Around,** p. 19). Get off at Antony-Orly and transfer to the VAL train. Reverse these instructions to enter the city from Orly. From the airport, buy a ticket at an RATP office (Ouest gate W level 1; Sud gate K). Weekly or monthly passes are not valid for Orlyval. (VAL trains run from Antony to Orly M-Sa 6am-8:30pm and Su and holidays 7am-11pm; trains arrive at Orly Ouest 2min. after reaching Orly Sud. Orly to Antony every 7min. M-Sa 6am-10:30pm, Su 7am-10:57pm; 30min. from Châtelet.)

DOOR-TO-DOOR SERVICE. See the listing for **Roissy-Charles de Gaulle** for information on **shuttle van service. Taxis** from Orly to town cost at least 120F during the day, 160F at night and on weekends. Allow at least 45 minutes for the trip, as traffic can be heavy.

TO AND FROM THE TRAIN STATIONS

Each of Paris's six train stations is a veritable community of its own, with resident street people and police, *cafés*, *tabacs*, banks, and shops. Locate the ticket counters (*guichets*), the platforms (*quais*), and the tracks (*voies*), and you will be ready to roll. Each terminal has two divisions: the *banlieue* (suburb) and the *grandes lignes* (big important trains). Some cities can be accessed by both regular trains and **trains à grande vitesse (TGV;** high speed trains). TGVs are more expensive, much faster, and require reservations that cost a small fee. For **train information** or to make reservations, contact SNCF at 08 36 35 35 35 (3F per min.), at www.sncf.fr, or use Minitel 3615 SNCF from 7am to 10pm daily. A telephone with direct access to the stations is to the right of the Champs-Elysées tourist office (see **Service Directory,** p. 277). Yellow **ticket machines** (*billetterie*) at every train station sell tickets to anyone who knows her PIN and has a MasterCard, Visa, or American Express (MC and V only at ticket booths). **SNCF** offers discounted round-trip tickets for travelers in France, which go under the name **tarifs Découvertes**—you should rarely have to pay full price.

> **ESSENTIAL INFORMATION**
>
> **RIDING THE RAILS**
>
> Take care: Gare du Nord and Gare d'Austerlitz can get rough at night, when drugs and prostitution emerge.
>
> Also, it is not advisable to buy tickets in the stations except at official counters. The SNCF doesn't have any outfits in refrigerator boxes, no matter what you're told.
>
> And finally, the most salient advice of all: Don't forget to *composter* your ticket (time-stamp it) at the orange machines on the platform before boarding the train. If you fail to do so, the *contrôleur* will severely reprimand you in fast-paced French, and you could be slapped in the face with a heavy fine.

TO AND FROM THE BUS STATIONS

International buses arrive in Paris at **Gare Routière Internationale du Paris-Gallieni** (M: Gallieni), just outside Paris at 28, av. du Général de Gaulle, Bagnolet 93170. **Eurolines** (☎08 36 69 52 52; Minitel 3615 Eurolines; www.eurolines.fr) sells tickets to most destinations in France and neighboring countries. Pick up schedules for departures from the station or the office at 55, r. St-Jacques, *5ème* (M: Maubert-Mutualité). The bus is typically about 50% cheaper than the train, though it takes longer.

GETTING AROUND PARIS

BY PUBLIC TRANSPORTATION

The **RATP** (Régie Autonome des Transports Parisiens) coordinates a network of subways, buses, and commuter trains in and around Paris. For info, contact **La Maison de la RATP,** right above M: Gare de Lyon; the **Bureau de Tourisme RATP,** pl. de la Madeleine, *8ème* (☎40 06 71 44; M: Madeleine; open M-Sa 8:30am-6:45pm, Su 6:30am-1pm); or the **RATP helpline** (☎08 36 68 77 14; 2,33F per minute; open daily 6am-9pm; www.ratp.fr). For wheelchair or seeing-impaired métro services, see **Travelers With Disabilities,** p. 240.

FARES. Individual tickets for the RATP cost 8F each, or can be bought in a *carnet* of 10 for 55F. Say, *"Un ticket, s'il vous plaît"* (AHN ti-KAY SEE VOO play), or *"Un carnet..."* (AHN CAR-nay...), to the person behind the window. Each métro ride takes one ticket, and the bus takes at least one, some-

ON Y GO!

The immortal phrase, "Let's go" has many literal translations in the French language, and can mean anything from "come on, lazy bottom" to "I'm a gonner unless you spirit me out of here in sixty seconds." **On y va?** is a nice way of asking if your partner is ready to accompany you to your next destination, while **On se casse?** has a more urgent, get-me-the-hell-out-of-here ring to it. **Allons-y!** betrays you to the world as a nerd from high school French class. **On y go** is used by a select group of trendy Anglophones—highly recommended (although somewhat suspect among true Francophiles).

times more, depending on connections you make and the time of day. For directions on using the tickets, see **Métro,** below.

PASSES. If you're staying in Paris for several days or weeks a **Carte Orange** can be very economical. Bring an ID photo (taken by machines in most major stations for 25F) to the ticket counter and ask for a weekly *carte orange hebdomaire* (82F) or equally swank monthly *carte orange mensuelle* (271F). These cards have specific start and end dates (the weekly passes run M-Su, and the monthly start at the beginning of the month). Prices quoted here are for passes in Zones 1 and 2 (the métro and RER in Paris and suburbs), and work on all métro, bus, and RER modes of transport. If you intend to travel to the distant 'burbs, you'll need to buy RER passes for more zones (they go up to 5). If you're only in town for a day or two, a cheap option is the **Mobilis pass** (32F for a one-day pass in Zones 1 and 2; ☎ 53 90 20 20), which provides unlimited métro, bus, and RER transportation within Paris. Always write the number of your *carte* on your coupon.

TOURIST STEALS. Paris Visite tickets are valid for unlimited travel on bus, métro, and RER, as well as discounts on sightseeing trips, bicycle rentals, and stores like Galéries Lafayette; they can be purchased at the airport or at métro and RER stations. These passes are available for 1 day (55F), 2 days (90F), 3 days (120F), or 5 days (175F), but the discounts you receive do not necessarily outweigh the extra cost.

MÉTRO

Métro stations are marked with an "M" or with the "*Métropolitain*" lettering designed by art nouveau dude Hector Guimard (See **Sights.**)

GETTING AROUND. The first trains start running around 5:30am, and the last ones leave the end-of-the-line stations (the "*portes de Paris*") for the center of the city at about 12:15am. For the exact departure times of the last trains, check the poster in the center of each station marked *Principes de Tarification* (fare guidelines), the white sign with the platform's number and direction, or the monitors above the platform. Transport maps are posted on platforms and near turnstiles; all have a *plan du quartier* (map of the neighborhood). Connections to other lines are indicated by orange *correspondance* signs, exits by blue *sortie* signs. Transfers are free if made within a station, but it is not always possible to reverse direction on the same line without exiting the station.

USING TICKETS. To pass through the turnstiles, insert the ticket into the small slit in the metal divider just to your right as you approach the turnstile. It disappears for a moment, then pops out about a foot farther along, and a little green or white circle lights up, reminding you to retrieve the ticket. If a small electric whine sounds and a little red circle lights up, your ticket is not valid; take it back and try another. When you have the right light, push through the gate and retrieve your ticket. **Hold onto your ticket** until you exit the métro, and pass the point marked **Limite de Validité des Billets;** a uniformed RATP *contrôleur* (inspector) may request to see it on any train. If caught without one, you must pay a hefty fine. Also, any *correspondances* (transfers) to the RER require you to put your validated (and uncrumpled) ticket into a turnstile. Otherwise you might need to buy a new ticket in order to exit.

LATE AT NIGHT. Do not count on buying a métro ticket home late at night. Some ticket windows close as early as 10pm, and many close before the last train is due to arrive. Always have one ticket more than you need, although large stations have machines that accept 8F in coins. Stay away from the most dangerous stations (Barbès-Rochechouart, Pigalle, Anvers, Châtelet-Les-Halles, Gare du Nord, Gare de l'Est). Despite the good neighborhoods in which some of these stops are located, they are frequented by hooligans looking to prey on tourists. When in doubt, take a taxi.

RER

The RER *(Réseau Express Régional)* is the RATP's suburban train system, which passes through central Paris. Introduced in 1969, the RER runs through deeper tunnels at higher speeds. Within the city, the RER travels much faster than the métro. There are five RER lines, marked A-E, with different branches designated by a number, such as the C5 line to Versailles-Rive Gauche. The brand-spanking-new line, the E, is called the Eole (Est-Ouest Liaison Express), and links Gare Magenta to Gare St-Lazare. The principal stops within the city, which link the RER to the métro system, are Gare du Nord, Nation, Charles de Gaulle-Etoile, Gare de Lyon, and Châtelet-Les-Halles on the Right Bank and St-Michel and Denfert-Rochereau on the Left Bank. To check for the right train, watch the electric signboards next to each track. These signs list all the possible stops for trains running on that track. Be sure that the little square next to your destination is lit up. To get to the suburbs, you'll need to buy special tickets (10-40F one-way). You'll need this ticket to *exit* RER stations. Insert your ticket just as you did to enter, and pass through. The RER runs, as does the métro, from 5:30am-1am.

BUS

Although slower and often more costly than the métro, bus rides can be cheap sight-seeing tours and helpful introductions to the city's layout.

TICKETS. Bus tickets are the same as those used in the métro, and can be purchased either in métro stations or on the bus from the driver. Enter the bus through the front door and punch your ticket by pushing it into the machine by the driver's seat. If you have a *carte orange* or other transport pass (Paris Visite, Mobilis, etc.), flash it at the driver. Inspectors may ask to see your ticket, so hold onto it until you get off. Should you ever wish to leave the earthly paradise that is the RATP autobus, just press the red button and the *arrêt demandé* sign will magically light up.

ROUTES. The RATP's *Grand Plan de Paris* includes a map of the bus lines for day, evening, and night time (available at métro stations, free). The free bus map *Autobus Paris-Plan du Réseau* is available at the tourist office and at métro information booths. Buses with **three-digit numbers** come from or are bound for the suburbs, while buses with **two-digit numbers** travel exclusively within Paris. Principle bus routes are listed below.

NIGHT BUSES. Most buses run daily 6:30am to 8:30pm, although those marked **Autobus du Soir** continue until 1am. Still others, ominously named **Noctambus,** run all night. Night buses (3 tickets needed, 4 if you use 2 buses, all travel passes valid) start their runs to the *portes* of the city from the "Châtelet" stop and leave Monday through Thursday every hour on the half hour from 1:30 to 5:30am, every half hour from 1-5:30am Friday to Saturday. Buses departing from the suburbs to Châtelet run every hour on the hour 1 to 6am. Noctambuses I through M, R, and S have routes along the Left Bank en route to the southern suburbs. Those marked A through H, P, T, or V have routes on the Right Bank going north. Look for bus stops marked with a bug-eyed moon. Ask at a major métro station or at Gare de l'Est for more information on Noctambuses.

TOUR BUS. **Balabus** stops at virtually every major sight in Paris (Gare de Lyon, Bastille, St-Michel, Louvre, Musée d'Orsay, Concorde, Champs-Elysées, Charles-de-Gaulle-Etoile, Porte Maillot, Pont de Neuilly, Grande Arche de La Défense; whole loop takes 1¼hr.). The fare is three tickets from the start points of the loop and one to three tickets on other points along the route. The bus runs daily from the first Sunday of April to the last Sunday of September on Sundays and holidays. The first bus leaves Grande Arche de la Défense at 12:30pm and Gare de Lyon at 1:30pm; the last bus leaves Grande Arche at 8pm and Gare de Lyon at 8:30pm. Buses run about every 20 minutes.

BY TAXI

For taxi companies, see **Service Directory,** p. 277. If you have a complaint, or have left a personal belonging behind, contact the taxi company, or write to **Service des Taxis de la Préfecture de Police,** 36, r. des Morillons, 75015 (☎55 76 20 00; M: Convention). Ask for a receipt; if you file a complaint, record and include the driver's license number.

RATES. Taxis in Paris are expensive. **Tarif A,** the basic rate, is in effect in Paris 7am to 7pm (4F per km). **Tarif B** is in effect Monday to Saturday 7pm to 7am, all day Sunday, and during the day from the airports and immediate suburbs (5,83F per km). **Tarif C,** the highest, is in effect from the airports 7pm to 7am (7,16F per km). In addition, there is a *prix en charge* (base fee) of about 13F. All taxis have lights on their roofs indicating the rate being charged. Should you call a taxi rather than getting one at a taxi stand, the base fee will increase according to how far away you are and how long it takes the driver to get there. For all cabs, stationary time (at traffic lights and in traffic jams) costs 2F per minute. Additional charges (6F) are added for luggage over 5kg, a fourth adult, or for taxis leaving from train stations and taxi stops. Taxis can and do refuse to take more than three people. For **tipping,** see p. 22. Some take credit cards (Amex, MC, V).

BY CAR

Irwin Shaw wrote, "One driver out of every twelve in Paris has killed a man. On foot, the Parisian is as courteous as the citizen of any other city. But mounted, he is merciless." The infamous rotary at the Arc de Triomphe is particularly nightmarish: police are stationed on the Champs-Elysées side to keep unwitting tourists from walking directly across eight lanes of traffic to the Arc. As a rule, the fastest and biggest car wins. **Priorité à droite** gives the right of way to the car approaching from the right, regardless of the size of the streets, and Parisian drivers make it an affair of honor to take this right even in the face of grave danger. Drivers are not allowed to honk their horns within city limits unless they are about to hit a pedestrian, but this rule is often broken. The legal way to show discontent is to flash the headlights. If you don't have a map of Paris marked with one-way streets, the city will be impossible to navigate. Parking is hard to find and expensive.

FINDING YOUR WHEELS. Expect to pay at least US$150 per week, plus 20.6% tax, for a teensy car; you'll probably have to purchase **insurance** as well (see below). Automatic transmission is often unavailable on cheaper cars. Reserve well before leaving for France and pay in advance if at all possible. It is always significantly less expensive to reserve a car from the US than from France. Always check if prices quoted include tax, unlimited mileage, and collision insurance; some credit card companies will cover this automatically. Ask about discounts and check the terms of insurance, particularly the size of the deductible. Non-Europeans should check with their national motoring organization (like AAA) for international coverage. Ask your airline about special fly-and-drive packages; you may get up to a week of free or discounted rental. The minimum age for renting in France is 21; those under 25 will often have to pay a surcharge. At most agencies, all that's needed to rent a car is a valid drivers' license and proof that you've had it for a year, but bring your passport just in case. For rental agencies, see **Service Directory,** p. 274.

INTERNATIONAL DRIVING PERMIT (IDP). Those in possession of an EU-issued driving license are entitled to drive in France with no further ado. While others may be legally able to drive in France on the strength of their national licenses for a few months, not all the police know; it's safest to get an International Driving Permit (IDP),

which is essentially a translation of your regular license into 10 languages, including French. The IDP, valid for one year, must be issued in your own country before you depart. You must be 18 years old to receive the IDP. The IDP is in addition to, not a replacement for, your home license, and is not valid without it. An application for an IDP usually needs to include one or two photos, a current local license, an additional form of identification, and a fee.

CAR INSURANCE. EU residents driving their own cars do not need any extra insurance coverage in France. For those renting, paying with a gold credit card usually covers standard insurance; if your home car insurance covers you for liability, make sure you get a **green card,** or **International Insurance Certificate** to prove it. If you have a collision abroad, the accident will show up on your domestic records if you report it to your insurance company. Otherwise, be prepared to shell out US$5-10 per day for insurance on a rental car. Leasing should include insurance and the green card in the price. Some travel agents offer the card; it may also be available at border crossings.

TWO-WHEELERS

During the métro strike of December 1995, bike stores sold out to car-less Parisians, and the community of cyclists dreaming of an autoless Paris became more vocal. The government promised that 1997 would bring 50km of Parisian streets reserved for motorless wheels. Nonetheless, if you have never ridden a bike in heavy traffic, don't use central Paris as a testing ground. The Bois de Boulogne and the Bois de Vincennes should be more your speed. Bicycles can be transported on all RER lines, but not on the métro. Ask for a helmet and inquire about insurance. For rental listings, see **Service Directory,** p. 273.

PARIS ETIQUETTE, ABRIDGED VERSION

> In Paris they simply stared when I spoke to them in French; I never did succeed in making those idiots understand their language.
>
> -Mark Twain

AUGUST. Be aware that Parisians clear out of their beloved city for nearly the entire month of August: most things shut down, and anglophones flood the city's monuments.

BLENDING IN. A good rule of thumb in Paris: don't evoke their stereotype of the American tourist and they won't evoke yours—that nasty, nasal Frenchman. With that in mind, try to blend in as much as possible. The French tend to dress more conservatively than people in other countries. Shorts shouldn't be too short, nor should they feature strategically ripped butt areas. Usually skirts or dresses for girls are more appropriate and just as good in hot weather. Don't worry about overdressing; Parisians are very stylish, and even students dress well. Closed shoes, solid colored pants, and plain shirts are ideal, not baggy pants, torn jeans, or your favorite "No Fear" t-shirt.

CHURCHES. Surprising as it may seem, churches are indeed places of worship before they are tourist attractions; it is important to keep proper conduct in mind, including mode of dress. Cutoffs, tight, short, bare-shouldered, sloppy, or dirty are words that should never be used in describing what you are wearing into a church. Do not walk into the middle of a mass unless you plan to give an impromptu homily, and don't yell or shriek, even if you feel inspired to speak in tounges. Do not take flash photographs , and don't walk directly in front of the altar unless directed to do so.

DRIVING. The French have a not undeserved reputation for aggressive, dangerous driving. Still, while they will zoom past slow cars or space cadets, they will in all likelihood not hit you. Parisians jaywalk for sport.

FLOORS. Keep in mind that the French call the ground floor the *rez-de-chaussée* and start numbering with the first floor above the ground floor *(premier étage)*. The button labeled "R" and not "1" is typically the ground floor. This system can cause unpleasant surprises, when your "fourth-floor hotel room" is in reality above the tree line.

GREETINGS AND SALUTATIONS. Although the Parisian concept of customer service leaves much to be desired, there is no end to the pleasantries that one encounters whenever entering or exiting a business, restaurant, or hotel. Always, always say *"Bonjour Madame/Monsieur"* when you come in, and *"Au Revoir"* when you leave, or face an even icier reception. If you bump into someone on the street or while awaiting/pushing your way into transportation, always say *"Pardon"* or *"Excusez-moi."* The proper way to answer the phone is *"Âllo,"* but if you use this on the street, your cover will be blown.

HOURS. As for hours of opening *(horaires)*, most restaurants and some small business close for "lunch," which clocking in at a hefty three hours, must include a sizable nap (typically noon-3pm). Many establishments and most museums are closed on Mondays, and other hours are characteristically protean: calling ahead is always a good idea.

POCKET CHANGE. Cashiers and tellers will constantly ask you *"Avez-vous la monnaie?"* ("Do you have the change?") as they would rather not break your 1000F note for a pack of gum. If you don't have it, smile ever-so-sweetly and say *"Non, désolée."* Number 274 on the list of "Things I Wish I Had Packed": a coin purse.

PUBLIC RESTROOMS. The streetside public restrooms in Paris are worth the 2F they require. For this paltry sum, you are guaranteed a clean restroom, as these magic machines are self-cleaning after each use. This kind of cleanliness should not be expected in your average cafe, as they tend to have squat toilets. In addition, don't feel you have to buy something in order to use the restroom. Just march right in, and if someone says something, feign frontal lobotomy.

SAFETY AND SECURITY. Personal safety in France is on par with the rest of Western Europe, with a far lower rate of violent crime than the US. As big cities go, Paris is relatively safe. It's best not to be complacent, though, especially since tourists are often seen as (and often are) easy victims. Be especially careful on public transport at rush hour and on the way to and from the airport. Theft is also common on métro line number one and at department stores; never leave your wallet, passport or credit card on the counter. Exercise caution and common sense—keep bags closed and under your arm if possible and be particularly vigilant in crowded areas—and you increase your chances of a trouble-free holiday. Certain areas of Paris can be rough at night, including Les Halles and the Bastille area. Travelers should not walk around Pigalle, Barbès-Rochechouart, Montmartre, r. St-Denis in the *2ème*, or Belleville alone at night. In general, the northern and eastern arrondissements are less safe than the southern and western ones, and the Right Bank less safe than the Left. Be especially aware when in the arrondissements outside the typical tourist loop. In an emergency, dial 17 for police. The distribution of people can reveal a great deal about the relative safety of the area; look for children playing, women walking in the open, and other signs of an active community. If you are traveling alone, be sure that someone at home knows your itinerary and never admit that you're traveling alone. *Ça va sans dire:* When walking at night, stick to busy, well-lit streets and avoid dark alleyways, parks, parking lots, and deserted areas. Keep in mind that a district can change character drastically between blocks. Whenever possible, *Let's Go* warns of unsafe neighborhoods, but always use your noggin.

TIPPING. Service is always included in meal prices in restaurants and cafés, and in drink prices at bars and clubs; look for the phrase *service compris* on the menu or just ask. If service is not included, tip 15-20%. Even when service is included, it is polite to leave a *pourboire* at a café, bistro, restaurant, or bar—a few francs to 5%.

THE MEDIA

TELEVISION AND RADIO

Television makes up for the lack of national papers. For most of the post-war period, French television was in the hands of a state-run monopoly, but in the mid-80s, several public stations were privatized. **TF1,** now the most popular station in France, was privatized in 1986. For the stubbornly intellectual, there is the public channel **ARTE.** Cable TV is also available; pay channel **Canal Plus** shows recent films and live sporting events. TV Guides are the most popular publications in France, with **Télé 7 jours** leading the pack while **Télérama** provides commentary not only on TV but also on culture in general. French **radio** went commercial in 1984, although the success of large conglomerates means few stations remain independent. National stations include **Fun Radio** for teens; **Skyrock,** a noisy and provocative rock station; and **Nostalgie,** adult-oriented with quiz shows and emotional music. Public stations include **France-Inter,** a quality general interest station, and **France Info,** an all-news station.

NEWSPAPERS

The weeklies **Pariscope** (3F) and **Officiel des Spectacles** (2F) are the most comprehensive listings of movies, plays, exhibits, festivals, clubs, and bars. *Pariscope* also includes an English-language section called **Time Out Paris.** *Pariscope* is easy to use online at *www.pariscope.fr.* The tourist office's free monthly **Where: Paris** highlights exhibits, concerts, walking tours, and events. The Mairie de Paris, 29, r. de Rivoli, *4ème* (☎42 76 42 42; M: Hôtel-de-Ville) publishes the free monthly, **Paris le Journal,** with articles about what's on around the city. On Wednesday, *Le Figaro* includes **Figaroscope,** a supplement about what's happening in Paris. **Free Voice,** a monthly English-language newspaper published by the American Church (see **English-Language Religious Services,** p. 277), and the bi-weekly **France-USA Contacts (FUSAC)** list jobs, housing, and information for English speakers and are available for free from English-speaking bookstores, restaurants, and travel agencies throughout Paris.

Libération (7F), a socialist newspaper, offers comprehensive news coverage of world events. Heavy on culture, including theater and concert listings, *Libé* has excellent, controversial, and thought-provoking editorials. Readers with a penchant for politics will disappear behind a copy of **Le Monde** (7F50), which is decidedly centrist with a tendency to wax socialist. **Le Figaro** (7F) leans to the right, with an entire section of financial news. **La Tribune** (7F) is France's *Wall Street Journal,* with an international view on finance. The Communist Party puts out **L'Humanité** (7F) for the good of the people. For a rundown of the latest on rap, hip-hop, industrial, and pop, fashion trends, and Paris street culture, pick up a copy of the well-designed and snidely amusing magazine **Technik Art** (18F), a monthly *communiqué* (in French) for the Parisian dandy. Gay and lesbian readers should consult **Têtu** (30F) for the latest in French queer politics, fashion, and events. **Marianne** is the French version of *Time* magazine, with world news and French gossip (15F). **Le Nouvel Observateur** is a news magazine with an inquisitive take on French culture and society (20F). For those who prefer the lighter side of things, **Le Canard Enchainée** (8F) is a satirical newspaper that comes out every Wednesday—read *Figaro* first to get all the jokes. There are two **newsstands open 24 hours:** 33, av. des Champs-Elysées, *8ème,* M: Franklin D. Roosevelt; 2, bd. Montmartre, *9ème,* M: r. Montmartre.

INSIDE

Life & Times

HISTORY

ANCIENT PARIS OR LET'S GO: LATIN

PARISII, Parisiorum, masc. pl., n. The **Île de la Cité** (see **Sights,** p. 55) at the center of the Seine offered both protection from invaders as well as easy access to fresh water and means of transportation, and trade. The Gallic **Parisii** clan settled the island at the end of the 2nd century BC and donated their name to the glory of generations to come.

CAESAR, Caesaris, masc. n. In 52 BC, Julius Caesar noted gleefully in his *Commentaries* that the Parisii burned their town down rather than surrender it to the Romans. His troops initiated 300 years of Roman rule while catapulting Jules himself to fame, power, and the eventual leadership of the up-and-coming Empire.

LUTETIA, Lutetiae, fem., n. The Romans, who elegantly named their new colonial outpost **Lutetia Parisiorum** ("the Midwater-Dwelling of the Parisii"), expanded the city to the Left Bank, building new roads (rue St-Jacques), public baths (**Musée de Cluny,** p. 126), and gladiatorial arenas, all of which can be seen in remarkably well-preserved ruins in the present-day *5ème* arrondissement (see **Sights,** p. 73). By AD 360, the Romans had shortened the name of the now-resplendent outpost to "Paris."

DIONYSIUS, Dionysii, masc., n. Despite Roman prosperity, the advance of **Christianity** and barbarians threatened goaty Roman-pagan rule. Paris's first bishop **St-Denis** (a.k.a., Dionysius) achieved martyrdom after being beheaded on Paris's northern hilltop, Mount Mercury, in AD 260, giving the area the name **Montmartre** (Mount of the Martyr, see **Sights,** p. 102). After the Romans had their way with St-Denis for his attempts at christianiz-

LE COQ

The rooster is the symbol of the French people, coming from gallus and signifying the Gauls, the progenitors of modern France. From this we get the conception of the French as proud, war-like people, who arise early and wake up everyone else. Sometimes, in the press, you will see a reference to *l'Hexagone*. This is another term for France itself, although the reasons behind this are a secret more closely guarded than the recipe for *crème brulée* (hint: it has to do with the shape of the country). The letters RF, much like the Roman SPQR, stand for République Française, and are often stitched into uniforms, and stamped on passports.

ing the city, he allegedly picked up his head and walked north; he collapsed on the site of the current Basilique de St-Denis, the traditional burial place of France's kings and queens.

ATTILA, Attilae, n. By the 3rd century AD, the fall of the Empire was imminent. Long-distance trade declined; the army, spread too thin, could not prevent invasions by German delinquents such as the Vandals, Visigoths, and Franks. When Attila and his marauding Huns tried to take the city in 450, the prayers of St-Geneviève diverted the invaders at Orléans and saved the city. The devout nun became Paris's patron saint and gave rise to the belief that Huns musn't mess with Nuns (see **Goths,** p. 208).

PARIS DELENDA EST, *Paris is to be destroyed.* By the time Rome finally fell in 476, Gaul had suffered invasions by Germanic tribes for centuries. Although the honor of sacking the Eternal City was left to the Goths, it was the **Franks** who eventually dominated Gaul and bequeathed it their name. In 476, **King Clovis** of the Franks defeated the Gallo-Romans and took control of Paris, founding France's first royal house, naming Paris capital, and converting the entire city to Christianity. The **Merovingian Dynasty** (400-751) enjoyed almost 300 years of rule before **Pepin the Short's** son, **Charlemagne,** took power in 768 and established the **Carolingian Dynasty** (751-987). On Christmas Day, 800, Charlemagne had himself crowned Holy Roman Emperor by **Pope Leo III.** Charlemagne expanded his territorial claims and, despite his own illiteracy, renewed interest in the art and literature of the ancients, initiating the **Carolingian Renaissance.** Paris suffered when Charlemagne moved his capital to Aix-la-Chapelle and again when a wave of invaders menaced Europe in the 9th and 10th centuries. Charlemagne's empire fell.

MEDIEVAL PARIS

As the first millennium approached, France was a disparate collection of independent kingdoms, each with its own customs, languages, and traditions. These kingdoms were organized in the **feudal system,** which bonded peasant-worker vassals to their lords.

Paris would not return to prominence until the election in 987 of the Count of Paris, **Hugh Capet,** to the throne. Under the rule of the **Capetian Dynasty** (987-1328), Paris flourished as a center of trade, education, and power. Capet's 12th-century descendants attempted to unite the various kingdoms into one centralized country. In 1163, construction began on **Notre-Dame cathedral** (see **Sights,** p. 55), which would take over 170 years to complete. The Capetians' most famous king, **Philip II** (1179-1223), expanded Paris's territory, refortified its walls, and paved the city's streets. With the establishment of the University of

Paris in 1215 and the Sorbonne in 1253 (see **Sights,** p. 73), Paris reorganized into two distinct parts: the merchant Rive Droite (Right Bank) and the academic Rive Gauche (Left Bank). One of the last Capetians, the holy **Louis IX** (St-Louis), began construction of the **Sainte Chapelle** (see **Sights**, p. 58) in 1245, just opposite the rising cathedral of Notre-Dame on Île de la Cité. Both trade and papal power transferred to France in the 14th century when Pope Clement V moved to Avignon in 1309.

Like most of France's cities, 14th-century Paris suffered the ravages of both the **Black Death** (1348-49) and the **Hundred Years' War** (1337-1453), in which the Burgundians allied with the English against the French and Paris was stuck in the middle. When the last Capetian, **Charles IV,** died in 1328, **Edward III** of England claimed his right to the French throne. Were it not for mythic **Joan of Arc,** who allied with the Valois King **Charles VII** against **Henry V** of England, Paris might have become an English colony. Joan, a French peasant girl from Orléans who heard angelic voices telling her to save France, revitalized the Valois troops, crowned Charles VII king in 1429, and led the Valois to a string of victories. Attempting to win Paris back from the Burgundians in 1429, she was wounded in what is now the *1er* arrondissement (see **Sights,** p. 61). Despite her successes, she was captured two years later by the English and burned at the stake in Rouen for heresy. Charles VII recaptured Paris in 1437 and drove the English back to Calais. The **Valois Dynasty** took over where the Capetians left off and moved toward a unified France.

THE RENAISSANCE

The influence of the **Italian Renaissance** sparked great interest in literature, art, and architecture in 16th-century Paris. In 1527, Charles VII's descendent **François I** commissioned Pierre Lescot to rebuild the **Louvre** (see **Museums,** p. 115) in the open style of the Renaissance and to begin work on the **Cour Carrée.** François I moved the official royal residence to the new Louvre and invited **Leonardo da Vinci** to his court, where the Italian painter presented **La Jaconde** (**Mona Lisa;** see **Ms. Mona's Wild Ride,** p. 118) as a gift to the French king. During the reign of François's successor, **Henri II,** new mansions were added to the **Place des Vosges** (see **Sights,** p. 72), a masterpiece of French Renaissance architecture. However, when Henri II died in the square's Palais des Tournelles in 1563 after a jousting accident, his wife, **Catherine de Medici,** ordered it destroyed and began work on the **Tuileries Palace,** the **Pont-Neuf,** and the **Jardins des Tuileries** (see **Sights,** p. 61).

Religious conflict between **Huguenots** (French protestants) and **Catholics** initiated the **Wars of Religion** between 1562 and 1598. After the death of her husband Henri II, Catherine de Medici effectively became France's ruler. A fervent Italian Catholic, she was ruthless in the wars against the French Protestants of the southwest kingdom of Navarre.

Influenced by his progressive grandmother **Marguerite de Navarre** (and her Renaissance masterpiece, *The Heptameron*), **Henri de Navarre** agreed to marry Catherine de Medicis's daughter **Marguerite de Valois (Queen Margot)** in an effort to create peace between the two warring kingdoms. But the wedding was a trap: when the leading Protestants in France had assembled in Paris for the royal union in 1572, Catherine signaled the start of the **St-Bartholomew's Day Massacre.** A wild Parisian mob slaughtered some 2000 Huguenots. Henri's life and throne were saved only by a temporary, not-exactly-voluntary conversion to Catholicism. In 1589, Henri de Navarre acceded to the throne as **Henri IV de Bourbon,** ensuring peace, uniting France, and establishing the last of France's royal houses, the **Bourbons.** Upon his ascension to the throne at St-Denis, Henri IV waved off the magnitude of his conversion with the remark, *"Paris vaut bien une messe"* ("Paris is well worth a mass," or, loosely, "Paris: what a mess!"). His heart still lay with the Huguenots, though: in 1598, he issued the **Edict of Nantes,** which granted tolerance for French Protestants and quelled religious wars for almost a century.

"THE STATE? THAT'S ME," OR, THE 17TH CENTURY

The French monarchy reached its height of power and extravagant opulence in the 17th century. First of the **Bourbon** line, Henri IV succumbed to an assassin's dagger in 1610 and was succeeded by **Louis XIII.** Louis' capable and ruthless minister, **Cardinal Richelieu,** consolidated political power in the hands of the monarch and created the centralized, bureaucratic administration characteristic of France to this day. He expanded Paris and built the **Palais du Luxembourg** (see **Sights,** p. 77) for the Queen mother, **Marie de Medici,** and the Palais Cardinal, today the **Palais Royal** (See **Sights,** p. 62) for himself. This absolutist state, however, strained the already taut social fabric of France as Richelieu manipulated nobles and teased the bourgeoisie with promises of social advancement.

When Richelieu and Louis died within months of each other in 1642, they were succeeded by another king-and-cardinal combo, **Louis XIV** and **Cardinal Mazarin.** Since Louis was only five years old at the time, the cardinal took charge, but by 1661 the 24-year-old monarch had decided he was ready to rule alone. Not known for his modesty, Louis adopted the motif of **Sun King** and took the motto *"L'état, c'est moi"* ("I am the state"). Following this, he brought a personal touch to national affairs, moving the government to his new 14,000 room palace, **Château de Versailles** (see **Daytripping,** p. 199). Louis made Versailles into a magnificent showcase for regal opulence and noble privilege. The King himself was on display: favored subjects could observe him and his Queen rise in the morning, groom, and dine. Royal births were also public events. Louis XIV strove to put down any form of dissent, operating on the principle of *"un roi, une loi, une foi"* ("one king, one law, one faith"). Louis reigned for 72 years, revoking the Edict of Nantes in 1685 at the behest of his mistress, and initiating the ruinous **War of the Spanish Succession** (1701-1713). The nobles vegetated at court, so most didn't even notice their complete loss of political power. From Versailles, Louis XIV commissioned the landscape architect André Le Nôtre to build a wide, tree-lined boulevard called the Grand Cours, today known as the **Champs-Elysées** (see **Sights,** p. 86). The Sun King also built the **Place Vendôme** (see **Sights,** p. 61) and his daughter, the Duchesse de Bourbon, commissioned the **Palais Bourbon,** which today houses the **Assemblée Nationale** (see **Sights,** p. 83).

Louis finally died in 1715, having outlasted even his grandsons. He was succeeded by the two-year old **Louis XV.** The light that had once emanated from the French throne could not eclipse serious domestic problems. The lavish expenditures of Louis XIV and his successors left France with an enormous debt, and Louis's manipulation of the nobility led to simmering resentment. Part of Louis XIV's decision to move his royal residence to Versailles was his fear of uprising in Paris.

THE FRENCH REVOLUTION

When **Louis XVI** succeeded to the throne in 1774, the country was in desperate financial straits. Peasants blamed the soon-to-be-*ancien régime* for their mounting debts, while aristo-fat-cats detested the King for his attempts at reform. In 1789, to get out of this no-win situation, Louis XVI called a meeting of the **Estates General,** an assembly of delegates from the three classes of society: aristocrats, clergy, and the bourgeois-dominated **Third Estate.** This anachronistic body had not met since 1614, and after weeks of legal wrangling, the Third Estate broke away and declared itself the National Assembly. Locked out of its chamber, the delegation moved to the Versailles tennis courts where the **Oath of the Tennis Court,** a promise to draft a new constitution, was sworn on June 20, 1789. The King did not dismiss the Assembly; instead he sent in troops to intimidate it and received the immortal riposte "the assembled nation cannot receive orders." As rumors multiplied, the initiative passed to the Parisian mob, known as the *sans-culottes* (those without breeches) who were angered by high bread prices and the disarray of government.

When they stormed the old fortress of the **Bastille** (see **Sights,** p. 93) on July 14th, a destructive orgy stormed across the nation as peasants burned the records of their debts and obligations. The French now celebrate **July 14** *(le quatorze juillet)* as the **Fête Nationale** (Anglos call it **Bastille Day;** see **Festivals,** p. 6). The Assembly joined in the revolution in August with the abolishment of feudal law and the **Declaration of the Rights of Man,** which embodied the principles of *liberté, égalité,* and *fraternité.* Major reforms, the abolition of guilds, and the dismantling of the Church transformed the nation but could not bring peace to Paris: Notre-Dame and Versailles were ransacked and vandalized.

When the petrified king, now under virtual house arrest, tried to flee the country in 1791 he was arrested and imprisoned; meanwhile, Austria and Prussia mobilized in order to stamp out the democratic disease. In 1793, as the revolutionary armies miraculously defeated the invaders, the radical **Jacobin** faction, led by **Maximilien Robespierre** and his **Committee of Public Safety,** took over the Convention and began a period of suppression and mass execution known as the **Terror.** In January, the Jacobins guillotined the King and his cake-savoring Queen, **Marie-Antoinette,** abolishing the monarchy. The ironically named **Place de la Concorde** (Harmony Square) was the site of more than 1300 beheadings (see **Sights,** p. 87). With a **Republic** declared, the *ancien régime* was history.

The Revolution had taken a radical turn. The Church refused to be subjugated to the National Assembly and was replaced by the oxymoronical **Cult of Reason.** A new calendar of 10-day weeks did not catch on, but the Revolutionary **metric** system of measurement is now the international standard. As counter-revolutionary paranoia set in, power lay with the 'incorruptible' **Robespierre** and his McCarthyesque Committee of Public Safety. The least suspicion of royalist sympathy led to the block; Dr. Guillotine himself did not escape the vengeance of his invention. Robespierre ordered the execution of his revolutionary rivals, including the popular **Danton,** before his own denunciation and death in 1794. The **Terror** was over and power was entrusted to a five-man Directory.

NAPOLEON AND EMPIRE

Meanwhile, war continued as a young Corsican general swept through northern Italy and into Austria. Fearful of his rising popularity, the Directory jumped at **Napoleon Bonaparte's** idea of invading Egypt to threaten Britain's colonies in India. Although successful on land, the destruction of his fleet at the Battle of the Nile left his disease-ridden army marooned in Cairo. Napoleon responded by hurrying back to France to salvage his political career. Riding a wave of public support, he deposed the Directory, first making himself First Consul of a triumvirate, then Consul for Life in an 1802 referendum, and ultimately **Emperor** in 1804. Napoleon crafted a civil code, his most lasting achievement; elements of it continue in French law today. Although faithful to revolutionary ideals, the **Napoleonic Code** incorporates an autocratic approach to life, re-establishing slavery and requiring wives to show total obedience to their husbands.

Paris benefitted from Napoleon's conquests and booty. His interest in the ancient Egyptian and Roman worlds brought countless sculptures from Alexandria and Italy into Paris, including the Louvre's *Dying Gladiator* and *Discus Thrower* (see **Louvre,** p. 115). He ordered the constructions of the two triumphal Roman arches, the **Arc de Triomphe** (see **Sights,** p. 84) and the **Arc du Carrousel** (see **Louvre,** p. 115) topping the latter with a gladiatorial sculpture stolen from St. Mark's Cathedral in Venice. Napoleon's many new bridges, like the **Pont d'Austerlitz,** the **Pont Iéna** (see **6ème,** p. 76), and the **Pont des Arts** (see **7ème,** p. 80) spanned the Seine in style. He ordered the construction of a neo-Greco-Roman style temple, the **Madeleine** (see **Sights,** p. 87) and he finished the **Cour Carrée** of the Louvre, originally ordered by Louis XIV. But the monument that perhaps best exemplifies Napoleon's Empire style is the **Château de Malmaison.** Napoleon and Empress Josephine set the tone for the Empire style, replete with Egyptian motifs and high-waist dresses. Their coronation ceremony was held in Notre-Dame and painted by the revolutionary painter **Jacques-Louis David** (and now on display in the Louvre, see **Fine Arts,** p. 40). When Josephine failed to produce an heir, she and Napoleon amicably annulled their marriage, and Josephine moved to Malmaison. The Emperor married **Marie Louise d'Autriche** and his armies pushed east to Moscow.

In 1812, after occupying a deserted Moscow, Napoleon was forced to withdraw at the onset of winter. The freezing cold decimated the French ranks, and of the 700,000 men he had led out to Russia, barely 200,000 returned. Napoleon lost the support of a war-weary people. In return for abdicating in 1814, he was given the Mediterranean island of **Elba,** and the monarchy was reinstated under **Louis XVIII,** brother of his headless predecessor. The story has a final twist: Napoleon left Elba and landed near Cannes on March 26th, 1815. He marched north as the King fled to England. The adventure of the **Hundred Days War** ended on the field of **Waterloo** in Flanders, Belgium, where the **Duke of Wellington** triumphed as much by luck as by skill. The ex-Emperor threw himself on the mercy of the English, who banished him to remote St. Helena in the south Atlantic, where he died

THE REVOLUTION MIGHT BE TELEVISED

The Revolutionaries brought with them, as any successful political regime does, a slew of symbols, paraphenalia, and catchy tunes. In 1789, Lafayette gave us the tricolor, made of three stripes, one each of blue, white, and red. (Random fact: contrary to what your eyes may tell you, the width of each stripe is not the same. The red is larger than the blue, in order to compensate for the different wavelengths of red and blue light.) Everyone worth a 10 Franc coin knows the slogan that was a hit on the dance floor, and matched the beat at beheadings: Liberté, Egalité, Fraternité! A lesser-known, and slightly less intimidating, icon of the new world order was Marianne, the "muse of the country," whose image is still found all over, from city hall sculptures to stamps. Her name, common among the commoners, was taken as a symbol of the Revolution's humble roots. She, although a worker, is typically surrounded by curious paraphenalia, like a lion, a tower, a sack of wheat, a Phrygian bonnet, and a baguette (just kidding). And lest we should forget, the Revolution brought a song that will instantly enamor you to Frenchies everywhere: *La Marseillaise*. *"Allons enfants de la Patrie, le jour de gloire est arrivé ..."*

in 1821. Napoleon is popularly regarded as a hero in France even today, and thousands still pay their respects at his tomb at **Les Invalides** (see **Sights,** p. 82). The **Restoration** of the monarchy saw Louis XVIII at the helm, as the **Bourbon** dynasty went on and on.

REPUBLIC, RESTORATION, AND MORE REVOLUTION

Although initially forced to recognize the achievements of the Revolution, the reinstated monarchy soon returned to its despotic ways. When **Charles X** restricted the press and limited the electorate to the landed classes, the people had had enough. Remembering the fate of his brother, Charles abdicated quickly following the **July Revolution** of 1830, and a constitutional monarchy was created under **Louis-Philippe,** Duke of Orleans, whose more modest bourgeois lifestyle garnered him the name **"the citizen king."** In a symbolic gesture, he kept his flag tricolor and his monarchy constitutional. The middle classes prospered, but the industrialization of France created a class of urban poor receptive to the new ideas of **socialism.** When the king and his bourgeois government refused to reform, the people were well practiced: there followed the **February Revolution** of 1848 and the declaration of the **Second Republic** and France's first universal male suffrage. The late Emperor's nephew, **Louis Napoleon,** was elected president. Since the constitution barred him from seeking a second term, he ignored it and seized power in a coup in 1851. Following a referendum in 1852, he declared himself **Emperor Napoleon III** to popular acclaim. Napoleon III's reign saw the industrialization of Paris and the rise of the urban population, pollution, and poverty that Balzac and Hugo's novels describe (see **Literature,** p. 36). Still, during his reign, France's prestige was restored: her factories hummed and **Baron Georges Haussmann** rebuilt Paris, replacing the medieval street plan (too conducive to street demonstrations) with grand boulevards along which an army could be deployed (see **Architecture,** p. 43). Despite Napoleon III's extraordinary reconstruction of Paris, his downfall came in July 1870 with the French defeat in the **Franco-Prussian War.**

The confident French did not notice the storm clouds gathering across the Rhine, where **Bismarck** had almost completed the unification of Germany. After tricking the French into declaring war, the Iron Chancellor's troops swiftly overran the country. The Emperor was captured and as German armies advanced the **Third Republic** was declared. Paris held out for four months, with the residents so desperate for food that they slaughtered most of the animals in the zoo (see **Sights,** p. 110).

When the government admitted defeat, placing a conservative regime led by **Adolphe Thiers** in power, the Parisian mob revolted again; in 1871 they declared the Paris **Commune.** For four months, a committee of leftist politicians, the *communards*, assumed power and rejected the Thiers government. These radical Parisians threw up barricades and declared the city a free Commune. When the city was invaded by vast numbers of French troops in an effort to recapture the city, the *communards* burned the Hôtel de Ville, the Palais Royal, and Catherine de Medici's Tuileries Palace before retreating to their last stand in the cemetery of Père Lachaise (see **Sights,** p. 105). The crushing of the Commune was quick and bloody. Many estimate that over 20,000 Parisians died, slaughtered by their compatriots in about a week. The last of the *communards* were shot against Père Lachaise's **mur des fédérés** on the morning of May 21, 1871. The defeat broke both the power of Paris over the provinces and that of the Parisian proletariat over the city.

BELLE ÉPOQUE

After over eighty years of revolutions, violence, and political instability, it is easy to understand why the period of peace, prosperity, and culture that followed between roughly 1890 and 1914 is called the **Belle Epoque** (the Beautiful Period). The colors of the **Impressionists** (see **Fine Arts,** p. 41), the novels of **Proust** (see **Literature,** p. 38) and the **World Expositions** of 1889 and 1900 (which gave Paris the **Eiffel Tower** (see **Sights,** p. 81) the **Pont Alexandre III,** the **Grand** and **Petit Palais** (see **Sights,** p. 86) and the first **métro** line, all reflected the optimism and energy of the Belle Epoque. At the same time, however, industrialization and urbanization introduced many new social problems that challenged the Third Republic. Although the government's reforms laid the foundation for the contemporary social welfare state, social tensions continued to grow.

The Third Republic was further undermined by the **Dreyfus affair.** Dreyfus was a Jewish army captain convicted in 1894 on trumped-up charges of treason and exiled. When the army refused to consider the case even after proof of Dreyfus's innocence was uncovered, France became polarized between the *Dreyfusards*, who argued for his release, and the reactionary right-wing *anti-Dreyfusards*, to whom Dreyfus was an unpatriotic traitor regardless of the evidence. These ethnic tensions foreshadowed the 20th-century conflicts that France would later confront in its colonial territories.

WORLD WAR I

After centuries of mutual dislike, the **Entente Cordiale** brought the British and the French into cooperation in 1904. Together with tsarist Russia, the three nations of the **Triple Entente** faced the **Triple Alliance** of Germany, Italy, and the Austro-Hungarian Empire. Tensions exploded in 1914 when a Serbian nationalist assassinated the Habsburg heir to the Austrian throne, **Archduke Franz-Ferdinand,** in Sarajevo. Germany did not persuade Austria to exercise restraint, and Austria marched on Serbia. Playing the champion of its fellow Slavs, Russia responded, and suddenly virtually all of Europe was at war.

After advancing within 50km of Paris, the German offensive stalled at the **Battle of the Marne.** Four years of agonizing trench warfare ensued. Germany's unrestricted submarine warfare on ships entering European waters provoked the **United States** to enter on the side of the Triple Entente. American troops tipped the balance of power in favor of the British and the French (Russia had withdrawn in 1917 in the midst of its own violent revolution), and on November 11, 1918, fighting ended. Of course, this was not before an entire generation of European men and boys was lost to the trenches.

The Germans were forced to sign the humiliating **Treaty of Versailles** in the Hall of Mirrors, where Prussian King Wilhelm I had been crowned Kaiser of the German Reich in 1870 at the end of Germany's victory in the Franco-Prussian War. The treaty contained a clause ascribing the blame for the war to Germany. The foundations for the great resentment that would aid Hitler's rise to power were laid in the Sun King's château.

ROARING 20S AND DEPRESSION IN THE 30S

Parisians danced in the streets with British, Canadian, and American soldiers to celebrate the end of WWI. The party continued into the **roaring 20s,** when artists like **Cocteau, Picasso, Chagall,** and **Man Ray;** intellectuals like **André Gide** and **Colette;** performers like

Josephine Baker; and expatriates like **Gertrude Stein, Ernest Hemingway, Ezra Pound,** and **F. Scott Fitzgerald** (see **Expatriate Literature,** p. 39) flooded Paris's cafés and saloons.

The party ended with the **Great Depression** in the 1930s, and was exacerbated by the violent right-wing **Fascist demonstrations** in which thousands of Parisians marched on Place de la Concorde and stormed the Assemblée Nationale. To combat the Fascists, Socialists and Communists united under **Léon Blum's** left-wing **Front Populaire,** seeking better wages, unionization, and vacation benefits. The Popular Front split over Blum's decision not to aid the Spanish Republicans against the Fascist Franco in the Spanish Civil War. Internal tensions between the right and the left, fascists and socialists, bourgeois and workers left France ill-equipped to deal with the dangers of Hitler's rapid rise to power and his impending mobilization on the opposite shores of the Rhine.

WORLD WAR II

After invading Austria, Czechoslovakia, Poland, Norway, and Denmark, Hitler's armies swept through the Ardennes in Luxembourg and blitzkrieged across Belgium and the Netherlands before entering Paris on June 13, 1940. Curators at the Louvre, sensing the inevitable **Nazi Occupation,** removed many works of art, including the Mona Lisa, and placed them in hiding. Photographs of Nazi footsoldiers and SS troops goosestepping through the Arc de Triomphe are as chilling as the images of shocked Parisians lined up along the Champs-Elysées watching the spectacle of Nazi power. The French signed a truce with the Germans ceding the northern third of the country to the Nazis and designating the lower two-thirds to a collaborating government set up in Vichy. The puppet **Vichy** government under **Maréchal Pétain** cooperated with Nazi policy, including the **deportation** of over 120,000 French and foreign Jews to **Nazi concentration camps** between 1942 and 1944.

Soldiers broke down doors on the streets surrounding the rue des Rosiers in the largely Jewish neighborhood of the Marais in the *4ème* arrondissement (see **4ème**, p. 68) and hauled Jewish families to the Vélodrome d'Hiver, an indoor winter cycling stadium. Here Jews awaited transportation to French concentration camps like **Drancy,** in the northeast industrial suburb of Paris near St-Denis, or to camps farther east in Poland and Germany (the **Mémorial de la Déportation** on the Île de la Cité honors those who perished in the Holocaust; see **Sights,** p. 58). France was plagued by many profiteering and anti-Semitic **collaborators** *(collabos)* who aided the **Gestapo.** Recently, the French government and the Roman Catholic Church in France have acknowledged some responsibility for the deportations and for their moral apathy, but the issue remains controversial.

Paris's theaters, cinemas, music-halls, and cafés continued to operate for the Nazi soldiers and officers who now flocked to the French capital for rest and relaxation. Many restaurants and entertainers who continued to serve and sing for Nazi clients, like the **Moulin Rouge, Maxim's** (see **Sights,** p. 90), **Yves Montand, Maurice Chevalier,** and **Edith Piaf,** were criticized as collaborators at the end of the war. French women who took German lovers had their heads shaved following liberation (as the film *Hiroshima Mon Amour* shows) and were forced to walk in the streets amid spitting and jeering.

Today France prefers to commemorate the brave men and women of the **Resistance,** who fought in secret against the Nazis throughout occupation. In Paris, the Resistance fighters (or *maquis*) set up headquarters below the boulevards, in the **sewers** (see **Museums,** p. 132) and **catacombs** (see **Sights,** p. 97). In London, **General Charles de Gaulle** established the **Forces Françaises Libres** (Free French Forces), declared his **Comité National Français** the government-in-exile, and broadcast inspirational messages to his countryman on the BBC (the first of which is now engraved above the **Tomb of the Unknown Soldier** under the Arc de Triomphe). On June 6, 1944, British, American and Canadian troops launched the D-Day invasion on the Normandy coast. On August 25th, after four years of occupation, Paris was free. Again, Parisian civilians and Resistance fighters danced and drank with the American, Canadian, and British soldiers. De Gaulle evaded sniper fire to attend mass at Notre-Dame and give thanks for the **Liberation of Paris.** His procession down the Champs-Elysées was met with the cheers of thousands of elated Parisians.

After the war, as monuments to French bravery were established in the Musée de l'Armée and the Musée de l'Ordre de la Libération (see **Museums,** p. 124), and as thousands of French Jewish survivors began to arrive at the main Repatriation Center in the **Gare d'Orsay** (see **Museums,** p. 119), there was a move to initiate change and avoid returning to the social and political stagnation of the pre-war years. De Gaulle promised new elections once the war's deportees and exiled citizens had been repatriated, and the country drafted a new constitution. In 1946, French women gained the right to vote, decades after English, American, Cuban, Brazilian, and Turkish suffragists.

Le Louvre

POST-COLONIAL PARIS, THE 1950S AND 60S

The **Fourth Republic** was proclaimed in 1944, but its wartime leader de Gaulle quit in 1946, unable to adapt to democratic politics. The Fourth lacked a strong executive to run the country when the legislature stalemated, and 14 years saw 25 governments. Despite these problems, the Fourth Republic presided over an economically resurgent France.

The end of the war also signaled great change in France's residual 19th-century **colonial empire.** France's defeat in 1954 at the Vietnamese liberation of **Dien Bien Phu** inspired the colonized peoples of France's other protectorates and colonies, which all gained their **independence** in rapid succession: Morocco and Tunisia in 1956, Mali, Senegal, and the Ivory Coast in 1960. But in Algeria, France drew the line in the sand when Algerian nationalists, backed by the resistance efforts of the **FLN** (Front Libération National), moved for independence. With a population of over one million French *colons*, or **pied-noirs** (literally "black feet" in French), who were either born in or had immigrated to Algeria, France was reluctant to give up a colony that it had come to regard as an extension of the French *hexagone* (see **Le Coq,** p. 26). The result was the **Algerian War** in 1962.

Les Halles

The Fourth Republic came to an end in the midst of this chaos overseas. De Gaulle was called out of retirement to deal with the crisis and voted into power by the National Assembly in 1958. Later that year, with a new **constitution** in hand, the nation declared itself the Fifth Republic. But the Algerian conflict was growing worse. Terrorist attacks in Paris by desperate members of the FLN were met by curfews for North African immigrants. At a peaceful demonstration against such restrictions in 1961, police opened fire on the largely North African crowd, killing hundreds and dumping their bodies into the Seine. Amid the violence in Paris and the war in Algeria, a 1962 referendum reluctantly granted Algeria independence. One hundred years of French colonial rule in Algeria abruptly came to an end, and the French colonial empire crumbled in its wake.

But the repercussions of French colonial exploitation continue to haunt Paris, where racial tensions today run high between middle-class French, Arab North Africans, Black West Africans, and Caribbeans, many of whom are second- and third-generation citizens.

Palais du Luxembourg

REVOLUTION OF 1968

De Gaulle's foreign policy was a success, but his conservatism brought growing domestic problems. In **May 1968,** what

PARIS IS(N'T) BURNING

As the Allied troops made their way to Paris after their successful embarkment on the beaches of Normandy, **Hitler** and the occupying Nazi forces in Paris prepared for a scorched-earth retreat. By August 23, 1944, in obedience to direct orders from Adolf Hitler, *Wehrmacht* engineers had placed mines at the base of every bridge in Paris. Despite Hitler's admiration of Napoleon's monumental tomb in the Invalides (see **Sights,** p. 82) during his smug visit in 1940, more **explosives** were crammed into the basement of the **Invalides,** the **Assemblé Nationale,** and **Nôtre-Dame.** The **Opéra** and **Madeleine** were on the list, and the **Eiffel Tower** was rigged so that it would topple and prevent the approaching Allies from crossing the Seine. A brief order from German commander **Dietrich von Choltitz** would reduce every major monument in Paris—ten centuries of history—to heaps of rubble and twisted iron. Although a loyal Nazi, the cultured general could not bring himself to destroy one of the most beautiful cities in the world. Pestered by Hitler's incessant question, "Is Paris burning?" von Choltitz stalled until the Allies had entered the city and relieved him of his burden. In 1968, he was awarded the French *Légion d'Honneur* for his bravery in the face of a screaming Hitler.

started as a student protest against the university system rapidly grew into a full-scale revolt as workers went on strike in support of social reform. Frustrated by racism, sexism, capitalism, an outdated curriculum, and the threat of a reduction in the number of students allowed to matriculate, university students seized the Sorbonne. **Barricades** were erected in the **Latin Quarter** (see **5ème,** p. 73), and an all-out student revolt had begun. Students dislodged cobblestones to hurl at riot police, and their slogan, *"Sous les pierres, la plage"* ("Under the stones lies the beach"), symbolized the freedom of shifting sand that lay beneath the rock-hard bureaucracy of French institutions. The situation escalated for several weeks. Police used tear gas and clubs to storm the barricades, while students fought back by throwing Molotov cocktails and lighting cars on fire. When 10 million state workers went on strike, paralyzing the country in support of the students, the government deployed tank and commando units into the city.

The Parisian university system was almost immediately decentralized, with various campuses scattered throughout the city and the nation so that student power could never again come together so explosively as it had in 1968. The National Assembly was dissolved and things looked to be heading for revolution yet again, averted only when fresh elections returned the Gaullists to power. However, the aging General had lost his magic touch, and he resigned following a referendum defeat in 1969.

THE 80S, 90S, AND PARIS TODAY: LA HAINE

Four political parties have dominated the French political scene since de Gaulle's resignation in 1969. On the (moderate) right are two parties formed when de Gaulle's old allies split in 1974: the **Union pour la Démocratie Française (UDF),** led by **Valéry Giscard d'Estaing,** and the **Rassemblement pour la République (RPR),** led by **Jacques Chirac.** On the left is the **Parti Socialiste (PS),** in power through the 1980s under **François Mitterrand,** and the **Parti Communiste Français (PCF),** with holds few seats and little political power.

After de Gaulle's exit, many feared the Fifth Republic's collapse. It has endured, but with change. De Gaulle's Prime Minister, **Georges Pompidou,** won the presidency, held a *laissez-faire* position toward business and a less assertive foreign policy than de Gaulle. In 1974, Pompidou died suddenly, and his successor was conservative **Valéry Giscard d'Estaing.** D'Estaing's term saw the construction of the **Centre Pompidou** (see **Museums,** p. 122), a center for the arts incorporating galleries and performance space. D'Estaing carried on de Gaulle's legacy by concentrating on economic development and strengthening French presence in international affairs.

In 1981, Socialist **François Mitterrand** took over the presidency and the Socialists gained a majority in the Assemblée Nationale. Within weeks they had raised the minimum wage and added a fifth week to the French worker's annual vacation. The political collapse of the Left during Mitterand's presidency forced him to compromise with the right. Mitterrand began his term with widespread nationalization, but the international climate could not support a socialist economy. In the wake of the 1983 recession, the Socialists met with serious losses in the **1986 parliamentary elections.** The right gained control of parliament, and Mitterrand had to appoint the conservative **Jacques Chirac** as Prime Minister.

At the same time, the **far right** began to flourish under the leadership of **Jean-Marie Le Pen.** He formed the **Front National (FN)** on an anti-immigration platform. The dissolution of France's colonial empire and healthy post-war economy led to the development of a new working class from North Africa and other former colonies. Le Pen was able to capitalize on racism toward these immigrants that is often phrased—euphemistically—as cultural difference. In the 1986 parliamentary elections, the FN picked up 10% of the vote by blaming France's woes (unemployment in particular) on immigrants and foreigners.

Meanwhile, in an unprecedented power-sharing relationship known as "cohabitation," Mitterrand withdrew to control foreign affairs, allowing Chirac to assume domestic power. Chirac privatized many industries, but a large-scale transport strike and widespread terrorism hurt the right, allowing Mitterrand to win a second term in 1988.

The Socialists recovered in the 1988 elections, giving Mitterrand another term (and a victory over Chirac). He proceeded to run a series of unpopular Socialist governments, one led briefly by **Edith Cresson,** France's first woman Prime Minister.

Mitterrand's **Grands Projets** (see **Architecture,** p. 43) transformed the architectural landscape of Paris with grand millennial style. Seeking immortality in stone, steel, concrete, and inspired by Giscard d'Estaing's **Centre Pompidou** (see **Museums,** p. 122); Mitterrand was responsible for the **Musée d'Orsay** (see p. 119), **Parc de la Villette** (see **Museums,** p. 126) the **Institut du Monde Arabe** (see **5ème,** p. 73), the **Louvre Pyramid,** the **Opéra de la Bastille** (see **12ème,** p. 94), the **Grande Arche de la Defénse** (see **Sights,** p. 112), and the new **Bibliothèque de France.** Although expensive and at times as controversial as the Eiffel Tower was in 1889, Mitterrand's vision for a 21st century Paris has produced some of the city's most breathtaking and experimental new architecture. Mitterrand's other great legacy was his Socialist project to decentralize financial and political power from Paris to local governments outside the Île-de-France. But the people were more concerned with scandals involving Mitterrand's ministers than his grandiose plans. In the mid-90s, Mitterrand revealed two startling facts. First, he had collaborated with the Vichy government in WWII before joining the Resistance. Second, he had been seriously ill with cancer since the beginning of his presidency.

In 1995, Mitterrand chose not to run again because of his failing health, and Jacques Chirac was elected president. With unemployment at 12.2% at the time of the election, Chirac faced a difficult year. The crisis ended in a prolonged **Winter Strike** by students, bus drivers, subway operators, electricians, and postmen, who protested against budget and benefit cuts proposed by Chirac and his unpopular Prime Minister, **Alain Juppé.** For weeks, Paris was paralyzed. Stores kept reduced hours, mail delivery came to a halt, and occasional blackouts and traffic jams plagued the city. Despite hardships, many Parisians were glad to see the spirit of 1968 still alive and to rediscover their neighbors, local cafés, and corner markets while grounded in their neighborhoods by the transport strikes. France moved slowly into 1996, recovering from the strike and mourning François Mitterrand, who died in early January. Later that year, Chirac was denounced around the globe for conducting underground **nuclear weapons tests** in the **South Pacific.**

The ascendancy of the right was short-lived; in 1997, Chirac dissolved the parliament, but elections reinstated a Socialist government. Chirac was forced to accept his one-time presidential rival **Lionel Jospin,** head of the Socialist majority, as Prime Minister in 1998. Although Chirac will remain in office until 2002, the left is firmly in control of France. Chirac's Gaullist **RPR** is the dominant conservative party, with Jospin's **PS** leading the socialist left. Anti-immigrant sentiment escalated in 1993 when Interior Minister Charles Pasqua proposed "zero immigration" and initiated the **"Law Pasqua,"** which gave police greater freedom to interrogate immigrants in France. A recent fragmentation of the far right has left two different parties competing for the extremist vote.

AN AFFAIR TO REMEMBER

Mitterrand broke so many hearts during his lifetime that speculation is rife about who wrote the anonymous 1998 novel about an affair with Monsieur le Président, *Un ami d'autrefois (A Former Friend)*. Attention focused initially on literary figures such as Françoise Sagan and Francoise Giroud. They have now been eclipsed by the actress Berangere Dautun, who claims the novel is based on an affair conducted by her late mother-in-law, Odette Dautun. One French political commentator said: "If all Mitterrand's former mistresses start writing books, then it's a jolly good thing he commissioned the *très grand bibliotheque* (the new national library in Paris)." The most enduring testament to Mitterrand's extramarital affairs is his illegitimate daughter, Mazarine, the fruit of his passion for Anne Pingeot, a museum curator. It was only in 1994, a year before his term ended, that M. Mitterrand appeared with his daughter. Photographs in Paris-Match magazine revealed what the media had known for years, that Mlle Pingeot lived with the President's family in the Elysée Palace. Mazarine Pingeot has stirred bitter controversy by going public to promote her first novel as a way of finally coming to grips with her own identity. The French response? Nobody's perfect. Not even the President.

One of the most important challenges in the 80s and 90s has been the question of European integration. Despite France's support of the creation of the **European Economic Community (EEC)** in 1957, the idea of a unified Europe has met considerable resistance. Since the inception of the 1991 **Maastricht Treaty,** which significantly strengthened economic integration by expanding the 13-nation EEC to the **European Union (EU),** the French have manifested fear of a loss of French national character and autonomy. Hoping that a united Europe would strengthen cooperation between France and Germany, Mitterrand led the campaign for a "Oui" vote in France's 1992 referendum on the treaty. This position lost him prestige; the referendum scraped past with a 51% approval rating. The **Schengen agreement** of 1995 created a six-nation zone without border controls. 1999 saw the extension of this zone to the entire E.U. (barring the UK, Ireland, and Denmark), as well as the birth of the European single currency, the **Euro.**

The good news is that immigrants, their children, and grandchildren are changing the face of France. Arabic expressions like *kif-kif* ("it's all the same") have become accepted in spoken French, black performers like MC Solaar and Teri Moïse top the French music charts, and multi-ethnic restaurants have changed the way Paris thinks about French cuisine. To get an idea of the racial climate in France, see **Post-Colonial Francophone Literature** (p. 39), **Post-Colonial Paris** (p. 33) **Film** (p. 45), or Mathieu Kassovitz's films *La Haine* and *Café Au Lait.*

LITERATURE

HUMANISM AND THE RENAISSANCE

The Renaissance in France produced literary texts that challenged Medieval notions of courtly love and Christian thought. Inspired by Boccaccio's *Decameron* and the Italian Renaissance, **Marguerite de Navarre's** *Héptaméron* used pilgrim tales to explore the innovative ideas of **Humanism. Rabelais's** novels *Gargantua* and *Pantagruel* were serial bestsellers in their time and explored Europe from giants' point of view. **Montaigne's** *Essais* pushed the boundaries of intellectual thought. The love poems of **Ronsard** and **Du Bellay,** the memoirs of **Marguerite de Valois,** and the works of **Louise Labé** contributed to the Renaissance's spirit of optimism and change.

CLASSICISM AND RATIONALISM

The founding of the **Académie Française** in 1635 assembled 40 men to regulate and codify French literature and language. The Académie has since acted as the church of French letters (see **Sights,** p. 79).

But 17th-century French literature was not all as strict as the Académie. French philosophers reacted to the mushy musings of humanists with **Rationalism,** a school of thought that championed logic and order. Map-lover **René Descartes** placed his trust in his own good sense, and set out to understand the world. In his 1637 *Discourse on Method*, Descartes proved his own existence with the catchy deduction, "I think, therefore I am." As the father of analytical geometry, Descartes also introduced the notation '*x*' for an unknown quantity. The equally diverse genius **Blaise Pascal** misspent his youth inventing the mechanical calculator and the science of probabilities. He later became a devotee of Jansenism, a Catholic reform movement that railed against the worldliness of the Jesuit-dominated Church. Retiring from public life, he expounded the virtues of solitude in his best-known work, *Pensées* (1658). **La Fontaine's** *Fables* and **Charles Perrault's** *Contes de ma mère l'oye* (Fairy Tales of Mother Goose) explored right and wrong in more didactic and animalistic ways. **Molière,** the era's comic relief, satirized the social pretensions of his age. Molière's actors formed the basis for the **Comédie Française,** the world's oldest national theatre company; it still produces the definitive versions of French classics at its theatre in Paris (see **Arts and Entertainment,** p. 150).

THE ENLIGHTENMENT

The Enlightenment in France was informed by advances in the sciences, aimed at the promotion of reason and tolerance in an often backward and bigoted world. The Bible of the Enlightenment philosophers was **Denis Diderot** and **Jean D'Alembert's** *Encylopedie* (1752-1780), a record of the entire body of human knowledge with entries by the philosophes themselves. This staggeringly modest corpus included entries by such luminaries as Jean-Jacques Rousseau and **Voltaire. François Marie Arouet** (aka Voltaire) illuminated the century with his insistence on liberty and tolerance. Voltaire is best known for his satire **Candide** (1758), a refutation of the claim that "all is for the best in the best of all possible worlds." Satire was also the pet medium of playwright **Beaumarchais,** whose incendiary comic masterpieces **Le Barbier de Seville** (1775) and **Le Mariage de Figaro** (1784) were banned by Louis XVI. Voltaire was all smiles and smooches compared to **Jean-Jacques Rousseau** who, something of a misfit, advocated a complete overhaul of society instead of happily satirizing it away. In his **Confessions** (1766-1769) and in novels like **Mile** (1762) and **Julie, ou La Nouvelle Heloise** (1761), Rousseau determines that leaving society behind is better than living in corrupt society.

LITERATURE SINCE THE ENLIGHTENMENT, OR THE LAND OF THE "ISM"

Q: What . . . uh, is, em . . . an "ism"?
A: An "ism" is a means of generalizing about the work of several authors of a particular period. These authors endure precisely because they defeat such categorization, but we like to categorize them anyway, because it's useful. And so much fun.

Romanticism \romantic-ism\ n 1. An artistic reaction to the tumultuous changes in 19th-century French government and society. 2. A mode of expression that highlights human sentiment over human reason. 3. A movement dominated by **Victor Hugo**, and his novels *The Hunchback of Notre-Dame* (1831) and *Les Misérables* (1862).

Realism \real-ism\ n 1. The Realist mode inspired novelists who meant to accurately record contemporary reality by focusing on detailed description. 2. **Honor de Balzac**'s *La Comédie humaine* renders an entire generation of French society. In *La Ville noire* (1860), **Georges Sand** firmly established herself as a Realist with a closely researched account of working-class life. **Gustave Flaubert**'s masterpiece *Madame Bovary*(1857) is the subtly rendered story of Emma Bovary, a woman tragically frustrated by her life and loves. 3. Of this period but not of the Realist school (though he told it like it is), Charles **Baudelaire** rocked Paris with his evil *Les Fleurs du mal* (1857), trying to transcend everyday life with a little help from our friends, prostitutes, and wine.

Symbolism \symbol-ism\ n 1. A movement that reacted against stale conventions and used new techniques to capture moments of perception. Led by poets **Stephane Mallarmé** and **Paul Verlaine,** the movement made modern poetry, largely through the work of precocious **Arthur Rimbaud.**

VILLON EN VILLE

Paris's first major poet was the great, the bawdy, the mysterious Francois Villon (1431-?), who wrote a number of *balades* from the point of view of aging prostitutes, as well as a will in verse, *Le Grand Testament*. Excess was never enough for Monsieur Villon, who theived, whored, drank himself silly, and spent too much time in prison. He narrowly escaped getting hanged in 1463. Leaving Paris soon after this incident (even if he liked death, he did not like to die), Villon disapeared, although one poem remains in which he describes his close encounter with the gallows. Behold one of the earliest mentions of Paris in poetry:

Quatraine

Je suis François, dont il me poise,
Né de Paris emprès Pontoise,
Et de la corde d'une toise
Saura mon col que mon cul poise.

[I'm Francois, that's what they
accuse me of,
Born in Paris near Pontoise,
And by the noose of a gallows,
My neck shall be no more than
what my ass can pull.]

Naturalism \natural-ism\ SYN. Emile Zola. 1. The late 19th century witnessed an explosion of novels, thanks in part to advances in printing technology and the *roman-feuilleton*, or serialized novel. **Zola** took full advantage of these developments, gaining a huge readership. Zola was also one of France's first 'public intellectuals,' taking a strong stance on the Dreyfus Affair (see **History**, p. 30) with his famous *J'accuse* ("Yeah I'm pointing at you") letter to the French government. 2. Also associated with the Naturalist movement (though utterly different from Zola) was **Guy de Maupassant,** most famous for *Bel-Ami* (1885), *Pierre et Jean* (1888), and a caustic sense of irony.

Surrealism \surreal-ism\ n 1. ??? 2. Before the Surrealists came other authors interested in issues of narrative structure and sexuality. With his seven-volume *A la Recherche du temps perdu* (In Search of Lost Time, 1913-1927), **Marcel Proust** called into question turn-of-the-century decadence and standards of narrative structure. Meanwhile, **André Gide** and **Colette** explored their sexual proclivities: Gide's homoerotic novels and Colette's sensual works inspired later 20th-century feminist and homoerotic writing. 3. Surrealists themselves, under the leadership of **André Breton,** shared Freud's obsession with the unconscious. **Guillaume Apollinaire's** visual poems used different fonts to create a pictorial poetry.

Existentialism \existential-ism\ n 1. **Jean-Paul Sartre's** Existentialism held that life itself was meaningless; only by committing yourself to a cause could existence take on a purpose. Sartre committed his ideas to the stage and dominated French theater in the 1940's and 1950's. Satre's *Being and Nothingness* (1943) declared that our lives are ruled by the absurd. He also wrote four novels but abandoned the medium to his companion **Simone de Beauvoir**. Most famous for *The Second Sex* (1949), de Beauvoir called into question the myth of femininity. **Albert Camus'**s Existentialism was marked by morality; commitment to an ideal was not enough if it was unfair to others. Camus's play *Caligula* (1945) was an early example of **Anti-Theater**, whose adherents laid bare the strangeness of life and exposed the inadequacies of language.

Feminism \femin-ism\ n 1. Numerous French *femmes-écrivains* have explored femininity and gender identity. Of particular import are **Marguerite Duras** (*L'Amant, The Lover,* 1984), **Marie Cardinal** (*Les Mots pour le dire*, 1975), **Christine Rochefort** (*Les Stances ... Sophie*, 1963), **Hélène Cixous** (*Le Rire de la Méduse*, 1975), **Luce Irigaray** (*Ce Sexe Qui n'en est Pas Un*, 1977), and **Marguerite Yourcenar** (*Le Coup de Grace*, 1957). The 1974 establishment of the publishing house **Editions des Femmes** ensured that French women writers would continue to have a means of expressing themselves in print.

LA PRÉSENCE AFRICAINE

Beginning in Paris in the 1920s with the foundation of the **Négritude** movement by African and Antilles intellectuals **Aimé Césaire** (Martinique) and **Léopold Sédar**

Senghor (Senegal), Francophone literature began to flourish. Césaire's *Cahiers d'un retour au pays natale* and Senghor's *Anthologie de la poésie nègre et malgache* attempted to define a shared history and identity among black peoples in Africa, the Caribbean, the Antilles, and North America. Their work and the subsequent founding of the press **Présence Africaine** (see **Shopping,** p. 146) inspired generations of Francophone intellectuals on both sides of the Atlantic, the most celebrated of whom is **Franz Fanon** *(Les Damnées de la Terre)*.

LATE 20TH CENTURY

Experimentation with narrative and perspective in the 50s and 60s led to the **nouveau roman** (the new novel), which abandoned conventional narrative techniques for new ones, such as *sous conversation* (what people think as they converse). One of its best known exponents is **Alain Robbe-Grillet** *(Projet pour une révolution à New York)*.

From the 70s to the 90s, criticism, theory, and philosophy have exerted a great influence over intellectual life in France. In the 60s, as Sartre's cigarette smoke ceased to cloud up cafés and classrooms, the **postmodernists** moved in. Among the greatest of these thinkers are historical "archaeologist" **Michel Foucault,** thinker turned sci-fi fan **Jean Baudrillard,** and more recently the feminist body Hélène Cixous. Theory was profoundly affected by **deconstruction**, a practice founded by masterful **Jacques Derrida,** whereby an author's text is rigorously examined for unconscious writing habits. To many, these intellectuals represent the most important thinkers in the post-war world.

The 80s and 90s have also seen the emergence of new writers in France such as **Annie Ernaux** and **Hervé Guibert,** as well as a growing number of works by authors of North African origin, such as **Mehdi Charef's** *Le thé au harem d'Archi Ahmed* (1983). Late 20th-century political conflicts over immigrants, racism, and xenophobia have renewed interest in post-colonial Francophone literatures.

FINE ARTS

MEDIEVAL MASTERPIECES

Much of Paris's surviving **medieval art** would instruct one on religious themes: as the average 12th-and 13th-century churchgoer was illiterate, brilliant stained glass and intricate stone facades, like those at **Chartres** (see **Daytripping,** p. 208), **Sainte-Chapelle,** and **Notre-Dame** (see **Sights** p. 55), had to serve as very large reproductions of the Bible. Monastic industry brought the art of illumination to its height, as monks added ornate illustrations to manuscripts. The Cluny, the Musée Marmottan (see **Museums,** p. 134), and the Chantilly Museum display manuscripts, including Chantilly's **Très Riches Heures du Duc de Berry,** an illuminated prayer book whose relatistic portrayal of peasants ushered in the **Northern Renaissance.**

THE RENAISSANCE

Inspired by the painting, sculpture, and architecture of the **Italian Renaissance,** 16th-century France imported its styles from Italy. François I had viewed such re-born art during his Italian campaigns, and when he inherited France in 1515, he decided the time had come to put France, artistically, on the map. The king implored friends in Italy to send him works by Titian and Bronzino. He also imported the artists themselves to create **Fontainebleau** (see **Daytripping,** p. 206). **Leonardo da Vinci** appeared soon after with the **Mona Lisa** (*La Jaconde;* see **Ms. Mona's Wild Ride,** p. 118) smilingly in tow as a gift to the French monarch at the Louvre (see **Museums,** p. 115). Rosso and Francesco Primaticcio arrived in France in the 1530's to introduce the French to Italian Mannerist techniques, which were soon adopted by the **Ecole de Fontainbleau.**

In the 17th century under Louis XIV, the **Baroque** style, which seduced the senses with grandeur, richness of design and materials, and good old-fashioned excess, swept up from Italy to France. The architecture of **Versailles** (see **Daytripping,** p. 199) benefitted from this Italian infusion. The palace, first built over a period of three years from 1631-1634, was extravagantly reimagined by Louis XIV during the second half of the century. But the Baroque period had room for realism, even as it indulged a monarch's penchant for gilt and high-heels—the brothers **Le Nain** (who worked together on all their canvases) and **Georges de La Tour** (1593-1652) produced canvases of everyday life.

Baroque exuberance was subdued by the more serious and classical works of **Nicolas Poussin** (1694-1665). Poussin believed that reason should be the guiding principle of art, and the French **Académie Royale,** founded in 1648, came to value his style above so much that subsequent French painters had to contend with his precepts. Under director **Charles le Brun** (1619-1690), the Academy became the sole arbiter of taste in matters artistic, holding annual **Salons,** "official" art exhibitions held in vacant halls of the Louvre.

The early-18th century brought on the **Rococo** style. Its asymmetric curves and profusion of ornamentation are more successful when kept in the closet, in **Louis XV** interior design, than in architecture. Catering to the tastes of the nobility, **Antoine Watteau** (1684-1721) painted the *fêtes* and secret *rendez-vous* of the aristocracy, and **François Boucher** (1703-1770) painted landscapes and scenes from courtly life. Napoleon I's reign saw the emergence of **Neoclassicism** as the emperor tried to model his empire, and his purple capes, on the Roman version. **Jacques-Louis David** (1748-1825) created giant canvases on Classical themes and facilitated the emergence of **Empire style** in fine and decorative art, which exploited Greek and Roman iconography.

CLASSICAL AND ROMANTIC SCHOOLS

The French Revolution inspired painters to create heroic depictions of scenes from their own time. Following David, and encouraged by the deep pockets of Napoleon, painters created large, dramatic pictures, often of the emperor as Romantic hero and god, all rolled into one *petit* package. But after Napoleon's fall, few artists painted nationalistic *tableaux*. One exception was **Theodore Géricault** (1791-1824), whose *Raft of the Medusa* (1819) can be seen in the Louvre (see **Museums,** p. 115).

Nineteenth century France was ready to settle into respectable, bourgeois ways after the troubling years of France's shift from Republic to Empire. The paintings of **Eugène Delacroix** (1798-1863) were a shock to the salons of the 1820s and 1830s. *The Massacre at Chios* (1824) and *The Death of Sardanapalus* (1827; see **Museums**, p. 120) both display an extraordinary sense of color, as well as an affection for melodrama. Delacroix went on to do a series of "Moroccan" paintings, and he soon shared this orientalist territory with another painter, **Jean-August-Dominique Ingres** (1780-1867). Ingres' most famous painting of Eastern inclination is the nearly liquid reclining nude, *La Grande Odalisque*. Another influential Romantic, **Paul Delaroche** (1797-1859) created charged narratives on large canvases. Delaroche's most famous work is *La jeune Martyre* (*The Young Martyr*, 1855).

IMPRESSIONISM

The late-19th and early-20th century saw the reinvention of painting in France: first, a shift of subject matter to everyday life, and then a radical change in technique. **Impressionism** found its beginnings in the mid-19th century with **Théodore Rousseau** (1812-1867) and **Jean-François Millet** (1814-1875) who were leaders of the **Ecole de Barbizon**, a group of artists who painted nature for its own sake. Landscape painting capturing a "slice of life" paved the way for **Realism**. The Realists were led by **Gustave Courbet** (1819-1877) who focused on everyday subjects but portrayed them larger-than-life on huge canvases. **Edouard Manet** (1832-1883) facilitated the transition from the Realism of Courbet to what we now consider **Impressionism,** as in the 1860's, he began to shift the focus of his work to color and texture. Perspective, used for the past five centuries in European art to create the appearance of three-dimensions, was replaced by attention to composition of color. Manet's *Déjeuner sur l'herbe* (Meal on the grass, 1863) (see **Museums**, p. 121) was refused by the Salon of 1863 due to its naughty Naked Lunch theme (two suited men and a naked woman are shown picnicking in the forest) and revolutionary technique; it was later shown at the Salon des Refusés, along with 7000 other rejected salon works.

By the late 1860's Manet's new aesthetic had set the stage for **Claude Monet** (1840-1926), **Camille Pissarro** (1830-1903), and **Pierre-Auguste Renoir** (1841-1919) who began to further explore Impressionist techniques. They strove to attain a sense of immediacy; colors were used to capture visual impressions as they appeared to the eye, and light became subject-matter. In 1874, these groundbreaking artists had their first group exhibition. A critic writing at the time snidely labeled the group "Impressionists." The artists themselves found the label accurate, as they were in fact trying to express visual impressions. The Impressionists' show became an annual event for the next seven years. In the late 1880's, the members of the group inspired **Edgar Degas** (1834-1917), **Gustave Caillebotte** (1848-1894), **Berthe Morisot** (1841-1895), **Henri Fantin-Latour** (1836-1904) and *Water Lilies* by Monet in the early 1900's (see **Museums**, p. 121).

The **Post-Impressionists,** or Neo-Impressionists,were loners. **Paul Cézanne** (1839-1906) painted landscapes using an early Cubist technique in isolation at Aix-en-Provence; **Paul Gauguin** (1848-1903) took up residence in Tahiti where he painted in sensuous, colonial color; while **Vincent van Gogh** (1853-1890), projected his emotions onto the countryside at Arles and, in solitude, removed his ear. **Georges Seurat** (1859-1891) revealed his **Pointillist** technique at the Salon des Indépendants of 1884. The sculptor **Auguste Rodin** (1840-1917) focused on energetic, muscular shaping of bronze (see **Museums,** p. 123).

As the 19th century drew to a close, Bohemia had moved its center to the cabarets and cafés of Montmartre (see **Sights,** p. 101), a refuge from the modern city below. **Henri de Toulouse-Lautrec** (1864-1901) captured the spirit of the Belle Epoque in vibrant silkscreen posters that covered Paris as well as in his paintings of brothels, circuses, and can-can cabarets. **Art Nouveau** transformed architecture, furniture, lamps, jewelry, fashion, and even the entrances to the Paris Métro (see the **Museums**, p. 122). Everything was in place, ready to be swept of its feet by the modernism of the 20th century.

TWENTIETH CENTURY

Pablo Picasso, one most prolific artists of the 20th century (he started drawing at the age of ten and continued working up until his death at the age of 86), first arrived in Paris from Spain in 1900 and made a reputation for himself with such collectors as **Gertrude Stein. Cubism** was a radical movement developed by Picasso and his friend **Georges Braque** (1882-1963), which built on Cézanne's geometric approach and emphasised an object's form by showing all its sides at once. The word "Cubism" was coined (cubed?) by **Henri Matisse** (1869-1964) as he described one of Braque's landscapes. Matisse himself moved to squeezing paint from the tube directly onto canvas. This agressive style earned the name **Fauvism** (from *fauves*, wild animals) and characterizes Matisse's mature works, like *The Dance* (1931-32; see **Museums**, p. 119).

Marcel Duchamp (1887-1968) put Cubism in motion with his *Nude Descending a Staircase* (1912). **Marc Chagall** (1887-1985) moved to Paris from Russia and found himself in La Ruche or "The Beehive" (an artists' colony on the outskirts of Montmartre) with artists like **Fernand Léger** (1881-1955) and **Jacques Lipchitz** (1891-1973). The disillusionment that pervaded Europe after WWI was Duchamp's dropcloth, as he led the **Dada** movement in Paris. The production of "non-art" was for Dadaists a rejection of artistic conventions and traditions. This culminated in the exhibition of Duchamp's *La Fontaine* (The Fountain, 1917), a urinal that Duchamp turned upside-down.

Surrealism's goal was a union of dream and fantasy with the everyday, rational world in "an absolute reality, a surreality," according to poet and leader of the movement, **André Breton**. The bowler-hatted men of **René Magritte** (1898-1967), the dreamscapes of **Joan Miró** (1893-1983), the textures and patterns of **Max Ernst** (1891-1976), and **Salvador Dalí's** (1904-1989) melting time-pieces and other imagery arose from time spent in Paris .

During the 30s, photographers like **Georges Brassaï** (1889-1984), **André Kertész** (1894-1985) and **Henri Cartier-Bresson** began using small cameras to record the streets and quartiers of Paris in black and white. But the arrival of World War II forced many artists working in Paris at the time across the continent or the ocean. The Nazi advance on Paris forced all of the Louvre's treasures into basements. On May 27, 1943, hundreds of "degenerate" paintings by Picasso, Ernst, Klee, Léger, and Miro were destroyed in a bonfire in the garden of the Jeu de Paume (see **Museums,** p. 130). Tens of thousands of masterpieces

EXPATRIATE LITERATURE

After WWI, a "lost generation" of writers round their way to Paris from Ireland, England, and America— **James Joyce, Ernest Hemingway, Ford Maddox Ford, Ezra Pound, Gertrude Stein,** and **F. Scott Fitzgerald** among them. These expatriates sought a freedom in Paris they could not find at home; as Gertrude Stein liked to say, "America is my country, but Paris is my hometown."

To read about Paris through smiling Irish—or otherwise Anglo—eyes, check the following list: Charles Dickens's **Tale of Two Cities,** Henry James's **The Ambassadors** and **The American,** Ernest Hemingway's **A Moveable Feast,** James Baldwin's **Giovanni's Room,** Henry Miller's **Tropic of Cancer,** Anaïs Nin's **Journals,** Gertrude Stein's **Autobiography of Alice B. Toklas,** Somerset Maugham's **The Moon and Sixpence,** and George Orwell's **Down and Out in Paris and London** are all expatriot classics. Patrick Suskin's big hit, **Perfume: The Story of a Murderer**, tells the tale of an olfactorily well-endowed killer. Art Buchwald's memoirs, **I'll Always Have Paris** and **Leaving Home** recount stories of post-WWII Paris after Liberation. And a singularly elegant expatriate yarn or two can be found in Edmund White and Hubert Sorin's **Our Paris: Sketches from Memory.**

belonging to Jewish collectors were appropriated and shipped to Germany, and only recently have serious inquiries into stolen art been made.

Later 20th-century experiments in photography, installation art, video, and sculpture can be seen in the collections and temporary exhibitions of the **Centre Pompidou** and the **Fondation Cartier pour l'Art Contermporain** (see **Museums,** p. 122).

ARCHITECTURE

Paris was conquered by Julius Caesar in 52 BC The **Romans** rebuilt Paris in the image of their own city. In the 17th century **Louis XIII** and **Louis XIV** used architecture as a screen on which to project royal authority. Not surprisingly, destruction outweighed construction during the French Revolution. Most of its architectural achievements were temporary: an artificial mountain on the Champ de Mars, a cardboard interior for Notre-Dame, and sundry plaster statues of Liberty. More lasting were defacements of churches and kings' statues. The 19th century was a prosperous time for Parisian architecture. Industrialization brought on innovations in the use of **glass and iron.** Commissioned by Napoleon III to modernize the city, city planner **Baron Georges Haussmann** tore long, straight boulevards through the tangled, narrow alleys of old Paris, creating a unified network of **grands boulevards.** But unchecked growth continued to swamp improvements, and much of Paris was a congested slum. In the early part of the 20th century, architects began to focus on new building materials, such as **concrete**. During the postwar years, the city expanded into its surroundings, continuing a trend that dates back to the emergence of working-class districts *(faubourgs)* in the late 18th century. During the 50s and 60s, the government sponsored housing developments for a ring of "new towns" surrounding Paris. As Paris enters the 21st century, new projects such as the renovation of the **Centre Pompidou** will continue to transform the capital.

GLOSSARY

Art Deco (*Art Decoratif*) 1920's geometric stylings.

Art Moderne Streamlined 1930's chrome and stucco architecture.

Art Nouveau The classic example is the viney *métro* entrance; 1890's trend.

Auguste, King Philippe made Paris into a defensive capital, responding to regular raids by beginning work on the fortress of the **Louvre** in 1190 and building the first walls around the city. The 12th century also saw the basic segregation that still characterizes the city's geography: Philippe Auguste's construction established political and ecclesiastical institutions on the **Île de la Cité,** academic ones on the **Left Bank,** and commercial ones on the **Right Bank.**

Baroque architecture was introduced from Italy by Louis XIII's mother, **Marie de Medici,** who commissioned the **Palais de Luxembourg** (1615; p. 77), but it reached its peak with the château of **Vaux-le-Vicomte** (1657; p. 212), which brought architect Louis **Le Vau**, artist Charles **Le Brun** and landscaper Louis **Le Nôtre** together for the first time.

Belle Epoque Interior design around 1900.

Calcaire Limestone.

Cathedral The church of a bishop. A cathedral is composed of the **Ambulatory,** a walkway; the **Apse,** the rounded east end-wall; the **Nave,** the roof, whose ribbed beams of which make it look like a ship (from Latin, *navis*); the **Transept,** the crossing arms; and the **Chevet,** the east end of the cathedral with its radiating chapels.

Château Before the 15th century, a fortress; thereafter, a country estate.

Classicism refers to architecture which imitates that of Ancient Rome and Greece. The ultimate expression of 19th-century classicism is to be found in Charles Garnier's Paris **Opéra** (1862-1875; p. 89), a vast, ornate, stone fantasy.

Cloître A cloister.

Coupole A small dome.

Eiffel, Gustave In 1876, Gustave Eiffel and architect Louis-Auguste Boileau designed a new building for Au Bon Marché, the world's first department store, creating large, skylit interior spaces in which to display merchandise. Nicknamed the 'magician of iron', Eiffel is most famous for the star of the Universal Exhibition of 1889, a certain tower that bears his name (see **Sights,** p. 81). Twice as tall as any other building in the world at the time, its framework construction excited violent passions: most Parisians thought it unspeakably ugly, not to mention unstable. Truly a monumental figure, Eiffel also designed the internal structure of the Statue of Liberty.

Empire Architecture and design from 1804-1814, the reign of Napoleon I.

Entresol The floor between the *rez de chausée* (ground floor) and the first floor.

Faubourg The nearer suburbs of Paris, between the central city and the *banlieue*, the former site of Charles V's city walls.

Flying Buttresses exterior supports which leap from the side-aisles to support the nave, allowed medieval cathedral ceilings to soar up to 15 meters into the air. The nave itself was constructed of a series of ribbed vaults, stronger and higher than the Romanesque counterpart, the barrel vault. See **Notre-Dame,** p. 55.

Futurism's most prominent member was Swiss citizen **Charles-Edouard Janneret**, who built a forward-looking Paris under the name, **Le Corbusier** from the 1930's until his death in 1965.

Gothic Increasing prosperity and a changing perception of religion led to the development of the Gothic style in the 12th century. Designing cathedrals to the glory of a "God of Light," rather than the punishing God of the Romanesque period, master builders created a "weightless" style of architecture.

Grands Projets President Mitterrand's 15-billion-franc *Grands Projets* has inspired a series of modern monuments at the dawn of the century (see p. 34). The old marketplace of **Les Halles,** now a subterranean shopping mall, was torn down, and the *quais* of the Left Bank, like those of the Right, were almost converted into expressways—acts that have inspired popular calls for conservatism. The new glass fronted **Opéra de Paris**, completed in 1989 and designed by Charles Ott as a post-modern addition to the historic pl. de la Bastille (see **Sights**, p. 93), has replaced Garnier's 19th century creation both musically and visually.

Haussmann, Georges Although traces of the past abound, today's Paris was virtually remade under Haussmann. From 1852 to 1870, Haussmann transformed Paris from an intimate medieval city to a centralized modern metropolis. Commissioned by Napoleon III, Haussmann tore long, straight boulevards through the tangled, narrow alleys of old Paris, creating a unified network of **grands boulevards.** These avenues were designed not only to increase circulation of goods and people but also to make Paris a work of art, reflecting the elegance of Second Empire style. Not incidentally, the wide avenues also impeded insurrection, limiting once and for all the effectiveness of street barricades. Haussmann redesigned the **Bois de Boulogne** (see **Sights,** p. 107) and the **Bois de Vincennes** (see **Sights,** p. 110), as well as the **Parc des Buttes de Chaumont** (see **Sights,** p. 104). The city doubled its area when Haussmann shifted the boundaries of the 20 existing *quartiers* into **20 arrondissements** (see **Orientation,** p. 11). Five of Paris's seven hills were leveled; only **Montmartre** and the **Montagne Ste-Geneviève** remain.

Henri IV had plans; after fighting for almost four years to get into Paris, he was not about to leave. He changed the face of Paris, building the **Pont Neuf** and the **Place des Vosges.** He widened the roads and banned merchant overflow into the streets to accommodate carriages. His efforts were not quite enough; obstacles blocking the street slowed his carriage and enabled François Ravaillac to leap in and assassinate him in 1610.

HLM The 1950s initiated the construction of large housing projects or **HLMs** *(habitations à louer modéré)*, concrete monstrosities originally intended as habitable, affordable housing, but that have since become sites of poverty, violence, and racial segregation.

Neoclassicism is exemplified by Jacques-Germain Soufflot's grandiose Eglise Ste-Geneviève (1757). The Neoclassical agenda was best fulfilled in the two architectural monuments dedicated to the Empire's glory: the **Eglise de la Madeleine** (see p. 87), a giant imitation of a Greco-Roman temple and the imposing Arc de Triomphe (see p. 84).

Rayonnant The circular rose window is an example of the well-named Rayonnant style. This style appeared around 1230, when architects reached the height limit for stone vaulting and turned their attention from structural innovation to decoration. Windows became still larger and the supporting stone was carved into delicate tracery; a delectable example is the Sainte-Chapelle (finished 1248; see **Sights,** p. 58), with an almost continuous glass curtain on three sides of the chapel. From this period, Paris also gained the Basilique de St-Denis, Europe's first Gothic cathedral, just outside the city (see **Daytripping,** p. 208).

Romanesque Roman basilicas and the residential excavations in the square in front of Nôtre-Dame blossomed into the massive Romanesque cathedrals of the 11th century, which are characterized by the immense walls and semicircular arches still visible at **St-Germain-des-Pres** (see **Sights**, p. 78).

ZAC project *(zone d'aménagement concerte)* plans to build a new university, sports complex, public garden, and métro in the 13*ème*, Paris's most rapidly redeveloping *arrondissement*.

MUSIC

MODERN

Music at the turn of the 20th century began a new period of intense, often abstract invention. **Claude Debussy** (1862-1918), whose style is called **Impressionist,** used tone color and non-traditional scales in his instrumental works *Prélude à l'après-midi d'un faune* (Prelude to the Afternoon of a Fawn, 1894) and *La Mer* (The Sea, 1905), as well as his opera *Pelléas et Mélisande* (1902). **Ravel's** use of Spanish rhythm betrayed his Basque origins. When a listener screamed "but he is mad!" at the 1928 premiere of his most famous work, *Boléro*, the composer retorted, "Aha! She has understood." The music of **Igor Stravinsky,** whose ballet *The Rite of Spring* caused a riot at its 1913 premiere (see p. 86), was violently dissonant and rhythmic, and began the **Modernist** movement.

Already famous for his monochromatic *Blue* paintings, in 1960 **Yves Klein** presented *The Monotone Symphony*. In this performance piece three naked models painted a wall blue with their bodies, while the artist conducted an orchestra on one note for 20 minutes. Somewhat less messy, although no less radical, composer **Pierre Boulez** (born 1925) was an adept of the **Neo-serialist** school, which uses the 12-tone system developed in the 1920s by Austrian Arnold Schoënberg. Always innovative, Boulez's work includes aleatory music, partial compositions, but his greatest influence on modern music has been as director of the **IRCAM** institute in the Pompidou Museum (see **Museums,** p. 122).

Boulez's teacher, the late **Olivier Messaien** (d. 1992) suffered from synesthesia, a sensory disorder which confuses sound and vision; different harmonies appeared to him in different colors, and this dual perception affected his composition. He was also fascinated by birdsong, as seen in *Chronochromie* (1960). Another of Messaien's students **Iannis Xenakis,** used computers to coordinate and even compose music according to mathematical techniques. His first major composition, *Metastasis* (1954), was a translation into sound of the design of the Philips Pavilion in the 1958 Brussels Exposition.

But the Parisian public has been happiest with the songs of crooner **Charles Aznavour** and the unregrettable **Edith Piaf. Jacques Brel's** and **Juliette Grecco's** popular *chansons* charmed smoky cabarets in the 1960s. Some of Paris's most famous song divas, Piaf, the Egyptian-born **Dalida,** and the Québecoise **Fabienne Thibeault** have now made way for such new *chanteuses* as **Patricia Kaas, Isabelle Boulay,** and the seductive **Mylène Farmer.**

JAZZ

France recognized the artistic integrity of jazz sooner than the United States. In the 1930s, French musicians copied the swing they heard on early Louis Armstrong sides, but the 1934 Club Hot pair of violinist **Stéphane Grapelli** and stylish Belgian-Romany guitarist **Django Reinhardt** were already innovators. After WWII, American musicians streamed into Paris. A jazz festival in 1949 brought the young **Miles Davis** across the pond for a dreamy April in Paris. Pianist **Bud Powell,** drummer **Kenny Clarke,** and others found the respect, dignity, and gigs accorded them too attractive to leave. **Duke Ellington** and others played clubs like the Left Bank hotspot, **Le Caveau de la Huchette** (see **Nightlife,** p. 196), and jazz classics helped the city's rain-slicked streets take on a saxophonic gloss.

ROCK, HIP-HOP, AND TODAY'S SCENE

In the late 50s and 60s, a unique French take on American rock emerged: the movement was termed, in a stroke of onomatopoetic genius, **yé-yé.** Teen idols like **Johnny Hallyday** and **François Hallyday** took the limelight, and youth-oriented **Salut les Copains** was the moment's rag. In the 80s a number of solid groups emerged. Look for **Téléphone, Marquis de Sade, Indochine,** or **Les Rita Mitsouki.**

In recent years, ethnic hybrids have had a huge influence on French pop music. Check out **Alabina, Karim Kacel, Cheb Kalad,** and **Mano Negra** for examples of African **raï. Techno** has not had the following in France that it's had elsewhere on the continent, but for some progressive-syntho fun, expose yourself to **Air.** Another phenomenally successful export has been the French disco house sound, with the 70s-influenced (and occasionally 70s-sampling) tunes of **Daft Punk, Bob Sinclar,** and **Cassius** burning up dance floors. Daft Punk's *Homework* album, Cassius's *1999* album, and Stardust's *Music Sounds Better With You* single are probably the best embodiment of the sound. Or just attend Respect, at Queen on Wednesday nights (see **Nightlife,** p. 191). Renowned **DJ Dimitri from Paris** combines house with touches of lounge, while the **Micronauts** and their acid house sound continue to be in demand. The Source label is one of the major underground dance music labels in France. Recent pop hits have come from groups like **Les Nubians, Les Négresses Vertes, Autour de Lucie, Dolly, Louise Attaque,** and soloists like **Axel Renoir, Etienne Daho,** and the Québecois **Jean LeLoup.** French R&B stars **Native** and **Teri Moïse** top the charts along with rap stars like **MC Solaar, Liaison Dangereuses, Manau, Passithe,** and controversial **NTM** (Nique Ta Mère) and the more recent **KDD** (Kartel Double Dentente), whose lyrics speak out against urban crime, racism, and anti-immigrant prejudice in France.

The bulk of popular music played on French radio will be familiar to anglophone travelers, despite a 1996 law requiring that **francophone music** make up 40% of radio playlists—much of that quota gets filled between 1 and 6 AM. The problem facing French music is not so much one of quality as it is of distribution; it still has a strong following in France outside the mainstream, but most of the music industry in France is in the hands of multinational corporations.

FILM

Not long after he and his brother Louis presented the world's first paid screening in a Paris café in 1895, **Auguste Lumière** remarked, "The cinema is a medium without a future." In defiance of this statement, the French strive to reveal the broadest possibilities of film. The French government subsidizes the film industry, and American studios, which dominate the French market, call this unfair. But Paris retains a vibrant film culture.

PAINT THE REVOLUTION

Jaques-Louis David was born in 1748 in Paris. Having demonstrated his talents while apprenticed to a historical painter, David enrolled at the Academie Royale de Peinture at age 18. Discouragement in school did not prevent his receipt of the Prix de Rome in 1774, which sent David to study in Italy and guaranteed him commissions in France. He returned to Paris in 1780 with the influence of Italian Classicists like Carravaggio in his pocket, and his career took off. Works like **Andromache Mourning Hector** (1784) earned him election to the prestigious Academie Royale, a position from which David could roll with the punches of his time and avoid forced separation from his head. Through the *ancien regime,* the French Revolution, and Napoleon's Empire, David painted with politics. From his pre-revolutionary paintings (**The Tennis Court Oath,** 1791), to his neo-classical revolutionary paintings (**The Oath of the Horatii,** 1784, **The Death of Socrates,** 1787, and **The Death of Marat**, 1793) that praise the Republican virtues of the Revolution using Greek and Roman themes (see **Musée du Louvre, p. 115**), David honored the mob and the monarch of the moment. In the early days of the First Empire, David moved to the camp of Napoleon, and painted **The Coronation of Napoleon** (1806), again using the Greek and Roman motifs for which the emperor had a soft spot in his brassy little heart. This new iconographycame to be known as **Empire style.**

BEGINNINGS

The trick cinema of magician-turned-filmmaker **Georges Méliès** astounded audiences with "disappearing" objects, but gave way by 1908 to an emphasis on narrative. At 14 minutes in length and with 30 scenes, Méliès's *Journey to the Moon* (1902) was the first motion picture to realize the story-telling possibilities of the medium. Paris was the Hollywood of the early days of cinema, dominating production and distribution worldwide. However, WWI stunted growth and allowed the Americans to sink their claws in for good, in France as elsewhere. Still, the creative climate in France was fertile: new movements in art engaged film and yielded the slapstick *Entr'acte* (1924) by **René Clair,** starring that grand-Dada of impertinence, **Marcel Duchamp,** and **Luis Buñuel's** *Un Chien Andalou* (1928), a marvel of jarring associations featuring **Salvador Dalí.** The Dane **Carl Dreyer's** *Passion of Joan of Arc* (1928) exhibits a passion for close-ups.

Although WWI allowed Hollywood to wrest celluloid dominance from a shattered Europe, in the 1920s and 1930s French cinema was the most critically acclaimed in the world under such great directors as **Jean Renoir,** son of the Impressionist painter. *La Grande illusion*, which he directed in 1937, is a powerful anti-war statement, set in the prisoner of war camps of World War I. Jean Renoir balanced social criticism with humanism, revealing in *The Rules of the Game* (1939) the erosion of the French bourgeoisie and his country's malaise at the doorstep of war.

The 1930s brought sound, crowned by **Jean Vigo's** *Zero for Conduct* (1933). This dark story of boarding school rebellion prefigured the growth of **Poetic Realism** under **Marcel Carné** and writer **Jacques Prévert** (*Daybreak*, 1939), with its concern for the gritty lives of the working class. Censorship during the Occupation led to a move from political films to nostalgia and escapist cinema. Carné and Prévert's epic *Children of Paradise* (1943-5) finds in 1840s Paris the indomitable spirit of the French.

NEW WAVE

Jean Cocteau carried the poetic into fantasty with *Beauty and the Beast* (1946) and *Orphée* (1950). The surrealist *Beauty and the Beast* featured an early use of special effects. A group of young intellectuals gathered by critic **André Bazin** for the magazine **Cahiers du Cinéma** took issue with "cinema of quality." Encouraged by government subsidies, in 1959 they swapped pen for the camera. **François Truffaut's** *The 400 Blows* and **Jean-Luc Godard**'s *Au Bout du Souffle* (Breathless) were joined the same year by **Alain Resnais's** *Hiroshima, Mon Amour* (written by Marguerite Duras) and announced the **French New Wave (Nouvelle Vague).** Aznavour starred in Truffaut's *Shoot the Piano Player* (1960). Three years earlier, a star was born when **Jean Vadim** sent the incomparable **Brigitte Bardot** shimmying naked across the stage in *And God Created Woman*.

Other directors of the New Wave are **Jean Rouch** (*Chronicle of a Summer*, 1961), **Louis Malle** (*The Lovers*, 1958), **Eric Rohmer** (*My Night with Maud*, 1969), **Agnès Varda** (*Cléo from 5 to 7*, 1961), and **Chris Marker** (*La Jetée*, 1962). These directors are unified by their interest in categories of fiction and documentary, the fragmentation of linear time, the thrill of youth, speed, cars, and noise, and Hitchcock and Lang's American films. The filmmaker as *auteur* (author) or essayist remains a notion in French film, and the term *"Art et Essai"* to describe what anglophones call "Art Cinema." Godard emerged as the New Wave oracle of the 60s. His collaborations with actors **Jean-Paul Belmondo** and **Anna Karina,** including *Vivre Sa Vie* (1962) and *Pierrot le Fou* (1965), inspired a generation of filmmakers.

CONTEMPORARY COMEDIES AND CLASSICS

The world impact of French cinema in the 60s brought wider recognition of French film stars in the 70s and 80s, such as stunning **Catherine Deneuve** *(Belle de jour, Les Parapluies de Cherbourg)*, gothic priestess **Isabelle Adjani** (*La Reine Margot*), and omnipresent **Gérard Depardieu** (*Danton, 1492, Camille Claudel*), as well as **Juliette Binoche** *(Blue)* and **Julie Delpy** (*Europa, Europa*). An extraordinary range of new French films are now available on video, and can serve as an introduction to French culture. **Edouard's Molinaro's** campy *La Cage aux Folles* (1975), **Colline Serraud's** *Trois hommes et un couffin* (Three Men and a Baby, 1985), and **Luc Besson's** action thriller *Nikita* (1990) have all inspired American remakes. **Jean-Jacques Beineix's** *Betty Blue* (1985), **Claude Berri's** *Manon des Sources* (1986) and *Jean de Florette* (1986), **Louis Malle's** WWII drama *Au Revoir les Enfants* (1987), **Marc Caro** and **Jean-Pierre Jeunet's** dystopic *Delicatessen* (1991), and Polish **Krzysztof Kieslowski's** three colors trilogy, *Blue* (1993), *White* (1994), and *Red* (1994), have all become instant classics of the late 20th-century French cinema. Several recent French films explore the issue of gay identity and sexual orientation, including Belgian **Alain Berliner's** transgender tragicomedy *Ma vie en rose* (1997). **Cédric Klapisch's** *Chacun cherche son Chat* (1996) featured the hip *quartier* of Bastille.

CINÉMA BEUR

Some of the most explosive recent Parisian films are the production of *cinéma beur*, the work of second-generation North Africans coming to terms with life in the HLMs (housing projects) of suburban Paris. Rich with graffiti art and rap music, films like **Mehdi Charef's** *Le Thé au harem d'Archi Ahmed* (1986) and **Mathieu Kassovitz's** *La Haine* (1995) expose the horrors of urban racism. Facing up to a history of colonialism, meanwhile, is a recent preoccupation, as in **Claire Denis's** *Chocolat* (1987). The art cinema continues to prosper under **Marcel Hanoun** (*Bruit d'Amour et de Guerre*, 1997) and **Jacques Doillon** (*Ponette*, 1997).

Sights

Paris is an ocean. Sound it: you will never touch bottom.
Survey it, report on it! However scrupulous your surveys and reports, however numerous and persistent the explorers of this sea may be, there will always remain virgin places, undiscovered caverns, flowers, pearls, monsters—there will always be something extraordinary.

—Honoré de Balzac, *Père Goriot,* 1834

WALKING PARIS

For all its grandeur, Paris is a small city. In just a few hours you can walk from the heart of the Marais in the east to the Eiffel Tower in the west, passing many of the city's principal monuments. If you would like to spend a day or an afternoon walking around a particular *arrondissement* (neighborhood) see the **Oh for a Day! sidebars** throughout the Sights section. For suggested week-long itineraries, see **Discover,** p. 5. For professional tours, see **Service Directory,** p. 278.

THE PASSAGEWAYS

Estimated Time: *3½ hrs. if you really look, more if you're buying.* ***Estimated distance:*** *1km., more if you circle the floor of each boutique multiple times.* ***Start:*** *M: Bourse. Exit the métro and walk against traffic down r. Vivienne.* ***Finish:*** *M: Etienne-Marcel.*

This is a tour of the 2*ème* Arrondissement's old-school shopping malls. In the early 19th century, speculators profitting from cheap land confiscated from the church and the aristocracy during the Revolution began to think of new ways to entice the rising middle class into their stores and boutiques. They built **passageways** designed to attract window

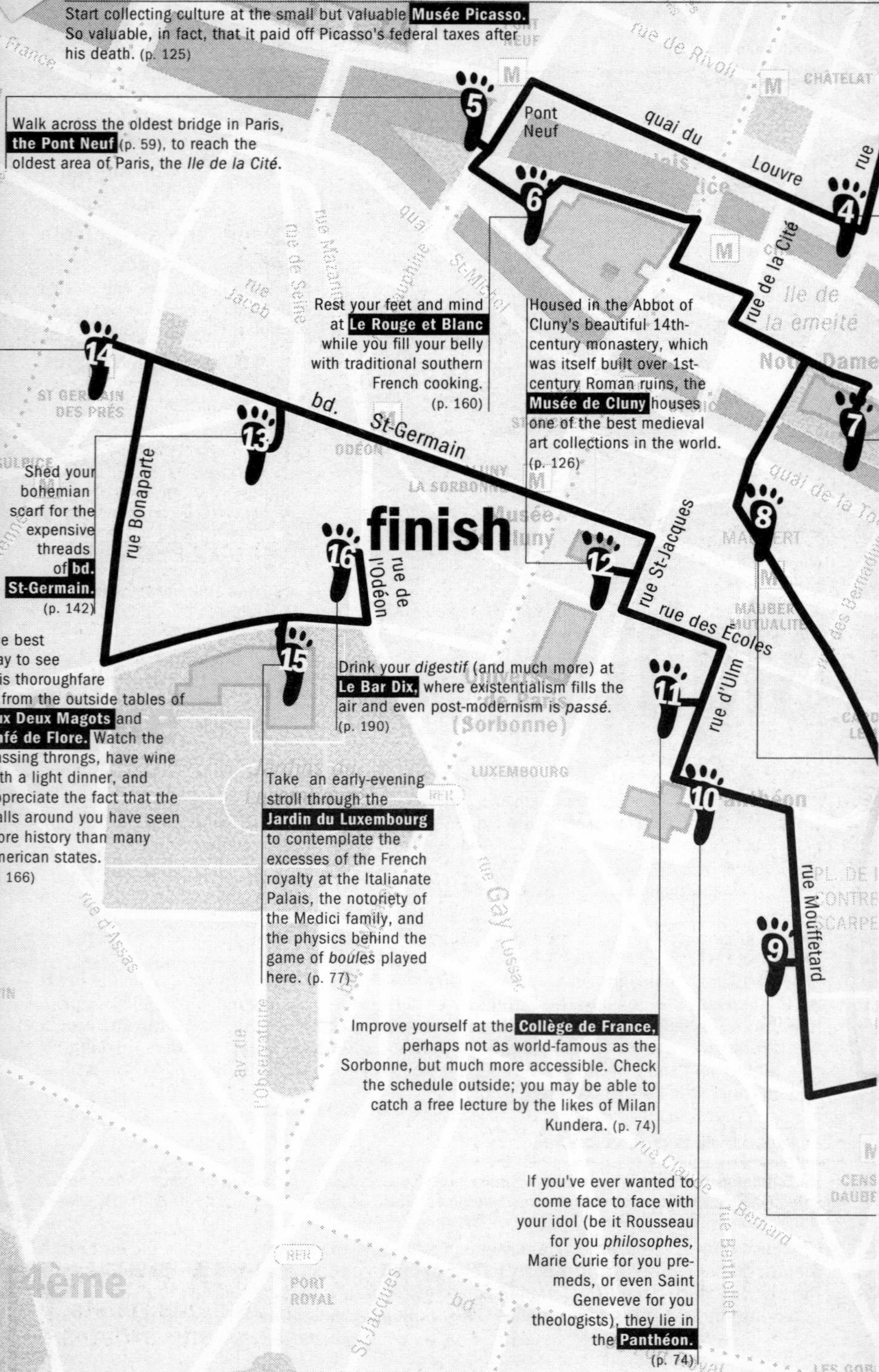

Start collecting culture at the small but valuable **Musée Picasso.** So valuable, in fact, that it paid off Picasso's federal taxes after his death. (p. 125)
Walk across the oldest bridge in Paris, **the Pont Neuf** (p. 59), to reach the oldest area of Paris, the *Ile de la Cité*.
Rest your feet and mind at **Le Rouge et Blanc** while you fill your belly with traditional southern French cooking. (p. 160)
Housed in the Abbot of Cluny's beautiful 14th-century monastery, which was itself built over 1st-century Roman ruins, the **Musée de Cluny** houses one of the best medieval art collections in the world. (p. 126)
Shed your bohemian scarf for the expensive threads of **bd. St-Germain.** (p. 142)
e best
ay to see
is thoroughfare
from the outside tables of
x Deux Magots and
afé de Flore. Watch the
assing throngs, have wine
th a light dinner, and
ppreciate the fact that the
alls around you have seen
ore history than many
merican states.
. 166)
Drink your *digestif* (and much more) at **Le Bar Dix,** where existentialism fills the air and even post-modernism is *passé*. (p. 190)
Take an early-evening stroll through the **Jardin du Luxembourg** to contemplate the excesses of the French royalty at the Italianate Palais, the notoriety of the Medici family, and the physics behind the game of *boules* played here. (p. 77)
Improve yourself at the **Collège de France,** perhaps not as world-famous as the Sorbonne, but much more accessible. Check the schedule outside; you may be able to catch a free lecture by the likes of Milan Kundera. (p. 74)
If you've ever wanted to come face to face with your idol (be it Rousseau for you *philosophes*, Marie Curie for you pre-meds, or even Saint Geneveve for you theologists), they lie in the **Panthéon.** (p. 74)
finish
Pont Neuf
quai du Louvre
rue de Rivoli
CHÂTELET
rue de la Cité
Ile de la emeité
Notre Dame
quai de la Tournelle
bd. St-Germain
rue Bonaparte
rue Jacob
rue de Seine
rue Mazarine
rue de l'Odéon
rue St-Jacques
rue des Écoles
rue d'Ulm
rue Mouffetard
rue Gay Lussac
rue d'Assas
rue Claude Bernard
rue Berthollet
av. de l'Observatoire
ST GERMAIN DES PRÉS
ODÉON
LA SORBONNE
Musée Cluny
MAUBERT MUTUALITÉ
LUXEMBOURG
(Sorbonne)
Panthéon
RER
PORT ROYAL
14ème

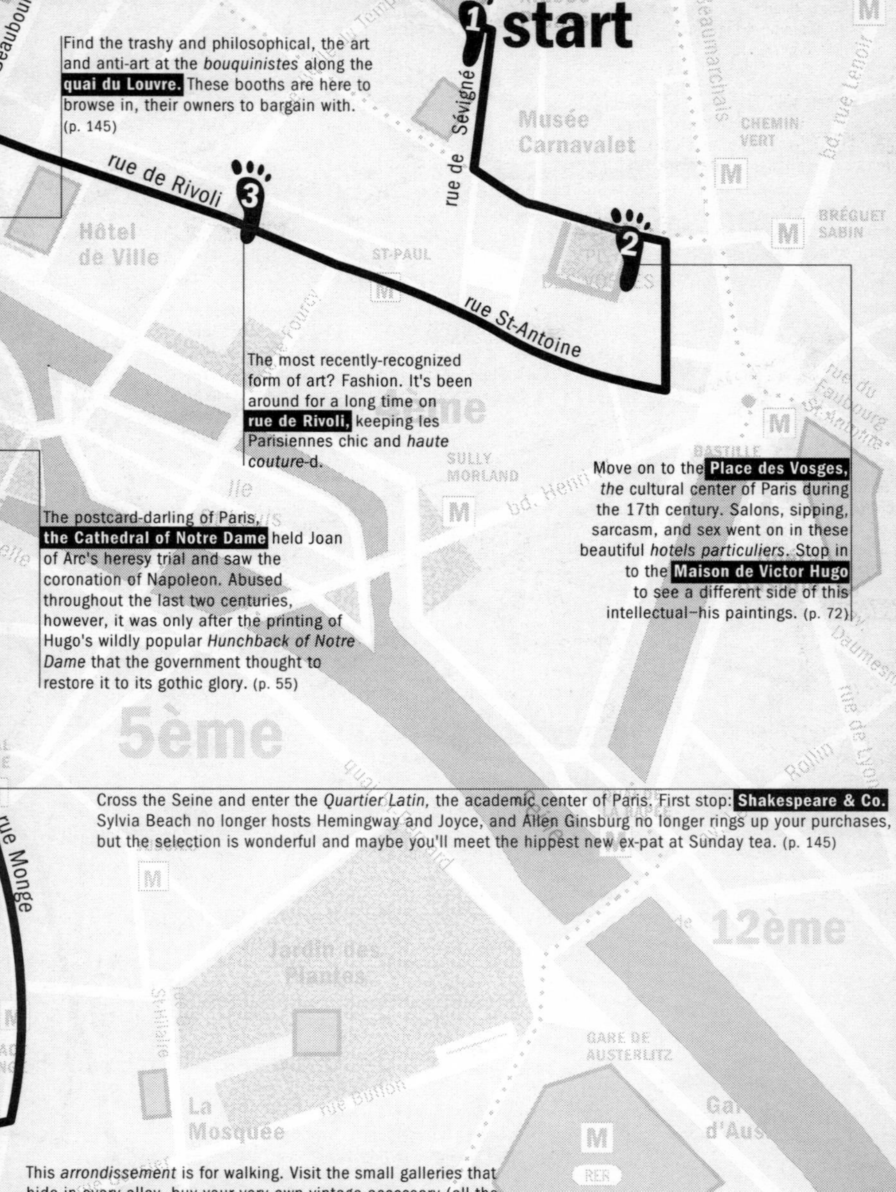

1 Find the trashy and philosophical, the art and anti-art at the *bouquinistes* along the **quai du Louvre.** These booths are here to browse in, their owners to bargain with. (p. 145)

2 Move on to the **Place des Vosges,** *the* cultural center of Paris during the 17th century. Salons, sipping, sarcasm, and sex went on in these beautiful *hotels particuliers*. Stop in to the **Maison de Victor Hugo** to see a different side of this intellectual–his paintings. (p. 72)

3 The most recently-recognized form of art? Fashion. It's been around for a long time on **rue de Rivoli,** keeping les Parisiennes chic and *haute couture*-d.

The postcard-darling of Paris, **the Cathedral of Notre Dame** held Joan of Arc's heresy trial and saw the coronation of Napoleon. Abused throughout the last two centuries, however, it was only after the printing of Hugo's wildly popular *Hunchback of Notre Dame* that the government thought to restore it to its gothic glory. (p. 55)

Cross the Seine and enter the *Quartier Latin*, the academic center of Paris. First stop: **Shakespeare & Co.** Sylvia Beach no longer hosts Hemingway and Joyce, and Allen Ginsburg no longer rings up your purchases, but the selection is wonderful and maybe you'll meet the hippest new ex-pat at Sunday tea. (p. 145)

This *arrondissement* is for walking. Visit the small galleries that hide in every alley, buy your very own vintage accessory (all the hip students are wearing them!) at Antiquités New-Puces at no. 45 (p. 143), or grab a crêpe like a real starving student along **rue Mouffetard,** the neighborhood's main drag. (p. 75)

TEENAGE MUTANT NINJA PARIS

For students, poets, bohemians and *artistes*

PARIS IN A HALF-SHELL

For revolutionaries, proletariats, and the otherwise discontent

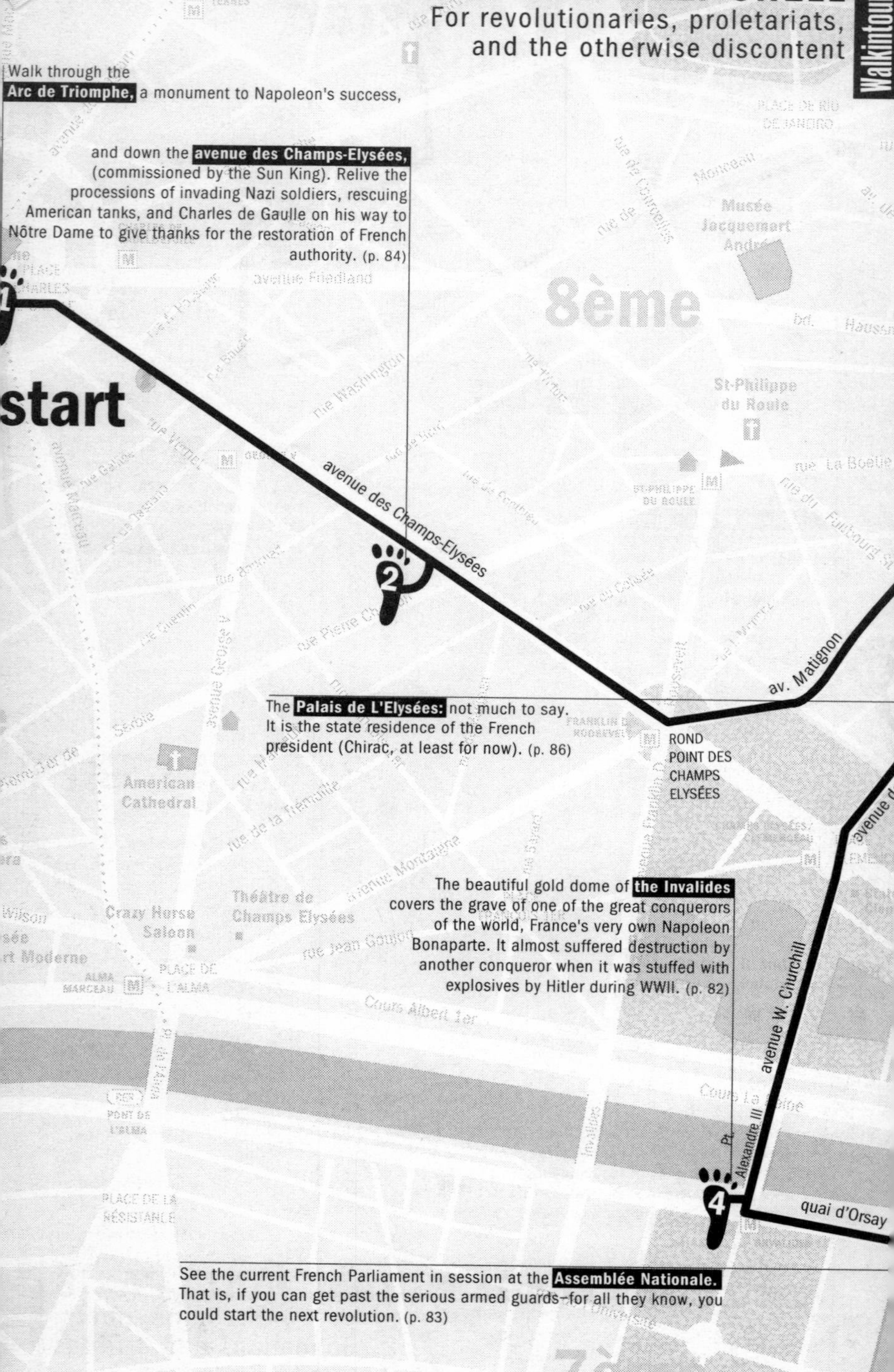

start

1 Walk through the **Arc de Triomphe,** a monument to Napoleon's success,

and down the **avenue des Champs-Elysées,** (commissioned by the Sun King). Relive the processions of invading Nazi soldiers, rescuing American tanks, and Charles de Gaulle on his way to Nôtre Dame to give thanks for the restoration of French authority. (p. 84)

2 The **Palais de L'Elysées:** not much to say. It is the state residence of the French president (Chirac, at least for now). (p. 86)

The beautiful gold dome of **the Invalides** covers the grave of one of the great conquerors of the world, France's very own Napoleon Bonaparte. It almost suffered destruction by another conqueror when it was stuffed with explosives by Hitler during WWII. (p. 82)

4 See the current French Parliament in session at the **Assemblée Nationale.** That is, if you can get past the serious armed guards—for all they know, you could start the next revolution. (p. 83)

finish

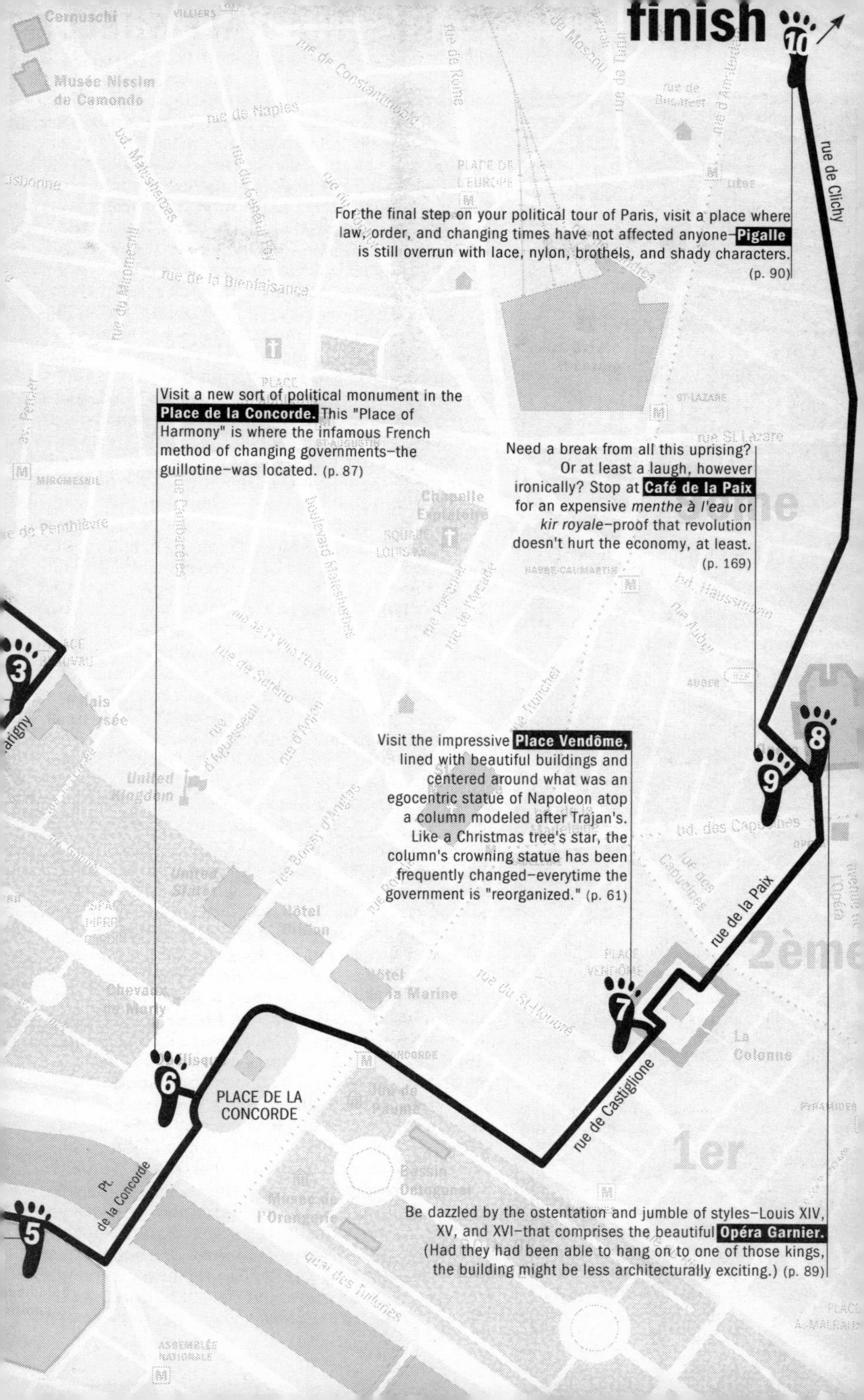

For the final step on your political tour of Paris, visit a place where law, order, and changing times have not affected anyone–**Pigalle** is still overrun with lace, nylon, brothels, and shady characters. (p. 90)

Visit a new sort of political monument in the **Place de la Concorde.** This "Place of Harmony" is where the infamous French method of changing governments–the guillotine–was located. (p. 87)

Need a break from all this uprising? Or at least a laugh, however ironically? Stop at **Café de la Paix** for an expensive *menthe à l'eau* or *kir royale*–proof that revolution doesn't hurt the economy, at least. (p. 169)

Visit the impressive **Place Vendôme,** lined with beautiful buildings and centered around what was an egocentric statue of Napoleon atop a column modeled after Trajan's. Like a Christmas tree's star, the column's crowning statue has been frequently changed–everytime the government is "reorganized." (p. 61)

Be dazzled by the ostentation and jumble of styles–Louis XIV, XV, and XVI–that comprises the beautiful **Opéra Garnier.** (Had they had been able to hang on to one of those kings, the building might be less architecturally exciting.) (p. 89)

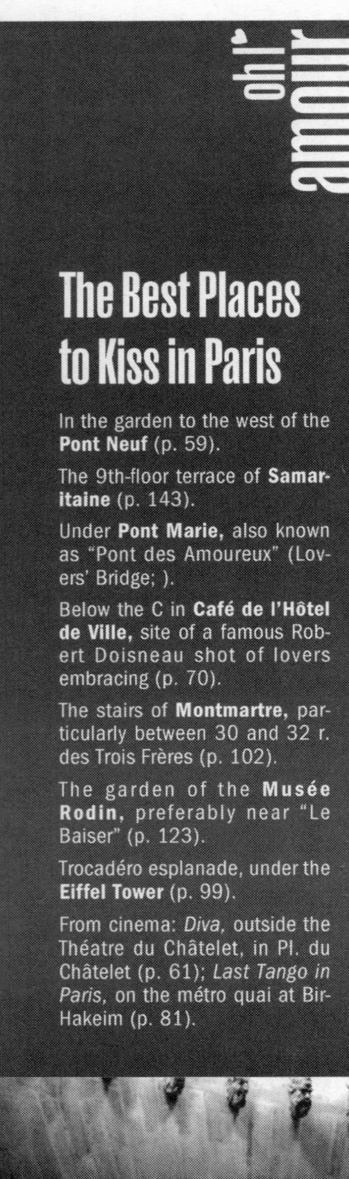

The Best Places to Kiss in Paris

In the garden to the west of the **Pont Neuf** (p. 59).

The 9th-floor terrace of **Samaritaine** (p. 143).

Under **Pont Marie,** also known as "Pont des Amoureux" (Lovers' Bridge;).

Below the C in **Café de l'Hôtel de Ville,** site of a famous Robert Doisneau shot of lovers embracing (p. 70).

The stairs of **Montmartre,** particularly between 30 and 32 r. des Trois Frères (p. 102).

The garden of the **Musée Rodin,** preferably near "Le Baiser" (p. 123).

Trocadéro esplanade, under the **Eiffel Tower** (p. 99).

From cinema: *Diva,* outside the Théatre du Châtelet, in Pl. du Châtelet (p. 61); *Last Tango in Paris,* on the métro quai at Bir-Hakeim (p. 81).

shoppers ("window lickers," in French), using sheets of glass held in place by lightweight iron rods. This startling new design allowed the daylight in, and gas lighting and electric heating ensured customers (of every sort) all night long. The passages might seem like quaint mini malls today, but these predecessors to the department store elicited a tirade from Marxist scholar Walter Benjamin, who believed they created a "fantasmagoria" of bourgeois wellbeing fed by an elusive promise of happiness through retail therapy. Right: so, like, shopping is fun. Today, they seem like a reminder of a more modest time when words like "Trump" and "Tower" had not yet entered the collective vocabulary. But however innocuous they may appear, these passageways have been restored to and lie in wait to attract a new generation of shopaholics.

Begin at the most fashionable *galleries* (posh passageways) of the 1820s. Inlaid marble mosaics swirl along the floor, and stucco friezes grace the entrance of **Galerie Vivienne.** Vivienne was built in 1823 as the grande dame of the passageways and is enjoying a revival. She boasts a showcase of pastel luxury, tiny shops, and the boutique of bad boy Jean-Paul Gaultier. *(4, r. des Petits Champs-2, r. Vivienne. Near the Palais Royal.)* **Galerie Colbert** is Vivienne's neglected little brother. Built to capitalize on her success, his glorious rotunda and classical sculpture never attracted the same lively crowds and has become an annex for shops and exhibitions of the Bibliothèque Nationale *(At the end of the corridor of Galerie Vivienne. Call 47 03 85 71 for exhibit info. Exhibitions open Tu-Su 10am-7pm. Prices vary some are free, others 20-40F.)* From Gallery Vivienne walk with traffic down r. des Petits Champs. **Passage Choiseul** was given a bad rap in Coline's *Mort à Credit* in which she called it, "more infected than a prison," and complained that "the ugly sunlight that does filter through is eclipsed by one movement." In reality more palatable and much less dramatic, Choiseul houses more practical shops than the others, with some bargain clothing stuffed in between the cafes, engravers and printers. Verlaine frequented Choiseul, and his work was printed at number 23. *(40 r. des Petits Champs-23 r. Augustin. M: Pyramides.)* Next take the métro to the Grands Boulevards stop and walk with traffic on bd. Montmartre. Between bd. Montmartre and r. St-Marc, is the oldest of Paris's remaining galleries, Passage des Panoramas. Built in 1799, it contains a 19th-century glass-and-tile roof and a more recently installed collection of ethnic restaurants. A chocolate shop (François Marquis), a printer (no. 8), and an engraver (no. 47), who have managed to stay open since the 1830s, are worth a visit, as they have conserved much of their old machinery. Street theatre also a grand tradition here. Across bd. Montmartre, find Passages Jouffry and Verdeau. Built fifty years after Panoramas, people tripped over each other and rushed in floods to see these naughty treats: passageways that were heated.

Toy shops, bookstores, and gift shops fairly bursting with charm are the current draw. (10 r. St-Marc and 11 bd. Montmartre. M: Rue Montmartre.) Now walk against traffic on r. de Turbigo and turn left onto r. St-Denis. Here you will find the most beautiful of the remaining passages, the **Grand Cerf.** Worth walking to for its stained-glass portal windows and the exquisite iron work—it has the highest glass and iron arches in Paris. But renovations haven't done for St Denis what they did for the Palais Royal *passages*, and the shops here can be disappointing. *(10 r. Dussoubs-145 r. St-Denis. M: Etienne Marcel.)*

Notre-Dame

SEINE ISLANDS

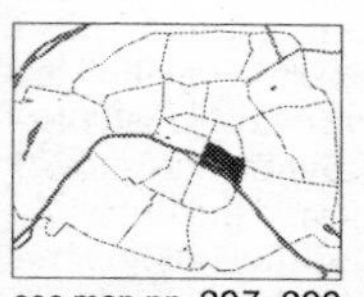
see map pp. 297–299

ÎLE DE LA CITÉ

Until the 5th century, when it became the first spot to be named "Paris," Île de la Cité was called Lutetia by the Gallic tribe who inhabited it (see **History,** p. 25). In the 6th century, Clovis crowned himself king of the Franks, and chose to rule from this tiny island, while his son, Childebert I, ordered the construction of a Christian church, which would eventually be replaced by Notre-Dame. In the 10th century, the Capetian dynasty created a Royal Council in the palace and from then until the 14th century when Charles V abandoned it in favor of the Louvre, Île de la Cite was the seat of the Monarchy.

Pont Neuf

NOTRE-DAME

> We climbed the spiral staircase. Atop this cathedral, I expected to see Quasimodo around some corner. "It's marvelous, marvelous" I kept exclaiming to myself. "Isn't it sir?" the fat woman replied, brimming with pride at being the concierge of Notre-Dame. "You don't see that anywhere else. We're at the heart of Paris. It beats the Eiffel Tower, doesn't it?"
>
> —Georges Brassaï, *Paris of the 30s*, 1932

M: Cité. ☎ 42 34 56 10; crypt ☎ 43 29 83 51. ***Open*** *M-F 8am-6:45pm, Sa-Su 8am-7:45pm.* ***Towers*** *open daily Apr.-Sept. 10am-6pm; Oct.-Mar. 10am-5pm. Free.* ***Tours*** *begin at the booth to the right as you enter. In English W-Th noon, Sa 2:30pm; in French M-F noon, Sa 2:30pm. Free.* ***Confession*** *can be heard in English. Priests also available to non-Christians who would like advice. Roman Catholic* ***Mass*** *M-F 6:15pm;* ***Vespers*** *sung 5:45pm in the choir.* ***Treasury*** *open M-Sa 9:30am-6pm; last ticket at 5:30pm. 15F, students and ages 12-17 10F, 6-12 5F, under 6 free.* ***High Mass*** *with Gregorian chant is celebrated Su 10am, with music at 11:30am, 12:30pm, and 6:30pm. After Vespers, one of the cathedral organists gives a free recital.* ***Crypt*** *open daily Apr.-Sept. 10am-6pm; Oct.-Mar. 10am-5pm; last ticket sold 30min. before closing. 35F, students 23F, under 12 free.*

Victor Hugo had it right when he said, "Great buildings, like great mountains, are the work of centuries." Notre-Dame was once the sight of a Roman temple to Jupiter, and its holy place housed three churches before Maurice de Sully began construction of the Catholic cathedral in 1163. De Sully, the bishop of Paris under King Philip II, was concerned with preventing the kind of poor interior design that had made

Quai D'Anjou

oh! for a day

Catching the Worm on Île de la Cité

Stroll over **Pont Neuf** on your way to Île de la Cité, perhaps even venture under the bridge to the romantic walkway by the Seine. Once on the island, stop in at the **pl. Dauphine,** and wander through the shady courtyard toward the **Palais de Justice.** Work your way down the island, starting with the delicate **Ste-Chapelle,** next to the Palais de Justice (p. 58). On your way out through the courtyard take a sharp left to the **Court d'Appel** to catch French lawyers in their traditional regalia. If you leave the Palais through the main gate and turn left, following the building around the block, you'll find the eery **Conciergerie** (p. 58). Shake off the goosebumps with a refreshing walk through the heady perfumes of the **flower market** on your way to the most impressive monument of all: **Notre-Dame.** Don't miss the climb to the top of the cathedral, where you can finish your tour among gargoyles, gazing over the cool blue tophats of Parisian town houses.

Notre-Dame's predecessor, St-Denis, claustrophobic and unbearable. His aim was to create an edifice filled with air and light, in a style that would later be dubbed **gothic** (see **Architecture,** p. 43). He died before his plan was completed, and it was up to later centuries to rework the cathedral into the composite masterpiece, finished in 1361, that stands today. Notre-Dame was used by royals for marriage ceremonies, most notably for Henri of Navarre to Marguerite de Valois; royal burials were performed at the St-Denis cathedral, coronations at Reims (although Henri VI was crowned at Notre-Dame in 1431), and important relics went to Ste-Chapelle (see p. 58). Nevertheless, Notre-Dame took pride of place in the public's attention.

The cathedral was the setting for Joan of Arc's trial for heresy in 1455 and Napoleon's papal coronation in 1804. Revolutionary secularists renamed the cathedral Le Temple de la Raison (The Temple of Reason). During this time, the Gothic arches were hidden behind plaster facades of virtuous Neoclassical design. Although reconsecrated after the Revolution, the building fell into disrepair and was used to shelter livestock. Victor Hugo's 1831 novel *Notre-Dame-de-Paris* (The Hunchback of Notre-Dame) revived the cathedral's popularity and inspired Napoleon III and Haussmann to invest time and money in its restoration. The modifications by Eugène Viollet-le-Duc (including a new spire, gargoyles, and a statue of himself admiring his own work) restored and reinvigorated the cathedral. Notre-Dame became a valued symbol of civic unity after its renovation. In 1870 and again in 1940 thousands of Parisians attended masses to pray for deliverance from the invading Germans. On August 26, 1944, Charles de Gaulle braved Nazi sniper fire to come here and give thanks for the imminent liberation of Paris. All of these upheavals seem to have left the cathedral unmarked, as have the hordes of tourists who invade its sacred portals every day. In the words of e. e. cummings, "The Cathedral of Notre-Dame does not budge an inch for all the idiocies of this world."

EXTERIOR. "Few architectural pages," Hugo proclaimed, "are as beautiful as this facade...a vast symphony in stone." Begun in the 12th century, work on the facade continued into the 17th century when artists were still adding Baroque statues. The carvings, designed to instill piety in a largely illiterate medieval population, were recently restored. The oldest work is found above the **Porte de Ste-Anne** (right), mostly dating from 1165-1175. The **Porte de la Vierge** (left), relating the life of the Virgin Mary, dates from the 13th century. The central **Porte du Jugement** (Door of Judgement) was almost entirely redone in the 19th century; the figure of Christ dates from 1885. Revolutionaries wreaked havoc on the facade during the ecstasies of the 1790s. Not content with decapitating Louis XVI, they attacked the statures of the Kings of Judah above the doors, which they thought were his ancestors. The heads were found languishing in the basement of the Banque Française du Commerce in 1977 and were installed in the Musée de Cluny (see **Museums,** p. 126).

TOWERS. The two towers—home to the cathedral's most famous fictional resident, Quasimodo the Hunchback—stare with grey solemnity across the square below. Streaked with black soot, the twin towers of Notre-Dame were a mysterious, imposing shadow on the Paris skyline for years. No more. After two years of sand-blasting, Notre-Dame has had its creamy complexion restored, and while the sinister effect of the blackened exterior has gone, the rosary windows, and rows of saints and gargoyles that line the cathedral have burst out into the sunlight. There's usually a line to make the climb, but it's well worth it. The claustrophobia-inducing staircase emerges onto a spectacular perch, where rows of gargoyles survey the heart of the city, particularly of the Left Bank's *quartier latin* and the Marais on the Right Bank. The climb generally deters the tour bus set; you may even have the towers to yourself if you come early. In the south tower, a tiny door opens onto the 13-ton bell that even Quasimodo couldn't ring: it requires the force of eight people to move. For a striking view of the cathedral, cross Pont St-Louis (behind the cathedral) to Île St-Louis and turn right on quai d'Orléans. At night, the buttresses are lit up, and the view from here is beautiful. The Pont de Sully, at the far side of Île St-Louis, also affords an impressive view of the cathedral.

INTERIOR. From the inside, the cathedral seems to be constructed of soaring, weightless walls. This effect is achieved by the spidery **flying buttresses** that support the vaults of the ceiling from outside, allowing for delicate stained glass walls. The transept's **rose windows,** nearly 85% 13th-century glass, are the most spectacular feature of the interior. At the center of the 21m north window is the Virgin, depicted as the descendent of the Old Testament kings and judges who surround her. The base of the south window shows Matthew, Mark, Luke, and John on the shoulders of Old Testament prophets, while in the central window Christ is surrounded by the 12 apostles, virgins, and saints of the New Testament. The cathedral's **treasury,** south of the choir, contains an assortment of glittering robes, sacramental cutlery, and other gilded artifacts from the cathedral's past. The famous Crown of Thorns, which is supposed to have been worn by Christ, was acquired by Saint Louis in 1239, and was moved from Ste-Chapelle to Notre-Dame at the end of the 18th century. The relic is "not ordinarily exposed" and is only presented on Fridays during Lent, from 5 to 6pm. Far below the cathedral towers, in a cool excavation beneath the pavement of the square in front of the cathedral, the **Crypte Archéologique,** pl. du Parvis du Notre-Dame, houses artifacts unearthed in the construction of a parking garage. Essentially an archeological dig, the crypt offers a self-guided tour through the history of Ile de la Cité, allowing you to wander among architectural fragments from Roman Lutèce up through the 19th-century sewers.

THE REST OF THE ISLAND

PALAIS DE JUSTICE

Within the structure called Palais de la Citée, 4, bd. du Palais, in the same courtyard as Ste-Chapelle. M: Cité. ☎44 32 51 51. Courtrooms open M-F 9am-noon and 1:30-5pm. Free.

The Palais de Justice harbors the infamous **Conciergerie,** a Revolutionary prison, and **Ste-Chapelle,** the private chapel of St-Louis. Since the 13th century, the buildings between the Conciergerie and the Ste-Chapelle have housed the **district courts** of Paris. After WWII, Maréchal Pétain was convicted in Chambre I of the Cour d'Appel. A wide set of stone steps leads to three doorways: you have the choice of entering through a door marked Liberty, Equality, or Fraternity, words that once signified Revolution and now serve as the bedrock of French tradition. All trials are open to the public as long as you can navigate your way through the marble hallways. Try entering through "Equality," and walk straight through a green door marked "Cour d'Appel" to the second floor. Immediately to your left is a gallery for the public, which is open to tourists. Even if your French is not up to legalese, the theatrical sobriety of the interior, with lawyers dressed in archaic black robes, makes a quick visit worthwhile.

STE-CHAPELLE

4, bd. du Palais. M: Cité. At the heart of the Palais du Justice, within the structure Palais de la Cité. ☎ 53 73 58 51 and 53 73 78 50. Open daily Apr.-Sept. 9:30am-6:30pm; Oct.-Mar. 10am-5pm. Last admission 30min. before closing. 35F, twin ticket with Conciergerie 50F, seniors and ages 18-25 23F, under 18 free.

Ste-Chapelle remains the foremost example of flamboyant Gothic architecture and a tribute to the craft of medieval stained glass. Construction of the chapel began in 1241 to house the most precious of King Louis IX's possessions: the Crown of Thorns from Christ's Passion. Bought along with a section of the Cross by the Emperor of Constantinople in 1239 for the ungodly sum of 135,000 pounds, the crown required an equally princely home. Although the crown itself—minus a few thorns that St-Louis gave away in exchange for political favors—has been moved to Notre-Dame, Ste-Chapelle is still worth exploring. The **Lower Chapel** looks bare, but a few "treasures," platter-sized portraits of saints, remain beneath the blue vaulted ceiling and gold stars. No mastery of the lower Chapel's dim gilt can prepare the visitor for the **Upper Chapel,** where twin walls of stained glass glow and frescos of saints and martyrs shine. Read from bottom to top, left to right, the windows narrate the Bible from Genesis to the Apocalypse. It's also worth stepping out onto the small stone balcony to the right of the stairwell: a statue of Jesus entwined in flowers and vines forms a pillar, and above his head gargoyles and humans wrassle in bas relief. Check for occasional concerts held in the Upper Chapel mid-March through October, or ask at the information booth.

MÉMORIAL DE LA DÉPORTATION

M: Cité. At the very tip of the island on pl. de l'Île de France, behind the cathedral, and down a narrow flight of steps. Open daily Apr.-Sept. 10am-noon and 2-7pm; Oct.-Mar. 10am-noon and 2-5pm. Free.

A simple but moving memorial erected for the French victims of Nazi concentration camps; two hundred thousand flickering lights represent the dead, and an eternal flame burns close to the tomb of an unknown deportee. The names of all the concentration camps glow in gold triangles that recall the Stars of David that French and European Jews were forced to wear on their clothing. A series of quotations is engraved into the stone walls—most striking of which is the injunction, "*Pardonne. N'Oublie Pas*" ("Forgive. Do Not Forget") engraved over the exit. Old men frequent the memorial and chant the kaddish, the Jewish prayer for the dead.

CONCIERGERIE

1, quai de l'Horloge. M: Cité. ☎ 53 73 78 50. Open daily Apr.-Sept. 9:30am-6:30pm; Oct.-Mar. 10am-5pm. Last ticket 30min. before closing. 35F, students 23F. Includes tour in French 11am and 3pm. For English tours, call in advance.)

Around the corner of the Palais de Justice from the entrance to the Ste-Chapelle, a dark but fascinating monument to the Revolution stands over the Seine. Built by Philip the Fair in the 14th century, the Conciergerie is a good example of secular medieval architecture. When Charles V moved the seat of Royal power from Île de la Cité to the Hôtel Saint-Pol and then to the Louvre, he left one man in charge of the Parliament, Chancery, and Audit Office on the island. The name Conciergerie refers to the adminstrative officer of the Crown who acted as the king's steward, the *Concierge* (keeper). Later this edifice became a royal prison, which was taken over by the Revolutionary Tribunal after 1793. The northern facade, blackened by auto exhaust, is an appropriately gloomy introduction to a building in which 2,700 people were sentenced to death between 1792 and 1794. At the farthest corner on the right, a stepped parapet marks the oldest tower, the **Tour Bonbec** (good beak), which once housed torture chambers. The modern entrance lies between the **Tour d'Argent,** stronghold of the royal treasury, and the **Tour de César,** used by the Revolutionary Tribunal.

Past the hall, stairs lead to rows of cells complete with preserved props and plastic people in the clothing of their day. Plaques explain how, in a bit of opportunism on the part of the Revolutionary leaders, rich men could buy themselves private cells with cots while the poor slept in "promiscuous" cells on straw. In a side room, a video with English subtitles explains the reality of daily life in the Conciergerie, if you can stand the melodramatic soundtrack. Farther down the hall is the cell where Maximilien de Robespierre, the mastermind behind the Reign of Terror, awaited his death. The cell has been converted into a display of his letters, and engraved on the wall are Robespierre's famous last words: "*Je vous laisse ma Mémoire. Elle vous sera chère, et vous la défendrez*" ("I leave you my memory. It will be dear to you, and you will defend it"). Marie-Antoinette was imprisoned in the Conciergerie for five weeks. Follow the corridor named for "Monsieur de Paris," the executioner during the Revolution, and you'll be tracing the final footsteps of Marie-Antoinette as she waited to have her head chopped off on October 16, 1793, for her comment about cake. Other exhibits tell the story of the Revolutionary factions. Concerts and wine tastings are occasionally held in the Salle des Gens d'Armes.

Notre-Dame

PONT NEUF

You can leave Île de la Cité by the oldest bridge in Paris, named the Pont Neuf (New Bridge). Stretching everyone's sense of novelty and completed in 1607, the bridge broke tradition since its sides were not lined by houses. Before the construction of the Champs-Elysées, the bridge was Paris's most popular thoroughfare, attracting peddlers, performance artists, and thieves. More recently, Christo, the Bulgarian performance artist, wrapped the entire bridge in 44,000 square meters of nylon. Comic gargoyle faces carved into the supports can be spotted from a Bateau Mouche.

Pont Neuf Garden

OTHER SIGHTS

HÔTEL DIEU. The Hôtel Dieu, behind Notre-Dame on r. d'Arcole, was a hospital built in the Middle Ages to confine the sick than to cure them. It had guards posted to keep the patients from getting out and infecting the city. More recently, Pasteur did much of his pioneering research inside. In 1871, the hospital's proximity to Notre-Dame saved the cathedral—*communards* were dissuaded from burning the cathedral for fear that the flames would engulf their hospitalized wounded. The hospital's serene gardens lie within the inner courtyard.

PRÉFECTURE DE POLICE. Across r. de la Cité is the Préfecture de Police, where at 7am on August 19, 1944, the Paris police began an insurrection against the Germans that lasted until the Allies liberated the city. *(Open daily 6:30am-8pm.)*

ÎLE ST-LOUIS

From Île de la Cité, a short walk across the **Pont St-Louis** will take you to the elegant enclave of Île St-Louis. Originally two small islands—the Île aux Vâches (Cow Island) and the Île de Notre-Dame, which were combined in the 17th century—it was considered suitable for duels, cows, and little else throughout the Middle Ages. In 1267, Louis IX departed for the Tunisian Crusade from the Île aux Vâches, never to return, and the island was renamed in memoriam. It became residential in the 17th century due to a contractual arrangement between Henri IV and the bridge entrepreneur Christophe Marie, after whom the **Pont Marie** is named. Architect Louis Le Vau gave the Île St-Louis an architectural unity in the mid-17th century. Today the island looks much as it did 300 years ago. Over the centuries, its *hôtels particuliers* have attracted an elite citizenry including Voltaire, Mme. de Châtelet, Daumier, Ingrès, Baudelaire, and Cézanne.

La Seine

PUTTIN' ON THE...

Founded by César Ritz at the turn of the century, the unaffordably opulent Ritz hotel (no. 15, pl. Vendôme) stands as a monument to both wealth and misery. It was here where Princess Diana had her last meal, where American Ambassador Pamela Harriman died in 1997 while swimming in the pool, and where Hemingway escaped the grind of the Left Bank to drink (and drink, and drink some more). After riding into Paris with the US Army in 1944, Hemingway gathered Resistance troops and went off to liberate the Ritz. Greeted by his old chum, the assistant manager, Hemingway proceeded to order 73 dry martinis. The bar in which the American writer lavished so much gin and vermouth upon himself has since been renamed the "Hemingway Bar." All in a day's work.

QUAI DE BOURBON

The quai wraps around the northwest edge of the island; it is to the left immediately after crossing the Pont St-Louis.

Sculptor **Camille Claudel** lived and worked at **no. 19** from 1899 until 1913, when her brother, the poet Paul Claudel, had her incarcerated in an asylum. Because she was the protegé and lover of sculptor Auguste Rodin, Claudel's most striking work is displayed in the Musée Rodin (see **Museums,** p. 123). At the intersection of the quai and r. des Deux Ponts sits the café **Au Franc-Pinot,** whose wrought-iron and grilled facade is almost as old as the island itself. The grapes that punctuate the ironwork gave the café its name; the *pinot* is a grape from Burgundy. Closed in 1716 after authorities found a basement stash of anti-government tracts, the café-cabaret reemerged as a treasonous address during the Revolution. Cécile Renault, daughter of the proprietor, mounted an unsuccessful attempt on Robespierre's life in 1794. She was guillotined the following year. Today the Pinot houses a mediocre jazz club and can no longer be denounced by the government.

QUAI D'ANJOU

The island's most beautiful old *hôtels* line quai d'Anjou, between Pont Marie and Pont de Sully. **No. 29** housed **Ford Madox Ford's** *Transatlantic Review*, the expatriate lit rag to which Hemingway contributed. **No. 9** was the address of Honoré Daumier, realist painter and caricaturist, from 1846 to 1863.

RUE ST-LOUIS-EN-L'ÎLE

To get there, loop around the end of the quai d'Anjou and walk down r. St-Louis-en-l'Ile.

The main thoroughfare of Île St-Louis harbors shops, art galleries, and traditional French restaurants as well as the famous Berthillon *glacerie*. The **Hôtel Lambert,** no. 2, was designed by Le Vau in 1640 for Lambert le Riche and was home to Voltaire and Mme. de Châtelet, his mathematician mistress.

EGLISE ST-LOUIS-EN-L'ÎLE

3, r. Poulletier. ☎ 46 34 11 60. Open Tu-Su 9am-noon and 3-7pm. Check with FNAC or call the church for details on concerts.

This church is more than just another Le Vau creation built between 1664 and 1726. If you get beyond the sooty, humdrum facade, you'll find a blazing Rococo interiorlit by more windows than seem to exist from the outside. The third chapel houses a splendid gilded wood relief, *The Death of the Virgin*. Legendary for its acoustics, the church hosts concerts throughout the year and every night in July and August.

QUAI DE BÉTHUNE

Marie Curie lived on the other side of r. des Deux Ponts at 36, quai de Béthune, until she died of radiation-induced cancer in 1934. French President **George Pompidou** died just a few doors down at no. 24.

FIRST ARRONDISSEMENT

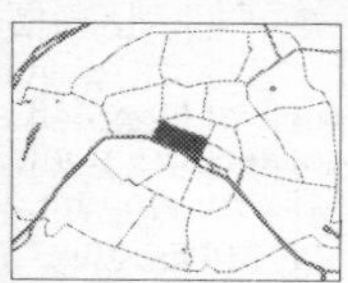

see map pp. 294–296

The first arrondissement stretches her culture flecked flanks under the shadow of the Louvre (see p. 115), former home to kings and queens. Today, the bed-chambers and dining rooms of innumerable rulers house the world's finest art, and the Sun King's well-tended gardens are filled with sunbathers, cafés, and carnival rides (for more on Louis XIV, see **History,** p. 27). The Ritz stands in the regal pl. Vendôme, while less-ritzy souvenir shops crowd r. du Louvre and Les Halles. Elegant boutiques line the r. Saint-Honoré, the street that passes the Comédie Française where actors still pay tribute to Molière, the company's founder. Farther west, smoky jazz clubs pulse on r. des Lombards while restaurants on r. Jean-Jacques Rousseau serve up France's most divine culinary finery.

Samaritaine

EAST OF THE LOUVRE

JARDIN DES TUILERIES

M: Tuileries. ☎ 40 20 90 43. ***Open*** *daily Apr.-Sept. 7am-9pm; Oct.-Mar. 7:30am-7:30pm. Free* ***tours*** *in English at varying times from the Arc de Triomphe du Carrousel. Call for details. Amusement park open late June to mid-Aug. and Dec. to early Jan. Rides 20F, under 12 15F.*

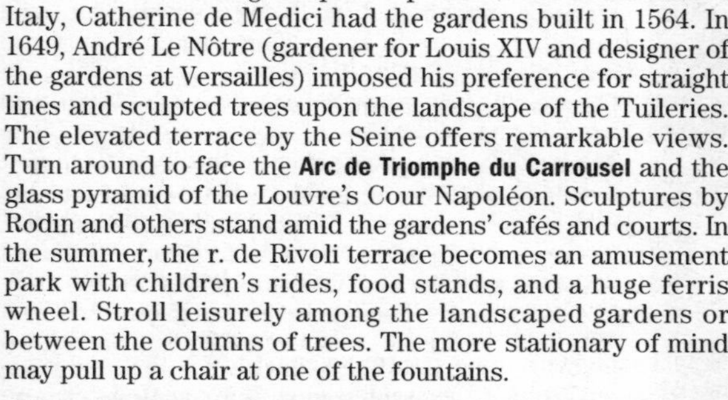

Sweeping down from the Louvre to the place de la Concorde, the Jardin des Tuileries celebrates the victory of geometry over nature. Missing the public promenades of her native Italy, Catherine de Medici had the gardens built in 1564. In 1649, André Le Nôtre (gardener for Louis XIV and designer of the gardens at Versailles) imposed his preference for straight lines and sculpted trees upon the landscape of the Tuileries. The elevated terrace by the Seine offers remarkable views. Turn around to face the **Arc de Triomphe du Carrousel** and the glass pyramid of the Louvre's Cour Napoléon. Sculptures by Rodin and others stand amid the gardens' cafés and courts. In the summer, the r. de Rivoli terrace becomes an amusement park with children's rides, food stands, and a huge ferris wheel. Stroll leisurely among the landscaped gardens or between the columns of trees. The more stationary of mind may pull up a chair at one of the fountains.

Place Vendome

JEU DE PAUME AND L'ORANGERIE. Flanking the pathway at the Concorde end of the Tuileries are the **Galérie National du Jeu de Paume** and the **Musée de l'Orangerie** (see **Museums,** p. 130).

PLACE VENDÔME

Stately pl. Vendôme, three blocks north along r. de Castiglione from the Tuileries, was begun in 1687 by Louis XIV. Designed by Jules Hardouin-Mansart, the square was built to house embassies, but bankers created lavish private homes for themselves within the elegant facades. Today, the smell of money is still in the air: bankers, perfumers, and jewelers, including Cartier (at no. 7), line the square.

In the center of pl. Vendôme, Napoleon stands atop a large **column** dressed as Caesar. In 1805, Napoleon erected the work, modeled after Trajan's Column in Rome and

Les Halles

WISH YOU WERE HERE

Parisians love to spend their days, especially during outbreaks of revolution, burning their beautiful buildings. These former landmarks are an excellent, if invisible, addition to any Parisian itinerary. Formerly closing off the quadrangle of the Louvre, and the sight of many an unsuccessful royal attempt to flee an angry mob, the **Palais des Tuileries** (below) was finally torched by the Communards in 1870. In the next year of Communard frenzy, they set the **Hôtel de Ville** (p. 70) ablaze, and for eight days burned it down to the frame. It has since been rebuilt, but only foreign heads of state can enter without joining a group tour. During the May 1968 riots, students broke into the **Théâtre de l'Odéon** (p. 77) and destroyed much of the interior, before police found them and quelled the party. Perhaps the most famous of no-longer-with-us sights is the king's former prison, the **Bastille** (p. 93). The anniversary of the storming is accompanied with life-threatening fireworks, pomp, and Jaques Chirac in person (p. 6).

fashioned out of the bronze from 1250 cannons he captured at the Battle of Austerlitz. After Napoleon's exile, the Royalist government arrested the sculptor and forced him, on penalty of death, to get rid of it. For all his pains, the return of Napoleon from Elba soon brought the original statue back to its perch. Over the next 60 years it would be replaced by the white flag of the monarchy, a renewed Napoleon in military garb, and a classical Napoleon modeled after the original. During the Commune, a group led by uppity artist Gustave Courbet toppled the entire column, planning to replace it with a monument to the "Federation of Nations and the Universal Republic." The original column was recreated with new bronze reliefs, at Courbet's expense (the painter was subsequently jailed and sent to Switzerland, where he died a few years later; see **History,** p. 28).

PALAIS-ROYAL AND SURROUNDINGS

PALAIS-ROYAL

Fountain open daily June-Aug. 7am-11pm; Sept. 7am-9:30pm; Oct.-Mar. 7am-8:30pm; Apr.-May 7am-10:15pm.

One block north of the Louvre along r. Saint-Honoré lies the once regal and racy Palais-Royal. It was constructed between 1628-1642 by Jacques Lemercier as Cardinal Richelieu's Palais Cardinal. After the Cardinal's death in 1642, Queen Anne D'Autriche moved in, preferring the Cardinal's palace to the Louvre. She brought with her a young Louis XIV and it was then that the palace became a royal one. Louis XIV was the first king to inhabit the palace, but fled during the Fronde uprising. In 1781, the broke Duc d'Orléans rented out the elegant buildings that enclose the palace's formal garden, turning the complex into an 18th-century shopping mall with boutiques, restaurants, theaters, wax museums, and gambling joints; its covered arcades were a favorite for prostitutes. On July 12, 1789, 26-year-old Camille Desmoulins leapt onto a café table here and urged his fellow citizens to arm themselves, shouting, "I would rather die than submit to servitude." The crowd filed out and was soon skirmishing with cavalry in the Tuileries garden. The Revolutions of 1830 and 1848 also began with angry crowds in these gardens. In the 19th century, Haussmann's boulevards re-gentrified the area and aristocrats moved back in.

In summer, the palace fountain becomes a mecca for tourists in need of a foot bath. In the central courtyard, the **colonnes de Buren**—a set of black and white striped pillars—are as controversial today as they were when installed by artist Daniel Buren in 1986.

COMÉDIE FRANÇAISE

Located on the southwestern corner of the Palais-Royal, facing the Louvre, the Comédie Française is home to France's leading dramatic troupe (see **National Theaters,** p. 150). Built in 1790 by architect Victor Louis, the theater became the first permanent home for the Comédie Française troupe, which was created by Louis XIV in 1680. The entrance displays busts of famous actors by celebrated sculptors, including Mirabeau by Rodin, Talma by David, and Voltaire by Houdon. Ironically, Molière, the company's founder, took ill here on stage while playing the role of the Imaginary Invalid. The chair onto which he collapsed can still be seen. At the corner of r. Molière and r. Richelieu, Visconti's **Fontaine de Molière** is only a few steps from where Molière died at no. 40.

LES HALLES AND SURROUNDINGS

EGLISE DE ST-EUSTACHE

M: Les Halles. Above r. Rambuteau. ☎42 36 31 05. Open June-Aug. M-F 10am-8pm, Su 9am-12:30pm and 2:30-7pm; Sept.-May M-F 9am-7pm. High Mass with choir and organ Su 11am. Organ tickets 80-150F.

The Eglise de St-Eustache towers over Les Halles. Eustache (Eustatius) was a Roman general who adopted Christianity upon seeing the sign of a cross between the antlers of a deer, although why he was looking there has never been settled. As punishment (for converting, not the antler fetish), the Romans locked him and his family into a brass bull that was placed over a fire until it became white-hot. Construction of the church in his honor began in 1532 and dragged on for over a century. In 1754, the unfinished facade was demolished and replaced with the Romanesque one that stands today—incongruous with the rest of the Gothic building but appropriate for its Roman namesake. Richelieu, Molière, and Mme de Pompadour were all baptized here. Louis XIV received communion in its sanctuary and Mozart chose to have his mother's funeral here. The glory days for St-Eustache seem long gone, however, as parts of the church are in need of renovation. The chapels contain paintings by Rubens, as well as British artist Raymond Mason's bizarre relief *Departure of the Fruits and Vegetables from the Heart of Paris*, commemorating the closing of the market at Les Halles in February, 1969. Summer concerts are played on the exquisite organ, commemorating St-Eustache's premiers of Berlioz's *Te Deum* and Liszt's *Messiah* in 1886. To the side of the church, Henri de Miller's 1986 sculpture *The Listener* brings together a huge stone human head and hand.

LES HALLES

The métro station Les Halles exits directly into the underground mall. To see the gardens above, use one of the four "Portes" and ride the escalators up toward daylight. Emile Zola called Les Halles *"le ventre de Paris"* ("the belly of Paris"). A sprawling food market since 1135, Les Halles received a much-needed face-lift in the 1850s with the construction of large iron-and-glass pavilions to shelter the vendors' stalls. Designed by Victor Baltard, the pavilions resembled the one that still stands over the small market at the Carreau du Temple in the *3ème.* In 1970, authorities moved the old market to a suburb near Orly. Politicians and city planners debated next how to fill *"le trou des Halles"* ("the hole of Les Halles"), 106 open acres that presented Paris with the largest urban redesign opportunity since Haussmannization. Most of the city adored the elegant pavilions and wanted to see them preserved. But planners destroyed the pavilions to build a subterranean transfer-point between the métro and the new commuter rail, the RER. The city retained architects Claude Vasconti and Georges Penreach to replace the pavilions with a subterranean shopping mall, the **Forum des Halles.** If the markets of Les Halles were once Paris's belly, then this underground maze is surely its bowels. Descend on one of the four main entrances to discover over 200 boutiques and three movie theaters. Putting the somewhat skanky mall underground allowed designers to landscape the vast Les Halles quadrangle with greenery, statues, and fountains. Both forum and gardens, however, present the danger of pickpockets. Hold onto your wallet, stay above ground and avoid the park at night.

oh! for a
day

Whirlwind 1er Tour

First things first. If it's Sunday, don't miss brunch at **Le Fumoir** (see p. 162). Early in the morning, the **Louvre** lines (see p. 115) shouldn't be terrible through I. M. Pei's glass pyramid. But stop feasting your eyes and break for lunch at **Café de L'Epoque** (see p. 161). After refuling, you could stroll the **Jardin des Tuileries** (see p. 61), ride the ferris wheel at the end of the garden, or ogle glitzy shops at **pl. Vendôme** (see p. 61). The **Palais-Royal** (see p. 62) has the galeries, the gardens, and the fountains for hours of wandering; sit and have a drink at one of the fancy cafés in the shade of the arcades. Dine at sparkling **Jules** (Let's see how much we can eat, p. 161). And for after-dinner fun and games, navigate towards r. de la Ferronnerie and r. des Lombards and choose from the many jazz options. A drink at friendly **Café OZ** (see p. 186) completes the I'm-not-in-Kansas-anymore feeling.

BOURSE DU COMMERCE

M: Louvre-Rivoli. ☎55 65 55 65; www.ccip.fr. Open M-F 9am-6pm. Tours in French and English.

Between r. du Louvre and the Forum des Halles, the large round Bourse du Commerce brokers commodities trading. The Bourse du Commerce's recently restored iron-and-glass cupola is surrounded by paintings and frescoes and worth the free peak inside. In the Middle Ages, a convent of repentant sinners occupied the site. Catherine de Medici threw out the penitent women in 1572, when a horoscope convinced her that she should abandon construction of the Tuileries, build her palace here instead. Catherine's palace was demolished in 1763, leaving only the observation tower of her personal astrologer as a memorial to her superstition. Louis XV replaced the structure with a grain market. It was transformed into a commodities market in 1889.

FONTAINE DES INNOCENTS

From the Châtelet métro station, walk down r. de la Ferronnerie to pl. J. du Bellay. Built in 1548 and designed by Pierre Lescot, the Fontaine des Innocents is the last trace of the Eglise and Cimetière des Sts-Innocents, which once bordered and overlapped Les Halles. Until its demolition in the 1780s, the edges of the cemetery were crowded by tombstones, the smell of rotting corpses, and vegetable merchants selling their produce. The cemetery closed during the Enlightenment's hygienic reforms, and the corpses were relocated to the city's catacombs (see **Sights,** p. 97). The fountain is now a rendezvous for alternateens and the overflow crowd from McDonald's.

EGLISE ST-GERMAIN L'AUXERROIS

Vespers nightly 5pm. Mass with organ Su 11am.

Tucked directly behind the Louvre along r. de l'Amiral de Coligny is the Gothic Eglise St-Germain l'Auxerrois. On August 24, 1572, the church's bell functioned as the signal for the St-Bartholomew's Day Massacre. Thousands of Huguenots were rounded up by the troops of the Duc de Guise and slaughtered in the streets, while King Charles IX shot at the survivors from the palace window. Today, visitors are allowed inside to view the violet stained-glass windows or listen to Sunday evening vespers.

OTHER SIGHTS

SAMARITAINE. Spanning three blocks along r. de Rivoli, Samaritaine is one of the oldest department stores in Paris. Founded in 1869, it ushered in the age of consumption. The building began as a delicate iron and steel construction in 1906 and was revamped in Art Deco style in 1928. The roof has one of the best free views of Paris in the city and is a painless elevator ride (see **Department Stores,** p. 142).

SECOND ARRONDISSEMENT

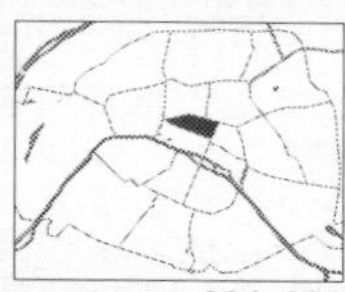

see map pp. 294–296

Passages

The *2ème* has a long history of trade and commerce, from 19th-century passageways full of goodies (see **Walking Paris,** p. 49) to the ancient Bourse where stocks and bonds were traded. The oldest and most enduring trade of the area, prostitution, has thrived on r. St-Denis (see p. 66) since the Middle Ages. Abundant fabric shops and cheap women's clothing stores line r. du Sentier and r. St-Denis while upscale boutiques keep to the streets in the *2ème's* western half. For men and women tired of chasing skirts and up for a bit of a laugh, the Opéra Comique, now the Théâtre Musicale, can be found between bd. des Italiens and r. de Richelieu.

TO THE WEST

GALERIES AND PASSAGES

Behold the world's first shopping malls. For a description and a walking tour of the passageways, see **Walking Paris,** p. 49.

BIBLIOTHÈQUE NATIONALE

58, r. de Richelieu. M: Bourse. Just north of the Galleries Vivienne and Colbert, across r. Vivienne. Main office ☎47 03 81 26; info line ☎53 79 59 59; galeries ☎47 03 81 10; cabinet ☎47 03 83 30. ***Library*** *open M-Sa 9am-5:30pm. Books available only to researchers who prove they need access to the collection. for info.* ***Galeries*** *open Tu-Su 10am-7pm. 35F, students 24F.* ***Cabinet des Médailles*** *open M-F 1-6pm, Sa 1-5pm. 22F, with student card 15F .*

Place de la Republique

With a 12 million volume collection that includes Gutenberg Bibles and first editions from the 15th century, the Bibliothèque Nationale is possibly the largest library in Continental Europe. Since 1642, every book published in France has been legally required to enter the national archives, which evolved out of the Bibliothèque du Roi, the royal book depository. To accommodate the ever-increasing volume of books, annexes were purchased near the library. At one point, books considered a little too titillating for public consumption descended into a room named "Hell," to which only the most qualified docents were granted access. In the late 1980s, the French government eschewed annexes as a short-term solution and resolved to build the mammoth **Bibliothèque de France** in the *13ème* (see p. 96), where the collections from the *2ème*'s Richelieu branch were relocated between 1996 and 1998.

Today Richelieu still holds collections of stamps, money, photography, medals and maps as well as original manuscripts written on everything from papyrus to parchment. Scholars must pass through a strict screening process to gain access to the main reading room; plan to bring a letter from your university, research advisor, or editor stating the nature of your research and two pieces of photo ID. For the public the **Galerie Mazarin** and **Galerie Mansart** host excellent temporary exhibits of books, prints, and lithographs.

Musée Picasso

Upstairs, the **Cabinet des Médailles** displays coins, medallions, and confiscated *objets d'art* from the Revolution.

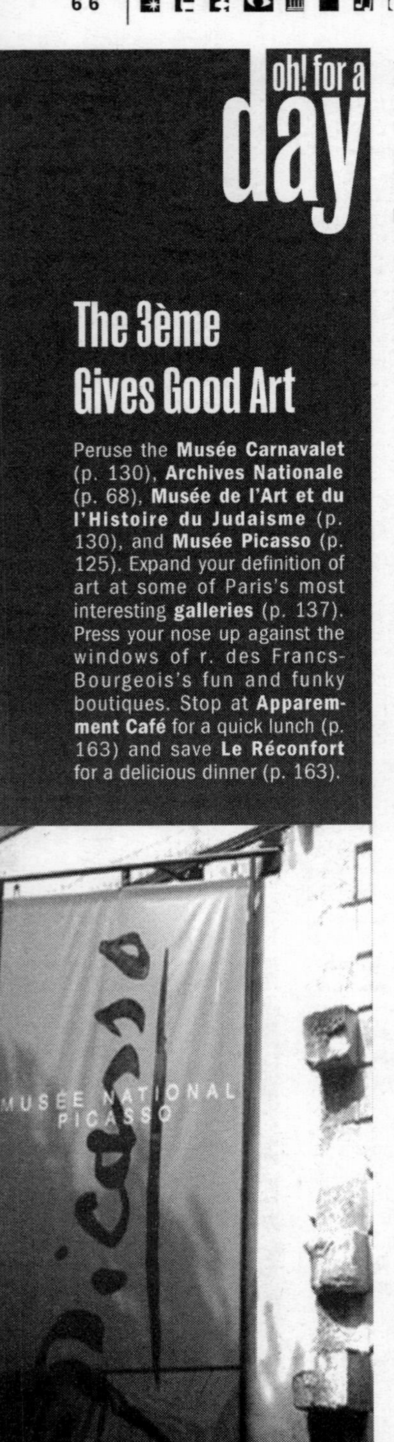

The 3ème Gives Good Art

Peruse the **Musée Carnavalet** (p. 130), **Archives Nationale** (p. 68), **Musée de l'Art et du l'Histoire du Judaisme** (p. 130), and **Musée Picasso** (p. 125). Expand your definition of art at some of Paris's most interesting **galleries** (p. 137). Press your nose up against the windows of r. des Francs-Bourgeois's fun and funky boutiques. Stop at **Apparemment Café** for a quick lunch (p. 163) and save **Le Réconfort** for a delicious dinner (p. 163).

Across from the library's main entrance, **pl. Louvois's** sculpted fountain personifies the four great rivers of France—the Seine, the Saône, the Loire, and the Garonne—as heroic women.

BOURSE DES VALEURS AND GALERIE JUNK BOND

R. Notre-Dame des Victoires. M: Bourse. ☎ 40 41 62 20. 30F, students 15F. Call ahead to book a tour.

The Bourse des Valeurs, Paris's stock exchange, had a rather frivolous beginning. Founded in 1724, it soon became a treasure chest for the Bourbon kings, who enjoyed issuing worthless bonds to finance their taste for palaces and warfare. Jacobins closed the exchange during the Revolution in order to fend off war profiteers. It was reopened under Napoleon, who loved all things Neoclassical and relocated it to its current somber building, complete with requisite Corinthian columns. Computers have made the edifice all but redundant—a fact that seems to have been missed by the **Galerie Junk Bond,** an artists' squat across from the Bourse. Junk Bond began as a colorful, if belated, protest in 1999, employing a paint-splattered facade to contrast its stately neighbor—only to be shut down the following summer. Both buildings now have a sleepy, abandoned feel. The Bourse houses a veritable museum of itself, explaining its history and ambiguous present function.

THÉÂTRE MUSICAL POPULAIRE (PREVIOUSLY OPÉRA COMIQUE)

M: Richelieu Drouot. To the west of the Bourse, between r. Favart and r. Marivaux. For performance information, see ***Classical Music, Opera, and Dance,*** *p. 152.*

Laughs and sobs resonated at the Opéra Comique for two centuries. Originally built as the Comédie Italienne, it burned down twice in the 1840s and was finally rebuilt in 1898. It was here that Bizet's *Carmen* first hitched up her skirts, cast a sweltering glance at the audience, and seduced Don José by trilling, "*Si tu m'aimes pas, je t'aime. Et si je t'aime prends garde à toi*" ("If you don't love me, I love you. And if I love you watch out"). Under new management, the opera has changed its name and expanded to embrace all kinds of musical theatre, including Broadway musicals and operettas.

TO THE EAST

RUE ST-DENIS

M: Strasbourg-St-Denis.

In the mid-1970s, Paris's prostitutes demonstrated in churches, monuments, and public squares demanding unionization. They marched down r. St-Denis, the central artery of the city's prostitution district, to picket for equal rights and protection under the law. Their campaign was successful and prostitution is now legal in France. Officially, sex workers are still not allowed to work the streets, and only the prostitutes themselves can use the money they earn on the job. This creates a problem, since even if a woman uses her earnings to support her family, her husband can be prosecuted as a procurer. Despite its legalization, however, prostitution in France is far less visible and common than in the Netherlands or Thailand. Except, of course, along r. St-Denis.

Hotel de Ville

OTHER SIGHTS

TOUR DE JEAN SANS PEUR. To the left of r. Montorgueil stand the well-preserved remnants of the 15th-century Tour de Jean Sans Peur (Tower of Fearless John), built next to the old city wall, which is now r. Etienne Marcel. Soon after ordering the successful assassination of the king's brother, Louis d'Orléans, in 1408, M Sans Peur erected a tower in his house, the Hôtel de Bourgogne. To crown this mountain of pride, he named it in his own honor. *(M: Sentier.)*

THE MARAIS

The *3ème* and *4ème arrondissements* comprise the area known as **the Marais.** Drained by monks in the 13th century, the Marais ("swamp") was land-filled to provide building space for the Right Bank. With Henri IV's construction of the **Place des Vosges** (see **Sights,** p. 72) at the beginning of the 17th century, the area became the city's center of fashionable living. Leading architects and sculptors of the period designed elegant *hôtels particuliers* with large courtyards. Under Louis XV, the center of Parisian life moved to the *faubourgs* (then considered suburbs) **St-Honoré** and **St-Germain,** and construction in the Marais ceased. During the Revolution, the former haunts of the sovereign gave way to slumlords and their tenements. Many *hôtels* fell into ruin or disrepair, but in the 1960s the Marais was declared an historic neighborhood and a thirty-year period of gentrification attracted trendy boutiques, cafés, and museums. The area's narrow streets nevertheless retain the stamp of a medieval village.

Place de la Bastille

THIRD ARRONDISSEMENT

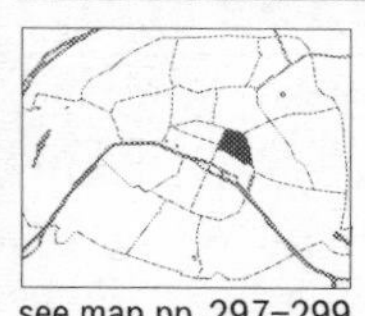

see map pp. 297–299

M: République.

PLACE EMILE-CHAUTEMPS

Pl. Emile-Chautemps lies between **bd. Sébastopol,** Haussmann's great thoroughfare, and the **Conservatoire National des Arts et Métiers,** 292, r. St-Martin (☎40 27 22 20), a technical institute whose immense **Foucault's Pendulum** swings against the earth's axis.

RUE DES ARCHIVES

The beautiful 18th-century **Fontaine des Haudriettes** on r. des Archives features a water-spouting lion.

Places des Vosges

RUE VIEILLE-DU-TEMPLE

Hôtel de Rohan *☎40 27 60 09; exhibits ☎40 27 60 00; research ☎40 27 64 19. Open M-F 9am-6pm.*

MERDE!

The French have a love affair with their dogs, and nearly 500,000 pooches call Paris home. According to official figures, the dogs of Paris leave over 11 tons of *déjections canines* on Paris's streets per day. Sidewalks are veritable mine fields; experienced Parisians keep one eye on the ground. Since 1977, the Paris government has been campaigning—under the title *"La lutte contre les polutions canines"* (The Fight Against Canine Pollution)—to encourage people to have their best friends defecate in street gutters. Inspiring slogans include: "Teach him the gutter" and "If you love Paris, don't let him do that!" Clean-up efforts are now aided by a technological triumph called the *Caninette*, or more informally the *Motocrotte* (crap mobile). You may see these hybrid motorcyle/vacuum cleaners sucking up *excreta* all around town. If you have the misfortune of stepping into some *crotte de chien*, hope it's with your left foot; according to Parisian superstition, it's good luck. For those who'd rather wring their little necks, take pleasure in the 17*ème*'s **Cimetière des Chiens** (see **Sights**, p. 101).

This street is lined with stately residences including the 18th-century **Hôtel de la Tour du Pin** (no. 75) and the more famous **Hôtel de Rohan** (no. 87). Built between 1705 and 1708 for Armand-Gaston de Rohan, Bishop of Strasbourg and alleged love-child of Louis XIV, the *hôtel* has housed many of his descendants. Frequent temporary exhibits allow access to the interior *Cabinet des Singes* and its original decorations. The Hôtel de Rohan, part of the National Archives, also boasts an impressive courtyard and rose garden. Equally engaging are the numerous art galleries that have taken root on the street (see **Galleries,** p. 137). Across r. Vieille-du-Temple, the **alleyway** at 38, r. Francs-Bourgeois, gives a sense of what Henri IV's dark and claustrophobic Paris felt like. At the corner of r. des Francs-Bourgeois and r. Vieille-du-Temple, the flamboyant Gothic **Hôtel Hérouët** and its turrets were built in 1528 for Louis XII's treasurer, Hérouët.

ARCHIVES NATIONALES

60, r. des Francs-Bourgeois. M: Rambuteau. ☎ 40 27 64 19 or 40 27 64 20. Scholars should apply to the Centre d'Accueil et de Recherche des Archives Nationales, 11, r. des Quatre-Fils.

Housed in the 18th-century Hôtel de Soubise, the **Musée de l'Histoire de France** (see **Museums,** p. 130) is the main exhibition space of the National Archives. The Treaty of Westphalia, the Edict of Nantes, the Declaration of the Rights of Man, Marie-Antoinette's last letter, Louis XVI's diary, letters between Benjamin Franklin and George Washington, and Napoleon's will are all preserved here. Like George III's diary entry for July 4, 1776 (the American Declaration of Independence), Louis XVI's entry for July 14, 1789 (Bastille Day) reads simply *Rien* (Nothing). Out at Versailles, far from the uprising in Paris, it had been a bad day for hunting. The only documents on display are featured in the museum's temporary exhibits. Call for upcoming events.

FOURTH ARRONDISSEMENT

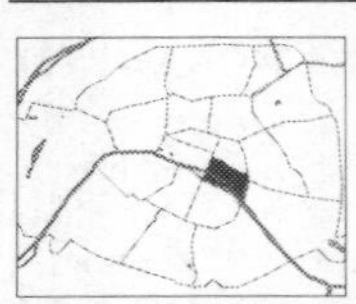

see map pp. 297–299

The **Lower Marais** is a supremely fun neighborhood. It's accessible. It's soft-core hip. It's red wine. It's just-barely-affordable, sort-of-designer shops. It's falafels—and knishes. It's gay men out for an afternoon snack. It's family-run goodness. Let the festivities begin. (Open on Sunday.)

TO THE NORTH: BEAUBOURG

CENTRE POMPIDOU

M: Rambuteau or Hôtel-de-Ville.

One of the most visible examples of renovation in the 4*ème* is the Centre Pompidou, the ultra-modern exhibition, performance, and research space considered alternately as an innovation or an eyesore (see **Museums,** p. 122). Dominating Beaubourg, a former slum *quartier* whose high rate of tuberculosis earned it the classification of an *îlot insalubre* (unhealthy block) in the 1930s, the Pompidou shocked Parisians when it opened in 1977. Its architects, Richard Rogers, Gianfranco Franchini, and Renzo Piano, designed a building whose color-coded electrical tubes (yellow), water pipes (green), and ventilation ducts (blue) highlight the exterior of the building. More people visit the Pompidou every year than visit the Louvre. Initially designed to accommodate 5,000 visitors a day, the center and its **Musée Nationale de l'Art Moderne** attract more like 20,000. Given this discrepancy and the impetus of the year 2000 celebrations, the center's directors re-enlisted Renzo Piano and architect Jean-François Bodin for a two-year renovation project that ended at the center's reopening on December 31, 1999. Head to the Pompidou to revel in their success or just to hang out in the cobblestone square out front, which gathers a mixture of artists, musicians, rebels, and passersby. Exercise caution: pickpockets frequent the area by day and rougher types hang out there by night.

RUE DES ROSIERS

Four blocks east of Beaubourg, parallel to r. des Francs-Bourgeois. M: St-Paul.

At the heart of the Jewish community of the Marais, the r. des Rosiers has kosher shops, butchers, bakeries, and falafel counters galore. Until the 13th century, Paris's Jewish community was concentrated in front of Notre-Dame. When Philippe-Auguste expelled the Jewish population from the city limits, many families moved to the Marais, just outside the walls. Since then, this quarter has been Paris's Jewish center, witnessing the influx of Russian Jews in the 19th century and new waves of North African Sephardim fleeing Algeria in the 1960s. This mix of Mediterranean and Eastern European Jewish cultures gives the area a unique flavor, with *kugel* and falafel served side-by-side. During WWII, many who had fled to France to escape the pogroms of Eastern Europe were murdered by the Nazis. Assisted by French police, Nazi soldiers stormed the Marais and hauled Jewish families to the Vélodrome d'Hiver, an indoor cycling stadium. Here, French Jews awaited deportation to work camps like Drancy, in a northeastern suburb of Paris, or to camps farther east in Poland and Germany. The Mémorial de la Déportation on the Île de la Cité commemorates these victims (see **Sights,** p. 58). Despite these atrocities, the Jewish community thrives in the Marais with two synagogues at 25, r. des Rosiers and 10, r. Pavée, designed by Art Nouveau architect Hector Guimard.

MÉMORIAL DU MARTYR JUIF INCONNU

17, r. Geoffroy de l'Asnier. M: St-Paul. Entrance to the left of the gates. ☎ 42 77 44 72; fax 48 87 12 50; email memcdjc@calva.net; www.calvacom.fr/calvaweb/memorial/cdjchome.html. ***Memorial*** *open Su-Th 10am-1pm and 2-6pm, F 10am-1pm and 2-5pm. 15F.* ***Documentation Center*** *open M-Th 2-6pm. 15F.*

The Memorial to the Unknown Jewish Martyr commemorates European Jews who died at the hands of the Nazis and their French collaborators. Due to a 1980 terrorist attack, visitors must now pass through a metal detector. The crypt and monument contain ashes brought back from concentration camps and from the Warsaw ghetto. Upstairs, the **Centre de Documentation Juive Contemporaine** (Jewish Contemporary Documentation Center) displays two permanent exhibits, "The Internment of the Jews under Vichy" and "Letters from Internment Camps in France," as well as temporary exhibits. The center's library holds more than 50,000 documents and one million items relating to the Nazi era.

RUE VIEILLE-DU-TEMPLE AND RUE STE-CROIX DE LA BRETTONERIE

Alongside the Jewish *quartier*, these streets form the heart of Paris's vibrant gay community. This is where the boys are. Paris's *super hyper chic* gay restaurants, shops, and bars rub elbows with bakeries in this area, and although many establishments fly the rainbow flag, both gay and straight convene to shop and brunch on the cobblestones.

oh! for a day

A Slow 4ème

Start the day off with shopping at the cute and quirky stores along the **r. des Francs-Bourgeois** (saving the more specifically gay stores of rue Ste-Croix de la Bretonnerie for later). Continue along Francs-Bourgeois to the **Place des Vosges** (see p. 72) for lounging, more window shopping, or a picnic lunch. Admire the one-time homes of Daudet and Hugo among the arcades around the *place*. Hungry? Swing back towards the **rue des Rosiers** (see p. 69) by way of the rue St Antoine for falafel at **l'As du Falafel** (see p. 176) in the Jewish *quartier*, not forgetting the **Eglise St-Paul-St-Louis** (see p. 68) on the way. Continue down Rosiers to the **rue Vieille du Temple** for people watching and an *aperatif* at **Au Petit Fer a Cheval** (see p. 163). Finish off the day with dinner and drinks at **Le Divin** (see p. 164).

HÔTEL DE VILLE AND SURROUNDINGS

HÔTEL DE VILLE

29, r. de Rivoli. M: Hôtel-de-Ville. ☎ 42 76 43 43, tours ☎ 42 76 50 49. **Open** *M-Sa 9am-6:30pm.* **Free tours** *offered the first M of each month at 10:30am; call in advance to reserve.*

Paris's grandiose city hall dominates a large square with fountains and Belle Epoque lampposts. The present edifice is a 19th-century creation built to replace the original medieval structure, a meeting hall for the cartel that controlled traffic on the Seine. In 1533 under King François I, the old building was destroyed. A new building was designed by Boccadoro in the Renaissance style of the Loire châteaux. The elegant building witnessed municipal executions on pl. Hôtel-de-Ville. In 1610, Henri IV's assassin Ravaillac was quartered alive here by four horses bolting in opposite directions.

On May 24, 1871, the *communards* doused the building with petrol and set it afire. Lasting a full eight days, the blaze spared nothing but the frame. The Third Republic built a virtually identical structure on the ruins, with a few significant changes. The Republicans integrated statues of their own heroes into the facade: historian Michelet flanks the right side of the building while author Eugène Sue surveys the r. de Rivoli. The Third Republic installed brilliant crystal chandeliers, gilded every interior surface, and created a Hall of Mirrors in emulation of Versailles. When Manet, Monet, Renoir, and Cézanne offered their services, they were all turned down in favor of ponderous, didactic artists whose work decorates the Salon des Lettres, the Salon des Arts, the Salon des Sciences, and the Salon Laurens. The Information Office holds exhibits on Paris in the lobby.

Originally called pl. de Grève, the **pl. Hôtel-de-Ville** made a vital contribution to the French language. Poised on a marshy embankment *(grève)* of the Seine, the medieval square served as a meeting ground for angry workers, giving France the useful phrase *en grève* (on strike). Strikers still gather here amid riot police. During the 1998 World Cup and the Euro 2000, fans watched the French victory on huge screens erected on the square.

TOUR ST-JACQUES

39-41, r. de Rivoli. M: Hôtel-de-Ville. Two blocks west of the Hôtel-de-Ville.

The Tour St-Jacques stands alone in the center of its own park. This flamboyant Gothic tower is the only remnant of the 16th-century Eglise St-Jacques-la-Boucherie. The 52m tower's meteorological station and the statue of Pascal at its base commemorate Pascal's experiments on the weight of air, performed here in 1648. The tower marks Haussmann's *grande croisée* of r. de Rivoli and the bd. Sébastopol, the intersection of his east-west and north-south axes for the city, only meters from where the earliest Roman roads crossed two thousand years ago.

SOUTH OF RUE ST-ANTOINE AND RUE DE RIVOLI

EGLISE ST-GERVAIS-ST-PROTAIS

R. François-Miron. M: Hôtel-de-Ville.

The Eglise St-Gervais-St-Protais was named after Gervase and Protase, two Romans martyred under Nero. The church's classical facade, flamboyant Gothic vaulting, stained glass, and Baroque wooden Christ by Préault are part of a working monastery. The public is welcome to matins (Tu-Sa 7am), vespers (Tu-Sa 6pm), and high mass (Su 11am) to hear the nave filled with Gregorian chant.

HÔTEL DE BEAUVAIS

68, r. François-Miron.

The Hôtel de Beauvais was built in 1655 for Pierre de Beauvais and his wife Catherine Bellier. Bellier, Anne d'Autriche's chambermaid, had an adolescent tryst with the Queen's son, 15-year-old Louis XIV. As the story goes, Anne was overjoyed to learn that her son would please his future wife more than Anne's impotent husband Louis XIII had pleased her. From the balcony of the *hôtel*, Anne d'Autriche and Cardinal Mazarin watched the entry of Louis XIV and his bride, Marie-Thérèse, into Paris. A century later, as a guest of the Bavarian ambassador, Mozart played his first piano recital here. Restored in 1967, the half-timbered 14th-century **Maison à l'Enseigne du Faucheur** (no. 11) and **Maison à l'Enseigne du Mouton** (no. 13) illustrate what medieval Paris looked like.

HÔTEL DE SENS

1, r. du Figuier. M: Pont Marie.

The Hôtel de Sens is one of the city's few surviving examples of medieval residential architecture. Built in 1474 for Tristan de Salazar, the Archbishop of Sens, its military features reflect the violence of the day. The turrets were designed to survey the streets outside, while the square tower served as a dungeon. An enormous Gothic arch entrance—complete with chutes for pouring boiling water on invaders—contributes to the mansion's intimidating air. The former residence of Queen Margot, Henri IV's first wife, the Hôtel de Sens has witnessed some of Paris's most daring romantic escapades. In 1606, the 55-year-old queen drove up to the door of her home, in front of which her two current lovers were arguing. One opened the lady's carriage door, and the other shot him dead. Unfazed, the queen demanded the execution of the other, which she watched from a window the next day. The *hôtel* now houses the **Bibliothèque Forney.**

LA MAISON EUROPÉENNE DE LA PHOTOGRAPHIE

5-7, r. de Fourcy. M: St-Paul. ☎44 78 75 00; fax 44 78 75 15; www.mep-fr.org. Open W-Su 11am-8pm. 30F, students 15F; free W 5-8pm. Wheelchair accessible.

Galleries, library, and *vidéothèque* are housed in the Hôtel Hénault de Cantobre. They host temporary exhibits of international photography. The permanent display, *Les Plus Beaux Plans du Monde*, displayed on 40 screens, presents photography and film from the late 1950s to the present.

ÉGLISE ST-PAUL-ST-LOUIS

99, r. St-Antoine. M: St-Paul. ☎42 72 30 32; fax 42 72 01 06. Open M 8am-8pm, Tu-W and F-Sa 7:30am-8pm, Th 7:30am-10pm, Su 9am-8pm. Free tours at 2:30pm, every 2nd Su of the month. Mass Sa 6pm, Su 9:30, 11:15am, and 7pm.

This church dates from 1627 when Louis XIII placed its first stone. Its large dome—a trademark of Jesuit architecture—is visible from afar, but hidden by ornamentation on the facade. Paintings inside the dome depict four French kings: Clovis, Charlemagne,

Robert the Pious, and St-Louis. The embalmed hearts of Louis XIII and Louis XIV were kept in vermeil boxes carried by silver angels before they were destroyed during the Revolution. The church's Baroque interior is graced with three 17th-century paintings of the life of St-Louis and Eugène Delacroix's dramatic *Christ in the Garden of Olives* (1826). The holy-water vessels were gifts from Victor Hugo.

OTHER SIGHTS

17, RUE BEAUTREILLIS. Jim Morrison died (allegedly of a heart attack) here in his bathtub on the third floor. His grave can be found at Père Lachaise (see **Sights,** p. 105).

PLACE DES VOSGES AND SURROUNDINGS

PLACE DES VOSGES

M: Chemin Vert or St-Paul.

At the end of r. des Francs-Bourgeois sits the magnificent pl. des Vosges, Paris's oldest public square. The central park, lined with immaculately manicured trees centered around a splendid fountain, is surrounded by 17th-century Renaissance townhouses. Kings built several mansions on this site, including the Palais de Tournelles, which Catherine de Medicis ordered destroyed after her husband Henri II died there in a jousting tournament in 1563. Henri IV later ordered the construction of a new public square.

Each of the 36 buildings has arcades on the street level, two stories of pink brick, and a slate-covered roof. The largest townhouse, forming the square's main entrance, was the king's pavilion; opposite, the pavilion of the queen is smaller. The marriage of Louis XIII's sister to the crown prince of Spain drew a crowd of 10,000 here in 1612. Originally intended for merchants, the pl. Royale attracted the wealthy, including Mme. de Sévigné and Cardinal Richelieu. Molière, Racine, and Voltaire filled the grand parlors with their bon mots. Mozart played a concert here at the age of seven. Even when the city's nobility moved across the river to the Faubourg St-Germain, pl. Royale remained among the most elegant spots in Paris. During the Revolution, however, the 1639 Louis XIII statue in the center of the park was destroyed (the statue there now is a copy), and the park was renamed pl. des Vosges after the first department in France to pay its taxes (in 1800). Follow the arcades around the edge of pl. des Vosges for an elegant promenade, window-shopping, and a glimpse of plaques that mark the homes of famous residents. Théophile Gautier and Alphonse Daudet lived at no. 8. Victor Hugo lived at no. 6, which is now a museum of his life and work (see **Museums,** p. 130). During the summer, the arcades fill with classical musicians. Leave pl. des Vosges through the corner door at the right of the south face (near no. 5), which leads into the garden of the Hôtel de Sully.

HÔTEL DE SULLY

62, r. St-Antoine. M: St-Paul. Caisse Nationale ☎ 44 61 21 50. Open M-F 9am-6pm, Sa 10am-1:15pm and 2-5pm.

Built in 1624, the Hôtel de Sully, was acquired by the Duc de Sully, minister to Henri IV. Often cuckolded by his young wife, Sully would say when giving her money, "*voici tant pour la maison, tant pour vous, et tant pour vos amants*" ("here's some for the house, some for you, and some for your lovers"), asking only that she keep her paramours off the staircase. The small inner courtyard offers the fatigued tourist several stone benches and an elegant formal garden. On the side of the *hôtel* along St-Antoine is the **Caisse Nationale des Monuments Historiques,** which distributes free maps and brochures on monuments and museums.

HÔTEL DE LAMOIGNON

22, r. Malher. M: St-Paul. ☎ 44 59 29 60. Open Tu-Sa 10am-6pm, Su noon-7pm. 20F, students and seniors 10F.

The Lamoignon is one of the finest *hôtels particuliers* in the Marais. Built in 1584 for Henri II's daughter, Diane de France, the facade is in the Colossal style, later used in the Louvre. Lamoignon and the adjacent buildings now house the **Bibliothèque Historique de la Ville de Paris,** a non-circulating library of Parisian history with 800,000 volumes. An exhibition hall next door focuses on the history of the *quartier*.

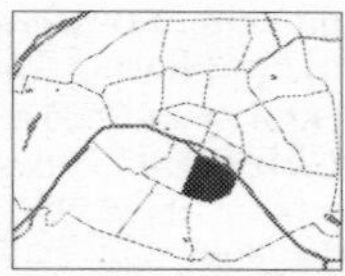
see map pp. 302–303

FIFTH ARRONDISSEMENT

TO THE WEST: THE LATIN QUARTER

Even as wave after wave of tourists breaks on the Rive Gauche, the 5*ème* maintains its reputation as the nerve of young Paris. The autumn influx of Parisian students is undoubtedly the prime cultural preservative of the Quartier Latin, which takes its name from the old-time language used in its prestigious *lycées* and universities prior to 1798 (for more **Latin in Paris,** see p. 25). Compared to the now opulent café scene of St-Germain-des-Prés, the Latin Quarter is relatively relaxed and more genuinely intellectual. Some say the Quarter has fallen into a sad state since the riots of May 1968 (see **History,** p. 33): the new, concrete sidewalk slabs that replaced the loose cobblestones used as missiles in the protests are proof enough. Indeed, in the 30 years since, many artists and intellectuals have migrated to the outer arrondissements as the *haute bourgeoisie* have moved in.

Mosquée de Paris

PLACE ST-MICHEL

M: St-Michel.

The busiest spot in the Latin Quarter, pl. St-Michel holds much political history: the Paris Commune began here in 1871, as did the student uprising of 1968. The 1860 fountain features a WWII memorial commemorating the citizens who fell here defending their *quartier* during the Liberation of Paris in August 1944. Ice cream shops and *crêpe* stands line r. St-Severin, while Greek *gyro* (say it with us now, "YEE-row") counters crowd r. de la Huchette.

The nearby **Eglise St-Julien-le-Pauvre** (a right off bd. St-Michel and another right onto r. St-Julien le Pauvre) was begun in 1170, and is one of the oldest churches in Paris. At the intersection of bd. St-Germain and bd. St-Michel, the **Hôtel de Cluny,** 6, pl. Paul-Painlevé, was once a medieval monastery, built on the ruins of a first-century Roman bath house. Today, the building houses the **Musée de Cluny's** collection of medieval art, tapestries, and illuminated manuscripts (see **Museums,** p. 126). As a major tourist thoroughfare, **bd. St-Michel** (or *boul' Mich'*) won't give you much of an impression of local life; however, many of the traditional bistros of the quarter hold their ground on the nearby streets.

Jardin des Plantes

LA SORBONNE

45-7, r. des Ecoles. M: Cluny-La Sorbonne or RER: Luxembourg. Open M-F 9am-5pm.

Walk away from the Seine on bd. St-Michel and make a left on r. des Ecoles. **Pl. de la Sorbonne's** cafés, students, and bookstores face out from the Sorbonne itself, one of Europe's oldest universities. Founded in 1253 by Robert de Sorbon as a dormitory for 17 theology students, the Sorbonne soon became the administrative base for the University of Paris. In 1469, Louis XI established France's first printing house here. As it grew in power and size, the Sorbonne often contradicted the authority of the French throne; it sided with England during the Hundred

Gallery of Comparative Anatomy

Years War. Today, the Sorbonne is officially known as *Paris IV*, the fourth of the University of Paris's 13 campuses. Commissioned in 1642 by Cardinal Richelieu, the university's main building, **Ste-Ursule de la Sorbonne,** located on r. des Ecoles is open to the public. The cardinal lies buried inside the **chapel,** his hat suspended above him by a few threads hanging from the ceiling. Legend has it that when Richelieu is freed from purgatory, the threads will snap and the hat will tumble down.

COLLÈGE DE FRANCE

Courses run Sept.-May. Info ☎ 43 29 12 11 or 44 27 12 11.

Created by François I in 1530 to contest the university's authority, the Collège de France stands behind the Sorbonne. The outstanding courses at the Collège, given by such luminaries as Henri Bergson, Paul Valéry, and Milan Kundera, are free and open to all. Check the schedules that appear by the door in September.

THE PANTHÉON

Pl. du Panthéon. M: Cardinal Lemoine. From the métro, walk down r. Cardinal Lemoine and turn right on r. Cujas; walk around to the front of the building to enter. ☎ 44 32 18 00. ***Open*** *daily 9:30am-6:30pm; last admission 5:45pm.* ***Admission*** *35F, students 23F.* ***Guided tours*** *in French of the history, architecture, and décor leave from inside the main door daily at 2:30 and 4pm.*

The inscription written in stone across the front of the Panthéon dedicates the building "To great men from a greatful fatherland," but originally, the Panthéon was simply a dedication from a man to his wife. In 507, King Clovis converted to Christianity and had a basilica designed to accommodate his tomb and that of his wife, Clotilde. In 512, the basilica became the resting place of Ste-Geneviève, who was believed to have protected Paris from the attacking Huns with her prayers (for more, see **History,** p. 25). Her tomb immediately became a pilgrimage site, and so many people came to pay homage to the patron saint of Paris that a set of worshippers dedicated themselves to the managment of her relics and remains, calling themselves Génovéfains.

Louis XV was also feeling pretty darn grateful after surviving a grave ilness in 1744, a miracle he ascribed to the powers of Ste-Geneviève. He vowed to build a prestigious monument to the saint and entrusted the design of the new basilica to the architect Soufflot in 1755. Louis laid the first stone himself in 1764 and after Soufflot's death, the neoclassical basilica was continued by architect Rondelet and completed in 1790. The walls of the basilica got a nice dressing-up in 1874 when the director of the Musée des Beaux Arts comissioned some of the finest artists of the time to depict the story of Ste-Geneviève.

The Revolution converted the church into a mausoleum of heroes on April 4, 1791, in an attempt to find a place for proleteriat poet Mirabeau's body. The

oh! for a day

Studying the 5ème

From **pl. St-Michel,** walk up bd. St-Michel away from the Seine to peek in at the gardens and ruins of the **Musée Cluny** (p. 126) on your left. If you make a left on r. des Ecoles, you might catch snippets of intellectual conversation as you pass **La Sorbonne** (p. 73) on your right. Make a right on r. St-Jacques and a left on r. Soufflot, and you'll be faced with the **Panthéon** (p. 73). Venture inside for **Foucault's Pendulm** and luminaries buried in the **crypt.** Relax in a café on **pl. de la Contrescarpe** and have a drink before wandering the tiny winding streets off the square, making sure not to miss **r. Mouffetard.** Walk back through the place and down r. Cardinal Lemoine, bearing right on r. des Fossés St-Bernard to visit the **Institut du Monde Arabe** (p. 76). Afterward, walk down r. Linné and stroll through the **Jardin des Plantes** (p. 75). For dinner, walk up r. Geoffroy and make a left on r. Lacépedé and visit **Au Jardin des Pâtés** (p. 164). For some relief from French speaking, wander back down r. Limé and make a right on r. des Boulangers and stop in for a pint at **Finnegan's Wake** (p. 189).

next year when his correspondence with King Louis XVI was revealed. In 1806, Napoleon reserved the crypt for the interrment of those who had given "great service to the State." The Panthéon is full of some of France's most valuable citizens: in the crypt you will find writers Voltaire, Rousseau, Hugo, and Zola (, scientists Marie and Pierre Curie, politician Jean Jaurès, and Louis Braille, inventor of the reading system for the blind. At Hugo's burial in 1885, two million mourners and Chopin's *Marche Funèbre* followed the coffin to its resting place.

FOUCAULT'S PENDULUM. The Panthéon's other attraction is a giant fifth-grade experiment taken to new extremes: the plane of oscillation of Foucault's Pendulum stays fixed as the Earth rotates around it. The pendulum's rotation is confirmation of the rotation of the Earth for non-believers, who included Louis Napoleon III and a large crowd in 1851.

EGLISE ST-ETIENNE DU MONT

While everyone's dying to get in, not all of France's luminaries are buried in the Panthéon. Pascal and Racine are buried next door in the Eglise St-Etienne du Mont. Built from 1492 to 1626, the Gothic interior features rose windows and relics.

OTHER SCHOLARLY SIGHTS

LYCÉE LOUIS-LE-GRAND. Just south of the Collège lies the Lycée Louis-le-Grand, where Molière, Robespierre, Victor Hugo, Baudelaire, and Pompidou spent part of their pre-university years. Sartre taught there as well.

ECOLE NORMALE SUPÉRIEURE. France's premier university, the Ecole Normale Supérieure, is located southeast of the Sorbonne on r. d'Ulm and is part of the Grands Ecoles, a consortium of France's best schools. Normale Sup' (as its students, the *normaliens*, call their alma mater) accepts only the most gifted students in its programs in literature, philosophy, and the natural sciences.

TO THE EAST: PLACE DE LA CONTRESCARPE

South on r. Descartes, past the prestigious Lycée Henri IV, **pl. de la Contrescarpe** is the geographical center of the 5*ème*.

RUE MOUFFETARD

South of pl. de la Contrescarpe, **r. Mouffetard** plays host to the liveliest street market in Paris (see **Food Markets,** p. 180). Today, r. Mouffetard and **r. Monge** bind much of the tourist and student social life, but r. Mouffetard wasn't always the snaking alley of gourmet shops and touristy jazz clubs you'll find here today. The most storied street of the Latin Quarter, running down the backside of Mt. Ste-Geneviève, it was the main thoroughfare of a wealthy villa from the 2nd century, when Romans ruled, until the 13th century. Hemingway lived down the Mouff' at 74, r. du Cardinal Lemoine.

ARÈNES DE LUTÈCE

At the intersection of r. de Navarre and r. des Arènes.

The Arènes de Lutèce (Lutèce Arenas) were built by the Romans in the 1st century AD to accommodate 15,000 spectators. Similar to oval amphitheaters in Rome and southern France, these ruins were unearthed in 1869 and restored in 1910; all the seats are reconstructions.

JARDIN DES PLANTES

☎40 79 37 94. ***Jardin des Plantes*** *and* ***Rosarie*** *open daily in summer 7:30am-8pm; winter 7:30am-5:30pm.* ***Jardin Alpin*** *and* ***Ecole de Botanique*** *open M-F 8-11am and 1:30-5pm. Free.* ***Serres Tropicales*** *open W-M Apr.-Oct. 1-6pm; Nov.-Mar. 1-5pm. 15F, students 10F.* ***Musée d'Histoire Naturelle*** *and* ***Ménagerie Zoo*** *open daily Apr.-Sept. 9am-6pm; Oct.-Mar. 9am-5pm. Last admission 30min. before closing. 30F, students and ages 4-16 20F.*

In the eastern corner of the 5*ème*, the Jardin des Plantes offers 45,000 square meters of carefully tended flowers and lush greenery. Opened in 1640 by Louis XIII's doctor, the gardens grew medicinal plants to promote His Majesty's health. The garden is divided into several sections: the **Ecole de Botanique** is a carefuly landscaped garden tended by students, horticulturalists and amature botanists; the **Roserie** is a lucious, fragrant display of roses from all over the world (in full bloom in mid-June); the two big, botanical boxes of the **Serres Tropicales** are full of tropical plants from rainforests; the **Jardin Alpin** contains more than 2000 plants from mountain ranges including the Alps, the Pyrenees, and the Himalayas.

The gardens also include the blockbuster **Musée d'Histoire Naturelle** (see **Museums,** p. 131) and the **Ménagerie Zoo.** Although no match for the Parc Zoologique in the Bois de Vincennes (see **Sights,** p. 110), the zoo will gladden anyone's day with its 240 mammals, 500 birds, and 130 reptiles. During the siege of Paris in 1871, the zoo was raided for meat, and elephants were served to starving Parisians. Mmmm...tusky.

ALONG THE SEINE

MOSQUÉE DE PARIS

Behind the Jardin des Plantes at pl. du Puits de l'Ermite. M: Jussieu. ☎ 45 35 97 33. Open June-Aug. Sa-Th 9am-noon and 2-6pm. Guided tour 15F, students 10F.

The Institut Musulman houses the beautiful Mosquée de Paris, a mosque constructed in 1920 by French architects to honor the role played by the countries of North Africa in WWI. Green-tiled arcades and cool courtyards provide a soothing setting for prayer, an afternoon in the exquisite *hammam* (see **Cafés,**), or mint tea in the café.

INSTITUT DU MONDE ARABE

1, r. des Fosses St-Bernard. M: Jussieu. Walk down r. Jussieu away from the Jardin des Plantes and make your first right onto r. des Fosses St-Bernard. ☎ 40 51 38 38. Open Tu-Su 10am-7pm. 25F, ages 12-18 20F, under 12 free.)

The Institut du Monde Arabe (IMA) is housed in one of the city's most striking buildings. Facing the Seine, the IMA resembles a ship, representing the boats on which Algerian, Moroccan, and Tunisian immigrants sailed to France. The southern facade is made up of 240 Arabesque portals that open and close, powered by light sensitive cells that determine just how much light is needed to illuminate the interior of the building without damaging the art. Inside, the IMA houses permanent and rotating exhibitions on Maghrebian, Near Eastern, and Middle Eastern Arab cultures as well as a library, research facilities, lecture series, film festivals, and a gorgeous rooftop terrace where you don't have to eat in the expensive restaurant to see the views of the Seine, Montmartre, and the Île de la Cité. For more on the IMA, see **Museums,** p. 131.

OTHER SIGHTS

JARDIN DES SCULPTURES EN PLEIN AIR. The beautiful Jardin des Sculptures en Plein Air, quai St-Bernard, boasts a collection of modern sculpture, including works by Zadkine and Brancusi, on a long stretch of green along the Seine. A nice place to read and sunbathe by day, but exercise caution at night.

SIXTH ARRONDISSEMENT

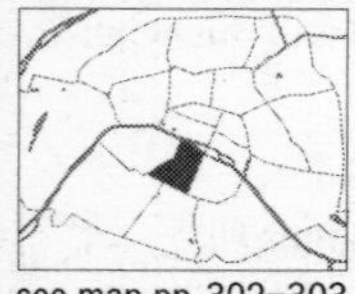

see map pp. 302–303

The 5*ème* contains Paris' Grandes Ecoles and much of the student population, but its western neighbor, the 6*ème*, rivals it in intellectual prowess—at least historically. The cafés of St. Germain-des-Prés are the former stomping grounds of Hemingway, Sartre, Picasso, Camus, Baudelaire, and almost any other intellectual or artistic giant you can think of who was in Paris during the first half of the 20th century. If you close your eyes, you might be able to picture them smoking, drinking absinthe, and contemplating modernity, but this can be difficult when surrounded by tourists or the current upscale set of inhabitants. Even so, the 6*ème* has a genuine art scene kept alive by its excellent galleries and the Ecole des Beaux-Arts.

JARDIN DU LUXEMBOURG AND ODÉON

JARDIN DE LUXEMBOURG

M: Odéon; RER: Luxembourg. Open daily Apr.-Oct. 7:30am-9:30pm; Nov.-Mar. 8:15am-5pm. The wrought-iron gates of the main entrance are on bd. St-Michel. Guided tours in French the first W of every month, Apr.-Oct., at 9:30am; depart from pl. André Honorat behind the observatory.

"There is nothing more charming, which invites one more enticingly to idleness, reverie, and young love, than a soft spring morning or a beautiful summer dusk at the Jardin du Luxembourg," wrote Léon Daudet in an absolute fit of sentimentality and mushiness in 1928. For those who care, a keg and booty music also do the trick. Parisians flock to these formal gardens to sunbathe, write, stroll, read, and gaze at the rose gardens, central pool, and each other. A residential area in Roman Paris, the site of a medieval monastery, and later the home of naughty 17th-century French royalty, the gardens were liberated during the Revolution and are now free to all. Children can sail toy boats in the fountain, ride ponies, and see the *grand guignol* (a puppet show; see **Guignols,** p. 153) while their parents and grandparents pitch *boules*. Feel free to saunter through the park's paths, passing sculptures of France's queens, poets, and heroes, and the romantic Fontaine Medici. A mammoth task-force of gardeners tends this most beloved of Parisian gardens; each spring they plant or transplant 350,000 flowers and move the 150 palm and orange trees out of winter storage.

PALAIS DU LUXEMBOURG

The Palais du Luxembourg, located within the park and now serving as the home of the French Senate, was built in 1615 at Marie de Medici's request. Homesick for her native Tuscany, she tried to recreate its architecture and gardens in central Paris. Her builders finished the Italianate palace in a mere five years and Marie moved in 1625. But a feud with the powerful Cardinal Richelieu made her time there brief. Marie's son, Louis XIII, promised that he would dismiss the cardinal, but he revoked his promise the following day. Wielding great power, Richelieu banished the Queen Mother in 1630 to Cologne, where she died penniless. The palace later housed members of the nobility, including the Duchesse de Montpensier (known as *la Grande Mademoiselle* because of her girth). Robert le Pieux made it the site of his pleasure dome, the Château de Vauvert: for years after its demolition, locals referred to *le diable de Vauvert*, due to rumors of the goings-on there. During the Terror, the palace was first a prison for nobles on deck for the guillotine and then for Revolutionary Jacobin perpetrators.

The Luxembourg again took center stage during the First and Second Empires. Imprisoned in the palace during the Revolution with her Republican husband, Beauharnais, the future Empress Josephine returned five years later to take up official residence with her second husband, the new Consul Napoleon Bonaparte. After the Emperor's exile to Elba, his young nephew was tried in the palace for leading several abortive rebellions against the July Monarchy. Sentenced to life imprisonment, he escaped and prepared his return to France. In 1851 he declared the Second Empire and became Emperor Napoleon III. During World War II, the palace was occupied by the Nazis, who made it the headquarters of the *Luftwaffe*.

In 1852 the palace first served its current function as the meeting place for the Sénat, the upper house of the French parliament. The president of the senate lives in Petit Luxembourg, originally a conciliatory gift from Marie de Medici to her nemesis Richelieu.

MUSÉE DU LUXEMBOURG

R. de Vaugirard. ☎ 42 34 25 95. Open M-Sa 11am-6:30pm.

Next to the Palace, **Musée du Luxembourg** shows free exhibitions of contemporary art.

THÉÂTRE DE L'ODÉON

M:Odéon. From the métro, walk down r. de L'Odéon to the pl. de l'Odéon.

The Théâtre Odéon is Paris's oldest and largest theater (see **National Theaters,** p. 150). Completed in 1782, the Odéon was purchased by Louis XVI and Marie-Antoinette for the

For all the Little People Out There

A world of parks awaits all those touring Paris too cool for Euro Disney and too young for Beaujolais and Chanel. The **Jardin du Luxembourg** (see p. 77) offers ponies, mini sail boats, and enough cotton candy to make a dentist see dollar signs. Explore **Parc Monceau** (see p. 88), among whose architectural *folies* half of France's ruling elite was wheeled as babies; the **Parc des Buttes-Chaumont** (see p. 104), whose cliffs and waterfalls will impress pre-teens, and whose *guignols* and explorable creeks are the favorites of many a muddy local child; the expansive **Parc de la Villette** (see p. 104), whose Cité des Science et de l'Industrie is fun and educational (but don't say the second word in front of the children), and whose other gardens are the best in the city for romping about; and the **Jardin d'Acclimatation** (see p. 107), which has pony rides, mini-golf, a zoo, bumper cars, and carousels.

Comédie Française. Founded by Molière in the 17th century, the celebrated theater troupe did not have a theater of its own. Beaumarchais's *Marriage of Figaro*, nearly banned by Louis XVI for its attacks on the nobility, premiered here in 1784 before delighted aristocratic audiences. In 1789, the actor Talma staged a performance of Voltaire's *Brutus* in which he imitated the pose of the hero in David's painting. As the Revolution approached, the Comédie Française splintered over the issue of political loyalties. Republican members followed Talma to the Right Bank, settling into the company's current location near the Louvre (see **National Theaters,** p. 150). Those actors who remained behind were jailed under the Terror and the theater was closed. It was later known as the *théâtre maudit* (cursed theater) after two fires and a chain of failures left it nearly bankrupt. Its present Greco-Roman incarnation dates from an 1818 renovation overseen by David (for more on the master, see **Fine Arts,** p. 46). The Odéon's fortunes changed after World War II, when it became a venue for contemporary, experimental theater. On May 17, 1968, student protesters seized the building and destroyed much of its interior before police quelled the rebellion.

EGLISE ST-SULPICE

M: St-Sulpice or Mabillon. From the Mabillon métro, walk down r. du Four and make a left on r. Mabillon which intersects r. St. Suplice at the church. 2 blocks west of the theater. ☎46 33 21 78. Open daily 7:30am-7:30pm. Guided visit in French daily 3pm.

Eglise St-Sulpice was designed by Servadoni in 1733, but remains unfinished. The church contains Delacroix frescoes in the first chapel on the right (*Jacob Wrestling with the Angel* and *Heliodorus Driven from the Temple*), a *Virgin and Child* by Jean-Baptiste Pigalle in a rear chapel, and an enormous Chalgrin organ. In the transept, an inlaid copper band runs along the floor from north to south, connecting a plaque in the south to an obelisk in the north. A ray of sunshine passes through a hole in the upper window of the south transept during the winter solstice, striking marked points on the obelisk at mid-day. A beam of sunlight falls on the copper plaque during the summer solstice and behind the communion table during spring and autumn equinox.

ST-GERMAIN-DES-PRÉS

Known as *le village de Saint-Germain-des-Prés*, the area around **bd. St-Germain** between St-Sulpice and the Seine is pocketed with cafés, restaurants, cinemas, and expensive boutiques, and is always crowded.

ÉGLISE DE ST-GERMAIN-DES-PRÉS

3, pl. St-Germain-des-Prés. M: St-Germain-des-Prés. From the métro, walk into pl. St-Germain-des-Prés to enter the church from the front. ☎43 25 41 71. Open daily 8am-7:45pm. Info office open Tu-Sa 10:30am-noon and 2:30-7pm.

The Eglise de St-Germain-des-Prés is the oldest standing church in Paris. King Childebert I commissioned a church on this site to hold relics he had looted from the Holy Land. Completed in 558, it was consecrated by St-Germain, Bishop of Paris, on the very day of King Childebert's death—the king had to be buried inside the church's walls.

The rest of the church's history reads like an architectural Book of Job. Sacked by the Normans and rebuilt three times, the present-day church dates from the 11th century. On June 30, 1789, the Revolution seized the prison in a dress rehearsal for the storming of the Bastille. The church then did a brief stint as a saltpeter mill and in 1794, the 15 tons of gunpowder that had been stored in the abbey exploded. The ensuing fire devastated the church's artwork and treasures, including much of its monastic library. Baron Haussmann destroyed the last remains of the deteriorating abbey walls and gates when he extended r. de Rennes to the front of the church and created place St-Germain-des-Prés.

The magnificent interior, painted in shades of terra-cotta and deep green with gold, was restored in the 19th century. In the second chapel—on the right after the apse—you'll find a stone marking the interred heart of 17th-century philosopher René Descartes, who died of pneumonia at the frigid court of Queen Christina of Sweden, as well as an altar dedicated to the victims of the September 1793 massacre in which 186 Parisians were slaughtered in the courtyard. Pick up a free map of the church with information in English on St-Germain's hstory, artifacts, and frequent concerts (see **Classical Music, Opera, and Dance,** p. 152). As in most medieval churches, built to accommodate an age without microphones, the acoustics are awesome.

Panthéon

rue Mouffetard

Sorbonne

ECOLE NATIONALE SUPÉRIEURE DES BEAUX-ARTS

14, r. Bonaparte, at quai Malaquais. M: St-Germain-des-Prés. From the métro, walk down r. Bonaparte. ☎47 03 50 00; application info ☎47 03 50 65; www.ensba.fr.

France's most acclaimed art school, the Ecole Nationale Supérieure des Beaux-Arts was founded by Napoleon in 1811 and soon became the stronghold of French academic painting and sculpture. The current building, the Palais des Etudes, was finished in 1838 and is a mix of architectural styles. The public is not permitted to tour the building itself nor to prowl around its gated courtyard, but you can get a look at the next Léger or Delacroix at the changing public shows in the Exhibition Hall at 13, quai Malaquais. If you have the talent to be the one on display, the school admits foreign students.

PALAIS DE L'INSTITUT DE FRANCE

Pl. de l'Institut. M: Pont Neuf. From the Pont Neuf métro, walk west on quai du Louvre and cross the Seine on the Pont des Arts. One block to the east of the ENSB-A on quai Malaquai.

The Palais de l'Institut de France broods over the Seine beneath its famous black and gold-topped dome, added to the building in 1663. Designed by Le Vau to lodge a college established in Cardinal Mazarin's will, it has served as a school (1688-1793), a prison (1793-1805), and is now home to the humorless Académie Française. The glorious building has housed this branch of the Institut de France since 1806 and is also home to La bibliothèque Mazarine. Although the building is not open to the public, peek inside the courtyard to the right and get a glimpse of Mazarine's enormous funeral sculpture.

ODÉON

After the arch of the **Cour du Commerce St-André,** a pedestrian passageway off bd. St-Germain, stands the **Relais Odéon,** a Belle Epoque bistro whose stylishly painted exterior, decked with floral mosaics and a hanging sign, is a fine example of Art Nouveau (see **Fine Arts,** p. 39), as is the doorway of #7, r. Mazarine, several blocks north. Farther down this passageway, on the top floor of the building on your left, was the site of the Revolutionary-era clandestine press that published Marat's *L'Ami du Peuple.* Marat was assassinated by Charlotte Corday in the bathtub of his home, which once stood where the courtyard meets r. de l'Ancienne Comédie.

OTHER SIGHTS

HÔTEL DES MONNAIES. Once the mint for all French coins, Hôtel des Monnaies, next door to the Palais de l'Institut de France (see above), proudly presents its austere 17th-century facade to the heart of the Left Bank.

PONT DES ARTS. The footbridge across from the Institut, appropriately called the Pont des Arts, is celebrated by poets and artists for its delicate ironwork, beautiful views of the Seine, and spiritual locus at the heart of France's prestigious Academy of Arts and Letters. Built as a toll bridge in 1803, it was the first bridge to be made of iron. On the day it opened, 65,000 Parisians paid to walk across it; today, it is less crowded, absolutely free, and just as lovely.

oh! for a day

Day and Night in the Seventh

Beat the crowds to the **Musée d'Orsay** (see p. 119) for a morning among the Impressionists. Then, pop your head into the **Musée de la Légion d'Honneur** (p. 124), across the road, before heading around the corner for lunch at the **Restaurant des Lettres** (p. 167). Wander down r. de l'Université and bd. des Invalides for an afternoon stroll among the rose gardens of the **Musée Rodin** (p. 123), before crossing the boulevard to investigate **Napoleon's Tomb.** For dinner, walk back up to r. de Bourgogne to hear French poetry and sip red wine after a satisfying meal. Catch the RER at Invalides, get out after two stops, and climb the **Eiffel Tower** (p. 81) for a view of the jeweled city in all her glittering splendor.

SEVENTH ARRONDISSEMENT

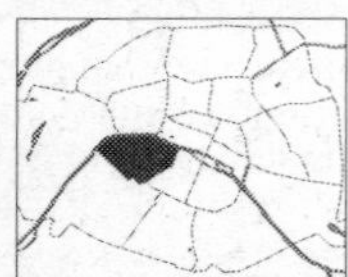

see map pp. 304–305

Since the 18th century, the *7ème* has stood its ground as the city's most elegant residential district. Home to the National Assembly, countless foreign embassies, the Invalides, the Musée d'Orsay (see **Museums,** p. 119), and the Eiffel Tower, this section of the Left Bank is a medley of France's diplomatic, architectural, and military achievements. In the home of the Musée Rodin's rose gardens and the public markets of the r. Cler, you can take in the most touristic and some of the most intimate sights in Paris in the same breath.

TO THE WEST

THE EIFFEL TOWER

M: Bir Hakeim. ☎ 44 11 23 45; www.eiffel-tower.com. ***Open*** *daily June-Aug. 9am-midnight; Sept.-May 9:30am-11pm.* ***Elevator*** *to 1st floor 22F, under 12 12F; 2nd floor 44F, under 12 22F; 3rd floor 62F, under 12 31F.* ***Stairs*** *to 1st and 2nd floors 18F. Under 4 free.*

The Eiffel Tower was created by the designer of the Statue of Liberty, Gustave Eiffel. Of the tower he wrote: "France is the only country in the world with a 300m flagpole." Designed in 1889 as the tallest structure in the world, the Eiffel Tower was conceived as a monument to engineering that would surpass the Egyptian pyramids in size and notoriety. Yet before construction had even begun, shockwaves of dismay reverberated through the city. Critics dubbed it "metal asparagus" and a Parisian tower of Babel. After the building's completion, writer Maupassant ate lunch every day at its ground-floor restaurant—the only place in Paris, he claimed, from which he couldn't see the offensive thing.

Nevertheless, when it was inaugurated in March, 1889 as the centerpiece of the Universal Exposition, the tower earned the love of Paris; nearly 2,000,000 people ascended during the event. Numbers dwindled by comparison during the following decades. As the 20-year property lease approached expiration, Eiffel faced the imminent destruction of his masterpiece. But the tower survived because of its importance as a communications tower, a function Eiffel had helped cultivate in the 1890s. The radio-telegraphic center atop the tower worked during WWI to intercept enemy messages, including the one that led to the arrest and execution of Mata Hari, the Danish dancer accused of being a German spy.

With the 1937 World Exposition, the Eiffel Tower again became a showpiece. Eiffel himself walked humbly before it, remarking: "I ought to be jealous of that tower. She is more famous than I am." Since then, Parisians and tourists alike have reclaimed the monument in over 150,000,000 visits. On everything from postcards to neckties and umbrellas, Eiffel's wonder still takes the heat from some who see it as Maupassant did: an "excruciating nightmare" overrun with tourists and their trinkets. Don't believe the anti-hype, though. The tower is a wonder of design, and all those kitschy replicas are just that. It is a soft brown, not the metallic steel gray that most visitors anticipate. And despite the 7,000 tons of metal and 2,500,000 rivets, which hold together its 12,000 replaceable parts, the tower appears light and elegant, especially at night, when artfully placed spotlights turn it into a lacy hologram.

As the world counted down to the year 2000, a tremendously expensive digital clock was mounted on the face of the Eiffel Tower, and for two years a pedestrian needed only glance up at the skyline to see the number of days remaining until the new century. But as millions watched Paris prepare to herald the Millennium by turning her famous landmark into a glorious candle of fireworks, the clock stopped. France held its breath as the whole operation was switched to manual—the show was saved, and no one noticed that Paris celebrated the Millennium a bit early. To commemorate this feat the tower will sparkle every night for the first ten minutes of every hour from sundown to 1am until the year 2001.

The cheapest way to ascend the tower is by walking up the first two floors (18F). The **Cinemax,** a relaxing stop on the first floor, shows films about the tower. Posters chronicling its history are a good excuse to catch your breath and rest your legs. Visitors must take an elevator to get to the third story, but tickets are only 21F. The top floor offers the obvious reward of an unparalleled view of the city, and captioned aerial photographs (in English) help you locate landmarks. On a clear day it is possible to see Chartres Cathedral 55 miles away.

NEAR THE TOWER

CHAMP DE MARS

Although close to the *7ème*'s military monuments and museums, the Champ de Mars (Field of Mars) celebrates the god of war for other good reasons. It was here that Julius

Caesar finally squelched the rebellious Parisii tribe in 53 BC. One hundred and forty years later, Viking ships were rolled over it. However, neither of these heroic encounters are the reason for the long, long lawn's name. Champs de Mars comes from the days of Napolean's Empire when it was used as a drill ground for the adjacent Ecole Militaire. In 1780, Charles Montgolfier launched the first hydrogen balloon from here. During the Revolution, the park witnessed civilian massacres and political demonstrations. At the Champ's 1793 Festival of the Supreme Being, Robespierre proclaimed Reason the new Revolutionary religion. During the 1889, 1900, and 1937 expositions, the space was used for fairgrounds. Today the God of War would be ashamed to see his parks turned into daisy strewn lawns stretching from the Ecole Militaire to the Eiffel Tower littered with lounging tourists looking up at a metal finger in the sky. Perhaps most disturbing for Mars would be the new, see-through monument to international peace that has been erected at the end of the Champs.

ECOLE MILITAIRE

1, pl. Joffre. M: Ecole Militaire. From the métro, head toward the Eiffel Tower on ave. de la Motte Piquet. Ecole Militaire will be on your left.

In 1751, Louis XV created the Ecole Militaire at the urging of his mistress, Mme. de Pompadour, who hoped to make educated officers of "poor gentlemen." In 1784, the 15-year-old Napoleon Bonaparte arrived from Corsica to enroll. A few weeks later he presented administrators with a comprehensive plan for the school's reorganization. By the time he graduated three years later, he was a lieutenant in the artillery. Teachers foretold he would "go far in favorable circumstances." The building was made into a barracks for the Swiss Guard by Louis XVI, but was converted back into a military school in 1848. Today, French and foreign officers attend the School of Advanced War Studies. As such, it belongs to the army, and no tours are available to the public.

UNESCO

7, pl. de Fontenoy. M: Ségur. ☎45 68 10 60 or 45 68 07 77; cinema ☎45 68 00 68; www.unesco.org. Bookstore open M-F 9am-1pm and 2-6pm. Exhibition hours vary.

The Ecole Militaire's architectural and spiritual antithesis, UNESCO (United Nations Educational, Scientific, and Cultural Organization) occupies the Y-shaped building across the road. Established in 1958 to foster science and culture throughout the world, the agency built this major international monument in Paris. It represents 186 nations and is the creation of three different architects: the American Breurer, the Italian Nervi, and the Frenchman Zehrfuss. Despite its dynamic symbolism, the entrance to the building from pl. de Fontenoy seems very understated and is easy to mistake for a private office building. Don't be deterred: the organization welcomes visitors and the exhibitions are often well worth the trouble of navigating the entrance.

In the outer courtyard a huge sculpture by **Henri Moore** called *Figure in Repose* is joined by a mobile by the American artist **James Calder** and a walking man by Swiss sculptor **Giacometti.** Inside the foyer of Room I is a painting by **Picasso** entitled *The Fall of Icharus*, and next door the Salle des Actes boasts a tapestry by the Swiss architect **Le Corbusier.** In the garden behind Segur Hall there is a lovely Japanese garden, a meditation area, and a set of metal sculptures by **Vassilakis Takis.** By the garden is an angel from the facade of a Nagasaki church destroyed by the atomic bomb during WWII. Unfortunately, UNESCO developed a reputation in the 60s and 70s for waste, cronyism, and Marxism, prompting the US, the UK, and Singapore to withdraw in 1984 (the UK rejoined in 1997). For information on internships with UNESCO, see **Alternatives to Tourism,** p. 267.

TO THE EAST

INVALIDES

2, av. de Tourville. M: Invalides.

The gold-leaf dome of the Hôtel des Invalides shines at the center of the *7ème.* The green, tree-lined **Esplanade des Invalides** runs from the *hôtel* to the **Pont Alexandre III,** a bridge with gilded lampposts from which you can catch a great view of the Invalides and the Seine. **Napoleon's tomb,** as well as the **Musée de l'Armée, Musée d'Histoire Contemporaine,** and **Musée de l'Ordre de Liberation,** are housed within the Invalides museum complex (see **Museums,** p. 124). Enter from either pl. des Invalides or pl. Vauban and av. de Tourville. To the left of the Tourville entrance, the **Jardin de l'Intendant** offers shady benches for rest when you've had your fill of guns and emperors. Lined with foreign cannons, the ditch used to be a moat and still makes it impossible to leave by any but the official entrance.

ASSEMBLÉE NATIONALE

33, quai d'Orsay; kiosque 4, r. Aristide-Briand. M: Assemblée Nationale. ☎ 40 63 64 08; kiosque ☎ 40 63 61 21; www.assemblée-nat.fr. Open Oct.-June while the Assembly is in session. Tours M and F-Sa 10am, 2, and 3pm. Free. Come 30min. early; entrance is first come, first serve. Reserve English tours in advance. Kiosque open Sept.-July M-F 9:30am-7pm, Sa 9:30am-1pm; Aug. M-F 10am-noon and 2-5pm.)

East of the Esplanade, the Palais Bourbon would probably not be recognized by its original occupants. Built in 1722 for the Duchesse de Bourbon, daughter of Louis XIV, today the palace is the well-guarded home of the French parliament. Machine-gun-toting police stationed every few yards are ostensibly there to prevent a replay of the unsuccessful 1934 Fascist coup, during which rioters stormed the building.

Free guided tours (in French, with pamphlet in English) of the Assembly's chambers include a visit to the **Salon Delacroix** and the library (both spectacularly painted by Eugène Delacroix). The library holds the original transcripts of Joan of Arc's trial, as well as busts of Voltaire and Diderot (for more on **French literature,** see p. 36). The tour continues in the Assembly chamber, the **Salle de Séances,** where the Président du Conseil presides. Behind him, a framed tapestry of Raphael's *School of Athens* depicts the republic of philosopher-kings. Members of the political right and left sit to the right and left of the president's seat. The **Kiosque de l'Assemblée Nationale** provides more info as well as souvenirs.

PALAIS DE LA LEGION D'HONNEUR

At the corner of r. de Lille and r. de Bellechasse. M: Solférino.

Once the elegant **Hôtel de Salm,** the Palais de la Legion d'Honneur was built in 1786 by architect Rousseau for the Prince de Salm-Kyrburgh. Unable to make payment, the prince later returned it to Rousseau but continued to live there as a tenant until he was decapitated in 1794. The state raffled the *hôtel* the following year to a wealthy wig maker named Lieuthraud who presented himself as Count Beauregard until 1797, when he was jailed as a forger. The mansion was then purchased by the Swedish ambassador and his wife, *salonnière* Mme. de Staël. Purchased again by Napoleon in 1804, the *hôtel's* current name bears the mark of its most recent owner. It was burned down during the Commune of 1871, but the members of the Legion rebuilt it soon after using the original plans. Now it houses the **Musée National de la Legion d'Honneur** (see **Museums,** p. 132). Although the museum's display of medals and military honoraria may not spark the interest of many tourists, admission allows a look at the 18th- and 19th-century interiors.

LA PAGODE

South of the Musée Rodin, at the intersection of r. de Babylone and r. Monsieur.

A Japanese pagoda built in 1895 by the Bon Marché department store magnate M. Morin as a gift to his wife, La Pagode endures as a testament to the 19th-century Orientalist craze in France. Incidentally, the marriage lasted as long as the orientalist fad: Mme. Morin left her husband for his colleague's son just prior to WWI. The building then became the scene of Sino-Japanese soirées, although these years saw a period of tension between the two countries. In 1931, La Pagode opened its doors to the public, becoming a cinema and swank café where the likes of silent screen star Gloria Swanson were known to raise a glass. The theater closed during the Nazi occupation, despite the Axis allegiance. Although it reopened in 1945, it was again closed in 1998 due to a lack of funds to maintain it. A campaign to save La Pagode is underway, but for now visitors must content themselves with the pagoda's exteriors.

GHOSTS OF PARIS'S PAST

Quai Voltaire, known for its lovely views of Seine bridges, also has an artistic heritage more distinguished than any other block in the city. At No. 27 **Voltaire** himself spent his last days. No. 19 housed **Baudelaire** in 1856-58 while he wrote *Les Fleurs du Mal* (Flowers of Evil), as well as **Richard Wagner** as he composed Die Meistersinger in 1861-62; No. 19 was also home to **Oscar Wilde** while he was in exile. **Delacroix** lived at No. 13 from 1829-1836, and the landscape painter **Corot** also resided at No.13. At No. 11, **Ingres** died in 1867. The famous Russian ballet dancer, **Rudolf Nureyev** lived at No. 23 from 1981 until his death in 1993. For more on Parisian literature and fine arts, see p. 36.

OTHER SIGHTS

HÔTEL MATIGNON. Once owned by Talleyrand, Hôtel Matignon is now the official residence of the prime minister. *(57, r. Varenne.)*

EGLISE ST-THOMAS D'AQUIN. The 17th-century Eglise St-Thomas d'Aquin was originally dedicated to St-Dominique, but was reconsecrated by Revolutionaries as the Temple of Peace. *(On r. de Gribeauval, off r. du Bac.* ☎ *42 22 59 74. Open M-F 9am-7pm, Su 9am-noon.)*

FONTAINE DES QUATRE SAISONS. Farther south, the **Fontaine des Quatre Saisons** (Fountain of Four Seasons) features a personified, seated version of the city of Paris near reclining figures of the Seine and the Marne. Bouchardon built the fountain in 1739-45 to provide water to this part of the city. Nearby at 202, bd. St-Germain, the poet Guillaume Apollinaire lived and died. *(55-57, r. de Grenelle. M: r. du Bac.)*

EIGHTH ARRONDISSEMENT

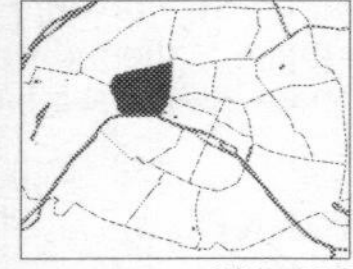

see map pp. 306–307

The showy elegance has a tendency to make tourists feel schlumpy; just remember that the *8ème* has a historical inferiority complex of its own. Faubourg St-Honoré was once an extension of the Tuileries, home of *nouveau riches* wannabes, while the residential Faubourg St-Germain on the left bank was the stomping ground of true blue bloods (aristocrats who felt they defined the opulant elegance of the ancien regime). The neighborhood didn't really take off until the turn of the 19th century, when the aristos had been chased out by the Revolution and Napoleon gave deserving officers and *haute bourgeoisie* titles and prestige of their own. Under his nephew, Louis-Napoleon, the *8ème* became a hub of social and commercial activity. Napoleon finished the construction of the pl. de l'Etoile centered around the Arc de Triomphe, from which radiate twelve grand Haussmanian boulevards, including the Champs-Elysées.

ALONG THE CHAMPS-ELYSÉES

> "Here there was a strange little exhibitionist who thought that if he could walk unclothed and unmolested from the Etoile to the Place de la Concorde he could solve many things—and, perhaps, Dick thought, he was quite right."
>
> —F. Scott Fitzgerald, *Tender is the Night*

ARC DE TRIOMPHE

M: Charles-de-Gaulle-Etoile. ☎ *55 37 73 77.* ***Open*** *daily Apr.-Sept. 9:30am-11pm; Oct.-Mar. 10am-10:30pm. Last entry 30min. before closing.* ***Admission*** *40F, ages 12-25 25F, under*

12 free. Expect lines even on weekdays. You will kill yourself trying to dodge the merry-go-round of cars unless you find the pedestrian underpass on the right side of the Champs-Elysées facing the monument. Buy your ticket in the pedestrian underpasses before going up to the ground level.

It is hard to believe that the Arc de Triomphe, looming gloriously above the Champs-Elysées at pl. Charles de Gaulle-Etoile, was first designed as a huge, bejeweled elephant. Oh those crazy Empire architects. The world's largest triumphal arch crowns a flattened hill between the Louvre and pont de Neuilly—an ideal vantage point that, in 1758, excited the imagination of the architect Ribart, whose ambition it was to erect an animal of monumental proportions. Fortunately for France, construction of this international symbol of her military prowess was not started until 1805, when Napoleon envisioned a monument somewhat more appropriate for welcoming troops home. Unfortunately for Napoleon, he was exiled before the monument was completed, but Louis XVIII ordered the completion of the work in 1823 and dedicated the arch to the war in Spain and to its commander, the Duc d'Angoulême. Designed in the end by Chalgrin, the Arc de Triomphe was consecrated in 1836, 21 years after the defeat of Napoleon's great army. There was no consensus on what symbolic figures could cap the monument, and so it has retained its simple unfinished form. The names of Napoleon's generals and battles are engraved inside; those generals whose names are underlined died in battle. The most famous of the Arc's allegorical sculpture groups depicting the military history of France is François Rude's *Departure of the Volunteers of 1792*, commonly known as *La Marseillaise*, to the right facing the arch from the Champs-Elysées.

Since Napoleon, the horseshoe-shaped colossus has been a magnet for various triumphal armies. The victorious Prussians marched through in 1871, inspiring the mortified Parisians to purify the ground with fire. On July 14, 1919, however, the Arc provided the backdrop for an Allied celebration parade headed by Maréchal Foch. His memory is now honored by the boulevard that bears his name and stretches out from the Arc into the 16*ème*. French sanctification of the Arc was frustrated once more during WWII; Frenchmen were reduced to tears as the Nazis goose-stepped through their beloved arch. After the torturous years of German occupation, a sympathetic Allied army made sure a French general would be the first to drive under the famous edifice.

The **Tomb of the Unknown Soldier** has been under the Arc since November 11, 1920. It bears the inscription, "Here lies a French soldier who died for his country, 1914-1918," but represents the 1,500,000 men who died during WWI. The **eternal flame** is rekindled every evening at 6:30pm, when veterans lay wreaths decorated with blue, white, and red. Inside the Arc, climb 205 steps up a winding staircase to the *entresol* between the Arc's two supports, and then 29 more to the *musée*. Or, tackle the lines at the elevator for a lift. Motion impaired visitors should be aware that the elevator is often out of service: call in advance to check. The **museum** explains (in French) the Arc's architecture and history. Just 46 steps beyond it, the **terrasse observation deck**, at the top of the Arc, provides a brilliant view of the Champs-Elysées, the tree-lined av. Foch (see **Sights**, p. 99), and the "Axe Historique"—from the Arc de Triomphe du Carrousel and the Louvre Pyramid at one end to the Grande Arche de la Défense at the other.

St-Germain-des-Prés

Palais du Luxembourg

St-Sulpice

AVENUE DES CHAMPS-ELYSÉES

"Paris is the Latin spirit expressing itself as Taste in a world already civilized, and conquering, not with man's will, but with feminine attraction."
—English journalist, 1929.

The av. des Champs-Élysées is the most famous of the 12 symmetrical avenues radiating from the huge rotary of pl. Charles de Gaulle-Étoile. Although the "Champs" has been a fashionable avenue since Marie de Medici ploughed its first incarnation, the Cours-la-Reine, through fields and marshland to the west of Paris in 1616, it was still pretty unkempt until the early 19th century, when the city built sidewalks and installed gas lighting. From that point on, the throughfare flourished, and where elegant houses, restaurants, and less subdued bars and panoramas sprung up, the *beau monde* was guaranteed to see and be seen. Balls, café-concerts, restaurants, and circuses drew enormous crowds. The infamous Bal Mabille opened in 1840 at no. 51. At no. 25, visitors have the rare chance of seeing a true *hôtel particulier* from the Second Empire—here the Marquise de Paiva, adventuress, famous courtesan, and spy, entertained the luminaries of the era. In the 1980s, the ostentatious boulevard was thoroughly commercialized and began to seem like little more than a series of chain stores and burger joints. In the last decade, Jacques Chirac has made a concerted effort to resurrect the Champs, widening the sidewalks, planting more trees, and creating urgently needed underground parking lots. Today it is an intriguing mixture of old and new, inviting swarms of tourists to tramp through mini mall, but still hiding pockets of greenery and glamour. Six big avenues radiate from the Rond Point des Champs-Elysées. Av. Montaigne runs southwest and shelters the houses of *haute couture.*

PALAIS DE L'ÉLYSÉE

M: Champs-Elysées-Clemenceau.

The guards pacing around the house at the corner of av. de Marigny and r. du Faubourg St-Honoré are protecting the Palais de l'Elysée. Built in 1718, the palais was later home to Mme. de Pompadour; after her divorce from Napoleon, Josephine Bonaparte lived here. Before he came into power, Napoleon III was also a resident. Since 1870, it has served as state residence of the French president, now Jacques Chirac. Entrance requires personal invitation. The guards here hold guns, bark at people, and are not amused by girls in bikinis trying to sneak into the garden.

GRAND AND PETIT PALAIS

At the foot of the Champs-Elysées, the Grand and Petit Palais face one another on av. Winston Churchill. Built for the 1900 World's Fair, they were widely received as a dazzling combination of "banking and dreaming," exemplifying the ornate Art Nouveau architecture. While the Petit Palais houses an eclectic mixture of artwork belonging to the city, its big brother has been turned into a space for temporary exhibitions on architecture, painting, sculpture, French history, and recently devoted its space to an overview of Paris at the Millenium. The Grand Palais also houses the **Palais de la Découverte** (see **Museums,** p. 132). Most beautiful at night, the glass dome of the Grand Palais glows greenly from within, and its statues are backlit.

OTHER SIGHTS

FOUQUET'S. Today, you can watch others cling desperately to the Champs' glorious past at Fouquet's, a famous and outrageously expensive café-restaurant where French film stars (ostensibly) hang out. The red-awninged eatery still hosts the French answer to the Oscars, the annual César awards (see p. 168).

THÉÂTRE DES CHAMPS-ELYSÉES. Built by the Perret brothers in 1912 with bas-reliefs by Bourdelle, the Théâtre des Champs-Elysées is best known for staging the controversial premiere of Stravinsky's *Le Sacre du Printemps.* Nijinsky had choreographed a ballet for dancers dressed in feathers and rags, hopping about pigeon-toed to evoke primitivism, and a riot ensued. The three large *salles* still host performances. *(15, av. Montaigne. M: Alma-Marceau. ☎ 49 52 50 15. See p. 153 for full listing.)*

CRAZY HORSE SALOON. Around the corner from the theater, the **Crazy Horse Saloon,** long famous for its cabaret, still entertains fans of the "Art du Nu," or art of the nude. *(12, av. Georges V.)*

PERSHING HALL. Pershing Hall is a 113-year-old, five-story piece of America. Given to the US government, the building has allegedly been used as a brothel, a brawling bar, a casino, a black-market exchange, and a Council Travel office. Now closed, it awaits its next incarnation. *(49, r. Pierre Charron.)*

AROUND PLACE DE LA CONCORDE

PLACE DE LA CONCORDE

M: Concorde.

Paris's largest and most infamous public square forms the eastern terminus of the Champs-Elysées. With your back to ave. Gabriel, the Tuileries Gardens are to your left; across the river lie the gold-domed Invalides and the columns of the Assemblée Nationale. Behind you stands the Madeleine. Constructed between 1757 and 1777 to provide a home for a monument to Louis XV, it soon became a billboard of public grievance and accusation against the King. It is not hard to imagine why this vast area was to become pl. de la Révolution, the site of the guillotine that severed 1,343 necks from their blue-blooded bodies. On Sunday, January 21, 1793, Louis XVI was beheaded by guillotine on a site near where the Brest statue now stands. The celebrated heads of Marie-Antoinette, Charlotte Corday (Marat's assassin), Lavoisier, Danton, Robespierre, and others rolled into baskets here and were held up to the cheering crowds who packed the pavement. After the Reign of Terror, the square was optimistically renamed **pl. de la Concorde** (place of Harmony).

Much favored by film crews for its views of Paris's monuments (and especially for the view of the Eiffel Tower in relief against the Paris sky), this square has been featured in many films, such as the dream sequence in Gene Kelly and Stanley Donen's *An American in Paris*. On Bastille Day, a military parade marches through pl. de la Concorde (usually around 10am) and down the Champs-Elysées to the Arc de Triomphe led by the President of the Republic (see **Festivals,** p. 8). In the evening, an impressive fireworks display lights up the sky over pl. de la Concorde. At the end of August, the Tour de France finalists pull into the home stretch on the Champs-Élysées and the pl. de la Concorde.

OBÉLISQUE DE LUXOR. Recalling a little scuffle called the Revolution that had been ignited by the pompous statue of his predecessor, it is not surprising that King Louis-Phillipe opted for a more apolitical monument when he chose the Obélisque de Luxor, offered by Mehemet Ali, Viceroy of Egypt, to Charles X in 1829. Getting the obelisk from Egypt to the center of Paris was no simple task—the monolith had to be transported by sea, and a special boat was built to transport it up the Seine. Erected in 1836, Paris's oldest monument dates back to the 13th century BC and recalls the deeds of Ramses II. At night the obelisk, fountains, and cast-iron lamps are illuminated, creating a romantic glow, somewhat eclipsed by the hordes of cars rushing by at breakneck speed.

CHEVEAUX DE MARLY. Flanking the Champs-Elysées at pl. de la Concorde stand Guillaume Coustou's Cheveaux de Marly. Also known as *Africans Mastering the Numidian Horses*, the original sculptures are now in the Louvre to protect them from the effects of city pollution. Perfect replicas graciously hold their places on the Concorde. Eight large statues representing France's major cities also grace the *place*.

THE MADELEINE

Pl. de la Madeleine. M: Madeleine. ☎44 51 69 00. Open daily 7:30am-7:15pm. Regular organ and chamber concerts; contact the church for a schedule, and Virgin or FNAC for tickets.)

Mirrored by the Assemblée Nationale across the Seine, the Madeleine—formally called Eglise Ste-Marie-Madeleine (Mary Magdalene)—was begun in 1764 by Louis XV and modeled after a Greek temple. Construction was halted during the Revolution, when the Cult of Reason proposed transforming the building into a bank, a theater, or a courthouse. Characteriscally, Napoleon decreed that it should become a temple to the greatness of his army, while Louis XVIII shouted, "It shall be a church!" Completed in 1842, the structure stands alone in the medley of Parisian churches, distinguished by its four ceiling domes that light the interior, 52 exterior Corinthian columns, and a curious altarpiece. An immense sculpture of the ascension of Mary Magdalene, the church's namesake, adorns the altar. A colorful flowermarket thrives along the right-hand side of the church; sometimes, their wares will appear upon the steps, making it look as though the Madeleine has just sprouted a flower-strewn lawn. Marcel Proust spent most of his childhood nearby at 9, bd. Malesherbes, which might explain his penchant for his aunt Léonie's *madeleines* with tea. You, too, can enjoy a few *madeleines* or pick up some chocolate *macarons* at the world-famous food shop, **Fauchon,** 24-30, pl. de la Madeleine, just behind the church (see **Specialty Stores,** p. 179).

OTHER SIGHTS

Directly north of pl. de la Concorde, like two sentries guarding the gate to the Madeleine, stand the **Hôtel de Crillon** (on the left) and the **Hôtel de la Marine** (on the right). Architect Jacques-Ange Gabriel built the impressive colonnaded facades between 1757 and 1770. On February 6, 1778, the Treaty of Friendship and Trade was signed by Louis XVI and American statesmen including Benjamin Franklin, making France the first European nation to recognize the independence of the United States of America. Chateaubriand lived in the Hôtel de Crillon (☎44 71 15 00) between 1805 and 1807. Today it is one of the most expensive, elegant hotels in Paris (single 3500F F; double 4500F). World-renowned **Maxim's** restaurant, 3, r. Royale, won't even allow you a peek into what was once Richelieu's home.

TO THE NORTH

CHAPELLE EXPIATOIRE

29, r. Pasquier, just below bd. Haussmann. M: Madeleine. Open Tu and F-Sa 1-4pm. 15F.

Pl. Louis XVI includes the improbably large Chapelle Expiatoire, its monuments to Marie-Antoinette and Louis XVI, and a lovely park. This was the sight of lime-filled trenches during the Revolution, when there was a great need for burial sights in a hurry. Although Louis XVIII had his brother and sister-in-law's remains removed to St-Denis in 1815, the Revolution's Most Wanted still lie here. Marat's assassin Charlotte Corday and Louis XVI's cousin Philippe-Égalité (who voted for the king's death only to be beheaded himself) are buried on either side of the staircase. Statues of the expiatory King and Queen, with their crowns at their feet, stand inside the Chapelle, on either side of a tomb-shaped altar (is anyone missing the symbolism here?). Their final letters are engraved in French on the base of the sculptures.

GARE ST-LAZARE

M: St-Lazare.

The Gare St-Lazare's platforms and iron-vaulted canopy are a bit grubby, but not to be missed by train riders and fans of Monet's painting *La Gare St-Lazare* (at the Musée d'Orsay) and Emile Zola's novel about the station and its trains, *La Bête Humaine.* Just outside the front entrance is a surrealist sculpture of a toppling tower of clocks. To the north of the station is pl. de Dublin, the setting for Gustave Caillebotte's famous urban impressionist painting, *A Rainy Day in Paris* (now at the Art Institute of Chicago).

PARC MONCEAU

M: Monceau or Courcelles. Open daily Apr.-Oct. 7am-10pm; Nov.-Mar. 7am-8pm. Gates close 15min. earlier.

The Parc Monceau, an expansive urban oasis guarded by gold-tipped, wrought-iron gates, borders the elegant bd. de Courcelles. The Parc Monceau is a pastoral setting for kids to play and parents to unwind or read in the shade. This park is also popular with joggers. The painter Carmontelle designed the park for the Duc d'Orléans; it was completed by Haussmann in 1862. The park boasts the largest tree in the capital: an oriental platane, 7m thick and two centuries old. An array of architectural follies—a pyramid, a covered bridge, an East Asian pagoda, Dutch windmills, and Roman ruins—make this formal garden and kids' romping ground (complete with roller rink) a Kodak commercial waiting to happen. As in other Parisian parks, frolicking, lying, or playing on the grass is forbidden and you are likely to be told to move *tout de suite* by the strangely clairvoyant park police.

CATHÉDRALE ALEXANDRE-NEVSKI

12, r. Daru. M: Ternes. ☎42 27 37 34. Open Tu, F, Su 3-5pm. Services Su at 10am and Sa 6-8pm.

Thanks primarily to Catherine the Great, French culture became a staple in the diet of Russian aristocrats. Almost all young, upper-class Russians came to Paris to seek culture, and many families owned vacation homes in the area. Built in 1860, the onion-domed Eglise Russe, also known as Cathédrale Alexandre-Nevski, is a Russian Eastern Orthodox church. The gold domes, spectacular from the outside, are equally beautiful on the inside. They were intricately painted by artists from St. Petersburg, and were recently restored to their former splendor.

NINTH ARRONDISSEMENT

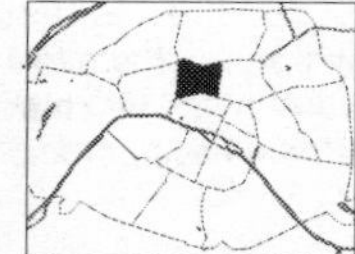

see map pp. 308–309

OPÉRA AND SURROUNDINGS

The boulevards and *quartier* surrounding the **Opéra Garnier** are simply called **l'Opéra.** On the southernmost border of the *9ème*, the Opéra is the arrondissement's most prosperous and visited area. For those less interested in the high art offerings of the Garnier's ballets, concerts, and opera, the *9ème* is filled with cinemas and is home to the legendary **Olympia,** one of Paris's most famous concert stages for American, European, and Brazilian pop, jazz, and rock performances. Perhaps the busiest sites of the *9ème*, however, are the arrondissement's department stores, **Au Printemps** and **Galeries Lafayette,** where thousands of Parisians and tourists seek out the fairest of the mall (see **Department Stores,** p. 142).

OPÉRA GARNIER

M: Opéra. ☎44 73 13 99, recorded info ☎08 36 69 78 68, reservations ☎08 44 73 13 00, tour info ☎40 01 22 63; www.opera-de-paris.fr. ***Open*** *daily 10am-5pm, last entry 4:30pm; museum 10am-noon and 2-5pm.* ***Admission*** *30F; ages 10-16, students, or over 60 20F.* ***English tours*** *12:30pm daily in summer. 60F; students, ages 10-16, or over 60 45F; under 10 25F. See also* ***Music, Opera, and Dance,*** *p. 152.*

Emerging from the Opéra métro, your eyes will be drawn to the newly renovated facade in the middle of pl. de l'Opéra, bright with multi-colored marble and glittering with gold. Designed by Charles Garnier under Napoleon III in the showy eclecticism of the Second Empire, the Opéra is perhaps most famous as home to the legend of the Phantom of the Opéra. Towering high above the grands boulevards of the southern *9ème*, the building epitomizes both the Second Empire's ostentation and its rootlessness; a mix of styles and odd details ties it to no formal tradition. Asked whether his building was in the style of Louis XIV, Louis XV, or Louis XVI, Garnier responded that his creation belonged to Napoleon III, who financed the project. Garnier's design outshined hundreds of other plans in an 1861 competition, including the entry of the "Pope of Architects" Viollet-le-Duc, who restored Notre-Dame. Garnier was just 35 and virtually unknown at the time, and the commission made him famous. The Opéra opened in 1875 after a 15-year long construction, and its magnificent interiors are adorned with Gobelin tapestries (for more on Gobelin tapestry, see p. 95), gilded mosaics, and an eight-ton chandelier that fell on the audience in 1896. The red and gold auditorium has 1,900 red velvet seats and a bright ceiling painted by Marc Chagall in 1964. This five-tiered auditorium was designed as a stage not only for operas but also for nineteenth-century bourgeois social life: balconies were constructed so the audience members could watch one another as well as the show.

Since 1989, when Opéra de la Bastille was inaugurated, most operas have been performed at the Bastille, while the Opéra Garnier has been used mainly for ballet. In 1992, Rudolf Nureyev made his last public appearance here, his home since his defection from the USSR, shortly before his death.

oh! for a day

Glam in the 9ème

Visit the **Opéra** (see opposite) during the day to tour the glamorous interior, then perhaps wander to the box office and pick up tickets to a performance in the grand auditorium for later that evening. Stop at the **Café de la Paix** (see p. 169) for a quick snack or for a more formal lunch and then swing by **Galeries Lafayette** and **Au Printemps** (see p. 142) on bd. Haussman to see if there is anything worth buying (something nice for the opera?). Put your best foot forward and mingle with Paris' upper crust at the Opéra performance in the evening. After the performance, walk down bd. Haussman, which becomes bd. Montmartre, and make a left on r. Faubourg Montmartre for an after-opera dinner at **Le Bistro de Galla** (see p. 169).

Guided tours are available in several languages, but they are in high demand during the summer; ask about availability at the entrance. The Opéra also houses a **library** and **museum** on the history of opera and dance that focus particularly on Nijinksy and the Ballet Russe, Diaghilev's innovative troupe.

CAFÉ DE LA PAIX

12, bd. des Capucines.

To the right of the Opéra, the Café de la Paix is the quintessential 19th-century café. Like the Opéra, it was designed by Garnier and sports mirrored walls and frescoed ceilings. A frequent haunt of Oscar Wilde, today the café caters to the after-theater crowd and anyone else who doesn't mind paying 26F for coffee (see **Cafés,** p. 169).

OTHER SIGHTS

OLYMPIA. Farther east down bd. des Capucines, the giant red glowing letters of the **Olympia** music hall signal the place where Edith Piaf achieved fame. Popular artists still perform here. *(☎47 42 25 49.)*

NORTH OF OPÉRA

EGLISE NOTRE-DAME-DE-LORETTE

M: Notre-Dame-de-Lorette. Exit the métro and the church will be in front of you on pl. Kossuth.

Eglise Notre-Dame-de-Lorette was built in 1836 to "the glory of the Virgin Mary." This Neoclassical church is filled with statues of saints and frescoes of scenes from the life of Mary. **R. Notre-Dame-de-Lorette,** however, is a whole other barrel of fish. Somewhat less saintly than its namesake, this street was the debauched hang-out of Émile Zola's *Nana* (whose name is now slang for chick or babe) and a thoroughfare of serious ill-repute in the late 1960s. *Lorette* came to be a term used to refer to the quarter's young prostitutes. The mere mention of Notre-Dame-de-Lorette made men look away and good girls blush.

PIGALLE

M: Pigalle.

Farther north, at the border of the 18*ème*, is the infamous area called Pigalle, the un-chastity belt of Paris. During World War II, American servicemen stationed in Paris, polite as ever, called Pigalle "Pig-alley." Stretching along the bd. de Clichy from pl. Pigalle to pl. Blanche is a salacious, voracious, and generally pretty naughty neighborhood. Sex-shops, brothels, porn stores, lace, leather, and latex boutiques line the streets. As a result, the area swarms with police. Although Pigalle is undergoing a slow gentrification, tourists (especially women) should be wary of walking alone here at night. The areas to the north of bd. Clichy and south of pl. Blanche are comparatively calmer.

EGLISE DE LA SAINTE-TRINITÉ

At the end of r. de la Chaussée. M: Trinité. Open daily 4:30-6:30pm.

Built at the end of the 19th century in Italian Renaissance style, this church has beautiful, painted vaults and is surrounded by a fountained park with tree-shaded benches.

Musée d'Orsay

TENTH ARRONDISSEMENT

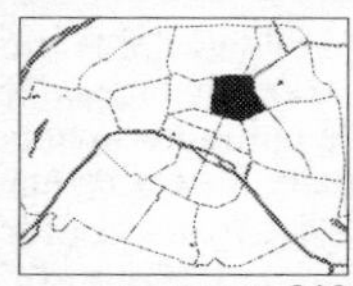

see map p. 310

Far from most tourist itineraries, the 10*ème*'s working-class neighborhoods offer a few hidden sights. The tree-lined **Canal St-Martin** is a refreshing break from the city, and the **Faubourg St-Denis** features North and West African markets, restaurants, and shops. Europe's train lines converge at the **Gare de l'Est** and the **Gare du Nord,** and the 3*ème*, 10*ème*, and 11*ème* converge at pl. de la République. One word of caution: bd. Magenta and bd. Faubourg tend to be risky at night. Beware of pickpockets.

GARE DU NORD

M: Gare du Nord.

Designed by Jacques-Ignace Hittorf in 1863, the Gare du Nord's beige Neoclassical exterior is topped by statues representing the cities of France. Inside, the platforms are covered by a vast vault of glass and steel, which Napoleon III called the station's umbrella.

GARE DE L'EST

M: Gare de l'Est.

The Gare de l'Est's 19th-century glass and ironwork spins a fanlike facade and latticed roof. Surrounding the station on pl. du 11 Nov. 1918 and bd. de Strasbourg, Alsatian restaurants serve specialties brought to this *quartier* by Alsatian refugess from WWI.

Eiffel Tower

PORTES ST-DENIS AND ST-MARTIN

M: Strasbourg/St-Denis. Porte St-Denis will be right in front of you when you get out of the métro; Porte St-Martin is one block east on bd. St Denis, which becomes bd. St-Martin.

At the end of r. Faubourg St-Denis, the grand **Porte St-Denis** looms triumphantly. Built in 1672 to celebrate the victories of Louis XIV in Flanders and the Rhineland, the gate imitates the Arch of Titus in Rome. Once the site of a medieval entrance to the city, the present arch serves only as a rotary for traffic. In the words of André Breton, *c'est très belle et très inutile* (it's very beautiful and very useless). On July 28, 1830, it was the scene of intense fighting as revolutionaries scrambled to the top and rained cobblestones on the monarchist troops below. Two blocks down bd. St-Denis, the 1674 **Porte St-Martin** is a smaller copy with a herculean Louis XIV on the facade wearing nothing but a wig and a smile.

Musée Rodin

PLACE DE LA RÉPUBLIQUE

M: République.

Pl. de la République is the meeting point of the 3*ème*, 10*ème*, and 11*ème* arrondissements and the disorienting junction of bd. Magenta, Voltaire, Temple, Turbigo, St-Martin and av. de la République. At its center, Morice's sculpture of *La République* glorifies France's many revolutionary struggles. Ironically, it was created by Haussman—who had to demolish several theaters for its expanse—to divide and conquer the rather revolutionary arrondissements that border it. Buzzing with crowds during the day, the area can be dangerous at night. See **Sights,** p. 67, for more on the *place.*

THÉÂTRE DE LA RENAISSANCE

M: République.

The stretch from Porte St-Martin to pl. de la République along r. René Boulanger and bd. St-Martin served as a lively theater district in the 19th century and has recently begun to retrieve some of its former sparkle. A shining example is the Théâtre de la Renaissance, with its sculpted facade of griffins and arabesques by Carrier-Belleuse. Newly refurbished, it has breathed new life into the neighborhood.

CANAL ST-MARTIN

M: République or Goncourt. From the métro, walk down r. du Faubourg du Temple.

The most pleasant area of the 10*ème* is the tree-lined Canal St-Martin. Measuring 4.5km, the canal connects to the Seine and has several **locks,** which can be traveled by boat on one of the Canauxrama trips (see p. 278). It was built in 1825 as a shortcut for river traffic on the Seine. It also served as a defense against the uppity, upstart eastern arrondissements. This currently residential area is being rediscovered by Parisians and tourists with the appearance of some upscale shops and restaurants. Apparently, the canal is not doing its job.

HÔPITAL ST-LOUIS

East of the canal, follow r. Bichat to the Hôpital St-Louis. Built in 1607 by Henri IV as a sanctuary/prison for victims of the plague, it was located across a marsh and downwind of the rotting Buttes-Chaumont (see **Sights,** p. 104). Its distance from any water-source suggests that it was intended more to protect the city from contamination than to help the unfortunates inside. Today, the hospital boasts the lovely **Quadrilatère Historique de St-Louis,** a flowered courtyard.

MONTFAUCON GALLOWS

53, r. de la Grange-aux-Belles.

A path uphill leads to the Montfaucon Gallows. Famous for its hanging capacity of 60, this system of pillars and chains once executed medieval prisoners with an efficiency unrivaled until the invention of the guillotine. The unlucky individuals were hung in clusters and left to rot. The stench of their corpses could poison the city on a windy day. In the 14th century, the gallows were replaced with a more efficient design by Pierre Rémy, treasurer to Charles IV, who in 1328 was hung by his own creation.

ELEVENTH ARRONDISSEMENT

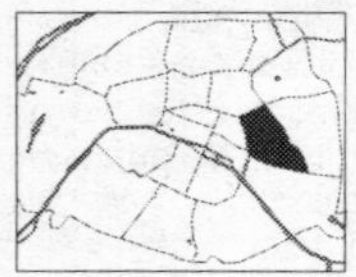

see map pp. 312-313

The 11*ème* is most famous for hosting the Revolutionary kick-off at the Bastille prison on July 14, 1789 (see **History,** p. 28). It was most recently reincarnated as a seedy working class area, but the 1989 opening of the glassy Opéra Bastille on the bicentennial of the Revolution has breathed new life into the 11*ème*. In the early 1990s, the neighborhood near the Opéra Bastille was touted as the next Montmartre, the next Montparnasse, and the next Latin Quarter: the city's latest Bohemia. But the Bastille's 15 minutes are over. In the scramble to find the next new "in" place, crowds have surged north toward rues Oberkampf and Ménilmontant, which burst with noise, restaurants, and bars.

THE BASTILLE PRISON

M: Bastille.

The Bastille prison was originally commissioned by Charles V to safeguard the eastern entrance to Paris. Strapped for cash, Charles 'recruited' a press-gang of passing civilians to lay the stones for the fortress. The Bastille towers rose 100 feet above Paris by the end of the 14th century. Under Henry IV they became the royal treasury; Louis XIII made them a state prison. Internment here, generally reserved for heretics and political dissidents, was the king's business, and, as a result, often arbitrary. But it was hardly the hellhole that the Revolutionaries who tore it down imagined it to be—Bastille's titled inmates were allowed to furnish their suites, have fresh linen, bring their own servants, and receive guests.: the Cardinal de Rohan held a dinner party for 20 in his cell. Notable and aristocratic prisoners included Mirabeau, Voltaire, and the Marquis de Sade (for more on these dandies, see **Literature,** p. 37).

Having sacked Invalides for weapons, Revolutionary militants stormed the Bastille for munitions. Supposedly an impenetrable fortress, the prison had actually been attacked during other periods of civil unrest (it had fallen during five). Surrounded by an armed rabble, too short on food to entertain a siege, and unsure of the loyalty of the Swiss mercenaries who defended the prison, the Bastille's governor surrendered. A passing English merchant later wrote in his journal that the crowd seemed to grow feverish as the bloody head of the governor, which had been severed from his body with a pocket knife, was paraded past on a pike. He wondered at the bloodlust of the crowd, exclaiming, "What a people!" Despite the gruesome details, the storming of the Bastille has come to symbolize the triumph of liberty over despotism. Its first anniversary was the cause for great celebration in Revolutionary Paris. Since the late 19th century, July 14 has been the official state holiday of the French Republic, and is usually a time of glorious firework displays and consumption of copious amounts of alchohol (see **Festivals,** p. 8). Demolition of the prison began the day after its capture and concluded in October 1792. Some of its stones were incorporated into the Pont de la Concorde.

PLACE HENRI GALLI

A commemorative pile of stones from the Bastille can also be found in pl. Henri Galli. A certain Citizen Palloy, the demolition contractor, used the stones to construct 83 models of the prison that he sent to the provinces as reminders of "the horror of despotism."

THE JULY COLUMN

M: Bastille. In the center of pl. de la Bastille.

Yes, the collumn topped by a conspicuous gold cupid doing an arabesque at the center of pl. de la Bastille is in fact a statue of Liberty. In 1831, King Louis-Philippe laid the cornerstone for the July Column to commemorate Republicans who died in the Revolutions of 1789 and 1830. Emblazoned names commemorate the 504 martyrs of 1830 buried inside along with two mummified Egyptian pharaohs.

MAISON DE RETRAITE ET DE SANTÉ

Take r. de Charonne a few blocks from the Metro. M: Alexandre Dumas.

Many of the Revolution's profiteers lived along the streets radiating from pl. de la Bastille. The *hôtel* at 157-161, r. de Charonne, housed Dr. Belhomme, whose Maison de Retraite et de Santé sheltered condemned aristocrats with ready cash during the Terror (1792-1795). For 1000 *livres* a month, Dr. Belhomme would rent a room in his sanatorium and certify his clients as too ill to brave the scaffold. Arrested himself after word got out, the savvy Dr. Belhomme holed up in a similar establishment on r. de Picpusin.

RUE DE LA ROQUETTE

M: Bastille/Voltaire.

More quiet than its neighbor, jumping r. de Lappe, the winding r. de la Roquette contains hidden gems. This 17th-century byway was home to poet Verlaine at no. 17 (for more, see **Literature,** p. 37), and is now lined with cafés, bars, elegant boutiques, and an avant-garde church.

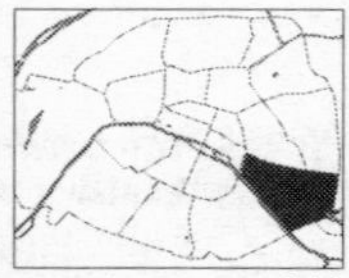

see map p. 311

TWELFTH ARRONDISSEMENT

The 12*ème* draws youthful momentum from the neighboring 4*ème* and 11*ème*. While its northwestern fringes are decidedly funky, its core is solid working class with a large immigrant population. The Opéra is but one of the recent architectural additions.

AROUND PLACE DE LA BASTILLE

OPÉRA BASTILLE

130, r. de Lyon. M: Bastille. ☎40 01 19 70; www.opera-de-paris.fr. Tours daily 1pm. 50F; students, under 16, and over 60 30F. For concert info, see **Classical Music, Opera, and Dance,** *p. 152.*

Once known as the "Red Belt" around Paris because of its participation in both the 1830 and 1848 Revolutions, the 12*ème* also saw its residents make up large sectors of the Parisian Resistance during WWII. But the only rebellions staged these days are over the Opéra Bastille, one of Mitterrand's *grands projets.* Presiding over the **pl. de la Bastille** and designed by Carlos Ott, a Canadian mall architect, the Opéra opened in 1989 to protests over its unattractive and questionable design (nets still surround parts of the building to catch falling tiles). The building is second only to Disneyland Paris in the minds of Parisians as an example of architectural Chernobyl: the "People's Opera" has been described as a huge toilet because of its resemblance to the coin-operated facilities in the streets of Paris. Also, many complain that the acoustics of the hall are defective. Worse yet, "the people," for whom the opera was supposedly designed, often can't afford to go there; as a result, the Opéra costs in taxes much more than it returns. On Bastille Day, all performances are free, but the queues are long. Your best shot is to join the line very early in the morning. The Opéra has not struck a completely sour note, though, as it has helped renew local interest in the arts.

VIADUC DES ARTS AND PROMENADE PLANTÉE

9-121, av. Daumesnil. M: Bastille.

Opened in 1995 in a renovated railway viaduct, the **Viaduc des Arts** provides workspace and showrooms for potters, painters, weavers, glass blowers, opera paraphernalia designers, and furniture manufacturers. Above the viaduct runs the **Promenade Plantée,** Paris's longest and skinniest park, perfect for a late-afternoon stroll with a loved one. Trees, roses, and shrubs line an old railroad track high above the avenue, the traffic, and the stores below.

OTHER SIGHTS

GAULTIER'S GALLERY. Clothing designer Jean-Paul Gaultier's gallery is at 30, r. Faubourg-St-Antoine. *(M: Bastille/Ledru-Rollin.)*

ELSEWHERE IN THE 12ÈME

PLACE DE LA NATION

M: Nation.

Its current reputation as a red-light district runs counter to pl. de la Nation's history: it was once the site of a white, royal wedding between Louis XIV and Marie-Thérèse in 1660. But during the Revolution, things got rawer: 1300 nobles were executed here. It became pl. de la Nation on July 14, 1880.

BOIS DE VINCENNES AND CHÂTEAU DE VINCENNES

At the eastern edge of the 12*ème* stands the expansive, green Bois de Vincennes (Vincennes Wood; see **Sights,** p. 110). Once a royal hunting ground, the Bois now contains the premier zoo in France, the Parc Zoologique and the royal Château de Vincennes.

THE BERCY QUARTER

M: Bercy.

East of the **Gare de Lyon,** the Bercy quarter has seen the rapid construction of Mitterand's new **Ministère des Finances** building, the mammoth grass-and-glass **Palais Omnisports** concert and sports complex, and Frank Gehry's 1994 **American Center.**

THIRTEENTH ARRONDISSEMENT

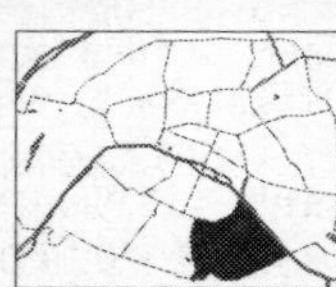

see map p. 314

Until the 20th century, the 13*ème* was one of Paris's poorest neighborhoods; Victor Hugo used parts of the 13*ème* as a setting for *Les Misérables.* Traversed by the **Bièvre,** a stagnant stream clogged with industrial refuse, it was notoriously the city's worst-smelling district. Environmentalists eventually won their campaign to close its tanneries and paper factories, and in 1910 the Bièvre was filled in. Today largely a working-class immigrant neighborhood, the 13*ème*—bordering the 14*ème*'s Cité Universitaire and scholastic 5*ème*—affordably houses a growing number of students in its northern and western areas, and is conveniently also the site of the new **Bibliothèque de France.** At the center of this large arrondissement is the modern **pl. d'Italie** and the young and bouncing **Butte aux Cailles;** below it **Chinatown** bustles. Most recently, a slew of restaurant-, club-, and bar-boats have docked on **Port de la Gare Quai François Mauriac** along the Seine. This trendy nightlife spot is crowded enough to be a safe place for evening strolls along the Seine, but is still quiet enough to be romantic. Kissy, kissy.

MANUFACTURE DES GOBELINS

42, av. des Gobelins. M: Gobelins. ☎44 08 52 00. 1½hr. tours in French with English handout Tu-Th 2 and 2:45pm. 45F, ages 7-24 25F, under 7 free.

The Manufacture des Gobelins, a tapestry workshop over 300 years old, is all that is left of the 13*ème*'s industrial past. In the mid-17th century, the Gobelins produced the priceless tapestries now displayed in the **Musée de Cluny** (see **Museums,** p. 126). Still an adjunct of the state, the factory receives commissions from French ministries and foreign embassies. Extensive and interesting guided tours (the only way inside) explain the intricacies of weaving.

BUTTE AUX CAILLES

M: Corvisart or Place d'Italie.

Farther southwest, the Butte aux Cailles (Quail Knoll) district features cobblestone streets, tree-shaded sidewalks, and street lamps. One of the first areas to fight during the Revolution of 1848, the area around r. des Cinq Diamants was the unofficial headquarters of the *soixante-huitards*, the student and intellectual activists of the 1968 riots. Today the fight continues in the Butte's cooperative bar, **La Folie en Tête** (see **Nightlife,** p. 193), and intellectual hang-out, **Le Temps des Cérises** (see **Restaurants,** p. 172). The nascent gentrification of the 13*ème* has attracted trend-setters, artists, and intellectuals, but residents are worried that once-affordable real estate may go the way of the now unaffordable Marais.

EGLISE SAINTE-ANNE DE LA MAISON BLANCHE.

M: Tolbiac. On r. Tolbiac.

This Byzantine church owes its completion to the Lombard family who in 1898 donated funds from their chocolate store on av. de Choisy to complete the construction. The front of the church is nicknamed *la facade chocolat* in their honor.

CHINATOWN

M: Porte d'Ivry, Tolbiac, or Maison Blanche.

East of Ste-Anne on av. de Choisy and av. d'Ivry lies Paris's Chinatown, home to large Chinese, Vietnamese, and Cambodian communities. Asian restaurants, shops, and markets like **Tang Frères** (see **Specialty Shops,** p. 144) on r. d'Ivry offer embroidered slippers, exotic fruits, fresh vegetables, and Asian specialties.

BIBLIOTHÈQUE DE FRANCE

M: Quai de la Gare or Bibliothèque François-Mitterrand.

Opened in 1996, the Bibliothèque de France is the last and most expensive of Mitterrand's *grand projets.* Replacing the old Bibliothèque Nationale in the *2ème* (still open to scholars), the new library is open to the public and houses 10 million volumes. Designed by Dominique Perrault, the four L-shaped towers are designed to look like open books from above. (See **Libraries,** p. 276.) The library is just one piece of the *13ème*'s urban renewal. A new project called ZAC (Zone d'Aménagement Concerte) plans to build a new university, five schools, a sports complex, a public garden, numerous office blocks, exhibitions spaces, cinemas, and a new métro.

FOURTEENTH ARRONDISSEMENT

see map pp. 315–317

Generations of newly arrived immigrants have called Montparnasse home. The first to arrive were Bretons who left Brittany in the 19th century after failed harvests. They settled in the neighborhood around the station, now known as Petite Bretange. Breton *crêperies,* handicraft shops, and cultural associations line **r. du Montparnasse.**

Like Montmartre and the *quartier latin,* the *14ème* has long been a haven for 20th-century artists and writers like Man Ray, Modigliani, and Henry Miller. While gentrification has forced struggling artists out of those *quartiers,* the *14ème*'s affordability and café culture still attract young artists and students, who debate at the **Cité Universitaire.** However, the arrondissement is largely an amalgam of cultures and styles, and emits more of a sense of serene fatigue than it does a *6ème*-style artistic vigor. There is no one street that best characterizes the area, but restaurants (both cheap and Lost Generation *chic*), galleries, cafés, and the **Montparnasse cemetery** make the *14ème* worth a visit.

BOULEVARD DE MONTPARNASSE

M: Montparnasse-Bienvenüe or Vavin.

In the early 20th century, Montparnasse became a center for avant-garde artists including Modigliani, Utrillo, Chagall, and Montmartre ex-pat Léger. Political exiles like Lenin and Trotsky talked strategy over cognac in the cafés along bd. Montparnasse. After WWI, Montparnasse attracted American expatriates and artistic rebels of all stripes. Man Ray transformed an apartment into a photo lab, Calder worked on his first sculptures, and Hemingway made merry (see *The Sun Also Rises* for Ernest's idea of *14ème* fun). Henry Miller produced the steamy *Tropic of Cancer* at Seurat's villa with the amorous assistance of Anaïs Nin. The Spanish Civil War and WWII ended this golden age of bohemia. To see where Lenin, Hemingway, and Sartre sat, racked their brains, and rocked the casbah, check out the café **La Coupole** (see **Cafés,** p. 172).

CIMETIÈRE MONTPARNASSE

3, bd. Edgar Quinet. M: Edgar Quinet. ☎44 10 86 50. Open mid-Mar. to Oct. M-F 8am-6pm, Sa 8:30am-6pm, Su and holidays 9am-6pm; Nov.-Mar. M-F 8am-5:30pm, Sa 8:30am-5:30pm, Su and holidays 9am-5:30pm. 2hr. guided visits in French 38F; call for times. Free.

In the shadow of the modern Tour Montparnasse, (see **Fifteenth Arrondissement,** p. 98) hides the beautiful Cimetière Montparnasse. Enter the cemetery off bd. Edgar Quinet (main entrance just east of M: Edgar Quinet), grab a free *Index des Célébrités* (available to the left of the entrance), and follow the exclusive *Let's Go* walk of fame. Hang a right on the av. du Boulevard, pausing to ponder the shared *tombeau* of no-longer-extant existentialists Jean-Paul Sartre and Simone de Beauvoir in the 20th *division* at right. Don't miss Durkheim in the 5th a bit farther ahead. Rounding the corner on av. de l'Ouest, you'll pass by the 6th, 7th, 8th, and 15th *divisions*, home to Charles Baudelaire, postmodern playwright Eugène Ionesco, Surrealist wizard Man Ray, Dadaist fool Tristan Tzara, and inspired automatist Robert Desnos. Farther east, you'll find composer Camille Saint-Saëns not far from shagadelic 70s pop singer, Serge Gainsbourg, whose graffitied grave resembles Jim Morrison's across town at Père Lachaise (see **Sights,** p. 105). Also in residence are Fantin-Latour, Samuel Beckett, Guy de Maupassant, and sculptors Constantin Brancusi and Frédéric Bartholdi (who did the Statue of Liberty). Finally, no visit would be complete without paying your respects to wrongly accused (and harshly punished) Jewish colonel Alfred Dreyfus, just across r. Emile Richard, and author Marguerite Duras (conveniently located in the 21st division on your way out.)

Place de la Concorde

THE CATACOMBS

1, pl. Denfert-Rochereau. M: Denfert-Rochereau. ☎ 43 22 47 63. ***Open*** *Tu-F 2-4pm, Sa-Su 9-11am and 2-4pm.* ***Admission*** *33F, under 25 22F, under 7 free.* ***Tour*** *lasts 45 min.*

At the intersection of six avenues, a lion sculpted by Bartholdi (who created the Statue of Liberty) and commemorating La Défense Nationale de 1870-1871 dominates **pl. Denfert-Rochereau.** Most visitors observe Bartholdi's Leo from their place in the line to visit the **Catacombs,** a series of tunnels 20m below ground and 1.7km in length. They were originally excavated to provide stone for building the city. By the 1770s, much of the Left Bank was in danger of caving in and digging promptly stopped. The former quarry was then used as a mass grave to relieve the stench emanating from Paris's overcrowded cemeteries. The entrance warns "Stop! Beyond Here Is the Empire of Death." In 1793, a Parisian got lost and became a permanent resident, so stick to the tour. During WWII, the Empire of Death was full of life when the Resistance set up headquarters among the departed. The catacombs are like an underground city, with street names on walls lined with femurs and craniums. The ghoulish arrangement features rooms with cheery proverbs—*"Pensez le matin que vous n'irez peut être pas jusques au soir et au soir que vous n'irez pas jusques au matin"* ("Think each morning that you may not be live 'til evening, and each evening that you may not be live 'til morning"). Beware the low ceilings and bring a sweater (and a flashlight if you have one). The catacombs are not recommended for the faint of heart or leg; there are 85 steep steps to climb on the way out.

Madeleine

PARC MONTSOURIS

Open M-F 7:30am-10pm, Sa-Su 9am-10pm.

Begun in 1867 by Haussmann, the Parc Montsouris features hundreds of rare and freakish trees, a gaggle of ducks and snow geese, and bright flowers in the summer. Sunbathers stretch out on the grass.

CITÉ UNIVERSITAIRE

On bd. Jourdan, upwards of 6,000 students from 122 countries study, argue, and drink themselves silly in the **Cité Universitaire,**

Opéra

a 40-hectare campus with 40 dorms, two of them designed by Le Corbusier (see p. 42). The **Pavilion Suisse** (1932) reflects the architect's dream of a vertical city; its roof garden housed anti-aircraft guns during WWII. In 1959, Le Corbusier returned to build the **Maison du Brésil.** While the **Maison des Etats-Unis** houses Americans in prison-like squalor, the **Maison Suédoise** and **Maison Japonaise** offer delightful accommodations. The swankiest addition is the luxurious **Maison d'Espagne.**

FIFTEENTH ARRONDISSEMENT

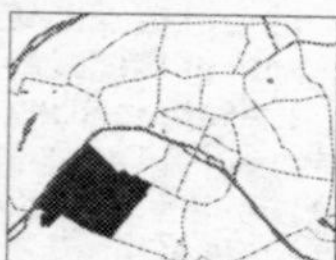

see map p. 315

The 15*ème* has few tourist sites—you'll probably only explore here if your stay extends beyond a week. Its varied neighborhoods, generally calm and safe at night, are similar to those of smaller French cities like Nantes or Rouen.

TOUR MAINE-MONTPARNASSE

33, av. du Maine. M: Montparnasse-Bienvenüe. ☎45 38 52 56; ciel ☎40 64 77 64. Tower open daily May-Sept. 9:30am-11:30pm; Oct.-April M-F 9:30am-10:30pm. Ciel open daily 8:30am-11pm. 48F, students 40F, seniors 45F, under 14 35F.

This modern tower dominates the quartier's northeast corner. Standing 59 stories tall and completed in 1973, the controversial building looks out of place amid Montparnasse's 19th-century architecture. Shortly after it was erected, the city forbid further sky-scraping, designating La Défense (see **Sights,** p. 112) the sole home for future *gratte-ciels* (sky-scrapers). For an open-air, all-encompassing view of the city, bypass the 52 floors of office space and ride the elevator to the 56th floor, then climb three flights to the rooftop terrace. The Tour is a good way to orient yourself as you explore the city.

PLACE DU 18 JUIN

At the intersection of r. de l'Arrivé and bd. Montparnasse. M: Montparnasse-Bienvenüe.

This traffic-ridden square commemorates two important events from WWII. On June 18, 1940, General de Gaulle broadcast his first BBC radio address from London, urging France to resist the Nazi occupiers. And it was here that General Leclerc, the leader of the French forces, accepted the surrender of General von Choltitz, the Nazi commander of the Paris occupation, on August 25, 1944.

INSTITUT PASTEUR

25, r. du Dr. Roux. M: Pasteur. Turn right on Bd Pasteur, and rue du Docteur Roux is the first left. Before entering the museum, obtain a name tag from the small office accross from the Institute. ☎45 68 82 82 or ☎45 68 82 83. Open Sept.-July M-F 2-5:30pm. 15F, students 8F. Guided tours in English easily arranged.

Founded by the French scientist Louis Pasteur in 1887, the institute is now a center for biochemical research, development, and treatment. It was here that Pasteur, a champion of 19th-century germ theory, developed pasteurization, his technique for purifying milk products and beer. This museum has preserved his somber and stately home, with grand portraits and the very instruments with which he found a vaccine for anthrax and the cure for rabies. It was also here in 1983 that Dr. Luc Montaigner (in conjunction with Robert Gallo) first isolated HIV, the virus that causes AIDS. You can visit Pasteur's tomb, an ornate marble construction dedicated to the virtues of faith, hope, charity, and science.

LA RUCHE

52, r. Danzig. M: Convention. Follow r. de la Convention toward pl. Charles Vallin, and r. Danzig will be on the right.

Built as a wine pavillion by Gustave Eiffel for the 1900 exhibition, "the Beehive" became home to industrious artists after it was bought and renovated by Alfred Boucher, himself a struggling sculptor. Chagall, Soutine, Modigliani, and Lèger were some of the more famous residents who vied for a "cell" here, and whose work is preserved in the gardens of la Roche, along with that of other residents, past and present. Today, the Fondation La Ruche still offers grants, studios, and housing to young artists.

SIXTEENTH ARRONDISSEMENT

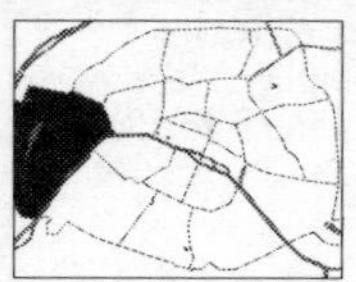
see map p. 318

When Notre-Dame was under construction, this elegant suburb was a tiny village in the woods. For the next few centuries, Kings and nobles chased deer and boar through its forests. Finally, in 1859, at the height of Haussmannization (for more on Haussmann, see **History,** p. 30) the area was transformed. The wealthy villages of Auteuil, Passy, and Chaillot banded together and joined Paris, forming what is now the 16*ème*. The area's original aristocratic families continue to hold their ground, making the 16*ème* a stronghold of conservative politics, fashion, and culture. It is rumored that some members of the local nobility forbid their children to sing *La Marseillaise*, the anthem of the Revolutionaries who beheaded their ancestors. *Allons enfants...*

TROCADÉRO AND SURROUNDINGS

PLACE D'IÉNA

M:Iéna. Open M-Sa 9:30am-12:30pm and 3-7pm, Su 9:30am-12:30pm.

The pl. d'Iéna positions you next to the rotunda of the **Conseil Economique** and in front of a sweep of popular museums, including the round facade of the **Musée Guimet,** the **Musée de la Mode et du Costume,** and the **Palais de Tokyo,** just down the street (see **Museums,** p. 134). Henri Bouchard's impressive facade for the **Eglise St-Pierre de Chaillot** (1937), is between r. de Chaillot and av. Pierre I de Serbie, five minutes away.

PALAIS DE TOKYO

11, av. du Président Wilson. M: Iéna.

The Palais de Tokyo houses the **Musée d'Art Moderne de la Ville de Paris** (see **Museums,** p. 134) and its world-class collection of 20th-century art. Built for the 1937 World Expo, the palace took its name from the quai de Tokyo, but after WWII and Japan's Axis role, it was renamed the quai de New York.

PALAIS GALLIERA

M: Iéna. Across from the Palais de Tokyo.

The sandy gardens and allegorical sculpture of the Palais Galliera draw sculpture enthusiasts and little kids alike. The Palais Galliera was built for the Duchess of Galliera by Louis Ginain as a repository for her collection of Italian Baroque art, although her collection was eventually sent to Genoa instead. The Italianate structure, completed in 1892, has housed the more unorthodox **Musée de la Mode et du Costume** (see **Museums,** p. 136) since 1977, and holds 10,000 costumes from around the world. Farther down the avenue at pl. d'Iéna, the **Musée Guimet** (see **Museums,** p. 135) contains a spectacular collection of Asian art.

PLACE DU TROCADÉRO

In the 1820s, the Duc d'Angoulême built a memorial to his Spanish victory at Trocadéro—hence the present name. Jacques Carlu's more modern design for the 1937 World Exposition features two stone wings cradling a gorgeous Art Deco courtyard that extends from the *place* over spectacular cannon-shaped fountains. Enigmatic gold inscriptions by Paul Valéry claim things like "the hand of the artist is equal and rival to thoughts of the artist, and each is nothing without the other." Surveyed by the 7.5m tall bronze *Apollo* by Henri Bouchard and eight other figures, the terrace attracts tourists, vendors, skateboarders, and in-line skaters and offers brilliant **views** of the Eiffel Tower and Champs de Mars, particularly at night (bring your camera). Be aware of pickpockets and traffic as you gaze upwards. As parts of the Jardins du Trocadéro are not well-lit at night, be careful and don't go alone.

PALAIS DE CHAILLOT

The Palais de Chaillot houses the **Musée de l'Homme** (see p. 136), the **Musée de la Marine** (see p. 136), the **Théâtre National de Chaillot** (see p. 151), and the **Cinémathèque Française** (see p. 152). The Palais de Chaillot is actually the last of a series of buildings built on this site. Catherine de Medici had a château here, later transformed into a convent by Queen Henrietta of England. Napoleon razed the convent and planned a palace for his son, but rotten luck at Waterloo brought construction to a screeching halt.

JARDINS DU TROCADÉRO

Below the palace, the Jardins du Trocadéro extend to the Seine. The **fountains** lining the central av. Gustave V de Suède and Albert I de Monaco are particularly striking at night. After a day of sight-seeing, children of all ages might enjoy the **carousel** (10F) in pl. de Varsovie in front of the Eiffel Tower.

oh! for a day

Curlicues and Concrete: Walking Auteuil

The aesthetic orgy that is Auteuil's architecture begins at the end of r. Raynouard as you pass from Passy into Auteuil (RER: Kennedy). The winsome **Castel Béranger** (1898), at no. 14, flaunts green iron flourishes, curling seahorses, and enigmatic faces. The architect, Hector Guimard, lived here briefly. Continue down r. La Fontaine toward rising numbers. More Guimard buildings cluster on r. La Fontaine, including no. 17 (1911). Within this building is **Café Antoine,** with a painted glass ceiling and art nouveau tiles; you might want to stop in for a *menthe à l'eau.* Off r. la Fontaine look for **r. Agar,** an odd, T-shaped street that is Art Nouveau all the way down to its street sign. Buildings undulate, and each wrought iron balcony has a unique design. **L'Oeuvre des Orphelins Apprentis d'Auteuil** (Society of Apprenticed Orphans), at no. 40, r. la Fontaine, was founded in 1866 to provide a home and future for local orphans.

(continued on p. 102)

PASSY AND AUTEUIL

Located south and southwest of Trocadéro, **Passy** was once famous for its restorative waters and later filled with avant-garde architecture. Now it's known mostly as the former set of *Last Tango in Paris* and, most of all, as a pricey shopping district.

RUE BENJAMIN FRANKLIN

This street commemorates the statesmen's one-time residence in Passy. Franklin lived at 66, r. Raynouard from 1777 to 1785 while negotiating a treaty between the new US and the old Louis XVI; the present building was built long after his stay. At the intersection of r. Benjamin Franklin and the pl. de la Palais Chaillot, there is a large statue of Franklin.

OTHER SIGHTS

STATUE OF LIBERTY. R. de Boulainvilliers will take you down to the miniature Bartholdi Statue of Liberty near the Pont de Grenelle. Donated by a group of American expatriates in 1885, it was moved to this spot for the 1889 World Exposition.

JARDIN DE RANELAGH. Take the métro to La Muette and follow the Chausée de la Muette to av. Ranelagh. The Jardin de Ranelagh has playgrounds, a carousel, and puppets.

SEVENTEENTH ARRONDISSEMENT

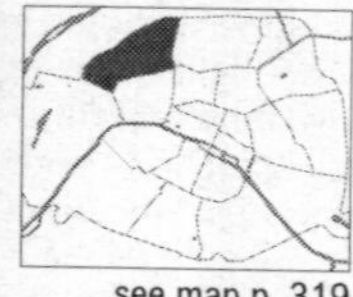

see map p. 319

While barricades were erected, nobles beheaded, and novels written in the heart of the city, **les Batignolles** of the 17*ème* was little more than farmers' fields until the mid-19th century. If you happen to be staying in the center of the 17*ème*, though, the **Musée Jean-Jacques Henner,** 43, av. de Villiers, might be worth a look (see

Museums, p. 136). Nearby, the **Banque de France,** 1, pl. Général Catroux, features a small garden, mosaic brickwork, and a facade with leering gargoyles and serpentine iron drainpipes that slither down the walls, spiralled with gold paint and capped with spitting-fish spouts. Inside, the lobby's vaulted ceilings rise to impossible heights.

VILLAGE BATIGNOLLES

RUE DES BATIGNOLLES

This street is considered the center of the **Village Batignolles,** a quiet village of shops and residences starting at av. des Batignolles and extending to pl. du Dr. Felix Lobligeois. To the west, restaurants and cafés line r. des Dames, while shops stand on r. des Lévis (M: Villiers). On the other side of r. des Batignolles, r. Lemercier (M: Brochant) has a daily covered market filled with meat, cheese, flowers, produce, and old women who have shopped here since WWII. Farther down, at no. 45, is yet another of Verlaine's Parisian addresses. Several blocks north, r. de la Jonquière (M: Guy Môquet) is lined with Moroccan, Tunisian, and Algerian shops and restaurants. La Cité des Fleurs, 59-61, r. de la Jonquière, boasts a row of exquisite private homes and gardens straight out of a Balzac novel. Designed in 1847, this prototypical condominium required each owner to plant at least three trees in the gardens.

CIMETIÈRE DES BATIGNOLLES

8, r. St-Just. M: Port-de Clichy. From the métro, walk south along av. Port-de-Clichy, make a left onto av. du Cimetière des Batignolles and then a right onto r. St-Just. ☎46 27 03 18. Open M-F 8am-6pm, Sa 8:30am-5:30pm, Su 9am-5:30pm. Free.

The Cimetière des Batignolles, sandwiched between a noisy *lycée* and the car horns of the Périphérique in the northwest corner of the 17*ème*, contains the graves of André Breton, Paul Verlaine, and Benjamin Peret. The guards at the entrance give out maps and can refer you to other sources of information on the resident stars.

CIMETIÈRE DES CHIENS

4, Pont de Clichy. M: Gabriel Péri Asnières-Gennevilliers. From the métro, take r. Gabriel Péri to bd. Voltaire to the cimetière. ☎40 86 21 11. Open W-M Mar. 16-Oct. 14 10am-6pm; Oct. 15-Mar. 15 10am-noon and 2-5pm. Free.

Across the Seine, the less famous **Cimetière des Chiens,** in Asnières, is the final resting spot for countless Parisian pets.

EIGHTEENTH ARRONDISSEMENT

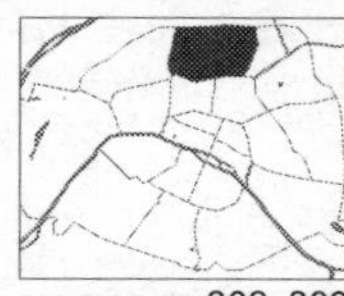
see map pp. 308–309

Built high above the rest of Paris on a steep hill, **Montmartre** gets its name from a history of Roman occupation and Christian martyrdom. A site of worship since before the arrival of the Druids, the hilltop was once home to an altar dedicated to Mercury and a shrine in honor of Mars. At different points in the Roman era, it was referred to as *Mons Mercurii* or *Mons Martis.* The mini-mountain suffered from this confused identity until a bishop named Dionysus, now known as St-Denis, came to introduce Christianity to the Gauls in the late 3rd century. Unimpressed, the Romans cut off his head. St-Denis then picked up his head and carried it north, until he collapsed on the spot that is now the Basilique de St-Denis. To honor his gumption, the hill's name was changed to *Mont Martyrum* (Hill of Martyrs), which then became **Montmartre.** During the Revolution, the hill was renamed *Montmarat* after the Revolutionary martyr Marat, but the change was so subtle that the name Montmartre has been used ever since.

Montmartre is one of the few Parisian neighborhoods Baron Haussmann left intact when he redesigned the city and its environs. A rural area outside the city limits until the 20th century, the hill used to be covered with vineyards, wheat fields, windmills, and gypsum mines. Its picturesque beauty and low rents attracted bohemians like

oh! for a day

Auteuil Walking Tour, Cont'd

Apprentice gardeners tend the beautiful grounds, and a shop sells second-hand clothing, including Pierre Cardin and fur coats. Continue down r. de la Fontaine; **no. 60** looks like the grotto of an old witch—even the fence is made of intertwining iron branches. Proust fans might want to pay homage at **no. 96,** where the writer was born on July 10, 1871. Continue down la Fontaine and turn left onto r. des Perchamps. Turn left onto r. d'Auteuil, lined with 17th-century *hôtels particuliers.* John Adams and his son John Quincy Adams lived at **no. 43-47.** Turn right off r. d'Auteuil onto r. Donzietti, right onto r. Poussin, and left onto Bosin until it becomes r. Raffet. Here, pink stucco, black marble, and mosaic-covered townhouses adjoin gray facades and iron grillwork. At the end of r. Raffet, turn right and look for 55, r. du Docteur-Blanche, where two Le Corbusier villas were constructed in 1925. **Villa La Roche** and **Villa Jeanneret** are stark white structures that now house the Fondation Le Corbusier. Villa La Roche contains a small collection of 20th-century paintings, sculpture, and furniture, although the real masterpiece is the building itself (see **Museums,** p. 243).

Toulouse-Lautrec and Eric Satie as well as performers and impresarios like Aristide Bruant. Toulouse-Lautrec, in particular, immortalized Montmartre through his paintings of life in disreputable nightspots like the Bal du Moulin Rouge (see below). A generation later, just before WWI smashed its spotlights and destroyed its crops, the *butte* welcomed Picasso, Modigliani, Utrillo, and Apollinaire into its artistic circle. Nowadays Montmartre is a mix of upscale bohemia above r. des Abbesses and sleaze along bd. de Clichy—not to mention the legions of panting tourists near Sacré Coeur, the front of which provides a dramatic panorama of the city. The northwest part of the *butte* retains some village charm, with breezy streets speckled with interesting shops and cafés. At dusk, gas lamps trace the stairways up the hillside to the basilica.

MOUNTING MONTMARTRE

Funicular open 6am-12:45am. 8F.

One does not merely visit Montmartre; one climbs it. The standard approach is from the south, via M: Anvers or M: Abbesses, although other directions provide interesting, less-crowded climbs. From M: Anvers, the walk up r. Steinkerque to the ornate switchbacked stairway is short and pretty but sometimes overcrowded with tourists and associated commerce. The longer climb from M: Abbesses, also the safest at night, leads one through more worthwhile cafés and shops; follow r. de la Vieuville to r. Drevet, turning right on r. Gabrielle and left up the stairs to r. du Cardinal Dubois.

For a less difficult ascent, use the glass-covered **funicular** from the base of r. Tardieu (from M: Anvers, walk up r. Steinkerque and take a left on r. Tardieu). Reminiscent of a ski lift, it is operated by the RATP and can be used with a normal métro ticket.

BASILIQUE DU SACRÉ-COEUR

35, r. du Chevalier de la Barre. M: Anvers, Abbesses, or Château-Rouge. ☎ 42 51 17 02. ***Open*** *daily 7am-11pm.* ***Free. Dome and crypt*** *open daily 9am-6pm.* ***Admission*** *to each 15F, students 8F.*

The Basilica of the Sacred Heart is like an exotic head-dress floating above Paris. In 1873, the Assemblée Nationale selected the birthplace of the *Commune* (see **History,** p. 30) as the location for Sacré-Coeur, "in witness of repentance and as a symbol of hope," although politician Eugène Spuller called it "a monument to civil war." It was hoped by the Catholic establishment that the Sacré-Coeur would "expiate the sins" of France after the bloody civil war in which thousands of *communards* (leftists who proclaimed a new populist government, known as the Commune of Paris) were massacred by government troops. After a massive fund-raising effort, the basilica was completed in 1914 and consecrated in 1919. Its hybrid style of onion domes and arches and white color set it apart from the smoky grunge of most Parisian buildings. Most striking inside the basilica are the **mosaics,** especially the depiction of Christ on the ceiling and the mural of the Passion at the back of the altar. The narrow climb up the dome offers the highest vantage point in Paris and a view that stretches as far as 50km on clear days. Farther down, the **crypt** contains a relic of what many believe to be a piece of the sacred heart of Christ.

Mirror Garden

LAPIN AGILE

22, r. des Saules.

Still going strong among quaint shuttered houses is the Lapin Agile cabaret. Frequented by Verlaine, Renoir, Modigliani, and Max Jacob, the establishment was first known as the "Cabaret des Assassins" until André Gill decorated its facade with a *lapin* (rabbit) striking a pose as it leaps out of a pot while balancing a hat on its head and a bottle on its paw. The cabaret immediately gained renown as the "Lapin à Gill," (Gill's rabbit). By the time Picasso began to frequent the establishment, walking over from his first studio at 49, r. Gabrielle, the name had contracted to "Lapin Agile."

DOWNHILL

Dragon Garden

RUES ABBESSES AND LEPIC

These days tasty restaurants, trendy cafés, and *boulangeries* crowd this corner of Montmartre around r. des Abbesses and r. Lepic. Tall iron gates hide the beautiful gardens of 18th-century townhouses. Walking down r. Lepic will carry you past the **Moulin Radet,** one of the last remaining windmills on Montmartre. Farther down is the site of the **Moulin de la Galette,** depicted by Renoir during one of the frequent dances held there, and one of van Gogh's former homes at 54, r. Lepic.

CIMETIÈRE MONTMARTRE

20, av. Rachel. M: Pl. de Clichy or Blanche. ☎ 43 87 64 24. Open daily 8am-5:30pm.

Parallel to r. Lepic, r. Caulaincourt leads downhill to the landscaped, secluded Cimetière Montmartre, where writers Alexandre Dumas and Stendhal, painter Edgar Degas, physicists André Ampère and Leon Foucault, composer Hector Berlioz, and filmmaker François Truffault are buried. Emile Zola also reposed here until his corpse joined the Panthéon in 1908. In 1871, this cemetery became the site of huge mass graves after the siege of the Commune.

Canal at La Vilette

BAL DU MOULIN ROUGE

M: Blanche. ☎ 53 09 82 82.

Along the bd. de Clichy and bd. de Rochechouart, you'll find many of the cabarets and nightclubs that were the definitive hangouts of the Belle Epoque, including the infamous cabaret Bal du Moulin Rouge immortalized by the paintings of Toulouse-Lautrec and the music of Offenbach. At the turn of the century, Paris's bourgeoisie came to the Moulin Rouge to play at being bohemian. After WWI, Parisian bohemians relocated to the Left Bank and the area around pl. Pigalle became a world-renowned seedy red-light district (see **Sights,** p. 90). Today, the

oh! for a day

Up and Down Montmartre

If you start your climb up **Montmartre** to **Basilique du Sacré-Coeur** early, you will escape the intensity of the miday heat and the miday crowds. Take the scenic route up from M: Abbesses following r. de la Vieuville to r. Drevet, turning right on r. Gabrielle and left up the stairs to r. du Cardinal Dubois. Visit the crypt and (for those who still have energy left) climb to the top of the tower for the extrodinary view. Descend the hill back towards M: Abbesses and stop for lunch at **Le Soleil Gourmand** located at 10, r. Ravignan. After lunch, you are in prime position to wander the streets around pl. Abbsesses and r. Lepic which will take you past **Moulin Radet,** one of the last remaining windmills in Paris as well as one of van Gogh's former homes at number 54, r. Lepic. Parallel to r. Lepic, r. Caulaincourt leads downhill to **Cimetière Montmartre** where you can visit the graves of French greats. Take r. Caulaincourt back uphill (no rest for the weary) to **Chez Ginette** for a delicous dinner. To sample the nightlife, walk back down towarrds M: Abbesses to **Chez Camille** on r. Ravignan, and further south on r. des Martyrs to **La Fourmi** which puts you in prime position to dance the night away across the street at **Divan du Monde.**

crowd consists of tourists out for an evening of sequins, tassels, and skin. The revues are still risqué, but the admission is prohibitively expensive.

LA GOUTTE D'OR

Farther east, the 18*ème* becomes an immigrant ghetto in the midst of urban renewal. Still filled with crumbling buildings, the quarter takes its name, "drop of gold," from the medieval vineyard that stood here. During the Algerian war for independence, the presence of the Algerian National Liberation Front (FLN) kept the area relatively segregated. Today, ambitious plans a change from its status as one of the few refuges of cheap housing in the city. Along bd. Barbés you'll find numerous discount clothing shops, as well as African cloth, food, and gift shops around r. Doudeauville and r. des Poissonniers. Those unfamiliar with the area should avoid it at night.

NINETEENTH ARRONDISSEMENT

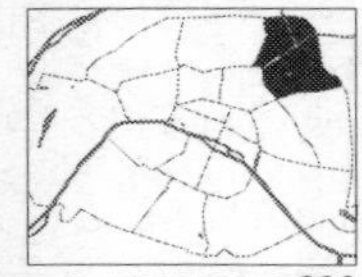

see map p. 320

Like Paris's other periphery arrondissements, the 19*ème* is a predominantly working-class quarter. But near the Parc des Buttes-Chaumont, wealthy Parisians pay handsomely for houses with views of one of Paris' finer parks. The 19*ème* is also home to a large part of Paris's Asian community, making it full of wonderful, inexpensive restaurants. At night, avoid r. David d'Angiers, bd. Indochine, and av. Corentin Cariou.

PARC DE LA VILLETTE

The best sight in the 19*ème* is the amazing Parc de la Villette (see **Museums,** p. 126).

PARC DES BUTTES-CHAUMONT

M: Buttes-Chaumont. Open daily May-Sep. 7am-11pm; Oct.-Apr. 7am-9pm. Gates close 15min. before.

To the south, Parc des Buttes-Chaumont is a mix of man-made topography and transplanted vegetation. Nostalgic for London's Hyde Park, where he spent much of his time in exile, Napoleon III built the Parc des Buttes-Chaumont. Before the construction of the Buttes-Chaumont, the *quartier* was (since the 13th century) host to a *gibbet* (an iron cage filled with the rotting corpses of criminals), a dumping-ground for dead horses, a breeding-ground for worms (sold as bait), and a gypsum quarry (the source of "plaster of Paris"). Making a park out of this mess took four years and 1000 workers. Designer Adolphe Alphand had all of the soil replaced and the quarried remains built up with new rock to create enormous fake cliffs surrounding a lake, waterfalls, caves with stalactites, and a Roman temple, from which there is a great view of the *quartier*.

TWENTIETH ARRONDISSEMENT

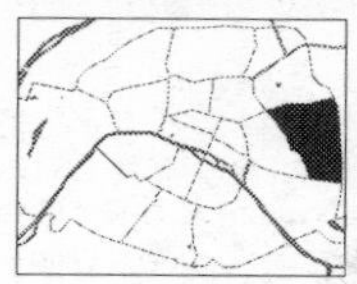

see map p. 321

As Haussmannization expelled many of Paris's workers from the central city, thousands migrated east to **Belleville** (the northern part of the 20*ème*), **Ménilmontant** (the southern), and **Charonne** (the southeastern). By the late Second Republic, the 20*ème* had come to be known as a "red" arrondissement, solidly proletarian and radical. Some of the heaviest fighting during the suppression of the Commune took place in these streets, where the communards made desperate last stands on their home turf. Caught between the Versaillais troops to the west and the Prussian lines outside the city walls, the Commune fortified the Parc des Buttes-Chaumont and the **Cimetière Père-Lachaise,** but soon ran out of ammunition. On May 28, 1871, the *communards* abandoned their last barricade and surrendered (see **History,** p. 30). After the Commune, the 20*ème* kept on as the fairly isolated home of those workers who survived the retributive massacres following the government's takeover. "Many a workman's child," historian Eugene Weber has observed, "grew to adolescence before World War I without getting out of Ménilmontant or Belleville." Today, the arrondissement has a similar feel, with busy residential areas and markets that cater not to visitors but to locals. The area is also the home to sizable Greek, North African, Russian, and Asian communities.

PÈRE LACHAISE CEMETERY

16, r. du Repos. M: Père-Lachaise. ☎43 70 70 33. ***Open*** *Mar.-Oct. M-F 8am-6pm, Sa 8:30am-6pm, Su and holidays 9am-6pm; Nov.-Feb. M-F 8am-5:30pm, Sa 8:30am-5:30pm, Su and holidays 9am-5:30pm. Last entrance 15min. before closing.* ***Free.*** *Free* ***maps*** *supposedly available at guard booths by main entrances, but they're usually out; it may be worth the 10F or so to buy a detailed map from a nearby tabac before entering. 2hr.* ***guided tour*** *in English June-Sept. Sa 3pm; in French Sa at 2:30pm, occasionally Tu at 2:30pm and Su at 3pm as well as numerous theme-tours. 37F, students 26F; meet at the bd. de Ménilmontant entrance (☎40 71 75 23 for info).*

With its winding paths and elaborate sarcophagi, Cimetière Père Lachaise has become the final resting place of French and foreign giants. Balzac, Colette, David, Delacroix, La Fontaine, Haussmann, Molière, and Proust are buried here, as are Chopin, Jim Morrison (see **Dying to Get In**), Gertrude Stein, and Oscar Wilde. With so many tourists, however, they're hardly resting in peace. The land for Père Lachaise was bought by Napoleon's government in 1803 from Père de la Chaise, Louis XIV's confessor, to create a "modern and hygienic necropolis" that would relieve the overcrowding of city cemeteries. At first, Parisians were reluctant to bury their dead so far from the city. To increase the cemetery's popularity, Napoleon ordered that the remains of a few famous figures be dug up and reburied in Père Lachaise. Thus abruptly arrived the remains of Molière, La Fontaine, those sexy medieval lovers Abélard and Héloïse, and several other luminaries.

The antithesis of the church cemetery, Père Lachaise is like a 19th-century garden party for the dead. Many of the tombs in this landscaped grove strive to remind visitors of the dead's many worldly accomplishments: the tomb of French Romantic painter Géricault wears a reproduction of his *Raft of the Medusa;* on Chopin's tomb sits his muse Calliope with a lyre in her hand. Oscar Wilde's grave is marked by a larger than life streaking Egyptian figure. Shortly after Wilde's burial, there was a scandal over the generous proportions of the Egyptian's Nile jewels. The director of the cemetery, exhausted by all the fuss, took matters into his own hands: he allegedly removed the offending parties with a small hammer, condemning them to eternal life as a paperweight. The well-endowed likeness of journalist Victor Noir that stands atop his tomb is said to have magical fertility powers. Haussmann, the man of the boulevards, wanted to destroy the cemetery as part of his urban-renewal project, but obviously relented; he now occupies a mausoleum in Père Lachaise. Remembered by plaques here are dancer Isadora Duncan, author Richard Wright, opera diva Maria Callas, and artist Max Ernst. The most-visited grave is that of Jim Morrison, the former lead singer of The Doors. His graffiti-covered bust was removed from the tomb, leaving his fans to fill the rest of the cemetery with their messages. In summer, dozens of young people bring flowers, joints, beer, poetry, and Doors paraphernalia to his tomb; the sandbox in front of the stone is now the sanctioned site for the creative expression of such pensive mourners. At least one guard polices the spot at all times.

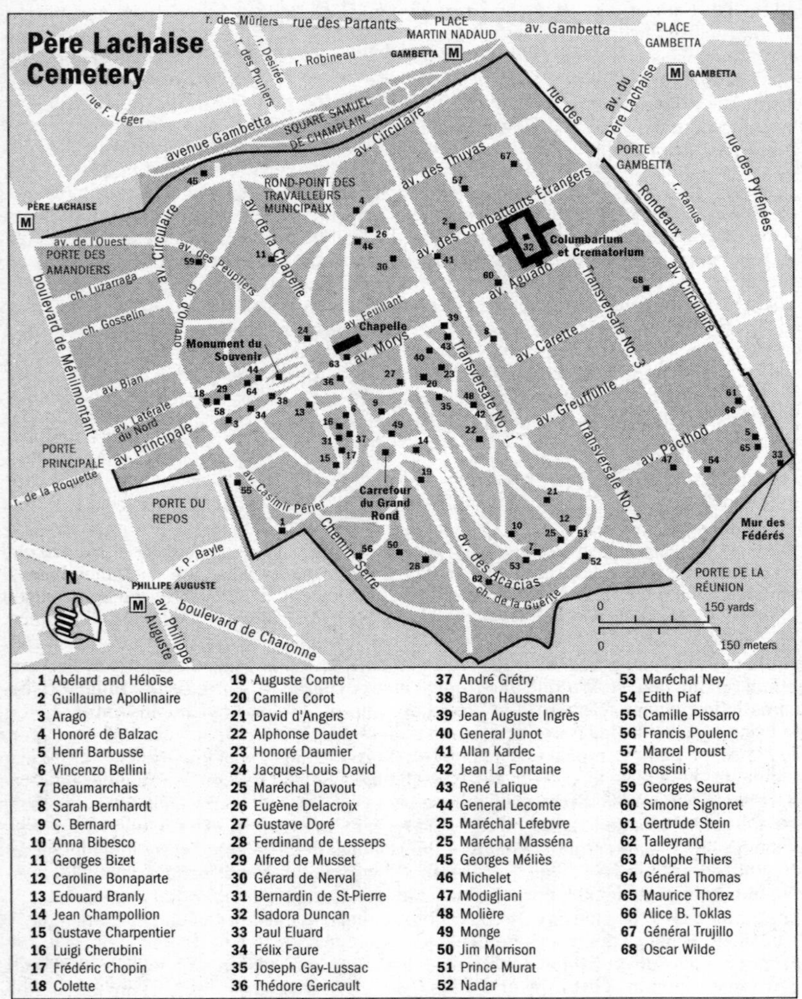

Over one million people are buried in the cemetery. Curiously, there are only 100,000 tombs. The discrepancy is due to the old practice of burying the poor in mass graves. Corpses are removed from these unmarked plots at regular intervals to make room for new generations of the dead. This grisly process is necessary in a densely populated city like Paris. Even with such purges, however, the 44 hectares of Père Lachaise are filled to bursting, so the government makes room by digging up any grave that has not been visited in a certain number of years. To avoid this fate, some solitary (and rich) souls who sense they are about to kick the bucket hire a professional "mourner."

Perhaps the most moving sites in Père Lachaise are those that mark the deaths of collective groups. The **Mur des Fédérés** (Wall of the Federals) has become a site of pilgrimage for left-wing sympathizers. In May 1871, a group of *communards* murdered the Archbishop of Paris, who had been taken hostage at the beginning of the Commune. They dragged his mutilated corpse to their stronghold in Père Lachaise and tossed it in a ditch. Four days later, the victorious *Versaillais* found the body. In retaliation, they lined up 147 Fédérés against the eastern wall of the cemetery, shot them, and buried them on the spot. Since 1871, the Mur des Fédérés has been a rallying point for the French Left, which recalls the massacre's anniversary every Pentecost. Ironically, Republican Adolphe Thiers, who ordered their execution, shares the cemetery with them; he died of natural causes in 1877. Near the wall, a number of moving monuments containing human remains commemorate the Resistance fighters of WWII as well as Nazi concentration camp victims.

PERIMETER SIGHTS

BOIS DE BOULOGNE

M: Porte Maillot, Sablons, Pont de Neuilly, Porte Dauphine, or Porte d'Auteuil. Open 24hr.

The Bois de Boulogne is an 846-hectare (over 2,000 acre) green canopy at the western edge of Paris and a popular place for walks, jogs, boating, and picnics. In a past life, it was the vast Foret de Rouvray, a royal hunting ground where deer and wild boar ran with wolves and bears. In 1852 the Bois had become "a desert used for dueling and suicides," and was given to the city of Paris by Napoleon III. Acting on imperial instructions, Baron Haussmann dug lakes, created waterfalls and cut winding paths through thickly wooded areas. By the turn of the century, the park was square enough that aristocratic families rode there to spend a Sunday afternoon "in the country." In harder times, the pleasure park also served its purpose—trees were felled for firewood during the Revolution; it was occupied by a "ragged army" of citizens scrounging for edible plants during the starvation of the Prussian seige in 1870; political undesirables ("men with intelligent faces") were shot here by the Communards in 1871; and during WWII people grew vegetable gardens to supplement meager rations. In 1991, a flood of newly liberated Eastern Europeans camped in the park. And more recently, the Bois by night has been a bazaar of sex and drugs, complete with transvestite prostitutes and violent crime. Police are stepping up patrols, but the boulevards around the periphery of the Bois continue to be lined with fleshly wares at night. *Let's Go* does not recommend moonlight strolls.

STADIUMS

The Bois de Boulogne contains several stadiums, the most famous of which are the **Hippodromes de Longchamp** and **d'Auteuil,** a flat racecourse and a steeplechase, respectively. The June Grand Prix at Longchamp was one of the premier events of the Belle Epoque social calendar. Also within the *bois*, the **Parc des Princes** hosts football (soccer) matches. The **Stade Roland Garros** is home of the **French Open** tennis tournament. The *bois*'s boathouses rent rowboats (see below).

LAKES

M: Porte Dauphine. Boathouses open late Feb. to early Nov. daily 10am-7pm, weather permitting. Rentals 45F per hr., 400F deposit; with insurance against damage to boat 52F per hr., 200F deposit.

There are two artificial lakes stretching down the eastern edge of the Bois. The manicured islands of the **Lac Inférieur** can be reached only by rowboat. Lake Superior will require an airplane. Between the two lakes you can stroll under a cascading waterfall.

JARDIN D'ACCLIMATATION

M: Sablons. Cross the street, pass Monoprix, and walk three blocks. ☎40 67 90 82. Open daily 10am-6pm; ticket office closes 5:45pm. 12F, under 3 free. No dogs allowed.

The Jardin d'Acclimatation offers a small zoo, some sports (mini-golf, riding, bowling), and carnival rides. Sneakily mixed in are educational museums that parents will adore (see below), picnic areas, and outdoor jazz concerts.

MUSÉE EN HERBE. The Musée en Herbe is a European art-history museum designed for children ages 4-11. Temporary exhibits range from farm animals to artists like Manet, Chagall, and Picasso. The museum also offers studio workshops on sculpture, pottery, papier mâché, painting and collage for children two and older. A participatory theater

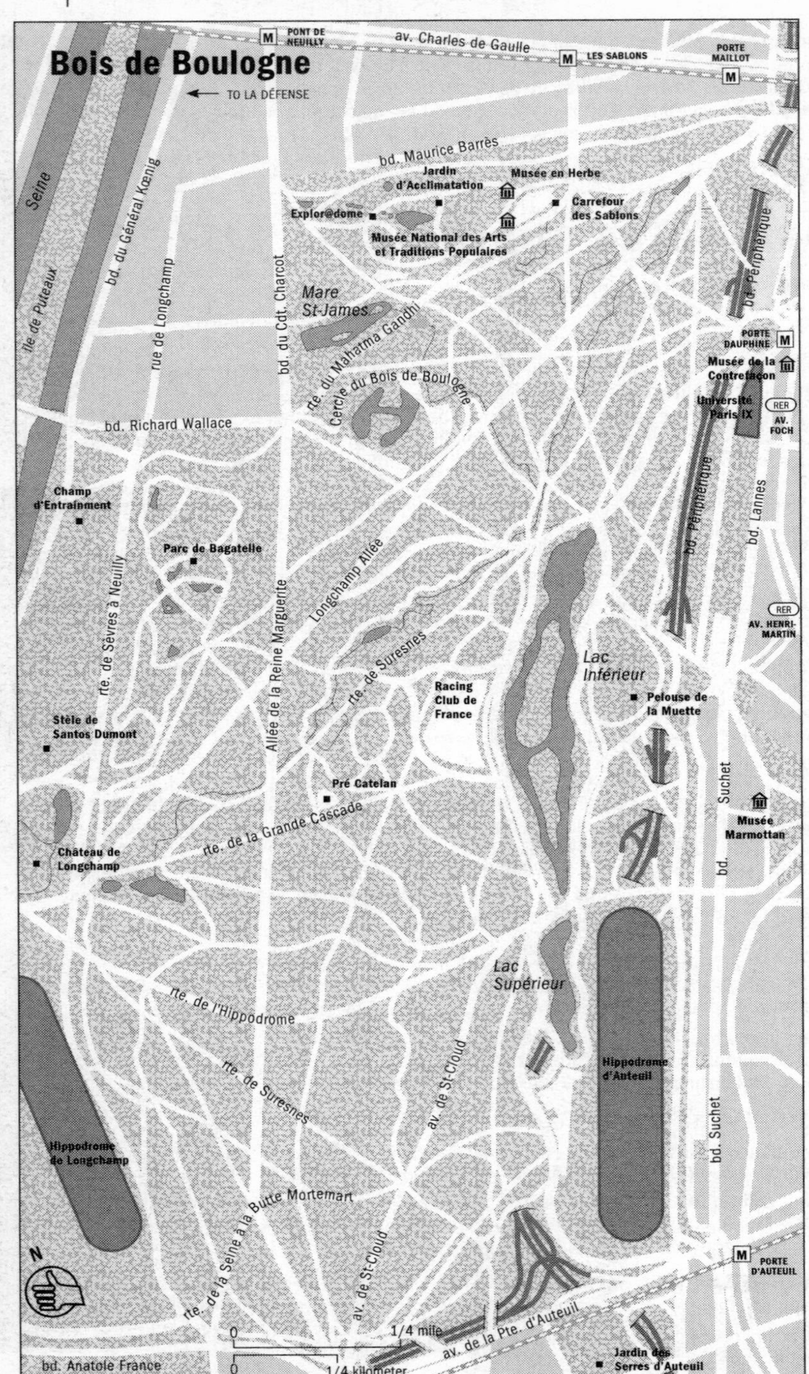
Bois de Boulogne
TO LA DÉFENSE
PONT DE NEUILLY
av. Charles de Gaulle
LES SABLONS
PORTE MAILLOT
Seine
Ile de Puteaux
bd. du Général Kœnig
rue de Longchamp
bd. du Cdt. Charcot
bd. Maurice Barrès
Jardin d'Acclimatation
Musée en Herbe
Carrefour des Sablons
Explor@dome
Musée National des Arts et Traditions Populaires
Mare St-James
rte. du Mahatma Gandhi
Cercle du Bois de Boulogne
bd. Périphérique
PORTE DAUPHINE
Musée de la Contrefaçon
Université Paris IX
RER
AV. FOCH
bd. Richard Wallace
Champ d'Entraînment
Parc de Bagatelle
rte. de Sèvres à Neuilly
Allée de la Reine Marguerite
Longchamp Allée
rte. de Suresnes
Racing Club de France
bd. Lannes
AV. HENRI-MARTIN
Lac Inférieur
Pelouse de la Muette
Stèle de Santos Dumont
Pré Catelan
rte. de la Grande Cascade
Château de Longchamp
bd. Suchet
Musée Marmottan
Lac Supérieur
rte. de l'Hippodrome
rte. de Suresnes
av. de St-Cloud
Hippodrome d'Auteuil
Hippodrome de Longchamp
rte. de la Butte Mortemart
rte. de la Seine à la Butte Mortemart
PORTE D'AUTEUIL
N
0
1/4 mile
1/4 kilometer
av. de la Pte. d'Auteuil
bd. Anatole France
Jardin des Serres d'Auteuil

company for children stages plays (Oct.-July W and Sa-Su) and puppet shows (W and Sa-Su 3:15 and 4:15pm). *(Directly on your left at the Entrée Sablons. ☎40 67 97 66. Open Su-F 10am-6pm, Sa 2-6pm. 16F. Studio sessions July-Aug. daily at 2 and 4pm; Sept.-June W, Sa, and Su at 2 and 4pm. Call to make reservations. Participation 25F.)*

EXPLOR@DOME. Inspired by a sister dome in San Francisco, this fun and perplexing set of displays provokes questions about human perception, gravity, and space. Special exhibitions change bi-monthly. A children's workshop is run by a set of very, very excited volunteers; kids create a gift to take home with them. A large computer area donated by Macintosh helps young ones get lost in the world wide web. *(Directly to the left of the Neuilly entrance, by the puppets and the dragon ride. ☎53 64 90 94. Open daily 10am-6pm. 30F. Call in advance for workshops.)*

PRÉ CATELAN

M: Porte Maillot. At the av. de Neuilly exit, take bus #244 to Bagatelle-Pré-Catelan. Open daily 8:30am-7:30pm.

The Pré Catelan could be named after Théophile Catelan, master of the hunt under Louis XIV, but legend likes to have it that this neatly manicured meadow was named after a murdered delivery boy. Arnault Catelan, who rode from Provence to Paris to deliver gifts to Philippe le Bel from Beatrice de Savoie, hired a group of men to protect him on his journey. The men robbed and murdered him in the dead of night, believing that Arnault carried gold. In fact, Arnault carried only rare perfumes from the South of France. Authorities later captured the marauders, who, doused in a rare Provençale scent, were easily identifiable.

JARDIN DE SHAKESPEARE. Inside the Pré Catelan, the Jardin de Shakespeare is a popular open-air theatre. There is Scottish highland vegetation in the **Macbeth** area, a Mediterranean section for **The Tempest,** and toasted cheese for **Lear.** *(☎46 47 73 20. Call ahead for performance times. Open daily for wandering 2-4pm. 5F, students 3F, under 10 2F.)*

PARC DE LA BAGATELLE

Same bus stop as Pré Catelan, above. ☎40 67 97 00. Open daily Jan. 1-15 9am-4:30pm; Jan. 16-Feb. 15 and Oct. 16-Nov. 30 9am-5:30pm; Feb. 16-28 and Oct. 1-15 9am-6pm; Mar. 1-15 8:30am-6:30pm; Mar. 16-Apr. 30 and Sept. 8:30am-7pm; June-July 8:30am-8pm. Ticket office closes 30min. earlier. 10F, ages 6-10 5F.

The Parc de la Bagatelle was once a private estate and became a public park in 1905. In 1777, in an impetuous act that could not have helped his image in pre-revolutionary Paris, the future Charles X bet his sister-in-law, Marie-Antoinette, that he could build the **Château de la Bagatelle** in three months. She was game, and Charles employed 1000 workers of all descriptions (including a Scottish landscape artist) to complete the job. The **Bagatelle garden** is famous for its June 21 rose exhibition (35F, seniors 25F, plus 10F park admission). Tulips are magnificent in April, irises bloom in May, and August is the month for the water lilies the gardener added in tribute to Monet.

JARDIN DES SERRES D'AUTEUIL

M: Porte d'Auteuil or Michel-Ange Molitor. Enter at 1, av. Gordon-Bennett, off bd. d'Auteuil. Open daily May-Aug. 10am-6pm; Sept.-Apr. 10am-5pm. 3F.

Victor Noir

Père-Lachaise

Jim Morrison

The Jardin des Serres d'Auteuil (Greenhouse Garden) is full of hothouse flowers and trees. The 19th century had a love affair with iron and glass (see the **Eiffel Tower,** p. 81) and a love of gardens, so it is not surprising that these two loves eventually merged. This was one of Paris' first hothouses, built between 1895 and 1898 to allow the green of summer gardens to bloom all winter long. It became so popular that tickets were rationed out according to a person's moral standards (but of course!), although an exception was made for drunkards, whose "condition" the garden was supposed to cure.

JARDIN DES POÈTES

Open Apr. 16-Oct. 15 daily 10am-7pm; Oct. 16-Apr. 15 W and Sa-Su 10am-7pm.

Free and prettier, if something of a make-out spot, is the neighboring **Jardin des Poètes.** Poems are attached to each flower bed: scan Ronsard, Corneille, Racine, Baudelaire, and Apollinaire. Rodin's sculpture of Victor Hugo is partially obscured by a thicket.

BOIS DE VINCENNES

BOIS DE VINCENNES

M: Château de Vincennes or Porte Dorée.

Like the Bois de Boulogne, the Bois de Vincennes was once a royal hunting forest. Today it is the largest expanse of greenery in Paris. Since it lay beyond the reach of Parisian authorities, it was also a favorite ground for dueling. The elder Alexandre Dumas dueled a literary collaborator here who claimed to have written the *Tour de Nesle.* Dumas's pistol misfired and the author had to content himself with using the experience as the basis for a scene in *The Corsican Brothers.* Like the Bois de Boulogne, the Vincennes forest was given to Paris by Napoleon III, to be transformed into an English-style garden. Not surprisingly, Haussmann (see **Architecture,** p. 43) oversaw the planning of lakes and pathways. Annexed to a much poorer section of Paris than the Bois de Boulogne, Vincennes was never quite as fashionable or as formal. Today, the Bois de Vincennes's bikepaths, horsetrails, zoo, and Buddhist Temple are wonderful escapes from the city.

PARC ZOOLOGIQUE DE PARIS

53, av. de St-Maurice. M: Porte Dorée. ☎ 44 75 20 10. Open daily May-Sept. 9am-6pm; Oct.-May 9am-5pm. Ticket office closes 30min. before zoo. 40F; ages 4-16, students 16-27, and over 60 30F; under 4 free. Kiddie train tour leaves from restaurant; 12F, under 10 10F. Guidebook to the zoo 30F.

In a country not known for its zoos, the Parc Zoologique de Paris is considered the best of the bunch. It is the Bois de Vincennes's most popular attraction and recently has been working hard to improve the animals' environment. The *phoques* (the French word for *seal* that is pronounced just as you think it is) are fed daily at 4pm. The park is also home to the **Grand Rocher,** an observatory. The 20F fee is a bit hefty, but the view is lovely.

CHÂTEAU DE VINCENNES

M: Château de Vincennes. On the northern edge of the park. Open daily May-Sept. 10am-noon and 1:15-6pm; Oct.-Apr. 10am-noon and 1:15–5pm. Admission by guided tour only; long tour 32F, students 21F; short tour 25F, students 15F; under 12 free to both tours.

Called "the Versailles of the Middle Ages," Château de Vincennes was the favored court of French kings as early as the 13th century, and although the Louvre was royalty's principal home, every French monarch from Charles V to Henri IV spent at least part of his time at Vincennes. On the spot that Louis VII chose for a royal hunting residence, Charles V built up a medieval fortress. Henri III found it a useful refuge during the Wars of Religion, and Mazarin and the court found its defenses useful in the wake of the Fronde. In the 18th century, Vincennes became a country-club prison for well-known enemies of the state like Mirabeau. When Diderot was imprisoned in the château, Rousseau walked through the forest to visit. In the 19th century, the complex resumed its military functions, serving as fortress, arsenal, and artillery park. In 1917, the infamous Mata Hari, convicted of spying for the Germans, faced a firing squad within its walls. In 1940, the château was headquarters for General Maurice Gamelin, Supreme Commander of

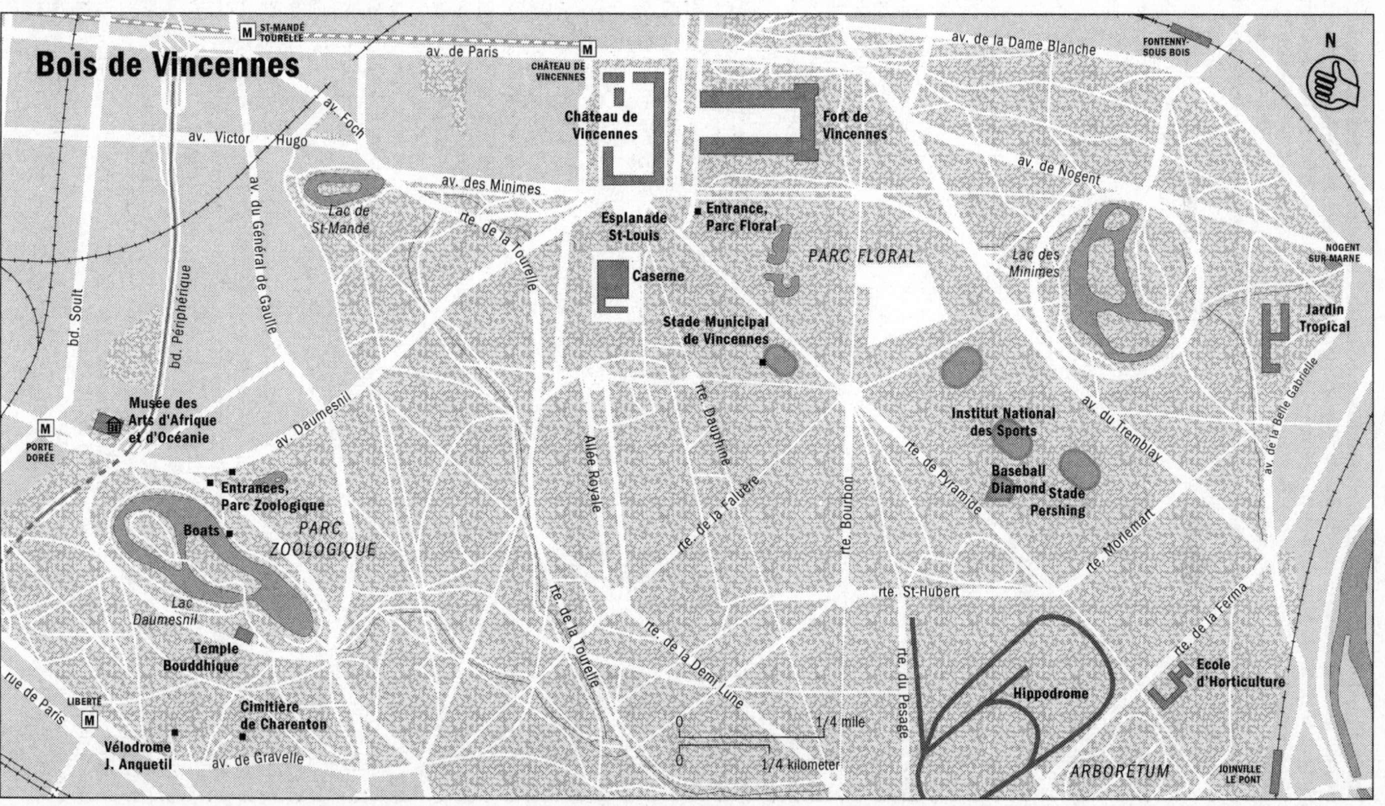

Bois de Vincennes
M
ST-MANDÉ TOURELLE
av. de Paris
M
CHÂTEAU DE VINCENNES
av. de la Dame Blanche
FONTENNY-SOUS BOIS
N
av. Foch
av. Victor Hugo
Château de Vincennes
Fort de Vincennes
av. de Nogent
av. des Minimes
Lac de St-Mandé
rte. de la Tourelle
Esplanade St-Louis
Entrance, Parc Floral
PARC FLORAL
Lac des Minimes
NOGENT SUR-MARNE
av. du Général de Gaulle
Caserne
bd. Soult
bd. Périphérique
Stade Municipal de Vincennes
Jardin Tropical
av. de la Belle Gabrielle
Musée des Arts d'Afrique et d'Océanie
M
PORTE DORÉE
av. Daumesnil
rte. Dauphine
Allée Royale
Institut National des Sports
av. du Tremblay
rte. de Pyramide
Baseball Diamond
Stade Pershing
Entrances, Parc Zoologique
Boats
PARC ZOOLOGIQUE
rte. de la Faluère
rte. Bourbon
rte. Morlemart
rte. St-Hubert
rte. de la Tourelle
Lac Daumesnil
Temple Bouddhique
rte. de la Demi Lune
rte. du Pesage
rte. de la Ferma
Ecole d'Horticulture
Hippodrome
rue de Paris
LIBERTÉ
M
Cimitière de Charenton
0
1/4 mile
0
1/4 kilometer
Vélodrome J. Anquetil
av. de Gravelle
ARBORÉTUM
JOINVILLE LE PONT

French Land Forces. De Gaulle criticized Gamelin for holing up in Vincennes, without even a radio to connect him with the front. Today, the 17th-century apartments house the archives of the French armed forces.

PARC FLORAL DE PARIS

Esplanade du Château. M: Château de Vincennes. ☎ 43 43 92 95; www.parcfloraldeparis.com. Open daily Mar. 27-Oct. 1 9:30am-8pm; Oct. 2-15 9:30am-7pm; Oct. 16-29 9:30am-6pm; Oct. 30-Feb. 28 9:30am-6pm. 10F, ages 6-17 and 60+ 5F, under 6 free.

One of the gems of the Bois de Vincennes is the Parc Floral de Paris, which can be reached by walking down r. de la Pyramide from the castle. The park has a library, a butterfly garden, miniature golf, and assorted games for kids.

LAC DAUMESNIL

Boat rental daily Mar.-Nov. 10:30am-5:30pm. 1-2 people 54F per hr., 3-4 people 60F per hr.; 50F deposit plus recommended tip.

Joggers, cyclists, and people-watchers share Lac Daumesnil; others row boats. Farther into the park are running and cycling paths. The **Vélodrome Jacques Anquetil,** the **Hippodrome de Vincennes,** and other sports facilities await.

FERME DE PARIS

☎ 43 28 47 63. Open Sa-Su and holidays in summer 1:30-7pm; in winter 1:30-5:15pm. 22F, under 18 11F.

If you're with the kids, or just feel the need to rue those lambchops you had for dinner, head to the Paris Farm.

SAINTE-CHAPELLE AND DONJON

Built between 1336 and 1370, the 52m-high donjon (big square tower) is a striking example of medieval architecture. It has been closed for restoration for the past five years, however, and unfortunately will probably not be open until 2002. The Ste-Chapelle was founded as a church in 1379, but the building was not inaugurated until 1552. Dainty in its decor and especially beautiful in late afternoon, the Ste-Chapelle is looking even better these days after restoration of the exterior. Guided tours are the only way to get in, but the church, stripped down to its bare bones over the centuries, is more impressive from the outside. There are archaeological digs to survey in the main courtyard, and the ramparts offer a pleasant, if unexciting, view of the area.

LA DÉFENSE

M/RER: La Défense, or the #73 bus. The RER is faster, but the métro is cheaper. If you take the RER, buy the RER ticket before going through the turnstile. A normal métro ticket may get you into the RER station in Paris, but won't get you out without a fine at La Défense. Grande Arche open daily 10am-7pm; roof closes 1hr. after ticket office, which closes at 6pm. ***Admission*** *43F; under 18, students, and seniors 33F. Beyond the small lawn, the* ***Info Défense*** *booth offers free maps, guides, and a permanent exhibit on the architectural history and future of La Défense. ☎ 47 74 84 24. Open M-F 10am-1pm and 2-5pm. For* ***French tours*** *call Défense-Evenement or take the petit train. ☎ 46 92 17 50. 35F, students 25F.* ***French petit train tours*** *every 40min. Apr.-Oct. daily 10am-6:30pm from under the Grande Arche; 27F, under 10 15F.*

Just outside Paris's most exclusive suburbs lies a gleaming, teeming space crammed with eye-popping contemporary architecture, enormous office buildings, and one very geometric arch. Great efforts have been made since La Défense's initial development in 1958, especially by Mitterrand and his grands projets program, to inject social spaces, monuments, and art into La Défense's commercial landscape. Shops, galleries, gardens, and sculptures by **Miró, Calder,** and **César** cluster around the **Grande Arche de la Défense,** a breathtaking 35-story building in the shape of a white hollow cube.

After the construction of the Tour Montparnasse in 1973 (see p. 98), Parisian authorities restricted further construction of skyscrapers *(gratte-ciels)* within the 20 arrondissements for fear that new highrises would alter the Paris skyline. As a result, new building projects moved to La Défense. To maintain the symmetry of the **Axe Historique** (the line that stretches from the Arc de Triomphe du Carrousel in front of the Louvre, down the Champs-Élysées to the Arc de Triomphe, and down the av. de la Grande Armée to La Défense), I.M. Pei suggested a plan for a monument to anchor the Défense end of the axis. Ultimately, Pei was asked to design the eastern terminus in the courtyard of the Louvre. Instead, Danish architect Otto von Spreckelsen's Grande Arche was chosen for La Défense. Spreckelsen backed out of the project before its completion, disheartened by red tape and by his own design, which he deemed a "monument without a soul." British engineer Peter Rice finished the work and designed the canvas tent "clouds" suspended to soften the arch's austere angles.

The Arche was inaugurated on the French Republic's bicentennial, July 14, 1989. The roof of this unconventional office building covers 2.5 acres—Notre-Dame could nestle in its hollow core. The arch's walls are covered with white marble and mirrors so that it shines brilliantly in sunlight. Ride the outdoor glass elevators for an unparalleled view at the top and a redux of the end of *Charlie and the Chocolate Factory.*

Other Défense buildings include the **Bull Tower,** the tent-like **Palais Défense,** and the **CNIT building,** a center for congresses, exhibitions, and conferences that, at 37 years old, is La Défense's oldest building. The **Musée de l'Automobile** features car-related accessories, exhibits on the history of the auto, and 110 vintage voitures. *(1, pl. du Dôme. Open daily 12:15-7:30pm. Admission 30F, students, seniors, and under 16 25F.)* The globe-shaped **Dôme IMAX** houses an omnimax theater (see **Cinema,** p. 151). To the right of the booth, the **Galerie de l'Esplanade** features temporary art exhibits. *(Open daily noon-7pm.)* The huge **Quatre Temps** shopping center—one of the largest shopping malls in Europe—contains cafés, supermarkets, and 30 restaurants. Enter from the Grande Arche métro stop, or from doors behind the Miró sculpture. The info desk on the first floor near the escalator to the métro distributes maps of the complex. *(Shops open M-Sa 10am-8pm. Supermarkets open M-Sa 9am-10pm.)*

You may want to invest in a **Carte Musées et Monuments,** which offers admission to 70 museums in the Paris area. This card will probably save you money if you are planning to visit more than three museums/sights every day and will enable you to sail past all of the frustrated tourists standing in line. At Versailles this card is indispensable: you will skip the 90-minute line in the summer heat. The card is available at major museums and in almost all métro stations. Ask for a brochure listing participating museums and monuments. A pass for one day is 80F; for three consecutive days 160F; for five consecutive days 240F. For more information, call **Association InterMusées,** 25, r. du Renard, *4ème* (☎44 78 45 81; fax 44 78 12 23; www.intermusees.com).

MAJOR MUSEUMS

MUSÉE DU LOUVRE

M: Palais-Royal/Musée du Louvre. ☎40 20 51 51 50 50; www.louvre.fr. ***Open*** *M and W 9am-9:45pm, Th-Su 9am-6pm. Last entry 45min. before closing, but people are asked to leave 15-30min. before closing.* ***Admission*** *W-Sa 9am-3pm 45F, W-Sa 3pm-close and Su 30F, under 18 and first Su of the month free. Prices include both the permanent and temporary collections.* ***Temporary exhibits*** *in the Cour Napoléon open at 10am.* ***English Tours*** *M and W-Sa 17F; ☎40 20 53 17, or check the special events board behind the info desk for exact times.* ***Bookstore*** *and* ***cafés*** *open same hours as the museum.*

Built on the foundations of a medieval castle that housed French kings for four centuries; restructured by a 20th-century Socialist politician and a Chinese-American architect; and filled with priceless objects from the tombs of Egyptian pharaohs, the halls of Roman emperors, the studios of French painters, and the walls of Italian churches, the Louvre is an intersection of time, space, and national boundaries. Explore the endless

in the galleries, enus de Milo, and

lass pyramid, where an escala- normous lobby. From the métro, by following signs through the Car- museum. **Tickets** for the museums are ıll-price tickets, save time by using coins et machines. You can also buy your tickets he hassle once in Paris. Simply go to the Lou- the tickets will be mailed to you. Website tickets ndar year in which they are purchased. Holders of a e **Museums,** p. 115) can skip the line by entering the nce (in the passage connecting the Cour Napoléon to the nd crowds, visit on weekday afternoons or on Monday and n the museum is open until 9:45pm.

ovations and conservation efforts, no guidebook can give you a walking tour of the museum. To find out which rooms will be open k the home page, ask the info desk, or call museum info (☎40 20 51 pick up an updated map at the circular info desk in the center of the Cour hatever your visiting pace, consider *The Guide for the Visitor in a Hurry* English-language brochure available in the bookstore of the Cour Napoléon. **ides,** available at the top of both the Denon and Sully escalators (rental 30F; sit of driver's license, passport, or credit card), describe over 350 of the museum's ghlights. **Tours** fill up quickly. The free plastic info cards *(feuillets)* found in gallery corners provide detailed commentary and historical context on art work in each gallery.

The Louvre is fully **wheelchair accessible.** You can borrow a wheelchair for free at the central information desk (passport deposit); call information for disabled visitors (☎40 20 59 90). The Louvre has begun a series of workshops for **children** in English (see the info desk in the Cour Napoléon). The auditorium in the Cour Napoléon hosts concerts (65-130F), films, lectures, and colloquia (all 25F). For more information, call ☎40 20 52 99. There is also a small theater in the hall with free one-hour films relating to the museum. (☎40 20 53 17. M-F 10am, Sa-Su every 1½hr. from 11am.)

If you're under 26 or a teacher and plan to visit the Louvre more than twice in the next twelve months, consider buying the *Carte Louvre Jeunes.* An amazing deal at 120F, it entitles its holder to one year's unlimited entrance (without waiting in line) to the permanent collection and temporary exhibits, visits with a guest on Monday nights 6-9:45pm, and discounts on all books, tours, concerts, movies, and classes offered at the Louvre. For more information, call ☎40 20 51 04 or inquire at the info desk for an application.

ORIENTATION

When visiting the Louvre, strategy is everything. Think like a four-star general: the goal is to come and see without being conquered. The Louvre is organized into three different wings—**Sully, Richelieu,** and **Denon**—each leading off the Cour Napoléon. Each wing is divided into different sections according to the artwork's date, national origin, and medium (for example, "18th-century French Painting"). The color-coding and room numbers on the Louvre's free maps correspond to the colors and numbers on the plaques at the entrances to every room within the wing. Getting lost is an inevitable part of the Louvre experience, but there are plenty of blue-jacketed docents who can point you in the right direction. The collection itself is divided into seven departments: Oriental Antiquities; Egyptian Antiquities; Greek, Etruscan, and Roman Antiquities; Painting; Sculpture; Decorative Arts; and Graphic Arts.

HISTORY

THE BEGINNING TO CHARLES V. Construction of the Louvre began in 1190, and it still isn't finished. King Philippe-Auguste built the original structure as a fortress connected

to a city wall to defend Paris while he was away on a crusade. In the 14th century, Charles V built a second city wall enclosing the first beyond what is now the Jardin des Tuileries (see **Sights**, p. 61), thus stripping the Louvre of its defensive utility. Not one to let a good castle go to waste, Charles converted the fortress into a residential château.

FRANÇOIS I. The monarchs of the 15th century avoided the narrow, dank, and rat-infested building. In 1528, however, François I returned to the Louvre in an attempt to flatter the Parisian bourgeoisie, whom he hoped to distract from recently raised taxes. François razed Charles's palace and commissioned Pierre Lescot to build a new royal palace in the open style of the Renaissance. All that remains of the old Louvre are its foundations, unearthed in the early stages of Mitterrand's renovations and displayed in an underground exhibit called **Medieval Louvre** on the ground floor of the Sully wing (admission included in museum ticket).

HENRY IV. François I was succeeded by Henry II whose widow, Catherine de Medici, had the Tuileries Palace built looking out on an Italian-style garden to give herself a little privacy (it was later burned by the *communards* in 1871; see **History**, p. 30). Henri IV completed the Tuileries and embarked on what he called the Grand Design—a project to link the Louvre and the Tuileries with the two large wings you see today in a "royal city." He only built a fraction of the project before his death in 1610.

LOUIS XIV. After fleeing the Palais Royale in 1650, Louis XIV moved back to Paris and into the Louvre, becoming the next king to take interest in the palace. Most of the **Cour Carrée** (Square Courtyard) owes its classicism to Louis XIV, who hired a trio of architects—Le Vau, Le Brun, and Perrault—to transform the Louvre into the grandest palace in Europe. Louis XIV eventually abandoned the Louvre in favor of Versailles, and construction did not get past the Cour Carrée. The main courtyard is the **Cour Napoléon,** begun by Catherine de Medici 200 years before it was completed by Napoleon III.

NAPOLEON I. Louis XIV's departure to Versailles marked the end of the Louvre as a royal residence. In 1725, after years of relative abandonment, the Academy of Painting inaugurated annual salons in the halls to show the work of its members. For over a century, French painting would revolve around the salons, and, in 1793, the Revolution made the exhibit permanent, thus creating the Musée du Louvre. Napoleon filled the Louvre with plundered art from continental Europe and Egypt. With his defeat at Waterloo, however, most of this art had to be returned to the countries from which it had been "borrowed." More durably, Napoleon built the **Arc de Triomphe du Carrousel,** a copy of Rome's Arch of Septimus Severus, to commemorate his victories. He happily continued Henri IV's Grand Design, extending the Louvre's two wings to the Tuileries palace and remodeling the facades of the older buildings.

I.M. PEI. For most of the 20th century, the Louvre was a confusing maze of government offices and inaccessible galleries. Until 1989, the Finance Ministry occupied the Richelieu wing of the Louvre. Mitterrand's *Grands Projets* campaign transformed the Louvre into an accessible, well-organized museum. Internationally renowned American architect I.M. Pei came up with the idea of moving the museum's entrance to the center of the Cour Napoléon, on an underground level surmounted by his stunning and controversial **glass pyramid.** At first, Pei's proposal met with intense disapproval; others consider Pei's pyramid a stroke of genius. The Cour Napoléon glows in the sun streaming through the glass. There are 666 panes of glass on the pyramid, each one seeming to contribute one more degree of intense heat in summer.

PAINTINGS

DUTCH. The **Flemish Gallery** (second floor, Richelieu) houses such masterworks as **Van Hemessen**'s *Young Tobias Gives Sight to His Father*, **Hieronymous Bosch**'s *Ship of Fools*, and **Jan Van Eyck**'s *Madonna of Chancellor Rolin*. **Peter Paul Rubens**'s 24-paneled *Médicis Cycle* (1621-25) occupies its own room. Returning from an exile imposed by her son Louis XIII, Marie de Medici hired Rubens to retell her personal history to the world (or at least to the treacherous French court). Not to be missed are the two great works by **Jan Vermeer,** *Lacemaker* and *Astronomer* as well as the the room

MS. MONA'S WILD RIDE

Lovely Mona is fortunate to be here at all. Louvre curators discovered her missing one morning in 1911. Poet Guillaume Apollinaire warned his friend Pablo Picasso, who owned two statues stolen from the Louvre, that a search for the *Mona Lisa* might uncover the contraband sculptures. The pair panicked, and at midnight struck out into the darkness with the statues packed into a suitcase, intending to dump them in the Seine. Near the *quais*, they suspected they were being followed and decided to leave the statues anonymously with a local newspaper. But the police soon tracked down and jailed Apollinaire as a suspect in the *Mona Lisa* heist. After two days of intense questioning, Apollinaire's resolve broke and he accused Picasso of stealing the painting. In spite of this treachery, Picasso cleared his name with a convincing plea. Only through the efforts of local artists, who attested to the fine quality of Apollinaire's character, was the poet released. The *Mona Lisa* turned up two years later in the possession of a former Louvre employee who had snuck it out under his overcoat, leaving only the frame and a fine impression of his left thumb. Unfortunately, the museum had recorded employees' right thumb prints only. The joyful, albeit embarrassed, museum directors returned the smiling lady to her proper place, where she now resides securely within a glass enclosure.

full of works by **Rembrant van Rijn** including three self portraits and the allegorical masterpiece, *Bathsheba.*

FRENCH. French works stretch from the Richelieu wing through the entire Sully wing and part of the Denon wing and include paintings from the Neoclassical, Rococo, and Romantic schools, from the 16th century through 1848 (after which time the Musée d'Orsay takes over; see p. 119). The Rococo works of **Antoine Watteau, Jean-Honoré Fragonard,** and **François Boucher** showcase aristocratic styles of architecture and dress. **Jacques-Louis David**'s 1785 work, *Le serment de Horaces (The Oath of the Horatii)*, was politically controversial, focusing on three brothers swearing allegiance to their country before going off to battle, an ominous theme for Paris on the eve of the Revolution. One of the largest paintings in the Louvre, and similarly political, his *Sacre de Napoleon 1er à Nôtre-Dame de Paris (The Coronation of Napoleon)* hangs across from *Mona Lisa* (for more on David, see **Fine Arts,** p. 46). **Théodore Géricault**'s *Le Radeau de la Méduse (Raft of the Medusa)* tells the true story of the survivors of the sunken ship Medusa, who were forced to resort to cannibalism to make it through two weeks on the open sea. **Delacroix**'s *La Liberté Guidant le Peuple (Liberty Leading the People)* personifies Liberty as a woman on the barricades of the French Revolution; King Louis-Philippe thought it so dangerous that he bought the painting and hid it from the public. Delacroix's *La Mort de Sardanapale (The Death of Sardanapalis)* depicts the final scene of a play by Byron in which King Sardanapalus slaughters his horses and concubines as the enemy surrounds his palace. Other important works in the collection include: **Georges de la Tour**'s candle-lit figures in paintings such as *Mary Magdalen* and *The Trick;* **Jean-Auguste-Dominique Ingres**'s *Le Bain turc;* and **Jean-Babtiste Corot**'s pensive *Lady in Blue*, a precursor to the Impressionists and a segue from the Louvre's collection to that of the **Musée D'Orsay** (see p. 247).

ITALIAN. The **Italian Renaissance** collection (on the first floor of the Denon wing) is rivaled only by that of the Uffizi museum in Florence. Rush to the 13th- and 14th-century works of **Cimabue** (*Virgin and Child in Majesty)* and **Giotto** (*Saint Francis of Assisi)*. The slender, willowy figures of **Sandro Botticelli,** a later disciple of the Renaissance, can be seen in *Venus and the Graces Offering Gifts to a Maiden.* For the best in Renaissance portraiture, look to **Raphael**'s *Portrait of Balthazar Castiglione* and **Titian**'s *Man with a Glove.* **Veronese**'s gigantic *Wedding Feast at Cana* occupies an entire wall. The models for the apostles were 16th-century aristocratic Venetians, with Veronese himself playing the cello. Another fan of live models, **Caravaggio** used the body of a girl drowned in the Tiber as his model for his work *Death of the Virgin.* Bought by

François I during the artist's visit to Paris, **Leonardo da Vinci**'s *Mona Lisa* (or *La Joconde, The Smiling One*) smiles mysteriously at millions of guests. In the struggle to elbow your way to a close-up view, don't forget to look at her neighbors. Da Vinci's *Virgin of the Rocks* uses the *sfumato* (smoky) technique for which he is famous.

GREEK, ETRUSCAN, AND ROMAN ANTIQUITIES

Although most visitors stumble into this section looking for two of the museum's most famous pieces, the **Venus de Milo** and the **Winged Victory of Samothrace,** the rest of the Louvre's collection of ancient sculpture is extraordinary. Despite polite yearly requests from the Greek Minister of Culture to return its collection of antiquities, the Louvre maintains that these sculptures are better off in Paris. The Louvre's collection of **Greek vases** is one of the finest in the world. Beautiful black and red *kylix's* and *kraters* (used to mix wine and water) depict nymphs and satyrs "exercising" heartily. The collection, acquired in 1861 by Napoleon III, includes the **Melos Amphora** with its painting of Hercules and Athena, surrounded by the Olympian bratpack.

Greek and Roman sculpture at the Louvre covers too many floors and periods to be tackled by all but classics junkies, but there are some standouts. The **Winged Victory of Samothrace** dominates the landing between the Denon and Sully wings. Originally situated on a rocky precipice overlooking the sea, the *Winged Victory* was excavated in 1863 on the Greek island of Samothrace. The statue commemorates a Rhodian naval victory and is one of the most important examples of Hellenistic sculpture. The recently restored **Borghesian Gladiator** pulses with ripples of Roman musculature and was imitated widely in works of the 17th and 18th centuries. Found in 1820 on the Greek island of Milos, the **Venus de Milo** (on the ground floor of the Sully wing) depicts the goddess of love wrapped in sculpted folds of cloth. The 8th-century BC Etruscan **Sarcophagus of a Married Couple** (in the Denon wing) details a couple reclining at a banquet. The **Sleeping Hermaphrodite** is sensual and sweet in almost translucent marble.

OTHER COLLECTIONS

The **Oriental Antiquities** department houses an impressive collection of pre-Christian antiques and sculpture from the Fertile Crescent. This collection includes the world's oldest legal document, a basalt slab from the 18th century BC on which is inscribed the **Code of King Hammurabi.** Room 4 presents the reliefs from the Palace of Khorsabad built by Sargon II in the 7th century BC and five winged bulls, which guarded the palace doors. The **Islamic Art** collection (in Richelieu and Sully) features rugs, tapestries, armor, and scientific instruments. Half of the first floor stands as a showcase for **Objets d'Art**—the jewelry, tapestries, furniture, dishes, and decorations belonging to centuries of ruling classes. The **sculpture** department includes everything after the Roman period until the 19th century. The stars of the collection are **Michelangelo**'s *Les Esclaves (The Slaves).*

MUSÉE D'ORSAY

62, r. de Lille, or 1, r. de Bellechasse. 7ème. M: Solférino; RER: Musée d'Orsay. ☎40 49 48 48; recorded info ☎45 49 11 11; www.musee-orsay.fr. ***Open*** *June 20-Sept. 20 Tu-W and F-Su 9am-6pm, Th 9am-9:30pm; Sept. 21-June 19 Tu-W and F-Su 10am-5:45pm, Th 10am-9:45pm. Last ticket sales 30min. before closing.* ***Admission*** *40F, ages 18-25 and all on Su 30F, under 18 free.* ***Tours*** *in English Tu-Sa, 90min., 36F.* ***Bookstore*** *and boutique open Tu-W and F-Su 9:30am-6:30pm, Th 9:30am-9:30pm.*

If only the old cronies who turned the Impressionists away from the Louvre could see the Musée d'Orsay today! Hundreds of people from around the world line up all year round to see these famous rejects a stone's throw away from the stronghold of the old Academy. Paintings, sculpture, decorative arts, architecture, photography, and cinema are presented in this former railway station, with works spanning the period from 1848 until the First World War.

PRACTICAL INFORMATION

The museum is least crowded on Sunday mornings and on Thursday evenings when it is open late. Avoid visiting on a Monday if at all possible, since this is the day the Louvre closes. The *Guide to the Musée d'Orsay* by Caroline Mathieu, the museum's director, is excellent (95F). Also available is the practical *Guide for the Visitor in a Hurry* (20F). Hand-held **audioguides,** available in English and other languages, provide anecdotal histories and analyses of 60 masterpieces throughout the museum. The recording lasts two hours, but you should set aside at least three to visit all the rooms. (30F; driver's license, passport, credit card, or 500F deposit required.) **Tours** leave regularly from the group reception area. In addition to the permanent collection, seven **temporary exhibition** spaces, called *dossiers*, are dispersed throughout the building. Call or pick up a free copy of *Nouvelles du Musée d'Orsay* to find out which temporary exhibitions are currently installed. The museum also hosts conferences, special tours, and concerts.

The **Café des Hauteurs** is situated on the upper level behind one of the train station's huge iron clocks. There is also a self-serve food stand directly above the café. The **Restaurant du Palais d'Orsay** on the middle floor is worth a peek, even if you don't plan on lunching. A Belle Epoque artifact designed by Gabriel Ferrier, the restaurant offers a view of the Seine and magnificent chandeliers in addition to pricey dining options. The **bookstore** downstairs offers reproductions, postcards, art books, and historical and architectural guides to Paris. The museum's **boutique** offers jewelry, scarves, and sculptures inspired by the museum's collection.

For all its size and bustle, the Orsay delights art lovers as one of the friendliest museums in Paris. A specially marked escalator at the far end of the building ascends directly to the Impressionist level, and maps and English-language information are available. A first visit to the museum begins on the ground floor, then goes to the top floor and ends on the middle floor, as signs and maps clearly indicate.

HISTORY

Built for the 1900 Universal Exposition, the Gare d'Orsay's industrial function was carefully masked by architect Victor Laloux behind glass, stucco, and a 370-room luxury hotel, so as to remain faithful to the station's elegant surroundings in the prestigious *7ème.* For several decades, it was the main departure point for southwest-bound trains, but newer trains were too long for its platforms, and it closed in 1939. After WWII, the station served as the main French repatriation center, receiving thousands of concentration camp survivors and refugees. Orson Welles filmed *The Trial* here in 1962. The Musée d'Orsay opened in 1986 as one of the *grands projets* of President Valéry Giscard d'Estaing, taking works from the Louvre, Jeu de Paume, Palais de Tokyo, Musée de Luxembourg, provincial museums, and private collections.

GROUND FLOOR: CLASSICISM AND REALISM

SCULPTURE. Three of **Jean-Baptiste Carpeaux**'s most expressive sculptures can be found on this ground level. His sculpture, *Ugolino* (1860), in the center of the gallery, was inspired by Dante's *Inferno.* Carpeaux sculpted a Count who was locked in a tower for treason and left to starve with his four sons, whose corpses he eventually ate. Another Carpeaux sculpture, *The Four Corners of the World*, is farther down the hallway. His most scandalous piece, *La Danse (The Dance)*, is tucked against the back wall of the gallery.

CLASSICISM. On the right-hand side of the central gallery, **Jean-Auguste-Dominique Ingres**'s *La Source* (*The Source*, 1820-1856) represents **Classicism.** Continuing to the **Romantic** painting in the next room, compare Ingres' smooth nude to the feverish brushwork of **Eugène Delacroix**'s sketch for *La Chasse aux Lions* (*The Lion Hunt*, 1854).

BARBIZON AND REALISM. Paintings in the first set of rooms to the left of the central gallery include landscapes by **Jean-François Millet, Jean-Baptiste-Camille Corot,** and **Théodore Rousseau.** Reacting to the urbanization of Paris, Corot moved out to Barbizon near Fontainebleu (see **Daytripping,** p. 207) in the 1830s to paint nature and rural life. Soon he was joined by others interested in documenting a way of life threatened by the Industrial era. They learned to paint outdoors, eventually inspiring the Impressionists. In the next gallery are works by **Realist** painter **Gustave Courbet.** Realists did not depict an idyllic vision of rural life: "How can it be possible to paint such awful people?" one critic demanded upon viewing the tired, imperfect faces of the funeral-goers in Courbet's *Un Enterrement à Ornans (A Burial at Ornans)* in 1850. Before leaving this room, take note that the guard positioned at the entrance is only there to protect one painting: the revealing *Origin of the World*, which is quite a departure from Corbet's other depictions of everyday life.

Edouard Manet's *Olympia* is housed in the next room on the left, adjacent to Courbet. This painting by the man who would later be considered a **father of Impressionism** caused a scandal at the 1865 salon. Inspired by Titian's *Venus of Urbino*, a standard for female nudes in Western art, Manet asked a prostitute to pose for him. But instead of painting a delectable goddess floating by on a cloud, Olympia was represented as a modern woman, wearing only high heels and a flower behind one ear while she stared brazenly out at her viewers. Caricatures of the painting covered Paris, showing the alarm people felt at viewing this confident prostitute in an atmosphere of high art. Manet was accused of creating pornography and insulted in the streets.

Louvre

UPPER LEVEL: IMPRESSIONISM AND POST-IMPRESSIONISM

The upper level of the Orsay features a series of rooms devoted to Impressionists and their successors, such as **Van Gogh, Gauguin,** and **Seurat.** Although considered mainstream today, Impressionism was an upheaval of artistic standards and the beginning of abstract art. When a group of radicals led by **Claude Monet** exhibited this new style in 1874, they were dubbed "Impressionistes." Artists like **Renoir, Manet, Degas, Pisarro,** and **Caillebotte** adopted the name and a new era in art history was born (see **Fine Arts,** p. 40).

Musée Rodin

The first room of the upper level features **Manet**'s *Déjeuner sur l'Herbe* (*Luncheon on the Grass*, 1863), **Monet**'s *La Gare St-Lazare*, and **Renoir**'s *Le bal du Moulin de la Galette*. Monet's experiments with light and atmospheric effects culminated in his *Cathédral de Rouen* series. Paintings by **Alfred Sisley** and **Camille Pissarro** use waving lines and dabs of color to evoke different seasons in the French countryside. Although relatively unknown today, **Berthe Morisot** was one of the most successful Impressionists during her lifetime. As it was not considered appropriate for her to wander the streets or to represent working class people, she used daring, loose brushstrokes to produce intimate portraits of the more secluded female sphere of late 19th-century French society. **Edgar Degas**'s dancers in *La classe de danse* are further developed in his electric **pastels,** a few rooms ahead. The *Petite danseuse de quatorze ans (Little fourteen-year-old dancer)* was the only one of Degas's sculptures exhibited before his death. At the time of the exhibition, the public was shocked by its realism; she has doll's hair, real ballet slippers, a real tutu, and polychrome skin.

Centre Pompidou

James Whistler's *Portrait of the Artist's Mother*, the American painting said to have inspired modern art, is among the Impressionist art on the upper level. More than a dozen diverse works by **Vincent Van Gogh** follow, including his tormented *Portrait de l'Artiste*. **Paul Cézanne**'s still lifes, portraits, and landscapes experiment with the soft colors and geometric planes that would open the door to **Cubism**.

The north wing focuses on the late 19th-century avant-garde. **Pointillists** like **Paul Signac** and **Georges Seurat** strayed from the blur of Impressionism to the dot-matrix precision of Pointillism. Like photography and film, their paintings are

IMPRESSIONIST PARIS

THE PONT NEUF. Monet and Renoir both painted the bridge looking from the southeast corner in 1872. Renoir's painting captures the bustle of carriages on a sun-drenched day, while Monet's depicts a crowd of grey and purple umbrellas on a misty, dreary one. Pissarro's 1901 view, more colorful and energetic, includes the newly-erected Samaritaine department store.

LUXEMBOURG GARDENS. Van Gogh's *Terrace of the Luxembourg Gardens* (1886) experiments with the bright colors of the grove of trees west of Pl. Edmond Rostrand. William Singer Sargent's more restrained *Luxembourg Gardens at Twilight* (1879) evokes the tranquility of the central fountain in the setting sun.

GRANDS BOULEVARDS. Pissaro's *Boulevard Montmartre* (1897) and Van Gogh's *Boulevard de Clichy* (1887) used the immense open spaces of the new boulevards to create more distant, abstract views of street life.

LE GARE ST-LAZARE. Manet, Monet, and Caillebotte all portrayed this fairly mundane location as a representative of modern, industrial life.

made up of thousands of tiny dots of color (see **Fine Arts,** p. 40). **Henri de Toulouse-Lautrec** left his aristocratic family behind to paint dancers and prostitutes. **Paul Gauguin** left his family and job as a stockbroker to join the School of Pont Aven, an artists' colony in Brittany. His *Belle Angèle* sets a Breton wife against a background reminiscent of Japanese art.

MIDDLE LEVEL: BELLE ÉPOQUE & ART NOUVEAU

Once the elegant ballroom of the Hôtel d'Orsay, the neo-Rococo *Salle des Fêtes* on the middle level displays late 19th-century salon sculpture, painting, and decorative arts. These works show what was going on in the sanctioned art world while Impressionists were off rebelling. Nearly one-third of the middle level's terrace is devoted to **Auguste Rodin.** Commissioned in 1880 to be the main doors to the new Ecole des Arts Décoratifs, the unfinished *Porte de l'Enfer (Gates of Hell)* is encrusted with figures from Dante's *Inferno;* Rodin recast many of these in larger bronzes, such as *Le Penseur (The Thinker)* and *Ugolino*. On the terrace stands *l'Age Mûr*, a sculpture by Rodin's lover, Camille Claudel. (For more on Rodin and Claudel, see the **Musée Rodin,** p. 123.)

Most of the western half of the middle level is devoted to the works of **Art Nouveau.** Modeled after the English Arts and Crafts movement, Art Nouveau's mantra was "unity in design": Art Nouveau techniques and styles sought a marriage of function and form. Artists from various disciplines—carpenters, glassblowers, and painters—joined together in close collaboration. One example of this joint effort can be seen in the Belle Epoque Dining Room of **Charpentier, Bigot,** and **Fontaine.** Objects like **René Lalique**'s delicately wrought *Flaçon à odeurs* (scent bottle, 1900), with a gold-leafed stopper, was a thing of beauty, but not an affordable one.

CENTRE POMPIDOU

R. Beaubourg, 4ème. M: Rambuteau or Hôtel de Ville; RER: Châtelet-Les-Halles. ☎44 78 12 33, wheelchair info ☎44 78 49 54; www.centrepompidou.fr. ***Centre open*** *W and F-M 11am-8pm, Th 11am-10pm;* ***museum open*** *W-M 11am-9pm;* ***library open*** *M and W-F noon-10pm, Sa-Su 11am-10pm. Library and Forum free;* ***museum*** *30F, students and over 60 20F, under 18 free, first Su of month free.*

Often called the Beaubourg, the **Centre National d'Art et de Culture Georges Pompidou** has inspired architectural controversy ever since its inauguration in 1977. Named after French president Georges Pompidou, it fulfills his desire for Paris to have a cultural center embracing music, cinema, books, and the graphic arts. Chosen from 681 competing designs, Richard Rogers and Renzo Piano's building-turned-inside-out bares its circulatory system to all. Piping and ventilation ducts in various colors run up, down, and sideways along the outside (blue for air, green for water, yellow for electricity, red for heating). Framing the building like a cage, huge steel bars support its weight. The Centre Pompidou attracts more visitors per year than any other museum or monument in France—eight million annually compared to the Louvre's three million.

The **Musée National d'Art Moderne,** the Pompidou's main attraction, houses a rich selection of 20th-century art, from the Fauvists and Cubists to Pop and Conceptual Art. Most of the works were contributed by the artists themselves or by their estates; Joan Miró and Wassily Kandinsky's wife number among the museum's founding members. The **Salle Garance** hosts an adventurous film series, and the **Bibliothèque Publique d'Information** is a free, non-circulating library. The **Institut de la Recherche et de la Coordination Acoustique/Musique (IRCAM)** is a musical institute where the public can research using a database of 20th-century music.

MUSÉE RODIN

77, r. de Varenne, 7ème. M: Varenne. ☎01 44 18 61 10; www.musee-rodin.fr. ***Open*** *Tu-Su Apr.-Sept. 9:30am-5:45pm; Oct.-Mar. 9:30am-4:45pm. Last admission 30min. before closing.* ***Admission*** *28F; students, seniors, under 18, and all on Su 18F.* ***Park*** *open Tu-Su Apr.-Sept. 9:30am-6:45pm; Oct-Mar. 9:30am-5pm. Admission to park alone 5F.* ***Audio tour*** *25F.* ***Temporary exhibits*** *housed in the chapel, to your right as you enter. Entrance included in the price of museum admission. Persons who are blind or vision-impaired may obtain advance permission to touch the sculptures.*

Located in the elegant 18th-century **Hôtel Biron,** where Auguste Rodin lived and worked at the end of his life, the Musée Rodin highlights the work of one of France's greatest sculptors. During his lifetime (1840-1917), Rodin was among the country's most controversial artists, classified by many as Impressionism's sculptor (Monet, incidentally, was a close friend and admirer). Today, almost all acknowledge him as the father of modern sculpture. Born in a working-class district of Paris, Rodin began study at the Petite Ecole, a trade school for technical drawing. He tried three times to get into the famous Ecole des Beaux-Arts (see **Sights**, p. 79) and failed each time. Frequenting the Louvre to study Classical sculpture, he later worked as an ornamental carver, setting up a small studio of his own. His travels away from Paris allowed him to articulate a definitive style, completely unlike the flowery academic style then in vogue. He refused the standard of "ideal beauty" for realism, which incorporated raw textures and tense, dynamic poses. Nonetheless, his technical skill was unequalled: one of his first major pieces, *The Age of Bronze,* was so anatomically perfect that he was accused of molding it directly from the body.

The museum houses many of Rodin's better known sculptures in plaster, bronze, and marble, such as *Le Main de Dieu (The Hand of God)* and *Le Baiser (The Kiss)*, along with nearly 500 other works. Rodin's training in drawing is evident everywhere; as he said, "my sculpture is but drawing in three dimensions." One room is dedicated to a rotating display of drawings and studies. In addition, the museum has several works by **Camille Claudel,** Rodin's muse, collaborator, and lover. Claudel's *L'Age Mûr* has been read as her response to Rodin's decision to leave her for another woman, here depicted as an angel of death; Claudel, on her knees, begs the Rodin to stay.

The *hôtel's* expansive garden is a museum unto itself. Flowers, trees, and fountains frame outdoor sculptures; the rose garden is at its most beautiful in June. If you're short on time or money, consider paying the smaller admission fee for the grounds only. You won't miss the collection's star: just inside the gates sits *Le Penseur (The Thinker). Balzac*, to the right of *Le Penseur*, was commissioned in 1891 by the Société des Gens de Lettres. A battle over Rodin's design and his inability to meet deadlines raged for years. Unlike the flattering portrait the Société expected, the finished product shows a dramatic, haunted artist with hollow eyes. Rodin canceled the commission and kept the statue himself. Later in his life, he noted, "Nothing that I made satisfied me as much, because nothing had cost me as much; nothing else sums up so profoundly that which I believe to be the secret law of my art." On the other side of the garden stands one version of Rodin's largest and most intricate sculpture, the unfinished *Porte de l'Enfer* (*The Gates of Hell*, 1880-1917). Inspired by Dante's *Inferno*, figures emerge from and descend into an endless whirlwind. Presiding above it all is the small *Thinker*, representing the author as he sits and contemplates man's fate. Originally commissioned as the entrance doors for the new Ecole des Arts Décoratifs, the sculpture was never finished. Rodin replied to his critics, "Were the cathedrals ever finished?"

THE GREEN PARTY

Degas's *L'absinthe* (1875) features the green concoction being downed at a café in Pigalle. Van Gogh, some think, owed much of his inspiration (and madness) to it. Like Baudelaire and Verlaine, Hemingway wrote about absinthe, "that opaque, bitter, tongue-numbing, brain-warming, stomach-warming, idea-changing liquid alchemy." Picasso, Toulouse-Lautrec, and hordes of Parisians drank it fanatically. First distilled in 1792 from the wormwood plant *(Artemisia absinthium)* and chlorophyll, which makes it green, the 120-proof, licorice-like drink was initially used by French soldiers in Algeria to foil dysentery. They came back to France in the 1830s with a taste for the stuff, and soon it seemed that all of Paris was riding the green wave. Bars had *l'heure vert* (green hour), where water was poured onto a sugar cube and into the clear green liquor, turning it a darker, cloudy hue. Drinkers talked about the *fée verte* (green fairy) that stole the drinker's soul, while others warned of *le péril vert,* and in 1915 absinthe was outlawed in France. Most countries followed suit, although it's still available in Spain and the Czech Republic. *Pernod* tastes similar, but for the real thing, most of us will probably have to settle for anecdotes. "After the first glass," wrote Oscar Wilde, "you see things as you wish they were. After the second, you see things as they are not. Finally you see things as they really are, and that is the most horrible thing in the world." (See the **Musée d'Absinthe** in **Auvers-sur-Oise,** p. 214.)

The small, upscale outdoor **cafeteria** is a superb place for lunch; it offers salads and sandwiches. *(Food 25-40F. Open daily Apr.-Sept. 10am-6pm; Oct.-Jan. 10am-4:30pm.)*

THE INVALIDES MUSEUMS

Esplanades des Invalides, 7ème; Musée de l'Ordre de la Libération at 51bis, bd. de Latour-Maubourg. M: Invalides. ☎ 44 42 37 72, Musée des Plans-Reliefs ☎ 45 51 95 05, Musée de l'Ordre de la Libération ☎ 47 05 04 10; www.invalides.org. ***Open*** *daily Apr.-Sept. 10am-7pm; Oct.-Mar. 10am-5pm. Last ticket sales 30min. before closing.* ***Musée de l'Armée, Musée des Plans-Reliefs, Musée de l'Ordre de la Libération*** *open daily Apr.-Sept. 10am-6pm; Oct.-Mar. 10am-5pm.* ***Admission*** *38F, students under 26 and ages 12-17 28F, under 12 free. MC, V for sales of 50F or more. Open daily Apr.-Sept.*

In 1989 the **Eglise du Dôme** was regilded using twelve kilograms of gold, making it the glorious Hôtel des Invalides, the only monument in Paris glinting with real gold. But recall that the Dome towers 107 meters into the sky before climbing up to get a souvenir. In 1670, Louis XIV decided to "construct a royal home, grand and spacious enough to receive all old or wounded officers and soldiers." Architect Libéral Bruand's building accepted its first wounded in 1674, and veterans still live in the Invalides today. For all his beneficence toward the wounded soldiers, Louis XIV requested the Dome Church have two separate entrances so that he could attend mass without mingling with the masses. Jules Hardouin-Mansart provided the final design for the double chapel within the Invalides complex, the Royal Dome church adjacent to a long hall dubbed St-Louis des Invalides where the soldiers could hear the priest but could enter through the inner courtyard. The restoration monarch, Louis Philippe, had Napoleon's remains returned to the French as a political move in 1840, but it wasn't until the reign of Napoleon's nephew, Louis Bonaparte, that the mosaic floor of the Dome Church was destroyed to build the huge, circular crypt for Napoleon I. His body was said to be perfectly preserved when exhumed from its original coffin before the service. Completed in 1861, **Napoleon's tomb** consists of six concentric coffins, made of materials ranging from mahogany to lead—perhaps to make sure he doesn't escape again, like he did from Elba (see **History,** p. 29). The tomb is placed on the lower level and viewed first from a round balcony above, forcing everyone who visits to bow down to the emperor even in his death (this delighted Adolf Hitler on his visit to Paris in 1940). Names of significant battles are engraved in the marble surrounding the coffins; oddly enough, Waterloo isn't there. Ten bas-reliefs recall Napoleon's institutional reforms of law and education. Bonaparte himself is depicted as a Roman emperor in toga and laurels. Six chapels dedicated to different saints lie off the main room, sheltering the tombs of famous French Marshals. Insert a 10F coin into one of the ancient contraptions near the door of the Church for a dry but informative five-minute explanation in English.

MUSÉE DE L'ARMÉE. More war trophies are housed in the Musée de l'Armée, which celebrates French military history. The museum lies in two wings on opposite sides of the Invalides's cobblestone main courtyard, the Cour d'Honneur. The **East Wing** *(Aile Orient)* houses war paraphernalia from the 17th, 18th, and 19th centuries and culminates in the First Empire exhibit on the second floor, with a special focus on Napoleon. Look out for his stuffed horse, or should we say, *pony*. The **West Wing** *(Aile Occident)* holds Prehistoric, Medieval, and Oriental armour, as well as 20th-century exhibits revolving around Charles de Gaulle and the two World Wars.

MUSÉE DES PLANS-RELIEFS. The Musée des Plans-Reliefs on the fourth floor is a collection of about 100 models of fortified cities. Spanning from 1668 to 1870, the exhibit is of special interest to architects, urban planners, and historians.

MUSÉE DE L'ORDRE DE LA LIBÉRATION. The Musée de l'Ordre de la Libération tells the story of those who fought for the liberation of France. A diverse collection of de Gaulle-related paraphernalia is complemented by tributes to the Resistance fighters of Free France. The exhibit juxtaposes journals and prisoners' drawings with camp uniforms and instruments of Nazi torture in an attempt to document the mental and physical horror endured by POWs and Holocaust victims.

MUSÉE D'HISTOIRE CONTEMPORAINE. Independent from the above museums, the Musée d'Histoire Contemporaine mounts two temporary exhibits per year. Originally constructed in 1914 to hold documents about the history of the unfolding World War, the three-room museum probes recent history, propaganda, and popular culture. The exhibits are in French, but the visual nature of the exhibits helps transcend the language barrier. *(Housed in a gallery off the Invalides' Cour d'Honneur. ☎ 44 42 54 91 or 44 42 38 39. Call for info regarding temporary exhibits and hours. 30F, students and ages 12-17 20F, under 12 free.)*

MUSÉE PICASSO

5, r. de Thorigny, 3ème. M: Chemin-Vert. ☎ 42 71 63 15 or 42 71 70 84. ***Open*** *W-M Apr.-Sept. 9:30am-6pm, last entrance 5:15pm; Oct.-Mar. 9:30am-5:30pm, last entrance 4:45pm.* ***Admission*** *30F, ages 18-25 and Su 20F, under 18 free.* ***Tours*** *Sa and Su in French 36F, ages 7-18 25F.*

When Picasso died in 1973, his family paid the French inheritance tax in artwork. The French government put this collection on display in 1985 in the 17th-century *Hôtel Salé* (see **Sights,** p. 67). Here is a catalogue of the life, work, and 70-year career of one of the most prolific and inventive artists of the 20th century. The museum leads the viewer chronologically through Pablo Picasso's earliest work in Barcelona to his Cubist and Surrealist years in Paris and his Neoclassical work on the French Riviera. In order to provide a clear understanding of the evolution of the artist's career, each room in the museum covers one period of Picasso's life, detailing the progression of his technique and his personal life, from his mistresses to his reactions to the two World Wars. You can follow the *Sens de Visite* arrows around the building and little numbers on each of the works—or, if you don't believe an artist's work should be defined by his time, not.

Born in Málaga, Spain in 1881, Picasso loved Paris and moved to the studios of the Bateau-Lavoir in Montmartre (see **Sights,** p. 101), where he painted his masterpiece, *Les Demoiselles d'Avignon* (1907), represented in the museum by various studies. In the late 20s, Picasso moved to Montparnasse (see **Sights,** p. 96), where he frequented the Café Sélect and La Closerie des Lilas along with Jean Cocteau and Surrealist guru André Breton. Unable to return to Spain during the Franco régime, Picasso adopted France as his permanent home in 1934. Later, he moved to the French Riviera, where he died in Cannes in 1973.

The collection begins with Picasso's arrival in Paris from Spain, when he experimented with various styles, including Impressionism. The first floor shows work from his Blue and Pink periods, including a haunting blue *Autoportrait.* Picasso initially gained attention and fame due to his collage and Cubist work. His guitar and musician collages, such as *Le violin et la musique (Violin with Sheet Music)*, moved his art toward abstraction. In his post-Cubist painting *Deux femmes courant sur la plage (Two Women Running on the Beach)*, Picasso painted thick-limbed, Neoclassical bodies. Picasso's dear friend, poet Paul Eluard, wrote in 1926, "Picasso loves intensely, but he kills what he loves." A collection of Picasso's sculptures in the 1930s demonstrate his experiments in rearranging bodily organs and human morphology; soon after, his disconcerted and somber paintings reflect the gloom he felt about the Spanish Civil War. His paintings at the time of the WWII are less energetic than his earlier work. The museum displays a selection of Picasso's last works, which incorporate a mix of Picasso's styles as well as those of other painters.

Picasso's experiments with abstraction often went hand-in-hand with his love affairs. Some of these experiments ended in *La femme qui lit (Woman Reading)*, a portrait of his lover Marie-Thérèse Walter; *La femme qui pleure (Woman Crying)*, inspired by the surrealist photographer Dora Maar; and *The Kiss*, painted later in his life while he was married to Jacqueline Roque. By their wedding, Clouzot's film *Le Mystère Picasso* and retrospectives at the Petit Palais were already celebrating his life's work.

MUSÉE DE CLUNY

6, pl. Paul Painlevé, 5ème. M: Cluny-Sorbonne. ☎53 73 78 00. **Open** *W-M 9:15am-5:45pm.* **Admission** *30F; students, under 25, over 60, and Su 20F; under 18 free.* **Tours** *in English W 12:30pm. 36F, under 18 25F.* **Concerts** *F 12:30pm, Sa 5pm, and summer evenings. 60F, students and seniors 50F, under 18 20F. Concert info ☎53 73 78 00.*

The **Hôtel de Cluny** houses the **Musée National du Moyen Âge,** one of the world's finest collections of medieval art, jewelry, sculpture, and tapestries. The *hôtel* itself is a flamboyant 14th-century medieval manor built on top of first-century Roman ruins. One of three ancient *thermae* (public baths) in Roman Lutèce (see **Life and Times,** p. 25), the baths were purchased in 1330 by the Abbot of Cluny, who built his residence upon them. In the 15th century, the *hôtel* became home to the monastic Order of Cluny, led by the powerful Amboise family. In 1843, the state converted the *hôtel* into the medieval museum; excavations after WWII unearthed the baths. Roman bathing was an important social ritual. After working out in the *palestre*, bathers would take a hot bath in the *caldarium*, then dip in the lukewarm *tepidarium* before plunging into the cold *frigidarium*. Only the *frigidarium* and swimming pool remain intact and open to visitors.

The medieval museum's collection includes art from Paris's most important medieval structures: Ste-Chapelle, Notre-Dame, and St-Denis. Panels of brilliant stained glass in ruby reds and royal blues from Ste-Chapelle line the ground floor. The brightly lit *galerie des rois* contains sculptures from Notre-Dame. A collection of medieval jewelry includes royal crowns, brooches, and daggers. The museum's collection of 15th- and 16th-century tapestries includes the famous series, *La Dame et la Licorne* (*The Lady and the Unicorn*).

The Jardin Médiéval, a 5000-square-meter replica of a medieval garden, is divided into four sections: The Forest of the Unicorn, which contains plants used in daily life; *Le Chemin Creux* dedicated to the Virgin Mary; a *terrasse* containing potted plants used for medicinal and aromatic purposes; and *Le Tapis de Mille Fleurs* (Carpet of a Thousand Flowers), which is supposed to work like an aphrodisiac. The museum also sponsors chamber music concerts in its Roman and medieval spaces.

LA VILLETTE

La Villette is the product of a successful urban renewal project. This former meat-packing district used to contain slaughterhouses that provided Paris with most of its pork and beef. With the advent of refrigerated trucks, it became more economical to kill cattle in the countryside and deliver the meat directly to butchers. It also became cheaper to have a neighborhood park for kids instead of a neighborood slaughterhouse where kids could play. Work began on La Villette in 1979, and in 1985, President Mitterrand inaugurated the complex with the motto, "The place of intelligent leisure."

The park was the product of much academic speculation: coming out of the métro at Porte de Pantin in the 19*ème*, you might think you've made a mistake and wandered into a theorist's wet dream. The lines of sight of this place are sliced by the angles of funny-shaped red buildings foolish enough to be called *folies;* architect Bernard Tschumi designed this 21st-century urban park along with a crackteam of intellectuals who thought right angles were for losers. If you dare, skulk toward the massive Cité des Sciences et de l'Industrie, but be warned: the *gosses* (little kids) are in full effect. Yes, this place is a *gosses*-magnet.

PARC DE LA VILLETTE

Info *☎40 03 75 10 or 40 03 75 64;* ***Grande Halle*** *☎08 03 30 63 06 or 08 03 07 50 75;* ***Hot Brass*** *☎42 00 14 14;* ***Zénith*** *☎42 08 60 00.* ***Info office open*** *daily 10am-7pm.* ***Promenade des Jardins open*** *daily May-Sept. 10am-8pm; Oct.-Feb. 10am-dusk. Free.*

Cut in the middle by the **Canal de l'Ourcq** and the **Canal St-Denis,** the **Parc de la Villette** separates the Cité des Sciences from the Cité de la Musique. Built in 1867 as the La Villette "big beef" building, the steel-and-glass **Grande Halle** features frequent plays, concerts, temporary exhibits, and films. Unifying the park is a set of red cubical structures that form a grid of squares, known as **folies.** One houses the fast-food restaurant, Le Quick, day-care centers, coffee shops, and education centers; another, at the entrance near M: Pte. de Pantin, is an **information office.** Every summer there is a free open-air **film festival** that shows foreign, art, and generally funky movies from July to August next to the Grande Salle. The **Zénith** concert hall hosts major rock bands. Directly behind Zénith is the **Hot Brass** jazz club; the park's great yearly jazz festival is extraordinarily popular (see **Festivals,** p. 6).

Finally, the **Promenade des Jardins** links several thematic gardens, such as the **Mirror Garden,** which uses mirrors to create optical illusions; the **Garden of Childhood Fears,** which winds through a wooded grove resonant with spooky sounds; and the rollercoaster **Dragon Garden.** The promenade ends at **Jardin des Dunes** and the **Jardins des Vents,** a playground for kids 12 and under (with parental accompaniment, lest the fun get out of control). Join a gaggle of moppets leaping on trampolines, running on rolling hills, and flying on a zip line in what will probably be the highlight of any kid's trip to Paris.

Musée d'Orsay

Louvre

CITÉ DES SCIENCES ET DE L'INDUSTRIE

M: Porte de la Villette. ☎40 05 80 00 in French; www.cite-sciences.fr.

EXPLORA SCIENCE MUSEUM

Museum *open M-Sa 10am-6pm, Su 10am-7pm. A one-day* ***Cité-Pass*** *covers entrance to Explora, the planetarium, the Louis Lumière 3-D cinema, and the Argonaute submarine; 50F.* ***Médiathèque*** *open daily noon-8pm; free.* ***Cité des Enfants*** *programs Tu and Th-F 9:30, 11:30am, 1:30, and 3:30pm; W and Sa-Su 10:30am, 12:30, 2:30, and 4:30pm; 1½hr. long; 25F.* ***Technocité*** *hours vary, inquire at the front desk or call ☎40 05 12 12; visits 1½hr; 25F.*

Dedicated to bringing science to the young layperson, the Explora science museum is la Villette's star attraction. The architecture of the buildings rocks on its own, but the exhibits can only be described as absolutely fabulous; kids will love them. There are close to 300 exhibits, ranging from astronomy and mathematics to computer science and sound. Dare to ask "What is a hunter-killer submarine used for?" or, "When will the sun burn out?" The museum also features a **planetarium** (Floor 2), the Cinéma Louis Lumière with 3D movies, a modest **aquarium** (Floor S2), and the Médiathèque, a multimedia scientific and technical library that has over 4000 films. If you're traveling with children, the Explora's **Cité des Enfants** offers one set of programs for kids ages 3-5 and another for ages 5-12. Both require adult accompaniment, but no more than two adults per family are admitted. Although programs are in French, the interactive exhibits are just as fun for

Gallery of Comparative Anatomy

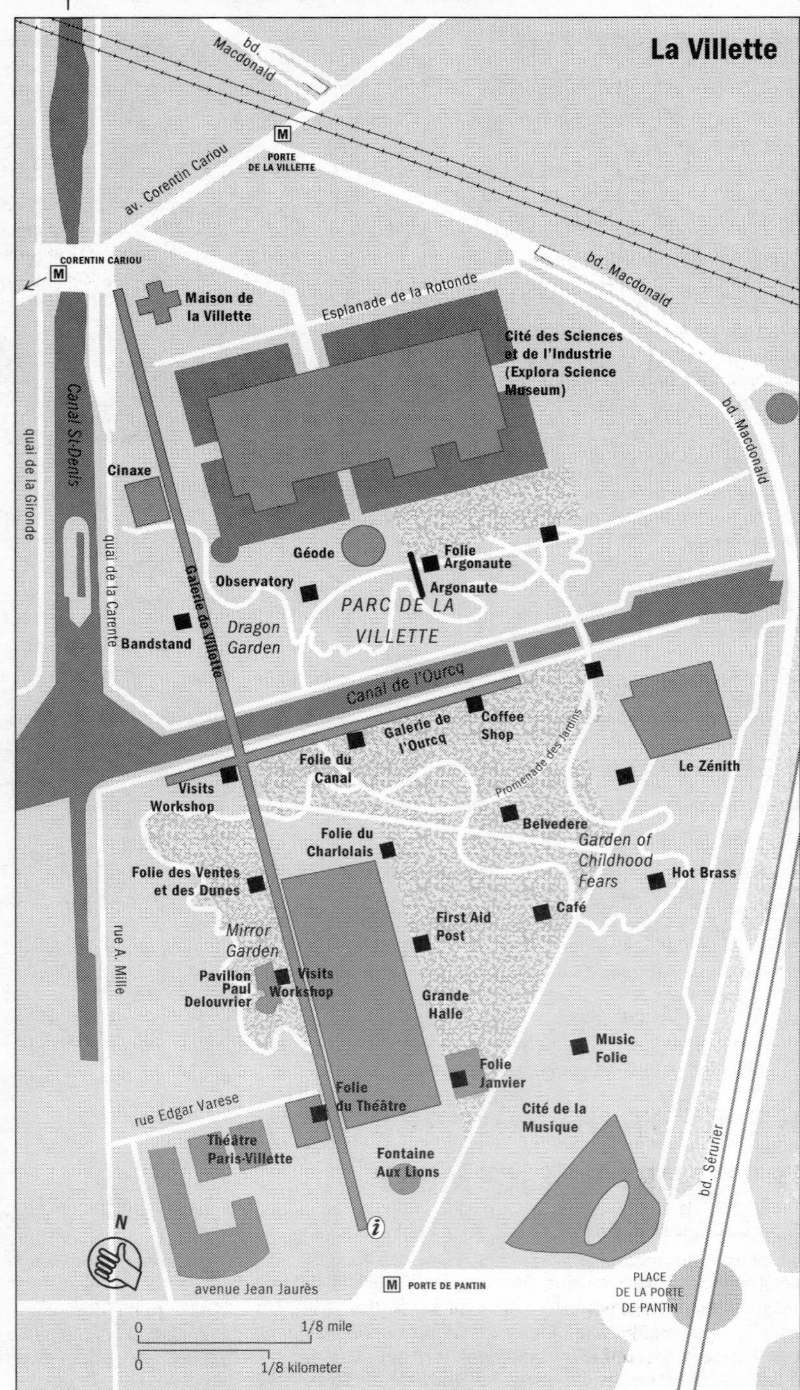

La Villette
bd. Macdonald
PORTE DE LA VILLETTE
av. Corentin Cariou
CORENTIN CARIOU
bd. Macdonald
Esplanade de la Rotonde
Maison de la Villette
Cité des Sciences et de l'Industrie (Explora Science Museum)
bd. Macdonald
Canal St-Denis
quai de la Gironde
quai de la Carente
Cinaxe
Géode
Folie Argonaute
Argonaute
Observatory
PARC DE LA VILLETTE
Bandstand
Dragon Garden
Galerie de Villette
Canal de l'Ourcq
Galerie de l'Ourcq
Coffee Shop
Promenade des Jardins
Le Zénith
Folie du Canal
Visits Workshop
Belvedere
Folie du Charlolais
Garden of Childhood Fears
Hot Brass
Folie des Ventes et des Dunes
Café
First Aid Post
Mirror Garden
rue A. Mille
Pavillon Paul Delouvrier
Visits Workshop
Grande Halle
Music Folie
Folie Janvier
Folie du Théâtre
rue Edgar Varese
Cité de la Musique
Théâtre Paris-Villette
Fontaine Aux Lions
bd. Sérurier
N
PORTE DE PANTIN
avenue Jean Jaurès
PLACE DE LA PORTE DE PANTIN
0
1/8 mile
0
1/8 kilometer

English-speaking explorers. The *vestiare* on the ground floor rents strollers and wheelchairs. Also located on the ground floor, **Technocité** (for those 11 and older) challenges visitors to program their own computer games, design a custom bicycle, work with computer animation, and experiment with industrial art.

GÉODE

☎ 40 05 12 12. Open Tu-Su 10am-9:30pm; shows every hour. Tickets 57F.

Outside the Cité, the enormous Géode is a huge mirrored sphere mounted on a water basin, like a disco ball in a birdbath. The exterior is coated with 6,433 polished, stainless-steel triangles that reflect every detail of the surroundings. Inside, **Omnimax movies** on volcanoes, glaciers, and other natural phenomena are shown on a 1000-square-meter hemispheric screen (see **Cinema,** p. 151 for more info).

ARGONAUTE

***Open** Tu-F 10:30am-5:30pm, Sa-Su 11am-6:30pm. 25F, under 7 free; an audioguide tour of the submarine, in English or French, is included.*

To the right of the Géode, the **Argonaute submarine** details the history of submersibles from Jules Verne to present-day nuclear-powered subs. This 400-ton, 50m-long fighter submarine was designed in 1950 as part of the French national fleet.

CINAXE

*☎ 40 05 12 12. **Open** Tu-F 1-5pm, Sa-Su 2-6pm; shows every 15min. 34F, 29F if bought with another exhibition ticket.*

Between the Canal St-Denis and the Cité, **Cinaxe** features inventive movies filmed in first-person perspective from vehicles like Formula One cars, low-flying planes, and Mars land-rovers, while hydraulic pumps simulate every curve and bump. Lunch beforehand is not recommended.

CITÉ DE LA MUSIQUE

*M: Porte de Pantin. ☎ 44 84 44 84; info ☎ 44 84 45 45; médiathèque ☎ 40 40 45 40; www.citemusique.fr. **Cité open** Tu-Th noon-6pm, F-Sa noon-7:30pm, Su 10am-6pm; last admission 45min. before closing. **Info center open** M-Sa noon-6pm, Su 10am-6pm. **Médiathèque open** M-F 12:30-5:30pm. **Admission** 35F, reduced 25F, children 6-18 10F, under 6 free; 10F more for temporary exhibits. **Guided tours in French** Sa at 2:30pm, thematic tours F at 7pm, kiddie tour Su at 11am. 60F, reduced 45F, children 6-18 20F, under 6 free. **Info center and médiathèque** free.*

At the opposite end of La Villette from the Cité des Sciences is the Cité de la Musique. Designed by Franck Hammoutène and completed in 1990, the complex of buildings is visually stunning, full of curves and glass ceilings. The highlight is the **Musée de la Musique,** a collection of paintings, sculptures, and 900 instruments. Visitors don a pair of headphones that tune into musical excerpts and explanations of each instrument. The Cité de la Musique's two performance spaces—the enormous 1200-seat **Salle des Concerts** and the 230-seat **Amphithéâtre**—host an eclectic range of shows and concerts year round (see **Music,** p. 152). The Cité de la Musique also contains a **music and dance information center** and the **Médiathèque Hector-Berlioz,** with 90,000 books, documents, music journals, and photographs.

THE BEST OF THE REST

FIRST ARRONDISSEMENT

MUSÉE DE LA MODE ET DU TEXTILE

107, r. de Rivoli, Palais du Louvre. M: Palais-Royal. ☎ 44 55 57 50. Open Tu and Th-F 11am-6pm, W 11am-9pm, Sa-Su 10am-6pm. 30F, students 20F. Wheelchair accessible.

Housed in the Louvre with the Musée des Arts Décoratifs, the Musée de la Mode et du Textile is a huge collection of all that has been *en vogue* since the 18th century. Exhibits rotate annually and tell changing stories of the history of costume, from 17th-century brocade evening dresses to pointy latex bras by Jean-Paul Gaultier.

GALÉRIE NATIONALE DU JEU DE PAUME

M: Concorde. From the métro, walk up the steps on r. Rivoli to the upper level of the Tuileries gardens. ☎ 47 03 12 50; recorded info ☎ 42 60 69 69. Open Tu noon-9:30pm, W-F noon-7pm, Sa-Su 10am-7pm. 38F, students under 26, seniors, and ages 13-18 28F, under 13 free. Tours in French W and Sa 3pm, Su 11am.

Huge windows bathe this spectacular exhibition space in afternoon sunlight. Connoisseurs and tourists alike come to appreciate the changing contemporary art exhibitions.

MUSÉE DE L'ORANGERIE

Southwest corner of the Jardin des Tuileries. M: Concorde. ☎ 42 97 48 16.

Opened in 1927, the museum is home to works by Renoir, Cézanne, Rousseau, Matisse, and Picasso, as well as Monet's *Les Nymphéas* (Water Lilies). Unfortunately, the museum is **closed until December 2002** for renovations.

THIRD ARRONDISSEMENT

MUSÉE DE L'ART ET D'HISTOIRE DU JUDAISME

71, r. de Temple. M: Hôtel de Ville. ☎ 42 72 97 47 or 53 01 86 60. Open M-F 11am-6pm, Su 10am-6pm. 40F, students 25F, includes excellent English audioguide. Wheelchair accessible.

Newly renovated and housed in a grand *hôtel* once used as a tenement for Jews fleeing Eastern Europe, this museum displays a history of Jews in Europe, France, and North Africa. An ornate 15th-century Italian ark, letters written to wrongly accused French general Dreyfus, a small collection of Chagall and Modigliani paintings, Lissitzky lithographs, and modern art collections looted from Jewish homes by the Nazis reside here.

MUSÉE CARNAVALET

23, r. de Sévigné. M: Chemin-Vert. ☎ 42 72 21 13. Open Tu-Su 10am-5:40pm. 30F, students 20F, seniors and under 18 free; free for all Su 10am-1pm.

Housed in Mme. de Sévigné's 16th-century *hôtel particulier*, this museum traces Paris's history from its origins to the present, with exhibits on the city from prehistory and the Roman conquest to Medieval politics, 18th-century splendor and Revolution, 19th-century Haussmannization, and Mitterrand's *grands projets*.

MUSÉE COGNACQ-JAY

8, r. Elzévir. M: St-Paul. Walk up r. Pavée and take a left on r. des Francs-Bourgeois and a right on r. Elzévir. ☎ 40 27 07 21. Open Tu-Su 10am-5:40pm; last admission 5:10pm. 22F, students and under 25 15F, seniors and under 18 free. Gardens open May-Sept. 10am-5:40pm.

The 16th-century Hôtel Donon houses Enlightenment art, including minor works by Rembrandt, Ingres, Rubens, Canaletto, and Fragonard.

MUSÉE DE L'HISTOIRE DE FRANCE

60, r. des Francs-Bourgeois. ☎ 40 27 60 96. M: Rambuteau. Walk up r. Rambuteau, which becomes r. des Francs-Bourgeois. Open M and W-F noon-5:45pm, Sa-Su 1:45-5:45pm. 20F, students, seniors, and Su 15F, under 18 free.

Housed in the Hôtel de Soubise, this museum is the main exhibition space of the Archives Nationales, featuring important documents including an edict drafted by Richard the Lionheart, an extract from Louis XVI's diary the day he was arrested by Revolutionaries, and a letter from Napoleon to Josephine.

FOURTH ARRONDISSEMENT

MAISON DE VICTOR HUGO

6, pl. des Vosges. ☎ 42 72 10 16. M: Chemin-Vert or Bastille. Open Tu-Su 10am-5:40pm. 22F, students 15F, under 18 free.

Dedicated to the father of the French Romantics and housed in the building where he lived from 1832 to 1848, the museum displays Hugo memorabilia. One room is devoted to paintings of scenes from *Les Misérables*, another to *Nôtre-Dame de Paris*.

MUSÉE ADAM MICKIEWICZ

6, quai d'Orléans. On the Île-St-Louis. ☎55 42 83 83. M: Pont Marie. Ring the doorbell and enter to your left in the courtyard. Library open Tu-F 2-6pm and Sa 10am-1pm. Museums open Th 2-6 and can only be visited with a guided tour at 2, 3:30, or 5pm. 30F, students 15F, children free.

Located in the **Bibliothèque Polonaise de Paris,** the museum is dedicated to Polish poet Adam Mickiewicz and includes letters from Goethe and Hugo as well as a sketch by Delacroix on George Sand's letter-head. In the same building are the **Musée Boleslas Bregas** and the **Salon Chopin,** with manuscripts, letters, and his death mask.

FIFTH ARRONDISSEMENT

MUSÉE D'HISTOIRE NATURELLE

In the Jardin des Plantes. ☎40 79 39 39. M: Gare d'Austerlitz. From the métro, enter the Jardin des Plantes from pl. Valhubert. ***All museums open*** *M and W-F 10am-5pm, Sa-Su 10am-6pm; last admission 30min. before closing.* ***Admission*** *30F, students 20F.* ***Grand Galerie open*** *until 10pm Th; 40F, students 30F; temporary exhibits 30F, students 20F.*

Three science museums in one, the star of which is the fantastic 4-floor **Grand Galérie d'Evolution,** which tells the story of evolution with gorgeous, stuffed critters and a state-of-the-art sound system. Children will worship you for bringing them here. Next door, the **Musée de Minéralogie,** surrounded by luscious rose trellises, contains some lovely diamonds, rubies, and sapphires, as well as an exhibit on volcanoes. At the other end of the garden, the **Gallery of Comparative Anatomy and Paleontology** houses a dinosaur exhibit and some other large skeletons (like those of elephants and whales) and fossils.

INSTITUT DU MONDE ARABE

1, r. des Fosses St-Jacques. ☎40 51 38 38. M: Jussieu. From the métro, walk down r. Jussieu away from the Jardin des Plantes; make your first right onto r. des Fosses St-Bernard. Museum open Tu-Su 10am-7pm; library open M-Sa 1-8pm. Museum admission 25F, ages 12-18 20F, under 12 free. 90min. tours Tu-F at 3pm, Sa-Su at 2 and 4pm; 55F.

The museum assembles 3rd- to 18th-century art from three Arab regions: the Maghreb, the Near East, and the Middle East. Level 4 is devoted entirely to contemporary Arab art. An extensive **public library** houses over 50,000 works as well as an audio-visual center. From September to June, the auditorium hosts Arab movies (subtitled in English and French; 25F, students 20F), music (100F), and theater (80F). The **rooftop terrace** has a fabulous and free view of Montmartre, Sacré Coeur, the Seine, and Île de la Cité.

SIXTH ARRONDISSEMENT

MUSÉE DELACROIX

6, pl. Furstenberg. M: St-Germain-des-Prés. Behind the Eglise St-Germain off r. de l'Abbaye. At the courtyard, follow the sign to the atelier Delacroix. ☎44 41 86 50. Open W-M 9:30am-5pm; last entry 4:30pm. 22F, ages 18-25 and over 60 15F, under 18 free.

Located in the 3-room apartment in which he lived until his death in 1863. One of the leaders of French Romanticism, Delacroix is most famous for his painting *Liberty Leading the People* (see **Musée du Louvre,** p. 115). Sketches, watercolors, engravings, and letters to Théophile Gautier and George Sand belie a rather gentle artist.

MUSÉE DE LA MONNAIE

11, quai de Conti. M. Odéon. From the métro, walk down r. Mazarine toward the Seine and make a right on r. Guénégaud; proceed to the entrance on r. Guénégaud. ☎40 46 56 66; tours ☎40 46 55 35; www.monnaideparis.fr. Open Tu-F 11am-5:30pm, Sa-Su noon-5:30pm. 20F, students 15F, free Su and to those under 16.

See more money than you'll ever make honestly. Located in the Hôtel des Monnaies, where coins were minted 'til 1973, the museum displays coins and historical documents.

MUSÉE ZADKINE

100bis, r. d'Assas. M: Vavin or Port-Royal. Just south of the Jardin du Luxembourg. ☎43 26 91 90. Open Tu-Su 10am-5:30pm. 27F, students 19F.

Installed in 1982 in the house and studio where he worked, the museum highlights the work of Russian sculptor Ossip Zadkine (1890-1967), whose work spans from the extremes of Cubism to neo-Classicism.

SEVENTH ARRONDISSEMENT

MUSÉE DES EGOUTS DE PARIS (THE SEWERS OF PARIS)

Across from 93, quai d'Orsay. M: Pont de l'Alma. ☎53 68 27 81. Open May-Sept. Sa-W 11am-4pm; Oct.-Apr. Sa-W 11am-5pm. Last tickets sold 1hr. before close. Closed last 3 weeks of January. 25F, students and under 10 20F, under 5 free.

A tour through the sewers illustrating the struggle for drinkable water and a clean Seine through the ages. Don't breath deep—the smell can be overwhelming.

MUSÉE-GALERIE DE LA SEITA

12, r. Surcouf. M: Invalides. On the corner of r. de l'Université and r. Surcouf. ☎45 56 60 17. Open M-Sa 11am-7pm. Permanent exhibit free, temporary exhibits 15F, students 10F.

While non-smoking grows in other countries, France celebrates its love affair with tobacco. Stages impressive temporary exhibits. Permanent exhibit on the story of tobacco includes pipe and cigarette holders depicting everything from nudes to nuns.

MUSÉE NATIONAL DE LA LÉGION D'HONNEUR ET DES ORDRES DE CHEVALERIE

2, r. de Bellechasse. M: Solférino. ☎40 62 84 25. Open Tu-Su 11am-5pm. 25F, students and seniors 15F.

Housed in an 18th-century mansion, this museum displays medals and uniforms of the French Legion of Honor. A tribute to the feudal loyalty of knights and noblemen to their Kings and Emperors through the ages, medals of enamel and gold depict everything from doves to Napoleon I.

EIGHTH ARRONDISSEMENT

MUSÉE CERNUSCHI

7, av. Velasquez, outside the gates of Parc Monceau. ☎45 63 50 75. M: Villiers or Monceau. Open Tu-Su 10am-5:30pm. 22F, seniors 15F, under 27 free; during exhibits students 18F, under 7 free.

A magnificent collection of Asian art. The collection he started in 1871 is still being expanded today. Second only to the **Musée Guimet** (see p. 135) in Asian art, the Cernuschi contains a rich collection of ancient to 18th-century Asian pieces, such as a three-ton Japanese Buddha, a Tang dynasty silk scroll entitled *"Horses and their Grooms,"* and an impressive array of funereal pottery, pen-and-ink drawings, and bronzes.

GRAND PALAIS

3, av. du Général Eisenhower. ☎44 13 17 30 or 44 13 17 17. M: Champs-Élysées-Clemenceau. Open Th-M 10am-8pm, W 10am-10pm; last entry 45min. before closing. Admission varies by exhibit and some require reservations. Anticipate something like 60F, students 35F, under 13 free.

Designed for the 1900 Universal Exposition, most of the building houses the Palais de la Découverte (see below), but the *palais* also hosts temporary exhibits.

PALAIS DE LA DÉCOUVERTE

In the Grand Palais, entrance on av. Franklin D. Roosevelt. ☎56 43 20 20, planetarium ☎40 74 81 73. M: FDR or Champs-Elysées-Clemenceau. Open Tu-Sa 9:30am-6pm, Su 9am-7pm. 30F, students, seniors, and under 18 20F. Planetarium entrance 15F. Family entrance 80F for two adults and two children over 5, then 15F for each additional child over 5.

Kids tear around the Palais's interactive science exhibits, pressing buttons that start comets on celestial trajectories, spinning on seats to investigate angular motion, and glaring at all kinds of creepy-crawlies. The **planetarium** has shows four times per day.

PETIT PALAIS

Av. Winston Churchill. ☎42 65 12 73. M: Champs-Elysées-Clemenceau or FDR.

Also called the Palais des Beaux-Arts de la Ville de Paris. Built for the 1900 Universal Exposition, the palais houses 17th- to 20th-century Flemish, French, and Dutch painting and sculpture, but will be closed for renovations until 2002.

MUSÉE JACQUEMART-ANDRÉ

158, bd. Haussmann. ☎42 89 04 91. M: Miromesnil. Open daily 10am-6pm; last visitors admitted at 5:30pm. 49F, students and ages 7-17 37F, under 7 free.

Nelie Jacquemart and her husband liked to impress: during their lifetime, eveyone had a chance to admire their double corniced marble and iron staircase, but only very special friends saw their precious collection of Renaissance artwork, including a Madonna and Child by Boticelli and *St. George and the Dragon* by Ucello. Have a light lunch in the tearoom under a fresco by Tiepolo.

MUSÉE NISSIM DE CAMONDO

63, r. de Monceau. ☎53 89 06 40. M: Villiers or Monceau. Open W-Su 10am-5pm. 27F, age 18-25 18F, under 18 free. Guided tours Sunday at 11:30am.

Another private collection gone public; dedicated by a Turkish count to the Musée des Arts Decoratifs in memory of his son who died in the Great War. Wander about the Chinese vases, over Svonnerie carpets, and past Sèvres porcelain.

NINTH ARRONDISSEMENT

MUSÉE GRÉVIN

0, bd. Montmartre. ☎47 70 87 99. M: Grands Boulevards. From the métro, walk west on bd. Montmartre. ***Open*** *daily Apr.-Aug. 1-7pm; Sept.-Mar. 1-6:30pm, last entry 6pm.* ***Admission*** *58F, ages 6-14 38F.* ***Guide book*** *10F. AmEx, V, MC (130F minimum).* ***Smaller branch*** *at level "-1" of the Forum des Halles, near the Porte Berger, 1er (☎40 26 28 50), M: Châtelet-Les-Halles.*

This wax museum's ornate halls feature Marie-Antoinette awaiting her execution in the Conciergerie, the cannibals from Géricault's *Raft of the Medusa*, and the King of Pop. Indeed, the photos of Mikey Mike visiting are worth the price of admission.

MUSÉE GUSTAVE MOREAU

14, r. de La Rochefoucauld. M: Trinité. From the métro, make a right on r. St-Lazare and then a left onto r. de La Rouchefoucauld. ☎48 74 38 50. ***Open*** *M and W 11am-5:15pm, Th-Su 10am-12:45pm and 2-5:15pm.* ***Admission*** *22F; students, over 60 and everyone on Sunday 15F; under 18 free.*

In the 19th-century home of symbolist painter Gustave Moreau, this museum contains thousands of Moreau's drawings and paintings, including a pleasant painting of Salomé dancing before the severed head of John the Baptist.

TENTH ARRONDISSEMENT

CRISTALLERIES BACCARAT

30bis, r. de Paradis. M: Gare de l'Est. Walk against traffic on bd. Strasbourg and turn right on r. de la Fidelité, which becomes r. de Paradis. ☎47 70 64 30. Open M-Sa 10am-6pm. 15F, students and groups 8F, under 12 free.

Since its founding in 1764 by Louis XV, Baccarat has been the most prestigious of crystal makers, patronized by kings, tsars, and shahs. The glittering display of every imaginable crystal object looks like an ice palace, or a scene from Balzac's *La Peau de Chagrin*.

TWELFTH ARRONDISSEMENT

MUSÉE DES ARTS AFRICAINS ET OCÉANIENS

293, av. Daumesnil. M: Porte Dorée. On the western edge of the Bois de Vincennes. ☎ 43 46 51 61. Open W-M 10am-5:30pm, Sa-Su 12:30-6pm; last entry 30min. before closing. 30F, students and children 20F; temporary exhibits 38F, 28F, Su 28F.

A stunning collection of several millennia of African and Pacific art. Impressive display of African statues, masks, jewelry, and wedding dresses from the Maghreb. Built for the 1931 Colonial Exposition, the building is still decorated with its original Eurocentric murals and friezes.

FOURTEENTH ARRONDISSEMENT

FONDATION CARTIER POUR L'ART CONTEMPORAIN

261, bd. Raspail. M: Raspail or Denfert-Rochereau. ☎ 42 18 56 51, reservations ☎ 42 18 56 72; www.fondation.cartier.fr. Open Tu-Su noon-8pm. 30F, students and seniors 20F, under 10 free. Soirées Nomades Sept.-June Th at 8:30pm.

Standard modern glass facade deceives from afar–this is not a building, but a mammoth bubble of glass sheets surrounding a crafted botanical garden and outdoor theater. Nestled in this flora, the *fondation* hosts exhibitions on subjects ranging from Warhol to the history of birds.

FIFTEENTH ARRONDISSEMENT

MUSÉE BOURDELLE

18, r. Antoine Bourdelle. M: Montparnasse-Bienvenüe. From av. du Maine, turn left onto r. Antoine Bourdelle. ☎ 49 54 73 73. Open Tu-Su 10am-5:30pm; last entry 5:15pm. 30F, students 20F.

A pupil of Rodin and mentor of Giacometti, Richier, and da Silva, Emile-Antoine Bourdelle (1861-1929) sculpted the reliefs that adorn the Théâtre des Champs-Élysées and the opera house in Marseilles. The museum presents 500 works in marble, plaster, and bronze, including Bourdelle's masterpiece, *Heracles as Archer*, and an impressive series of 40 busts of Beethoven.

MÉMORIAL DE LA LIBÉRATION DE PARIS

23, allée de la 2eme D-B, Jardin Atlantique. M: Montparnasse-Bienvenüe. Above the tracks of the Gare Montparnasse. Follow signs to the Jardin Atlantique from the train station, pl. du Pont des Cinq Martyrs du Lycée Buffon, or r. Commandant René Mouchotte. ☎ 40 64 39 44. Open Tu-Su 10am-5:40pm; last ticket 5:15pm. 22F, under 26 15F; during exhibitions 30F, under 26 20F.

These two joint museums were opened in 1994 for the 50th anniversary of the French resistance. One is a memorial to Maréchal Leclerc, a French Commander who fought in North Africa, and led his small army against the Germans to liberate Paris in August of 1944. The other is a museum commemorating the founder, president, and martyr of the French Resistance, Jean Moulin. From Africa to the beaches of Normandy, from liberated Paris to the capture of Berchtesgaden, this museum traces the military maneuvers of the two men.

SIXTEENTH ARRONDISSEMENT

MUSÉE D'ART MODERNE DE LA VILLE DE PARIS

11, av. du Président Wilson. M: Iéna. From Iéna, follow av. du Président Wilson. ☎ 53 67 40 00. Open Tu-F 10am-5:30pm, Sa-Su 10am-6:45pm. Special exhibits 30-45F, students and seniors 20-35F; permanent exhibitions 14F; free Su morning.

Housed in the magnificent Palais de Tokyo (see **Sights,** p. 84), this museum contains one of the world's foremost collections of 20th-century art, but on a smaller scale than that of the Centre Pompidou. Matisse's "La Danse Inachêvé," which was executed with the help of a brush attached to a bamboo stick, dominates its own room. Other striking pieces include Raoul Dufy's fauvist epic of electricity, "La Fée Électricité," and Amedeo Modigliani's haunting mannerist painting, "La Femme aux yeux bleus."

MUSÉE MARMOTTAN MONET

2, r. Louis-Boilly. M: La Muette. Follow Chaussée de la Muette, which becomes av. Ranelagh, through the Jardin du Ranelagh park. ☎ 44 96 50 33. Wheelchair accessible. Open Tu-Su 10am-5:30pm. 35F, students and seniors 15F, under 8 free.

Owing to generous donations by the family of Monet and others, the Empire-style house has been transformed into a lucrative shrine to Impressionism. The top floor is dedicated to paintings by Berthe Morisot. Known as the First Lady of Impressionism, she was a great friend of Monet and Renoir, a successful painter in her own right, and a student and model for Manet (she is the pretty brunette in "On the Balcony").

Museum of Evolution

MUSÉE NATIONAL DES ARTS ASIATIQUES (MUSÉE GUIMET)

6, pl. d'Iéna. M: Iéna. ☎56 52 53 00.

A large collection of Asian art representing 17 different countries. Closed until spring 2001 for renovations. Some pieces have been moved to the Musée Guimet's annex, the **Musée du Panthéon Bouddhique** (below).

MUSÉE DU PANTHÉON BOUDDHIQUE

19, av. d'Iéna. M: Iéna. ☎45 05 00 98. Open W-M 9:45am-6pm. 16F, students and seniors 12F, under 18 free.

This small museum is packed with over 300 pieces of art that trace the religious history of Japan and China. There is a tranquil Japanese garden out back.

MAISON DE BALZAC

47, r. Raynouard. M: Passy. ☎55 74 41 80. Open Tu-Su 10am-5:45pm. 20F, students 15F, over 60 free; free Su 10am-1pm.

Home of Honoré de Balzac from 1840-47. Here he sought refuge from bill collectors. Visitors can see the desk where he edited *La Comédie Humaine* for 17 hours a day and wrote new novels including *Cousine Bette.* Several rooms of famous portraits and memorabilia; the museum is more fun if you've read a Balzac novel or two.

La Joconde

MUSÉE HENRI BOUCHARD

25, r. de l'Yvette. M: Jasmin. ☎46 47 63 46; www.musee-bouchard.com. Open July-Sept. 15, Oct.-Dec. 15, Jan. 2-Mar. 15, and Apr.-June 15 W and Sa 2-7pm. 25F, students 15F.

Housed in the workshop of Henri Bouchard (1875-1960), sculptor of the Palais de Chaillot's *Apollo* as well as 1,300 other pieces. The workshop has been left in its original state with displays of the plasters, tools, and moulds used to make the sculptures. Bouchard's son and daughter-in-law are the curators, available to explain his style and technique.

MUSÉE CLEMENCEAU

8, r. Benjamin Franklin. M: Passy. ☎45 20 53 41. Open Tu, Th, and Sa-Su 2-5pm; closed Aug. 20F, students and seniors 15F.

The museum thoroughly documents the life of revered and vilified journalist and statesman, Georges Clemenceau (1841-1929). Publisher of Emile Zola's *J'accuse*, Prime Minister of France, and much-criticized negotiator of the Treaty of Versailles, Clemenceau lived here from 1895 until his death in 1929.

Musée d'Orsay

FONDATION LE CORBUSIER

Villa la Roche 8-10, pl. du Docteur-Blanche. M: Jasmin. Walk up r. de l'Yvette and turn left on r. du Docteur-Blanche and left again at no. 55 into pl. du Docteur-Blanche. ☎42 88 41 53. Open Sept.-July M-Th 10am-12:30pm and 1:30-6pm, F 10am-12:30pm and 1:30-5pm; library open after 1:30pm. 15F, students 10F.

The foundation is located in Villas La Roche and Jeanneret, both designed and furnished by the Swiss architect Le Corbusier (1887-1965). He once exclaimed to his mentor, "A house is a machine one lives in!" a concept he realized in these creations.

MUSÉE DE L'HOMME (MUSEUM OF MAN)

17, pl. du Trocadéro. M: Trocadéro. In the Palais de Chaillot, on the left-hand side if facing the Eiffel Tower. ☎44 05 72 00 or 44 05 72 72. Open W-M 9:45am-5:15pm. 30F, under 27 and seniors 20F, under 4 free. Films Sept.-July W and Sa at 3 and 4pm.

Anthropology museum illustrating world cultures from 250,000 BC to the present, via ethnological artifacts such as prehistoric tools, a painted cart from Sicily, a Turkish store, Eskimo fishing boats, and hats from Cameroon. Dioramas abound.

MUSÉE DE LA MARINE (MUSEUM OF THE NAVY)

17, pl. du Trocadéro. M: Trocadéro. In the Palais de Chaillot. ☎53 65 69 69. Open W-M 10am-6pm; last entry 5:30pm. No tours in English, except for those who call the Service Culturelle on M to arrange a group tour. 38F, under 25 and seniors 25F.

Model ships of incredible detail and a few real boats from the 17th-19th centuries are anchored here, including the golden dinghy built for Napoleon in 1810. Sailing equipment and oil paintings of stormy sea battles round out the collection.

MUSÉE DE LA MODE ET DU COSTUME (MUSEUM OF FASHION AND CLOTHING)

In the Palais Galleria, 10, av. Pierre I-de-Serbie. M: Iéna. ☎47 20 85 23. Open Tu-Su 10am-6pm; last entry 5:30pm. 45F, students and seniors 35F.

With 30,000 outfits and 70,000 accessories, the museum has no choice but to rotate temporary exhibitions showcasing fashions of the past three centuries. A fabulous place to visit to see the history of Paris fashion, haute couture, and society.

MAISON DE RADIO FRANCE

116, av. du Président Kennedy. M: Passy or RER: Av. du Pt. Kennedy/Maison de Radio France. Head for the Seine and enter through Door A of the big, white, cylindrical building. ☎42 30 15 16. Tours M-Sa 10:30, 11:30am, 2:30, 3:30, and 4:30pm; English tours at 3pm Tu-F during the summer (check by phone). 20F, students and seniors 15F.

The museum, accessible only by guided tour, presents the history of communications compressed into one hour at the headquarters of France's public radio stations (programs broadcast live at www.radio-france.fr). Attractions range from ancient radio specimens to studios and a concert hall. Inquire about attending free tapings of TV programs.

MUSÉE DU VIN

R. des Eaux, or 5-7, pl. Charles Dickens. M: Passy. Go down the stairs, turn right on pl. Alboni, and then turn right on r. des Eaux. ☎45 25 63 26. Open Tu-Su 10am-6pm. 35F, seniors 30F, students 29F.

This mildly amusing cave is peopled with strange wax models engaged in the process of wine-making, including one of Balzac fleeing his creditors. You may have to remind the receptionist to give you your free tasting of red, rosé, or white.

SEVENTEENTH ARRONDISSEMENT

MUSÉE JEAN-JACQUES HENNER

43, av. Villiers. M: Malsherbes. ☎47 63 42 73. Open Tu-Su 10am-noon and 2-5pm. 21F, students and seniors 17F, under 18 free.

Three floors of the works of Jean-Jacques Henner (1829-1905), on the periphery of Realism with his soft-focus subjects with haunting, luminous, bone-white skin.

EIGHTEENTH ARRONDISSEMENT

MUSÉE D'ART NAÏF MAX FOURNY

2, r. Ronsard. M: Anvers. Walk up r. de Steinkerque, turn right at pl. St-Pierre, then left onto r. Ronsard. ☎42 58 72 89. Open Sept.-July daily 10am-6pm. 25F.

Within a former Parisian marketplace, this museum contains folk art ranging from childlike scrawls to raw, moving tableaux. Participatory games for visitors ages 3-12.

MUSÉE SALVADOR DALÍ (ESPACE MONTMARTRE)

11, r. Poulbot. M: Anvers or Abbesses. From pl. du Tertre, follow r. du Calvaire toward the view, then turn right onto r. Poulbot. ☎42 64 40 10. Open daily Nov.-Mar. 10am-6pm; Oct.-Apr. 10am-9:30pm; last entrance 30min. before closing. 40F, students 26F.

Something of a tourist trap, the museum is full of lesser-known lithographs and sculptures. "Surrealist surroundings" amount to erotic artwork and space-music.

MUSÉE DU VIEUX MONTMARTRE

12, r. Cortot. M: Lamarck-Caulaincourt. Turn right on r. Lamarck, right again up steep r. des Saules, then left onto r. Cortot. ☎46 06 61 11. Open Tu-Su 11am-6:30pm. 25F, students and seniors 20F.

Dedicated to the political, artistic, cultural, and religious past of the *butte*, the museum occupies a 17th-century house overlooking Paris's only vineyard.

TWENTIETH ARRONDISSEMENT

LA MAISON DE L'AIR

27, r. Piat. ☎43 28 47 63. Open Apr.-Sept. Tu-F 1:30-5:30pm, Sa-Su 1:30-6:30pm; Oct.-Mar. Tu-Su 1:30-5pm. 22F, ages 11-18 and over 60 11F, ages 6-10 5F.

This kid-ready municipal museum allows you to touch, hear, and smell your way into a broader understanding of the air around you. Exhibits investigate the wonders of flight, the atmosphere, meteorology, and the evils of air pollution (a growing problem in Paris).

GALLERIES

The highest concentration of contemporary art galleries is in the Marais, especially on r. Vieille-du-Temple and r. Quincampoix, and in the *6ème*/St-Germain-des-Prés area, on r. Mazarine, r. de Seine, r. des Beaux-Arts, and r. Jacob. These galleries exhibit primarily contemporary art. The *8ème*, on the other hand, is loaded with Old Masters. Those near M: Franklin Roosevelt on the Champs-Elysées, av. Matignon, r. du Faubourg St-Honoré, and r. de Miromesnil focus on Impressionism and post-Impressionism. The *Portes Ouvertes* festival allows visitors to witness artists in action in their studios (see **Festivals,** p. 6). Almost all galleries close in August.

ÎLE ST-LOUIS

Galerie Clorinde Martin, 77, r. St-Louis-en-l'Île (☎43 29 08 09). M: Pont Marie. Tiny but airy gallery showing the work of contemporary French landscape and still-life painters. Some of the most interesting art on the island. Open M-Sa noon-7pm.

Galerie Félix, 54, r. St-Louis-en-l'Île (☎40 46 05 58). M: Pont Marie. Small space showing contemporary work by artists who still aren't over Impressionism. Open daily 11:30am-7:30pm.

THIRD ARRONDISSEMENT

The swank galleries in the Marais display some of Paris's most exciting and avant-garde art, and the *3ème* is saturated with them. Cutting-edge art peeks out of storefront windows along **r. de Perche, r. Debellyme, r. Vieille-du-Temple, r. de Poitou,** and **r. Beaubourg.**

Galeries Michèle Chomette, 24, r. Beaubourg (☎42 78 05 62). M: Rambuteau. From the métro, walk north on r. Beaubourg. Enter at no. 24 by ringing the buzzer and proceed upstairs. Contemporary and historic photography. 6-8 exhibitions per year. Artists include Arnaud Claass, Henri Foucault, and Mikael Levin. Open Tu-Sa 2-7pm. Closed Aug.

Galerie Daniel Templon, 30, r. Beaubourg (☎42 72 14 10). M: Rambuteau. From the métro, walk north on r. Beaubourg. Enter at no. 30; the gallery is at the back of the courtyard. Tucked securely away from the tourist bustle near the Centre Pompidou—one of Paris's most respected contemporary galleries. 20th-century painting and sculpture and an impressive roster of artists including Ross Bleckner, Arman, Eric Fischl, and Jim Dine. Open M-Sa 10am-7pm; closed Aug.

Galerie Sabine Puget, 108, r. Vielle-du-Temple (☎42 71 04 20; *www.officedesarts.com/spuget*). M: Filles du Calvaire. Walk down r. des Filles du Calvaire, which becomes r. Vieille-du-Temple. This contemporary gallery in the heart of the Marais boasts high ceilings, lots of natural light, and gorgeous contemporary artists. Open Tu-Sa 10:30am-7pm; closed Aug.

Galerie Zürcher, 56, r. Chapon (☎42 72 82 20). M: Arts and Métiers. From the métro, walk south on r. Beaubourg and make a right on r. Chapon; enter through no. 56 and the gallery is at the back of the courtyard. Specializes in abstract, European artists. Open Tu-Sa 11am-7pm.

Galerie Askéo, 19, r. Debellyme (☎42 77 17 77). M: Filles du Calvaire. This three-story metallic gallery displays engaging installation art on a grand scale. Open Tu-Sa 2:30-7pm.

Galerie Sanguine, 26, r. Beaubourg (☎53 65 12 44). M: Rambuteau. This two-floor gallery specializes in post-1960 painting, photography, and graphics, and regularly includes works by Lichtenstein, Cesar, Christo, Goldin, and Klasen. Open M-Sa 2-7pm.

Galerie Eterso, 108, r. Vieille-du-Temple (☎42 72 65 20). M: Filles de Calvaire. Suave leather couches, glass-topped tables, and small installations. Open Tu-Sa 11am-1pm and 2-6pm.

FOURTH ARRONDISSEMENT

Galerie Rachlin Lemaire, 23, r. de Renard (☎44 59 27 27). M: Rambuteau or Châtelet. Adventurous contemporary art. Open M-Sa 10:30am-1pm and 2:30pm-7pm.

Fiesta Galerie, 45, r. Vieille-du-Temple (☎42 71 53 34). M: St-Paul. Retro-pop fun. Giant stuffed M&Ms and miniature Yodas. Open Tu-Sa noon-7pm, Su-M 2-7pm.

Galerie Gana Beaubourg, 3, r. Pierre au Lard (☎42 71 00 45). M: Rambuteau. Capacious international contemporary art space. Open Tu-Sa 10am-7pm.

SIXTH ARRONDISSEMENT

R. de Seine, r. Mazarine, r. Bonaparte, and r. Dauphine are home to art gallery after art gallery, all providing an amazing glimpse at cutting-edge contemporary art.

Galerie de L'Europe, 55, r. de Seine (☎55 42 94 23; *www.galerie-europe.net*). M: Mabillon. From the métro, walk with traffic on bd. St-Germain and make a left on r. de Seine. A huge, multilevel space hosting changing contemporary group and individual exhibits. One of the most prominent contemporary galleries in St-Germain-des-Prés. Open Tu-Sa 10:30am-1pm, 2:30pm-7pm.

Atlantis Gallery, 33, r. de Seine (☎43 26 89 62). M: Mabillon. See directions for Galerie de l'Europe. This smaller contemporary gallery with a friendly, approachable staff exhibits work of established artists. Open Tu-Sa 11am-1pm and 2:30-7pm.

Galerie Barès, 32, r. de Seine (☎55 42 93 95). M: Mabillon. See directions above for Galerie de l'Europe. Small gallery specializes in prints, engravings, and lithographs and has a changing selection of works by artists such as Miró and Picasso. Open M-Sa 10:30am-1pm and 2:30-7pm.

Galerie Albert Loeb, 12, r. des Beaux Arts (☎46 33 06 87). M: St-Germain-des-Prés. From the métro, walk toward the Seine on r. Bonaparte and make a right onto r. des Beaux-Arts. The austere marble front of this gallery hides a large, well-laid-out space that hosts quality contemporary individual exhibitions. Open Tu-Sa 10am-1pm and 2-7pm.

EIGHTH ARRONDISSEMENT

Galerie Lelong, 13, r. de Téhéran (☎45 63 13 19). M: Miromesnil. A standard display of famous (Miró, Koons) 20th-century art. Open Tu-F 10:30am-6pm, Sa 2-6:30pm. Closed July-Sept.

Galerie Louis Carré et Cie, 10 av. de Messine (☎45 62 57 07). M: Miromesnil. A satisfying and often novel array of contemporary French painting and sculpture (Ceuco, Arroyo, Buery, Telemaque). Open M-Sa 10am-12:30pm and 1:30-6:30pm. Only open Saturday for exhibitions.

ELEVENTH ARRONDISSEMENT

Galerie J. et J. Donguy, 57, r. de la Roquette (☎47 00 10 94). M: Bastille or Voltaire. Performance pieces and installations. Experimental poetry festival every June. Open daily 1-7pm.

Glassbox, 113bis, r. Oberkampf. M: Oberkampf. Attracts politically engaged artists.

Bo Plastic, 31, r. de Charonne (☎53 36 73 16; e-mail boplas@club-internet.com). M: Ledru-Rollin. Innovative plastic creations like egg-shaped chairs with the yolk-sized seat scooped out. Sells retro 60s-70s furniture and accessories. Open M-Sa 11am-8pm.

Espace d'Art Yvonamor Palix, 13, r. Keller (☎48 06 36 70; fax 40 21 82 95). M: Ledru-Rollin. Small gallery displays international art. Open Tu-F by appointment, for public viewing Sa 2-7pm. Call ahead, exhibitions are not always happening. Closed Mondays.

Galerie Jousse Séguin, 34, r. de Charonne (tel. 01 47 00 32 35; e-mail jousse.seguin@world-net.fr). M: Ledru-Rollin. A gallery of minimalist 50s furnishings that may bring back bad memories of school days. Open M-F 11-1:30 and 2:30-7pm, Sa 11-7pm.

Ateliers de Ménilmontant, 42, r. Alexandre Dumas. M: Alexandre Dumas. To preserve the area's old buildings, the Ateliers hold open studios and bring artists together to paint outdoor frescoes.

TWELFTH ARRONDISSEMENT

The 12*ème* has a few galleries; most of them are located among workshops and studios in the **Viaduc des Arts** (see **Sights,** p. 94). They showcase design, contemporary art, leather, glass, furniture, and architectural models. And fabulous, fabulous **Jean Paul Gaultier** has a gallery at 30, Faubourg St-Antoine.

Galerie Claude Samuel, 69, av. Daumesnil (☎53 17 01 11). M: Bastille. One of the only contemporary art spaces in the Viaduc. Opening hours variable.

Fireworks, 101, av. Daumesnil (☎46 28 46 46). M: Bastille. Intriguing colored glass; some are even affordable. Open M 2-6pm, Tu-F 9:30am-6:30pm, Sa 2-7pm.

THIRTEENTH ARRONDISSEMENT

The 13*ème*'s art scene is cutting edge. Galleries are lodged into a building of the Minister of Finance complex along **r. Louise-Weisse** (M: Chevarelet).

Galerie Emmanuel Perrotin, 30, r. Louise-Weiss (☎42 16 79 79). M: Chevarelet. Radical European and Japanese multimedia art. Open Tu-Sa 11am-7pm.

FOURTEENTH ARRONDISSEMENT

Gallerie 213, 213, bd. Raspail (☎43 22 83 23.) M: Vavin or Raspail. Displays works of young photographers. Open Tu-Sa 11am-7pm.

Gallerie Camera Obscura, 12, r. Ernest Cresson (☎45 45 67 08; email cameraobscura@clara-net.fr). M: Denfert-Rochereau. A simple and elegant gallery which exhibits the works of international photographers. Open Tu-Sa 2-7pm.

Christian
Dior

INSIDE

Shopping

Paris is the Latin spirit expressing itself as taste in a world already civilized, and conquering, not with man's will, but with feminine attraction.
-Diane Lewis

SHOPPING BY ARRONDISSEMENT

ÉTIENNE-MARCEL AND LES HALLES (1ER AND 2ÈME)

Sugar and spice, and all things naughty. Fabrics are a little cheaper, and the style here is younger. At the **Agnés B.** empire on r. du Jour, the black classics still rule, and **Claude Pierlot** at 3, r. de Turbigo does button-up cardigans with a well-bred touch. The stores on r. Etienne Marcel and r. Tiquetonne are best for technicolor clubwear, and outrageously sexy outfits. (M: Etienne-Marcel.) **Forum Les Halles,** a subterranean shopping mall (see p. 142) located just south of the Etienne Marcel area, and the streets that surround it contain a large range for a full urban warrior aesthetic.

MARAIS (4ÈME AND THE LOWER 3ÈME)

The Marais gives less lip than the Etienne Marcel area, trading street wise edge for a consistent line-up of affordable, trendy boutiques. Shopping in the Marais is a complete aesthetic experience as boutiques of all colors and flavors pop out along medieval streets and among welcoming, tree-shaded cafes. What the Marais does best is the mid-priced clothing chains, independent designer shops, as well as vintage stores that line **r. Vieille-du-Temple, r. de Sévigne, r. Roi de Sicile** and **r. des Rosiers.** Lifestyle and shops line **r. de Bourg-Tibourg** and **r. des Francs-Bourgeois.** The best selection of affordable-chic men's wear in Paris can be found here, especially along **r. Ste-Croix-de-la-Bretonnerie.** Most stores are open late on weekdays and on Sundays. *(M: St-Paul or Hôtel-de-Ville.)*

oh! for a day

Just looking...

It could take five minutes or several hours to complete this deadly little stroll among fabulous boutiques and cafes in the medieval byways of the Marais, in fact it might take all day. From M: St. Paul, turn right and walk along until r. de Rivoli becomes r. St. Antoine. Turn left on r. de Sévigne. Stop in at no. 12, **Loft,** if you need a dishy gift for a handsome bloke. Pop by **MKDM** at no. 24 for a funky japanese style t-shirt —or five. Turn onto r. des Francs Bourgeois and pause at the corner to peruse those sexy satins at **Plein Sud,** no.21. Turn left down r. Pavée and then right onto r. des Rosiers to visit the oceanic glamour of **Paola Afrani,** no. 3bis. Continue down r. des Rosiers and cross r. Vielle du Temple to reach r. Ste Croix de la Bretonnerie. Yiddish treats pack the tiny cafes and delis along the way and provide refueling. At no. 5, **Boy'z Bazaar** has the leather jacket of any boy's dreams, and **Zadig and Voltaire,** at no. 12, is the perfect way to round up your wardrobe, from wickedly cool bags to DKNY at a discount.

ST-GERMAIN-DES-PRÉS (6ÈME AND EASTERN BORDER OF 7ÈME)

Post-intellectual, materialistic St-Germain-des-Prés, particularly the triangle bordered by bd. St-Germain, r. St-Sulpice and r. des Saints-Pères, is super saturated with high-budget names. But don't just settle for *lécher les vitrines* (*window shopping;* literally, licking the windows)—r. du Four hosts fun and affordable designers such as **Paul and Joe** (no. 40, ☎45 44 97 70; open daily 11am-7:30pm) and **Sinéquanone** (no. 16, ☎56 24 27 74; open M-Sa 10am-7:30pm). *(M: St Germain des Pres.)* Closer to the Jardin du Luxembourg, calm r. de Fleurus hosts **A.P.C.** as well as the interesting designs of **t***** at no. 7. *(M: St-Placide.)* In the *7ème*, visit r. de Pré-aux-Clercs and r. de Grenelle to witness avant-garde jewelry at **Stella Cadente,** no. 22. In general, the *7ème* is very expensive, but there are some impressive little boutiques around the Bon Marché department store on r. de Sevres, and r. du Cherche Midi. *(M: Vaneau, Duroc, Sèvres-Babylone, Rue du Bac.)*

DEPARTMENT STORES

Au Bon Marché, 22, 38 r. de Sèvres, *7ème* (☎44 39 80 00). M: Sèvres-Babylone. Paris's oldest department store (supposedly Eiffel advised on its ironwork), Bon Marché has it all, from scarves to smoking accessories, designer clothes to a wonderful back-to-school children's section. Across the street is *La Grande Epicerie de Paris,* Bon Marché's celebrated gourmet food annex. Open M-W and F 9:30am-7pm, Th 10am-9pm, Sa 9:30am-8pm. MC, V.

Au Printemps, 64, bd. Haussmann, *9ème* (☎42 82 50 00). M: Chaussée d'Antin-Lafayette or Havre-Caumartin. Also at 30, pl. d'Italie, *13ème* (☎40 78 17 17), M: pl. d'Italie; 21-25, cours de Vincennes, *20ème* (☎43 71 12 41), M: Porte de Vincennes. One of the two biggies in the Parisian department store scene, containing mostly goods far beyond the budget category. Caters more to women's fashion than men's. Most hotels have 10% discounts for use in the store. Haussmann open M-W and F-Sa 9:30am-7pm, Th 9:30am-10pm. MC, V.

Forum des Halles, M: Les Halles or RER: Châtelet-Les Halles, *2ème* (☎44 76 96 56). An immense and shabby underground shopping mall. Descend from one of the 4 main entrances to discover over 200 boutiques. There is a branch of the FNAC music and CD store, a branch of the cosmetics wonderland, Sephora, a movie theater complex, and a swimming pool. All stores open M-Sa 10am-7:30pm.

Galeries Lafayette, 40, bd. Haussmann, *9ème* (☎42 82 34 56). M: Chaussée d'Antin. Also at 22, r. du Départ, *14ème* (☎45 38 52 87), M: Montparnasse. Chaotic (the equivalent of Paris's entire population visits here each month), but carries it all, including mini-boutiques of Kookaï, Agnès B., Gap, and Benetton. Most hotels offer 10% discount coupons for the store. Open M-W, F, Sa 9:30am-7pm, Th 9:30-9pm. AmEx, MC, V.

Monoprix, branches all over Paris. Standard daily hours 9:30am-7:30pm, but some locations open until 10pm. Good value for groceries, fashion, and housewares. MC, V.

Samaritaine, 67, r. de Rivoli, 1*er* (☎40 41 20 20). M: Pont-Neuf, Châtelet-Les-Halles, or Louvre. 4 large historic art deco buildings between r. de Rivoli and the Seine, connected by tunnels and bridges. Not as chic as Galeries Lafayettes or Bon Marché, as it dares to sell souvenirs (gasp!) and merchandise at down-to-earth prices (the horror!). The rooftop observation deck provides one of the best views of the city; take the elevator to the 9th floor and climb the short, spiral staircase. Open M-W and F-Sa 9:30am-7pm, Th 9:30am-10pm. AmEx, MC, V.

Tati, 13, pl. de la République, 3*ème* (☎48 87 72 81). M: République. Also at 106, r. Faubourg du Temple, 11*ème* (☎43 57 92 80), M: Belleville; and 4, bd. de Rochechouart, 18*ème* (☎55 29 50 00), M: Barbès-Rochechouart. A fabulously kitschy, chaotic, crowded, and cheap department store. Generally low-end, but worth rummaging. Get your sales slip made out by one of the clerks (who stand around for just that purpose) before heading to the cashier. All branches open M-Sa 10am-7pm. MC, V.

Galeries Lafayette

CLOTHES

OUTLET STORES

Stock is French for outlet store, with big names for less—often because they have small imperfections or are from last season. Widen your stock portfolio and invest! Many are on r. d'Alésia in the 14*ème* (M: Alésia), including **Cacharel Stock,** no. 114 (☎45 42 53 04; open M-Sa 10am-7pm; AmEx, MC, V); **Stock Chevignon,** no. 122 (☎45 43 40 25; open M-Sa 10am-7pm; MC, V); **Stock Daniel Hechter,** no. 92 (☎47 07 88 44; open M-Sa 10am-7:30pm; MC, V). A large **Stock Kookaï** bustles at 82, r. Réamur, 2*ème*. (☎45 08 93 69. Open M-Sa 10:30am-7:30pm.)

rue Mouffetard

SLIGHTLY USED

SECOND-HAND

La Clef des Marque, 20, pl. du Marché St-Honoré, 1*er* (☎47 03 90 40). M: Pyramides. Two stories of designer merchandise, including lingerie, swimwear, basic cotton tops, and shoes. You just might stumble upon Prada pumps or Gaultier jeans for less than your hotel room. Open M 12:30-7pm, Tu-F 11am-2:30pm and 3:30-7pm, Sa 11am-1pm and 2-7pm. MC, V.

Mouton à Cinq Pattes, 8-10-18, r. St-Placide, 6*ème* (☎45 48 86 26). M: Sèvres-Babylone. Also at 19, r. Grégoire de Tours, 6*ème* (☎43 29 73 56), M: Odéon; 15, r. Vieille de Temple, 4*ème* (☎42 71 86 30), M: St-Paul; and 130 av. Victor Hugo (☎47 55 42 25), M: Victor Hugo. Piles of designer clothing and accessories at low prices. Everything for the stylin' Parisian woman. Victor Hugo open M-Sa 10:30am-7:30pm; all other locations M-Sa 10am-7pm. AmEx, MC, V.

VINTAGE

Antiquités New-Puces, 45, r. Mouffetard, 5*ème* (☎43 36 15 75). M: Monge. Although a bit on the beat tip, New-Puces goes from camp to class, and from *très cher* upstairs (100-300F) to dirt-cheap down (50-150F). Open daily 11am-8pm.

Guerrisold, 9, 21, and 21bis, bd. Barbès, 18*ème* (☎42 55 95 68), M: Barbès-Rochechouart; 17bis bd. Rochechouart, 9*ème* (☎42 80

Champs-Elysées

66 18), M: Cadet; and 22, bd. Poissonière, 9*ème* (☎47 70 35 02), M: Bonne Nouvelle. Popular chain has racks upon racks for men and women. Silk shirts and leather coats, jeans, and more. Most branches open M-Sa 9:30am-7pm.

MID-PRICED

WOMEN'S AND MEN'S

MKDM, 24 r. de Sévigne, 4*ème* (☎42 77 00 74). M: St-Paul. Two young Japanese designers display their latest creations in trendy casual wear. Paris-Tokyo tendencies. T-shirt mania. Innovation doesn't come cheap: creations range from 180-700F. Open daily *1:30-7:30pm*.

Le Shop, 3, r. d'Argout, 2*ème* (☎40 28 95 94). M: Etienne-Marcel. Two levels, 1200 square meters and 24 corners of club wear. Plus, a live DJ. Open M 1-7pm, Tu-Sa 11am-7pm.

Zadig & Voltaire, 15, r. du Jour, 1*er* (☎42 21 88 70). M: Etienne-Marcel. Also at 1, r. des Vieux Colombiers, 6*ème* (☎43 29 18 29), M: Odéon and 12 r. Ste-Croix-de-la-Bretonnerie (☎42 72 15 20), M: St-Paul. Men's and women's designs by DKNY, T. Gillier as well as items from Helmut Lang, etc. Their own label does soft, feminine designs; sweater sets and jerseys. A wonderful selection of handbags. Opening hours change per branch. Main branch open Tu-Sa 10:30am-7:30pm. M 1-7:30pm.

WOMEN'S

Paola Frani, 3bis, r. des Rosiers, 4*ème* (☎42 74 65 66). M: St-Paul. Featuring imaginative designs and a staggering range of materials, these clothes are designed to look stylish and totally original at an art opening, a posh dinner, or a very trendy club. Pricey, but well worth a splurge. Open Su, M 3-7pm, Tu-Sa 11am-7pm.

Plein Sud, 21, r. des Francs-Bourgeois 4*ème* (☎42 72 10 60) M: St Paul. A sweep of delicate, shimmering tops and dead sexy dresses. Adds a spark to any wardrobe. Again, a splurge—but likely to supply favorite clothing that will be classic for years to come. Also at 2 r. Vide Gousset 2*ème* (☎42 36 75 02). Open Tu-Sa 11am-1pm, 2pm-7pm.

MEN'S

Boy'z Bazaar, 5, r. Ste-Croix-de-la-Bretonnerie, 4*ème* (☎42 71 94 00). M: Hotel de Ville. A large selection of all that's elegant and trendy in casual men's wear from Energie to Paul Smith. Caters largely to a gay clientele, and they sell a CD called "Compilation Gay" (179F). Open M-Sa noon-midnight, Su 2pm-7pm.

Loft Design By Paris, 12, r. du Faubourg-St-Honoré, 8*ème* (☎42 65 59 65). M: Concorde or Madeleine. Mostly for men, Loft sells well-tailored men's shirts and casual sweaters and pants. Elegant and minimalist, it boasts refinement and style rather than innovation. Open M-Sa 10am-7pm. AmEx, MC, V. There is also a branch in the Marais, at 12, r. de Sévigné (☎48 87 13 07). Open M-Sa 10am-7pm, Su 11:30am-7pm.

SPECIALTY SHOPS

Colette, 213, r. St-Honoré (☎55 35 33 90; www.colette.tm.fr). M: Concorde. An "anti-department store" whose bare display tables feature an eclectic selection of scuba watches, Japanese vases, and mineral water. Some cutesy items are affordable and make for interesting souvenirs, but the best way to shop minimalist is to buy nothing at all. Open M-Sa 10:30am-7:30pm.

Sephora, 70-72, av. des Champs-Elysées, 8*ème* (☎53 93 22 50). M: Charles-de-Gaulle-Etoile. An overwhelming array of cosmetic products designed to awaken your secret vanity. The rainbow arrangements and the sheer magnitude of perfumes, powders, pungents, and exfoliaters at Sephora could convince even Snow White that she needed Shiseido's help. Prices run the gamut from very reasonable to quite absurd. Open M-Sa 10am-1am, Su 11am-1am. AmEx, V, MC.

Muji, 27, r. St-Sulpice, 6*ème* (☎46 34 01 10). M: Odéon. Made in Japan: this bric-à-brac is affordable, modern, and minimalist. Tons under 30F. Furniture and clothing as well. Open M-Sa 10am-8pm.

Totale Eclipse, 40, r. de la Roquette, 11*ème* (☎48 07 88 04). A small boutique with a wonderful collection of funky jewelry and handbags. Open M-Sa 11am-7:30pm.

Marais Plus, 20, r. des Francs-Bourgeois, 4*ème* (☎48 87 01 40). From novelty books to fluorescent cutlery, this *tchatchkerie* sells high quality fun stuff and is a wonderful place to buy gifts. Open daily 10am-7:30pm.

BOOKS

As a proud bearer of the literary vanguard and a well-read populace, Paris overflows with high-quality bookstores. Large and small, they fall into two categories: the efficient shop, with large windows and black paneling, bearing sleek new editions with nary a place to sit as you browse through them; or the gallery of curiosities—crooked shelves crammed with equal parts moth-fodder and lost treasures—more a lifestyle than a business for the owner and his clients.

The *5ème* and *6ème* are particularly bookish: interesting shops line every large street in the Latin Quarter, not to mention the endless stalls *(bouquinistes)* along the quais of the Seine. Some specialty bookshops serve as community centers for students, intellectuals, and travelers with special concerns. English bookshops like **The Village Voice** have bulletin boards where you can post and read events and housing notices. **Les Mots à la Bouche** offers gay, bi, and lesbian information. **Présence Africaine** can direct you to Caribbean, Maghrébin, and West African resources.

Samaritaine

ENGLISH-LANGUAGE

W.H. Smith, 248, r. de Rivoli, *1er* (☎44 77 88 99). M: Concorde. Large general selection and many scholarly works. Large selection of magazines. Sunday *New York Times* available by Tu. Open M-Sa 9am-7:30pm, Su 1pm-7:30pm. AmEx, MC, V.

Brentano's, 37, av. de l'Opéra, *2ème* (☎42 61 52 50). M: Opéra. An American and French bookstore with an extensive selection of English literature, guidebooks, and greeting cards in English. Paperbacks 40-75F. Open M-Sa 10am-7:30pm. AmEx, MC, V.

Hats

Shakespeare and Co., 37, r. de la Bûcherie, *5ème.* M: St-Michel. Across the Seine from Nôtre-Dame. Run by *bon vivant* George Whitman (alleged great-grandson of Walt), this shop seeks to reproduce the atmosphere of Sylvia Beach's establishment at 8, r. Dupuytren (later at 12, r. de l'Odéon), a gathering place for expatriates in the 20s. Beach published James Joyce's *Ulysses* in 1922. The current location has no link to any Lost Generation notables. It has, however, accumulated a quirky and wide selection of new and used books. Bargain bins outside include French classics in English (30F). Profits support impoverished writers who live and work in this literary cooperative–former residents include beatniks Allen Ginsberg and Lawrence Ferlinghetti. If you're interested in living here and serious about writing, the Sunday evening tea party is a good way to introduce yourself. Live poetry M nights. Open daily noon-midnight.

Tea and Tattered Pages, 24, r. Mayet, *6ème* (☎40 65 94 35). M: Duroc. The place to go for second-hand English-language books. The crazy-quilt, mostly pulp fiction selection is subject to barter and trade. Sell books at 2-5F a paperback and get a 10% discount on your next purchase. Books cost 25-45F. If they don't have what you want, sign the wish list and you'll be called if it comes in. Tea room serves root beer floats, brownies, lunch, and American coffee with free refills. Regular poetry readings and photo exhibits. Open daily 11am-7pm.

The Village Voice, 6, r. Princesse, *6ème* (☎46 33 36 47). M: Mabillon. Takes its name less from the Manhattan paper than from the Parisian neighborhood that was known as "le village de St-Germain-des-Prés." An excellent Anglophone bookstore and the locus of the city's English literary life, featuring 3-4 readings, lectures, and discussions every month (always at 7pm). Paperbacks 48-90F. Many newspapers and magazines. Open daily 10am-8pm. AmEx, MC, V.

Au Printemps

GENERAL FRENCH

Gibert Jeune, 5, pl. St-Michel, 5*ème* (☎56 81 22 22). M: St-Michel. Main branch plus 6 specialized branches clustered around the Fontaine St-Michel. The main location for books in all languages including lots of reduced-price books. Extensive stationery department downstairs; used books bought down here, too. The branch at 27, quai St-Michel (☎43 54 57 32), M: St-Michel, sells university texts. Additional branch at 15bis, bd. St-Denis, 2*ème* (☎55 34 75 75) sells general books and texts; open 10am-7pm. Main branch open M-Sa 9:30am-7:30pm. AmEx, MC, V.

Gibert Joseph, 26-30-32-34, bd. St-Michel, 6*ème* (☎44 41 88 88). M: Odéon or Cluny-Sorbonne. A gigantic *librairie* and music store all rolled into one with both new and used selections. Frequent sidewalk sales with crates of books, notebooks, and old records starting at 10F. Good selection of used dictionaries and guidebooks. Open M-Sa 10am-7:30pm. MC, V.

Librairie Gallimard, 15, bd. Raspail, 7*ème* (☎45 48 24 84). M: Rue du Bac. The main store of this famed publisher of French classics features a huge selection of pricey Gallimard books. Basement is filled with Folio paperbacks. Open M-Sa 10am-7pm. AmEx, MC, V.

FNAC (Fédération Nationale des Achats de Cadres), 109, r. St-Lazare, 9*ème* (☎55 31 20 00). M: St-Lazare. Open M-Sa 10am-7:30pm, Th 10am-9:30pm. See also **Forum des Halles** (1*er*, the largest), **Montparnasse** (6*ème*), and **Etoile** (17*ème*) branches listed under **Music,** p. 146. Large bookstores carrying most subjects with particularly large travel and map selections. MC, V.

MUSIC

Highly taxed in France, CDs are considered luxury goods. In addition to expensive, imported American and British pop, grunge, rock, rap, alternative, R&B, and classical, you'll find great selections of French pop, rap, rock, techno, house, punk, and cabaret as well as huge supplies of classic jazz, acid jazz, jungle, raï, African, Arabic, and fusion. *Disques d'occasion* (used CDs), at 20-60F, are generally no more expensive than in the US and UK and can often be found at flea markets (see below), as well as at a growing number of second-hand music stores.

B.P.M. (Bastille Paris Musique), 1, r. Keller, 11*ème* (☎40 21 02 88). M: Bastille. Catering to your rave needs, this address is a clubhouse, information point, and music store for house and techno fans. From groovy French House to jungle. Record players so you can listen before buying. Check posters and fliers for upcoming parties. Open M-Sa noon-8pm. MC, V.

FNAC (Fédération Nationale des Achats de Cadres). Several branches. **Forum des Halles:** 1-7, r. Porte Lescot, 1*er* (☎40 41 40 00); M: Les Halles. **Montparnasse:** 136, r. des Rennes, 6*ème* (☎49 54 30 00); M: Rennes. **Champs-Elysées:** 74, av. des Champs-Elysées, 8*ème* (☎53 53 64 64); M: Franklin D. Roosevelt. **Italiens:** 24, bd. des Italiens, 9*ème* (☎48 01 02 03); M: Opéra. **Bastille:** 4, pl. de la Bastille, 12*ème* (☎43 42 04 04); M: Bastille. **Etoile:** 26-30, av. des Ternes, 17*ème* (☎44 09 18 00); M: Ternes. Huge selection of tapes, CDs, and stereo equipment. The branch at Les Halles contains a well-stocked shelf of books about music. The Champs-Elysées, Bastille, and Italiens branches have particularly large selections. Box office sells concert and theater tickets. **Montparnasse, Etoile,** and **Forum des Halles** branches open M-Sa 10am-7:30pm. **Italiens** branch open M-Sa 10am-midnight. **Bastille** branch open M-Sa 10am-8pm, W and F until 10pm. **Champs-Elysées** branch open M-Sa 10am-midnight, Su noon-midnight. MC, V.

Rough Trade, 30, r. Charonne, 11*ème* (☎40 21 61 62). M: Bastille. Parisian branch of the British record label that brought you the Smiths, Stiff Little Fingers, Wire, Père Ubu, and countless other pop and punk bands. Techno, hip hop, and house downstairs; rock, pop, noise, and CDs upstairs. They also sell tickets to concerts around town and to all the major European music festivals. Open M-Sa noon-7pm. MC, V.

PUCES DE ST-OUEN

Located in St-Ouen, a town just north of the 18ème. M: Porte de Clignancourt. ***Open*** *Sa-M 7am-7:30pm; many of the official stalls close early, but renegade vendors may open at 5am and stay open until 9pm.*

The granddaddy of all flea markets, the Puces de St-Ouen is an overwhelming smorgasbord of stuff. It opens early and shuts late, and serious hunters should allow themselves the better part of a day in order to cover significant ground, although the market tends to be least crowded before noon. You'll find everything you need (and don't) in the many acres of criss-crossing pedestrian alleys. There is a definite divide in terms of prices and quality: much of the merchandise is either dirt-cheap and low-quality or expensive and antique. This market began during the Middle Ages, when merchants resold the cast-off clothing of aristocrats (crawling with its namesake insects) to peasant-folk, so it's used to such feudal divides.

RENEGADE MARKET. The 10-minute walk along av. de la Porte de Clignancourt, under the highway, and left on r. Jean Henri Fabre to the official market is jammed with tiny **unofficial stalls.** These stalls sell flimsy new clothes, T-shirts, African masks, and teenage jewelry at exorbitant prices. If this renegade bazaar turns you off, continue to the official market where you'll be able to browse leisurely in a much less crowded setting.

OFFICIAL MARKET. Located on r. des Rosiers and r. Jules Vallès, the regular market is officially divided into a number of sub-markets, each specializing in a certain type of item.

From r. Jean Henri Fabre, slip into the **Marché Malik,** a warehouse filled with discount clothing, leather jackets, sneakers, vintage clothing dealers, and a tattoo parlor. Exiting onto r. Jules Vallès, and walking away from the bongo drums and hard-sell banter of r. Fabre, you'll encounter the indoor **Marché Jules Vallès** with its overwhelming collection of old trinkets and antique miscellany. **Marché Paul Bert,** on r. Paul Bert, has more antiques as well as a large collection of furniture. Next door at the more posh **Marché Serpette,** specialized antique art deco furniture stores reign side-by-side with shops dealing in antique firearms. **Marché Biron** on r. des Rosiers will help you plan what to buy for your home when you're rich and famous. **Marché Dauphine** on r. Fabre is home to 300 dealers on two levels and has stalls specializing in leather armchairs, costume dresses, jewlery, and antique kitchenware. **Marché Vernaison,** located between r. des Rosiers and av. Michelet, has more upper-class *tchatchkes*, prints, beads, buttons, and musical instruments.

The **Marché des Rosiers,** r. Paul Bert (lamps, vases, and 20th-century art), and the **Marché Autica,** r. des Rosiers (paintings, furniture), are small, paler shadows of the large markets. The **Marché Malassis** sells Disney and Tintin memorabilia, vintage cameras, perfume bottles, couture, and furniture.

ESSENTIAL
INFORMATION

COMMENT DIT-ON "RIP-OFF"?

First-time flea market visitors should note some important tips. First, there are no five-franc diamond rings here. If you find the Hope Diamond in a pile of schlock jewelry, the vendor planted it there. Second, be prepared to bargain; sellers don't expect to get their starting price. Third, pickpockets love crowded areas, especially the one around the unofficial stalls. Fourth, the Three Card Monte con artists proliferate. Don't be pulled into the game by seeing someone win lots of money: he's part of the con, planted to attract suckers. Finally, if you are a savvy rock-and-roll connoisseur with a cultivated sense of patience, this is the place to find rare records. Record peddlers seem not to know what they have, and if you look long enough, you might just find a priceless LP for next to nothing.

INSIDE

Entertainment

Alors, something groovy, you know?
—Maya Angelou, 1976.

Les temps changent, mec.
—MC Solaar, 1995.

Paris can satisfy all tastes and all desires. When looking for something to do, consult the bibles of Paris entertainment, the weekly bulletins **Pariscope** (3F) and **Officiel des Spectacles** (2F), both on sale at newsstands. Even if you don't understand French, you should be able to decipher the listings of times and locations. Contact **Info-Loisirs,** a recording that keeps tabs on what's on in Paris (English/French, ☎08 36 68 31 12; 2.23F/min).

You don't need to speak fluent French to enjoy the theater scene. Paris's theaters present productions whose music, physical comedy, and experimental abstraction lend themselves to any audience. The comedy-oriented **café-théâtres** and the music-oriented **cabarets** perpetuate the ambiance of 1930s Paris. Paris's ballet and modern dance companies often host performances by visiting companies, including the Kirov Ballet, the Alvin Ailey Dance Company, and the Dance Theater of Harlem. Paris's new **Stade de France** and other athletic venues offer **spectator** and participatory sports galore.

Among Paris's many treasures, music and film top the list. West African music, Caribbean calypso and reggae, Latin American salsa, North African raï, European house, techno, and rap are fused by the heppest of DJ's in the coolest of Paris's **clubs.** Classical concerts are staged in both expensive concert halls and churches, particularly during the summer. Parisians are inveterate film-goers, greedy for film from all over the world. Frequent English-language film series and festivals make Parisian cinema accessible, inventive, challenging, and entertaining.

CIRCUS MAXIMUS

Circus is not just for children. Circus is high art. If you're sick of pretentious Parisian theater, try these cutting-edge establishments for a bit of techno music and a bit of somersaulting: **Zingaro** in the Fort d'Aubervilliers (☎49 87 59 59) is an equestrian circus whose mega-artsy shows are like ballet on horseback; **Espace Chapiteaux,** (☎08 03 07 50 75, 2,23F/min) in La Vilette (see p. 126) holds circuses of all varieties year-round in its giant tent, with tickets ranging from 60-110F, depending upon your age and willingness to put your head in a lion's mouth; **Archaos** (☎06 61 89 65 77) in suburb Neuilly-sur-Seine is pantomime and house music, dealing with modern issues.

THEATER

Thankfully for the non-fluent, Parisian theater is still highly accessible, thanks in part to its dependence on French and international classics, and also thanks to its love of a grand spectacle. Four of France's five **national theaters,** those bastions of traditional French drama, are located in Paris (the fifth is in Strasbourg). Unless you're banking on last-minute rush tickets, make reservations 14 days in advance. Paris's **private theaters,** although less celebrated than their state-run counterparts, often stage outstanding productions. Risky performances sometimes misfire, so check the reviews and entertainment weeklies before investing in a seat. Many theaters do not offer performances on Mondays, and many more close in July and August. *Pariscope* and *l'Officiel des Spectacles* provide listings of current shows, as well as one of the best ways to see theater in Paris: **half-price previews**. For **Ticket Services,** see **Service Directory,** p. 277.

Bouffes du Nord, 37bis, bd. de la Chapelle, 10*ème* (☎46 07 34 50). M: La Chapelle. This experimental theater, headed by the British director Peter Brook, produces cutting-edge performances and occasional productions in English. Closed July and Aug. Box office open M-Sa 11am-6pm. Tickets 70-140F. Wheelchair accessible.

La Comédie Française, 2, r. de Richelieu, 1*er* (☎44 58 15 15; www.comedie-francaise.fr). M: Palais-Royal. Founded by Molière, now the granddaddy of all French theaters. Expect wildly gesticulated slapstick farce; you don't need to speak French to understand the jokes. Performances take place in the 892-seat Salle Richelieu. Expect several plays by Molière in the coming season. Box office open daily 11am-6pm. Tickets 70-190F, under 27 65F (remainders). Rush tickets (30F) available 45min. before show; line up an hour in advance. They also have special package deals, often for students under a certain age, with reduced prices for tickets to three plays or more; call for details. The *comédiens français* also mount plays in the 330-seat **Théâtre du Vieux Colombier,** 21, r. des Vieux Colombiers, 6*ème* (☎44 39 87 00 or 44 39 87 01). M: St-Sulpice. 2000 will feature *The Misanthrope* by Molière and George Feydeau's *Chat en Poche*. Tickets 160F, over 60 110F; student rush tickets 65F sold 45min. before performances, available to students under 27 and anyone under 25.

Odéon Théâtre de l'Europe, 1, pl. Odéon, 6*ème* (☎44 41 36 36; www.theatre-odeon.fr). M: Odéon. Programs in this elegant Neoclassical building range from classics to avant-garde, but the Odéon specializes in foreign plays in their original language. 1042 seats. Also **Petit Odéon,** an affiliate with 82 seats. In 2000-2001, the theatre will present the poetry of Robert Wilson and Lou Reed, *Medea* by Euripides, and *L'Avare* by Molière. Open Sept.-July. Box office open M-Sa 11am-6:30pm. Tickets 30-180F for most shows; student rush tickets 50F, available 90min. before performance. Petit Odéon 70F, students 50F. Call ahead for wheelchair access. MC, V.

Théâtre de la Huchette, 23, r. de la Huchette, 5*ème* (☎43 26 38 99). M: St-Michel. 100-seat theater where Ionesco's *La cantatrice chauve (The Bald Soprano)* and *La leçon (The Lesson)* premiered and continue to play today, 43 years later. A bastion of Left Bank intellectualism, but still a good choice for people with functional high school French. Shows M-Sa. *La cantatrice chauve* starts at 7pm, *La leçon* at 8pm. No one admitted after curtain. Box office open M-Sa 5-7pm. Tickets 100F, students under 25 M-F 80F; both shows 160F, students M-F 120F. Wheelchair accessible.

Théâtre National de Chaillot, pl. du Trocadéro, 16*ème* (☎53 65 30 00). M: Trocadéro. In the Palais de Chaillot. Plays, music, and dance concerts take place in 2 rooms, one with 1000 and the other with 400 seats. 2000-2001 season includes: *Top Dog* by Urs Ween and a Pinter play. Can arrange spiffy translation into English for non-francophones. Call to arrange wheelchair access. Box office open M-Sa 11am-7pm, Su 11am-5pm. Tickets 160F, under 25 and seniors 120F, same-day student rush 80F. MC, V.

Théâtre de la Huchette, 23, r. de la Huchette, 5*ème* (☎43 26 38 99). M: St-Michel. 100-seat theater where Ionesco's *La cantatrice chauve (The Bald Soprano)* and *La leçon (The Lesson)* premiered and continue to play today, 43 years later. A bastion of Left Bank intellectualism, but still a good choice for people with functional high school French. Shows M-Sa. *La cantatrice chauve* starts at 7pm, *La leçon* at 8pm. No one admitted after curtain. Box office open M-Sa 5-7pm. Tickets 100F, students under 25 M-F 80F; both shows 160F, students M-F 120F. Wheelchair accessible.

CABARET

Au Lapin Agile, 22, r. des Saules, 18*ème* (☎46 06 85 87). M: Lamarck-Coulaincourt. Turn right on r. Lamarck, then right again up r. des Saules. Picasso, Verlaine, Renoir, and Apollinaire hung out here during the heyday of Montmartre; now a mainly tourist audience crowds in for comical poems and songs. Originally called the *Cabaret des Assassins,* this *chansonnier* inspired Steve Martin's 1996 hit play *Picasso at the Lapin Agile.* In 1875, when the artist André Gill painted a rabbit on the theater's facade, it came to be known as *le lapin à Gill* (Gill's Rabbit), a name that eventually morphed into *Le lapin agile* (the nimble rabbit). Shows Tu-Su at 9:15pm. Admission and first drink 130F, students 90F. Subsequent drinks 30-45F.

Caveau de la République, 1, bd. St-Martin, 3*ème* (☎42 78 44 45). M: République. A Parisian crowd fills the 482 seats of this 96 year-old venue for political satire. Shows consist of 6 separate comedy and song acts; the sequence is called the *tour de champs* (tour of the field). Good French skills and knowledge of French politics needed to get the gags. Tickets sold up to 6 days in advance, daily 11am-6pm. Shows mid-Sept. to June Tu-Sa 9pm, Su 3:30pm. Admission M-Th 145F, F-Sa 180F, Tu-Th students 85F and over 60 110F. MC, V.

CINEMA

The French love affair with cinema is reflected in the fact that there are probably more films shown in Paris—over 300 a week—than in any other city in the world. You'll find scores of cinemas throughout the city, particularly in the *quartier latin* and on the Champs-Elysées. Many theaters in Paris specialize in programs featuring classic European film, current independent film, Asian classics, American classics, and Hollywood blockbusters. The two big theater chains—**Gaumont** and **UGC**—offer *cartes privilèges*, discounts for five visits or more. In late June, the wonderful two-day **Fête du Cinéma** offers great discounts and interesting films (see **Festivals,** p. 8).

Check *Pariscope* or *l'Officiel des Spectacles* (available at any newsstand, 3F) for weekly film schedules, prices, and reviews. The notation V.O. *(version originale)* after a non-French movie listing means that the film is being shown in its original language with French subtitles; watching an English-language film with French subtitles is a great way to pick up new vocabulary. V.F. *(version française)* means that the film has been dubbed—an increasingly rare phenomenon. Paris's cinemas offer student, senior, and family discounts. On Monday and Wednesday, prices drop about 10F for everyone.

Musée du Louvre, 1*er* (info ☎40 20 51 86; schedules and reservation ☎40 20 52 99). M: Louvre. Art films, films on art, and silent movies. 25-70F, students 15-50F. Open Sept.-June.

Les Trois Luxembourg, 67, r. Monsieur-le-Prince, 6*ème* (☎46 33 97 77). M: Odéon. High-quality independent, classic, and foreign films, all in V.O. Purchase tickets early. 40F, students 30F.

Action Christine, 4, r. Christine, *6ème* (☎43 29 11 30). M: Odéon. Off r. Dauphine. Eclectic, international selection of art and cult films from the 40s and 50s. Always V.O. 40F, early show (usually 6 or 7pm) 25F; M and students 30F. For 180F, buy a 1-year pass for 6 movies.

L'Arlequin, 76, r. de Rennes, *6ème* (☎45 44 28 80). M: St-Sulpice. A revival cinema with occasional visits from European directors and first-run previews. Some films V.O., others dubbed. Buy tickets in advance. 46F, students M-F 36F, W all tickets 36F. Su matinée 30F. MC, V.

Cinémathèque Française, pl. du Trocadéro, *16ème* (☎45 53 21 86). M: Trocadéro. At the Musée du Cinéma in the Palais de Chaillot; enter through the Jardins du Trocadéro. Also 18, r. du Faubourg-du-Temple, *11ème*. M: République. Recording (☎47 04 24 24) lists all shows. A must for film buffs. 2-3 classics, near-classics, or soon-to-be classics per day. Foreign films usually in V.O. Buy tickets 15-20 min. early. Open W-Su 5-9:45pm. 28F, students 17F.

Dôme IMAX, pl. de la Défense (☎08 36 67 06 06; 2.23F/min.). M: Grande Arche de la Défense. The big dome to the right with your back to the Grand Arche. IMAX cinema. Documentaries in French, but who listens to an IMAX anyway? 55F; students, seniors, and under 16 40F. For 2 shows 75F; students, seniors, and under 16 65F.

MUSIC, OPERA, AND DANCE

Acclaimed foreign and provincial dance companies visit Paris frequently; watch for posters and read *Pariscope*. Connoisseurs will find the thick and indexed *Programme des Festivals* (free at tourist offices) an indispensable guide to seasonal music, dance series, and celebrations. The monthly publication *Paris Selection*, also free at tourist offices, keeps track of concerts in churches and museums, many of which are free or reasonably priced. Beware of rock-bottom prices to performances, as seats are often obstructed (like at **Opéra Garnier**) or the venue's acoustics bad (as at **Opéra Bastille**). For seasonal events, consult **Festivals,** p. 6.

FREE CONCERTS. Free concerts are often held in churches and parks, especially during summer festivals. These concerts are extremely popular, so get there early. The **American Church in Paris,** 65, quai d'Orsay, *7ème* (☎40 62 05 00; M: Invalides or Alma Marceau), sponsors free concerts (Sept.-June Su at 6pm). **Eglise St-Merri,** 78, r. St-Martin, *4ème* (M: Hôtel-de-Ville), is also known for its free concerts (Sept.-July Sa at 9pm and Su at 4pm); contact Accueil Musical St-Merri, 76, r. de la Verrerie, *4ème* (☎42 71 40 75 or 42 71 93 93; M: Châtelet). Concerts take place W-Su in the **Jardin du Luxembourg** band shell, *6ème* (☎42 34 20 23); show up early for a seat or prepare to stand. Infrequent concerts in the **Musée d'Orsay,** 1, r. Bellechasse, *7ème* (☎40 49 49 66; M: Solférino), are occasionally free.

VENUES AND COMPANIES

Cité de la Musique, La Villette, *19ème* (☎44 84 44 84; www.cite-musique.fr). M: Porte-de-Pantin. Hosts everything from lute concerts to American gospel year-round in its enormous *salle des concerts* and smaller *amphithéâtre*. Tickets 65-200F; *carnet* of 4 tickets for 160F. Shows at 8pm; box office opens 30min. prior.

L'Etoile du Nord, 16, r. Georgette Agutte, *18ème* (☎42 26 47 47; fax 42 26 63 98). M: Guy-Môquet. An independent dance space with impressive modern choreographers. Tickets 50-120F.

Institut de Recherche et Coordination Acoustique/Musique (IRCAM), Centre Pompidou, 1, pl. Igor-Stravinsky, *4ème* (☎44 78 47 44; http://mediatheque.ircam.fr). M: Rambuteau. Often holds concerts. Contemporary works sometimes accompanied by film or theater. Stop by the office at the Stravinsky fountain or at the Centre Pompidou for schedules. There are 2 computers in the lobby that allow you to "visit" IRCAM and play musical games. 20F per afternoon; 300F per year, students 150F.

Opéra de la Bastille, pl. de la Bastille, *11ème* (☎08 36 69 78 68; fax 44 73 13 74; www.opera-de-paris.fr). M: Bastille. Opera and ballet with a modern spin. Because of acoustical problems, it's not the place to go all-out for front row seats. Subtitles in French. Tickets 60-670F. Call, write, or stop by for a free brochure of the season's events. Tickets can be purchased by Internet, mail, fax, phone (M-Sa 9am-7pm), or in person (M-Sa 11am-6pm). Rush tickets for students under 25 and anyone over 65 15min. before show; opera 120F, ballets 70F, and concerts 50F. Wheelchair accessible, but call ahead. MC, V.

Opéra Comique, 14, r. Favart, *2ème* (☎42 44 45 46; fax 49 26 05 93). M: Richelieu-Drouot. Operas on a lighter scale—from Rossini to Offenbach. Box office open M-Sa 11am-7pm. Tickets 50-550F. Student rush tickets available 15min. before show starts; 50F.

Opéra Garnier, pl. de l'Opéra, *9ème* (☎08 36 69 78 68; fax 44 73 13 74; www.opera-de-paris.fr). M: Opéra. Hosts Ballet de l'Opéra de Paris, symphonies, and chamber music. Tickets available 2 weeks before. Box office open M-Sa 11am-6pm. Ballet tickets 30-420F; opera tickets up to 670F. Last-minute, discount tickets available 1hr. before showtime. MC, V.

Orchestre de Paris, 252, r. du Faubourg St-Honoré, *8ème* (☎45 61 65 60; www.orchestredeparis.com). M: Ternes. Internationally renowned orchestra. Season runs Oct.-June; call or stop by for concert calendar. 2-4 concerts per week W-Sa. Box office open M-Sa 11am-6pm. Shows at 8pm. Tickets 60-320F. Student rush tickets 30min. before; 50F. MC, V.

Théâtre des Champs-Elysées, 15, av. Montaigne, *8ème* (☎49 52 50 50). M: Alma Marceau. Top international dance companies and orchestras, from world music to chamber music, as well as opera. Season runs Sept.-June. Buy tickets 3 weeks in advance. Reserve by phone M-F 10am-noon and 2-6pm; box office open M-Sa 1-7pm. Tickets 40-750F.

Théâtre Musical de Paris, pl. du Châtelet, *1er* (☎40 28 28 40). M: Châtelet. A superb 2300-seat theater featuring orchestras, ballet companies, opera, and dance. Magnificent acoustics. Season Oct.-June. Tickets 60-775F. Last-minute discount tickets 15min. before showtime (opera 110F, all others 60F). AmEx, MC, V.

Théâtre de la Ville, 2, pl. du Châtelet, *4ème* (☎42 74 22 77). M: Châtelet. Primarily known for its innovative theatrical and dance productions, this venue also offers a selection of classical and world music concerts. Shows 95-190F, students 70-80F. Call for program and discounts. Tickets sold by phone M-Sa 11am-7pm; box office open M 11am-7pm, Tu-Sa 11am-8pm. AmEx, MC, V.

GUIGNOLS

Grand guignol is a traditional Parisian marionette theater featuring the *guignol*, its classic stock character. It's like Punch and Judy, but without the domestic violence. Although the puppets speak French, they're very urbane, and you'll have no trouble understanding the slapstick, child-geared humor. Nearly all parks, including Jardin du Luxembourg (see Sights, p. 77) have *guignols*; check *Pariscope* for more info.

Montmartre

Au Lapin Agile

Opéra

PATISSERIES MAISON
Tarte aux fruits 28F
Crème brûlée 34F
Tarte aux Pommes 24F

INSIDE

Food & Drink

You got very hungry when you did not eat enough in Paris because all the bakery shops had such good things in the windows, and people ate outside at tables on the sidewalks so that you saw and smelled the food.
—Ernest Hemingway, *A Moveable Feast,* 1964

FRENCH CUISINE

A BRIEF HISTORY

Italian monarch Catherine de Medici brought the tradition of **haute cuisine** from Florence, along with her cooks, who taught the French to appreciate the finer aspects of sauces and seasonings. Great 19th-century chefs made fine food an essential art of civilized life and much of their wisdom on sauces and glazes is collected in the voluminous *Larousse Gastronomique*, a standard reference for French chefs today. The style made famous in the US by Julia Child is **cuisine bourgeoise,** quality home-cooking. A glance through her *Mastering the Art of French Cooking I & II* will give you ideas for dishes to try in France. Both *haute cuisine* and *cuisine bourgeoise* rely heavily on the **cuisine de province** (also called *cuisine campagnarde*), since they are basically sophisticated versions of regional cuisine. Trendy **nouvelle cuisine**—tiny portions of delicately cooked, artfully arranged ingredients with light sauces—became popular in the 1970s. Immigrant communities have shaken up the traditionally spiceless French culinary scene. In addition to ubiquitous Greek *gyro* sandwiches, there are a number of outstanding Moroccan, Algerian, Tunisian, Senegalese, Ivory Coast, and Caribbean restaurants in Paris. Many bistros have menus with foreign dishes or visiting chefs. North African couscous is the most assimilated foreign dish. Chinese, Thai, Vietnamese, Cam-

YOUR DAILY BREAD

Among the 1300 *boulangeries* in Paris, how to separate the wheat from the chaff? Start with the definition. According to the craft, a baguette must weigh between 250 and 300 grams, measuring about 70cm in length and 6cm in diameter. The crust must be smooth and golden, ready to crackle under moderate finger-pressure (ask for it *"bien cuit"*). The underside, or "sole," should never be charred; beware also a honeycomb imprint, indicating accelerated cooking in a rotating oven—the taste will be cut short as well. The inside should be light and soft, subtly doughy and salty. The true connoisseur eats at least one whole baguette per day (twice the national average) for enough practice to judge for herself.

bodian, Korean, Tibetan, Japanese, Indian, and Pakistani restaurants, especially in the "Chinatowns" of the *9ème*, *13ème*, and *19ème*, offer many affordable and delicious vegetarian options.

MEALTIMES

BREAKFAST. *Le petit déjeuner* is usually light, consisting of bread, croissants, or *brioches* (buttery breads) with jam and butter, plus an espresso with hot milk *(café au lait)* or a hot chocolate (*le chocolat*, often served in a bowl, or *bol*).

LUNCH. *Le déjeuner*, the largest meal of the day, is served between noon and 2:30pm, although some cafés and restaurants in tourist areas stay open throughout the day. Restaurants are most crowded from 1-2pm when everyone takes their lunch break. During lunch, some shops, businesses, and government offices close; linger over a two-hour lunch a few times and you'll be hooked too.

DINNER. *Le dîner* begins quite late. Most restaurants open at 7pm, with 8:30pm the typical time to dine; revelers sometimes extend their meals into the early morning. A complete French dinner includes an *apéritif*, an *entrée* (appetizer), *plat* (main course), salad, cheese, dessert, fruit, coffee, and a *digestif* (after-dinner drink, typically a cognac or other local brandy). The French usually take wine with their restaurant meals. You might hear the story of the famous director who dared to order a Coke with his 1500F meal; he was promptly kicked out of the restaurant. Of him it was said, *"Il manque de savoir vivre"*—he doesn't know how to live.

ETIQUETTE

HOW TO ORDER. Always greet your server by looking him or her attentively in the face and saying, *"Bonjour, Monsieur,"* or *"Bonjour, Mademoiselle."* In the evening, brush off your smartest *"Bon soir."* Failure to employ these simple phrases (even if you plan to order in English) will be rewarded with cool treatment and melodramatic, reprimanding glares. In Paris, the position of waiter or waitress is not a temporary job; it's a career. Your server requires you to acknowledge her services with a gracious *"s'il vous plaît"* or *"merci beaucoup."* Also, do not ask for any unfinished food to go, and don't ask to split a dish with your dining partner. Unless, of course, you enjoy the drama. And to demand the bill (again, with a deep current of *politesse* in your voice) say, *"L'addition, s'il vous plaît."*

TIPPING. You will usually see the words *service compris* (service included) on a menu, which means the tip is automatically added to the check. Otherwise you should tip 15-20%. If you are particularly pleased with the service, feel free to leave a small cash tip in addition to what is normally expected (anywhere from a few francs to 5% of the check), but don't feel obligated.

THE MENU

Most restaurants offer *un menu à prix fixe* (fixed-price meal) that costs less than ordering *à la carte* (when you pick individual items out). Importantly, lunch *menus* are often cheaper than dinner menus—if there is a pricier restaurant that you'd particularly like to try, consider going for lunch. A *menu* may include an *entree* (appetizer), a main course *(plat)*, cheese *(fromage)*, and dessert. Some also include wine or coffee. For lighter fare, try a *brasserie*, which has a fuller menu than a café but is more casual than a restaurant.

DRINKS

Mineral **water** is everywhere; order sparkling water (*eau pétillante* or *gazeuse*) or flat mineral water *(eau plate)*. Ice cubes *(glaçons)* are rare. To order a pitcher of tap water, ask for *une carafe d'eau fraîche*. There are five major *apéritifs* (pre-meal drinks): *kir*, a blend of white wine with *cassis*, black currant liqueur (*kir royale* substitutes champagne for the wine); *pastis*, a licorice liqueur; *suze*, which is fermented *gentiane*, a sweet-smelling mountain flower that yields a wickedly bitter brew; *picon-bière*, beer mixed with a sweet liqueur; and martinis.) Finish the meal with **espresso** *(un café)*, which comes in lethal little cups with blocks of sugar. When *boisson compris* is written on the menu, you are entitled to a free drink (usually wine) with the meal.

WINE

In France, wine is not a luxury; it's an everyday necessity. During WWI, French infantry pinned down by heavy shell-fire subsisted on the barest of rations: bread and wine. When France sent its first citizen into orbit on a Soviet space craft, he some *vin* with him. Obviously, wine is an institution in France; it is served at almost every occasion.

WINE-PRODUCING REGIONS. The **Loire Valley** produces a number of whites, with the major vineyards at Angers, Chinon, Saumur, Anjou, Tours, and Sancerre. **Cognac,** farther south on the Atlantic coast, is famous for the double-distilled spirit of the same name. Centered on the Dordogne and Garonne Rivers, the classic **Bordeaux** region produces red and white Pomerol, Graves, and sweet Sauternes. *Armagnac*, similar to cognac, comes from **Gascony,** while Jurançon wines come from vineyards higher up the slopes of the **Pyrénées.** Southern wines include those of **Languedoc and Roussillon** on the coast and **Limoux and Gaillac** inland. The vineyards of **Provence** on the coast near Toulon are recognized for their rosés. The **Côtes du Rhône** from Valence to Lyon in the Rhône Valley are home to some of the most celebrated wines of France, including Beaujolais. **Burgundy** is especially famous for its reds, from the wines of Chablis and the Côte d'Or in the north to the Mâconnais in the south. **Alsatian** whites tend to be

MENU READER

l'agneau (m)	lamb
l'ail (m)	garlic
l'andouillette (f)	tripe sausage
l'apéritif (m)	pre-dinner drink
l'asperge (f)	asparagus
l'assiette (f)	plate
l'aubergine (f)	eggplant
la bavette	flank
le beurre	butter
bien cuit	well done
la bière	beer
le bifteck	steak
le blanc de volaille	chicken breast
bleu/saignant	rare
le boeuf	beef
la boisson	drink
la bouillebaisse	fish soup of Provence
la brioche	pastry-like bread
la brochette	shish-ka-bab
le canard	duck
la carafe d'eau	pitcher of tap water
le cassoulet	meat and bean stew
les cervelles	brain
le champignon	mushroom
chaud	hot
la chèvre	goat cheese
choix	choice
la choucroute	sauerkraut
le chou-fleur	cauliflower
la ciboulette	chive
le citron	lemon
le citron vert	lime
le civet	stew
la compote	stewed fruit
le confit	preserve
le confit de canard	duck cooked and preserved in its own fat
coq au vin	rooster stewed in wine
la côte	rib or chop
la courgette	zucchini/courgette
la crème brulée	custard dessert with carmelized sugar
la crème Chantilly	whipped cream
la crème fraîche	fresh heavy cream
la crêpe	thin pancake
les crêpes Suzette (f)	warm dessert of crêpe flamed in orange liqueur
la crevette	shrimp
la croque-madame	*croque-monsieur* with fried egg
la croque-monsieur	toasted ham and cheese sandwich
les crudités (f)	raw vegetables

continued on p. 161

spicier and more pungent. Many areas produce sparkling wines, but the only one that can legally be called "Champagne" is distilled in the **Champagne** area surrounding Reims.

SELECTING WINE. There is a specific wine for every meal and occasion, a pairing dictated by draconian rules. Don't worry too much about these rules; go with your own taste preferences. **White wines** tend to be lighter, drier, and fruitier. They go with fish, and many of the white dessert wines, like Barsac, Sauternes, or Coteaux du Layon are great with fruit. **Red wines** tend to be heavier, more fragrant, and considerably older. Red meat and red wine is a fine combination. When confused about which wine to choose, simply ask. Most waiters in good restaurants and employees in wine shops will be more than happy to recommend their favorites to you. Or, fall back on the *vin de maison* (house wine) of the restaurant, but beware: they can be bitter and grainy. Wine bars will let you sample expensive wines by the glass (see **Wine Bars,** p. 177).

RESTAURANTS AND CAFÉS BY TYPE

Restaurants By Type provides a list of restaurants followed by an arrondissement label. Turn to **Restaurants By Location,** which groups restaurants by arrondissement, for the full write-up. The arrondissement listings rank restaurants in order of value: the top entry may not be the cheapest, but it will be the best in its price range and area.

ALL-YOU-CAN-EAT

Restaurant Natacha	16*ème*
Lao-Thai	19*ème*

AMERICAN

Coffee Parisien	6*ème*
Haynes Bar	9*ème*

BASQUE

Le Caveau de Palais (p. 160)	Île de la Cité
Chez Gladines	13*ème*

BISTRO

Les Fous de l'Isle	Île St-Louis
Les Noces de Jeanette (p. 162)	2*ème*
Le Petit Bofinger	4*ème*
Le Divin	4*ème*
Le Temps des Cérises	4*ème*
Restaurant Perraudin	5*ème*
Au Pied de Fouet	7*ème*
Restaurant du Bourgogne	10*ème*
Au Trou Normand	11*ème*
Chez Paul	11*ème*
Le Bistrot du Peintre	11*ème*
Le Square Trousseau	12*ème*
La Route du Château	14*ème*
Le Café du Commerce	15*ème*
Le Zéphyr	20*ème*

BRUNCH

Le Fumoir (p. 162)	1*er*
Le Dénicheur	2*ème*
Le Loup Blanc	2*ème*
En Attendant Pablo	3*ème*
L'Apparemment Café	3*ème*
Les Fous de l'Isle	Ile St-Louis
Amnésia Café	4*ème*
Café Beaubourg	4*ème*
Le Loir dans la Théière	4*ème*
Les Enfants Gâtés	4*ème*

BRUNCH

Le Troisième Bureau	11*ème*
James Joyce Pub	17*ème*
L'Endroit	17*ème*

CAFÉS

See below for full listings.

CAMBODIAN, THAI & VIETNAMESE

Le Lotus Blanc	7*ème*
Indochine	13*ème*
La Lune	13*ème*
Lao Thai	13*ème*
Wassana	18*ème*
Lao Thai	19*ème*

CARIBBEAN

Babylone Bis	2*ème*
Le Rocher du Diamant	12*ème*

CORSICAN

Sampieru Corsu	15*ème*

CREOLE

Papou Lounge (p. 161)	1*er*
Babylone Bis	2*ème*
La Théière dans Les Nuages	4*ème*
Chez Lucie	7*ème*

CRÊPERIE

La Crêpe Rit du Clown	6*ème*
Crêperie Saint Germain	6*ème*
Crêperie de Josselin	14*ème*
Ty Breiz	15*ème*

EASTERN EUROPEAN

Chez Marianne	4*ème*
Un Saumon à Paris	11*ème*

FRENCH

Au Petit Fer à Cheval (p. 163)	4*ème*
Café de l'Epoque	1*er*

FRENCH, CONT.

Le Dénicheur (p. 162)	2ème
En Attendant Pablo (p. 163)	3ème
Le Hangar (p. 163)	3ème
Jules (p. 161)	1er
Le Loup Blanc (p. 162)	2ème
Le Réconfort (p. 163)	3ème
Taxi Jaune (p. 163)	3ème
Restaurant Chez Max	1er
Le Rouge et Blanc (p. 160)	Île de la Cité
Au Gamin de Paris	4ème
L'Excuse	4ème
Le Grizzli	4ème
Le Tapis Franc	4ème
Le Vieux Comptoir	4ème
Au Bistrot de la Sorbonne	5ème
Café Le Volcan	5ème
L'Apostrophe	5ème
Le Truffière	5ème
Restaurant Perraudin	5ème
La Cambuse	6ème
Le Machon d'Henri	6ème
Le Petit Vatel	6ème
La Varangue	7ème
Le Club des Poètes	7ème
La Menu de Margot	8ème
Occitanie	11ème
Chez Paul	11ème
Pause Café	11ème
L'Ebauchoir	12ème
Le Temps des Cérises	13ème
Café du Commerce	13ème
Au Rendez-Vous Des Camionneurs	14ème
Le Colvert	14ème
Le Jeroboam	14ème
Les Petites Sorcières	14ème
L'Armoise	15ème
Restaurant Les Listine	15ème
Chez Ginette	18ème
Refuge des Fondues	18ème
Chez Claude et Claudine	18ème
Rendez-Vous des Chauffeurs	18ème
Le Baratin	20ème

FRIGHTENING CLOWN THEME

La Crêpe Rit du Clown	6ème
Le Clown Bar	11ème

GREEK

Sans Frontières	6ème
Le Colvert	14ème
Chez François	15ème
Mozlef	15ème

INDIAN

Le Réconfort	3ème
Kamala Inde	6ème
Nirvana	8ème
Sarangiu Anarkali	9ème
La Ville de Jagannath	11ème

IRISH

The James Joyce Pub	17ème

ITALIAN

Il Delfino (p. 161)	Île de la Cité
Signorelli (p. 161)	1er
Pizza Sicilia	1e
La Castafiore	Ile St-Louis
Le Jardin des Pâtes	5ème
Pizzéria King Salomon	9ème
Piccola Italia	15ème

JAPANESE

Japanese Barbecue (p. 162)	2ème

KOSHER

l'As du Falafel	4ème
Café des Psaumes	4ème
Pizzéria King Salomon	9ème

MALAYSIAN

Chez Foong	15ème
Mexi and Co.	5ème
Ay, Caramba!	19ème

MEXICAN AND TEX-MEX

Mexi and Co.	5ème
Ay, Caramba!	19ème

MEDITERRANEAN

Café Med	Ile St-Louis

MIDDLE EASTERN

Chez Omar	3ème
Le Réconfort	3ème
Chez Marianne	4ème
l'As du Falafel	4ème
Café des Psaumes	4ème
Sans Frontières	6ème
Byblos Café	16ème

NORTH AFRICAN

Café Moderne	11ème
Le Souk	11ème
P'tit Cahoua	13ème
L'Atlantide	18ème
Café Flèche d'Or	20ème

OPEN LATE (MIDNIGHT OR LATER)

Papou Lounge	1er
L'Epi d'Or	1er
Le Dénicheur	2ème
Babylone Bis	2ème
Le Hangar	3ème
l'As du Falafel	4ème
Café des Psaumes	4ème
Chez Marianne	4ème
L'Apostrophe	5ème
Crêperie Saint Germain	6ème
Le Club des Poètes	7ème
Haynes Bar	9ème
Chez Paul	11ème
Chez Gladines	13ème
Le Samson	13ème
N'Zadette-M'foua	14ème
Casa Tina	16ème
The James Joyce Pub	17ème

OUTDOOR DINING

Le Hangar	3ème
Chez Marienne	4ème
Le Grizzli	4ème
Le Bistrot du Peintre	11ème
Le Patio Provençal	17ème

PERUVIAN

Restaurant Pachamama	3ème

PROVENÇALE

Le Divin	4ème
Grannie	7ème
Occitanie	11ème
Au Produits du Sud-Ouest	11ème
Restaurant Les Listines	15ème
Le Patio Provençal	17ème

QUÉBECOIS

Equinox	4ème

RUN BY A GURU

La Victoire Suprême du Coeur (p. 161)	1er
Chez Papa	14ème

SANDWICH SHOPS

Così	6ème
Guen maï	6ème
Antoine's: Les Sandwichs des 5 Continents	8ème
Vitamine	8ème
Barry's	8ème
Deli's Café	9ème
Le 25ème Image	10ème

SPANISH

La Casita Tapas	1er
Casa Tina	16ème

TIBETAN

Le Singe d'Eau	8ème

TRENDY INTELLIGENTSIA

Chez Omar (p. 162)	3ème
Le Fumoir (p. 162)	1er
L'Apparemment Café	3ème
Les Enfants Gâtés	4ème
Café de Flore	6ème
Le Sélect	6ème
Café de l'Industrie	11ème
Chez Paul	11ème
Le Troisième Bureau	11ème
La Folie en Tête	13ème

TURKISH

Le Cheval de Troie	12ème
Aux Îles des Princes	17ème

VEGETARIAN

La Victoire Suprême du Coeur	1er
Aquarius	4ème
Piccolo Teatro	4ème
Le Grenier de Notre Dame	5ème
Le Jardin des Pâtes	5ème
Guen maï	6ème
Le Kitch	11ème
Phinéas	14ème
Aquarius Café	14ème
Au Grain de Folie	18ème
Rayons de Santé	18ème

WEST AND EAST AFRICAN

Babylone Bis (p. 162)	2ème
Paris-Dakar	10ème
À la Banane Ivoirienne	11ème
N'Zadette-M'foua	14ème
Le Dogon	10ème

RESTAURANTS AND CAFÉS BY LOCATION

Do not approach French dining with the assumption that chic equals *cher.* Recent economic hard times have led to the return of the *bistro*, a more informal, less expensive restaurant. Even more casual are *brasseries;* often crowded and action-packed, *brasseries* are best for large groups and high spirits. The least expensive option is usually a *crêperie*, a restaurant specializing in the thin Breton pancakes filled with meats, cheeses, chocolates, fruits, and condiments. Surprisingly, you can often eat at a *crêperie* for the price of a fast-food chain. A number of North African restaurants also serve affordable couscous dishes. At *nouveau bistros*, French, Mediterranean, Asian, and Spanish flavors converge in a setting that is usually modern and artsy.

ÎLE DE LA CITÉ

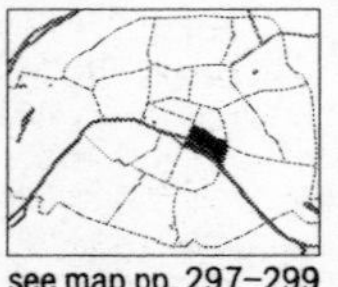
see map pp. 297–299

Le Caveau de Palais, 19, pl. Dauphine (☎43 26 04 28). M: Cité. Le Caveau is a chic, intimate restaurant serving traditional French food from an old-style brick oven. Two prix fixe menus (140F and 220F) include appetizer, entree, and desert. The proprietor is proud of his Basque specialties, including the *côte du boeuf* (side of beef) with mustard sauce and *escargot* (snails) with pesto and garlic. Fish lovers should not miss the grilled monkfish. Reservations encouraged.

Le Rouge et Blanc, 26, pl. Dauphine (☎43 29 52 34). M: Cité. This simple, provençale bar and bistro is the creation of proprietor Rigis Fillet, a friendly young man who is proud of his southern roots and treats his customers like old friends. There are two prix fixe menus (98 or 150F). On sunny days, tables are set out along the sidewalk. Open M-Sa 11am-3pm and 7pm-10:30pm. Closed when it rains.

Il Delfino, 74, quai d'Orfèvres (☎43 54 16 71). M: Cité. A simple pizzeria on the corner of Place Dauphine; offers an affordable alternative to the traditional French restaurants of the area. Pizza and pasta dishes are 39-49F, and fish dishes 69-139F.

FIRST ARRONDISSEMENT

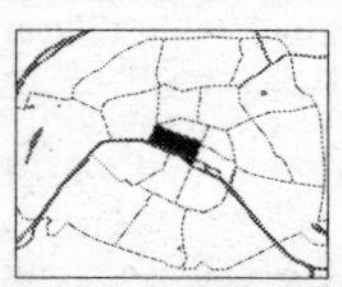

see map pp. 294–296

The arcades overlooking the Louvre along **r. de Rivoli** are filled with the chic and expensive, but tea or *chocolat chaud* at a *salon de thé* (see p. 177) are affordable. **Les Halles** features louder eateries, everything from fast-food to four-course Italian feasts. Diverse lunch and diner options run along **r. Jean-Jacques Rousseau.**

Jules, 62, r. Jean-Jacques Rousseau (☎ 40 28 99 04). M: Les Halles. Walk toward the church St-Eustache, then take a right onto r. Coquillère and a right on r. J.-J. Rousseau. Jules is the name of Chef/owner Eric Teyant's daughter, and if dad cooks as well at home, she's a very lucky little girl. Subtle blend of modern and traditional French cooking; selections change by season. 4-course menu 120F; includes terrific cheese course. Open M-F noon-2:30pm and 7-10:30pm.

Papou Lounge, 74 r. J.-J. Rousseau (☎44 76 00 03). M: Les Halles. Walk toward the church St-Eustache, then take a right onto r. Coquillère, then a right on r. J.-J. Rousseau. With house music, black-and-white tile floors, and photographs of tribal warriors, the Papou is a cross between a Tahitian lounge and a French café. Good for a change of pace and cheap lunch. Salads (50F) appear on the menu next to substantial beef *brochette* with tomatoes, rice, and green beans (70F). Daily special 55F. Beer 16-20F. Open daily 10am-2am with nonstop food service. MC, V.

La Victoire Suprême du Coeur, 41, r. des Bourdonnais (☎40 41 93 95). M: Châtelet. Follow traffic on r. des Halles then turn left on r. des Bourdonnais. Run by the devotees of guru Sri Chinmoy who have both body and soul in mind when creating dishes like *gratinée aux champignons* (mushrooms and green beans in cheese sauce). Never mind that the photos of their Yul Brynner-esque guru up to his elbows in dough are a little weird. It's vegetarian, and very tasty. All-day 3-course *formule* 89F. Entrees 47-67F. Open M-F noon-2:30pm and 6:30-10pm, Sa noon-10pm.

Signorelli, 35, r. St-Honoré (☎40 13 91 41). M: Les Halles. From Les Halles, head down r. St-Honoré toward the Louvre. Takes its name from copied paintings of Luca Signorelli, Michelangelo's master, that hang on its walls. Daily *prix fixe menu* 78F. Pastas include homemade tortellini with prosciutto (69-82F). Desserts like chocolate fondue with orange-infused cream (51F). Open M-F noon-2:30pm and 7-10:30pm, Su 7-10:30pm. AmEx, MC, V.

MENU READER, CONT.

eau de robinet	tap water
l'échalote (f)	shallot
l'entrecôte (m)	chop (cut of meat)
l'escalope (f)	thin slice of meat
l'escargot (m)	snail
farci	stuffed
le faux-filet	sirloin steak
le feuilleté	puff pastry
le flan	custard
le foie gras d'oie/ de canard	liver of fattened goose/duck
forestière	with mushrooms
frais	fresh
la fraise	strawberry
la framboise	raspberry
les frites	French fries
le fromage	cheese
le gâteau	cake
le gésier	gizzard
le gibier	game
la glace	ice cream
le granité	icy sorbet
la grenouille	frog (legs)
l'haricot vert (m)	green bean
l'huitre (f)	oyster
le jambon	ham
le kir	white wine and cassis
le lait	milk
le lapin	rabbit
le légume	vegetable
le légume	vegetable
le magret de canard	duck breast
maison	home-made
le marron	chestnut
le miel	honey
la moule	mussel
la moutarde	mustard
nature	plain
les noix (f)	nuts
l'oeuf	egg
l'oie	goose
l'oignon	onion
le pain	bread
les pâtes (f)	pasta
la pâtisserie	pastry, pastry shop
le plat	main course
le pétoncle	scallop
poêlé	pan-fried
à point	medium
le poisson	fish
le poivre	pepper
la pomme	apple
la pomme/la pomme de terre	potato
le potage	soup
le poulet	chicken

continued on p. 163

CAFÉS

Le Fumoir, 6, r. de l'Admiral Coligny (☎42 92 05 05). M: Louvre. On r. du Louvre, cross r. de Rivoli and r. du Louvre will become r. l'Admiral Coligny. Decidedly untouristy types drink their chosen beverage in deep green leather sofas. Part bar, part tea house in feel, Le Fumoir serves the **best brunch in Paris,** 120F; coffee, 15F. Open daily 11am-2am. AmEx, MC, V.

Café de L'Epoque, 2, r. du Bouli (☎42 33 40 70). M: Louvre Rivoli. Walk towards the Louvre on r. de Rivoli, go right on r. de Marengo, cross r. Saint-Honore and bear left on r. Croix des Petits Champs. The café is on the right. Fast service, good food, and traditional French atmosphere. Main courses 40-50F. Open daily Apr.-Nov. 7am-11pm; Dec.-Mar. 7am-9pm.

SECOND ARRONDISSEMENT

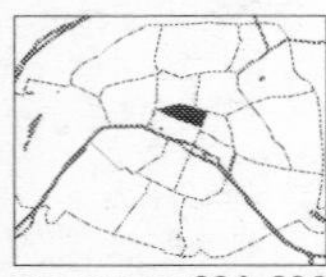
see map pp. 294–296

The 2*ème* provides inexpensive meals. **R. Montorgueil** is lined with excellent bakeries, fruit stands, and specialty stores (see **Food Markets,** p. 178). Side streets like **r. Marie Stuart** and **r. Mandar** hide worthwhile dining options. The **Passage des Panoramas** and **Passage des Italiens** (see **Passageways,** p. 49) showcase fast, cheap food.

Les Noces de Jeannette, 14, r. Favart, and 9, r. d'Amboise (☎42 96 36 89). M: Richelieu Drouot. Exit onto bd. des Italiens, turn left, and go left onto r. Favart. Jeanette's elegance and wonderfully mixed clientele will impress your date. *Menu du Bistro* (162F) includes large salad *entrées;* roasted fish, duck, and grilled meat *plats;* and desserts to make you faint with delight. Free kir with meal. Reservations recommended. Open daily noon-1:30pm and 7pm-9:30pm.

Le Dénicheur, 4, r. Tiquetonne (☎42 21 31 01). M: Etienne-Marcel. Walk against traffic on r. de Turbigo and go left on r. Tiquetonne. Diner turned disco/junkyard café, filled with lawn gnomes and an affable crowd. 2-course *menu* 50-55F; 3-course *menu* 70F; dinner *menu* 98F. Omelettes, sandwiches, and quiches 43F. Su brunch 85F. Open daily noon-3:30pm, 7:30pm-1am.

Le Loup Blanc, 42, r. Tiquetonne (☎40 13 08 35). M: Etienne-Marcel. Walk against traffic on r. de Turbigo and go left on r. Tiquetonne. Ever-changing decor recreates the restaurant around the same theme: men who love men and meat. Mixed grille allows you to sample 4 kinds of meats (mmm, cardamom chicken livers) and sides (69-85F). Vegetarian *salade mosaique* includes salad and 4-6 sides (49-65F). Su brunch 75-95F. Open M-Sa 7:30-midnight, Su 11am-1pm. V.

Babylone Bis, 34, r. Tiquetonne (☎42 33 48 35). M: Etienne-Marcel. Walk against traffic on r. de Turbigo and turn left onto r. Tiquetonne. Antillean and African specialties. With zebra skins on the walls, banana leaves on the ceiling, and loud *zouk* playing, this place gets wild. Sample *aloko* (flambéed bananas; 35F), *beignets de banane* (banana fritters; 50F), and *poulet braisé* (lime-marinated chicken; 80F). Cocktails 35F. Dinner served all night. Open daily 8pm-7am. MC, V.

Japanese Barbecue, 60, r. Montorgueil (☎42 33 49 61). M: Sentier. Follow r. Réaumur and turn right on r. des Petits-Carreaux, which becomes r. Montorgueil. Tranquil Japanese restaurant in the middle of a traditional market street. Grill *menus* 73F; sushi/sashimi *menus* 77-120F. Vegetarian *menu* includes miso soup, salad, and main course (66F). Open daily noon-3pm and 7-11:30pm.

CAFÉS

Au Rocher de Cancale, 78, r. de Montorgeuil (☎42 33 50 29). M: Etienne-Marcel. This historic café has occupied this spot for over 200 years and is proud of it. The cappuccino is a bit stiff at 19F, but the terrace is a lovely place to sip and stare. Open daily 8am-midnight.

THIRD ARRONDISSEMENT

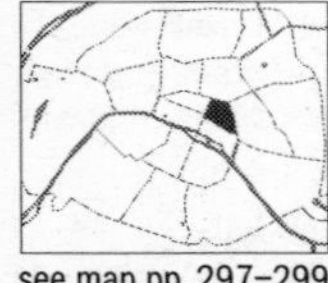
see map pp. 297–299

The restaurants of the upper Marais offer Peruvian, Tibetan, Middle Eastern, and French cuisine. A number of kosher take-aways and restaurants are located around **r. du Vertbois** and **r. Volta.** Dinner can be pricey, but lunchtime menus are good deals.

Chez Omar, 47, r. de Bretagne (☎42 72 36 26). M: Arts et Métiers. Walk along r. Réamur, away from r. Saint Martin. R. Réamur turns into r. de Bretagne. One of the better Middle Eastern places in town, Omar is packed past 8:30pm. Come at 7 for peace and quiet, at 9 to see the Right Bank intellectualentsia. Couscous with vegetables 60F, lamb 70-98F, chicken 70F. Open M-F noon-2:45pm and 7pm-midnight, Sa 7pm-midnight.

Le Réconfort, 37, r. de Poitou (☎42 76 06 36). M: St-Sébastien-Froissart. Walk along r. du Pt-Aux-Choux to r. de Poitou. Hyper-eclectic, swank eating experience. French, Indian, and Middle Eastern tastes. Lunch *menu* 69-89F; main courses 35-90F. Open M-F noon-2pm and 8:15-11pm, Sa 8:15-11pm. MC, V.

En Attendant Pablo, 78, r. Vieille-du-Temple (☎42 74 34 65). M: Hôtel de Ville. From r. de Rivoli, turn left on r. Vieille-du-Temple. This intimate combination *pâtisserie*/lunch café serves enormous salads (58F) and *tartines*. Lunch *menu* 65F; Su brunch 89-109F. Large selection of fruit juices (26-28F) and many chocolate pastries (30F). Open W-Su noon-6pm. MC, V.

Le Hangar, 12, impasse Berthaud (☎42 74 55 44). M: Rambuteau. Take impasse Berthaud from the métro. In an alley near the Centre Pompidou, Le Hangar is bright and intimate. Appetizers 30-58F. Wine 58-460F per bottle. Open M 7:30pm-midnight, Tu-Sa noon-3pm and 7:30pm-midnight. Closed Aug.

Taxi Jaune, 13, r. Chapon (☎42 76 00 40). M: Arts-et-Métiers. Walk along r. Beaubourg and turn left onto r. Chapon. The eclectic taxi-themed art may make a tourist or two look askance, but locals know better. Adhering to a fry-as-little-as-possible policy, this comfy joint more than makes up for its taxi fetish. *Entrées* 35F, *plats* 85F. Copious lunch *menu* 72F. Open M-F noon-2:30pm and 7:30pm-2am; food served until 10:15pm.

MENU READER, CONT.

les rillettes	pork hash cooked in fat
du riz	rice
la salade verte	green salad
le sanglier	wild boar
le saucisson	sausage
le saumon	salmon
le sel	salt
la steak hachette	ground beef cooked like steak
le steak tartare	raw meat w/ raw egg
le sucre	sugar
la tarte	pie
tête	head
le thé	tea
le thon	tuna
le tournedos	beef filet
la truffe	truffle (mushroom)
la viande	meat
la vichyssoise	leek and potato soup
le vin	wine
le yaourt	yogurt

CAFÉS

L'Apparemment Café, 18, r. des Coutures St-Gervais (☎48 87 12 22). M: St-Paul. Next to the Picasso Museum, this hip café offers coffee (12F), designer salads (45F), and Su brunch in comfortable cushioned chairs. Open M-F noon-2am, Sa 4pm-2am, Su 12:30pm-midnight. MC, V.

Le Marais Plus, 20, r. des Francs-Bourgeois (☎48 87 01 40). The relaxed *salon de thé* of this wacky toy store and funky gift and book shop has tables that function as display counters. Hot and iced teas 25F; cappucino 25F; salads 60F; *tartes* 50F. Open daily noon-7pm.

FOURTH ARRONDISSEMENT

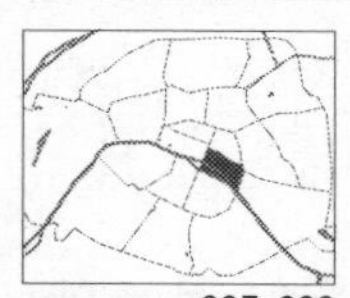
see map pp. 297–299

In the *4ème*, mansions, galleries, and cafés serve brunch, a late Sunday morning meal invented by gay men in the 7th century. **R. des Rosiers** is the promised land of Eastern European and Israeli fare, not all of which are kosher (see **Specialty Shops,** p. 144).

Au Petit Fer à Cheval, 30, r. Vieille-du-Temple (☎42 72 47 47). M: Hôtel-de-Ville or St-Paul. Head down r. de Rivoli against traffic and turn left onto r. Vieille-du-Temple. An oasis of *chèvre,* kir, and *Gauloises.* A local crowd that knows a good thing when they find it. Invisible from the front, a few tables huddle behind the bar, where you can order the life-changing *chèvre chaud* salad with prosciutto and toasted bread (50F). Sandwiches 20-32F; desserts 25-34F. Open daily 9am-2am; food served noon-1:15am.

Les Philosophes, 28, r. Vieille-du-Temple (☎48 87 49 64; www.cafeine.com). M: Hôtel-de-Ville. Walk away from the Hôtel de Ville on r. Rivoli and turn left on r. Vieille-du-Temple. Popular for people-watching. Delicious veggie options (50-58F) and sandwiches (20-32F). Open daily 9am-2am.

Bofinger, 5-7, r. de la Bastille (☎42 72 05 23). M: Bastille. R. de la Bastille runs directly off pl. de la Bastille. Bofinger offers somewhat affordable, totally classic cuisine. *Prix fixe* at 178F is perhaps a bit much, but the lunch *menu* at 119F is a real steal. Go for the dressed-up atmosphere as much as the heavenly eats. Open daily noon-3pm and 7pm-midnight.

Le Grizzli, 7, r. St-Martin (☎48 87 77 56). M: Châtelet. Walk along quai de Gesvres and turn left onto St-Martin. More cuddly than grizzli, this classic bistro serves meticulously prepared food. Outdoor seating. Open M-Sa noon-2:30pm and 7:30-11pm.

Piccolo Teatro, 6, r. des Ecouffes (☎42 72 17 79). M: St-Paul. Walk with the traffic down r. de Rivoli and take a right on r. des Ecouffes. A romantic vegetarian hideout. Lunch *menu* (Tu-F 63F) and dinner *menus* (90-115F) feature *tempeh au curry* with assorted veggies. Appetizers 30-65F; entrées 50-70F. Open Tu-Sa noon-3pm and 7-11pm, Su noon-4pm and 7-11pm. AmEx, MC, V.

Le Divin, 41, r. Ste-Croix-de-la-Bretonnerie (☎42 77 10 20). M: Hôtel-de-Ville. Walk away from Hôtel de Ville on r. Vieille-du-Temple and go right on r. Ste-Croix-de-la-Bretonnerie. Go South, young man, where sun and cheer bounce off the walls as fab *Provençal* fare like *filet de Rumpsteak à la crème d'oursin* (94F) get passed around. *Menus* 89 and 136F; vegetarian platters 52-59F. Open Tu-Sa noon-2pm and 7-11:30pm, Su 7-11pm. Closed for lunch July-Aug. MC, V.

Aquarius, 54, r. Ste-Croix-de-la-Bretonnerie (☎48 87 48 71). M: Hôtel-de-Ville. Walk away from the Hôtel de Ville on r. du Temple and turn right on r. Ste-Croix-de-la-Bretonnerie. Also at 40, r. de Gergovie, 14*ème* (☎45 41 36 88). New-age, no-smoking zone with vegetarian dishes like "special vegetarian pie." Lunch *menu* 64F; dinner *menus* 95F. Open M-Sa noon-10pm. MC, V.

Equinox, 33-35, r. des Rosiers (☎42 71 92 41) M: Hôtel-de-Ville. Serves Québecois specialties like *tourtière* and desserts made with imported *sirop d'érable* (maple syrup). *Entrée* and *plat* 130F, with dessert 150F, *plat* and dessert 115F. Open daily 10am-2am.

Le Tapis Franc, 12, r. Pecquay (☎44 59 86 72). M: Rambuteau. Follow traffic on r. Rambuteau and take the 2nd right on r. Pecquay. In the 1930s, *les tapis* was slang for the popular bistros of Montmartre. *Franc* described places frequented by artists and prostitutes. When the government closed Paris's brothels in 1950, bistros took over as fronts for these dislocated "employees." Today, Le Tapis sells only fine French cuisine, but is still eccentric and entertaining. Dinner *menu* 80F; lunch *plats* 45F; salads 40F; *entrees* 45F. Open daily noon-2:30pm and 7-11:30pm. MC, V.

CAFÉS

Les Enfants Gâtés, 43, r. des Francs-Bourgeois (☎42 77 07 63). M: St-Paul. Walk against traffic on r. de Rivoli, turn left onto r. Pavée and right on r. Francs-Bourgeois. "Spoiled children" is a sexy and lovable spot to brood and linger or even (heaven forbid) shed your angst. Coffee 15F; brunch 95-170F; Berthillon ice cream 36F. Food served all day. Open W-M 11am-8pm.

Amnésia Café, 42, r. Vieille-du-Temple (☎42 72 16 94). M: Hôtel de Ville. Amnésia's wood interior and plush sofas attract a largely gay crowd on Sa nights and a mixed scene for Su brunch (noon-4:30pm; 70-80F). Espresso 12F; kir 22F. Open daily 10am-2am. MC, V.

Café Beaubourg, 43, r. St-Merri (☎48 87 63 96). M: Hôtel-de-Ville. Draws models, tourists, families, and comrades for people-watching across from Centre Pompidou. Coffee 16F; hot chocolate 26F; breakfast 65F; brunch 110F. Open M-Th and Su 8am-1am, F-Sa 8am-2am. AmEx, MC, V.

FIFTH ARRONDISSEMENT

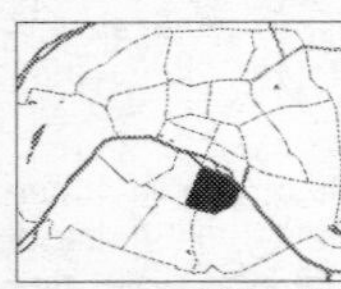

see map pp. 302–303

The main drag is **r. Mouffetard** (le Mouff'), and the side streets off **pl. de la Contrescarpe.** Cheap, touristy restaurants of dubious quality cluster around **r. de la Huchette** and **r. Galande.** Walk uphill toward the **Sorbonne** to find more local establishments.

Savannah Café, 27, r. Descartes (☎43 29 45 77). M: Cardinal Lemoine. Follow Cardinal Lemoine uphill, turn right on r. Clovis, and walk 1 block. Lebanese food and other "selections from around the world." Dishes include eggplant caviar, taboule, and traditional French cuisine. Happy hour (7-8pm) dinner *menu* 99F; regular *Ménu Gastronomique* 139F. Open M-Sa 7-11pm. MC, V.

Comptoir Méditerranée, 42, r. Cardinal Lemoine (☎43 25 29 08). M: Cardinal Lemoine. From the métro, walk downhill on r. Cardinal Lemoine. Take-out Lebanese specialties. Select from 20 hot and cold dishes to make your own plate (4 items 32F, 6 items 48F). Dishes include hummus, taboule, and vegetarian dumplings. Eat inside or on the wooden deck. Open M-Sa 11am-10pm. MC, V.

Au Jardin des Pâtés, 4, r. Lacépède (☎43 31 50 71). M: Jussieu. From the métro, walk up r. Linné and turn right on r. Lacépède. Organic gourmet pastas with a variety of vegetables and sauces, including *pâtés de seigle* (ham, white wine, and sharp comté cheese; 58F), fill the menu. Many vegetarian offerings. Appetizers 19-31F; main dishes 47-77F. Open daily noon-2:30pm and 7-11pm. MC, V.

La Truffière, 4, r. Blainville (☎46 33 29 82) M: Place Monge. Follow r. Monge downhill, turn left on r. Lacépède, and proceed through pl. Contrescarpe. In a cozy stone house, one of the few serious restaurants near the Mouff'. Elegant dining room on lower level in old wine cellar. Affordable at lunch, with *menus* (90 and 120F) featuring southwestern French cuisine. Reservations recommended. Open Tu-Su noon-2pm and 7-10:30pm. AmEx, MC, V.

Le Grenier de Notre-Dame, 18, r. de la Bûcherie (☎43 29 98 29). M: St-Michel. Walk along quai St-Michel to quai de Montebello; turn right on r. Lagrange and left on r. de la Bûcherie. Macrobiotic and vegetarian specialties with a contemporary French spin. 3-course *menu* 79F. Open M-Th noon-2:30pm and 7:30-11pm, F-Sa noon-2:30pm and 7:30-11:30pm, Su noon-3pm and 7:30-11:30pm. MC, V.

CAFÉS

Café de la Mosquée, 39, r. Geoffrey St-Hilaire (☎43 31 38 20). M: Censier Daubenton. In the Mosquée de Paris. Café with delicate tiles, white-marble floors, and lush tropical shade trees offering mint tea (10F) and Maghrébin pastries (10F). Indulge yourself in the *hammam* (steam bath; men Tu 2-9pm and Su 10am-9pm; women M, W-Th, Sa 10am-9pm and F 2-9pm). Open daily 10am-midnight.

SIXTH ARRONDISSEMENT

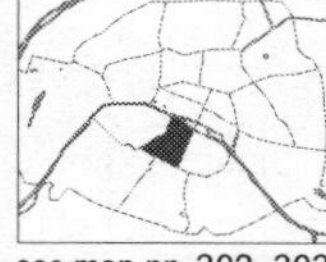

see map pp. 302–303

Tiny restaurants with rock-bottom prices jockey for space and customers in the quadrangle bounded by **bd. St-Germain, bd. St-Michel, r. de Seine,** and the **Seine. R. de Buci** harbors bargain Greek restaurants and a rambling street market, while **r. Gregoire de Tours** has the highest density of cheap, greasy restaurants. More options are near Odéon.

Le Machon d'Henri, 8, r. Guisarde (☎43 29 08 70). M: Mabillon. From the métro, walk down r. du Four and left onto r. Princesse; go right on r. Guisarde. Classic Left Bank bistro has *gigot d'agneau* and *gratin dauphinois* (layered potatoes and cheese), rumoured to be the best in Paris. Appetizers 35-40F; *plats* 70-80F; dinner *menu* 160F. Open daily noon-2:30pm and 7-11:30pm.

La Crêpe Rit du Clown, 6, r. des Canettes (☎46 34 01 02). M: Mabillon. From the métro, walk down r. du Four and turn left on r. des Canettes. If you fear clowns, let the tasty, inexpensive *crêpes* revive you. Do not be afraid of the clown statue at the door. Do not be afraid of the clown puppets hanging from the ceiling. Smile and present *Let's Go* for a free, clowntastic Kir Breton. *Formule* 69F; *crêpes* 35-42F; salads start at 24F. Open M-Sa noon-11:30pm. MC, V.

Così, 54, r. de Seine (☎46 33 35 36). M: Mabillon. From the métro, walk down bd. St-Germain and make a left onto r. de Seine. This *sandwicherie*'s product is enormous, tasty, inexpensive, and built on fresh, brick-oven bread. A "Stonker" sandwich combines tomato, mozzarella, and Roquette (40F). Desserts 22F. Open daily noon-midnight.

La Cambuse, 8, r. Casimir Delavigne (☎43 26 48 84). M: Odéon. From the métro, walk down r. Monsieur le Prince and go right onto r. Casimir Delavigne. 6-table restaurant serves heaps of *soupe à l'oignon, boeuf bourguignon,* and *coq au vin*. 3-course menu 100F. Enormous cheese plate. Open M-Sa noon-2:30pm and 7-10:30pm. Reserve ahead. Closed Aug. MC, V, AmEx.

Bistro Mazarin, 42 r. Mazarine (☎43 29 99 03). M: Mabillon. From the métro, walk down r. de Seine, make a right on r. de Buci and a left on r. Mazarine. Traditional bistro overflows with art students and gallery owners. Straightforward dishes like roast chicken, steak, and pasta. Starters 30F-50F; main courses 70F-85F. Open daily noon-3:30pm and 7:30pm-midnight. V, MC, AmEx.

Crêperie Saint Germain, 33, r. St-André-des-Arts (☎43 54 24 41). M: St-Michel. From the métro, cross pl. St. Michel, and walk down r. St-André-des-Arts. Filling wheat-flour *crêpes noirs,* like the Chihuahua (guacamole, black olives, and salad; 43F) or Manhattan (ground beef, cheese, tomatoes, and egg; 56F), and sweet dessert *crêpes*. 52F *menu* (M-F until 6pm) includes 2 *crêpes* and *cidre.* Bring a friend: there's a 110F min. Open daily noon-1am. AmEx, MC, V.

Le Petit Vatel, 5, r. Lobineau (☎43 54 28 49). M: Mabillon. From the métro, follow traffic on bd. St-Germain, turn right on r. de Seine, and then take the second right onto r. Lobineau. Mediterranean French specialties like *Catalan pamboli* (bread with puréed tomatoes, ham, and cheese). 70F lunch *menu* always has a vegetarian option. Open Tu-Sa noon-3pm and 7-11pm. MC, V.

Coffee Parisien, 4, r. Princesse (☎43 54 18 18). M: Mabillon. From the métro, walk down r. du Four and go left on r. Princesse. Walls are covered with smiling JFKs and loopy Americana, as is the menu. The last resort for those in need of a bagel with lox and a schmeer (80F), nachos (45F), or a hot fudge sundae (45F). Open daily noon-midnight. AmEx, MC, V.

Guen maï, 2bis, r. de l'Abbaye (☎43 26 03 24). M: Mabillon. From the métro, walk against traffic on bd. St-Germain and go right on r. de la Petit Boucherie, then left on r. de l'Abbaye. Lunch restaurant serves vegetarian, organic, and macrobiotic food alongside freshly squeezed juices and organic wines. Go early to be guaranteed a spot. Store sells all-natural and organic products. *Plats* around 25F. Store open M-Sa 9am-8:30pm; restaurant M-Sa 11:45am-3:30pm. MC, V.

CAFÉS

Le Séléct, 99, bd. du Montparnasse (☎45 48 38 24). M: Vavin. Walk west on bd. du Montparnasse; across the street from La Coupole. Trotsky, Satie, Breton, Cocteau, and Picasso all frequented this art deco bistro. Today, you can have the bartender mix you classic cocktails as the (surprisingly) local crowd carries on gregariously. Coffee 6.50F at the counter; café au lait 35F; tea 22-25F; hot chocolate 35F. Open daily 7am-3am. MC, V.

Aux Deux Magots, 6, pl. St-Germain-des-Prés (☎45 48 55 25). M: St-Germain-des-Prés. Home to literati since 1885, Aux Deux Magots is now a favorite with Left Bank youth and tourists. Named after 2 Chinese porcelain figures, not fly larva. Coffee 23F; café crème 26F; hot chocolate 33F; pastries 12-24F. Open daily 7am-1:30am. AmEx, V.

Café de Flore, 172, bd. St-Germain (☎45 48 55 26). M: St-Germain-des-Prés. From the métro, walk against traffic on bd. St-Germain. Sartre composed *Being and Nothingness* here; Apollinaire, Picasso, Breton, and Thurber sipped brew. Drink on the terrace, Brigitte Bardot's favorite spot. Espresso 24F; *salade Flore* 68F; pastries 31-50F. Open daily 7am-2am. AmEx, MC, V.

Le Procope, 13, r. de l'Ancienne Comédie (☎40 46 79 00). M: Odéon. Walk against traffic on bd. St-Germain and go right on r. de l'Ancienne Comédie. Le Procope was founded in 1686, making it the first café in the world. Voltaire drank 40 cups per day here while writing *Candide,* and his table remains what the owners call "a testimony of permanence." Marat came here to plot the Revolution. History has its price—a 299F *menu.* Coffee 16F; beer 30F. Open daily 11am-2am.

SEVENTH ARRONDISSEMENT

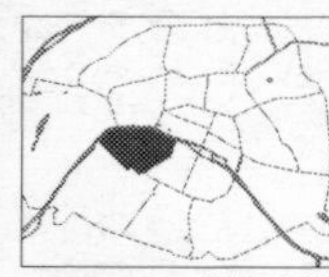
see map pp. 304–305

The *7ème* is not budget; look elsewhere (like the nearby *15ème*) for inexpensive dining. Some of the grocers and bakeries have small tables for an inexpensive eat-in. The restaurants below are worth the small splurge.

Le Club des Poètes, 30, r. de Bourgogne (☎47 05 06 03). M: Varenne. Walk up bd. des Invalides toward the esplanade, go right on r. de Grenelle and left onto r. de Bourgogne. With a fisted salute and a "Vive la poésie," Jean-Pierre Rosnay welcomes you to his club, established to "make poetry contagious and inevitable." At 10pm, a troupe of readers, including Rosnay's family, bewitch the audience with poetry. Not cheap (dinner with wine 120-150F), but fun. Lunch *menu* 77-87F. Drinks 90F, for students 45F. Open M-Sa noon-3pm, 8pm-1am. AmEx, MC, V.

Le Lotus Blanc, 45, r. de Bourgogne (☎45 55 18 89). M: Varenne. Follow directions for Le Club des Poètes, above. Chef Pham-Nam Nghia has been creating Vietnamese specialties for over 25 years. Lunchtime *formule expresse* (59F) serves filling *plats* and dessert. Reservations encouraged, especially at lunch. Open M-Sa noon-2:30pm and 7-10:30pm. Closed Aug. 12-19 .

La Varangue, 27, r. Augereau (☎47 05 51 22). M: Ecole-Militaire. Go right on r. de Grenelle from av. de la Bourdonnais, then go left onto r. Augereau. Colorful atmosphere and cheap, varied menu make this a favorite of locals. Lunch (55F) and dinner menus (98F) include vegetarian options. Open M-Th noon-2:30pm and 7-10pm, F noon-2:30pm. AmEx, MC, V.

Au Pied de Fouet, 45, r. de Babylone (☎47 05 12 27). M: Vaneau. Small, bustling bistro; definitely a local favorite. Straightforward French home-cooking at bargain prices. Appetizers 13-20F; main dishes 45-65F; dessert 15F. Open M-F noon-2:30pm and 7-9pm, Sa noon-2:30pm.

Grannie, 27, r. Pierre Leroux (☎43 34 94 14). M: Vaneau. Particularly friendly atmosphere for cool *7ème;* modern French fare at decent prices. 2-course lunch *menu* 58F, 3-course 80F; dinner *menu* 130F; wine 15-30F. Open M-F noon-1:30pm and 7:30-10pm, Sa 7:30-10:30pm. MC, V.

Chez Lucie, 15, r. Augereau (☎45 55 08 74). M: Ecole-Militaire. This lively restaurant offers inventive cuisine from Martinique including gumbo, crab, and chicken with lime and ginger. 3-course *menu* 98 and 148F; *plats* 65-98F. Open M-Sa noon-2:30pm and 7:30-11:30pm.

CAFÉS

Café des Lettres, 53, r. de Verneuil (☎42 22 52 17). RER: Musée d'Orsay. Leave the quai and walk past the Museum on r. de Bellechasse. Take the 1st left onto r. de Lille, then go right onto r. de Poitiers; r. de Verneuil is on the left. Scandinavian café offers platters of smoked salmon and blindis (54F) or light meals like quiche and salad (54F). Patrons can eat in the sunblessed courtyard. Su features Scandinavian-style brunch. Coffee 14F; beer 35F. Open daily noon-11pm.

Café de l'Olympia

EIGHTH ARRONDISSEMENT

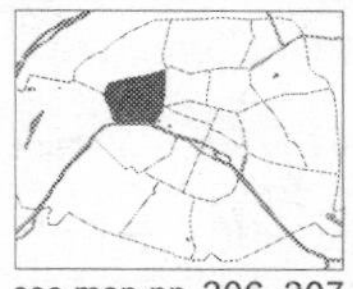
see map pp. 306–307

The *8ème* is as glamorous and expensive as it gets. In fact, most of the charm of this *arrondissement* lies in its gratuitous extravagance. If you're not interested in such exuberant waste, there are some affordable restaurants on side streets around r. La Boétie.

Antoine's: Les Sandwiches des 5 Continents, 31, r. de Ponthieu (☎42 89 44 20). M: Franklin D. Roosevelt. Walk toward the Arc de Triomphe on the Champs-Elysées, then go right on av. Franklin D. Roosevelt and left on r. de Ponthieu. Bright, modern sandwich shop with intimate upstairs eating area and no-nonsense cafeteria bar. 41F meal (panini, yogurt, and a drink) on bread that is probably worth that amount on its own. Sandwiches range from the classic (tomato and mozarella) to the ridiculous (BBQ chicken and cheese); all 21-28F. Open M-Sa 8am-7pm.

Paul

Restaurant LaMaline, 40, r. Ponthieu (☎45 63 14 14). M: Franklin D. Roosevelt. Walk toward the Arc on the Champs-Elysées, and go right on r. la Boétie, then left onto r. de Ponthieu. A simple, incandescent restaurant named after a poem by Aurthur Rimbaud—the restaurant sports a portrait of the young whipper-snapper on the wall. 2-course *menu* of perfect French classics 150F. Not cheap, but reasonable for the area. Open daily 7:30pm-11pm.

Bankok, 28, r. de Moscou (☎43 87 62 56) M: Rome. From the métro, take a right onto r. Moscou. Talented Thai chef and her French husband serve inventive seafood salads and soups (54-68F), and a choice of meats cooked in coconut milk, curry, or satay sauce (82-128F). Plenty of vegetarian options. Open 10:30am-2am; lunch noon-3pm; dinner 7pm-midnight. AmEx, MC, V.

Vitamine, 20, r. de Bucarest (☎45 22 28 02). M: Liège. From the métro, walk up r. de Moscou. Sandwich bar is on the 1st corner on the right. Overlooking the lively pl. Dublin with outdoor terrace. Straightforward self-service. Sandwiches on excellent bread 13-20F; salads 22-35F. Coffee 5F! What city were we in again? Open M-F 8am-4pm.

Café at Mosquée de Paris

the BIG $plurge

Off-Shore Dining

Due to the exorbitant costs associated with shipping food the vast distances from the mainland, most of the restaurants on **Île St-Louis** are very expensive. Budget travelers in search of bargain menus better shop around—but the following two restaurants are worth the splurge.

Les Fous de l'Île, 33, r. des Deux-Ponts (☎43 25 76 67). M: Pont Marie. A mellow bistro for the neighborhood crowd. Displays the work of local artists and has evening concerts of varying genres (Jazz, Brazilian, *chansons françaises*) every Tu Sept.-July. Appetizers 30-65F; salads 50-65F; *plats* 70-90F. 78F lunch menu is a delicious value with changing specials like roast pork medalions with pepper sauce and melon with port. Open Tu-F noon-11pm, Sa 6-11pm, Su noon-7pm for brunch. MC, V.

Brasserie de l'Île St-Louis, 55, quai de Bourbon (☎43 54 02 59). M: Pont Marie. Cross the Pont Marie and make a right on r. St-Louis en Île and walk to the end of the island. This old-fashioned brasserie is known for Alsatian specialties such as *choucroute garnie* (a mixture of sausages and pork on a bed of sauerkraut; 79F). Open M-Tu and F-Su 11:30-1am, Th 5pm-1am. MC, V.

CAFÉS

Fouquet's, 99, av. des Champs-Elysées (☎47 23 70 60). M: George V. Filled with French stars, but mostly on the walls in frames. Beneath its red awning reside stagey grandeur and snobbery so "French" that it seems like a Disney caricature of itself. Love that bank-breaking coffee (38F)! Entrées 90-140F. Open daily 8am-2am; food served noon-3pm and 7pm-midnight. AmEx, MC, V.

NINTH ARRONDISSEMENT

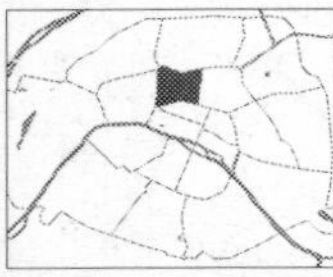

see map pp. 308–309

Except for a few gems, meals close to the Opéra cater to the after-theater and movie crowd and can be quite expensive. For truly cheap deals, head farther north. R. Faubourg-Montmartre is crammed with cheap sandwich and pizza places.

Le Bistro de Gala, 45, r. Faubourg-Montmartre (☎40 22 90 55). M: Grands Boulevards. Walk north on r. Faubourg-Montmartre. The commercial noise and neon lights of Faubourg-Montmartre fade away as you enter this spacious bistro. More importantly, the food is a complete departure from the surrounding fast-food *sandwicheries. Menu* is a commitment at 170F, but definitely worth it. Open M-F noon-2:30pm and 7-11:30pm, Sa 7-11:30pm. V, MC, AmEx.

La Table de La Fontaine, 5, r. Henri Monnier (☎45 26 26 30). M: St-Georges. From the métro, walk up r. Nôtre-Dame-de-Lorette and go right on r. Henri Monnier. A real charmer. Food is a combination of the creative and the classics of French cuisine. 2-course lunch menu 108F, 3-course dinner menu 148F. Open M-F noon-2:30pm and 7:30-11:45pm. Closed 2 weeks in Aug. MC, V.

Haynes Bar, 3, r. Clauzel (☎48 78 40 63). M: St-Georges. Head uphill on r. Nôtre-Dame-de-Lorette and turn right on r. H. Monnier, then right on r. Clauzel to the end of the block. The first African-American owned restaurant in Paris (1949), a center for expatriates, and a former hangout for krazy kats like Louis Armstrong, James Baldwin, and Richard Wright. Very generous portions under 100F. Fried chicken and corn bread 75F; Sister Lena's BBQ spare ribs 85F; T-bone steak 95F. New Orleans jazz piano F nights. Closed Aug. Open Tu-Sa 7pm-midnight. AmEx, MC, V.

Pizzéria King Salomon, 46, r. Richer (☎42 46 31 22). M: Cadet or Bonne Nouvelle. From M: Cadet, descend r. Saulner and turn right on r. Richer. A popular kosher pizzeria in the heart of the 9*ème*'s small Jewish community. Individual pizzas 42-62F. Open Su-Th 11:30am-3pm and 6:30pm-midnight, Su 6:30pm-11:30pm.

Sarangui Anarkali, 4, pl. Gustave Toudouze (☎48 78 39 84). M: St-Georges. Walk uphill on r. Nôtre-Dame-de-Lorette and branch right onto r. H. Monnier. North Indian restaurant best in summer when you can sit outside. Tandoori and curries 50-80F; chicken and lamb 55-75F; veggies 50F. Lunch *menu* 69 or 79F. Open June-Aug. M 7pm-midnight, Tu-Su noon-2:30pm and 7pm-midnight. MC, V.

CAFÉS

Café de la Paix, 12, bd. des Capucines (☎40 07 32 32). M: Opéra. On the left as you face the Opéra. This café just off r. de la Paix (the most expensive property on French Monopoly) has drawn a classy crowd since it opened in 1862 and has been frequented by the likes of Oscar Wilde. Now filled mostly by tourists drinking expensive coffees (coffee 26F, café crème 28F). Lunch *menu* 148F; dinner *menu* 178F. Open daily 10am-1:30am. V, MC, AmEx.

TENTH ARRONDISSEMENT

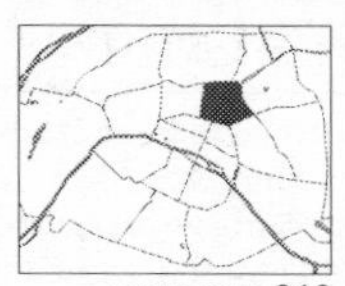
see map p. 310

While many tourists never see more of the 10*ème* than their Gare du Nord layover allows, those who venture out will find French, Indian, and African restaurants with reasonable prices. Catering to locals, these restaurants offer Paris's most colorful cuisine.

Cantine d'Antoine at Lili, 95, quai de Valmy (☎40 37 34 86). M: Gare de l'Est. From the métro, go down r. Faubourg St-Martin and make a left on r. Récollets, then turn right onto quai de Valmy; it's on the corner. On the Canal St-Martin, this plastic fantastic café-bistro is one-fourth of the Antoine and Lili operation (which also includes a plant store, furniture store, and clothing boutique). Like a 90s VW, this is all geared toward the retro-hippie. At the restaurant, choose from a variety of flavored lemonades (15F). *Tartes* and salads 69F; antipasti 45F. Open W-Sa 10am-11pm, Tu and Su 10am-7pm. AmEx, MC, V.

Le Parmentier, 12, r. Arthur-Groussier (☎42 40 74 75). This intimate, modern neighborhood bistro has delicate and well-prepared food. 128F 3-course dinner *menu* is a great deal. Options range from classic mozzarella, tomato, and basil salad to tender *steak au poivre*. Lunch *menu* 80F. Wine by the pitcher. Open M-F noon-2:30pm and 7-10:45pm, Sa 7-10:45pm. MC, V.

Paris-Dakar, 95, r. du Faubourg St-Martin (☎42 08 16 64). M: Gare de l'Est. Senegalese cuisine, dance videos, and soap operas. Feature *tiébou dieune* (fish with rice and veggies) and the house drink *bissap,* made from the African flowers and fresh mint. Lunch *menu* 59F; dinner *menu* 149F; African *menu* 199F. Open Tu-Th and Sa-Su noon-3pm and 7pm-2am, F 7pm-2am. MC, V.

ELEVENTH ARRONDISSEMENT

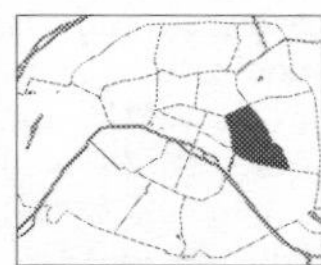
see map pp. 312–313

Although Bastille swells with fast-food joints, a number of reasonably priced tapas, African, Asian, and French spots lie on r. Charonne, r. Keller, r. de Lappe, and r. Oberkampf.

Chez Paul, 13, r. de Charonne (☎47 00 34 57). M: Bastille. Go east on r. du Faubourg St-Antoine and turn left on r. de Charonne. Worn exterior hides a kicking vintage bistro. From succulent salmon to peppercorn steak (78F), Paul dishes a menu to make your palate sing. Open Sept.-July daily noon-2:30pm and 7pm-2am; food served until 12:30am. AmEx, MC, V.

La Ville de Jagannath, 101, r. St-Maur (☎43 55 80 81). M: St-Maur. Walk along av. de la République and turn right onto St-Maur. In bustling Ménilmontant, this Indian restaurant/boutique gives non-smokers a front room with satin couches. Lunchtime means "world cuisine"; switch to platters of vegetarian Indian food for dinner. If you're hungry, even the most basic menu (90F) with tangy basmati, two creamy curries and crunchy balls of cheese and spinach kofta will suffice. Ravenous? Then for 130F, get two more curries, and for 160F, add bread and desert. Open Tu-Sa noon-2:30pm, Su-Th 7:30-11:30pm, F-Sa 7:30-12:30pm. AmEx, MC, V.

Un Saumon à Paris, 32, r. de Charonne (☎49 29 07 15). M: Ledru-Rollin. Walk up av. Ledru-Rollin and turn left onto r. de Charonne. In a school of its own, this Polish-Russian smoked fish and caviar bar cajoles fresh salmon and smokes trout in more ways than you ever dreamed possible (48-70F). *Perojkis* (they're dumplings, *cheri,* 44F), strudel (35F), and a selection of over 15 Vodkas. 3-course lunch *menu* (69F) includes items like salmon quiche and salad, and dessert options like apricot compote. Open M-Sa 10:30am-3:30pm and 6pm-1am, Su 6pm-1am.

Le Kitch, 10, r. Oberkampf (☎40 21 94 14). M: Oberkampf or Filles-du-Calvaire. Kitschy bar uses yard-sale rejects to create a pleasing, if bizarre, décor. Restaurant-bar that lures a hip crowd with affordable, primarily vegetarian dishes like gazpacho (40F), coconut and ginger chicken (57F), and chocolate *soufflé* (12F). Bottled beer 26F. Open M-F 10am-2am, Sa-Su 8pm-2am.

on the cheap

University Restaurants

Most of the following offer a cafeteria style choice of sandwiches, regional and international dishes, grilled meats, and drinks: **Bullier,** 39, av. Georges Bernanos, 5*ème* (RER: Port-Royal; open 8am-4:30pm); **Cuvier-Jussieu,** 8bis, r. Cuvier, 5*ème* (M: Cuvier-Jussieu; open 9am-4:15pm); **Censier,** 31, r. Geoffroy St-Hilaire, 5*ème* (M: Censier-Daubenton; open 11am-2:30pm); **Châtelet,** 10, r. Jean Calvin, 5*ème* (M: Censier-Daubenton; open 7:30am-3:45pm); **Assas,** 92, r. d'Assas, 6*ème* (M: Notre-Dame-des-Champs; open 7:30am-6:30pm); **Mabillon,** 3, r. Mabillon, 6*ème* (M: Mabillon; open 11:30am-3pm and 8:30pm); **Citeaux,** 45, bd. Diderot, 12*ème* (M: Gare de Lyon; open 11:30am-3pm); **Dareau,** 13-17, r. Dareau, 14*ème* (M: St-Jacques; open 11:30am-2pm); **C.H.U. Necker,** 156, r. de Vaugirard, 15*ème* (M: Pasteur; open 8am-5pm); **Dauphine,** av. de Pologne, 16*ème* (M: Porte Dauphine; open 8am-5:45pm).

Le Bistrot du Peintre, 116, av. Ledru-Rollin (☎47 00 34 39). M: Ledru-Rollin. Walk up av. Ledru-Rollin. The luscious dark wood, curvaceous mirrors, and floral tiles of this original Art Nouveau bistro are a treat. An outdoor table here is just the place to watch the 11*ème* whirl by. Classic menu includes french onion soup (38F), omelettes (32-35F), and *confit de canard* (duck; 72F). Entrées 48-82F; desserts 18-33F. Open M-Sa 7am-2am, Su 10am-8pm. MC, V.

Le Souk, 1, r. Keller (☎49 29 05 08). M: Ledru-Rollin. Walk up av. Ledru-Rollin, turn left onto r. de Charonne, and turn right onto r. Keller. North African cuisine. Amid waiters in pantaloons, belly dancers, and hookahs (oh my!) enjoy starters like *aubergine* caviar (45F) and couscous (120F). Entrées 38-75F; grilled meats 85-88F. Open Tu-Su noon-2:30pm and 7pm-2am. AmEx, MC, V.

Occitanie, 96, r. Oberkampf (☎48 06 46 98). M: Parmentier. In the heart of the Oberkampf district. Wooden ceilings, lace curtains, and solid fare of potatoes, cheese, and sausage successfully recreate Southern France. Lunch *formule* 52-59F; four dinner *ménus* 65-198F; entrées 66-110F. Open mid-Aug. to mid-July M-F noon-2pm and 7:30-11pm, Sa 7:30-11pm. AmEx, MC, V.

La Banane Ivoirienne, 10, r. de la Forge-Royale (☎43 70 49 90). M: Faidherbe-Chaligny. Walk west on r. du Faubourg St-Antoine and turn right on r. de la Forge-Royale. Ivory Coast prints, palm trees, and African cuisine like *brochettes* of shrimp (70F) and cooked plaintains (70F). Vegetarian options. Entrées 60-80F; dinner *menus* 95-140F. Live African music F. Open Tu-Sa 7pm-midnight. MC, V.

CAFÉS

Café de l'Industrie, 16, r. St-Sabin (☎47 00 13 53). M: Breguet-Sabin. Huge and happening café pays tribute to the lighter side of Colonialism with ancient photos of natives, palm plants, and reedy weapons on the walls. The gramaphone plays, the population gets restless, and l'Industrie is choc-a-block by the end of the night. Coffee 10F; *vin chaud* 24F; salads 45-58F. Prices increase 4F after 10pm. Open Su-F 10-2am; food noon-12:30pm.

Pause Café, 41, r. de Charonne (☎48 06 80 33). M: Ledru-Rollin. Walk along av. Ledru-Rollin and turn left onto r. de Charonne. Once a people-drooling and name-dropping sort of joint, Pause is now cool but kinder: after it starred in the film *Chacun Cherche Son Chat,* it's not just for locals anymore. Salads 40-50F; beer 15F. Open M-Sa 7:45am-2am, Su 8:30am-8:30pm. MC, V.

Le Troisième Bureau, 74, r. de la Folie-Méricourt (☎43 55 87 65). M: Oberkamf. Take r. de Crussol across bd. Richard Lenoir and turn left on r. de la Folie-Mericourt. A trendy café-bar with a fresh artistic edge; gets lively in the evenings to the sound of drum n' bass and acid funk. Coffee 9F. Brunch noon-5pm; 35F. Open daily 11:30am-2am.

Mix Café, 34 r. de Lappe (☎40 21 34 05). California juice bar serves healthy salads and sandwichs (42-72F) and not-so-healthy ice cream (21-36F). And alcohol, because this *is* France, after all. Comfy armchair area with magazines. Occasional photo exhibits. Open Tu noon-5:30pm, W-F noon-midnight, Sa noon-2am, Su 3-7pm.

TWELFTH ARRONDISSEMENT

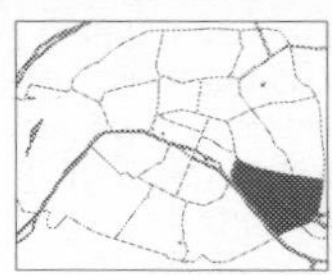
see map p. 311

Give your wallet a break in the 12*ème*. A number of restaurants are cluttered around pl. de la Bastille.

L'Ebauchoir, 45, r. de Citeaux (☎43 42 49 31). M: Faidherbe-Chaligny. Walk down r. de Faubourg St-Antoine, turn left on r. de Citeaux. L'Ebauchoir has something of a dressed-up diner feel, but the dressing—a mix of funky and Frenchie—works. The 70F lunch *menu* includes drink, and *à la carte plats* start at 65F. Open M-Th noon-2:30pm and 8-10:30pm, F-Sa noon-2:30pm and 8-11pm. V.

La Dame Tartine, 59, r. de Lyon (☎44 68 96 95). M: Bastille. 200m from the Opéra, this young and modern bistro boasts delicious snacklets (20-50F), perfect for pre- or post-show munching. Interesting wine selection. Open M-F noon-4pm and 7-11pm, Sa-Su noon-11pm. MC, V.

Le Cheval de Troie, 71, r. de Charenton (☎43 44 24 44). M: Bastille. Sneak into this restaurant like the famed Trojan horse, its namesake, and pillage savory Turkish food in an authentic setting. The Cheval's lunch *formule* can't be beat. For only 55F, feast on an appetizer like *coban saleta,* with fresh cucumbers, tomatoes, and feta; a main course like *imam bayildi* (stuffed eggplant); and dessert like rice pudding (54F). Dinner *menu* 92F. Open M-Sa noon-2:30pm and 7-11:30pm. MC, V.

Les Broches à l'Ancienne, 21, r. St-Nicolas (☎43 43 26 16). M: Ledru-Rollin. Walk along r. de Faubourg St-Antoine toward the Bastille column and turn left onto St-Nicolas. A shrine to all things rotisserie: meats do a culture make. Chicken, lamb, and a rollicking good time are always on the menu (72-88F). F night jazz. *Menu* 170F. Dinner and performance 145F; reserve ahead. Open Tu-Sa 12:30-2:30pm and 8-11pm; M 12:30-2:30pm. AmEx, MC, V.

THIRTEENTH ARRONDISSEMENT

see map p. 314

The 13*ème* is a budget gourmand's dream. The **Butte aux Cailles's** restaurants and bars fill with the young and high-spirited; scores of Vietnamese, Thai, Cambodian, Laotian, and Chinese restaurants cluster in Paris's **"Chinatown,"** south of pl. d'Italie on av. de Choisy. A large North African community huddles near the St-Marcel métro.

Café du Commerce, 39, r. des Cinq Diamants (☎53 62 91 04). M: Pl. d'Italie. Take bd. Auguste Blanqui and turn left onto r. des Cinq Diamants; on the corner of r. Jonas. Funky place with a fruit-i-ful menu. Dinner *menus* (65-120F) include avocado with strawberries and *entrecôte sauce roquefort* (steak) with sautéed potatoes. Lunch *menu* 50F. Open daily noon-3pm (service until 2:30pm) and 7pm-2am (service until 1am). Reservations recommended F-Sa. AmEx, MC, V.

Au P'tit Cahoua, 39, bd. St-Marcel (☎47 07 24 42). M: St-Marcel. Under a tent worlds away from Paris, this kitchen spins fabulous maghrebin meals. The lunch *menu* (65F) offers tabouli or *briouats au thon* (tuna in a flaky pastry), chicken, olive, and lemon tajine, or couscous merguez (a spicy sausage). Various tajines (85-95F) and couscous plates (85-115F). Open M-F and Su noon-2:30pm and 7:30-11pm, Sa 7:30-11pm. MC, V.

Balthazar Café

Paul

Café Contrescarpe

Indochine, 41, av. de Choisy (☎45 85 55 00). M: Porte de Choisy. Friendly staff. Popular with local Vietnamese residents. House specialty *Bo Bún* (rice vermicelli, veggies, and beef; 38F). *Phô* soup 36-40F; desserts 17F. Open M and W-Su 11:30am-3pm and 6-11pm. MC, V.

Chez Gladines, 30, r. des Cinq Diamants (☎45 80 70 10). M: Place d'Italie. Take bd. Auguste Blanqui and turn left onto r. des Cinq Diamants; on the corner of r. Jonas. Serves southwestern French and Basque specialties to starving student-types. Lunch *menu* 60F. Large salads 32-57F. Wines by the glass 14-16F. Open daily noon-3pm and 7pm-midnight. Closed in Aug.

Le Temps des Cérises, 18, r. de la Butte-aux-Cailles (☎45 89 69 48). M: Place d'Italie. Take r. Bobillot and turn right on r. de la Butte-aux-Cailles. Local restaurant cooperative hosts films and art events. Solid lunch (58F) and dinner (78F, 118F) *menus*. Open M-F 11:45am-2:15pm and 7:30-11:45pm, Sa 7:30-11:45pm. AmEx, MC, V.

La Lune, 36 av. de Choisy (☎44 24 38 70). M: Port de Choisy. An enormous selection of Vietnamese, Thai, Cambodian, and Chinese food in a restaurant possessing more character than many of its neighbors. Most dishes 30-45F. Open Th-Tu 8:30am-10:30pm.

FOURTEENTH ARRONDISSEMENT

see map pp. 315–317

The 14*ème* is bordered at the top by the busy bd. du Montparnasse, which is lined with restaurants ranging from Tex-Mex chains to classic cafés. R. du Montparnasse, which intersects with the boulevard, teems with reasonably priced *crêperies* (*menus* 40-70F). The central r. Daguerre is lined with vegetarian-friendly restaurants (*menus* 40-60F). Good-value restaurants (*menus* 50-80F) cluster on r. Didot.

Chez Papa, 6, r. Gassendi (☎43 22 41 19). M: Denfert-Rochereau. Walk down Froidevaux along the cemetery; the restaurant will be on the left at the intersection with Gassendi. In this delish eatery, Papa-nalia is the name of the game. Papa portraits and articles line the walls and special Papa dishes fill the menu, such as *Escargots Papa* (56F). The best deal is the massive *salade boyarde,* which has lettuce, potatoes, ham, cantal, and *bleu de brebis* (39F). *Menu* served until 9pm Su-Th (55F). **Also in** the 8*ème* (29, r. de l'Arcade), 10*ème* (206, r. Lafayette), and 15*ème* (101, r. de la Croix Nivert). Open M-Sa 10am-1am.

Crêperie Josselin, 67, r. du Montparnasse (☎43 20 93 50). M: Edgar Quinet. On a street full of *crêperies,* this one stands out. Locals crowd the dining room. Outstanding food at reasonable prices: *crêpes salées* 22-70F, *sucrées* 22-42F. Open Tu-Su noon-3pm and 6-11:30pm.

Au Rendez-Vous Des Camionneurs, 34, r. des Plantes (☎45 40 43 36). M: Alésia. Cross av. du Maine, walk down r. du Moulin Vert, and turn right onto r. des Plantes. Vibrant local watering hole for artists, young couples, and anyone looking for a value. The menus consist of simple, delicate dishes (77F). Reservations recommended. Open M-F noon-2:30pm and 7:30-9:30pm. Closed Aug.

La Bélière, 74, r. Daguerre (☎43 20 25 84). M: Denfert-Rouchereau. Follow av. du Général Leclerc south, and take a right on r. Daguerre. Join a loyal local following in celebrating the 78F *menu* and frequent live music after 10pm, and hope that the city doesn't tear this old building down. Open M-Sa 8pm-midnight. MC, V.

Aquarius Café, 40, r. de Gergovie (☎45 41 36 88). M: Pernety. Walk against traffic on r. Raymond Losserand and turn right on r. de Gergovie. A vegetarian oasis. The "mini mixed grill" dish includes tofu sausages, wheat pancakes, brown rice, and vegetables in a mushroom sauce (65F). Desserts are light and almost feel healthy (16-37F). Open M-Sa noon-3pm and 7:30-10pm. AmEx, MC, V.

Phinéas, 99, r. de l'Ouest (☎45 41 33 50). M: Pernety. Follow the traffic on r. Pernety and turn left on r. de l'Ouest. Specializing in *tartes sucrées et salées* made before your eyes, this restaurant doubles as a comic book shrine. *Entrées* include vegetarian options (58-80F). Desserts 10-36F. Open Tu-Sa 9am-noon for take-away, noon-11:30pm for dine-in. AmEx, MC, V.

CAFÉS

La Coupole, 102, bd. du Montparnasse (☎43 20 14 20). M: Vavin. Half-café, half-restaurant, La Coupole's Art Deco chambers have hosted Lenin, Stravinsky, Hemingway, and Einstein. The *menus* are expensive, but you can probably still afford coffee (11F), hot chocolate (21F), or a *croque monsieur* (28F). Dancing Tu, F, and Sa 9:30pm-4am; cover 100F. Open daily 7:30am-2am. AmEx, DC, MC, V.

FIFTEENTH ARRONDISSEMENT

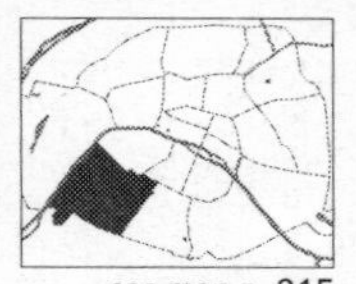
see map p. 315

Cheap eats crowd r. du Commerce, r. de Vaugirard, bd. de Grenelle, and Gare Montparnasse. Inexpensive Middle Eastern abounds—**Mozlef,** 18, r. de l'Arrivée, and **Samaya,** 31, bd. de Grenelle, are two of the best (both open daily noon-midnight). Asian food also has a presence; locals lunch at **Thai Phetburi,** 31, bd. de Grenelle. (Open M-Sa noon-2:45pm and 7-11:15pm.

Chez Foong, 32, r. Frémicourt (☎45 67 36 99). M: Cambronne. Walk across pl. Cambronne; turn left onto Frémicourt. After a walk on the white beaches that fill the posters in this restaurant, this next best thing is dinner from this superb Malaysian kitchen. Try grilled fish in banana leaves with coconut (59F), mango and shrimp salad (56F), and exquisite pastries (35F). 3-course lunch and dinner *menus* 85F (M-F). Worth the trek. Open M-Sa noon-2:30pm and 7-11pm. MC, V.

Restaurant Les Listines, 24, r. Falguière (☎45 38 57 40). M: Falguière. Upscale cuisine that won't break the bank. Delicately prepared seafood and meat. 2-course *menu* 85F, 3-course 120F. Loire wine 14-21F. Open M-F noon-2:30pm and 7pm-1am, Sa noon-2:30pm. AmEx, MC, V.

Chez François, 106, r. St-Charles (☎45 77 51 03). M: Charles Michels. Canteen-style restaurant with speed-challenged wait staff and a phenomenal goat cheese salad. Go for the 3-course *menu* (98F); avoid meat for fish. Good desserts. Open M-Sa noon-2:30pm and 7-10:30pm. MC, V.

CAFÉS

Aux Artistes, 63, r. Falguière (☎43 22 05 39). M: Pasteur. Follow Pasteur away from the rails for 2 blocks and make a right. One of the arrondissement's coolest spots. Modigliani was a regular. Professionals, students, and artists (not to mention American tourists) mix at this lively café. Lunch *menu* 58F; dinner *menu* 80F. Open M-F noon-12:30am, Sa noon-2pm. MC, V.

SIXTEENTH ARRONDISSEMENT

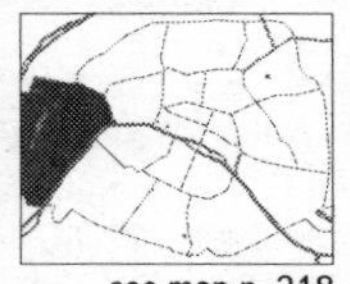
see map p. 318

A good greasy spoon (or even a cheap bistro) has a hard time in the wealthy 16*ème*, but try the restaurants along r. de l'Annonciation or r. de Lauriston. Food shops on r. Passy and av. Mozart and the *marchés* on av. du Président Wilson, r. St-Didier, and at the intersection of r. Gros and r. La Fontaine (see **Marchés,** p. 180) will afford a gourmet picnic.

Casa Tina, 18, r. Lauriston (☎40 67 19 24). M: Charles-de-Gaulle-Etoile. Walk up av. Victor Hugo, turn left on r. Presbourg and right on r. Lauriston going uphill. Warm and lively. Good for an intimate celebration, but skip the romance in favor of garlic potatoes. Serves tapas, paella, and sangria in an 89F lunch menu. Dinner menu 110F. Open daily noon-2:30pm and 7-11pm. Reservations recommended. AmEx, MC, Visa.

Byblos Café, 6, r. Guichard (☎42 30 99 99). M: La Muette. Walk down r. Passy one block and turn left on r. Guichard. Spacious, modern Lebanese restaurant. Cold *hors d'oeuvres* good for pita-dipping and mainly vegetarian: tabouli, moutabal, moussaka, and a variety of hummus dishes all 34F. Warm *hors d'oeuvres* less PC, including hot Lebanese sausages (44F). Takeout available for 10-20% less than eating in. Open daily noon-2:30pm and 7-10:30pm. AmEx, MC, V.

CAFÉS

Café du Musée de l'Art Moderne de la Ville Paris (☎53 67 40 47). M: Iéna/Alma Marceau. Follow directions to the Palais de Tokyo (see p. 99). Situationally superior: on a patio beneath the columns of the Palais, this café offers lunch overlooking the Seine and the Eiffel Tower. Salads 65F; quiches 55F; Sushi 88F. Open May-Oct. Tu-F 10am-5pm, Sa-Su 10am-6:30pm.

La Rotunde de la Muette, 12, Chaussée de la Muette (☎45 24 45 45). M: La Muette. 2min. from the métro down Chaussée de la Muette. A good place for a bite before heading to the Musée Marmottan. Outdoor patio. Sandwiches 25-50F. AmEx, MC, V.

on the cheap

Counter Culture

Café drinks are cheaper at the *comptoir* (or *zinc*) than seated inside the *salle* or on the *terrasse.* Both of these prices should be posted. Aside from coffee, other popular café drinks include *citron pressé,* freshly squeezed lemon juice (with sugar and water on the side). Cafés also serve *croques monsieur* (grilled ham-and-cheese sandwiches), *croques madame* (the same with a fried egg), and assorted omelettes.

SEVENTEENTH ARRONDISSEMENT

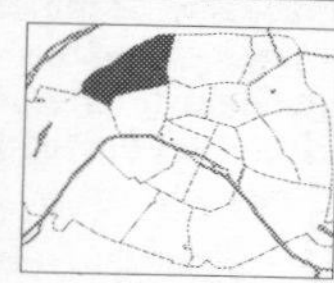
see map p. 319

Far from the tourists, no restaurant in the 17*ème* can survive without strong support from the locals. Fortunately, the variety of neighborhoods here implies an equal variety of cuisine. The best area to look for cheap eats is in Batignolles, extending northward from r. des Dames. R. de la Jonquière (M: Guy-Môquet) is lined with Moroccan, Tunisian, and Algerian shops and restaurants.

The James Joyce Pub, 71, bd. Gouvion St-Cyr (☎44 09 70 32). M: Porte Maillot. Take bd. Gouvion St-Cyr past Palais de Congrès. Upstairs from the pub itself is a restaurant with stained-glass windows depicting scenes from Joyce's novels. The spectacular brunch on Su (noon-3pm) is a full Irish fry: eggs, bacon, sausage, mushrooms, black and white puddings, beans, chips, and coffee (65F). Downstairs, the pub pulls pints of what Joyce called "...Ghinis. Foamous bomely brew bebattled by bottle gagerne de guergerre..." Also serves as a tourist office for English speaking ex-pats. Televised sporting events and monthly concerts; weekly advertisement in *Pariscope* lists times. Pub open M-Th 7pm-1:30am, F-Su 11am-2am; restaurant M-Sa noon-3pm and 7:30-10:30pm, Su noon-5pm. MC, V.

Le Patio Provençal, 116, r. des Dames (☎42 93 73 73). M: Villiers. Follow r. de Lévis away from the intersection and go right on r. des Dames. Staples of southern French fare 35-65F. Glass of wine 25F. Busy, making service a bit slow and reservations necessary. Open M-F noon-2:30pm and 7-11pm. MC, V.

Restaurant Natacha, 35, r. Guersant (☎45 74 23 86). M: Porte Maillot. Take bd. Gouvion St-Cyr past the Palais de Congrès and turn right on r. Guersant. Follow the gray flannel suits to this local gem. Great for lunch: all-you-can-eat buffet for 85F. 2-course *menu* 65F; dinner *menu* 110F. Open M-F noon-2:30pm and 7:30-11pm, Sa 7:30-midnight. Reservations recommended. MC, V.

Aux Îles des Princes, 96, r. de Saussure (☎40 54 01 03). M: Wagram. Turn left off av. de Villiers onto r. Jouffroy, then left onto r. de Saussure. A hopping Turkish spot specializing in charcoal-grilled meats (50-80F). Friendly owner speaks a bit of French and no English, but hand gestures will get you fed (*menus* 70-120F). Open M-Sa noon-3pm and 7-11pm, Su 7-11pm. MC, V.

CAFÉS

L'Endroit, 67, pl. du Dr-Félix-Lobligeois (☎42 29 50 00). M: Rome. Follow r. Boursault to r. Legendre, and turn right. As cool during the day as it is at night. 4-course Su brunch (12:30-3:30pm; 100F) heads a long *menu*. See **Nightlife,** p. 194, for the full listing.

EIGHTEENTH ARRONDISSEMENT

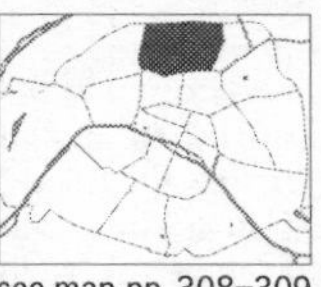
see map pp. 308–309

During the siege of Paris in 1814, Russian cossacks occupied Montmartre. They came to call the restaurants, where they grabbed quick bites between battles, *bistro* (Russian for "quick"). The Russians are gone, but the tourists are here in force, particularly around pl. du Tertre and pl. St-Pierre. Charming bistros and cafés are common between r. des Abbesses and r. Lepic. In addition to the listings below, **Chez Louisette** and **Au Baryton,** which are located within the St-Ouen flea market just north of the 18*ème*, offer *moules marinière*, *frites*, and live French *chanson* entertainment (see **Markets,** p. 180).

Chez Ginette, 101, r. Caulaincourt (☎46 06 01 49). M: Lamarck-Caulaincourt. Upstairs from the métro. An unspoiled slice of Montmartre. Locals come for inventive and inexpensive French cooking, like monkfish with prawn sauce (100F). Open M-Sa noon-2:30pm and 7:30pm-2am. Closed Aug. MC, V.

Le Soleil Gourmand, 10, r. Ravignan (☎42 51 00 50). M: Abbesses. Facing the church in pl. des Abbesses, go to the right end and take the right-most of the three streets that diverge there. 2 sisters run this local favorite with artistic flare. The food is refreshingly light. Try 5-cheese tart with salad (58F), oriental seafood salad (65F), and house-baked cakes (30-44F). Open daily 12:30-2:30pm and 8:30-11pm.

Rendez-vous des Chauffeurs, 11, r. des Portes Blanches (☎42 64 04 17). M: Marcadet-Poissoniers. Walk one block north on bd. des Barbès and make a right. Off the beaten track. Maintains its earthy character despite rave reviews for a 65F *menu* served at lunch and 7:30-8:30pm. Reservations recommended. Open Th-Tu noon-2:30pm and 7:30-11pm. MC, V.

Refuge des Fondues, 17, r. des Trois Frères (☎42 55 22 65). M: Abbesses. Walk down r. Yvonne le Tac and take a left on r. des Trois Frères. Only two main dishes: *fondue bourguignonne* (meat fondue) and *fondue savoyarde* (cheese fondue). The wine is served in baby-bottles with rubber nipples; leave your Freudian hang-ups at home. *Menu* with *apéritif,* wine, appetizer, fondue, and dessert 92F. Reserve or show up early. Open W-M 7pm-2am. Closed for part of July and Aug.

Wassana, 10, r. Ganneron (☎44 70 08 54). M: Pl. Clichy. Walk up av. de Clichy and make the fifth right. Pink dining room serves delicious Thai food five minutes from the corpse of Stendhal. Lunch *menus* (65 and 85F), and a dinner *menu* (130F) include fish and lemon soup, chicken in coconut milk sauce, and sautéed beef with ginger and mushrooms. Appetizers 35-49F; main course 48-75F. Open M-F noon-2:30pm and Sa 7:30-11pm.

CAFÉS

Halle St-Pierre, 2, r. Ronsard (☎42 58 72 89). A quiet café open the same hours as the Musée d'Art Naïf Max Fourny (see **Museums,** p. 137), with assorted coffee and tea (7-20F), cookies, brownies, and cakes (15F), salads, and the major French newspapers. A very pleasant setting unnoticed by the tourists outside. Open Tu-Su 10am-6pm.

Le Sancerre, 35, r. des Abbesses (☎42 58 08 20). M: Abbesses. Classic Montmartre café with some interesting dishes, from chili con carne (49-80F) to hearty crêpes maison (25-35F). Hopping at night as well. Terrace. Open daily 7am-2am. MC, V.

Le Bonaparte

Place de la Contrescarpe

Café in Montmarte

on the cheap

Falafel in the Fourth

L'As du Falafel, 34, r. des Rosiers (☎48 87 63 60). M: St-Paul. This kosher falafel stand and restaurant displays pictures of Lenny Kravitz, who credited it with "the best falafel in the world, particularly the special eggplant falafel with hot sauce." Go his way. Falafel special 25F. Open Su-Th 11:30am-11:30pm. MC, V.

Café des Psaumes, 14-16, r. des Rosiers (☎48 04 74 77). M: St-Paul. A lip-smacking kosher restaurant. *Menus* (with fries and a drink or pastry, 35-45F) are a super value. *Couscous douceur* (sweet, sweet couscous with beef, raisins, chick peas, almonds, and cinnamon, 85F—do me right! Do me right!). Open Su-Th 11am-11pm. MC, V.

Chez Marianne, 2, r. des Hospitalières-St-Gervais (☎42 72 18 86). M: St-Paul. Sample 5, 6, 7, or 9 specialties (55-75F), including tzatziki, falafel, and tarama at this Jewish/Eastern European/Mediterranean Marais institution. Homemade desserts like strudel (30F) and *vatrouchka,* a white cheese cake (35F). Reservations recommended. Take-out falafel available. Open daily 11am-12:30am. MC, V.

NINETEENTH ARRONDISSEMENT

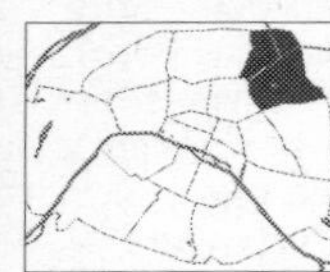

see map p. 320

The ethnically diverse *19ème* offers budget dining in "Little Chinatown," where Chinese, Vietnamese, Thai, and Malaysian restaurants cluster along r. de Belleville (M: Belleville). Greek sandwich shops line av. Jean Jaurès and r. de Crimée. The Parc des Buttes-Chaumont is a winning spot for a picnic.

Lao-Thai, 34, r. de Belleville (☎43 58 41 84). M: Belleville. Thai and Laotian specialties on an all-you-can-eat buffet with 12 different dishes, rice, and dessert. Perfect for the poor and hungry traveler. At 15F, a martini is only 3F more than a Coke. Lunch M-F 49.50F, Sa-Su 55.50F. Dinner Su-Th 74F, F-Sa 80F. Open Tu-Su noon-2:30pm and 7-11:15pm. MC, V.

Aux Arts et Sciences Réunis, 161 av. Jean-Jaurès (☎42 40 53 18). M: Ourcq. Serving up hearty meals family-style, Aux Arts hosts a local crowd. Saucy staff sure to please after a morning at La Villette (see **Sights,** p. 104). *Entrées* 42F; *menu* 60F. Open M-Sa 11:30am-2pm and 7-9pm.

CAFÉS

La Cascade, 2, pl. Armand-Carrel (☎40 40 08 10). M: Laumière. Maybe it's the nautical theme or the bumpin' samba beats, but wandering into La Cascade after a morning in the Parc des Buttes-Chaumont, you'll swear you've taken a sudden vacation from your vacation. Enjoy the cruise. 3-course menu 69.90F. Open daily 9am-8pm; hot food served noon-4pm. AmEx, MC, V.

Ay, Caramba!, 59, r. de Mouzaïa (☎42 41 23 80; fax 01 42 41 50 34). M: Pré-St-Gervais. From the métro, turn right on r. Mouzaïa. With piñatas and a Mariachi band, Ay, Caramba! fits right in in this quiet, residential, French neighborhood. Menu includes fajitas and tacos (84-89F) and nachos caramba (43F). Margaritas 43F. Adjoining Tex-Mex grocery and liquor store. Open M-Th 7:30-11:30pm, F-Su noon-2:30pm and 7:30-11:30pm. AmEx, MC, V.

TWENTIETH ARRONDISSEMENT

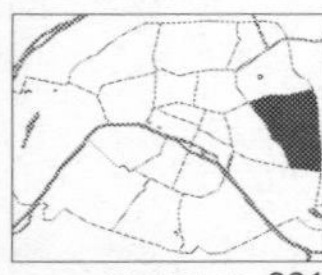

see map p. 321

A traditional meal amid Belleville's cobblestones is a breath of fresh air after Paris's crowded center. A number of trendy cafés and bistros line r. St-Blaise in the south. Come for lunch if you're in the neighborhood, visiting Père Lachaise, or just plain lost.

Café Flèche d'Or, 102, r. de Bagnolet (☎43 72 04 23). M: Alexandre-Dumas. Follow r. de Bagnolet until it crosses r. des Pyrénées; café is on right. Near Porte de la Réunion at Père Lachaise. This bar/performance space/café is housed in a defunct train station. North African, Caribbean, and South American cuisine with nightly jazz, ska, folk, samba (cover 10-25F), and Su morning psychology cafés. Lunch *menu* 69F; dinner *menus* 110-125F. Open M 6pm-2am, Tu-Su 10am-2am; lunch Tu-Su noon-2:30pm; dinner daily 8pm-midnight. MC, V (100F minimum).

Le Zéphyr, 1, r. Jourdain (☎46 36 65 81). M: Jourdain. Walk along Belleville and turn left onto r. Jourdain. An authentic Parisian bistro with fabulous food and 1930s decor. Unique dishes: *ravioli d'aubergine et cumin à la vinaigrette de menthe* (eggplant ravioli with cumin and mint vinaigrette, 48F). 4-course dinner *menu* 160F; lunch *menu* 72F. Open M-F noon-2pm and 8-11pm, Sa 8-11pm. Reservations recommended. MC, V.

CAFÉS

Rital & Courts, 1, r. des Envierges (☎47 97 08 40). M: Pyrénées. This pleasantly funky Italian restaurant-café-bar perches on a corner across from Parc de Belleville. *Ravioli maison* 70F; coffee 12F. Open daily 11am-midnight; lunch noon-3pm; dinner 8-10pm; crowded bar 10pm-midnight.

WINE BARS

Although wine bistros have existed since the early 19th century, the budget-friendly, wine-by-the-glass bar emerged with the invention of a machine that pumps nitrogen into the open bottle, protecting wine from oxidation. Rare wines have become affordable (25-30F a glass). The owners carefully select the wines that constitute their *caves* (cellars) and are available to help out less-knowledgeable patrons. The wine shops in the **Nicolas** chain are reputed for having the world's most inexpensive cellars, although Nicolas himself owns the fashionable and expensive wine bar **Jeroboam,** 42, r. Artois, *8ème* (☎ 42 89 29 75; M: Opéra). For a crash-course on French wine, see **Wine,** p. 157.

Le Clown Bar, 114, r. Amelot, 11*ème* (☎43 55 87 35). M: Filles du Calvaire. Cross Boulevard du Filles du Calvaire to r. Amelot. There are many imitators, but there is only one Clown Bar. Across from the Cirque d'Hiver, and frequented by real live carnies. By the glass starts at 20F. Open M-Sa noon-3:30pm and 7pm-1am. MC, V.

Willie's Wine Bar, 13, r. des Petits Champs, 1*er* (☎42 61 05 09). M: Palais-Royale. Behind the Palais. Popular since its opening in 1980. Exposed wood beams, chic decor, and huge windows looking out onto the Palais and apartment of author Colette. International clientele. Huge selection of French wines 30-50F a glass. Open M-Sa noon-2:30pm and 7pm-12am. MC, V.

Le Baron Rouge, 1 r. Théophile-Roussel, 12*ème* (☎43 43 14 32). M: Ledru-Rollin. Follow the r. du Faubourg Saint Antoine away from the opera and take a right on r. Charles Baudelaire. Théophile-Roussel is your first left. The boisterous bartender will happily suggest one of the dozens of wines on the menu (7F-20F/glass), and for around 25F, he'll bring you a light snack to boot. Open Tu-Th 10am-2pm, 5-9:30pm, F and Sa 10am-9:30pm, Su 10am-3pm. MC, V.

Jacques Mélac, 42, r. Léon Frot, 11*ème* (☎43 70 59 27). M: Charonne. From the métro, walk down r. Charonne to r. Léon Frot. A family-owned wine bar. In Sept., Mélac lets children harvest, tread upon, and extract wine from grapes grown in vines hanging from the bar's storefront. Wine 22F per glass; bottle 90-120F. Open Sept.-July M 9am-5pm, Tu-Sa 9am-midnight. MC, V.

SALONS DE THÉ

Zis iz not a tea party.

-high school French teacher attempting to relay the meaning of life

Parisian *salons de thé* (tea rooms) fall into three categories: those stately salons straight out of the last century piled high with macaroons, Seattle-inspired joints for pseudo-intellectuals, and cafés that simply want to signal that they also serve tea.

the BIG $plurge

Living Large in the Marais

L'Excuse, 14, r. Charles V (☎42 77 98 97). M: St-Paul. Walk against traffic on r. de Rivoli, turn right onto the narrow r. St-Paul, and then left onto Charles V. For those seeking a serious splurge, deluxe is the name of the game at this magical bistro. In other words, the 185F dinner *menu* is well worth it. Lunch *menu* (120-150F) is an even better deal, with larger portions for less dough. Weekly specialities like *roulé de sole à l'étuvée* (braised sole rolled with layers of tomato, basil, and cream of vanilla, 169F). Open M-Sa noon-2pm and 7:30-11pm.

Angelina's, 226, r. de Rivoli, 1*er* (☎42 60 82 00). M: Concorde, Tuileries. Where *Grandmère* takes little Delphine after playing in the Tuileries. And Audrey Hepburn's favorite. *Chocolat africain* (hot chocolate; 36F) and *Mont Blanc* (meringue with chestnut nougat; *37F*) are the dangerous house specialties. Afternoon tea 33F. Open M-F 9am-7pm, Sa-Su 9:30am-7:30pm. AmEx, MC, V.

Marriage Frères, 30, r. du Bourg-Tibourg, 4*ème* (☎42 72 28 11). M: Hôtel de Ville. Also at 13, r. des Grands Augustins, 6*ème* (☎40 51 82 50), M: St-Michel; and 260, r. Faubourg St-Honoré, 8*ème* (☎46 22 18 54). Founded by 2 brothers who found British tea shoddy, this exquisite salon offers 400 varieties of tea (35-41F) poured in kidgloves under palm fronds in an attempt to bring back the Empire. Tea *menu* includes sandwich, pastry, and tea (115F). Classic brunch *menu* (brioche, eggs, tea, cakes; 135F). Reserve for brunch. Open daily 10:30am-7:30pm; lunch M-Sa noon-3pm; afternoon tea 3-6:30pm; brunch Su 12:30-7:30pm. AmEx, MC, V.

Ladurée, 16, r. Royale, 8*ème* (☎42 60 21 79). M: Concorde. Also at 75, av. des Champs-Elysées, 8*ème* (☎40 75 08 75). M: FDR. Ever wondered what it would be like to dine in a Fabergé egg? Famed for the mini macaroons stacked in the window (7.50F). Scrumptious specialty tea "Ladurée mélange" 35F. Open daily 8:30am-7pm; lunch served until 3pm.

Le Loir Dans la Théière, 3, r. des Rosiers, 4*ème* (☎42 72 90 61). M: St-Paul. From the métro, cross r. de Rivoli, follow r. Pavée, and take a right on r. des Rosiers. The famed door mouse from *Alice in Wonderland* (after whom the teashop is named) drowns in his teapot on the mural gracing this downbeat, artsy salon. Serves curiouser and curiouser caramel and jasmine tea (20F), coffees (12-30F), and Su brunch (120F). Open M-F 11:30am-7pm, Sa and Su 10am-7pm. MC, V.

Muscade, 36, r. de Montpensier, 1*er* (☎42 97 51 36). M: Palais-Royale. In the Palais-Royale's northwest corner, Muscade has mirrored walls and art by Cocteau. *Le Chocolat Muscade* (26F) is a recently melted chocolate bar parading as a liquid. An assortment of pastries (30F) and 26 kinds of tea (22F). Book a table on the terrace in summer. Open Tu-Su tea 10-11:30am; lunch 12:15-3:30pm; dinner 6:30-11:30pm.

SHOPS AND MARKETS

Something you can never do too often in Paris is assemble inexpensive meals yourself: go from one shop to another to make a picnic. A *charcuterie* is the French version of a delicatessen, a *crémerie* sells dairy products, and the corner *fromagerie* may stock over 100 kinds of cheese. Buy bread in the morning or just before mealtimes from *boulangeries* when the baguettes are steaming hot. A *pâtisserie* sells pastries; a *confiserie* stocks candy and ice cream. Buy your produce at a *primeur*. *Boucheries* sell meat and poultry. A *traiteur* has *plats cuisinés* (prepared meals). *Epiceries* (grocery stores) carry staples, wine, and produce. *Marchés,* open-air markets held at least once a week (see p. 180), remain the best places to buy fresh produce, fish, and meat. Finally, you can grab simple food items, cigarettes, and lotto tickets at any corner *dépaneur* (convenience store). Note that French storeowners are fantastically touchy about people handling their fruits and vegetables; unless there's a sign that says *libre service,* ask inside before you start handling the goods displayed. *Supermarchés* (supermarkets) have it all under one roof, although they make shopping less interesting. If you're in the mood for a five-and-dime complete with men and women's clothing, photocopiers, telephone cards, and a supermarket, go to any of the 48 **Monoprix** and **Prisunics** that litter the city. They are usually open during the week until 9pm, although the Prisunic at 52, av. Champs-Elysées, is open until midnight. Starving students swear by the ubiquitous **Ed l'Epicier** and **Leader Price.** Buy in bulk and watch the pile of francs you save grow. **Picard Surgelés,** with 50 locations in the city, stocks every food ever frozen—from *crêpes* to calamari.

SPECIALTY STORES

Food shops in Paris are ubiquitous; *boulangeries* and *pâtisseries* seem to tempt on every corner. Should, for some reason, you decide that your corner *chocolaterie* is no longer cutting it, the following listings are the best specialty food shops that Paris has to offer; all deserve a .

Boulangerie: Poujauran, 20, r. Jean-Nicot, *7ème* (☎47 05 80 88). M: La Tour-Maubourg. Various country and herb breads, in addition to the standards; miniatures sold also. Tarts, cookies, and confections of superior quality as well. Open Tu-Sa 8:30am-8:30pm.

Chocolatier: La Maison du Chocolat, 8, bd. de la Madeleine, *9ème* (☎47 42 86 52). M: Madeleine. Also at other locations, including 52, r. François 1er, *8ème* (☎47 23 38 25). The whole range, from milk to dark, and, for those tired of the usual consumption of solid chocolates, La Maison offers a mysterious distilled chocolate essence drink. Standard solid bar 28-39F. Open M-Sa 9:30am-7pm. MC, V.

Confiserie: Confiserie Rivoli, 17, r. de Rivoli, *4ème* (☎42 72 80 90). M: St-Paul. Tubs of Haribo candy 50F. *Let's Go* does not recommend eating too many gummies. Open M-Sa 10am-7pm.

Epicerie Chinoise: Tang Frères, 44 or 48, av. d'Ivry, *13ème* (☎45 70 80 00). M: Porte d'Ivry. Look for no. 44 and go down a few steps to this huge grocery in the heart of Chinatown; or look for no. 48 and follow the sign through a parking lot to the much larger Tang next door. Rice, spices, teas, soups, and noodles in bulk. Sassy selection of exotic fruit. Stocks high-quality, hard-to-find Eastern and Western produce. Cheap Asian beers (Sapporo and Kirin 7.80F), rice wines, and sake. No. 44 open M-Sa 10am-8:30pm; no. 48 Tu-Su 9am-7:30pm.

Fromagerie: Androuet, 19, r. Daguerre, *14ème* (☎43 21 19 09). Amid the galleries of r. Daguerre is this gallery of cheese. The brightly colored cheeses are decorated in patterns of leaves or layers of raisins (*vendangeur*, 26.50F per piece). Open Tu-F 9am-1pm and 3:30-8pm, Su 9am-1:30pm.

Glacerie: Berthillon, 31, r. St-Louis-en-l'Île, *4ème* (☎43 54 31 61), on Île-St-Louis. M: Cité or Pont Marie. The best and most famous ice cream and sorbet in Paris. Choose from dozens of *parfums* (flavors), ranging from passion fruit and gingerbread to the standard chocolate. Sitting down is more expensive (double 32F), but you would probably be willing to sell your children to pay for this stuff: it's that good. Since lines are long in summer, look for stores nearby that sell Berthillon products; the wait is shorter and they're open in late July and Aug., when the main outfit closes. A list of the 6 stores is posted on the Berthillon window after it closes. Singles 9F; doubles 16F; triples 20F. Open Sept.-July 14: takeout W-Su 10am-8pm; eat-in W-F 1-8pm, Sa-Su 2-8pm. Closed 2 weeks in Feb. and Apr.

Glacerie: Jadis et Gourmande, 39, r. des Archives, *3ème* (☎48 04 08 03). M: Rambuteau. Some of the richest ice cream in town. Also a *chocolaterie.* 1 scoop 10F, 2 scoops 15F, 3 scoops 20F. Open M 1-7:30pm, Tu-Sa 10am-7:30pm.

Pâtisserie: Au Panetier, 10, pl. des Petits Pères, *2ème* (☎42 60 90 23). M: Bourse. Known for its wide selection, the modest and beautifully tiled Au Panetier—one of the oldest pastry shops in

on the cheap

In the 15ème

Sampieru Corsu, 12, r. de l'Amiral Roussin. M: Cambronne. Walk into the pl. Cambronne, take a left on r. de la Croix Nivert, then turn left on r. de l'Amiral Roussin. This communist-inspired restaurant, serves each guest according to his or her means. The patron and his wife invite workers and tourists alike to share a table with other members of the proletariat. Eat your fill of roast chicken, or "Isabella" paella, and pay as much as you can, though the suggested price for the copious 3-course *menu* is 45F (*pâté*, cheese, and wine included). Laborers eat for free. Open M-F 11:30am-1pm and 6:30-pm.

Ty Breiz, 52, bd. de Vaugirard (☎43 20 83 72). M: Pasteur. Authentic Breton *crêperie* brings a taste of the North to Paris, from fine and filling *crêpes* to clogs on the wall. Dinner *crêpes* 17-51F, including the 48F "*savoyarde*" (cheese, bacon, onions, potatoes). They're very serious about their pancakes here, but use the "p" word and you may be forced to read educational pamphlets on *crêpe* vocabulary, history, and the definition of a *galette*. Dessert *crêpes* 16-43F. Show them *Let's Go* for a free *kir breton*. Open M-Sa 11:45am-2:45pm and 7-10:45pm. MC, V.

Paris—also creates delectable and affordable tarts (10-12F). Open M-F 10am-7pm.

Pâtisserie: Gérard Mulot, 76, r. de Seine, 6*ème* (☎43 26 85 77). M: Odéon, St-Sulpice. Classic service, outrageous selection of handmade pastries, from flan to marzipan with virtually any kind of fruit. Heaven on earth is Mulot's *macaron. Tartes* 15F; eclairs 13F. Open Th-Tu 7:15am-8pm.

Wine Store: Nicolas, 132, bd. Raspail, 6*ème* (☎43 26 64 36). M: Vavin. When you think of France, you think of wine, and so will Mom. But the overwhelming variety can be difficult to sort through. At Nicolas, the super-friendly English-speaking staff is happy to help you pick the perfect Burgundy and pack it in travel boxes with handles. Wines 20-250F. Numerous branches throughout the city. Open M-F 10am-8pm. AmEx, MC, V.

MARKETS (MARCHÉS)

In the 5th century, ancient Lutèce held the first market on what is now Île de la Cité. More than a millennium and a half later, markets exude conviviality and neighborliness in every arrondissement, despite the ongoing growth of the *supermarché*. Most are open two to six days per week (always on Sunday). The freshest products are often sold by noon, when many stalls start to close. Quality and price can vary significantly from one stall to the next; you might want to stroll through the market before buying.

Marché r. Montorgueil, 2*ème*. A center of food commerce and gastronomy since the 13th century, the marble Mount Pride Market is composed of wine, cheese, meat, and produce shops.

Marché Port Royal, 5*ème*. M: Censier-Daubenton. Make a right on bd. du Port-Royal in front of the Hôpital du Val de Grâce and make a right. Toward the intersection of bd. du Port-Royal. Colorful, fun, and busy. Find your favorite fresh produce, meat, fish, and cheese here; other tables are loaded with shoes, cheap chic, and housewares. Open Tu, Th, and Sa 8am-1:30pm.

Marché Mouffetard, 5*ème*. M: Monge. Walk through Pl. Monge and follow r. Ortolan to r. Mouffetard. Cheese, meat, fish, produce, and housewares sold here. Visit the bakeries of high reputation. Open Tu-Su 8am-1:30pm.

Marché Monge, 5*ème*. M: Monge. Strong on produce and breads, but with all the basics, including Vietnamese and African prepared foods. Open W, F, Su 8am-1:30pm.

Marché Biologique, on bd. Raspail between r. Cherche-Midi and r. de Rennes, 6*ème*. M: Rennes. French New-Agers peddle everything from organic produce to 7-grain bread and tofu patties. Open Su 7am-1:30pm.

Marché St-Quentin, 85bis, bd. de Magenta, 10*ème*. M: Gare de l'Est or Gare du Nord. Outside: a massive construction of iron and glass, built in the 1880s, renovated in 1982, and covered by a glorious glass ceiling. Inside: stalls of all varieties of produce, meat, cheese, seafood, and wine. Open Tu-Sa 8am-1pm and 4-7:30pm, Su 8am-1pm.

Marché Bastille, on bd. Richard-Lenoir from pl. de la Bastille north to r. St-Sabin, 11*ème*. M: Bastille. Produce, cheese, exotic mushrooms, bread, meat, and housewares stretch from M: Richard Lenoir to M: Bastille. Popular Su morning family outing. Open Th and Su 7am-1:30pm.

Marché Popincourt, on bd. Richard-Lenoir between r. Oberkampf and r. de Jean-Pierre Timbaud, 11*ème*. M: Oberkampf. An open-air market close to many hotels fills with fresh, well-priced perishables. Less expensive than the Marché Bastille. Open Tu and F 8am-1:30pm.

Marché Beauvau St-Antoine, on r. d'Aligre between r. de Charenton and r. Crozatier, 12*ème*. M: Ledru-Rollin. One of the largest Parisian markets. Cheap produce, the quality of which is wildly variable. Produce market open Tu-Sa 8am-1pm and 3:30-7:30pm, Su 8am-1pm. Tag sale daily 8am-1pm. Busiest on weekends.

Marché Président-Wilson, on av. Président-Wilson between r. Freycinet and pl. d'Iéna, 16*ème*. M: Iéna or Alma-Marceau. An alternative to the 16*ème*'s exorbitant restaurants. Competitively priced agricultural and dairy products, meat, and fish. Flower stalls, clothing, table linens, and other household goods. Open W and Sa 8:30am-1pm.

Marché Berthier, on bd. de Reims between r. de Courcelles and r. du Marquis d'Arlandes, along pl. Ulmann, 17*ème*. M: Porte de Champerret. Turn left off bd. Berthier onto r. de Courcelles then right on bd. de Reims. Probably has the cheapest produce in Paris. North African and Middle Eastern specialties like fresh mint, Turkish bread, and baklava. Open W and Sa 8am-1pm.

INSIDE

Nightlife

I like the nightlife, I like to boogie.
—Sun King Louis XIV

Le Roi s'amuse, alors pourquoi pas moi?
—anonymous drunken French barfly

BARS AND PUBS

Bars in Paris are either nighttime cafés bursting with Parisian people-watching potential or more laid-back Anglo havens. In the *5ème* and *6ème*, bars cater to French and foreign students, while the Bastille and Marais teem with Paris's young and hip, gay and straight. Near Les Halles you'll find a slightly older set, while the outer arrondissements cater to the full range of locals in tobacco-stained bungalows and yuppie drinking holes. Of course, Let's Go researchers are not allowed to drink while on duty, which, ramble they be gin to ?drinking much merry, vodka be good.

CLUBS

Clubbing is less about hip DJs and cutting-edge beats, and more about dressing up, getting in, and being seen. Although admission can be selective, once inside, clubs are soft-core and rarely intimidating. Drinks are expensive and people drink little. At most clubs, regulars buy bottles of liquor which are kept at the bar for a couple of weeks; they then reserve tables for specific nights and work on their bottles. Note that many clubs accept reservations, which means that on busy nights, there will be no available seating. To help get into selective clubs (see **Glamorama,** below), it is advisable to dress well, to come early, to be confident but not aggressive about getting in, and to come in a couple if you

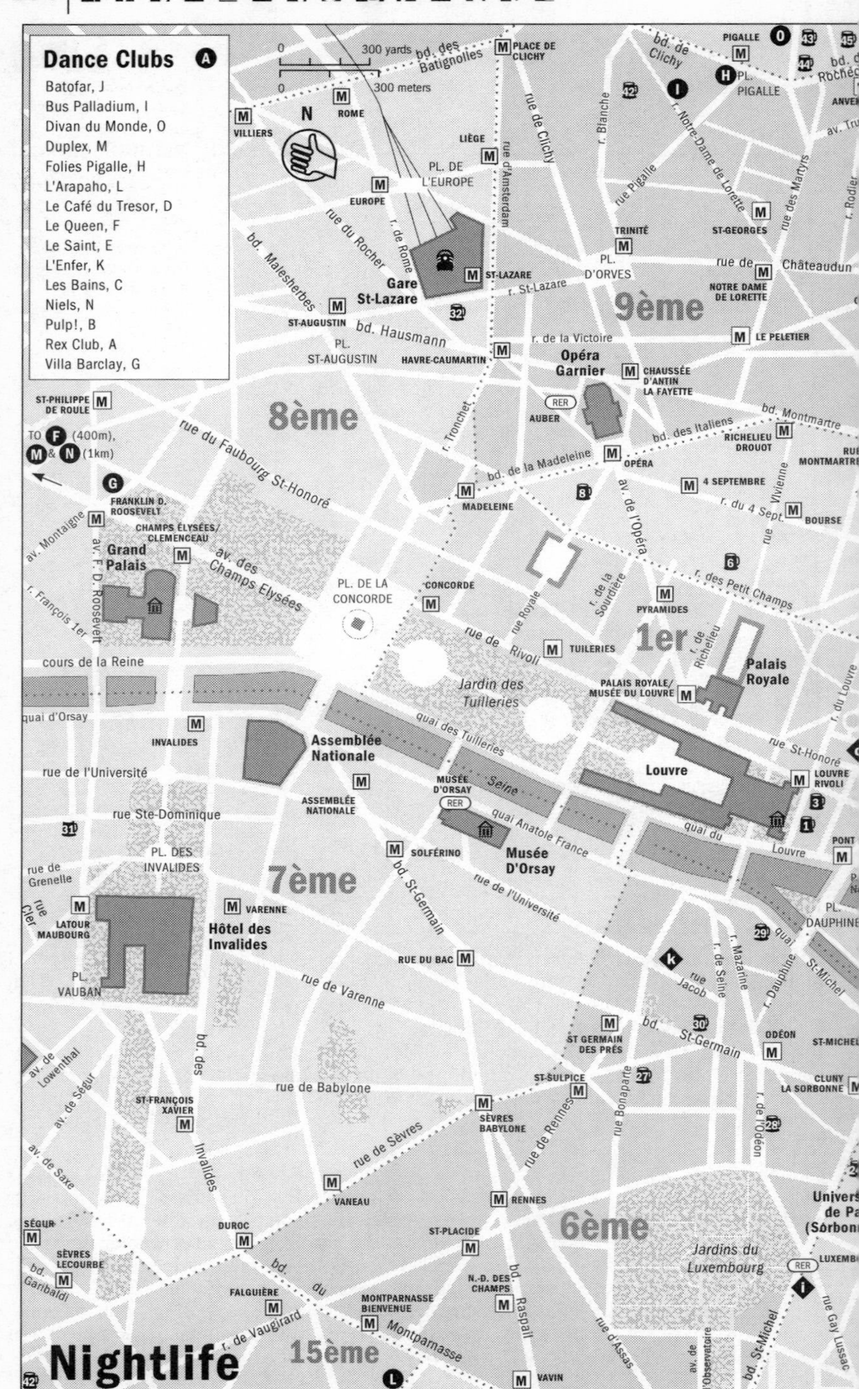
Dance Clubs A
Batofar, J
Bus Palladium, I
Divan du Monde, O
Duplex, M
Folies Pigalle, H
L'Arapaho, L
Le Café du Tresor, D
Le Queen, F
Le Saint, E
L'Enfer, K
Les Bains, C
Niels, N
Pulp!, B
Rex Club, A
Villa Barclay, G
0
300 yards
0
300 meters
N
TO F (400m),
M & N (1km)
bd. des Batignolles
PLACE DE CLICHY
bd. de Clichy
PIGALLE
PL. PIGALLE
ROME
VILLIERS
LIÈGE
PL. DE L'EUROPE
EUROPE
rue de Clichy
r. Blanche
r. Notre-Dame de Lorette
rue Pigalle
rue des Martyrs
rue d'Amsterdam
rue du Rocher
r. de Rome
bd. Malesherbes
Gare St-Lazare
ST-LAZARE
TRINITÉ
ST-GEORGES
PL. D'ORVES
rue de Châteaudun
NOTRE DAME DE LORETTE
r. St-Lazare
9ème
ST-AUGUSTIN
bd. Hausmann
PL. ST-AUGUSTIN
HAVRE-CAUMARTIN
r. de la Victoire
LE PELETIER
Opéra Garnier
CHAUSSÉE D'ANTIN LA FAYETTE
RER
AUBER
ST-PHILIPPE DE ROULE
8ème
r. Tronchet
bd. Montmartre
bd. des Italiens
RICHELIEU DROUOT
rue du Faubourg St-Honoré
bd. de la Madeleine
OPÉRA
G
FRANKLIN D. ROOSEVELT
MADELEINE
4 SEPTEMBRE
r. du 4 Sept.
BOURSE
av. Montaigne
CHAMPS ÉLYSÉES/ CLEMENCEAU
Grand Palais
av. F. D. Roosevelt
av. des Champs Elysées
av. de l'Opéra
rue Vivienne
r. François 1er
PL. DE LA CONCORDE
CONCORDE
rue Royale
r. de la Sourdière
PYRAMIDES
r. des Petit Champs
rue de Rivoli
TUILERIES
1er
r. de Richelieu
Palais Royale
cours de la Reine
Jardin des Tuilleries
PALAIS ROYALE/ MUSÉE DU LOUVRE
r. du Louvre
quai d'Orsay
INVALIDES
Assemblée Nationale
quai des Tuilleries
rue St-Honoré
rue de l'Université
Louvre
LOUVRE RIVOLI
MUSÉE D'ORSAY
Seine
RER
ASSEMBLÉE NATIONALE
rue Ste-Dominique
quai Anatole France
quai du Louvre
PONT
SOLFÉRINO
Musée D'Orsay
PL. DES INVALIDES
rue de Grenelle
7ème
bd. St-Germain
rue de l'Université
rue Cler
VARENNE
LATOUR MAUBOURG
Hôtel des Invalides
PL. DAUPHINE
quai St-Michel
r. Mazarine
r. de Seine
rue Jacob
RUE DU BAC
r. Dauphine
PL. VAUBAN
rue de Varenne
ST GERMAIN DES PRÉS
bd. St-Germain
ODÉON
ST-MICHEL
av. de Lowenthal
bd. des Invalides
av. de Ségur
ST-SULPICE
rue Bonaparte
CLUNY LA SORBONNE
rue de Babylone
ST-FRANÇOIS XAVIER
SÈVRES BABYLONE
r. de l'Odéon
rue de Sèvres
rue de Rennes
av. de Saxe
VANEAU
RENNES
Univers de Pa (Sorbon
SÉGUR
DUROC
ST-PLACIDE
6ème
SÈVRES LECOURBE
Jardins du Luxembourg
RER
LUXEMB
bd. Garibaldi
bd. du Montparnasse
FALGUIÈRE
MONTPARNASSE BIENVENUE
N.-D. DES CHAMPS
bd. Raspail
rue d'Assas
rue Gay Lussac
r. de Vaugirard
15ème
av. de l'Observatoire
bd. St-Michel
Nightlife
VAVIN

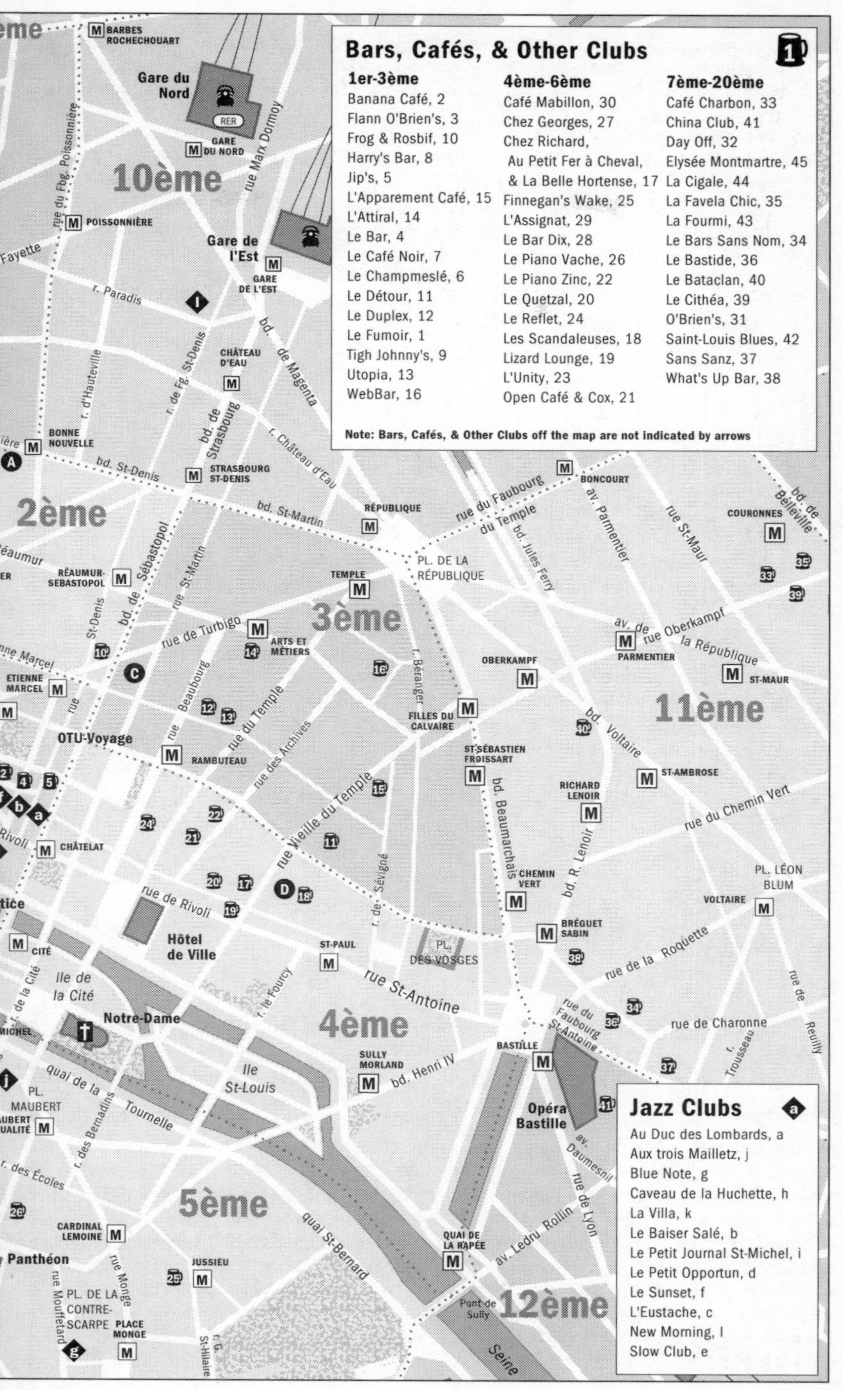

Bars, Cafés, & Other Clubs
1er-3ème
Banana Café, 2
Flann O'Brien's, 3
Frog & Rosbif, 10
Harry's Bar, 8
Jip's, 5
L'Apparement Café, 15
L'Attiral, 14
Le Bar, 4
Le Café Noir, 7
Le Champmeslé, 6
Le Détour, 11
Le Duplex, 12
Le Fumoir, 1
Tigh Johnny's, 9
Utopia, 13
WebBar, 16
4ème-6ème
Café Mabillon, 30
Chez Georges, 27
Chez Richard,
Au Petit Fer à Cheval,
& La Belle Hortense, 17
Finnegan's Wake, 25
L'Assignat, 29
Le Bar Dix, 28
Le Piano Vache, 26
Le Piano Zinc, 22
Le Quetzal, 20
Le Reflet, 24
Les Scandaleuses, 18
Lizard Lounge, 19
L'Unity, 23
Open Café & Cox, 21
7ème-20ème
Café Charbon, 33
China Club, 41
Day Off, 32
Elysée Montmartre, 45
La Cigale, 44
La Favela Chic, 35
La Fourmi, 43
Le Bars Sans Nom, 34
Le Bastide, 36
Le Bataclan, 40
Le Cithéa, 39
O'Brien's, 31
Saint-Louis Blues, 42
Sans Sanz, 37
What's Up Bar, 38
Note: Bars, Cafés, & Other Clubs off the map are not indicated by arrows
Jazz Clubs
Au Duc des Lombards, a
Aux trois Mailletz, j
Blue Note, g
Caveau de la Huchette, h
La Villa, k
Le Baiser Salé, b
Le Petit Journal St-Michel, i
Le Petit Opportun, d
Le Sunset, f
L'Eustache, c
New Morning, l
Slow Club, e
10ème
2ème
3ème
4ème
5ème
11ème
12ème
Gare du Nord
Gare de l'Est
BARBES ROCHECHOUART
GARE DU NORD
POISSONNIÈRE
GARE DE L'EST
CHÂTEAU D'EAU
BONNE NOUVELLE
STRASBOURG ST-DENIS
RÉPUBLIQUE
PL. DE LA RÉPUBLIQUE
TEMPLE
RÉAUMUR-SEBASTOPOL
ARTS ET MÉTIERS
ETIENNE MARCEL
OTU-Voyage
RAMBUTEAU
FILLES DU CALVAIRE
OBERKAMPF
PARMENTIER
ST-MAUR
COURONNES
GONCOURT
ST-SÉBASTIEN FROISSART
RICHARD LENOIR
ST-AMBROSE
CHÂTELAT
CHEMIN VERT
VOLTAIRE
PL. LÉON BLUM
BRÉGUET SABIN
Hôtel de Ville
CITÉ
ST-PAUL
PL. DES VOSGES
Ile de la Cité
Notre-Dame
Ile St-Louis
SULLY MORLAND
BASTILLE
Opéra Bastille
PL. MAUBERT
CARDINAL LEMOINE
Panthéon
JUSSIEU
PL. DE LA CONTRE-SCARPE
PLACE MONGE
QUAI DE LA RAPÉE
Pont de Sully
Seine
rue Marx Dormoy
rue du Fbg. Poissonnière
r. Paradis
r. de Fg. St-Denis
bd. de Magenta
bd. de Strasbourg
r. d'Hauteville
r. Château d'Eau
bd. St-Denis
bd. St-Martin
rue du Faubourg du Temple
bd. Jules Ferry
av. Parmentier
rue St-Maur
bd. de Belleville
bd. de Sébastopol
rue St-Martin
rue de Turbigo
rue Beaubourg
rue du Temple
rue des Archives
r. Béranger
av. de la République
rue Oberkampf
bd. Voltaire
rue Vieille du Temple
bd. Beaumarchais
bd. R. Lenoir
rue du Chemin Vert
rue de Rivoli
r. de Sévigné
rue St-Antoine
rue de la Roquette
rue de Charonne
r. Trousseau
rue de Reuilly
rue du Faubourg St-Antoine
bd. Henri IV
quai de la Tournelle
r. des Bernadins
r. des Écoles
quai St-Bernard
av. Ledru Rollin
rue de Lyon
av. Daumesnil
rue Monge
rue Mouffetard
r. G. St-Hilaire
r. le Fourcy

can. In general, women tend to dress more formally than men. Further, clubs are usually busiest between 2 and 4am. Clubs have very different feels on different evenings, so you might want to check what type of music and scene is scheduled before heading out.

BISEXUAL, GAY, & LESBIAN ENTERTAINMENT

The center of lesbian and gay life is the Marais (see the **4ème Arrondissement,** p. 67). Most gay establishments cluster around r. du Temple, r. Ste-Croix de la Bretonnerie, r. des Archives, and r. Vieille du Temple in the *4ème.* For the most comprehensive listing of gay and lesbian restaurants, clubs, hotels, organizations, and services, consult Gai Pied's *Guide Gai* (79F at any kiosk), *Illico* (free at gay bars and restaurants), *Le Guide Paris* (28F at gay shops), *e.m@le* (free at gay extablishments) are all chock-full of up-to-date events listings. *Pariscope* has an English-language section called *A Week of Gay Outings.* **Les Mots à la Bouche,** Paris's largest gay and lesbian bookstore serves as an unofficial information center for queer life and can also tell you what's hot and where to go

NIGHTLIFE BY ARRONDISSEMENT

FIRST ARRONDISSEMENT

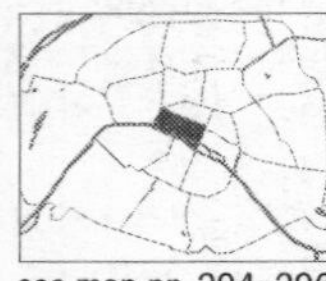

see map pp. 294–296

Le Fumoir, 6, r. de l'Admiral Coligny (☎42 92 05 05). M: Louvre. As cool by night as it is by day. Extra dry martini 58F. See **Cafés,** p. 162.

Banana Café, 13-15 r. de la Ferronerie (☎42 33 35 31). M: Châtelet. From the Porte du Pont Neuf of Les Halles, go straight, left on r. St. Honoré; r. de la Ferronerie is straight ahead past the Châtelet métro stop. This *très branché* (way cool) evening arena is the most popular gay bar in the *1er.* Two floors include a piano bar. Legendary theme nights. During "Crazy Time" from 4:00-9pm, drinks are two for one, except for cocktails. Open daily 4pm-dawn. AmEx, MC, V.

Café Oz, 18 r. St. Denis (☎40 39 00 18). M: Châtelet. From the métro walk down r. Rivoli and make a left onto St. Denis. Friendly Australian bar with pine benches, big tables, and happy-to-be-of-service bar tenders. Ask about nude pie-eating championships. All-day brunch Sundays. Happy hour daily 6-8pm. Pints 25-35F. Open Su-Th 3pm-2am; F 3pm-3am; Sa 12pm-3am. MC, V.

Flann O'Brien's, 6, r. Bailleul (☎42 60 13 58). M: Louvre-Rivoli. From the métro, walk away from the Seine on r. du Louvre and make the first right after crossing r. de Rivoli. Arguably the best Irish bar in Paris, Flann is often packed, especially on live music nights. Go for the Guinness—stay for Thursday Quiz night. Demi 20F, full pint 37F. Happy hour daily, 4-8pm. Ask about the live music schedule. Open daily 4pm-2am.

SECOND ARRONDISSEMENT

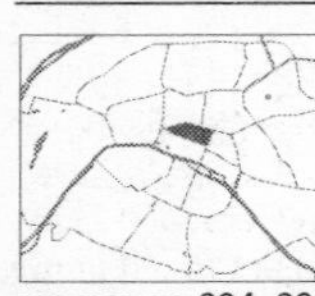

see map pp. 294–296

Le Champmeslé, 4, r. Chabanais (☎42 96 85 20). M: Pyramides or Quatre Septembre. From the métro, walk down av. de l'Opéra and make a right on r. des Petits Champs. Make another right onto r. Cabanais. This comfy lesbian bar is Paris's oldest and most famous. Mixed crowd in the front, but women-only in back. Drinks 30-45F. Popular cabaret show every Thursday at 10pm. On your birthday month, you get a free drink. No cover. Open M-W 5pm-2am, Th-Sa 5pm-5am. MC, V.

Le Café Noir, 65, r. Montmartre (☎40 39 07 36). M: Sentier. Paper maché creatures hang from the ceiling, crazy tiling tiles the floor, and bartenders leap onto the bar to perform comedy. A real mix of locals and anglophones: patrons seem willing to overcome the language barrier to meet someone new. Beer 12-14F M-F 8am-2am, Sa 5pm-2am.

Le Scorp, 25, bd. Poissonnière (☎40 26 01 93). M: r. Montmartre. The legendary lesbian L'Entr'acte has been through several incarnations in the past few years, and is now Le Scorp, though no one seems to mind what you call it anymore. House, techno, and Latin are the pulpy mainstays. Drinks 30F-60F. Weekdays are more mixed with men admitted if they accompany a woman. Weekends are women-only. Open W-Sa midnight-5am. Su-Th no cover, F and Sa 50F. AmEx, MC, V.

Harry's Bar, 5, r. Daunou (☎42 61 71 14). M: Opéra.The kitsch birthplace of the Bloody Mary hosts businessmen, tourists and couples in their 30s and 40s. Claiming to be the "oldest bar in Europe" Harry's does its best to make international students feel at home by pinning college flags on the wall and making wallpaper out of international currency. Open daily 11am-4am. AmEx, DC, V.

Frog & Rosbif, 116, r. St-Denis (☎42 36 34 73). M: Etienne Marcel. At the corner of r. St-Denis and r. Tiquetonne. As if a slice of High Street had been plugged in next to the peep shows. Live rugby and football broadcasts, three happy hours (6-9pm), house ales, and the typical entourage of Englishmen. Open daily noon-2am.

DANCE CLUBS

Rex Club, 5, bd. Poissonnière (☎42 36 10 96). M: Bonne-Nouvelle. A non-selective club which presents a most selective DJ line-up. Young break-dancers and veteran clubbers fill this casual, subterranean venue to hear cutting-edge techno, break beats, and hip hop fusion from international DJs on one of the best music systems in Paris. Large dance floor and lots of seats as well. Open Tu-Sa 11:30pm-6am. Shots 25-30F, Soft drinks 35F, Beers 30-45F.60-80F. Cover varies; W are free, Th-Sat 60-80F. MC, V.

Le Scorp, 25, bd. Poissonnière (☎40 26 01 93). M: r. Montmartre. See above.

THIRD ARRONDISSEMENT

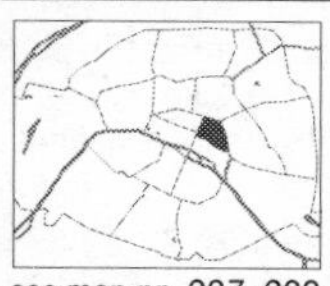
see map pp. 297–299

Nightlife in the *3ème* is more subdued than that of the neighboring *4ème*, as the *3ème* offers only a few discrete nocta-spots. A number of gay and lesbian bars are located on r. aux Ours, r. Saint Martin, and r. Michel Le Comte.

L'Apparemment Café, 18, r. des Coutures St-Gervais. M: St-Paul. Lounge with board games. See p. 187 for full listing.

Le Détour, 5, r. Elizéver (☎40 29 44 04). M: St-Paul. Swank neo-couchical lounge beats with soul, jazz, and deep house. Hookahs (strawberry, apple, or apricot tobacco) 35F. Cocktails 50F, beer 18F. Open daily 7pm-1:30am.

Le Duplex, 25, r. Michel Le Comte (☎42 72 80 86) M: Rambuteau. This gay bar d'art has a funky mezzanine, yet feels small and intimate. Not an exclusively male bar, but few women hang out here. Beer 15F. Open daily 8pm-2am. AmEx, MC, V.

Utopia, 15 r. Michel Le Comte. (☎42 71 63 43). M: Rambuteau. Displaying the slogan *le bar des filles qui bougent* (the bar for girls who move), Utopia boasts house beats, pool, pinball, and occasional out-there dress-up parties. Beer 18F. Happy hour M-W 5-8pm. Open M-Sa 5pm-2am.

L'Attirail, 9 r. au Maire (☎42 72 44 42). M: Arts et Métiers. This casual and unpretentious bar welcomes concerts and performances from Celtic chanting to accordion music, oriental jazz, and Tzigane rap. Play your cards right and your drink may come with a freebie (french fries, not ass). Beer 15F. Open daily 6pm-2am.

DANCE CLUBS

Les Bains, 7, r. du Bourg l'Abbé (☎48 87 01 80). M: Réaumur-Sébastopol or Etienne-Marcel. Ultraselective, super-crowded, and expensive. Used to be a public bath, visited at least once by Marcel Proust. More recently, Mike Tyson, Madonna, and Jack Nicholson have stopped in, but only to bathe in their glory. And then the Artist Once-Again Known as Prince boosted its reputation with a surprise concert a few years back. Lots of models on the floor. House and garage grunge. Mirrored bar upstairs. Cover and 1st drink M-F 100F; Sa-Su 120F. Subsequent drinks 70F. Open daily 11:30pm-6am. AmEx, MC, V.

FOURTH ARRONDISSEMENT

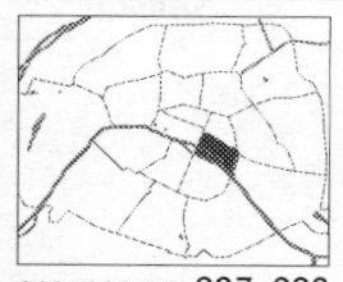
see map pp. 297–299

No matter where you are in the *4ème*, a bar is nearby. With the exception of *Les Enfants Gâtés*, all of the cafés listed under **Cafés**, p. 158, also double as bars. Spots with outdoor seating are piled on top of each other on r. Vieille-du-Temple, from r. des Francs-Bourgeois to r. de Rivoli. Gay bars crowd r. Ste-Croix-de-la-Bretonnerie.

TONIGHT, GET WHAT YOU WANT

Ordering anything in Paris can be a trying experience, and ordering a beer particularly so. Harried waiters bop around crammed cafés, and you are expected to know just what you want (and how to say it) at a moment's notice. Perhaps your simplest choice is a **draught beer**—simply say, *"Une pression, s'il vous plaît"* (OON PRESS-yawn, SEEL VOO PLAY). You don't even have to specify the brand: they'll just bring you the cheapest option. They may ask if you want 50cl (*cinquante*, SANK-aunt) or 25 (*vingt-cinq*, VAN-sank); if you're looking for less than the full dose, "un demi" is also a key phrase. On the lighter side, **cider** is also often an option. That's an easy one—just "*un cidre*" (AHN CEE-dra), followed, as always, by "s'il vous plaît." As for beer brands, Heineken and Hoegarten are sure bets (French beer, fortunately, is not all that popular). Both of these non-French options, however, are extremely difficult to say if you're trying to put on your sassiest French accent. For Heineken, you've just got to suck it up and try your best, but for Hoegarten or a similar super-light, lemon-accompanied drinking pleasure, simply say *"Une blanche, s'il vous plaît"* (OON BLON-sha...yada yada). Strange but true—no one will think you've asked for white wine (*vin blanc*), and you'll get just what you wanted.

Le Café du Trésor, 5, r. du Trésor (☎44 78 06 60). M: St-Paul. Walk along r. de Rivoli in the direction of traffic, turn right onto r. Vieille-du-Temple and right onto the pedestrian r. du Trésor. Color, boom, style, and youth. DJs spin house, deep house, and funk. Th-Sa 8pm-1:30am. Open daily 9am-2am; food served M-F 12:30-3pm and 7:30-10:30pm, Sa-Su 12:30-10:30pm. MC, V.

La Belle Hortense, 31, r. Vieille-du-Temple (☎48 04 71 60). M: St-Paul. Walk in the direction of traffic along r. de Rivoli and turn right onto r. Vieille-du-Temple. A breath of fresh air for those worn-out by the oft' scene-y scene along the rest of the *rue*. Wide wine selection from 18F a glass, 90F a bottle. Walls and walls of books (literature, art, philosophy) and (surprise!) some really mellow music to go with your merlot. Frequent exhibits, readings, and discussions in the small leather-couch-filled back room. Open daily 1pm-2am.

Les Etages, 35, r. Vieille-du-Temple (☎42 78 72 00). M: St-Paul. Set in an 18th-century hotel-turned-bar, Les Etages boasts three floors of tapas fun. Come en masse to this close, cool space around 8pm to snag an entire floor and quaff 25F margaritas and sangria. Eat like a bird at rock bottom prices: tapas from 15F and free honey-roasted nuts. Open daily 5pm-2am. MC, V.

Le Bar du Palmier, 16, r. des Lombards (☎42 78 53 53). M: Chatelet. With an absolutely fa-bulous cast of waiters and a nice terrace for people watching on weekends, the Palmier is nothing but fun. Ignore or indulge in the tropical theme, but for God's sake, don't miss the opportunity to banter with your barman or waiter. Happy hour 6-8pm. Open daily 5pm-5am. Beer 20-30F. AmEx, MC, V.

Les Scandaleuses, 8, r. des Ecouffes (☎48 87 39 26). M: St-Paul. Walk along r. de Rivoli in the direction of traffic and turn right onto r. des Ecouffes. A vibrant, ultra-hip lesbian bar set to techno beats. Men welcome if accompanied by women. Beer 22F. Happy hour 6-8pm. Open daily 6pm-2am. MC, V.

L'Unity, 176/178, r. St-Martin (☎42 72 70 59). M: Rambuteau. Walk down r. Rambuteau and look right. Next to the Pompidou, this studenty women's club features a pool table, cards and boardgames at the bar, and a loud soundtrack including reggae, folk, rock, and techno. Men welcome if accompanied by women. Happy hour M-F 4-8pm. Drinks 17-40F. Open daily 4pm-2am.

Lizard Lounge, 18, r. du Bourg-Tibourg (☎42 72 81 34). M: Hôtel-de-Ville. A split-level steel-sleek space for anglo/franco late 20-something hipsters. The underground cellar has a happy hour (8-10pm) where all cocktails and pints are 25F. Beer 17-40F, cocktails 40-50F. Open daily noon-2am. MC, V.

Open Café, 17, r. des Archives (☎42 72 26 18). M: Hôtel-de-Ville. Recently redone, the Open Café is the most popular of the Marais gay bars, often drawing a large crowd of loiterers to its corner. Grit your teeth, grip your handbag, and bitch your way onto the terrace. Beer 18F, cocktails 35F. Open daily 11am-2am; Su brunch (70-105F). Happy hour 6-8pm. MC, V.

Chez Richard, 37, r. Vieille-du-Temple (☎42 74 31 65). M: Hôtel-de-Ville. Inside a courtyard off r. Vieille-du-Temple, this super-sexy bar and lounge screams drama. The secret: on a slow night (read: not the weekend) it's an ideal chill spot, with hip bartenders and nice n' smooth beats. Beer 22-40F, cocktails 50-60F. Open daily 5pm-2am. MC, V.

Au Petit Fer à Cheval, 30, r. Vieille-du-Temple (☎42 72 47 47; www.cafeine.com). M: Hôtel-de-Ville. A Marais institution with a horseshoe bar, sidewalk terrace, and small restaurant in the back. Paradise on earth. Beer 14-18F, cocktails 48F. For more on food at the Petit Fer, see **Restaurants,** p. 189. Open daily 9am-2am.

Cox, 15, r. des Archives (☎42 72 08 00). M: Hôtel-de-Ville. As the name suggests, this is a buns-to-the-wall men's bar with bulging and beautiful boys. So crowded, the boys who gather here block traffic on the street. Very cruisy; this isn't the place for a quiet cocktail. Happy hour (with beer half-off) M-Sa 6-8pm, Su 6-9pm. Beer 16-25F 9F. Open daily 2 1pm-2am.

Le Piano Zinc, 49, r. des Blancs Manteaux (☎40 27 97 42). M: Rambuteau. A mature crowd gathers nightly to enjoy the hysterical cabaret performances of the gifted bar staff. Campy homage is paid to Liza, Eartha, Madonna, Bette, and Edith Piaf. All are welcome to perform (although attendance at 10pm rehearsals is recommended). Happy Hour 6-8pm. Beer 10-14F, cocktails 37-44F. Open Tu-Su 6pm-2am. AmEx, MC, V.

Le Quetzal, 10, r. de la Verrerie (☎48 87 99 07). M: Hôtel-de-Ville. Nicknamed l'Incontournable (a must), this neon techno bar runs the gamut from stylish to shady. The cruisy Quetzal is opposite the r. des Mauvais Garçons (bad boys). Beer 18F, cocktails 15-45F. Happy Hour 5-8pm. Open daily 5pm-5am. V.

Le Sunset

Le Fumoir

Au Duc des Lombards

FIFTH ARRONDISSEMENT

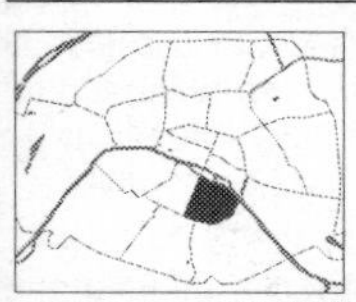
see map pp. 302–303

Le Reflet, 6, r. Champollion (☎43 29 97 27). M: Cluny-La Sorbonne. Walk away from the river on bd. St-Michel, then make a left on r. des Ecoles. Take the first right. Small, low key, crowded with student and younger Frenchies. Pictures of Woody Allen, Hitchcock, Orson Welles, and decent oil paintings by local artists populate the black walls. Beer 11-16F, cocktails 12-32F at bar. Open M-Sa 10am-2am, Su noon-2am. MC, V.

Le Piano Vache, 8, r. Laplace (☎46 33 75 03). M: Cardinal Lemoine or Maubert-Mutualité. From the métro, walk up r. de la Montagne Saint Geneviève and make a right on r. Laplace. Dark, Poster-plastered bar hidden beind the Panthéon. Relaxed, student-geared atmosphere with a bartender who takes his music choices seriously. Beer 20-30F, cocktails 40F. Open July-Aug. daily 6pm-2am, Sa-Su 9pm-2am; Sept.-June noon-2am, Sa-Su 9pm-2am.

Finnegan's Wake, 9, r. des Boulangers (☎46 34 23 65). M: Cardinal Lemoine. From the métro, walk up r. des Boulangers to this Irish pub set in a renovated ancient wine cellar with low, black-beamed ceilings. Have a pint (25-35F) with the boisterous crowd and soak up some Irish culture. Open M-F 11am-2am, Sa-Su 6pm-2am.

Sarl Le Salon Egyptien, 77, r. Carinal Lemoine (☎43 25 58 99). M: Cardinal Lemoine. From the métro, walk uphill on Cardinal Lemoine. Little leather seats surround low, brass tables on tiled floors. The

SIROP, YOU MAKE MY HEART SING, YOU MAKE EVERYTHING ... GROOVY

Have you ever felt so smashed, you thought the huge construction worker at the bar was sipping a pink beer? Fear no more! In Paris, this happens all the time, as the local fetish for **raspberry, grenadine, mint** and **peach sirop** knows no bounds. **Raspberry beer** is actually good, and you'll kick yourself for thinking you're too macho to try it. Perhaps the best kept Froggie secret is **Menthe à l'eau.** Warning, it is bright green, and you will think your waiter accidentally dropped some nuclear waste in your glass. But it is oh-so-refreshing after the long, hot toil of the tourist day. Of course, **Kir Royal** (champagne with grenadine), gets a party going and looks festive waving in your hand as you attempt to climb the Eiffel Tower in your stillettos—these drinks go directly to your head, they do not pass go, and they do collect your two hundred dollars.

smoke wafting into the street smells of apricot, apple, cherry and the various other fruity tobaccos you can request when you order your hookah (25F). Matching fruit juices 18F, mint tea 10F, and bottled beer 20F. The downstairs room can get uncomfortably smokey. Open everyday, 11am-2am.

Greuze, 19, r. Soufflot (☎43 54 63 00). M: Cluny-La Sorbonne. From the métro, walk up Boulevard St-Michel, make a left on r. Soufflot. This festive bar/restaurant specializes in Beligian beer (Greuze being a Beligian brew) and has over 100 bottled beers available, from cherry-flavored Kriek to Trappist beer brewed by swingin' monks (35-90F). Each beer comes in a specially shaped glass. Street seating; the large rooms towards the back are great for large groups. Open daily, 11am-12pm. MC, V.

DANCE CLUBS

Le Saint, 7, r. St. Severin (☎43 25 50 04). M: St-Michel. Reggae to techno to R&B. No saints here, only hostelers and the occasional angel-faced student from the latin quarter. Set it 13th C. caves, the club slowly evolves from an intimate bar to a warm set of coves and ends in a tiny, flashy dance floor that is nearly too close for comfort. Cover Tu-Th 60F, F 80F, S 90F. Drinks 15-50F. Open daily 11pm-6am.

SIXTH ARRONDISSEMENT

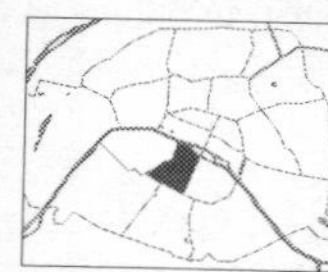

see map pp. 302–303

Le Bar Dix, 10, r. de l'Odéon (☎43 26 66 83). M: Odéon. From the métro, walk against traffic on bv. St. Germain and make a left on r. de l'Odéon. A classic student hangout where you might be forced to eavesdrop on existentialist discussions in the former coal cellar downstairs. No matter, because after enough sangria (15F), you'll feel pretty OK about being condemned to freedom. Open daily 6pm-2am.

Chez Georges, 11, r. des Cannettes (☎43 26 79 15). M: Mabillon. From the métro, walk down r. du Four and make a left on r. des Cannettes. This former cabaret lives a double life: upstiars it's a wine bar full of old men playing chess; downstairs it's a candlelit cellar rampant with bebopping Anglo students. Open Tu-Sa noon-2am (upstairs), 10pm-2am (cellar).Closed August.

L'Assignat, 7, r. Guénégaud (☎43 54 87 68). M: Mabillon or Odéon. From the métro, walk down r. Mazarine off bv. St-Germain and make a right on r. Guénégaud. Very neighborhood-oriented and very cheap (12F beer), this little pub named after a Revolutionary bank note draws a crowd. Irregular jazz happenings. Open M-Sa 9am-2am. Closed July.

Café Mabillon, 164 bd. St-Germain (☎43 26 62 93). M: Mabillon. Dimly lit equals trendy and hip? You decide. Clientele surges onto the street on weekend nights. Drinks a bit pricey (fancy cocktails 60F), but it's a fine place to nurse a beer for a couple of hours. Open daily 7am-6am. V.

SEVENTH ARRONDISSEMENT

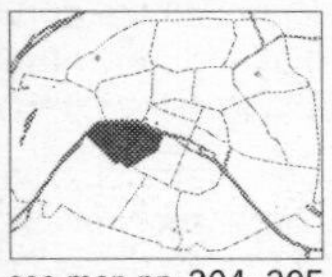
see map pp. 304–305

O'Brien's, 77, r. St-Dominique (☎45 51 75 87). M. Latour-Maubourg. Handsome Irish pub with a horseshoe shaped bar where local students, businessmen and tourists are drawn by the Guiness sign on the door. Gather before their big screen TV for soccer matches, but supporting the US during the World Cup match could make you very unpopular. During the winter months you can win yourself a bottle of Champagne on quiz night, Sundays at 9pm. Happy hour M-F 6-8pm, pints 29F. Otherwise, 25cl beer 25F, 50cl beer 40F, cocktails 35-50F. Open M-Th 6pm-2am, F-Su 4pm-2am.

Master's Bar, 64, av. Bosquet (☎45 51 08 99). M: Ecole-Militaire. Central location and easy-going atmosphere. Here you'll find the Frenchman who's not averse to Anglo-American culture. Relax in the cracked white leather chairs with moderately priced drinks: beer 28-35F, cocktails 35-50F. Happy hour 5-7pm. A good place to stop for a late-night coupe-faim, they serve club sandwiches (50F) or smoked salmon (52F). Open M-F noon-2am, Sa 7pm-2am.

EIGHTH ARRONDISSEMENT

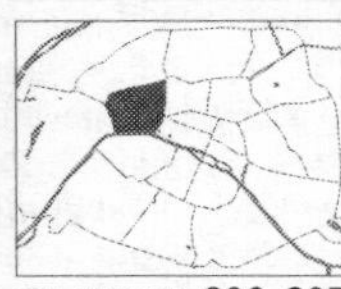
see map pp. 306–307

Chesterfield Cafe, 124, r. de la Boétie (☎42 25 18 06) M: Franklin D. Roosevelt. Walk toward the Arc on the Champs-Elysées, and r. de la Boétie will be the second street on your right. Friendly American bar with first-class live music. Americans and Frenchies mix happily with the attractive waitstaff. Snack bar has good ol' yankee fare: hamburgers 62F; brownies 34F; and key lime pie 36F. Cocktails 46F; beer 23-48F; coffee 12F. No cover Su-Th. Open daily 10am-5am.

Day Off, 10, r. de l'Isly (☎45 22 87 90). M: St-Lazare. Off r. de Rome, near the Gare St-Lazare, this mellow bar/*resto* features a dark wood interior, long bar, and walls covered with divas. Good for a relaxed evening with friends. Drinks 18-45F. Open M-F 11am-3pm and 5pm-3am.

DANCE CLUBS

Le Queen, 102, av. des Champs-Elysées (☎53 89 08 90). Come taste the fiercest funk in town where drag queens, superstars, models, moguls, and buff Herculean go-go boys get down to the mainstream rhythms of a 10,000 gigawatt sound system. Some nights here are rumored to end in a rambunctious bath of shaving cream. Her majesty is at once one of the cheapest and one of the most fashionable clubs in town, and thus the toughest to get in to—especially for women. M disco; W "Respect"; Th house; F-Sa house; Su "Overkitsch." Cover Su-Th 50F, F-Sa 100F. All drinks 50F. Open daily midnight to dawn. Pray to Madonna that you get in.

Villa Barclay, 3, av. Matignon (☎53 89 18 91). M: Franklin D. Roosevelt. Freshly pressed Frenchies explore the wilds outside of the 16*ème*. A plush, if slightly claustrophobic, living room, motors the pushing-30 scene. The crowd loosens up in the wee hours and elegant beauties clamber onto tables to shake that booty. Restaurant *menu* 250F. Downstairs is a crowded, sticky inferno which doesn't stop bopping until someone drops. Drinks 60-80F. Cover 100F. Ladies: show a little attitude and some skin, and they may comp you. Disco open Th-Sat 11:30pm-dawn.

NINTH ARRONDISSEMENT

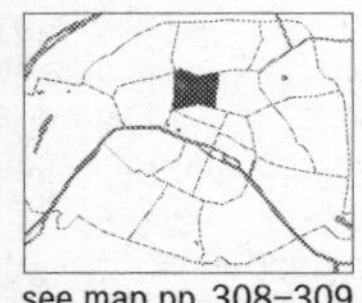
see map pp. 308–309

DANCE CLUBS

Bus Palladium, 6, r. Fontaine (☎53 21 07 33). M: Pigalle. The classiest of the mainstream clubs, Le Bus fills with a young and trendy crowd who rock the party that rocks the ex-rock 'n' roll club, still sporting vintage posters and faded gilded décor. Cover 100F. Free for ladies Tu; free for all W. Drinks 60F. Open Tu-Sa 11pm-6am. AmEx, V.

Folies Pigalle, 11, pl. Pigalle (☎48 78 25 56). M: Pigalle. This club is the largest in the once-sleazy Pigalle *quartier.* A former strip joint, the Folies Pigalle is popular among gay and straight clubbers, with some special girls-only events. Mostly house and techno. Very crowded at 4am. Open Tu-Sa 11pm-7am, Su 3-8pm. Cover 100F. Drinks 60F. AmEx, MC, V.

ELEVENTH ARRONDISSEMENT

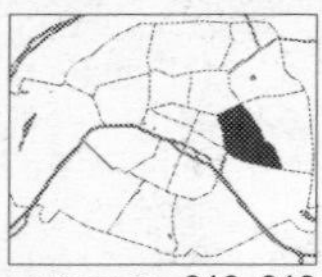
see map pp. 312–313

Gritty but groovy, the bars on r. Oberkampf and r. de Lappe are definitely "downtown." The 11*ème* is a neighborhood that moves to the beat under waves of rich spices; it hosts a comfortable, energetic crowd of internationals and real, live Parisians.

Café Charbon, 109, r. Oberkampf (☎43 57 55 13). M: Parmentier or Ménilmontant. A spacious bar that proudly wears traces of its *fin-de-siècle* dance hall days, but still manages to pack in the punters. If that beer looks pink, you might still be sober–a specialty is sweet beer with *cassis* (raspberry cordial; 15F). Beer 15-20F. Open 9pm-2am. MC, V.

Le Bar Sans Nom, 49, r. de Lappe (☎48 05 59 36). M: Bastille. Facing the Mix Café, a blank red front is all that distinguishes the sneaky No-Name bar from others along the packed r. de Lappe. Dim, jazzy lounge famous for its inventive cocktails, some even *flambé.* A favorite is the Morgeto, a Cuban cocktail with mint, lemon, and rum. Beer 30-40F; shots 40F; cocktails 50F. Open M-Sa 7pm-2am.

Boteco, 131, r. Oberkamf (☎43 57 15 47). M: Parmentier. Popular, techno-generation Brazilian bar/restaurant with trendy wait staff, grafitti art, and flip-up benches transforms itself into a dance space. Beer 18F. Open daily 9-2am.

Sans Sanz, 49, r. du Faubourg St-Antoine (☎44 75 78 78). M: Bastille. Popular, upbeat bar with bouncer control. A large baroque-framed screen projects scenes from the bar like a black and white movie. Outdoor seating; indoor A/C. Beer 10F; drink prices go up after 9pm. Open daily 9:30pm-2am.

Bar bat, 23, r. de Lapppe (☎43 14 26 06). M: Bastille. A busy bar and restaurant that attracts all sorts of twentysomethings. No pout necessary. Sleek chill-out area near entrance. Restaurant serves Corsican menu. *Plats* 42-79F. Long mirrored bar with friendly waiters and happy hour from 5-8pm at the back. Beer 19F. DJ plays R 'n' B. Open daily 4pm-2am; dining 6pm-1am.

CLUBS

What's Up Bar, 15, r. Daval (☎48 05 88 33). M: Bastille. From the métro, walk north on bd. Richard Lenoir and make a right on r. Duval. One of those rare Paris miracles: a place that is (almost always) free and funky. Set up in a concrete bunker, this bar/club has DJ competitions and its own magazine. M drum and bass, W Electronic, F Garage, Sa Freestyle. Open M-F 10pm-2:30am, Sa-Su 10pm-5am. Cover F-Sa 50F. Drinks 25-50F. MC, V, AmEx.

Le Cithéa, 114, r. Oberkampf (☎40 21 70 95). M: Parmentier. More of a bar with live music than a pulsing, flash-dancing club. In the very hip Oberkampf *quartier* and full of young, artsy folk, Le Cithéa features a wide variety of jazz, hip hop, and free jack fusion bands, as well as DJs spinning drum 'n' bass. Drinks 25-60F. Open daily 9:30pm-5am. Cover W-Th 30F, F-Sa 60F. MC, V.

Le Bataclan, 50, bd. Voltaire (☎43 14 35 35). M: Oberkampf. A concert space and café-bar that hosts indie rock bands like Guided By Voices and Beck. Funky sliding toward trendy. Tickets start at 100F and vary with show. Th (free) is low-key, F (80F) is gay night, and Sa (80F) is house. Call for schedules and reservations. Open Sept.-July Th-Sa 11pm-dawn.

TWELFTH ARRONDISSEMENT

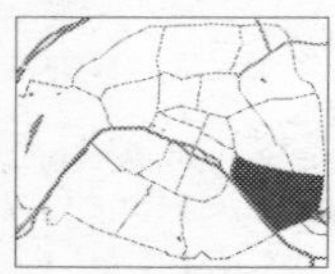
see map p. 311

China Club, 50, r. de Charenton (☎43 43 82 02). M: Ledru-Rollin or Bastille. Swank Hong Kong club with a speakeasy-style cellar and lacquered *fumoir chinois* look. High-class prices, but a Chinatown (gin fizz with mint) is hard to resist. Cocktails (70-90F) and periodic, free jazz (call ahead for details). Open M-Th 7pm-2am, F-Sa 7pm-3am. Happy hour 7-9pm. Reservaions (and a trust fund) recommended for dinner. AmEx, MC, V.

Viaduc Cafe, 43, Daumesnil (☎44 74 70 70; www.viaduc-cafe.fr). M: Reuilly-Diderot. Built right into the Viaduc des Arts (see **Sights,** p. 212). Decorations caught somewhere between Chagall and cave painting, American pop music and a palm tree or two are the accompaniments to a late-night stop-over in this massive, cement café. An excellent choice for after the opera. Outdoor seating. Coffee 12F. Open daily 9am-4am, food served until 3am. Jazz brunch Su noon-4pm.

Factory Café, 20 r. du Faubourg St-Antoine (☎44 74 68 74). M: Bastille. Heading down r. du Faubourg St Antoine from the Place de la Bastille, the club is on your right. A perfect place to test the waters of Paris club-land just outside the reaches of the most obnoxious *au centre* bouncers. Just a little bit of attitude at the door. Admission (50F) comes complete with first drink; subsequent drinks 35-45F. Open daily 9pm-2am. AmEx, DC, MC, V.

Le Piano Vache

THIRTEENTH ARRONDISSEMENT

see map p. 314

Les Oiseaux de Passage, 7, passage Barrault (☎45 89 72 42). M: Corvisart. From r. de la Butte aux Cailles, turn right on r. des Cinq Diamants, then left on passage Barrault. Young, hip, and laid-back. Art openings, live music, multiple board games, and theme evenings, including "silent discussion night." Beer and kir 12F; most food under 55F. Open M-F 11am-2am, Sa-Su 4pm-2am. Closed three weeks in Aug.

La Folie en Tête, 33, r. de la Butte aux Cailles (☎45 80 65 99). M: Corvisart. 'The' artsy axis mundi of the 13*ème*. Magazines, writing workshops, and musical instruments. Crowded concerts on Saturday nights. Beer 10-14F; coffee 7F; selection of 10F cocktails before 8pm; all prices increase by 2F after 10pm. Open M-Sa 5pm-2am. MC, V.

Bateau El Alamein, Port de la Gare (☎45 86 41 60). M: Quai de la Gare. This calm, plant-filled boat lodged on the Seine is the perfect spot for a nightcap. Beer 20F. Open daily 6pm-2am.

Le Merle Moqueur, 11, r. de la Butte aux Cailles (☎45 65 12 43). M: Corvisart. Take r. Bobillot south until r. de la Butte aux Cailles branches right. Bamboo walls, African music, and a shabby-cool ambiance. Cheap beer (14F) and food (nothing over 50F). No frills and few tourists. Most customers head for the terrace but the back room is cooler. Happy hour 5-8pm. Open daily 5pm-2am. AmEx, DC, MC, V. Wheelchair accessible.

Le Baiser Sale

DANCE CLUBS

Batofar, facing 11, Quai François-Mauriac (☎56 29 10 33). M: Quai de la Gare. A club on a light-boat! The boat's innards have been transformed into cavernous bar areas and a sizeable dance floor. Friendly industrial environment. Jungle, dub, drum n' bass, eccentric electronic, and Su "blue note groove" live jazz. Open in summer Tu-Su 6pm-2am. Tapas 20F. Cover up to 100F.

L'Arapaho, 30, av. d'Italie, Centre Commercial Italie 2 (☎45 89 65 05). M: Pl. d'Italie. The gray door on the right, just past Au Printemps. Since 1983, this place has built up a reputation for hosting some of the best hard-core, rap, pop, and metal bands to come through Paris. A pitstop on most indie rock bands' tour itineraries. Tickets usually around 60-130F. Beer 20F, cocktails 50F. F "Asian Folly" night, Sa Cuban. Cover and first drink 100F. Open F-Sa 11pm-dawn.

Le Bar Dix

FOURTEENTH ARRONDISSEMENT

see map pp. 315–317

L'Entrepôt, 7-9, r. Francis de Pressensé (☎45 40 78 38; film schedule ☎08 36 68 05 87; restaurant reservations ☎45 40 60 70). M: Pernety. Walk down r. Raymond Losserand and turn right onto r. Francis de Pressensé. An alternative cinema coupled with a plush, trendy bar that features live music and a garden patio. Beer 14-37F. Ciné-Philo, a screening and discussion café, is held Su 2:30pm and occasionally other days; 42F, students 32F. Open Su-M 11:30am-10pm, Tu-F 11am-2am, Sa 4pm-2am; food served noon-2pm and 7pm-closing. AmEx, MC, V.

Smoke Bar, 29, r. Delambre (☎43 20 61 73). M: Vavin. Unpretentious yet stylish. Dark wood, red ceilings, blue lights, jazz posters, blues music. A perfect place to hang out with a drink, a game of chess, and a cigarette. Cocktails 30-45F; beer 22-26F. Happy hour 3-7pm. Open M-F noon-2am, Sa 6pm-2am. MC, V.

Mustang Café, 84, bd. du Montparnasse (☎43 35 36 12). M: Montparnasse-Bienvenüe. What's a poor boy to do in a city that closes up at 2am? Head to Mustang, where 20F beer and Tex Mex munchies flow freely 'til 5. This place is all-American, with juke box, occasional wet T-shirt competitions, and Anglophones (and Anglophiles) a plenty. Happy hour M-F 4-8pm. Open daily 11am-5am. Food served 11:30am-5pm and 7pm-5am. MC, V.

DANCE CLUBS

L'Enfer, 34, r. de Départ (☎42 79 94 94). M: Montparnasse-Bienvenüe. Pretty, pretty young clubbers get down with their bad selves to mainstream hip hop, house, and techno. More mature crowd on Saturdays, and less attitude at the door than at more central clubs. Cover 100F with drink; subsequent drinks 50F. Open Th-Sa 11:30pm-10am. V.

SIXTEENTH ARRONDISSEMENT

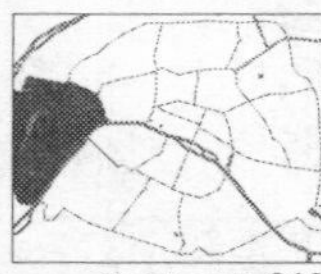

see map p. 318

L'Etoile, 12, r. de Presbourg (☎45 00 78 70). M: Charles-de-Gaulle-Etoile. Just across from the entrance to Duplex on av. Foch. Vibrant techno, hip-hop, and funk from DJ Jean-Jean from St-Tropé. The tropics span a dance floor, bar area, plush VIP lounge, and lush outdoor courtyard. Pouty (the girls) or panty (the boys), the clientele tends to be in their 20s or 30s, but still very much the ex-Duplex *Jeunesse Dorée*. Entrance and drink 100F. At the door: Just walk it baby, walk it! Open daily 11:30pm to dawn.

Duplex, 2bis, av. Foch (☎45 00 93 93). M: Charles-de-Gaulle-Etoile. Walk around the Arc to this chic nightclub where young glamouratzi party to techno-fied pop, funk, and occasionally hip-hop. Bouncers friendlier and crowd more laid back on weekdays. Businessmen stick to the bar and seated area. Remember, the path to a bouncer's heart runs through his libido. Also houses expensive restaurant (open Tu-Su 9pm-1am). Cover and first drink Su and Tu-Th 100F, F-Sa 120F. Club open Tu-Su midnight-dawn.

SEVENTEENTH ARRONDISSEMENT

see map p. 319

L'Endroit, 67, pl. du Dr-Félix-Lobligeois (☎42 29 50 00). M: Rome. Follow r. Boursault to r. Legendre, and make a right. The purveyor of cool in work-a-day Batignolles. On a square facing the church. Beer (22-30F), wine (20-25F), cocktails (50-65F) and liquor (45F) are just for starters. Try the Black Honduras (a Kahlua-Amaretto mixture). Open daily noon-2am. MC, V.

La Main Jaune, pl. de la Porte-de-Champerret (☎47 63 26 47). M: Porte de Champerret. The metro lets you out right in the middle of he pl. de la Porte-de-Champerret. A roller disco (with regular dancing as well) popular with the high school crowd. Open W and Sa-Su 2:30-7pm, F-Sa and holidays 10pm-dawn. Admission W and Sa-Su 50F (includes a drink), skate rental 10F; F-Sa night it becomes a disco with Portuguese music and a no-wheels clientele.

EIGHTEENTH ARRONDISSEMENT

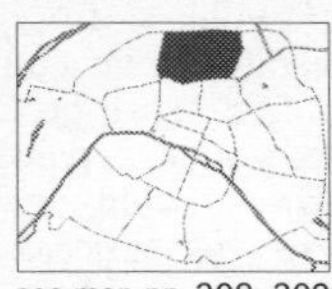

see map pp. 308–309

Chez Camille, 8, r. Ravignan (☎46 06 05 78). M: Abbesses. From the métro, walk down r. de la Veuville and make a left on r. Drevet and another left on r. Gabrielle which becomes r. Ravignan. Small and trendy bar with a pretty terrace looking down the *butte* to the Invalides dome. Cheap coffee and tea. Beer 23-30F, wine 22-28F, and cocktails 30-50F. Open M-Sa noon-2am.

La Fourmi, 74, r. des Martyrs (☎42 64 70 35). M: Pigalle. From the métro, walk east on bd. Rochechouart and make a left on r. des Martyres. Popular stop-off before clubbing at Divan du Monde, this bar has artsy character with a large zinc bar and industrial decor. More spacious than other bars, and more energetic as well. Crowd is young and scrappy. Beer 25-35F, wine 25-40F, cocktails 30-60F. Open M-Sa 8:30am-2am, Su 10:30am-2am. MC, V, AmEx.

LIVE MUSIC CLUBS

La Cigale, 120, bd. Rochechouart (☎49 25 89 99). M: Pigalle. The métro puts you right on bd. Rochechouart. One of the two large rock clubs in Pigalle, seating 2000 for international indie, punk, hard-core bands. Concerts 100-180F. The converted theater also brings in modern dance shows. Music starts 8:30pm, box office open M-Sa noon-showtime. MC, V.

Elysée Montmartre, 72, bd. Rochechouart (☎44 92 45 42). M: Anvers. The métro lets you out right on bd. Rochechouart. The biggest-name rock, reggae, and rap venue in a neighborhood fixture. Featuring well-known British and American groups in addition to home-grown talent, and a large dance floor for disco and salsa nights. Drinks 30-50F, shows 80-150F. AmEx, MC, V.

DANCE CLUBS

Divan du Monde, 75, r. des Martyrs (☎44 92 77 66). M: Pigalle. From the métro, walk east on bd. Rochechouart and make a left on r. des Martyres. Not quite global, but this grungy den does try with Brazilian music, live bands, English DJs, funk, and "Creative Relaxation" evenings. Youngish crowd varies; frequent week-long festivals. Sa is Brazillian night, Su is gay tea dance. Open daily 7:30pm-dawn. Cover 40F-100F. Drinks from 20F. MC, V.

NINETEENTH ARRONDISSEMENT

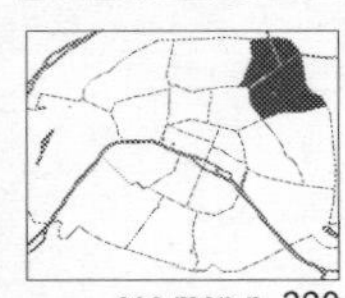

see map p. 320

Pub de l'Ecrin, 57, r. d'Hautpoul (☎42 45 30 73). M: Ourcq. One of the few meeting spots in the 19th, this locals' bar hosts a mixed gay/straight crowd. Come to play pool, enjoy the fun, relaxed atmosphere, and snack on 15F sandwiches. Drinks 15-35F. Happy hour 6-9pm. Open M-Sa 5pm-2am. MC, V.

TWENTIETH ARRONDISSEMENT

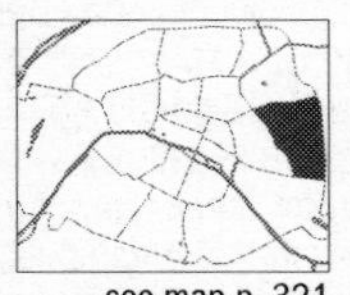

see map p. 321

La Flèche d'Or, 102bis, r. de Bagnolet (see **Restaurants,** p. 177). Live music from ragga hip hop to Celtic rock every night, art videos, dance classes, Sunday *bals*, and crazy theater on the tracks below the terrace. Open daily 10pm-2am.

Lou Pascalou, 14, r. des Panoyaux (☎46 36 78 10). M: Ménilmontant. Follow bd. de Ménilmontant; make a left on r. des Panayaux. A bit out of the way, Lou Pascalou features open-air terrace seating, a pool table, occasional concerts, and art displays. Beer 14, cocktails 22-45F, add 2F after 10pm. Open daily 10am-2am.

JAZZ

Nearly every type of jazz is represented in Paris, from New Orleans to cool jazz, from acid jazz to hip hop and fusion. Brazilian samba and bossa nova are steadily growing in popularity together with music from the West Indies and Francophone Africa. Paris jazz clubs charge either through inflated drink prices or a cover charge. Once you have paid your cover, you are not required to drink and will likely not be disturbed should you choose to nurse one drink for the rest of the night. Frequent summer festivals sponsor free or nearly free jazz concerts. The **Fête du Marais** often features free Big Band jazz, while the **La Villette Jazz Festival** offers very big names and a few free shows (see **Festivals,** p. 6). In the fall, the **Jazz Festival of Paris** comes to town as venues high and low open their doors to celebrity and up-and-coming artists. French mags *Jazz Hot* (45F) and *Jazz Magazine* (35F) are great sources, as is the bimonthly *LYLO* (*Les Yeux, Les Oreilles;* free). If you can't find them in bars or FNACs, try the main office, 55, r. des Vinaigriers, 10*ème*. *Pariscope* and *l'Officiel des Spectacles* also have jazz listings.

Au Duc des Lombards, 42, r. des Lombards, 1*er* (☎42 33 22 88). M: Châtelet. From r. des Halles, walk down r. de la Ferronerie and make a right on r. Saint-Denis and another right on r. des Lombards. Murals of Ellington and Coltrane cover the exterior of this premier jazz joint. Still the best in French jazz, with occasional American soloists, and hot items in world music. Cover 80-100F, music students 50-80F. Beer 28-48F, cocktails 55F. Music starts either 8:30pm or 10pm and wails on until 3am (4am on weekends). Open daily 7:30pm-4am. V.

Le Baiser Salé, 58, r. des Lombards, 1*er* (☎42 33 37 71). M: Châtelet. From r. des Halles, walk down r. de la Ferronerie and make a right on r. Saint-Denis and another right on r. des Lombards. Lower-key than Lombards. Cuban, African, Antillean music featured together with modern jazz and funk. Month-long African music festival Oct.-Nov.; bass festival June. Concerts start at 9:30pm, music until 3am (typically 3 sets). Cover 40-80F, depending on performers; mainly new talent. Free Monday jam sessions with 1 drink min. Beer 26F, cocktails 46F. Bar open daily 4pm-dawn.

L'Eustache, 37 r. Berger, 1*er* (☎40 26 23 20). M: Châtelet-Les Halles. From the métro stop, follow traffic along Les Halles garden on r. Berger. Fun and relaxed bar near Les Halles featuring good, free jazz on the weekend Sept.-June. Open daily 11am-2am, music starts around 9:30 pm. MC, V.

Le Petit Opportun, 15, r. des Lavandières-Ste-Opportune, 1*er* (☎42 36 01 36). M: Châtelet. From the métro, walk r. des Halles and a right onto r. des Lavandières-Ste-Opportune. Basement cave venue in three rooms; to see the band, show up early for a spot in the front room. Some of the best modern jazz around, including Americans. Cover 50-80F depending on act. Drinks 30-60F. Open Sept.-July Tu-Sa 9pm-5am; music begins at 10:30pm.

Slow Club, 130, r. de Rivoli, 1*er* (☎42 33 84 30). M: Châtelet. In a cellar that used to be a banana-ripening warehouse. An old favorite of Miles Davis hosts Big Band, Dixieland, and rock 'n' roll in a rock-around-the-clock vein. Older crowd than la Huchette. Lessons offered (☎42 53 14 49). Expect dancing and a crowd in their 30s. Weekday cover 60F, students 55F; weekend cover from 75F. Drinks from 25F. Open Tu-Th 10pm-3am, F-Sa 10pm-4am.

Le Sunset, 60, r. des Lombards, 1*er* ☎40 26 46 60). M: Châtelet. From r. des Halles, walk down r. de la Ferronerie and make a right on r. Saint-Denis and another right on r. des Lombards. An easy-going club with an old and widespread reputation, Le Sunset is where musicians come to unwind and jam into the wee hours after their gigs around Paris. Mostly French and European acts. Cover 70-100F, with a 20% discount for *Let's Go* readers; drinks 30-65F. Concerts M-Sa 10pm-3am; Su 9pm-2am. Hang around past 2am to catch the jam scene. MC, V.

Le Petit Journal St-Michel, 71, bd. St-Michel, 5*ème* (☎43 26 28 59). M: Saint-Michel. From the métro, walk down Boulevard St-Michel away from the Seine. Another of the early strongholds, though more traditional and with an older crowd (40s-50s). First-class New Orleans and Big Band performers play in this Parisian center of the "Old Style." Open M-Th 9:30pm-12:30am, F-Sa till 2am. Closed the month of August. Obligatory 1st drink 100F, subsequent drinks 40F.

Caveau de la Huchette, 5, r. de la Huchette, 5*ème* (☎43 26 65 05). M: St-Michel. From Boulevard St-Michel, make a right onto r. de la Huchette. Come prepared to listen, watch, and dance the jitterbug, bebop, swing, and jive in this extremely popular, if somewhat touristy jazz club. Be-

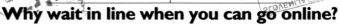

bop dance lessons offered before club opens; call 42 71 09 09. Varied age-group (ages 20-60). Crowded on weekends. Cover Su-Th 60F, F-Sa 75F. Students 55F during the week. Drinks 26-35F. Open daily 9:30pm-2:30am, F till 3:30am, Sa till 4am.

Aux Trois Mailletz, 56, r. Galande, 5*ème* (☎43 54 00 79). M: St-Michel. From the métro, walk along the Seine on the Quai St-Michel, make a right on r. du Petit Pont and a left on r. Galande. The basement houses a crowded café featuring world music and jazz vocals. The upper floor is packed with a strange mix of well-dressed students and well-dresed forty somethings. 80-100F admission to club on weekends; admission to bar is free. Beer 36-50F, cocktails 70F. Bar open daily 5pm-dawn; cave 8:30pm to dawn.

New Morning, 7-9, r. des Petites-Ecuries, 10*ème* (☎45 23 51 41). M: Château d'Eau. 400-seat former printing plant with the biggest American headliners in the city. Dark, smoky, and crowded, it's everything a jazz club should be. Sit in the lower front section or near the wings for the best acoustics. All the greats have played here—from Chet Baker to Stan Getz and Miles Davis—and the club still attracts big names like Wynton Marsalis, Betty Carter, John Scofield, and Archie Shepp. Open Sept.-July from 8pm; times vary; concerts usually at 9pm. Tickets available at box office, the FNAC, or Virgin Megastore; 110-140F. Drinks 35-65F. MC, V.

Streetlife

Le Sunset

Chez Georges

INSIDE

Daytripping

These miraculous escapes from the toils of a great city give one a clearer impression of the breadth with which it is planned, and of the civic order and elegance pervading its whole system.

—Edith Wharton, *A Motor-Flight Through France,* 1908

VERSAILLES

By sheer force of ego, the Sun King converted a hunting lodge into the world's most famous palace. The sprawling château stands as a testament to the despotic playboy-king, Louis XIV, who lived, entertained, and governed on the grandest of scales. A century later, while Louis XVI and Marie-Antoinette entertained in lavish style, the peasants of Paris starved. The opulence of Versailles makes clear why they lost their heads (see **History,** p. 28).

TRAVEL TIME (MIN.)	
Versailles	30-40
Fontainebleau	55-65
Chartres	65-75
Giverny	60-70
Disneyland Paris	45-50
Vaux-le-Vicomte	75-120
Saint-Germain-en-Laye	15-20
Auvers-sur-Oise	60-90

PRACTICAL INFORMATION

Trains: The **RER** runs from M: Invalides or any stop on RER Line C5 to the Versailles Rive Gauche station (30-40min., departs every 15min., 28F round-trip). From the Invalides or other RER Line C stop, take trains with labels beginning with "V" (i.e., Vick, Vora, and so on). Buy your RER ticket

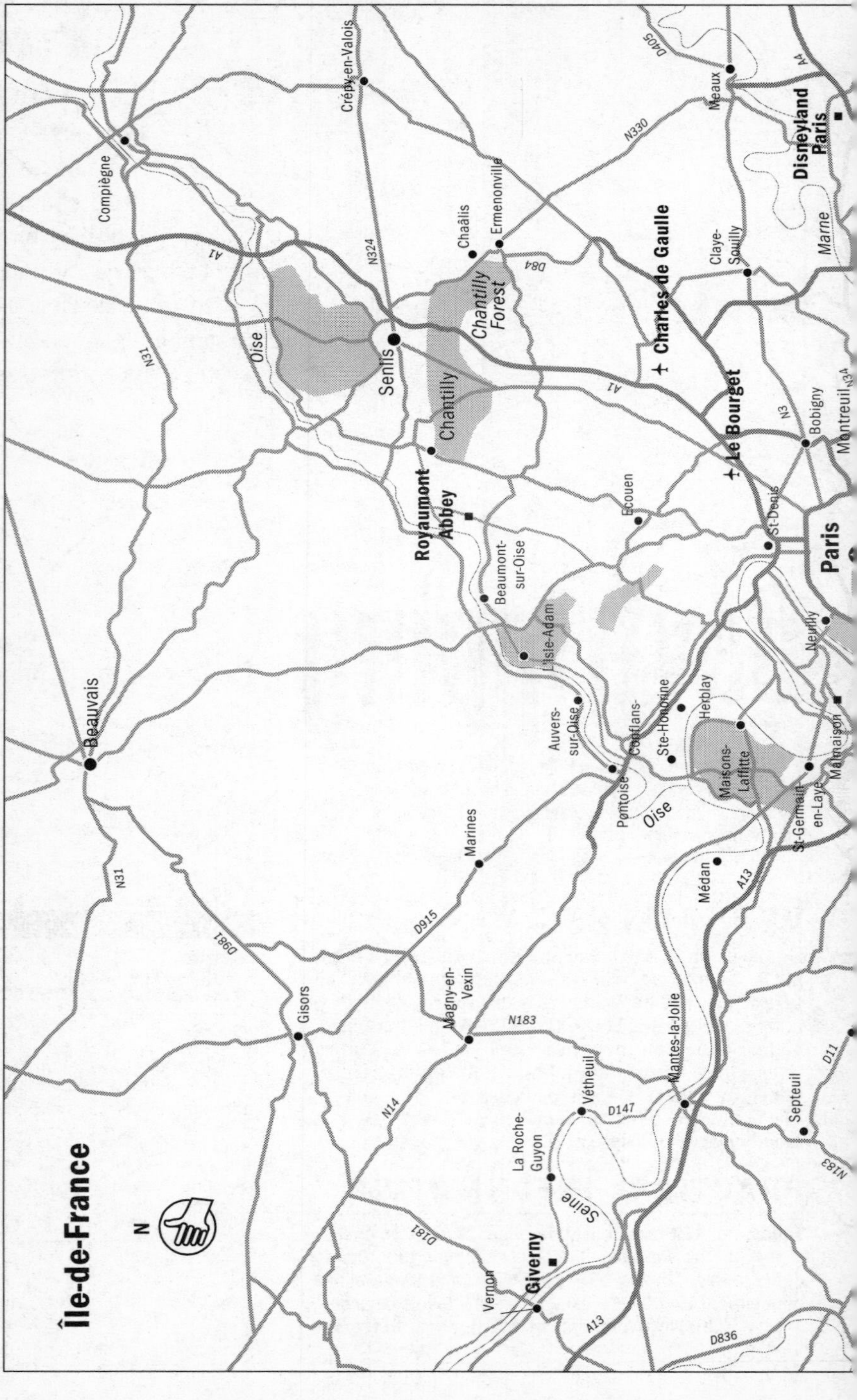

Île-de-France

N

Beauvais
Compiègne
Crépy-en-Valois
Senlis
Chantilly
Chantilly Forest
Chaâlis
Ermenonville
Royaumont Abbey
Beaumont-sur-Oise
L'Isle-Adam
Ecouen
Charles de Gaulle
Le Bourget
Meaux
Disneyland Paris
Claye-Souilly
Marne
Bobigny
Montreuil
St-Denis
Paris
Neuilly
Malmaison
Herblay
Conflans-Ste-Honorine
Auvers-sur-Oise
Pontoise
Oise
Maisons-Laffitte
St-Germain-en-Laye
Médan
Marines
Gisors
Magny-en-Vexin
Vétheuil
Mantes-la-Jolie
Septeuil
La Roche-Guyon
Seine
Giverny
Vernon
A1
A4
A13
N31
N324
N330
N3
N34
N183
N14
D405
D84
D915
D981
D147
D181
D11
D836

Versailles
Sèvres
Meudon
A4
Créteil
St-Maur
Champigny
N12
N12
D91
Sceaux
N7
Rambouillet Forest
N10
Orly
N4
Palaiseau
Dampierre
N306
Chevreuse
Brie-Comte-Robert
Breteuil
A6
N6
N306
Rambouillet
A10
Evry
N19
Melun-Sénart
N36
Maintenon
Le Marais
Corbeil-Essonnes
N154
A10
D6
Vaux-le-Vicomte
Melun
Dourdan Forest
A11
D906
N7
A11
A6
Seine
N105
Chartres
Barbizon
Étampes
A10
Fontainebleau
D837
N152
Montereau
N6
Fontainebleau Forest
Moret-sur-Loing
Loing
0
10 miles
0
10 kilometers

Versailles

Visiting Versailles is a mammoth undertaking. One day will allow thorough visits of all the major attractions. At least two days are needed to see everything. A standard day-long visit: The first **3 hours** should be spent in the **Château,** on the tours commencing at entrances A and C, with an option to substitute some of that time with one of the **1- to 2-hour guided tours** (in French and English) leaving from Entrance D. After lunch, spend **an hour or two** in the **gardens,** either walking through the Hameau, or on one of the daily guided walks. Finally, spend **1 hour** in the **Grand Trianon,** the best furnished of the royal quarters, and if time permits, **30 minutes** in the **Petit Trianon.**

before going through the turnstile to the platform; although a métro ticket will get you through these turnstiles, it will not get you through RER turnstiles at Versailles and could get you in trouble with the *controlleurs*.

Tourist Office: Office de Tourisme de Versailles, 7, r. des Reservoirs (☎39 50 36 22; fax 39 50 68 07), down the street from the *château* on the Opéra side.

HISTORY

A child during the aristocratic insurgency called the Fronde (see **History,** p. 27), Louis XIV is said to have entered his father's bedchamber one night only to find (and frighten away) an assassin. Fearing noble conspiracy the rest of his life, Louis chose to move the center of royal power out of Paris and away from potential aristocratic insubordination. In 1661, the Sun King renovated the small hunting lodge in Versailles and enlisted the help of architect Le Vau, painter Le Brun, and landscape architect Le Nôtre (see **Vaux-le-Vicomte,** p. 210). The court became the mandatory nucleus of noble life, where France's aristocrats vied for the king's favor (see **History,** p. 27).

No one knows just how much it cost to build Versailles; Louis XIV burned the accounts to keep the price a mystery. At the same time, life there was less luxurious than one might imagine: courtiers wore rented swords and urinated behind statues in the parlors, wine froze in the drafty dining rooms, and dressmakers invented the color *puce* (literally, "flea") to camouflage the insects crawling on the noblewomen. Louis XIV died on September 1, 1715 and was succeeded by his great-grandson Louis XV in 1722. He commissioned the Opéra, in the North Wing for the marriage of Marie Antoinette and Louis VXI. The newlyweds inherited the throne and Versailles when Louis VX died of smallpox at the château in 1774. The Dauphin and Marie Antoinette changed little of the exterior of the château, redecorating inside and creating Marie Antoinette's personal pretend playland, the Hamlet. On October 5, 1789, 15,000 Parisian fishwives and National Guardsmen marched out to the palace and brought the royal family back to Paris, where they were guillotined in 1793.

During the 19th century, King Louis-Philippe established a museum to preserve the château, against the wishes of most French people, who wanted Versailles demolished just as the Bastille had been. In 1871, the château took the limelight once again, when Wilhelm of Prussia became Kaiser Wilhelm I of Germany in the Hall of Mirrors. That same year, as headquarters of the Thiers regime, Versailles sent an army against the Parisian Commune. The *Versaillais* pierced the city walls and crushed the *communards*. On June 28, 1919 at the end of WWI, France forced Germany to sign the ruinous Treaty of Versailles in the Hall of Mirrors, the very room of modern Germany's birth.

TOURS

☎30 84 74 00; www.chateauversailles.com. Open Tu-Su May-Sept. 9am-6:30pm; Oct.-Apr. 9am-5:30pm. Last admission 30min. before closing. Admission to palace and ***self-guided tour, entrance A:*** *45F; ages 18-25, over 60, and after 3:30pm 35F. Supplement for* ***audio tour, entrance C****: 1hr., ages 7 and up, 25F, under 7 free. Supplement for* ***guided tour, entrance D:*** *1hr., 25F, ages 7-17 17F; 1½hr., 37F, ages 7-17 26F; 2hr., 50F, ages 7-17 34F; under 7 free.*

Arrive early in the morning to avoid the crowds, which are worse on Sunday from May to September and in late June. From the Versailles Rive Gauche RER train stop, take a right. Proceed 200m, and the gilt-fenced outer courtyard of the château will be on your left. Most of Versailles's visitors enter at **Entrance A,** located on the right-hand side in the north wing, or **Entrance C,** located in the archway to the left. **Entrance B** is for groups, **Entrance D** is where tours with a living, breathing guide begin, and **Entrance H** is for visitors in wheelchairs. **General admission** allows entrance to the following rooms: the *grands appartements*, where the king and queen received the public; the War and Peace Drawing Rooms; the *Galerie des Glaces* (Hall of Mirrors); and Marie Antoinette's apartment. Head for Entrance C to purchase an **audioguide**. From Entrance D, at the left-hand corner as you approach the palace, you can choose between seven **guided tours** of different parts of the château. **Sign-language tours** are available, but reservations must be made in advance with the Bureau d'Action Culturelle (☎30 83 77 88).

Versailles

Inside the Palace

SELF-GUIDED TOUR: ENTRANCE A

The general admission ticket starts your visit in the **Musée de l'Histoire de France,** created in 1837 by Louis-Philippe to celebrate his country's glory. Along its textured walls hang portraits of men and women who shaped the course of French history. The 21 rooms (arranged in chronological order) seek to construct a historical context for the château, which is helpful for those not taking an audio or guided tour.

Up the staircase to the right is the dual-level **royal chapel** constructed by architect Hardouin-Mansart from 1699-1710 where the king heard mass. Back toward the staircase and to the left is a series of gilded **drawing rooms** in the **State Apartments** that are dedicated to Hercules, Mars, and the ever-present Apollo (the Sun King identified with the sun god). The ornate **Salon d'Apollo** was Louis XIV's throne room. Framed by the **War and Peace Drawing Rooms** is the **Hall of Mirrors,** which was originally a terrace until Mansart added a series of mirrored panels and windows to double the light in the room and reflect the gardens outside. These mirrors were the largest that 17th-century technology could produce and were an unbelievable extravagance. Le Brun's ceiling paintings (1679-1686) tell the history of Louis XIV's heroism, culminating with *The King Governs Alone*. The Treaty of Versailles was ratified here, effectively ending the First World War.

The **Queen's Bedchamber,** where royal births were public events, is now furnished as it was on October 6, 1789, when Marie Antoinette left the palace for the last time. A version of the David painting depicting Napoleon's self-coronation dominates the **Salle du Sacré** (also known as the Coronation Room). The **Hall of Battles** installed by Louis-Phillippe is a monument to 14 centuries of France's military.

On the Water

MIRROR, MIRROR

The Hall of Mirrors, perhaps the centerpiece of any visit to Versailles, united the best of available artistic talent. 73 meters long and 10.5 meters wide, it was begun by Jules Hardouin Mansart in 1678 and worked in turn by Le Brun, Le Comte, Caffieri, and Coysevox until its completion eight years later. 17 mirrors, each an incredible expense at the time, face 17 windows that look out onto the gardens. The ceiling paintings, elevating the military triumphs of Louis XIV to biblical significance, were conceived by Le Brun.

THE GARDENS

Open *daily sunrise-sundown.* ***Free. Fountains*** *turned on for special displays mid-Apr. to mid-Oct. Sa-Su 3:30-5:30pm. 28F.* ***Tours:*** *June-Oct.; call ☎30 83 77 88; 2hr.; 18F.*

Numerous artists—Le Brun, Mansart, Coysevox—executed statues and fountains, but master gardener André Le Nôtre provided the overall plan for Versailles's gardens. Louis XIV wrote the first guide to the gardens himself, entitled the *Manner of Presenting the Gardens at Versailles.* Tours should begin, as the Sun King commanded, on the terrace. The two-hour **Discovering Groves Tour** provides a history of Le Nôtre's work.

To the left of the terrace, the **Parterre du Midi** graces the area in front of Mansart's **Orangerie,** once home to 2000 orange trees; the temperature inside still never drops below 6°C (43°F). In the center of the terrace lies the **Parterre d'Eau,** while the **Bassin de Latone** fountain below features Latona, mother of Diana and Apollo, shielding her children as Jupiter turns villains into frogs.

Past the fountain and to the left is the **Rockwork Grove,** built between 1680 and 1683. The south gate of the grove leads to the magnificent **Bassin de Bacchus,** one of four seasonal fountains depicting the God of wine crowned in vine branches reclining on a bunch of grapes. The **Bassin du Miroir d'Eau** spurts near the the **Bassin de Saturne** and the peaceful **Jardin du Roi,** an English-style garden plated with exotic trees. The king used to take light meals amid the **Colonnade's** 32 violet and blue marble columns, sculptures, and white marble basins. The north gate to the Colonnade exits onto the 1099-foot-long **Tapis Vert** (Green Carpet), the central mall linking the château to the **Char d'Apollon** (Chariot of Apollo). Pulled by four prancing horses, the Sun God rises to enlighten the world.

On the north side of the garden is Marsy's incredible **Bassin d'Encelade.** When the fountains are turned on, a 25m jet bursts from Enceladus's mouth. Flora reclines on a bed of flowers in the **Bassin de Flore,** while a gilded Ceres luxuriates in sheaves of wheat in the **Bassin de Cérès.** The **Parterre du Nord,** full of flowers, lawns, and trees, overlooks some of the garden's most spectacular fountains. The **Allée d'Eau,** a fountain-lined walkway, provides the best view of the **Bassin des Nymphes de Diane.** The path slopes toward the sculpted **Bassin du Dragon,** where a dying beast slain by Apollo spurts water 27m into the air. Ninety-nine jets of water attached to urns and seahorns surround Neptune in the **Bassin de Neptune,** the gardens' largest fountain.

Beyond Le Nôtre's classical gardens stretch wilder woods and farmland. Stroll along the **Grand Canal,** a rectangular pond beyond the Bassin d'Apollon measuring 5118-feet long. To explore further, rent a **bike** to the right of the canal, just outside the garden gates (32F per hr.). Rent a **boat** for four people at the boathouse to the right of the canal. (Open Tu-F noon-5:30pm, Sa-Su 11am-6pm. 72F per hr., 52F per 30min.; 50F refundable deposit.)

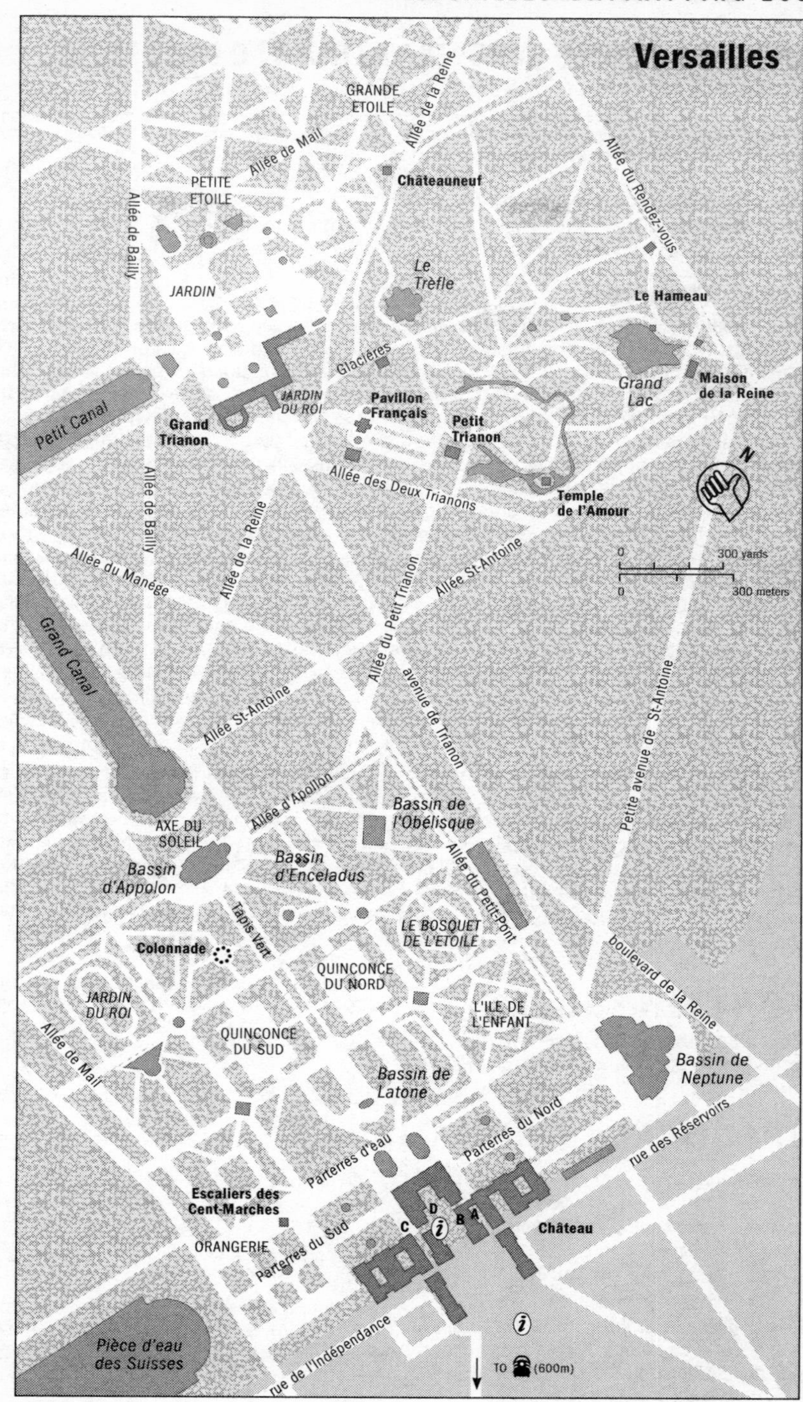
Versailles
GRANDE ETOILE
Allée de la Reine
Allée de Mail
PETITE ETOILE
Châteauneuf
Allée du Rendez-vous
Allée de Bailly
Le Trèfle
JARDIN
Le Hameau
Glacières
Grand Lac
Maison de la Reine
JARDIN DU ROI
Pavillon Français
Petit Canal
Grand Trianon
Petit Trianon
Allée des Deux Trianons
Temple de l'Amour
N
Allée de Bailly
Allée de la Reine
Allée St-Antoine
0
300 yards
300 meters
Allée du Manège
Allée du Petit Trianon
Grand Canal
avenue de Trianon
Petite avenue de St-Antoine
Allée St-Antoine
Allée d'Apollon
Bassin de l'Obélisque
AXE DU SOLEIL
Bassin d'Appolon
Bassin d'Enceladus
Allée du Petit-Pont
Tapis Vert
LE BOSQUET DE L'ETOILE
boulevard de la Reine
Colonnade
QUINCONCE DU NORD
JARDIN DU ROI
L'ILE DE L'ENFANT
Allée de Mail
QUINCONCE DU SUD
Bassin de Neptune
Bassin de Latone
Parterres du Nord
rue des Réservoirs
Parterres d'eau
Escaliers des Cent-Marches
D
C
B
A
Château
ORANGERIE
Parterres du Sud
rue de l'Indépendance
Pièce d'eau des Suisses
TO (600m)

THE TRIANONS AND MARIE-ANTOINETTE'S HAMEAU

Shuttle trams from the palace to the Trianons and the Hameau leave from behind the palace: round-trip 33F, ages 3-12 20F. The walk takes about 25min. Both Trianons: ***Open*** *Tu-Sa Nov.-Mar. noon-5:30pm; Apr.-Oct. noon-6pm; last entrance 30min. before closing.* ***Admission*** *to Grand Trianon 25F, reduced tariff 15F; Petit Trianon 15F, reduced tariff 10F. Combined ticket to the Trianons 30F, reduced tariff 20F.*

The Trianons and Hameau provide a racier counterpoint to the château: it was here that kings trysted with lovers, and Marie-Antoinette lived like the peasant she wasn't.

PETIT TRIANON

On the right down the wooded path from the château, is the **Petit Trianon,** built between 1762-68 for Louis XV and his mistress Madame de Pompadour. Marie-Antoinette took control of the Petit Trianon in 1774, and it soon earned the nickname "Little Vienna." The Petit Trianon was later inhabited by Napoleon's sister and the Empress Marie-Louise. In 1867, the Empress Eugénie, who worshipped Marie-Antoinette, turned it into a museum.

Exit the Petit Trianon, turn left, and follow the marked path to the libidinous **Temple of Love,** a domed rotunda with 12 white marble columns. Marie-Antoinette held many intimate nighttime parties in the small space, during which thousands of torches would be illuminated in the surrounding ditch. The Queen was perhaps at her happiest and most ludicrous when spending time at the **Hameau,** her own peasant village down the path from the Temple of Love. Inspired by Jean-Jacques Rousseau's theories on the goodness of nature, the Queen aspired to a more simple life. She commissioned Richard Mique to build a compound of 12 buildings (including a mill, dairy, and gardener's house, all surrounding a quaint artificial lake) in which she could play at country life. At the center is the **Queen's Cottage.** Any illusions of her slumming it disappear after crossing through her cottage doors. The rooms contained ornate furniture, marble fireplaces, and walk-in closets for all that silver and monogrammed linen, and all those footmen.

GRAND TRIANON

The single-story, stone-and-pink-marble Grand Trianon was intended as a château-away-from-château for Louis XIV. Here the King could be reached only by boat along the **Grand Canal.** The palace, which consists of two wings joined together by a central porch, was designed by Mansart and erected in 1687-88. **Formal gardens** are located behind the colonnaded porch. The mini-château was stripped of its furniture during the Revolution but was later restored and inhabited by Napoleon and his second wife. Charles de Gaulle installed presidential apartments and rooms for visiting heads of state in the Grand Trianon, and the constitutional amendment for Maastricht was written here.

FONTAINEBLEAU

More digestible than Versailles, the Château de Fontainebleau achieves nearly the same grandeur, with a charm unique among the great châteaux. With lush surrounding gardens, the estate ranks among the best day-trips from Paris.

PRACTICAL INFORMATION

Trains: Hourly trains run to Fontainebleau from Gare de Lyon, *banlieue* level (45min., 94F round-trip). From the station, **Car Vert A** (☎64 22 23 88) runs buses (9.50F) after each train arrival from Paris; take the bus in direction "Château-Lilas" and get off at the Château stop. You can also rent a bike from **MBK** (☎64 22 36 14; fax 60 72 64 89) at the train station. (60F per half-day; mountain bikes 120F per half-day. Helmets 10F. Open M-F 10am-6pm, Sa-Su 10am-7pm. MC, V.) The château is a 30min. **walk** away.

Tourist Office: 4, r. Royal (☎60 74 99 99; fax. 60 74 80 22). Across from the château. Organizes tours of the village, finds accommodations, sells audio tours of the château, and has maps of Fontainebleau and Barbizon. Open M-Sa 9:30am-6:30pm, Su 10am-4pm.

HISTORY

Kings of France have hunted on these grounds since the 12th century, when the exiled Thomas à Becket consecrated Louis VII's manor chapel. In 1528, François I rebuilt the castle to be closer to the game he loved to hunt. Italian artists designed and decorated the palace, and their paintings, including the *Mona Lisa*, filled François's private collections. Subsequent kings commissioned magnificent rooms and new wings. Louis XIII was born here in 1601, Louis XIV revoked the Edict of Nantes here in 1685, and Louis XV was married here in 1725. Napoleon, who visited Fontainebleau frequently, called it "La Maison des Siècles" (the House of Centuries). In 1814, Napoleon bid goodbye to the Empire from the central courtyard, now called the **Cour des Adieux** in his honor. More recently, Fontainbleau hosted a 1999 summit on Kosovo.

Versailles Gardens

CHÂTEAU DE FONTAINEBLEAU

☎60 71 50 60. ***Open*** *July-Aug. W-M 9:30am-6pm; May-June and Sept.-Oct. W-M 9:30am-5pm; Nov.-Apr. W-M 9:30am-12:30pm and 2-5pm. Last entry 45min. before closing. 35F; students, seniors, and Sundays 23F, under 18 free.*

The pamphlet handed out with your admission is of little use: you may want to invest in a small printed **guide** (25F) available down the hall from the ticket booth. **Audio tours** (36F, 90min.) are sold in town at the Fontainebleau Tourist Office (see above). Most rooms feature information placards with a few sentences in English.

Daytripping

GRANDS APPARTEMENTS. The Grands Appartements provide a lesson on the history of French architecture and decoration. Dubreuil's **Gallery of Plates** tells the history of Fontainebleau on a remarkable series of 128 porcelain plates. In the long **Galerie de François I,** muscular figures by Il Rosso (known in French as Maître Roux) tell mythological tales of heroism, brilliantly illuminated by windows that look out onto the **Fountain Courtyard.** Similarly, the **Ball Room**'s magnificent octagonal ceiling, heavy wood paneling, and bay windows face out onto the **Oval Courtyard.** The **King's Cabinet** (also known as the **Louis XIII Salon** because Louis XIII was born there) was the site of *le débotter*, the king's post-hunt boot removal. Napoleon pored over the volumes of the sunlit **Bibliothèque Diana.** Since the 17th century, every queen and empress of France has slept in the gold and green **Queen's Bed Chamber;** the gilded wood bed was built for Marie-Antoinette. The N on the red and gold velvet throne of the **Throne Room** is a testament to Napoleon's humility in what is today the only existing throne room in France. Sandwiched between two mirrors, **Napoleon's Bed Chamber** is a monument to either narcissism or eroticism, while the Emperor's austere **Small Bed Chamber** contains a small military bed. In the **Emperor's Private Room,** known today as the **Abdication Chamber,** Napoleon signed off his empire in 1814. The tour ends with the 16th-century, Italian-frescoed **Trinity Chapel.**

MUSÉE CHINOIS DE L'IMPÉRATRICE EUGÉNIE. This museum was created in 1863 by the Empress to house her collection of Chinese decorative art. *(Admission is included in price of the château.)*

Versailles

PETITS APPARTEMENTS. Parts of the château can be seen only by guided tour. The tour of the Petits Appartements features the private rooms of Napoleon and the Empress Josephine, as well as the impressive **map room** and **Galerie des Cerfs**. *(4 1hr. tours W-M 2-5pm. 16F. Call ahead.)*

MUSÉE NAPOLÉON. The Musée Napoléon features an extensive collection of the Emperor's personal effects: his wee toothbrush, his tiny shoes, his field tent, his son's toys, and gifts from European monarchs. *(2 1hr. tours per morning M, Th, Sa. 16F under 26 and over 60 12F, under 18 free. Call ahead ☎ 60 71 50 60.)*

THE GARDENS. Fontainebleau's serene **Jardin Anglais** and **Jardin de Diane** shelter quiet grottos guarded by statues of huntress Diana and the **Etang des Carpes,** a carp-filled pond that can be explored by rowboat. *(Boat rental June-Aug. daily 10am-12:30pm and 2-7pm; Sept. Sa-Su 2-6pm. 50F per 30min., 80F per hr.)* The **Forêt de Fontainebleau** is a thickly wooded 20,000-hectare preserve with hiking trails, bike paths, and sandstone rock-climbing. The tourist office provides maps.

CHARTRES

Were it not for a piece of fabric, the cathedral of Chartres and the town that surrounds it might be only a sleepy hamlet. Because of this sacred relic—the cloth that the Virgin Mary supposedly wore when she gave birth to Jesus—Chartres became a major medieval pilgrimage center. The spectacular cathedral that towers above the surrounding rooftops and wheat fields is not the only reason to visit the city: the *vieille ville* (old town) is also a masterpiece of medieval architecture.

PRACTICAL INFORMATION

Trains: Chartres is accessible by frequent trains from **Gare Montparnasse, Grandes Lignes** (☎ 08 36 35 35 35, 7am-10pm, 2,23F per min. Roughly 1 train per hr. during the summer; call ahead for winter schedule. Slightly over 1hr.; round-trip 144F, under 26 and over 60 108F). To reach the cathedral from the train station, walk straight along r. Jehan de Beauce to pl. de Châtelet and turn left into the place, right onto r. Ste-Même, and left onto r. Jean Moulin. Or, just head toward the massive gothic spires.

Tourist Office: (☎ 02 37 18 26 26; fax 02 37 21 51 91; email Chartres.Tourism@wanadoo.fr). In front of the cathedral's main entrance at pl. de la Cathédrale, the tourist office helps find accommodations (10F fee) and supplies visitors with a list of restaurants, brochures, and two good maps, one with a walking tour and the other with hotels and other sites. (Open Apr.-Sept. M-Sa 9am-7pm, Su and holidays 9:30am-5:30pm; Oct.-Mar. M-Sa 10am-6pm, Su and holidays 10am-1pm and 2:30-4:30pm Closed Jan. 1, Nov. 1 and 11, and Dec. 25.)

THE CATHEDRAL

*☎ 02 37 21 75 02 or 02 37 28 15 58. **Open** M-Sa 7:30am-7:15pm, Su and holidays 8:30pm-7:15pm. No casual visits during mass. **Masses** M, W-Th, and Sa at 11:45am and 6pm; T and F at 9am, 11:45am, and 6pm; Su 9:30am (Latin), 11am, and 6pm. Call the tourist office for info on concerts in the cathedral, the annual student pilgrimage in late May, and other pilgrimages and festivals throughout the year. **Treasury** closed indefinitely at time of publication. **Tower** open May-Aug. M-Sa 9am-6pm, Su 1-6:30pm; Sept.-Oct. and Mar.-Apr. M-Sa 9:30-11:30am and 2-5pm, Su 1-2pm; Nov.-Feb. M-Sa 10-11:30am and 2-4pm, Su 1-2pm. **Admission** 25F, ages 12-25 15F, under 12 free. Leave a piece of identification in order to rent English audioguides from the gift shop (15-30F for various tours). **English tours of the cathedral** begin at the rear of the church nave and last 1¼hr. Apr.-Jan. M-Sa noon and 2:45pm; 30F, students 20F. **French tours of the crypt** leave from La Crypte, 18, Cloître Notre-Dame. ☎ 02 37 21 56 33. Tours 30min. Apr.-Oct. M-Sa 11am, 2:15, 3:30, 4:30, and 5:15pm; Nov.-Mar. 11am and 4:15pm. 15F, students 10F, under 7 free.*

The Cathédrale de Chartres is the best-preserved medieval church in Europe, miraculously escaping major damage during the Revolution and WWII. A patchwork masterpiece of Romanesque and Gothic design, the cathedral was constructed by generations of unknown masons, architects, and artisans who labored for centuries.

SANCTA CAMISIA. The year after he became emperor in 875, Charlemagne's grandson, Charles the Bald, donated to Chartres the Sancta Camisia, the cloth believed to be worn by the Virgin Mary when she gave birth to Christ. Although a church dedicated to Mary had existed on the site as early as the mid-700s, the emperor's bequest required a new cathedral to accommodate the growing number of pilgrims. In the hope that the sacred relic would bring healing and answer prayers, thousands flocked to the church on their knees. The sick were nursed in the crypt below the sanctuary, usually for a period of nine days. The powers of the relic were confirmed in AD 911 when the cloth saved the city; under attack from invading Goths and Vikings, the viking leader Rollon converted to Christianity. He became the first duke of Normandy.

STAINED GLASS. At a time when books were rare and the vast majority of people illiterate, the cathedral was a multimedia teaching tool. Most of the stained glass dates from the 13th century and was preserved through both World Wars by heroic town authorities, who dismantled over 2000 square meters and stored the windows pane by pane in Dordogne. The medieval merchants who paid for each window are shown in the lower panels, providing a record of daily life in the 13th century. The famous Blue Virgin, Tree of Jesse, and Passion and Resurrection of Christ windows are among the surviving 13th-century stained glass. The center window shows the story of Christ from the Annunciation to the ride into Jerusalem. Bring binoculars if you can (or rent them for 10F per hr. plus ID or 300F deposit). Stories should be "read" from bottom to top, left to right.

LABYRINTH. The windows of Chartres often distract visitors from the treasures below their feet. A winding labyrinth is carved into the floor in the rear of the nave. Designed in the 13th century, the labyrinth was laid out for pilgrims as a substitute for a journey to the Holy Land. By following this symbolic journey on their hands and knees, the devout would act out a voyage to heavenly Jerusalem.

TOUR JEHAN-DE-BEAUCE. The adventurous can climb the cathedral's north tower, Tour Jehan-de-Beauce (named after its architect and completed in 1513) for a stellar view of the cathedral roof, the flying buttresses, and the city below. The tower is a wonderful example of flamboyant Gothic, a late medieval style. Built to replace a wooden steeple that repeatedly burned down, it provides a striking counterpart to its more sedate partner, the **octagonal steeple,** built just before the 1194 fire.

CRYPT. Parts of Chartres's **crypt,** such as a well down which Vikings tossed the bodies of their victims during raids, date back to the 9th century. You can enter the subterranean crypt only as part of a tour that leaves from La Crypte, the store opposite the cathedral's south entrance. The tour is in French, but information sheets are available in English.

ELSEWHERE IN THE CATHEDRAL. The Gothic and Romanesque exterior of the church is marked by three entrances. The 12th-century statues of the **Portale Royale** present an assembly of Old Testament figures. The 13th-century **Porche du Nord** depicts the life of Mary while the **Porche du Sud** shows the life of Christ. Inside the church, the Renaissance **choir screen,** begun by Jehan de Beauce in 1514, depicts the Virgin Mary's life.

The only English-language **tours** of the cathedral are given by campy British tour-guide Malcolm Miller, an authority on Gothic architecture who has been leading visitors through the church for the past 40 years. His presentations on the cathedral's history and symbolism are intelligent, witty, and enjoyable for all ages. If you can, take both his morning and afternoon tours—no two are alike.

THE TOWN

Founded as the Roman city *Autricum,* Chartres is a medieval village at heart. Clustered around its mammoth house of God, the town's oldest streets are named for the trades once practiced there. Chartres is built on a hill, and some of the best views of the cathedral are found by walking down the well-marked tourist circuit. Chartres's medieval tangle of streets can be maddening; free maps are available from the tourist office. For those with difficulty walking or who want a more relaxed tour of the town, a *petit train* runs from April to October with 30-minute narrated tours (in French only) of the old city. *(☎ 02 37 21 87 60. Tours begin in front of the tourist office. 30F, kids under 12 18F.)*

MUSÉE DES BEAUX-ARTS. The Musée des Beaux-Arts resides in the former Bishop's Palace. Built mainly in the 17th and 18th centuries (on a site occupied by bishops since the 11th century), the palace houses an eclectic collection of painting, sculpture, and furniture. *(29, r. du Cloître Notre-Dame. Next to the cathedral. ☎02 37 36 41 39. Open May-Oct. M and W-Sa 10am-noon and 2-6pm, Su 2-6pm, Nov.-Apr. M and W-Sa 10am-noon and 2-5pm, Su 2-5pm. 15F, students and seniors 7.5F.)*

MONUMENT TO JEAN MOULIN. A monument to Jean Moulin, the famous WWII Resistance hero who worked closely with de Gaulle, stands on r. Jean Moulin, off r. Cheval Blanc. Prefect of Chartres before the war, Moulin attempted suicide rather than sign a Nazi document accusing French troops of atrocities. Tortured and killed by the Gestapo in 1943, he was eventually buried in the Panthéon.

CENTRE INTERNATIONAL DU VITRAIL. The 13th-century barn in which the center is housed was once used to store wine and grains for the clergy. It now hosts temporary exhibitions on stained glass. *(5, r. du Cardinal Pie. ☎02 37 21 65 72. Open M-F 9:30am-12:30pm and 1:30-6pm, Sa-Su 10am-12:30pm and 2:30-6pm. 20F, students 12F.)*

CHURCHES. Rebuilt in the 16th century, the feudal **Eglise St-Aignan,** on r. des Greniers, offers summer concerts. *(Open daily 9am-noon and 2-6:30pm)* The 12th-century Romanesque **Eglise St-André** sits on r. St-André on the banks of the Eure River. *(Open daily 10am-noon and 2-6pm.)* Once part of the Benedictine monastery of St-Père-en-Vallée, the **Eglise St-Pierre,** on pl. St-Pierre, is a 13th-century Gothic masterpiece. *(Open daily 10am-noon and 2-5pm.)*

GIVERNY

Drawn by the verdant hills, haystacks, and lily pads on the Epte river, Impressionist Claude Monet and his eight children settled in Giverny in 1883. By 1887, John Singer Sargent, Paul Cézanne, and Mary Cassatt had placed their easels beside Monet's and turned the village into an artists' colony. (For more on Impressionism, see **Fine Arts,** p. 40.)

GETTING THERE AND GETTING AROUND

Trains: The SNCF runs erratically from Paris **Gare St-Lazare** to **Vernon,** the nearest station. Check the fickle timetables posted in the Grandes Lignes reservation rooms at St-Lazare; SNCF ☎08 36 35 35 35, or look the schedule up on the web at www.sncf.fr. 132F round-trip.

Other Transport: Rent a **bike** from the Vernon station (☎02 32 51 01 72; 55F per day; deposit of 1000F or credit card; MC, V) or take a **bus** (☎02 32 71 06 39; 10min.; M-Sa 6 per day each way, Su and holidays 4 per day each way; look for the schedule inside the information office in the train station; 12F, round-trip 2120F). Make sure you coordinate train and bus schedules before you start your trip to avoid 3hr. delays. **Taxis** in front of the train station are another option. (One-way 65F weekdays, 80F weekends.) The 6km, hour-long **hike** from the Vernon station to Giverny along a pedestrian and cyclist path is unmarked: it begins as the dirt road that intersects r. de la Ravine above the highway. Get a free **map** at the Vernon tourist office.

SIGHTS

FONDATION CLAUDE MONET. Today, Monet's house and gardens are maintained by the Fondation Claude Monet. From April to July, Giverny overflows with roses, hollyhocks, poppies, and the scent of honeysuckle. The water lilies, the Japanese bridge, and the weeping willows look like—well, like Monets. Such serenity is broken only by the crowds of tourists and school children. The only way to avoid the rush is to go early in the morning and, if possible, early in the season. In Monet's thatched-roof house, big windows, solid furniture, and pale blue walls house his collection of 18th- and 19th-century Japanese prints. (*84, r. Claude Monet. ☎02 32 51 28 21; www.fondation-monet.com. Open Apr.-Oct. Tu-Su 10am-6pm. 35F, students and ages 12-18 25F, ages 7-12 20F. Gardens 25F.)*

MUSÉE D'ART AMÉRICAIN. Near the foundation, the new and spacious Musée d'Art Américain is the sister institution to the Museum of American Art in Chicago and houses a small number of works by American expatriates. *(99, r. Claude Monet. ☎02 32 51 94 65; www.maag.org. Open Apr.-Oct. Tu-Su 10am-6pm. 35F; students, seniors, teachers, and ages 12-18 20F; under 12 15F.)*

DISNEYLAND PARIS

It's a small, small world and Disney is hell-bent on making it even smaller. When Euro-Disney opened on April 12, 1992, Mickey Mouse, Cinderella, and Snow White were met by the jeers of French intellectuals and the popular press, who called the Disney theme park a "cultural Chernobyl." Resistance seems to have subsided since Walt & Co. renamed it Disneyland Paris and started serving wine. Pre-construction press touted the complex as a vast entertainment and resort center covering an area one-fifth the size of Paris. In truth, Disney owns (and may eventually develop) 600 hectares, but the current theme park doesn't even rank the size of an *arrondissement*. From the gate it takes only 10 minutes to walk to the farthest point inside the park, a fact disguised by the park's maze-like design. Despite its dimensions, this Disney park is the most technologically advanced yet, and the special effects on some rides will knock your socks off.

PRACTICAL INFORMATION

Everything in Disneyland Paris is in English and French. The detailed guide called the *Park Guide Book* (free at Disney City Hall to the left of the entrance) has a map and info on everything from restaurants and attractions to bathrooms and first aid. The *Guests' Special Services Guide* has info on wheelchair accessibility throughout the park. In case you hadn't planned on a full day and night of magic, Disney now offers *FastPast*, a free service that rewards those motivated enough to pick up a ticket with reduced wait times at specific rides at specific times. For more info on Disneyland Paris, visit their website at **www.disneylandparis.com.**

Train: RER A4 from either M: Gare de Lyon or Châtelet-Les-Halles and take the train (direction: "Marne-la-Vallée") to the last stop, "Marne-la-Vallée/Chessy." Before boarding the train, check the boards hanging above the platform to make sure there's a light next to the Marne-la-Vallée stop; otherwise the train won't end up there (45min., departs every 30min., round-trip 78F). The last train to Paris leaves Disney at 12:22am, but you may have trouble getting the métro once you get back—it closes at midnight. **TGV** service from de Gaulle reaches the park in a mere 15min., making Disneyland Paris fantastically accessible for travelers with Eurail passes. Certain **Eurostar** trains now run directly between Waterloo Station in London and Disneyland (departure usually around 9:15am returning at 7:30pm; prices vary between 750 and 2090F; reserve far in advance; ☎08 36 35 35 39).

Car: Take the A4 highway from Paris and get off at exit 14, marked "Parc Disneyland Paris," about 30min. from the city. You can park for 40F per day in any one of the 11,000 spaces in the parking lot.

Bus: Disneyland Paris buses make the rounds between the terminals of both Orly and de Gaulle airports and the bus station near the Marne-la-Vallée RER (40min.; departs every 45-60min. 8:30am-7:45pm, 8:30am-10pm at CDG on weekends; round-trip 85F).

Tickets: Instead of selling tickets, Disneyland Paris issues **passeports,** available at the ground floor of the Disneyland Hotel. You can also buy *passeports* at the Paris tourist office on the Champs-Elysées (see **Tourist Offices,** p. 277), FNAC, Virgin Megastores, the Galeries Lafayettes, or at any of the major stations on RER line A, such as Châtelet-Les-Halles, Gare de Lyon, or Charles-de-Gaulle-Etoile. Pursue either of these options if you plan on coming out on a weekend, so you won't risk wasting a couple of hours while the windows remain closed due to crowds. The *passeport* is valid for 1 day; have your hand stamped if you plan to leave but return later.

Admission: Apr.-Oct. 220F, ages 3-11 170F; Jan. 2 -Mar. and Nov.-Dec. 22 170F, ages 3-11 140F; Dec. 23-Jan. 1 225F, ages 3-11 175F. 2- and 3-day *passeports* also available.

Hours: Open daily July 8-Sept. 3 9am-11pm; Sept. 4-Oct. 20 and Nov. 6-Dec. 22 M-F 10am-8pm, Sa-Su 9am-8pm; Oct. 21-Nov. 5 and Dec. 23-Jan. 1 daily 9am-8pm; Dec. 31 9am-1am. Hours subject to change in the winter when snow and sleet make the experience less magical.

VAUX-LE-VICOMTE

Nicolas Fouquet, Louis XIV's Minister of Finance, assembled the triumvirate of Le Vau, Le Brun, and Le Nôtre (architect, artist, and landscaper) to build Vaux in 1641. On August 17, 1661, upon the completion of what was then France's most beautiful château, Fouquet threw an extravagant 6,000-guest party in honor of Louis XIV. The King and Anne d'Autriche were but two of the witnesses to a regal bacchanalia that premiered poetry by La Fontaine and a comedy-ballet, *Les Facheux*, by Molière. After novelties like elephants in crystal jewelry, the evening concluded in a "Chinese" fireworks extravaganza featuring the King and Queen's coat of arms and pyrotechnic squirrels (Fouquet's family symbol). But the housewarming bash was the beginning of the end for Fouquet. Shortly thereafter, young Louis XIV—supposedly furious at having been upstaged—ordered Fouquet arrested. In a trial that lasted three years, the judges voted narrowly for banishment over death. Louis XIV overturned the judgement in favor of life imprisonment—the only time in French history that the head of state overruled the court's decision in favor of a more severe sentence. Fouquet was to remain imprisoned at Pignerol, in the French Alps, until his death in 1680. Many suspected that Fouquet was the man in the iron mask, including Alexandre Dumas, who fictionalized the story in *Le Vicomte de Bragelonne*.

PRACTICAL INFORMATION

Vaux is exquisite and much less crowded than Versailles, but getting there is an exquisite pain, as there is no shuttle service from the train station in Melun to the château 7km away. **Paris Vision** (☎42 60 30 01) runs a day or half-day coach tour to the château.

Driving: The castle is 50km out of Paris. Take Autoroute A4 or A6 from Paris and exit at Val-Maubué or Melun, respectively. Head toward Meaux on N36 and follow the signs.

By Train: Take the **RER** to Melun from Châtelet-Les-Halles or Gare du Nord (45min., round-trip 90F).

Taxi: ☎64 52 51 50. 100-150F each way.

Tourist Office: 2, av. Gallieni (☎64 37 11 31). By the train station in Melun. They can help you with accommodations and sight-seeing, and give you a free map. If the tourist office is closed, do not fear. Although the highway is perilous (and the walk takes 1½-2hr.), the directions are relatively simple: just follow av. de Thiers through its many name changes to highway 36 (direction: "Meaux") and follow signs to Vaux-Le-Vicomte. Open Tu-Sa 10am-noon and 2-6pm.

CHÂTEAU AND GARDENS

☎64 14 41 90; email chateau@vaux-le-vicomte.com; www.vaux-le-vicomte.com. ***Open*** *daily Mar. 11-Nov. 11 10am-6pm; visits by appointment for groups of 20 or more the rest of the year.* ***Admission*** *to château and gardens 63F; students, seniors, and ages 6-16 49F; under 6 free.* ***Admission*** *to gardens and équipages 30F, students, seniors, and ages 6-16 27F. On Sa evenings from May to the end of Sept., the château is candle-lit for* ***nightime visits*** *8pm-midnight; 82F; ages 6-16, students, and seniors 70F.* ***Fountains*** *on 3-6pm, second and last Sa of each month in summer. Château* ***tour*** *includes good audio presentation in English using actor's voices.*

THE CHÂTEAU

The château is covered with ornate scripted "F"s and squirrels (Fouquet's symbol); the tower with three battlements has his second wife's crest engraved on it. **Madame Fouquet's Closet** once had walls lined with small mirrors, the decorative forerunner of Versailles's Hall of Mirrors. Over the fireplace of the **Square Room** hangs Le Brun's portrait of Fouquet. Le Brun's **Room of the Muses** is one of his most famous decorative schemes. Le Brun had planned to crown the cavernous, Neoclassical **Oval Room** (or **Grand Salon**) with a fresco entitled *The Palace of the Sun*, but Fouquet's arrest halted all decorating activity, and only a single eagle was completed. The tapestries once bore Fouquet's menacing squirrels, but Colbert seized them and replaced the rodents with his own adders. The ornate **King's Bedchamber** boasts an orgy of cherubs and lions fluttering around the centerpiece, Le Brun's *Time Bearing Truth Heavenward.*

GARDENS

With Vaux, Le Nôtre gave birth to a truly French style of garden—shrubs were trimmed, lawns shaved, bushes sculpted, and pools strategically placed. Vaux owes its most impressive *trompe l'oeil* ("fools the eye") to Le Nôtre's adroit use of the laws of perspective. From the back steps of the château, it looks as if you can see the entire landscape at a glance. The grottos at the far end of the garden appear directly behind the large pool of water. Yet as you approach the other end, the grottos seem to recede, revealing a sunken canal known as **La Poêle** (the Frying Pan), which is invisible from the château. The right-hand *parterre* (literally "on the ground," referring to the arabesques and patterns created with low, clipped box plants) was originally a flowerbed, but today it is dominated by a statue of the classical goddess Diana. The **Round Pool** and its surrounding 17th-century statues mark an important intersection; to the left, down the east walkway, are the **Water Gates,** likely the backdrop for Molière's performance of *Les Facheux.* The **Water Mirror,** farther down the central walkway, was designed to reflect the château perfectly, but you may have some trouble positioning yourself to enjoy the effect. A climb to the **Farnese Hercules,** is the vanishing point when you look out from the castle. Today, the old stables, **Les Equipages,** house a fantastic carriage museum.

SAINT-GERMAIN-EN-LAYE

More a wealthy Parisian suburb than a provincial town, St-Germain-en-Laye offers a break from the intensity of Paris. The winding streets of the town center are packed with restaurants, cafés, and shops. Home to François I's 16th-century château and Claude Debussy's birthplace, this chic little hamlet is worth a visit, especially in the summer during the **Fête des Loges**.

PRACTICAL INFORMATION

Trains: St-Germain is 25min. from M: Charles-de-Gaulle on RER Line A1 (trains leave every 10-25min., round-trip 39F).

Office Municipal de Tourisme: Maison Claude Debussy, 38, r. au Pain (☎34 51 05 12; fax 34 51 36 01). From the RER station, exit at *Eglise,* turn right onto the pedestrian r. de la Salle, and then left onto r. au Pain. Provides all that you need to know about the festival as well as lists of restaurants and hotels, a free map, and info about the town in English. Open Mar.-Oct. Tu-F 9:15am-12:30pm and 2-6:30pm, Sa 9:15am-6:30pm, Su 10am-1pm; Nov.-Feb. closed Su.

SIGHTS

CHÂTEAU DE ST-GERMAIN-EN-LAYE

☎39 10 13 00. ***Museum*** *open W-M 9am-5:15pm. 25F, students 17F; temporary exhibits 25F, 17F; combined ticket 38F, 28F; 1hr. tour in French 24F, 17F; under 18 free.* ***Garden*** *open daily May-July 8am-9:30pm; Aug.-Apr. 8am-5pm.*

Louis VI "Le Gros" built the first castle here in the 12th century. Rebuilt by Charles V after its destruction during the Hundred Years' War, the castle took on its present appearance in 1549 under François I. Lover of all things Italian, François I ordered his architects Chabiges and Delormé to construct a Renaissance palace (the current **château vieux**) on the foundations of the old castle. Henri II added the **château neuf,** home to Louis XIII and birthplace in 1638 of the future Louis XIV. During the period from the Revolution to the July Monarchy, St-Germain was used as a civilian prison, a cavalry school, and a military prison. In the 19th century, it became a popular weekend outing, and the first railroad in France was built between here and Paris in 1837. In 1919, St-Germain-en-Laye served as the site of the official dismantling of the Austro-Hungarian Empire.

Long ago in 1867 Napoleon III created a museum of "antiquity" in St-Germain-en-Laye. Today, the **Musée des Antiquités Nationales** claims to have the richest collection of its kind in the world, tracing the history of early man in France. Unfortunately, the display looks a bit like someone's pet rock collection.

The château's **garden** terrace, probably the town's greatest asset, was designed by Le Nôtre. The current gardens and nearby forest provide a panoramic view of western Paris, the Grande Arche de la Défense (see p. 112), and the *banlieue.* A map of forest trails (50F) is available from the tourist office.

EGLISE ST-GERMAIN. The Eglise St-Germain was consecrated in 1827 on the site of the 11th-century priory that gave St-Germain its name. Large and stately pillars support the Romanesque structure, the fourth church to be built on this site since 1028. The church's 14th-century stone statue of Nôtre-Dame-de-Bon-Retour (Our Lady of Safe Return) was found when they dug the foundations for the church in 1775. James II's tomb is at the front. *(Across from the château. ☎34 51 99 11. Open daily 9:30am-noon and 2:30-6pm. Mass M-F 7:15pm; Sa 6:30pm; Su 10:15am, 11:30am, and 6:30pm.)*

MAISON CLAUDE DEBUSSY. The Maison Claude Debussy is the Impressionist composer's birthplace. An autographed copy of *Il pleut doucement sur la ville* (It Rains Softly on the Town) is among the eclectic array of documents and pictures. The museum's auditorium hosts two concerts per month. *(38, r. au Pain. Follow r. de la Salle to r. au Pain and turn left. Open Tu-Sa 2-6pm. Free. Concerts 30-70F.)*

MUSÉE DÉPARTEMENTAL MAURICE DENIS LE PRIEURÉ. The Musée Départemental Maurice Denis le Prieuré is dedicated to the works of Maurice Denis (1870-1943), the Symbolists, the Nabis, the Post-Impressionists, and the Pont-Aven group. *(2bis, r. Maurice-Denis. ☎39 73 77 87. Open W-F 10am-5:30pm, Sa-Su 10am-6:30pm. 25F, students 15F, under 12 free. Tours Su at 3:30pm. 10F.)*

AUVERS-SUR-OISE

> I am entirely absorbed by these plains of wheat on a vast expanse of hills—like an ocean of tender yellow, pale green, and soft mauve.
>
> —Vincent van Gogh, 1890

The seventy canvases van Gogh produced during his ten week stay in Auvers bear testimony to what he called the "medicinal affect" of this bit of countryside, only 30 km northwest of Paris. Fleeing Provence where he had been diagnosed with depression and possible epilepsy, van Gogh arrived at Auvers-sur-Oise in May 1890, where he would be treated by Dr. Gachet. But neither the doctor nor the countryside were enough to lift his depression. On the afternoon of July 27, van Gogh set off with his paints to the fields above the village, crawling back into his room that evening with a bullet lodged deep in his chest. Gachet, Theo van Gogh, and even the police had a chance to demand an explanation from the painter as he lay bleeding, smoking his pipe, for two days. "Sadness goes on forever" he told his brother, and died.

PRACTICAL INFORMATION

Trains: Take the **SNCF train** from Gare St-Lazare (☎30 36 70 61) or Gare du Nord to Pontoise (this may involve intermediate changes; consult the station's information desk), then switch to the Persau-Creil line and get off at Gare d'Auvers-sur-Oise. The connection can take up to 30min. *(*1-1½hr., every hr., 58F roundtrip). Go to ticket desks marked "Paris Banlieue;" ask about the departure time and platform of your connecting train when you buy your tickets. Should you hit the afternoon lull in return train service, catch the **bus** to Pontoise. Or you can take the **RER** express 'A' line from Châtelet or Etoile toward Cergy-le-Haut. Get off at Cergy-Prefecture and take bus #9507 toward Parmain. Ask to stop at "Auvers-sur-Oise-Mairie."

Tourist Office: Manoir des Colombières, r. de la Sansonne, the Office de Tourisme d'Auvers-sur-Oise (☎30 36 10 06). Helpful walking maps (1-3F) and souvenirs. 90min. guided **tours** of the village depart from here. Open daily 10am-12:30pm and 2-5pm. Tours Apr.-Oct. Su 3pm; 30F, under 14 10F.

SIGHTS

The following walk should take around two hours. Begin facing up the hill from the train station, and take a left.

On your right you will find the **Raveaux Inn,** which once housed van Gogh. While the **Maison de van Gogh,** 8, r. de la Sansonne, is just around the corner and a good place to start your tour, it has little to offer beyond a glimpse of van Gogh's bare room and a pretty slideshow. However, the cost of admission includes an elegant, souvenir "passport" to Auvers-sur-Oise that details the history of the *auberge* and van Gogh's sojourn here. You might want to just buy the booklet, which also gives information on the town's other museums and self-guided walking tours, as well as discounts to four of the museums. (☎34 48 05 47. Open daily 10am-6pm. 30F; family ticket 60F.)

The 10-minute walk from the Maison to the **Cimetière d'Auvers** is worth the rural beauty. Follow the path behind the museum as it curves to the right. Continue along r. Daubigny and turn left up the narrow steps leading to **Nôtre-Dame d'Auvers** (open daily 9am-6pm), the 12th-century subject of Van Gogh's 1890 *Eglise d'Auvers*, which hangs in the Musée d'Orsay (see **Museums,** p. 119).

Past the church, the *chemin du cimetière* leads up the hill and through the fields where van Gogh painted his *Champ de blé aux corbeaux* (*Wheatfields with Crows*, 1890). Circle up and to your left on the track through the fields; it emerges near the **Atelier de Daubigny,** 61, r. Daubigny, once the home and studio of pre-Impressionist painter Charles-François Daubigny. (☎34 48 03 03. Open Apr. 10.-Nov. 1 Tu-Su 2-6:30pm. 20F, under 12 10F.) Mount r. Daubigny and turn left onto r. de Lery. On a side street off r. de Léry, the **Musée de l'Absinthe,** 44, r. Callé, is yet another memorial to the Impressionists, this one devoted to the drink that Manet and Degas immortalized (see **The Green Party,** p. 124). (☎30 36 83 26. Open June-Sept. W-Su 11am-6pm; Oct.-May Sa-Su 11am-6pm. 25F, students 20F, under 14 10F.) To continue, follow r. de Lery up to the **Château de Lery** (☎34 48 48 36). Turn right onto r. Victor Hugo and r. du Dr Gachet and pass Gachet's house, painted by van Gogh and Cézanne.

INSIDE

Planning Your Trip

WHEN TO GO

While **summer** heat does nothing to soften the blow of Paris's pollution, high temperatures usually don't hit until July; June is notoriously rainy. In August, tourists move in and Parisians move out on vacation. Smaller hotels, shops, and services may close—when tourists flood those that remain open, frustration is about the only thing available to all. Still, if you avoid the Champs-Elysées, Versailles, and the Eiffel Tower, August in Paris can be pleasingly calm. In the **fall**, the tourist-madness begins to calm down. Despite **winter** cold and rain, there isn't much snow. In the off season airfares and hotel rates drop, travel is less congested, and museum lines are short(er).

AVG TEMP (LOW/HI)	JANUARY		APRIL		JULY		OCTOBER	
	°C	°F	°C	°F	°C	°F	°C	°F
	0/7	32/45	4/15	40/59	13/25	56/77	10/22	51/71

DOCUMENTS AND FORMALITIES

FRENCH EMBASSIES AND CONSULATES ABROAD

If your country is not listed here try visiting **www.expatries.org** or **www.embassyworld.com** for a complete, updated list of consulates. For **Consular Services in Paris**, see p. 274.

Australia, Consulate General, Level 26 St. Martins Tower, 31 Market St., Sydney NSW 2000. ☎(02) 92 61 57 79, fax (02) 92 83 12 10, www.france.net.au/frames_fr.htm. Open M-F 9am-1pm.

Canada, Consulate General, 1 pl. Ville Marie, 26th floor, Montréal QC H3B 4SE. ☎(514) 878 43 81, fax: (514) 878 39 81. Open M-F 8:30am-noon. Consulat général de France à Québec, Maison Kent, 25 rue Saint-Louis, Québec Qc, G1R 3Y8. Tel: (418) 694 22 94, fax: (418) 694 22 97. Open M-F 9am-12:30pm. Consulate General, 130 Bloor St. West, Suire 400, Toronto, Ontario M5S 1N5. ☎(416) 925 80 41. Open M-F 9am-1pm.

Ireland, French Embassy, Consulate Section, 36 Ailesbury Rd., Ballsbridge, Dublin 4. ☎(1) 260 16 66, www.ambafrance.ie. Open M-F 9am-noon.

New Zealand, New Zealand Embassy and Consulate, 34-42 Manners St. PO box 11-343, Wellington. ☎64 4 384 5042/3, fax. 64 4 384 5298. Consulate Anite House, Level 1, 48-62 Greys Ave., Auckland NZ, mail: P.O. Box 8000, Symonds St. ☎6 493 799 788, fax. 6 493 024 043, www.dree.org/nouvelle-zelande.

South Africa, General Consulate, PO Box 11278, Johannesburg 2000 (if you live in Gauteng, KwazuluNatal, Free State, Mpumalanga, Northern Province, North West Province or in Lesotho). ☎011 331 3468. Visas, ☎011 331 3478. If you live in the Northern Cape, Eastern Cape or Western Cape, consult Consulate, 2 Dean St., PO box 1702 Cape Town 8000. ☎(21) 4 231 575, fax (21) 424 8470. Open M-F 9am-12:30pm.

United Kingdom, Consulate General, 21 Cromwell Rd., London SW7 2EN. ☎(171) 838 2000, www.ambafrance.org.uk/db.phtml?id=consulat. Open M-W 8:45am-3pm, Th-F 8:45am-noon. Visa service, PO Box 57, 6a Cromwell Pl., London sw7 2 EN. ☎(207) 838 2050, fax. (207) 838 2046. Open 9-10am, 1:30-2:30pm M-F.

United States, Consulate General, 4101 Reservoir Rd. NW, Washington DC 20007. ☎(202) 944-6000, www.france-consulat.org/dc/dc.html. Open 8:45am-12:30pm. Visa sevice: fax. (202) 944-6212, answering machine (8:45am-12:45pm) (202) 944-6200, ☎(2-5pm W-Th, 2-4:30pm F) (202) 944-6200, e-mail visas-washington@amb-wash.fr Consulates also located in Atlanta, Boston, Chicago, Honolulu, Houston, New Orleans, Los Angeles, Miami, New York, San Francisco, and San Juan. See www.info-france usa.org/america/consulate for more information.

PASSPORTS

REQUIREMENTS. Citizens of Australia, Canada, Ireland, New Zealand, South Africa, and the U.S. need valid passports to enter France and to re-enter their own country. France does not allow entrance if the holder's passport expires in under three months after the expected date of departure; returning home with an expired passport is illegal, and may result in a fine.

LOST PASSPORTS. If you lose your passport in France, immediately notify the local police and the nearest embassy or consulate of your home government. To expedite replacement, you will need to know all information contained in the lost passport and show identification and proof of citizenship. A replacement may take weeks to process, and it may be valid only for a limited time. Any visas stamped in your old passport will be irretrievably lost. In an emergency, ask for immediate temporary traveling papers that will permit you to re-enter your home country. Your passport is a public document belonging to your nation's government. You may have to surrender it to a foreign government official, but you are entitled to get it back in a reasonable amount of time.

NEW PASSPORTS. All applications for new passports or renewals should be filed several weeks (or months) in advance of your planned departure date. Most passport offices do offer emergency passport services for an extra charge. Citizens residing abroad who need a passport or renewal should contact their nearest embassy or consulate.

VISAS AND WORK PERMITS

French visas are valid for travel in any of the states of the EU common travel area (the entire Union except the UK and Ireland, plus Iceland and Norway); however if the primary object of your visit is a country other than France you should apply to their consulate for a visa. **British** and **Irish** citizens do not require a visa to visit, reside in, or work in France; however there are some formalities to complete for stays of over 90 days (see below). All visitors to France are required to register their presence with the Police in the town in which they are staying; this is normally done automatically by hotels and hostels, and when signing a lease with a landlord.

VISITS OF UNDER 90 DAYS. Citizens of South Africa need a **short-stay visa** (*court séjour*). To apply, your passport must be valid for three months past the date you intend to leave France. In addition, you must submit two passport-sized photos, proof of a hotel reservation or an organized tour, or, if you intend to stay with relatives or friends, a certificate of accommodation stamped by the police station or town hall (2 copies), or if you intend to work, a letter from your employer, a return ticket and proof of medical insurance. A transit visa (1 or 2 entries of 1 or 2 days each) costs R54.2;, single/multiple entry visa for 30 days or under costs R137.61; for 31-90 days, the cost is R162.63, for single entry, or R191.82 for multiple entries. Apply for a visa at your nearest French consulate; short-stay visas for South African nationals usually take 2 days to process.

VISITS OF OVER 90 DAYS. All non-EU citizens need a **long-stay visa** (*long séjour)* for stays of over 90 days. Requirements vary according to the nature of your stay; contact your French consulate. The visa itself can take two months to process and costs 650F. U.S. Citizens can take advantage of the Center for International Business and Travel (CIBT) (☎800-925-2428), which will secure visas for travel to almost all countries for a service charge. Within 60 days of their arrival, all foreigners (including EU citizens) who plan to stay over 90 days must apply for a **temporary residence permit** *(carte de séjour temporaire).* For more information on long-term stays in Paris, see **Living in Paris,** p. sxx. For more information on long-term stays in Paris, see **Living in Paris**, .

STUDY AND WORK PERMITS. Only EU citizens have the right to work and study in France without a visa. Others wishing to study in France must apply for a special student visa. For more information, see p. 218.

IDENTIFICATION

French law requires that all people carry a form of official identification—either a passport or an EU government-issued identity card. The police have the right to demand to see identification at any time and you risk running a large fine if you do not comply. Minority travelers, especially black and Arab travelers, should be especially careful to carry proof that they are in France legally. In general when traveling it is advisable to carry two or more forms of identification, including a photo ID. A passport combined with a driver's license or birth certificate usually serves as adequate proof of your identity and citizenship. Many establishments, especially banks, require several IDs before cashing traveler's checks. Never carry all your forms of ID together, however; you risk being left entirely without ID or funds in case of theft or loss. It is useful to carry extra passport-size photos to affix to the various IDs or railpasses you may acquire, although photo booths can be found in just about every métro station.

ESSENTIAL INFORMATION

ENTRANCE REQUIREMENTS

Members of the European Union may enter with a **valid national ID card**.

Passport (p. 218). Required for citizens of Australia, Canada, Ireland, New Zealand, South Africa, and the USA.

Visa (p. 219). For stays of under 90 days, required of citizens of South Africa. For stays over 90 days, a visa (*Carte de Sejour Temporaire*) is also required of citizens of Australia, Canada, New Zealand and the USA.

Work Permit (p. 218). Required for citizens of Australia, Canada, New Zealand, South Africa and the USA.

Driving Permit (p. 20). Required for all those planning to drive. You must be at least 18 years old to drive in France.

STUDENT AND TEACHER IDENTIFICATION

The **International Student Identity Card (ISIC),** the most widely accepted form of student ID, provides discounts on sights, accommodations, food, and transport. The ISIC is preferable to an institution-specific card (such as a university ID) because it is more likely to be recognized (and honored) abroad. All cardholders have access to a 24-hour emergency helpline for medical, legal, and financial emergencies (in North America call (877) 370-ISIC, elsewhere call US collect +1 (715) 345-0505), and US cardholders are also eligible for insurance benefits. Many student travel agencies issue ISICs, including STA Travel in Australia and New Zealand; Travel CUTS in Canada; usit in the Republic of Ireland and Northern Ireland; SASTS in South Africa; Campus Travel and STA Travel in the UK; Council Travel (www.counciltravel.com/idcards/default.asp) and STA Travel in the US (see p. 233). The card is valid from September of one year to December of the following year and costs AUS$15, CDN$15, or US$22. Applicants must be degree-seeking students of a secondary or post-secondary school and must be of at least 12 years of age. Because of the proliferation of fake ISICs, some services (particularly airlines) require additional proof of student identity, such as a school ID or a letter attesting to your student status, signed by your registrar and stamped with your school seal. The **International Teacher Identity Card (ITIC)** offers the same insurance coverage as well as similar but limited discounts. The fee is AUS$13, UK£5, or US$22. For more info, contact the **International Student Travel Confederation (ISTC),** Herengracht 479, 1017 BS Amsterdam, Netherlands (☎+31 (20) 421 28 00; fax 421 28 10; email istcinfo@istc.org; www.istc.org).

YOUTH IDENTIFICATION

The International Student Travel Confederation issues a discount card to travelers who are 25 years old or under, but are not students. This one-year **International Youth Travel Card** (**IYTC**; formerly the **GO 25** Card) offers many of the same benefits as the ISIC. Most organizations that sell the ISIC also sell the IYTC (US$22).

CUSTOMS

ARRIVING IN FRANCE. Upon entering France from a non-EU country, you must declare items which exceed the legal allowance and pay duty on them as established by French customs law. Keeping receipts for purchases made abroad will help establish values when you return. It is wise to make a list, including serial numbers, of any valuables that you carry with you from home; if you register this list with customs before your departure and have an official stamp it, you will avoid import duty charges and ensure an easy passage upon your return. Be especially careful to document items manufactured abroad.

RECLAIMING VALUE-ADDED TAX. Most purchases in France include a 20.6% value-added tax (TVA). Non-EU residents (including EU citizens who reside outside the EU) can in principal reclaim the tax on purchases for export worth over 1200F made in one store. Only certain stores participate in this *vente en détaxe* refund process; ask before you pay. You must show a non-EU passport or proof of non-EU residence at the time of purchase, and ask the vendor for a tripartite form called a *bordereau de vente à l'exportation;* make sure that they fill it out, including your bank details. When leaving the country, present the receipt for the purchase together with the completed form to a French customs official. If you're at an airport, look for the window labeled *douane de détaxe*, and budget at least an hour for the intricacies of French bureaucracy. On a train, find an official or get off at a station close to the border. Once home, you must send a copy back to the vendor within 6 months; eventually the refunds will work their way into your account. Some shops exempt you from paying the tax at the time of purchase; you must still complete the above process. Note that food products, tobacco, medicine, unmounted precious stones, cars, means of transportation (i.e. bicycles and surfboards), and 'cultural goods' do not qualify for a TVA refund.

GOING HOME. Upon returning home, you must declare all articles acquired abroad that exceed the allowance established by your country's customs service, and pay duty on them. There is normally a smaller allowance for goods and gifts purchased at **duty-free** shops abroad; if you exceed this you must declare and pay duty and possibly sales tax on them as well. "Duty-free" merely means that you need not pay a tax in the country of purchase. Note that from June 30th, 1999, Duty Free has been abolished for trips starting and ending within the EU For more specific information on customs requirements, contact your home country's customs office.

MONEY

Money may be the root of all evil, but in Paris it's a necessary one. Even a modest daily budget will probably fall between 250-300F. If you stay in hostels and prepare your own food, you may be able to spend from 100-140F per person per day. Hotels start at about 130F per night for a double room, and a basic sit-down meal with wine costs 65F. Personal checks from home will meet with blank refusal, and even traveler's checks are not widely accepted outside tourist-oriented businesses; moreover, many establishments will only accept franc- or euro-denominated travelers checks. The bottom line is, carry enough cash to take you through the day, and take care.

CURRENCY AND EXCHANGE

The national currency of France is the *franc français* or **French Franc** (abbreviated to FF or just F), though it has now been superseded by the **euro** (symbol €; see above for more information). Each franc is divided into 100 **centimes**. The franc is available in brightly colored 50F, 100F, 200F and 500F notes, smart two-tone 10F and 50F coins, as well as silvery 5F, 2F, 1F and ½F coins and pale copper 5, 10 and 20 *centimes* pieces. There are a still a few old 20F notes around, too.

The currency chart below is based on published exchange rates from August 2001, except for the Euro rate which is fixed permanently at the value given. Note that one euro is approximately equal to one dollar. For current exchange rates, see **www.finance.yahoo.com** or **letsgo.com.**

EURO€1 = 6.55957 FF 1F = EURO€0.152449
US$1 = 6.15 FF 1 FF = US$0.16
CDN$1 = 4.13 FF = CDN$0.24
UK£1 = 9.92 FF = UK£0.10
IR£1 =8.33 FF= IR£0.12
AUS$1 = 4.01 FF = AUS$0.25
NZ$1 = 3.26 FF = NZ$0.31
SAR1= 1.00 FF = SAR1.00

As a general rule, it's cheaper to convert money in France. It's good to bring enough foreign currency to last for the first 24-72 hours of a trip to avoid being penniless after banking hours or on a holiday. Watch out for commission rates and check newspapers for the standard rate of exchange. Banks generally have the best rates. Since you lose money with each transaction, convert in large sums. Also, using an ATM card or a credit card (see p. 223) will normally get you better rates. If you use traveler's checks or bills, carry some in small denominations (US$50 or less), especially for times when you are forced to exchange money at disadvantageous rates.

ESSENTIAL INFORMATION

EUROPEAN UNION CUSTOMS

There are **no customs** at internal E.U. borders (travelers arriving in one EU country from another by air should take the **blue channel** when exiting the baggage claim), and travelers are free to transport whatever legal substances they like across the Union provided they can demonstrate that it is for personal (i.e. non-commercial) use. In practice this means quantities in excess of 800 cigarettes, 10L of spirits, 90L of wine (60 of sparkling wine) and 110L of beer—quite enough for most people! Correspondingly, on June 30, 1999, **duty-free was abolished** for travel between EU member states. Those arriving in the EU from outside will still have a duty-free allowance. January 1 1999 saw the launch of the **Euro**, a common currency for 11 of the EU nations. While it exists only in electronic form as yet, in the future it will mean far fewer money-changing headaches for travelers in Europe (see **Money**, p. 221).

Beware *bureaux de change* at airports, train stations, and touristy areas like the Champs-Elysées, which generally have less favorable rates; going off the beaten path may stretch your dollar. Many banks will exchange money from 9am-noon and 2-4:30pm. Banks near the Opéra (see **Sights**, p. 89) exchange money from 9am-5pm during the week and have 24-hour exchange machines. For more information, see **Service Directory: Currency and Exchange**, or, for information on opening a bank account, see **Living in Paris**,

TRAVELER'S CHECKS

Traveler's checks are one of the safest and least troublesome means of carrying funds, since they can be refunded if lost or stolen. A number of places in France only accept traveler's checks in francs or euros so keep that in mind when buying your checks. (Members of the American Automobile Association, and some banks and credit unions, can get American Express checks commission-free; see **Driving Permits and Insurance**). **American Express** and **Visa** are the most widely recognized. If you're ordering checks from a bank, do so in advance, especially if you are requesting large sums. American Express offices often sell traveler's checks in major currencies over the counter.

American Express: Call (800) 251 902 in Australia; in New Zealand (0800) 441 068; in the UK (0800) 521 313; in the US and Canada (800) 221-7282. Elsewhere call US collect +1 (801) 964-6665; www.aexp.com. Traveler's checks are available in Francs at 1-4% commission at AmEx offices and banks, commission-free at AAA offices. *Cheques for Two* can be signed by either of 2 people traveling together.

Citicorp: In the US and Canada call (800) 645-6556; in Europe, the Middle East, or Africa call the UK +44 (020) 7508 7007; elsewhere call US collect +1 (813) 623-1709. Traveler's checks available in 7 currencies at 1-2% commission. Call 24hr.

Thomas Cook MasterCard: In the US and Canada call (800) 223-7373; in the UK call (0800) 62 21 01; elsewhere call UK collect +44 (1733) 31 89 50. Checks available in 13 currencies at 2% commission. Thomas Cook offices cash checks commission-free.

Visa: In the US call (800) 227-6811; in the UK call (0800) 89 50 78; elsewhere call UK collect +44 (1733) 31 89 49. Call for the location of their nearest office.

CREDIT CARDS

Credit cards are generally accepted in Paris. Major credit cards can be used to extract cash advances in francs from associated banks and cash machines throughout France. Credit card companies get the wholesale exchange rate, which is generally 5% better than the retail rate used by banks and other currency exchange establishments. The most commonly accepted cards, in both businesses and cash machines, are **Visa** (also known as **Carte Bleue**), and **MasterCard** (also called **Eurocard**). Heavy surcharges keep small businesses out of the **American Express** loop. American Express cards do work in some ATMs, as well as at AmEx offices and major airports.

French-issued credit cards are fitted with a micro-chip (such cards are known as *cartes à puces*) rather than a magnetic strip *(cartes à piste magnétiques);* in untouristed areas, cashiers may attempt (and fail) to scan the card with a microchip

ESSENTIAL INFORMATION

ATM ALERT

All automatic teller machines require a four-digit **Personal Identification Number (PIN),** which credit cards in the United States do not always carry. You must ask your credit card company to assign you one before you leave. Without this PIN, you will be unable to withdraw cash with your credit card abroad. Also, if your PIN is longer than four digits, ask your bank whether the first four digits will work, or whether you need a new number. There are no letters on the keypads of most European bank machines, so work out your PIN here: QZ correspond to 1, ABC correspond to 2; DEF to 3; GHI to 4; JKL to 5; MNO to 6; PRS to 7; TUV to 8; and WXY to 9. If you mistakenly punch the wrong code into a French ATM three times it will eat your card. If you **lose your card** in Paris, call for help at the following numbers, all of which have English-speaking operators: **Mastercard** (☎08 00 90 13 87); **Visa** (☎08 00 90 20 33); **American Express** (☎01 47 77 72 00).

reader. In such circumstances you should ask for a more senior staff member who (hopefully) will know to swipe your card through the magnetic strip reader. If in doubt, explain: say *"Ceci n'est pas une carte à puce, mais une carte à piste magnétique"* (This card does not have a microchip, but a magnetic-strip).

All ATM machines require a **Personal Identification Number** (**PIN**, see **ATM Alert**). Ask your credit card company for a PIN before you leave; without it, you will be unable to withdraw cash outside your home country. If you already have a PIN, make sure it will work in France. Credit cards often offer an array of other services, from insurance to emergency assistance. Check with your company to find out what is covered.

CASH CARDS

24-hour **Cash machines** (also called **ATMs**) are widespread in France. Depending on the system that your home bank uses, you can probably access your own personal bank account. ATMs get the same wholesale exchange rate as credit cards. Despite these perks, do some research before relying too heavily on automation. There is often a limit on the amount of money you can withdraw per day (usually about US$500, depending on the type of card and account), and computer networks sometimes fail. Your home bank may also charge a fee for using ATM facilities abroad.

The two major international money networks are **Cirrus** (U.S. ☎800-4-CIRRUS (424-7787)) and **PLUS** (U.S. ☎800-843-7587 for the "Visa Plus Locator Service"). Institutions supporting PLUS are: Crédit Commercial de France, Banque Populaire, Union de Banque à Paris, Point Argent, Banque Nationale de Paris, Crédit du Nord, Gie Osiris, and ATMs in many post offices. To locate ATMs around the world, use **www.visa.com/pd/atm** or **www.mastercard.com/atm.**

GETTING MONEY FROM HOME

AMERICAN EXPRESS. Cardholders can withdraw cash from their checking accounts at any of AmEx's major offices and many representative offices (up to US$1000 every 21 days; no service charge, no interest). AmEx "Express Cash" withdrawals from any AmEx ATM in France are automatically debited from the cardholder's checking account or line of credit. Green card holders may withdraw up to US$1000 in any seven-day period (2% transaction fee; minimum US$2.50, maximum US$20). To enroll in Express Cash, cardmembers may call (800) 227-4669 in the US; elsewhere call the US collect +1 (336) 668-5041.

WESTERN UNION. Travelers from the US, Canada, and the UK can wire money abroad through Western Union's international money transfer services. In the US, call (800) 325-6000; in Canada, (800) 235-0000; in the UK, (0800) 833 833. To wire money within the US using a credit card (Visa, MasterCard, Discover), call (800) CALL-CASH (225-5227). The rates for sending cash are generally US$10-11 cheaper than with a credit card, and the money is usually available at the place you're sending it to within an hour. To locate the nearest Western Union location, consult **www.westernunion.com**.

US STATE DEPARTMENT (US CITIZENS ONLY). In dire emergencies only, the US State Department will forward money within hours to the nearest consular office, which will then disburse it according to instructions for a US$15 fee. Contact the Overseas Citizens Service, American Citizens Services, Consular Affairs, Room 4811, US Department of State, Washington, D.C. 20520 (☎(202) 647-5225; nights, Sundays, and holidays 647-4000; http://travel.state.gov).

TAXES

All goods and services bought in France include a **Value Added Tax (TVA)** in the purchase price; this must also be included in all advertised or posted prices. The standard rate is 20.6%, although foodstuffs are taxed at 5.5% and newspapers and medicines 2.1%. Non-EU residents may be able to reclaim part of the tax they have payed on leaving the country: see **Reclaiming value-added tax,** p. 220. **Hotels** may levy a *taxe de séjour* (see **Accommodations,** p. 245).

SAFETY AND SECURITY

PROTECTING YOUR VALUABLES. To prevent theft, don't keep all your valuables (money, important documents) in one place. Label every piece of luggage both inside and out. **Don't put a wallet with money in your back pocket.** Never count your money in public and carry as little as possible. If you carry a purse, buy a sturdy one with a secure clasp, and carry it crosswise on the side, away from the street with the clasp against you. A **money belt** is the best way to carry cash; you can buy one at most camping supply stores. A **neck pouch** is equally safe, although far less accessible. Keep some money separate from the rest to use in an emergency or in case of theft.

PICKPOCKETS. In city crowds and especially on public transportation, **pickpockets** are amazingly good at their craft. Rush hour is no excuse for strangers to press up against you on the métro. If someone stands uncomfortably close, move to another car and hold your bags tightly. Be alert in public telephone booths. If you must say your calling card number, do so very quietly; if you punch it in, make sure no one can see you.

DRUGS AND ALCOHOL. A meek "I didn't know it was illegal" will not suffice. Possession of **drugs** in France can end your vacation abruptly; convicted offenders can expect a jail sentence and fines. Never bring any illegal drugs across a border (for more information, see **Le Drug**, p. 225). It is vital that **prescription drugs,** particularly insulin, syringes, or narcotics, be accompanied by the prescriptions themselves and a statement from a doctor and left in original, labeled containers. In France, police may stop and search anyone on the street—no reason is required. Also, a positive result of the gentlemanly drinking age (16) is that public drunkenness is virtually unseen, even in younger crowds. In general, raucous chest-beating and sidewalk stumbling will earn the disdain of locals.

LE DRUG

Drugs are not as much a social problem in France as in the U.S., England, Germany, or Holland. In Paris, the area around Métro Stalingrad has become the most drug exposed area with the recent arrival of crack. A majority of hard drug users and addicts are Antillais and African, and the correlation between drugs, crime, and illegal immigration causes the police, special police (RG), and the Ministry of the Interior (currently run by extreme right winger, Charles Pasqua) to use drug control as a pretext for cracking down on foreigners (including tourists). Although Paris is no Amsterdam, late at night in the métro, as in certain bars and clubs, a whiff of hash may waft your way. Let's Go does not recommend buying on the street or crossing international borders with drugs, especially from Amsterdam, where charter buses are often searched with the aid of police dogs.

HEALTH

BEFORE YOU GO

There is no shortage of pharmacies in Paris, and almost everything for minor health problems, from headaches to hangovers, is readily available. Some travelers swear by their own **first-aid kit,** containing bandages, aspirin or other pain killer, antibiotic cream, a thermometer, a Swiss army knife with tweezers, moleskin, decongestant for colds, motion sickness remedy, medicine for diarrhea or stomach problems (Pepto Bismol tablets and Immodium), sunscreen, insect repellent, and burn ointment. **Contact lens** wearers should bring an extra pair, a copy of the prescription, a pair of glasses, extra solution, and eyedrops. People with **asthma** or **allergies** should be aware that Paris has visibly high levels of air pollution, particularly during the summer, and that non-smoking areas are almost nonexistent. Call 01 44 59 47 64 for information on air quality in Paris (Open M-F 9am-5:30pm). Consider bringing an over-the-counter antihistamine, decongestant, inhaler, etc., since there may not be a French equivalent with the correct dosage.

NO PRÉSERVATIFS ADDED

Having invented the French kiss and the French tickler, the speakers of the language of love have long had *savoir faire* in all things sexual—safety included. French pharmacies provide 24-hour condom (*préservatif* or *capote*) dispensers. In wonderful French style, they unabashedly adorn the sides of buildings on public streets and vending machines in the métro. When dining out, don't ask for foods without *préservatifs* or mistake your raspberry compote for a *capote*. Funny looks will greet you, as the French have not yet caught on to the international craze for condom-eating, and will think you a bit odd.

In your **passport**, write the names of any people you wish to have contacted in case of a medical emergency, and also list any **allergies** or medical conditions you want doctors to be aware of. Allergy sufferers might want to obtain a full supply of any necessary medication before the trip. Matching a prescription to a foreign equivalent is not always easy, safe, or possible. Carry up-to-date, legible prescriptions or a statement from your doctor stating the medication's trade name, manufacturer, chemical name, and dosage. While traveling, be sure to keep all medication with you in your carry-on luggage.

MEDICAL CONDITIONS

Those with medical conditions (e.g., diabetes, allergies to antibiotics, epilepsy, heart conditions) may want to obtain a stainless steel **Medic Alert** identification tag ($35 the 1st year, and $15 annually thereafter), which identifies the condition and gives a 24-hour collect-call information number. Contact the Medic Alert Foundation, 2323 Colorado Ave., Turlock, CA 95382 (800-825-3785; www.medicalert.org). Diabetics can contact the **American Diabetes Association,** 1660 Duke St., Alexandria, VA 22314 (800-232-3472), to receive copies of the article "Travel and Diabetes" and a diabetic ID card, which carries messages in 18 languages explaining the carrier's diabetic status.

BIRTH CONTROL

Contraception is readily available in most pharmacies (for some 24-hr pharmacies, see p. 276). To obtain **condoms** in France, visit a pharmacy and tell the clerk, *"Je voudrais une boîte de préservatifs"* (zhuh-voo-DRAY oon BWAHT duh PREY-zehr-va-TEEF). The French branch of the International Planned Parenthood Federation, the **Mouvement Français pour le Planning Familiale** (MFPF; ☎42 60 93 20), can provide more information. Women on the pill should bring enough to allow for possible loss or extended stays. Bring a prescription, since forms of the pill vary a good deal. Women who use a diaphragm should bring enough contraceptive jelly. You might want to bring your favorite brand of condoms with you, as availability and quality vary.

INSURANCE

Travel insurance generally covers four basic areas: medical/health problems, property loss, trip cancellation/interruption, and emergency evacuation. Although your regular insurance policies may well extend to travel-related accidents, you may consider purchasing travel insurance if the cost of potential trip cancellation/interruption is greater than you can absorb. Prices for travel insurance purchased separately generally run about US$50 per week for full coverage, while trip cancellation/interruption may be purchased separately at a rate of about US$5.50 per US$100 of coverage.

Medical insurance (especially university policies) often covers costs incurred abroad; check with your provider. **US Medicare** does not cover foreign travel. **Canadians** are protected by their home province's health insurance plan for up to 90 days after leaving the country; check with the provincial Ministry of Health or Health Plan Headquarters for details. **Homeowners' insurance** (or your family's coverage) often covers theft during travel and loss of travel documents (passport, plane ticket, railpass, etc.) up to US$500.

ISIC and **ITIC** (see p. 219) provide basic insurance benefits, including US$100 per day of in-hospital sickness for up to 60 days, US$3000 of accident-related medical reimbursement, and US$25,000 for emergency medical transport. Cardholders have access to a toll-free 24-hour helpline for medical, legal, and financial emergencies overseas (US and Canada ☎(877) 370-4742, elsewhere call US collect +1 (713) 342-4104). **American Express** (US ☎(800) 528-4800) grants most cardholders automatic car rental insurance (collision and theft, but not liability) and ground travel accident coverage of US$100,000 on flight purchases made with the card.

INSURANCE PROVIDERS

Council and **STA** (see p. 233) offer a range of plans that can supplement your basic coverage. Other private insurance providers in the **US and Canada** include: **Access America** (☎(800) 284-8300); **Berkely Group/Carefree Travel Insurance** (☎(800) 323-3149; www.berkely.com); **Globalcare Travel Insurance** (☎(800) 821-2488; www.globalcare-cocco.com); and **Travel Assistance International** (☎(800) 821-2828; www.worldwide-assistance.com). Providers in the **UK** include **Campus Travel** (☎(01865) 258 000) and **Columbus Travel Insurance** (☎(020) 7375 0011). In **Australia,** try **CIC Insurance** (☎9202 8000).

KEEPING IN TOUCH

BY MAIL

SENDING MAIL FROM PARIS

Post offices are marked on most Paris maps by their abstract flying-letter insignia; on the streets, look for the yellow and blue PTT signs. In general, post offices in Paris are open Monday to Friday 8am to 7pm (they stop changing money at 6pm) and on Saturday 8am to noon, though the **Poste du Louvre,** 52, rue du Louvre, 1*er* (☎01 40 28 20 40 for postal info, 01 40 28 20 00 for telegrams; M: Louvre; closes daily 6:20-7am) is open almost 24 hours even on holidays, and takes MasterCard and Visa. Buy stamps at *tabacs* or from vending machines inside post offices.

Air mail between Paris and North America takes five to ten days and is fairly dependable. Send mail from the largest post office in the area. To airmail a 20g (about 1 oz.) letter or postcard from France to the U.S. or Canada costs 4F40, to Australia or New Zealand 5F20. It is vital to distinguish your airmail from surface mail by labeling it clearly **par avion.** To airmail a **package,** you must complete a green customs slip. In France there are two grades of express mail: letters sent **prioritaire** cost the

ESSENTIAL INFORMATION

THE EURO

On January 1, 1999, 11 countries of the European Union, including France, officially adopted the **euro** as their common currency. Euro notes and coins will not be issued until January 1, 2002, and until that time the Euro will exist only in electronic transactions and travelers checks. On June 1, 2002 the Franc will be entirely withdrawn from circulation and the Euro will become the only legal currency in France. *Let's Go* lists all prices in French Francs, as these will still be most relevant in 2000. However, all French businesses must by law quote prices both in Francs and euros.

Travelers who will be passing through more than one nation in the euro-zone should note that exchange rates between the 11 national currencies were irrevocably fixed on January 1, 1999. Henceforth Bureau de Change will be obliged to interchange euro-zone currencies at the official rate and with **no commission,** though they may still charge a nominal service fee. Euro-denominated traveler's checks may also be used throughout the euro-zone, and can also be exchanged commission-free throughout the 11 euro nations.

same as regular airmail letters and arrive within four or five days to North America, although anything heavier than a letter will cost more than regular airmail; **chronopost** arrive in one to three days at a soaring cost of 230F for a letter. Chronopost is only available until 6pm in most post offices, until 8pm at major branches; call 0 800 43 11 00. You must go up to a window for *prioritaire* or chronopost. No worries about how much postage to use, as the caring, idiot-proof machines in the lobbies of most post office hold your hand through the process, weighing your package/letter, and printing out a sticker with just the right amount of postage. The **aerogramme,** a sheet of fold-up, pre-paid airmail paper, requires no envelope and costs more (5F to the U.S. or Canada, no enclosures allowed). **Registered mail** is called *avec recommandation* and costs between 26 and 30F, depending upon where the mail is going. To be notified of a registered letter's receipt, ask for an *avis de récéption* and pay an additional 8F. **Surface mail** is by far the cheapest way but takes one to three months to cross the Atlantic. It's adequate for getting rid of books or clothing you no longer need; a special book rate makes this option even more economical.

RECEIVING MAIL IN PARIS

There are several ways to arrange pick-up of letters sent to you by friends and relatives while you are abroad. If you do not have a mailing address in Paris, you can receive mail through the **Poste Restante** system, handled by the 23-hour Louvre post office (see above). To ensure the safe arrival of your letters, they should be addressed with your last/family name in capital letters, followed by a comma and your first name, followed by *Poste Restante*, the address of the specific post office, and Paris, FRANCE. You will have to show your passport as identification and pay 3F for every letter received.

General Delivery: Mail can be sent to France through **Poste Restante** (the French phrase for General Delivery) to almost any city or town with a post office. Address *Poste Restante* letters to: NOIR, Victor; Poste Restante: Recette Principale; [750xx where xx is the arrondissement you want to send to, e.g. 06 for the 6*ème,* 16 for the 16*ème*] PARIS; FRANCE; mark the envelope 'hold'. When picking up your mail, bring a form of photo ID, preferably a passport. There is generally a small charge per item to pick up, which in many cases is overlooked anyway. If the clerks insist that there is nothing for you, have them check under your first name as well.

American Express: AmEx's travel offices throughout the world offer a free **Client Letter Service** (mail held up to 30 days and forwarding upon request) for cardholders who contact them in advance. Address the letter in the same way shown above. Some offices will offer these services to non-cardholders (especially AmEx Travelers Cheque holders), but call ahead to make sure. *Let's Go* lists AmEx office locations for most large cities in **Practical Information** sections; for a complete, free list, call (800) 528-4800.

BY PHONE

CALLING PARIS FROM HOME

To call France direct from home, dial:

1. The international access code of your home country. **International access codes** include: Australia 011; Ireland 00; New Zealand 044; South Africa 09; U.K. 00; U.S. 011. City and country codes are sometimes listed with a zero in front (e.g., 033), but after dialing the international access code, drop successive zeros.

2. 33 (France's country code).

3. The 10-digit French number **minus the first zero**.

Thus if a number was listed as 01 23 45 67 89, you would dial the international access code followed by 33 1 23 45 67 89. For help **using a Parisian payphone** see .

BILLED CARDS. Calls are billed either collect or to your account. **MCI WorldPhone** also provides access to MCI's Traveler's Assist, which gives legal and medical advice, exchange rate information, and translation services. Other phone companies provide similar services to travelers. **To obtain a calling card** from your national telecommunications service before you leave home, contact the appropriate company below.

Australia: Telstra Australia Direct (☎13 22 00)
Canada: Bell Canada **Canada Direct** (☎(800) 565-4708)

AT&T Direct® Service

The easy way to call
home from anywhere.

AT&T Access Numbers

Austria●	0800-200-288	France	0800-99-00-11
Belarus×	8◆800-101	Gambia●	00111
Belgium●	0-800-100-10	Germany	0800-2255-288
Bosnia▲	00-800-0010	Ghana	0191
Bulgaria▲	00-800-0010	Gibraltar	8800
Cyprus●	080-900-10	Greece●	00-800-1311
Czech Rep.▲	00-42-000-101	Hungary●	06-800-01111
Denmark	8001-0010	Iceland●	800-9001
Egypt●(Cairo)ǂ	510-0200	Ireland✓	1-800-550-000
Finland●	0800-110-015	Israel	1-800-94-94-949

Italy ● **172-1011**	**Russia (Moscow) ▸▲●755-5042**
Luxembourg ✚ ..**800-2-0111**	**(St. Petersbg.) ▸▲●** ..**325-5042**
Macedonia ● ..**99-800-4288**	**Slovakia ▲** ..**00-42-100-101**
Malta.......... 0800-890-110	**South Africa** ..**0800-99-0123**
Monaco ●........**800-90-288**	**Spain** **900-99-00-11**
Morocco........002-11-0011	**Sweden** **020-799-111**
Netherlands ●...**0800-022-9111**	**Switzerland ● 0800-89-0011**
Norway **800-190-11**	**Turkey ●** **00-800-12277**
Poland ▲● ..**00-800-111-1111**	**Ukraine ▲**..........**8◆100-11**
Portugal ▲ **800-800-128**	U.A. Emirates ●......800-121
Romania ●......**01-800-4288**	**U.K.**............**0800-89-0011**

FOR EASY CALLING WORLDWIDE

1. Just dial the AT&T Access Number for the country you are calling from. *2.* Dial the phone number you're calling. *3.* Dial your card number.

For access numbers not listed ask any operator for **AT&T Direct®** Service. In the U.S. call 1-800-331-1140 for a wallet guide listing all worldwide AT&T Access Numbers.

Visit our Web site at: **www.att.com/traveler**

Bold-faced countries permit country-to-country calling outside the U.S.

- ● Public phones require coin or card deposit to place call.
- ▲ May not be available from every phone/payphone.
- ✚ Public phones and select hotels.
- ◆ Await second dial tone.
- ▸ Additional charges apply when calling from outside the city.
- † Outside of Cairo, dial "02" first.
- ✖ Not available from public phones or all areas.
- ✔ Use U.K. access number in N. Ireland.

When placing an international call ***from*** the U.S., dial 1 800 CALL ATT.

EMEA © 8/00 AT&T

Ireland: Telecom Éireann **Ireland Direct** (☎(800) 25 02 50)

New Zealand: Telecom New Zealand (☎(0800) 00 00 00):

South Africa: Telkom South Africa (☎09 03)

UK: British Telecom **BT Direct** (☎(800) 34 51 44)

US: AT&T (☎(888) 288-4685), **Sprint** (☎(800) 877-4646), or **MCI** (☎(800) 444-4141).

PREPAID CARDS. You can buy prepaid cards at home or in France which can be used anywhere in the world; the number of varieties available is bewildering but beware: the cheaper the calls offered, the more likely you are to have trouble getting through. Most major telecommunications companies issue them too; these are generally widely available in news agents and travel stores. Common prepaid cards you can buy at home include the Telstra **PhoneAway** (Australia), the Telecom Eireann **Ireland Direct Prepaid**, AT&T **Global Prepaid Card** (USA), the Telecom New Zealand **talkaway**, and the Canada Direct **Hello!**.

CALLING HOME FROM PARIS

If you are using a public pay phone in Paris, you will always need to insert a functioning *Télécarte* to make your call (though it will not be billed if you call collect or use a billed card). Many tiny *épiceries* and *restos* offer lesser-known cards like the *Phonepass*, which give great rates (3hr. to US or 4hr. to the UK, 100F). The best way to find these is to look for posters listing rates in windows.

BILLED CARDS. To call home with a calling card, contact the France operator for your service provider.

Australia: Telstra (0 800 99 00 61).

Canada: Bell Canada (0 800 99 00 16 or 0 800 99 02 16).

Ireland: Telecom Éireann (0 800 99 03 53).

New Zealand: Telecom New Zealand (0 800 99 00 64).

South Africa: Telkom South Africa (0 800 99 00 27).

UK: British Telecom (0 800 99 02 44).

US: AT&T (0 800 99 00 11); Sprint (0 800 99 00 87); or MCI (0 800 99 00 19).

South Africa: Telkom South Africa Direct (0 800 99 00 27).

PREPAID CARDS. For general information, see **Prepaid Cards** above. You can also buy prepaid cards in France; the most popular is the **Carte Intercall Monde**, available in most *tabacs* and news agents. These are available in 50F and 100F denominations, and give up to 75% off standard French international call rates.

DIRECT DIAL. If you must use a pay phone, prepare yourself in advance with a fully-charged *Télécarte* (see below), and be ready to watch the numbers drop. Calls are cheaper between 7pm and 8am Monday to Friday, noon-midnight Saturday and all Sunday. Expect to pay about 3F per minute to the UK, Ireland and North America, and about 10F per minute to Australia and New Zealand. Use only public *France Télécom* pay phones, as private ones often charge more. Although convenient, in-room hotel calls invariably include an arbitrary and sky-high surcharge (as much as US$10).

If you do dial direct, you must first insert a *Télécarte* (see **calling within France** below), then dial 00 (the international access code for France), the country code and then number of your home. **Country codes** include: Australia 61; Ireland 353; New Zealand 64; South Africa 27; U.K. 44; U.S. and Canada 1. Note that when calling the UK from abroad you should drop the first zero of the area code.

Telephone rates are reduced Monday to Friday 7pm-8am, noon Saturday to Monday 8am for calls to the EU; M-F 7pm-1pm, and all day Sa and Su to the U.S. and Canada. Remember time differences when you call—Paris is one hour ahead of Greenwich Mean Time and six hours ahead of New York (Eastern Standard Time) (For more on this, see the **Appendix**,.)

CALLING COLLECT. The expensive alternative to dialing direct or using a calling card is using an international operator to place a **collect call** (also called reverse-charges; *faire un appel en PCV* in French). An English-speaking operator from your home nation can be reached by dialing the appropriate service provider (see **Billed Calls,** p. 229), who will typically place a collect call even if you don't possess one of their phone cards.

CALLING WITHIN FRANCE

Almost all French pay phones accept only stylish microchip-toting phonecards called **Télécartes;** in many cafés and bars, some phones are still coin-operated; some also take credit cards. You may purchase the card in two denominations: 49F for 50 *unités*, and 97F for 120 *unités*, each worth anywhere from six to 18 minutes of conversation. The *Télécarte* is available at post offices, métro stations, and *tabacs*. Don't buy cards from street vendors who recycle discarded cards and cheat you. If your credit isn't good at home, the 120 *unités Télécarte* will serve you well (call to the U.K. 20min. for 120 units; call to the U.S. or Canada 12min. for 120 units). Emergency and collect calls require neither coins nor *Télécartes*.

Phone numbers in Paris and the Ile-de-France require **01** in front, in the northwest of France **02,** in the northeast **03,** in the southeast and Corsica **04,** and in the southwest **05.** Emergency calls and numbers beginning with **0 800** (formerly 05) are free. Most numbers beginning with **08** (formerly 36) are expensive (the equivalent of 900 numbers in the U.S.).

Directory information: ☎ 12. English rarely spoken.

International information: 00 33 12 + country code (Australia 61; Ireland 353; New Zealand 64; U.K. 44; U.S. and Canada 1).

International Operator: ☎ 00 33 11.

EMAIL

For those who desire an internet fix, there is no shortage of cyber cafés in Paris. If you feel the need to plan ahead, a good first step is to visit the **Cybercafé Guide** (www.cyberiacafe.net/cyberia/guide/ccafe.htm#working_france) which can help you find cybercafés in France and all over the world. Cybercafés tend to be expensive. Your best strategy is to compose email letters on your laptop or home computer, then download and send them at the café. Save them to a disk as a text or word processing program file, then they can be opened on the café computer, and cut and pasted into your email. This will reduce your login time and your expense. Some tourist offices (see **Tourist Offices,** p. 277) and smell-mecca Sephora (see p. 144) have free internet access. Many a hostel has access in its lobby, but prepared for slow connections, lengthy lines, and comparatively high fees. For Cybercafé listings, see **Service Directory,** p. 276.

GETTING THERE

BY PLANE

When it comes to airfare, a little effort can save you a bundle. If your plans are flexible enough to deal with the restrictions, courier fares are the cheapest. Tickets bought from consolidators and standby seating are also good deals, but last-minute specials, airfare wars, and charter flights often beat these fares. The key is to hunt around, to be flexible, and to persistently ask about discounts. Students, seniors, those under 26 and those who plan ahead should never pay full price for a ticket.

ESSENTIAL INFORMATION

BUYING TICKETS OVER THE INTERNET

Buying cheap tickets to Paris online

There are many advantages to browsing for travel bargains on the Web. Many airline sites offer special last-minute deals to internet customers, and you can make leisurely selections at any hour of the day or night. Make sure that the site uses a secure server before handing over any credit card details. **STA online** (www.sta-travel-com) offers student-rate flights and insurance. **Travelocity** (www.travelocity.com) offers a comprehensive range of services including flights and car hire. **Cheaptickets** (www.cheaptickets.com) offers just that, with a minimum of hassle and free browsing before you buy. At **Priceline** (www.priceline.com) you choose how much you want to pay, though you are obliged to buy the ticket if it finds one; be prepared for antisocial hours and odd routes.

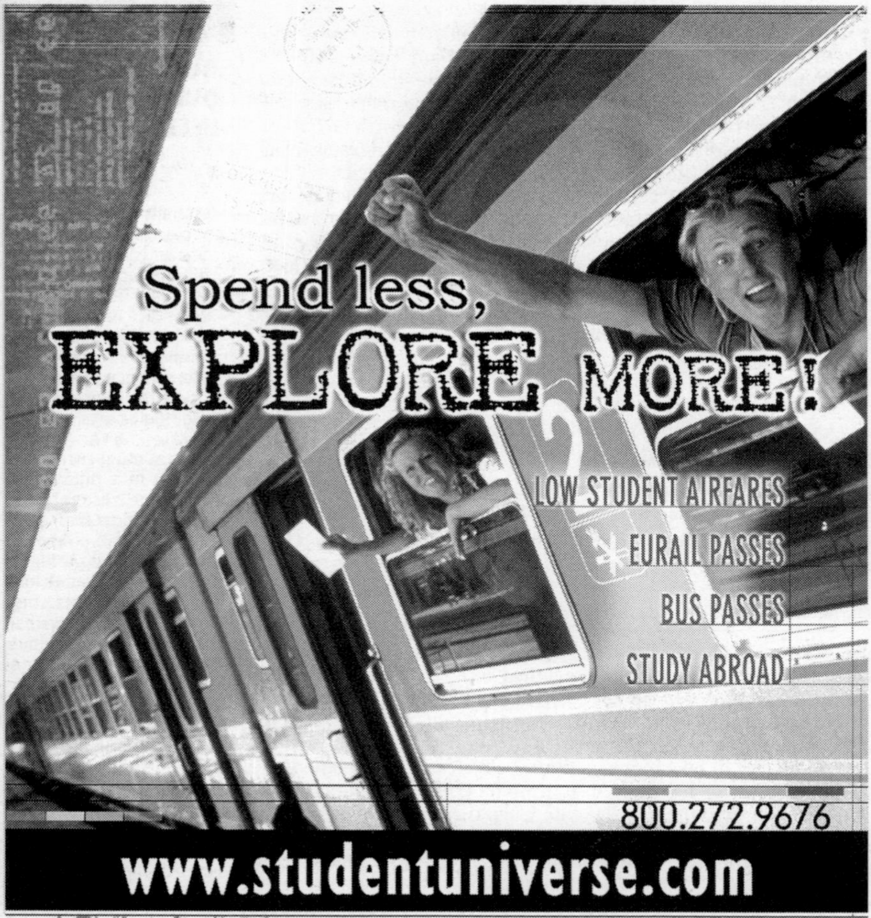

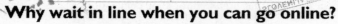

Timing: Airfares to France peak between June and September; and Easter and Christmas are also expensive periods in which to travel. Most cheap fares require a Saturday night stay. Flexibility is usually not an option for the budget traveler; traveling with an "open return" ticket can be pricier than fixing a return date when buying the ticket and paying later to change it. Most budget tickets, once bought, allow no date or route changes to made; student tickets sometimes allow date changes for a price.

Fares: Round-trip fares to Paris from the U.S. range from US$250-400 (during the off-season) to US$200-700 (during the summer). From Australia, count on paying between AUS$1600 and AUS$3000, depending on the season. From New Zealand, fares start at about NZ$5000 and climb to $9000. Flights from the U.K. to France are a comparative snip at UK£80-UK£140 for London-Paris, while a return flight from Dublin to Paris can cost as little as IR£120 return.

BUDGET AND STUDENT TRAVEL AGENCIES

Students and under-26ers holding **ISIC and IYTC cards** (see **Identification,** p. 219), respectively, qualify for big discounts from student travel agencies. Most flights from budget agencies are on major airlines, but in peak season some may sell seats on less reliable chartered aircraft.

Campus/Usit Youth and Student Travel (www.usitcampus.co.uk). In the U.K. call (0171) 730 34 02; in North America call (0171) 730 21 01; worldwide call (0171) 730 81 11. Offices include: 19-21 Aston Quay, O'Connell Bridge, **Dublin** 2 (☎(01) 677-8117; fax 679-8833); 52 Grosvenor Gardens, **London** SW1W 0AG; New York Student Center, 895 Amsterdam Ave., **New York,** NY, 10025 (☎212-663-5435; email usitny@aol.com). Additional offices in Cork, Galway, Limerick, Waterford, Coleraine, Derry, Belfast, and Greece.

Cheap Tickets (☎800-377-1000, www.cheaptickets.com) flies worldwide to and from the US. Choose itineraries by destination, price, and airline.

Council Travel (www.counciltravel.com). U.S. offices include: Emory Village, 1561 N. Decatur Rd., **Atlanta,** GA 30307 (☎404-377-9997); 273 Newbury St., **Boston,** MA 02116 (☎617-266-1926); 1160 N. State St., **Chicago,** IL 60610 (☎312-951-0585); 10904 Lindbrook Dr., **Los Angeles,** CA 90024 (☎310-208-3551); 205 E. 42nd St., **New York,** NY 10017 (☎212-822-2700); 530 Bush St., **San Francisco,** CA 94108 (☎415-421-3473); 1314 NE 43rd St. #210, **Seattle,** WA 98105 (☎206-632-2448); 3300 M St. NW, **Washington, D.C.** 20007 (☎202-337-6464). **For U.S. cities not listed,** call 800-2-COUNCIL (226-8624). Also 28A Poland St. (Oxford Circus), **London,** W1V 3DB (☎(0171) 287 3337), **Paris** (144 41 89 89), and **Munich** (089 39 50 22).

CTS Travel, 44 Goodge St., **London** W1 (☎(0171) 636 00 31; fax 637 53 28; email ctsinfo@ctstravel.com.uk).

STA Travel, 6560 Scottsdale Rd. #F100, Scottsdale, AZ 85253 (☎800-777-0112 fax 602-922-0793; www.sta-travel.com). A student and youth travel organization with over 150 offices worldwide. Ticket booking, travel insurance, railpasses, and more. U.S. offices include: 297 Newbury Street, **Boston,** MA 02115 (☎617-266-6014); 429 S. Dearborn St., **Chicago,** IL 60605 (☎312-786-9050); 7202 Melrose Ave., **Los Angeles,** CA 90046 (☎323-934-8722); 10 Downing St.,

ESSENTIAL INFORMATION

PACKING FOR PARIS

Pack lightly; the rest is commentary. You can buy anything you'll need in Paris. But, a few notes: In France, **electricity** is 220 volts AC, enough to fry any 110V North American appliance. 220V Electrical appliances don't like 110V current, either. Visit a hardware store for an adapter (which changes the shape of the plug) and a converter (which changes the voltage). Don't make the mistake of using only an adapter (unless appliance instructions explicitly state otherwise). Machines which heat-disinfect **contact lenses** will require a small converter (about US$20) to 220V, as well as a plug adapter. Consider switching temporarily to a chemical disinfection system, but check with your lens dispenser; some lenses may be damaged by a chemical system. Lens care supplies may be expensive and difficult to find, so bring enough for your entire vacation. Expect to pay at least US$4 for a 24-exposure ISO200 35mm color **film**. If you're not a serious photographer, you might want to consider bringing a **disposable camera.** Airport carry-on X-ray machines should not affect film speeds of 400 and under; always pack film in your carry-on luggage, since higher-intensity X-rays are used on checked luggage.

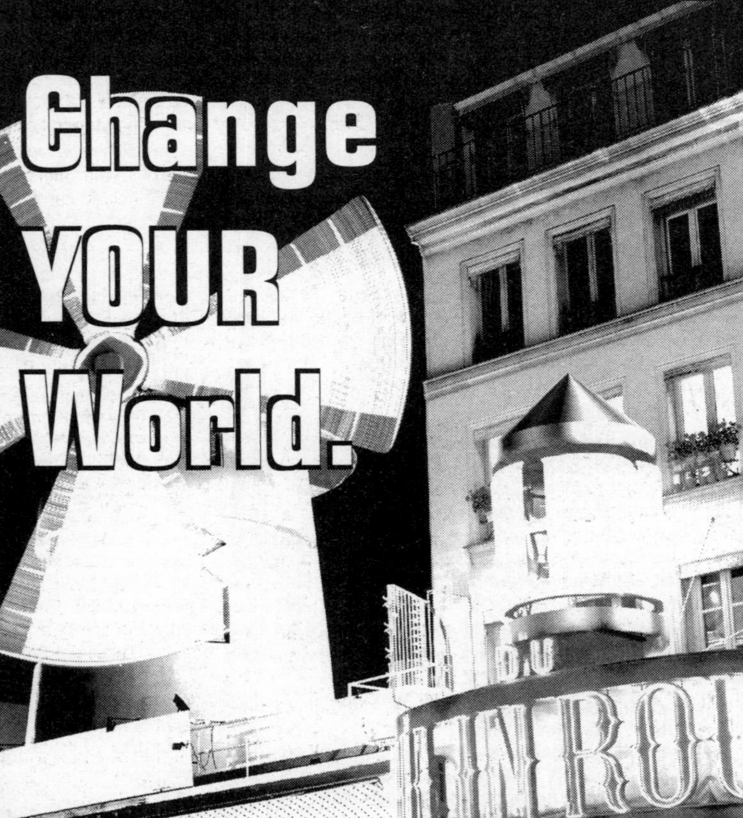
Change
YOUR
World.

New York, NY 10014 (☎212-627-3111); 4341 University Way NE, **Seattle,** WA 98105 (☎206-633-5000); 2401 Pennsylvania Ave., Ste. G, **Washington, D.C.** 20037 (☎202-887-0912); 51 Grant Ave., **San Francisco,** CA 94108 (☎415-391-8407). In the U.K., 6 Wrights Ln., **London** W8 6TA (☎(0171) 938 47 11 for North American travel). In New Zealand, 10 High St., **Auckland** (☎(09) 309 04 58). In Australia, 222 Faraday St., **Melbourne** VIC 3053 (☎(03) 9349 2411).

Travel CUTS (Canadian Universities Travel Services Limited), 187 College St., Toronto, Ont. M5T 1P7 (☎416-979 2406; fax 979 8167; www.travelcuts.com). 40 offices across Canada. Also in the U.K., 295-A Regent St., **London** W1R 7YA (☎0171 255 19 44).

Wasteels, Victoria Station, London, U.K. SW1V 1JT (☎(0171) 834 70 66; fax 630 76 28; www.wasteels.dk/uk). A huge chain in Europe, with 203 locations. Sells the Wasteels BIJ tickets, which are discounted (30-45% off regular fare) 2nd class international point-to-point train tickets with unlimited stopovers (must be under 26); sold only in Europe.

Travel Avenue (☎800-333-3335) rebates commercial fares to or from the U.S. and offers low fares for flights anywhere in the world. They also offer package deals, which include car rental and hotel reservations, to many destinations.

COMMERCIAL AIRLINES

The commercial airlines' lowest regular offer is the **APEX** (Advance Purchase Excursion) fare, which provides confirmed reservations and allows "open-jaw" tickets. Generally, reservations must be made 7 to 21 days in advance, with 7- to 14-day minimum-stay and up to 90-day maximum-stay restrictions, and hefty cancellation and change penalties (fees rise in summer). Book peak-season APEX fares early, since by May you will have a hard time getting your desired departure date. Although APEX fares are not the cheapest possible fares, they will give you a standard against which you can compare bargain fares. Low-season fares should be appreciably cheaper. **Air France** (☎0 802 802 802 in France; from abroad call +33 8 36 64 08 02; www.airfrance.com) is France's national airline, connecting France to the world. If flying in tricolor glory will make your vacation, it may be worth paying a bit more.

DISCOUNT AIRLINES

British Midland (Belfast (01232) 241188; Dublin (01) 283 0700; London (0345) 554554 ☎(0870) 607 0555 for reservations; U.S. ☎(800) 788-0555; www.britishmidland.com) has services from Belfast, Dublin, Edinburgh, Glasgow, Leeds, London, Manchester, Teesside. Prices start at UK£45 one-way.

Debonair Airways (☎(0541) 50 03 00; www.debonair.co.uk). Return tickets from London(UK£73-143).

Icelandair (☎800-223 5500; www.centrum.is/icelandair) has last-minute offers and standby fares on some flights between North America and Europe. Reservations must be made within three days of departure.

OTHER CHEAP ALTERNATIVES

AIR COURIER FLIGHTS. Couriers help transport cargo on international flights by guaranteeing delivery of the baggage claim slips from the company to a representative overseas. Generally, couriers must travel light (carry-ons only) and deal with flight restrictions. Most flights are round-trip only with short, fixed-length stays (usually one week) and a limit of a single ticket per issue. Most operate only out of the biggest U.S. cities. You must be over 21 (in some cases 18), have a valid passport, and procure your own visa, if necessary. Groups such as the **Air Courier Association** (☎800-282-1202; www.aircourier.org) and the **International Association of Air Travel Couriers,** 220 South Dixie Hwy., P.O. Box 1349, Lake Worth, FL 33460 (☎561-582-8320; email iaatc@courier.org; www.courier.org) provide their members with lists of opportunities and courier brokers worldwide for an annual fee. For more information, consult *Air Courier Bargains* by Kelly Monaghan (The Intrepid Traveler, US$15) or the *Courier Air Travel Handbook* by Mark Field (Perpetual Press, US$10).

CHARTER FLIGHTS. Charters are flights a tour operator contracts with an airline to fly extra loads of passengers during peak season. Charters can sometimes be cheaper than flights on scheduled airlines, some operate nonstop, and restrictions on minimum advance-purchase and minimum stay are more lenient. However, charter flights fly less frequently than major airlines, make refunds particularly difficult, and are almost always fully booked. Schedules and itineraries may also change or be cancelled at the last moment (as late as 48 hours before the trip, without a full refund), and check-in, boarding, and baggage claim are much slower. As always, pay with a credit card if you can, and consider traveler's insurance against trip interruption.

Discount clubs and **fare brokers** offer members savings on last-minute charter and tour deals. Study their contracts closely; you don't want to end up with an unwanted overnight layover. **Travelers Advantage,** Stamford, CT (☎800-548-1116; www.travelersadvantage.com; US$60 annual fee includes discounts, newsletters, and cheap flight directories) specializes in European travel and tour packages.

STANDBY FLIGHTS. Traveling standby requires considerable flexibility in the dates and cities of your arrival and departure. Companies that specialize in standby flights don't sell tickets, but the promise that you will get to your destination (or near your destination) within a certain window of time (anywhere from 1-5 days). Do not be surprised if you are stranded for several days, especially during tourist high season. You may only receive a refund if all available flights which depart within your date-range from the specified region are full. Future travel credit is always available. Carefully read agreements with any company offering standby flights, as the fine print can leave you in the lurch. To check on a company's service record, call the Better Business Bureau of New York City (☎212-533-6200). It is difficult to receive refunds, and clients' vouchers will not be honored when an airline fails to receive payment in time. **Airhitch,** 2641 Broadway, 3rd Fl., New York, NY 10025 (☎800-326-2009 or 212-864-2000; fax 864-5489; www.airhitch.org) and Los Angeles, CA (☎310-726-5000), runs coordinates standby flights between Europe and the US (to Europe US$159 each way when departing from the Northeast, $239 from the West Coast or Northwest, $209 from the Midwest, and $189 from the Southeast; travel within Europe possible with rates ranging from $79-$139).

TICKET CONSOLIDATORS. Ticket consolidators, or **"bucket shops,"** buy unsold tickets in bulk from commercial airlines and sell them at discounted rates. The best place to look is in the Sunday travel section of any major newspaper, where many bucket shops place tiny ads. Call quickly, as availability is typically extremely limited. Not all bucket shops are reliable establishments, so insist on a receipt that gives full details of restrictions, refunds, and tickets, and pay by credit card. For more information, check the website **Consolidators FAQ** (www.travel-library.com/air-travel/consolidators.html) or the book *Consolidators: Air Travel's Bargain Basement*, by Kelly Monaghan (Intrepid Traveler, US$8). Also try the **Air Travel Advisory Bureau** in London (☎(020) 76 36 50 00; www.atab.co.uk), which provides free referrals to specialist travel agencies and consolidators who offer discounted airfares out of major UK airports.

BY TRAIN

Each of Paris's six train stations is a veritable community of its own, with resident street people and police, *cafés*, *tabacs*, banks, and shops. Locate the ticket counters *(guichets)*, the platforms *(quais)*, and the tracks *(voies)*, and you will be ready to roll. Each terminal has two divisions: the *banlieue* and the *grandes lignes*. **Grandes lignes** depart for and arrive from distant cities in France and other countries—each of the six stations serves destinations in a particular region of France or Europe. Trains to the **banlieue** serve the suburbs of Paris and make frequent stops. Within a given station, each of these divisions has its own ticket counters, information booths, and timetables; distinguishing between them before you get in line will save you hours of frustration. **Don't forget to "composter" your ticket** (time-stamp it) at the orange machines on the platform before boarding the train, or you may be slapped with a heavy fine. All train stations are reached by at least two métro lines; the métro stop bears the same name as the train station. For **train information** or to make reservations, call the SNCF at 08 36 35 35 35 (3F per min.), or use Minitel 3615 SNCF 7am to 10pm daily. The SNCF line is perpetually busy (try in the evening). You can also book tickets at a local travel agency. There is a free telephone with direct access to the stations on the right-hand side of the Champs-Elysées tourist office. In addition, there are yellow **ticket machines** known as Billetterie at every train station; if you know your PIN, you can use a MasterCard, Visa, or American Express to buy tickets. MasterCard and Visa are also accepted at the ticket booths. Some cities can be accessed by both regular trains and **trains à grande vitesse (TGV;** fast speed trains). TGVs are more expensive but much faster; they also require reservations that cost a small fee. Regular trains require no reservations; this means that tickets for regular trains can be used as far after purchase date as you wish, though once stamped they must be used within 24 hours.

SNCF offers a wide range of discounted roundtrip tickets for travelers in France which go under the name **tarifs Découvertes**—you should rarely have to pay full price. While further discounts are available with the purchase of a special card, for those under 25, children, and adults traveling together. Get a calendar from a train station detailing *période bleue* (blue period), *période blanche* (white period) and *période rouge* (red period) times and days; blue gets the most discounts, while red gets none. Even without the cards, all of the above groups are automatically entitled to lesser reductions (usually 25% rather than 50%).

Note: The following prices are the **undiscounted fares** for one-way, second-class tickets unless otherwise noted. Summer schedules are listed. In general, prices, and number of trips per day, vary according to the day of the week, season, and other criteria. A word on **safety:** each terminal shelters its share of thieves. Gare du Nord and Gare d'Austerlitz become rough at night, when drugs and prostitution emerge. It is not advisable to buy tickets in the stations except at official counters.

Gare du Nord: Trains to northern France, Britain, Belgium, the Netherlands, Scandinavia, the Commonwealth of Independent States, and northern Germany (Cologne, Hamburg). To: Brussels (18 per day (spring), 2hr., 287F); Amsterdam (15 per day, 5hr., 378F); Cologne (7 per day, 5-

6hr., 364F); Boulogne (5 per day, 2½hr., 180F); Copenhagen (1 direct, 3 indirect per day, 16hr., 1265F); London (by the Eurostar chunnel, approx. 17 per day, 2hr., 350-1080F).

Gare de l'Est: To eastern France (Champagne, Alsace, Lorraine), Luxembourg, parts of Switzerland (Basel, Zürich, Lucerne), southern Germany (Frankfurt, Munich), Austria, and Hungary. To: Zürich (4 per day, 6hr., 418F); Munich (6 per day, 8hr., 685F); and Vienna (5 per day, 14hr., 970F).

Gare de Lyon: To southern and southeastern France (Lyon, Provence, Riviera), parts of Switzerland (Geneva, Lausanne, Berne), Italy, and Greece. To: Geneva (5 per day, 3½hr., 508F); Florence (4 per day, 11hr., 655F); Rome (4-5 per day, 12hr., 630F); Lyon (23 per day, 2hr., 295-398F); Nice (12 per day, 6hr., 340-945F); Marseille (13 per day, 4-5hr., 373F).

Gare d'Austerlitz: To the Loire Valley, southwestern France (Bordeaux, Pyrénées), Spain, and Portugal. (TGV to SW France leaves from Gare Montparnasse.) To: Barcelona (2 per day, 9hr., 500-810F) and Madrid (1 per day, 12-13hr., 530-850F).

Gare St-Lazare: To Normandy. To: Caen (29 per day, 2hr., 154F); Rouen (17 per day, 1hr., 103F).

Gare Montparnasse: To Brittany, and the TGV to southwestern France. To: Rennes (33 per day, 2-2½hr., 283F).

BY BUS

British travelers may find buses the cheapest way of getting to Paris, with return fares starting around UK£50. Obviously, the bus trip will also entail a ferry trip or occasionally a descent into the Channel Tunnel; these are included in the price of a ticket. On the downside, buses take longer than trains and planes and are more susceptible to delays.

Eurolines, 4 Cardiff Rd., Luton LU1 1PP (☎(08705) 14 32 19; fax (01582) 40 06 94; in London, 52 Grosvenor Gardens, Victoria; (☎(01582) 40 45 11); email welcome@eurolines.uk.com; www.eurolines.co.uk). Europe's largest operator of international coach services. Roundtrip fares between London and Paris start at UK£49.

BY CHANNEL TUNNEL

Though still dogged by huge debts, the Channel Tunnel is increasing in popularity every year as people have overcome their fears of traveling for 27 miles under the sea. Undoubtedly the fastest, most convenient and least scenic route from England to France, the 'Chunnel' offers two types of service. **Le Shuttle** is a drive-on train service which ferries cars and coaches between Folkestone and Calais; **Eurostar** is the high-speed train which links London to Paris and Brussels, with stops at Ashford in England and Calais and Lille in France. On the Eurostar, traveling at close to 150mph, the whole journey takes a snappy three hours. What's more, you board and exit the train right in the middle of each city—no added transportation time or cost is needed. Trains leave London Waterloo for Gare du Nord, where you can catch the metro and the RER. It is prudent to buy your ticket a week in advance. You must check-in at the station at least **20 minutes before departure**. Attach the nifty and required tag to all baggage items (available at terminals and travel agencies). You are allowed to transport two bags and one carry-on; you will be required to pay 90F for each additional piece of baggage. Enquire at Eurostar ticket offices or at Campus Travel in London for special promotions.

Eurostar: Reservations ☎01233 61 75 75 (UK); 01 49 70 01 75 (France); www.eurostar.co.uk. Eurostar tickets can also be bought at most major travel agents. **London-Paris Gare du Nord**: 3hr., 18-23 departures daily. roundtrip fares: UK£249 standard; under 25 UK£79; over 60 UK£119; child (4-11) UK£55; restricted fares from UK£79. **London-Disneyland Paris:** 3hr., 1 per day, departing UK in the morning, returning early evening. Round-trip UK£89-119; youth UK£79; child UK£59. Slightly fewer departures from Ashford; fares are same as for London departures.

Le Shuttle: ☎0800 096 9992 (UK); 03 21 00 61 00 (France); www.eurotunnel.co.uk. 20 min.; 1-3 departures per hour. Services run throughout the night. Roundtrip prices for car and all passengers: day UK£110-150; Economy (open) UK£219-299; mini-breaks (5-day return) UK£139-195.

SPECIFIC CONCERNS

WOMEN TRAVELERS

Women traveling alone, or even with other women, and even in busy areas, can expect to be hassled by men, especially at night. Women should exercise caution, maintain a confident gait, and avoid direct eye contact with intimidating men. Sunglasses will serve you well. Parisian women often respond to verbal harassment with an icy stare, but you should do your best to avoid conflict. Speaking to *drageurs* (as the French call them), even to say "NO!", is only to invite a reply, but if you feel threatened don't hesitate to call out to others or to draw attention to yourself. A loud *"laissez-moi tranquille!"* (LAY-say mwa trahnk-EEL; "leave me alone!") or *"au secours!"* (awe-S'KURE; "help!") will embarrass them and hopefully send them on their way. Harassment can be minimized by making yourself as inconspicuous as possible; see **Blending In,** for tips, though in some cities you may be harassed no matter how you're dressed. Wearing a conspicuous **wedding ring** may dissuade unwanted overtures. *Let's Go: Paris* lists crisis numbers on p. 275. **In an emergency, dial 17 for police assistance**.

TRAVELING ALONE

There are many benefits to traveling alone, among them greater independence and challenge. You will have greater opportunity to interact with the residents of the region you're visiting. Without distraction, you can write a great travel log in the grand tradition of Mark Twain, John Steinbeck, and Charles Kuralt.

On the other hand, any solo traveler is a more vulnerable target of harassment and street theft. Lone travelers need to be well-organized and look confident at all times. Try not to stand out as a tourist, and be especially careful in deserted or very crowded areas.

If questioned, never admit that you are traveling alone. Maintain regular contact with someone at home who knows your itinerary.

For more tips, pick up *Traveling Solo* by Eleanor Berman (Globe Pequot, US$17) or subscribe to **Connecting: Solo Travel Network,** P.O. Box 29088, Delamont RPO, Vancouver, BC V6J 5C2 (tel./fax (604) 737-7791; www.cstn.org; membership US$25-35), or the **Travel Companion Exchange,** P.O. Box 833, Amityville, NY 11701, USA (☎(631) 454-0880 or 800-392-1256; www.whytravelalone.com; US$48).

OLDER TRAVELERS

In Paris, most museums, concerts, and sights offer reduced prices for visitors over 60. If you don't see a senior citizen price listed, ask, and you may be delightfully surprised. Tour buses and Seine-river boat tours, such as the **Bateaux Mouches** (see **Tours,** p. 278) enable you to see a large number of sights without walking great distances. *Let's Go: Paris* tries to list at least one hotel in every arrondissement that is accessible to those with limited mobility (see **Travelers with Disabilities,** p. 240). When booking your hotel, ask for a room on the first floor or inquire about access to the lift. We've also tried to list at least one mid-priced quality hotel in each arrondissement so you can avoid the sometimes noisy young crowd at the hostels.

Elderhostel, 75 Federal St., Boston, MA 02110-1941 (☎877 426 8056 M-F 9am-9pm; email registration@elderhostel.org; www.elderhostel.org). Programs at colleges, universities, and other learning centers in Europe on varied subjects lasting 1-4 weeks. Must be 55 or over (spouse can be of any age).

Walking the World, P.O. Box 1186, Fort Collins, CO 80522 (☎970 498 0500; fax 970 498 9100; email walktworld@aol.com; www.walkingtheworld.com), sends trips to France.

Unbelievably Good Deals and Great Adventures That You Absolutely Can't Get Unless You're Over 50, Joan Rattner Heilman. Contemporary Books (US$13).

BISEXUAL, GAY, AND LESBIAN TRAVELERS

Next to Berlin, London, and Amsterdam, Paris has one of the largest gay populations in Europe. Despite homophobia and the ravages of AIDS, Paris' gay and lesbian communities are vibrant, politically active, and full of opportunities for fun (see **Festivals**, and **Nightlife**,). Listed below are contact organizations, mail-order bookstores and publishers which offer materials addressing some specific concerns. **Out and About** (www.planetout.com) offers a bi-weekly newsletter addressing travel concerns.

Gay's the Word, 66 Marchmont St., London WC1N 1AB (☎(020) 7278 7654; email sales@gaystheword.co.uk; www.gaystheword.co.uk). The largest gay and lesbian bookshop in the UK, with both fiction and non-fiction titles. Mail-order service available.

Giovanni's Room, 345 S. 12th St., Philadelphia, PA 19107, USA (☎(215) 923-2960; fax 923-0813; www.queerbooks.com). An international lesbian/feminist and gay bookstore with mail-order service (carries many of the publications listed below).

International Gay and Lesbian Travel Association, 4331 N. Federal Hwy., #304, Fort Lauderdale, FL 33308, USA (☎(954) 776-2626; fax 776-3303; www.iglta.com). An organization of over 1350 companies serving gay and lesbian travelers worldwide.

International Lesbian and Gay Association (ILGA), 81 rue Marché-au-Charbon, B-1000 Brussels, Belgium (tel./fax +32 (2) 502 24 71; www.ilga.org). Not a travel service; provides political information, such as homosexuality laws of individual countries.

TRAVELERS WITH DISABILITIES

Many of Paris's museums and sights are fully accessible to wheelchairs and some provide guided tours in sign-language. Unfortunately, budget hotels and restaurants are generally ill-equipped to handle the needs of handicapped visitors. Handicapped accessible bathrooms are virtually non-existent among hotels in the one-to-two star range and many elevators could double as shoe-boxes. Change is slowly coming to Paris. The invaluable brochure *Paris-Ile-de-France for Everyone* (available in English for 60F at most tourist offices and through the CNRH (see below), and 80F from abroad) lists accessible sites, hotels, and restaurants as well as indispensable practical tips.

Let's Go: Paris tries to list at least one wheelchair-accessible hotel in each arrondissement. Please see "handicapped accessible" in the index for a full list of **handicapped accessible hotels.** Note that the hotels described as such in this book are those with reasonably wide (but not regulation size) elevators or with ground-floor rooms wide enough for wheelchair entry. To ask restaurants, hotels, railways, and airlines if they are wheelchair accessible, say: *"Etes-vous accessibles aux fauteuils roulants?"* (ET VOO ax-es-EEB-luh OH foh-TOY roo-LON?). If transporting a **seeing-eye dog** to France, you will need a rabies vaccination certificate issued from home.

The RATP and its personnel are generally well equipped to assist blind or deaf passengers. Very few métro stations are wheelchair-accessible, but RER lines A and B are. For a guide to métro accessibility, pick up a free copy of the RATP's brochure, *Handicaps et déplacements en région Ile-de-France* (☎01 36 68 41 41 for help in English), which provide a list of stations equipped with escalators, elevators, and moving walkways. Public buses are not yet wheelchair accessible except for line 20, which runs from Gare de Lyon to Gare St-Lazare. Taxis are required by law to take passengers in wheelchairs. The following offer transport for the motion impaired: **Airhop** (☎01 41 29 01 29; open M-F 8am-noon and 1:30am-6pm) and **GiHP,** 24 ave. Henri Barbusse, 93000 Bobigny, (☎01 41 83 15 15; open M-F 7:30am-8pm) can help you get to and from the airports (See **To and From the Airports,** p. 15).

Those with disabilities should inform airlines and hotels of their disabilities when making arrangements for travel; some time may be needed to prepare special accommodations. Call ahead to restaurants, hotels, parks, and other facilities to find out about the existence of ramps, the widths of doors, the dimensions of elevators, etc. The following organizations provide information or publications that might be of assistance:

USEFUL ORGANIZATIONS

Mobility International USA (MIUSA), P.O. Box 10767, Eugene, OR 97440, USA (☎(541) 343-1284 voice and TDD; fax 343-6812; email info@miusa.org; www.miusa.org). Sells *A World of Options: A Guide to International Educational Exchange, Community Service, and Travel for Persons with Disabilities* (US$35).

Moss Rehab Hospital Travel Information Service (☎(215) 456-9600 or (800) CALL-MOSS; email netstaff@mossresourcenet.org; www.mossresourcenet.org). An information resource center on travel-related concerns for those with disabilities.

Society for the Advancement of Travel for the Handicapped (SATH), 347 Fifth Ave., #610, New York, NY 10016 (☎(212) 447-7284; www.sath.org). An advocacy group that publishes the quarterly travel magazine *OPEN WORLD* (free for members, US$13 for nonmembers). Also publishes a wide range of info sheets on disability travel facilitation and destinations. Annual membership US$45, students and seniors US$30.

TOUR AGENCIES

Directions Unlimited, 123 Green Ln., Bedford Hills, NY 10507, USA (☎(914) 241-1700 or (800) 533-5343; www.travel-cruises.com). Specializes in arranging individual and group vacations, tours, and cruises for the physically disabled.

AGENCIES IN PARIS

L'Association des Paralysées de France, Délégation de Paris, 22, r. de Père Guérion, 13*ème* (☎40 78 69 00). M: Place d'Italie. Publishes *Où ferons-nous étape?* (85F), which lists French hotels accessible to persons with disabilities. Open M-F 9am-12:30pm and 2-5:30pm.

Audio-Vision guides, at Parisian theaters such as the Théâtre National de Chaillot, 1, pl. Trocadéro, 11 Novembre, 16*ème* (☎53 65 31 00), the Comédie Française, 2, rue de Richelieu, 1*er* (☎44 58 15 15), and the Théâtre National de la Colline, 15, r. Malte-Brun, 20*ème* (☎44 62 52 00). Spoken service for the blind or vision-impaired, which describes the costumes, sets, and theater design.

Comité National Français de Liaison pour la Réadaption des Handicapés (CNFLRH), 236bis, r. de Tolbiac, 13*ème* (☎53 80 66 66; fax 01 53 80 66 67; www.handitel.org). Publishes *Paris-Ile-de-France for Everyone,* an English-language guide to hotels and sights with wheelchair access (60F in France, 80F from abroad).

MINORITY TRAVELERS

Despite Paris's extraordinary diversity, its large African, Maghreban, East Asian, and South Asian populations, and its wealth of multi-ethnic restaurants and cultural events, racism is as big a problem here as it is in London, Sydney, and New York. Immigrants are frequently blamed for France's high unemployment rate and expensive state welfare system, though socioeconomic studies do not support such claims (see **History,** p. 25). However, French prejudice is more cultural than color-oriented; the most common complaint is that immigrants do not adopt French culture and customs. Minority travelers are likely to be treated simply as foreigners; it wasn't for nothing that James Baldwin and Charles Mingus fled the US for Paris in the 1950s.

Those of Arab, North African, or West African descent may face suspicious or derogatory glances from passersby. Should you confront race-based exclusion or violence, you should make a formal complaint to the police. We encourage you to work through either SOS Racisme or MRAP in order to facilitate your progress through a confusing foreign bureaucracy.

S.O.S. Racisme, 28, rue des Petites Ecuries, 10*ème* (☎01 53 24 67 67; www.sos-racisme.org). Occupied primarily with helping illegal immigrants and people whose documentation is irregular. They provide legal services and are used to negotiating with police.

MRAP (Mouvement contre le racisme et pour l'amitié entre les peuples), 43, bd. Magenta, 10*ème* (☎01 53 38 99 99; fax 01 40 40 90 98; www.mrap.asso.fr/mrap.htm). Handles immigration issues and monitors racist publications and propaganda.

TRAVELERS WITH CHILDREN

Regardless of the fact that Paris offers a dizzying array of sights, sounds, and above all, smells, those traveling with children will need to plan their day's ahead. Children, whose legs and attention spans are generally shorter than those of adults, will soon tire and cease to care who painted the Mona Lisa, or who used to hang out in the Latin Quarter.

Thankfully, there are a plethora of sights and attractions that are just for kids in Paris. For a Let's Go thumb in the right direction, see **Guignols,** p. 153. A good way to plan the day with children is in bite-sized segments, allowing for an afternoon nap (especially in the August heat), and frequent, strategic breaks for the other great pacifier: Parisian sweets (for more on this, your secret weapon, see p. 179). The other good news is that while the French might love to hate you, the attitude barrier does not apply to little ones, who will most often be accommodated in restaurants, cafés, and (heaven forbid) bars. Cheaper restaurants and chains often have children's menus. Hotels generally have a minimal charge for an extra bed or cot, called a *lit supplementaire.* Travelers with babies should have no problem finding the necessary supplies in supermarkets and pharmacies.

The Paris magazine *L'Officiel des Spectacles* (2F) has a section entitled *Pour Les Jeunes* that lists exhibits, programs, and movies appropriate for children (see **Newspapers,** p. 23).

KEEPING KOSHER

In Paris, **kosher** delis, restaurants, and bakeries abound in the *3ème* and *4ème* arrondissements, particularly on rue des Rosiers and rue des Écouffes. Contact the **Union Libéral Israélite de France Synogogue** (see **Religious Services,** p. 277) for more information on kosher restaurants. For a list of vegetarian and kosher restaurants, see **Restaurants by Type,** p. 158. If you are strict in your observance, you may have to prepare your own food on the road. **The Jewish Travel Guide,** which lists synagogues, kosher restaurants, and Jewish institutions in over 100 countries, is available in Europe from

Vallentine Mitchell Publishers, Newbury House 890-900, Eastern Ave., Newbury Park, Ilford, Essex IG2 7HH, UK (☎(020) 8599 8866; fax 8599 0984) and in the US ($16.95 + $4 S&H) from ISBS, 5804 NE Hassallo St., Portland, OR 97213 (☎(800) 944-6190).

OTHER RESOURCES

French or Foe? Getting the Most Out of Visiting, Living and Working in France, Polly Platt. Distribooks Intl, 1998 (US$16.95). A popular guide to getting by in France

Cultural Misunderstandings: The French-American Experience, Raymonde Carroll, transl. Carol Volk. University of Chicago Press, 1990 (US$11.95). For Americans baffled by the French outlook on life.

Fragile Glory: A Portrait of France and the French, Richard Bern stein, 1991 (US$14.95). A witty look at France by the former New York Times Paris bureau chief.

Wicked French, Howard Tomb. Workman, 1989 (US$4.95). A hilarious guide to everything you really didn't need to know how to say in French.

A Traveller's Wine Guide to France, Christopher Fielden. Traveller's Wine Guides, 1997. (US$17.95). Exactly what it says it is, by a well-known oenophile.

Traveller's Literary Companion: France, Ed. John Edmonson. Passport Books, 1997 (US$17.95). For those rare times when *Let's Go* doesn't reach that literary high, these 120 extracts from great French writers provide another perspective on France.

Michelin Green Guides, Michelin. Around US$20. The authoritative guide to France, this series covers the country in 24 regional books with unbeatable information on towns and sights. You'll still need your trusty *Let's Go* for all your practical information, accommodations, and food needs.

THE WORLD WIDE WEB

Maison de la France (www.maison-de-la-france.com:8000/) is the main government tourist site. Up-to-date information on tourism in France, including a calendar of festivals and major events, regional info with links to local servers, and a host of tips on everything from accommodation to smoking laws. English version available.

France Diplomatie (www.france.diplomatie.fr/) is the French Department of Foreign Affairs site, with information on visas and other official matters as well as comprehensive presentations on French history, culture, geography, politics, and current affairs. Most information is available in English.

Secretariat for Tourism (www.tourisme.gouv.fr) has a number of governmental documents and press releases relating to the state of tourism in France, plus links to all the national, regional and departmental tourist authorities. In French.

Tourism in France (www.tourisme.fr) has information on all types of tourism in France, an extensive directory of links to local resources and features on "unwonted stays to discover France." In French and mildly amusing English.

Nomade (www.nomade.fr) and French Excite (www.excite.fr) are a popular French search engines—though they're not very useful if you can't read French.

TF1 (www.TF1.com) is the home page of France's most popular TV station, and with news, popular culture, and weather and traffic reports in French.

Météo-France (www.meteo.fr) has 2-day weather forecasts and maps for France.

Let's Go (www.letsgo.com) is where you can find our newsletter, information about our books, up-to-the-minute links, and more.

INSIDE

Accommodations

Ninotchka, it's midnight. One half of Paris is making love to the other half.
-Leon

TYPES OF ACCOMMODATIONS

HOTELS

Small Parisian hotels are a long-time institution in this city; they are almost all proudly shabby and of eccentric character. Hotels offer total privacy, no curfew, and (usually) concerned managers. Most importantly, they routinely accept reservations. Groups of two, three, and four may find it more economical to stay in a hotel since hotels rent doubles by the room and not by the body. Double rooms can be made into triples with the use of a *lit supplementaire* (pull out bed, 50-150F). This system perfectly suits families with small children. Some rooms are *mansarde*, which means they have a sloping roof and are on the top floor. These are often quite charming, with more space for extra beds.

The French government employs a ratings system that graces hotels with zero to four stars depending on the services offered, the percentage of rooms with bath, and other such indicators. Most hotels listed by *Let's Go* are zero, one- or two-star, with a smattering of inexpensive three-stars. *At the absolute minimum, e*xpect to pay at least 130F for a single room and 160F for a double.

If you want a room with twin beds, make sure to ask for *une chambre avec deux lits* (a room with two beds); otherwise you may find yourself in *une chambre avec un grand lit* (room with a double bed). In our listings, doubles refer to rooms with one full-size bed; two-bed doubles refer to the rare room with two separate (usually twin) beds.

Rooms in cheap hotels normally have no showers or toilets; they are in the hallway. Occasionally, you will have to pay extra for a hot shower (10-25F). Otherwise, rooms may come with a variety of add-ons: *avec bidet-lavabo* means a sink and a bidet, but no toilet; *avec WC* or *avec cabinet* means with sink and toilet; *avec douche* means with shower; and *avec salle de bain* is with a full bathroom. All French hotels display on the back of each room's door a list showing the prices of rooms, breakfast, and any residency tax. It is illegal to charge you more than is shown, although you can try to bargain for a lower rate if you are staying for more than a few days.

HOSTELS AND FOYERS

Many of Paris's **hostels** don't bother with the restrictions, such as sleepsheets, that characterize most international hostels. They do have maximum stays, age restrictions, and lockouts, but these are often flexible. According to French law, all hostels have a curfew of 2am, although some places are more flexible than others. Accommodations usually consist of single-sex rooms with two to eight beds, but you may be asked whether you're willing to be in a co-ed room. You *will* share a room with strangers. Most rooms are simply furnished with metal or wood frame bunkbeds, thin sheets and cheap blankets. Most have sinks and mirrors; showers and toilets are in a courtyard or communal hallway.

Foyers are intended for university students or workers during the academic year and are available for short- or long-term stays during the summer. *Foyers*, often comprised of single rooms, offer the security and privacy of a hotel while providing the lower prices and camaraderie of a youth hostel.

Hostels of Europe cards cost 100F, and many hostels are members. These cards are not obligatory, but usually offer 5% off your bill. Despite the hype, there are only six official **Hostelling International** hostels in Paris. Most of the hostels and *foyers* in the city are privately run organizations, usually with services comparable to those at HI and often preferable to the HI hostels because of their more central locations. To stay in a **Hostelling International (HI)** hostel, you must be a member.

RESERVATIONS

Make reservations at least two weeks in advance and up to a couple of months in advance for the summer. English may not be spoken at some smaller accommodations, but this shouldn't dissuade a non-French-speaker from calling; most proprietors are used to receiving calls from non-French-speakers. If the place where you wish to reserve a room asks for a deposit, they usually expect you to fax them your credit card number. Ask about a hotel's cancellation policy before giving a credit card number and whether or not your card will be billed. If you can avoid leaving a number (which is often the case if you just send written confirmation or say you don't have one), don't leave one. Either way, make sure the fax is clear about your anticipated dates and type of room. If you decide to leave Paris early, or if you want to switch hotels, don't expect to get back all of your deposit. On the flip side, if you change your plans before you even get started, you should certainly call and cancel your reservation. If you plan to arrive late, call and ask a hotel to hold your room. Once in Paris, the **Office du Tourisme** on the Champs-Elysées or one of its other bureaus should be able to find you a room, although the lines may extend to the horizon and the selections are not necessarily the cheapest (see **Tourist Offices,** p. 277). For accommodation agencies, see **Service Directory,** p. 273.

ACCOMMODATIONS BY PRICE

Accommodation prices are based on the cost of the lowest-end single available at each hotel or hostel. If an establishment does not rent singles, the price is based on the next cheapest room (in most cases a dormitory); this price is difference is noted with a *.

UNDER 150F

Aloha Hostel* (261)	15ème
Association des Etud. Protestants (254)	6ème
Auberge de Jeun. Le D'Artagnan* (263)	20ème
Auberge de Jeunesse Jules Ferry* (258)	11ème
BVJ/Paris Louvre* (249)	1er
CISP Kellerman (259)	13ème
Foyer de Chaillot* (255)	8ème
Foyers des Jeunes Filles (259)	13ème
Grand Hôtel de Clermont (262)	18ème
Henri IV (248)	Île de la Cité
Hôtel de Belfort* (258)	11ème
Hôtel Lafayette (256)	10ème
Hôtel du Marais (250)	3ème
Hôtel Moderne du Temple (256)	10ème
Hôtel Palace (257)	10ème
Hôtel Tiquetonne (250)	2ème
La Maison Hostel (261)	15ème
Ouest Hôtel (260)	15ème
Three Ducks Hostel (261)	15ème
Village Hostel* (263)	18ème
Woodstock Hostel* (257)	9ème
Young and Happy Hostel* (253)	5ème

150-200F

BVJ/Paris Quartier Latin (253)	5ème
Cambrai Hôtel (257)	10ème
CISP Ravel (259)	12ème
L'Ermitage (263)	20ème
Foyer International des Etudiantes (254)	6ème
Hôtel André Gill (262)	8ème
Hôtel de l'Aveyron (259)	12ème
Hôtel Caulaincourt (262)	18ème
Hôtel le Central (253)	5ème
Hôtel d'Esmerelda (253)	5ème
Hôtel La Marmotte (250)	2ème
Hôtel des Medicis (253)	5ème
Hôtel de Milan (257)	10ème
Hôtel de Printemps (261)	15ème
Hôtel de Nevers (258)	11ème
Hôtel Nôtre-Dame (258)	11ème
Hôtel de la Paix (255)	7ème
Hôtel Printania* (259)	12ème
Hôtel du Progrès (252)	5ème
Hôtel de Reims (258)	12ème
Hôtel Rhetia (257)	11ème
Hôtel du Séjour (250)	3ème
Maison des Clubs UNESCO (259)	13ème
Maisons des Jeunes de Rufz (249)	1er
Nièvre-Hôtel (259)	12ème
Perfect Hôtel (256)	9ème
Plessis Hôtel (258)	11ème
Résidence Bastille (258)	11ème
UCJF (256)	8ème

200-250F

Castex Hôtel (251)	4ème
Eden Hôtel (263)	20ème
Hôtel Belidor (262)	7ème
Hôtel des Boulevards (250)	2ème
Hôtel Camélia (261)	15ème
Hôtel de Chevreuse (254)	6ème
Hôtel Eiffel Rive-Gauch (255)	7ème

200-250F, CONT.

Hôtel Gay-Lussac (253)	5ème
Hôtel des Jeunes (251)	4ème
Hôtel Louvre-Richelieu (249)	1er
Hôtel Marignan (252)	5ème
Hôtel Picard (251)	3ème
Hôtel Ribera (262)	16ème
Luna-Park Hôtel (258)	11ème
Mistral Hôtel (258)	12ème

250-300F

Centre Parisien de Zen* (259)	12ème
Crimée Hôtel (263)	19ème
Dhely's Hotel (253)	6ème
Hôtel des Argonauts (253)	5ème
Hôtel d'Artois (255)	8ème
Hôtel de Blois (260)	14ème
Hôtel Broussais (260)	14ème
Hôtel du Midi (260)	14ème
Hôtel Montpensier (248)	1er
Hôtel Moderne (257)	11ème
Hôtel du Palais (248)	1er
Hôtel du Parc (260)	14ème
Hôtel Paris France (251)	3ème
Hôtel Practic (251)	4ème
Hôtel Riviera (262)	17ème
Hôtel Stella (254)	6ème
Hôtel St-Honoré (248)	1er
Hôtel St-Jacques (252)	5ème
Le Perdrix Rouge (263)	19ème
Practic Hôtel (261)	15ème
Rhin et Danube (263)	19ème
Style Hôtel (262)	18ème
Villa d'Auteuil (261)	6ème

300-350F

FIAP Jean-Monnet (260)	14ème
Grand Hôtel Jeanne d'Arc (251)	4ème
Hôtel Bellevue et du Chariot d'Or (251)	3ème
Hôtel Beauharnais* (256)	9ème
Hôtel Jouffrey (262)	17ème
Hôtel de Neslé (253)	6ème
Hôtel de Roubaix (250)	3ème
Hôtel St-André des Arts (254)	6ème
Pacific Hôtel (261)	15ème
Royal Phare Hôtel (255)	7ème

350-400F

Hôtel Andréa (251)	4ème
Hôtel des Arts (257)	9ème
Hôtel Beaumarchais (257)	11ème
Hôtel Bonne Nouvelle (250)	2ème
Hôtel Champerret Héliopolis (262)	17ème
Hôtel du Champs de Mars (254)	7ème
Hôtel Chopin (256)	9ème
Hôtel Europe-Liège (255)	8ème
Hôtel de France (255)	7ème
Hôtel Lion d'Or (248)	1er
Hôtel de Nice (251)	4ème
Hotel du Square (261)	15ème
Hôtel Vivienne (250)	2ème
Palym Hôtel (259)	12ème

400-450F		**500-550F**	
Hôtel Amelie (255)	7ème	Hôtel Favart (249)	2ème
Hôtel Keppler (262)	16ème	**OVER 600F**	
Hôtel du Lys (252)	6ème	Hôtel Madeleine Haussmann (255)	8ème
450-500F		Timhotel Le Louvre (249)	1er
Hôtel du Parc des Buttes-Ch. (263)	19ème		
Hôtel Malar (254)	7ème		
Hôtel de la Place des Vosges (252)	4ème		

ACCOMMODATIONS BY NEIGHBORHOOD

For more information on each neighborhood, see **Once in Paris: Orientation,** p. 11.

ÎLE DE LA CITÉ

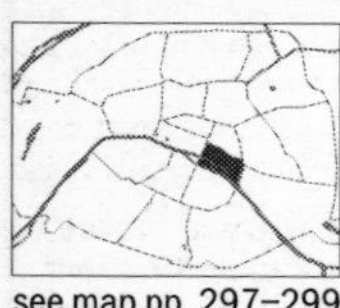

see map pp. 297–299

Henri IV, 25, pl. Dauphine (☎43 54 44 53). M: Cité. Walk toward the Conciergerie and turn right on bd. du Palais, left on quai de l'Horloge, and left at the front of the Conciergerie onto pl. Dauphine. Henri IV is one of Paris' best located, least expensive hotels. Named in honor of Henri IV's printing presses which once occupied the 400-year-old building, the hotel has big windows and charming views of the tree-lined pl. Dauphine. The spacious rooms have a mixture of sturdy but mismatched furnishings. Showers 15F. Reserve 1 month in advance. Singles 130-170F; doubles 170-205F, with shower 260F; triples 245-285F; quads 295F 290F. No wheelchair access.

FIRST ARRONDISSEMENT

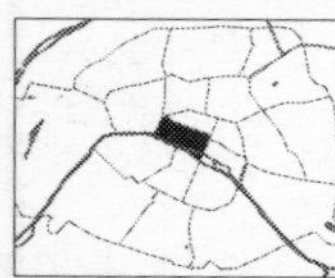

see map pp. 294–296

Hôtel Montpensier, 12, r. de Richelieu (☎42 96 28 50; fax 42 86 02 70). M: Palais-Royal. Walk around the left side of the Palais-Royal to r. de Richelieu. Clean rooms, lofty ceilings, bright decor, and English-speaking staff welcome the clientele. Its good taste distinguishes it from most hotels in this region and price range. Small elevator. TVs in rooms with shower or bath. Breakfast 40F. Shower 25F. Reserve 4 weeks in advance in high season. AmEx, MC,V. Singles with toilet 295F; doubles with toilet 305F. Rooms with toilet and shower 435F; with toilet, bath, and sink 515F. Extra bed 80F.

Hôtel du Palais, 2, quai de la Mégisserie (☎42 36 98 25; fax 42 21 41 67). M: Châtelet-Les-Halles. Located by the Seine at the corner of pl. du Châtelet and quai de la Mégisserie, all rooms (except on the top floor) have truly exceptional views of the Seine and Left Bank. They are also within earshot of the traffic below. The rooms are very basic but large and clean. Breakfast 30F. Reserve 3 weeks in advance. AmEx, MC, V. Singles with shower 283F, with shower or bath and toilet 353F; doubles 326F, with shower and toilet 356F, with bath and toilet 386F; triples 429F; large quad 462F; quint with 2-sink bathroom and huge windows 535F. Extra bed 70F.

Hôtel Lion d'Or, 5, r. de la Sourdière (☎42 60 79 04; fax 42 60 09 14 *www.123france.com*). M: Tuileries or Pyramides. From M: Tuileries walk down r. du 29 Juillet away from the park and turn right on r. St-Honoré then left on r. de la Sourdière. Clean and carpeted. You'll hear the bells toll from nearby Eglise St-Roch but little else. Phone and TV in most rooms. Friendly staff speaks English. Only 20 rooms; reserve 1 month in advance in high season. Breakfast 35F. 5% discount for stays of more than 3 nights. AmEx, MC, V. Singles with shower 380F, with bath and toilet 480F; doubles with shower 480-560F. Triples with shower 560F, with bath and toilet 680F. Extra bed 60F.

Hôtel Saint-Honoré, 85, r. St-Honoré (☎42 36 20 38 or 42 21 46 96; fax 42 21 44 08). M: Louvre, Châtelet, or Les Halles. From M: Louvre, cross r. de Rivoli on r. du Louvre and turn right on r. St-Honoré. Recently renovated, with new reception, breakfast area, and sizeable modern rooms. Friendly, English-speaking staff, and young clientele. Refridgerator access. All rooms have shower, toilet, and TV. Breakfast 29F. Reserve by fax or phone and confirm the night before. AmEx, MC, V. Singles 290F; doubles 410F, with bathtub 450F; triples and quads 490F.

Hôtel Louvre-Richelieu, 51, r. de Richelieu (☎42 97 46 20; fax 47 03 94 13). M: Palais-Royal. See directions for Hôtel Montpensier, above. 14 large, simple but comfortable and very clean rooms. Noise from the busy r. de Richelieu below is suprisingly negligable as the rooms are all above the second floor. English spoken. Breakfast 35F. Showers 10F. Reserve 3 weeks ahead in summer. MC, V. Singles 230F, with shower 345F. Doubles 280F, with shower 420F; triples with shower and toilet 490F. Extra bed 50F.

Timhotel Le Louvre, 4, r. Croix des Petits-Champs (☎42 60 34 86; fax 42 60 10 39). M: Palais-Royal. From the métro, cross r. de Rivoli to r. St-Honoré; take a left onto r. Croix des Petits-Champs. Although more expensive, this 2-star hotel has the only wheelchair-accessible rooms at reasonable prices in the 1*er*. Mystery man Tim offers clean, modern rooms with bath, shower and cable TV. Great location next to the Louvre. Small *jardin*. Breakfast 50F. AmEx, MC, V. Singles 800F; doubles 800F; one triple 1000F.

HOSTELS AND FOYERS

Centre International de Paris (BVJ)/Paris Louvre, 20, r. J.-J. Rousseau (☎53 00 90 90; fax 53 00 90 91). M: Louvre or Palais-Royal. From M: Louvre, take r. du Louvre away from the river, turn left on r. St-Honoré and right on r. J.-J. Rousseau. Courtyard hung with brass lanterns and strewn with brasserie chairs. 200 beds. Bright, dorm-style rooms with 2-10 beds per room. 2-course lunch or dinner 40F, 4-course 60F. English spoken. Internet 1F per min. Breakfast and showers included. Lockers 10F. Reception 24hr. Weekend reservations up to 1 week in advance; reserve by phone only. Rooms held only 10min. after your expected check-in time; call if you'll be late. 130F per person.

Maisons des Jeunes de Rufz de Lavison, 18, r. J.-J. Rousseau (☎45 08 02 10). M: Louvre or Palais-Royal. Next door to BVJ Louvre. During the academic year, it's a private residence for male college students. In summer (mid-June to mid-Aug.) it's a co-ed foyer, primarily for long-term stays. Quiet, spacious rooms for 50 students. Flower-filled, open-air courtyard. During winter, Shower and breakfast included. 5 night min. stay. Reception 9am-7pm. No curfew; entrance code given. Reservations starting June 15; 1 night's payment required. Singles 165F; doubles 145 per person. Monthly: singles 4,600F; doubles 3,460F per person; both require 500F deposit.

ESSENTIAL INFORMATION

PAY FOR WHAT YOU GET...

Be aware that the city of Paris has a **Taxe de Séjour** of approximately one to six francs flat-rate per person per night: this does not have to be included in advertised or quoted prices, but must be listed along with the room price on the back of the hotel room door.

It is adviseable to check for other add-on expenses such as **direct telephone service** (some hotels will even charge you for collect calls) before making a reservation.

Also, **always insist on seeing a room first,** before you settle in, even if the proprietor is not amenable.

SECOND ARRONDISSEMENT

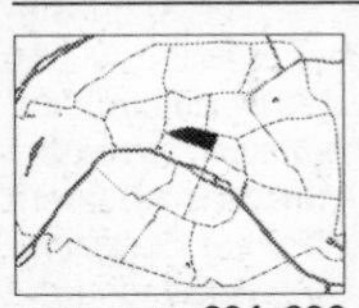

see map pp. 294–296

Hôtel Favart, 5, r. Marivaux (☎42 97 59 83; fax 40 15 95 58). M: Richelieu Drouot. From the métro, turn left down bd. des Italiens and left on Marivaux. Handsome hotel on a quiet, well-located street, it was once the home of Spanish painter Francisco Goya. Rooms are a cut above the rest: sizeable and very comfortable. Some boast satin wallpaper, mirrored ceilings, and views of the Opéra Comique. All rooms have cable TV, phone, shower, toilet, and hair dryer. One wheelchair accessible room on first floor with a very large bathroom. Large elevator. Breakfast included. Listed below are *Let's Go* prices at substantial discounts, so be sure to mention the guide. Singles 540F; doubles 685F; extra bed 100F. AmEx, MC, V.

on the cheap

IN THE 2ÈME

Hôtel Tiquetonne, 6, r. Tiquetonne (☎42 36 94 58; fax 42 36 02 94). M: Etienne-Marcel. Walk against traffic on r. de Turbigo; turn left on r. Tiquetonne. Near *Marché Montorgueil*, some tasty eateries on r. Tiquetonne, the rowdy English bars near Etienne Marcel, and St-Denis's sex shops—what more could you want in a location? This affordable 7-story hotel is a study in faux finishes: from fake-marble corridors to "I-can't-believe-it's-not-wood" doors. Elevator. Breakfast 25F. Hall showers 30F. Closed Aug. and 1 week at Christmas. MC, V. Singles with shower 143-213F; doubles with shower and toilet 246F.

IN THE 3ÈME

Hôtel du Marais, 16, r. de Beauce (☎42 72 30 26). M: Temple or Filles-du-Calvaire. From M: Temple, follow r. du Temple south, taking a left on r. de Bretagne and a right on r. de Beauce. A real bargain. No frills, but a nice pre-war place with an old-fashioned feel. 2am curfew. 3rd floor showers 10F. Singles with sink 130F; doubles 180F.

Hôtel Vivienne, 40, r. Vivienne (☎42 33 13 26; fax 40 41 98 19). M: r. Montmartre. Follow the traffic on bd. Montmartre past the Théâtre des Variétés and turn left on r. Vivienne. From its hardwood-floored reception area to its spacious rooms with armoires, this hotel adds a touch of refinement to budget digs. Some rooms with balconies. Elevator. Breakfast 40F. MC, V. Singles with shower and no toilet 390F; doubles with bath 490F, with shower 470F; 3rd person under 10 free, over 10 add 30%.

Hôtel La Marmotte, 6, r. Léopold Bellan (☎40 26 26 51). M: Sentier. From the métro take r. Petit Carreaux (the street market) and then turn right at r. Léopold Bellan. Reception located in cheerful ground-floor bar. Quiet rooms with TVs, phones, and free safe-boxes. Many restaurants nearby. Breakfast 25F. Shower 15F. Reserve a month in advance. AmEx, MC, V. Singles and doubles 180-220F, with shower 270-310F; 2-bed doubles 340F; extra bed 80F.

Hôtel des Boulevards, 10, r. de la Ville Neuve (☎42 36 02 29; fax 42 36 15 39). M: Bonne Nouvelle. From the métro, turn right on r. Poissonnière then left on r. de la Lune and right onto r. de la Ville Neuve. In a funky neighbourhood that's become a little run down. Quiet rooms with TVs, phones, and wooden wardrobes. The higher the room, the brighter it gets. Reserve 2 weeks ahead and confirm with credit card deposit. 10% *Let's Go* discount. AmEx, MC, V. Singles and doubles 240F, with shower 305F, with bath 330-340F; 3rd person 60F.

Hôtel Bonne Nouvelle, 17, r. Beauregard (☎45 08 42 42; fax 40 26 05 81). M: Bonne Nouvelle. From the métro, follow traffic down r. Poissonnière and turn left on r. Beauregard. On a medieval street in a working-class neighborhood, this hotel is a bizarre mixture of a kitschy Swiss chalet and a 70s motel (complete with fuzzy zebra skin stools). Being colorblind will make yours a more enjoyable stay. All rooms have TVs, hairdryers, and tidy bathrooms with toilet, shower, or bath. Tiny elevator. Breakfast 30-35F. Reserve by credit card. MC, V. Single 300F; singles and doubles with bath 350-500F; triples with bath 550-650F.

THIRD ARRONDISSEMENT

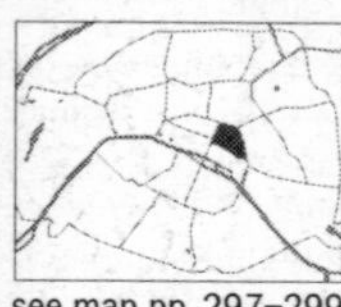

see map pp. 297–299

Hôtel du Séjour, 36, r. du Grenier St-Lazare (☎/fax 48 87 40 36). M: Etienne-Marcel or Rambuteau. From M: Etienne-Marcel, follow the traffic on r. Etienne-Marcel, which becomes r. du Grenier St-Lazare. One block from Les Halles and the Centre Pompidou, this family-run hotel is the perfect pick for travelers craving a clean, bright room and a warm welcome. 20 rooms. Showers 20F. Reception 7am-10:30pm. Singles 180F-200F; doubles 280F, with shower and toilet 340F; third person 150F extra.

Hôtel de Roubaix, 6, r. Greneta (☎42 72 89 91; fax 42 72 58 79). M: Réaumur-Sébastopol or Arts-et-Métiers. From the métro, walk opposite traffic on bd. de Sébastopol and turn left on r. Greneta. Or, take bus #20 from Gare de Lyon to St-Nicolas des Champs. Advice-dispensing staff, clean rooms with flowered wallpaper, soundproofed windows, and new bathrooms unite at the Roubaix. Large breakfast room and 2 lounges. All rooms have shower, toilet, telephone, locker, and TV. Some with balconies. Breakfast included. MC, V. Singles 310-330F; doubles 380-410F; triples 430-490F; quads 520F; quints 550F.

Hôtel Picard, 26, r. de Picardie (☎48 87 53 82; fax 48 87 02 56). M: Temple. From the métro, walk against traffic down r. du Temple, take the first left on r. du Petit Thouars, and at the end of the street turn right. Next door to cyber café WebBar. Simple pastel rooms; TVs in rooms with showers. Elevator. Breakfast 30F. Hall showers 20F. Apr.-Sept. reserve 1 week ahead. Tax 5F. MC, V. 10% *Let's Go* discount. Singles 210F, with shower and toilet 260F; doubles 250-270F, 330F; triples 520F.

Hôtel Paris France, 72, r. de Turbigo (☎42 78 00 04, reservations 42 78 64 92; fax 42 71 99 43). M: République or Temple. From M: République, take r. de Turbigo. The large lobby has soft sofas and a big TV. Some rooms have TV, phone, hair dryer, and locker. Some noisy rooms, but those on the top floor are renovated and bright with balconies, clean bathrooms, and super views. Elevator. Sunny breakfast 30F. AmEx, MC, V. Singles 250-405F; doubles 320-560F; triples 445-615F.

Hôtel Bellevue et du Chariot d'Or, 39, r. de Turbigo (☎48 87 45 60; fax 48 87 95 04). M: Etienne-Marcel. From the métro, walk against traffic on r. de Turbigo. A Belle Epoque lobby, with bar and breakfast room, gives a great first impression. Clean and modern rooms give a good second impression. All have phones, TVs, toilets, and baths. 59 rooms. Singles 315F; doubles 350F; triples 425F; quads 460F.

FOURTH ARRONDISSEMENT

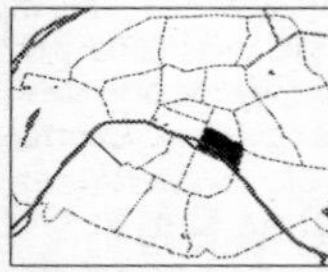

see map pp. 297–299

Grand Hôtel Jeanne d'Arc, 3, r. de Jarente (☎48 87 62 11; fax 48 87 37 31; www.hoteljeannedarc.com). M: St-Paul or Bastille. From M: St-Paul walk opposite traffic on r. de Rivoli and turn left on r. de Sévigné, then right on r. de Jarente. On a quiet side-street. Jeanne d'Arc blesses her visionary rooms with showers, toilets, and TVs. Praise the electric candles in the lobby. 2 rooms on the ground floor are wheelchair accessible. Elevator. Breakfast 38F. Reserve 2 months in advance. MC, V. Singles 325F; doubles 330-660F; triples 600F; quads 660F. Extra bed 75F.

Castex Hôtel, 5, r. Castex (☎42 72 31 52; fax 42 72 57 91). M: Bastille or Sully-Morland. Exit M: Bastille on bd. Henri IV and take the 3rd right on r. Castex. Modern stucco decor and peaceful rooms. TV room. Check-in 1pm. All rooms with telephone and sink. Breakfast 30F. Reserve by sending a fax with a credit card number 1 month in advance. AmEx, MC, V. Singles 240-320F; doubles 320-360F; triples 460F. Extra bed 70F.

Hôtel de Nice, 42bis, r. de Rivoli (☎42 78 55 29; fax 42 78 36 07). M: Hôtel-de-Ville. Walk opposite traffic on r. de Rivoli for about 4 blocks; the hotel is on the left. Nice, nice rooms feature vintage catalogue illustrations, TVs, toilets, showers, and phones. A few have balconies with great views. Hot in the summer (fans provided). Elevator. Breakfast 35F. Rooms ready at 2pm, but you can leave your bags earlier. Check-out 11am. Reserve by fax or phone with 1 night's deposit 1 month ahead for summer. MC, V. Singles 380F; doubles 550F; triples 680F. Extra bed 130F.

Hôtel Practic, 9, r. d'Ormesson (☎48 87 80 47; fax 48 87 40 04). M: St-Paul. Walk opposite the traffic on r. de Rivoli, then turn left on r. de Sévigné and right on r. d'Ormesson. A clean hotel on a cobblestone square in the heart of the Marais. Rooms are modest, but all have TVs and hairdryers. English spoken. Breakfast 25F. Reserve by fax 2-4 weeks in advance. Visa, AmEx, MC. Singles 250F; doubles 305-450F. Extra bed 80F. Tax 3F.

Hôtel Andréa, 3, r. St-Bon (☎42 78 43 93; fax 44 61 28 36). M: Hôtel-de-Ville. Follow traffic on r. de Rivoli and turn right on r. St-Bon. On a quiet street 2 blocks from Châtelet. Recently renovated, the Andréa has all the conveniences. Clean and comfortable rooms with phones, toilets, showers, TVs, A/C, and Internet connections. Elevator. Top floor rooms have balconies. Breakfast 35F. Reserve 3 weeks in advance with a credit card number. MC, V. Singles 360-380F; doubles 470F, with twin beds 490F.

HOSTELS

Hôtel des Jeunes (MIJE) (☎42 74 23 45; fax 40 27 81 64; www.mije.com/; email MIJE@Wanadoo.fr) books beds in Le Fourcy, Le Fauconnier, and Maubuisson (see below), 3 small hostels located on cobblestone streets in old Marais residences. No smoking. English spoken. Internet 1F per minute at Le Fourcy. Public phones and free lockers (with a 2F deposit). Ages 18-

30 only. 7-day max. stay. Reception 7am-1am. Lockout noon-3pm. Curfew 1am. Quiet after 10pm. Breakfast, shower, and sheets included. Arrive before noon the first day of reservation (call in advance if you'll be late). Groups may reserve 1 year in advance. Individuals should reserve at least 1 month in advance. Restaurant La Table d'Hôtes (at Le Fourcy) offers a main course with drink (50F) and coffee and 3-course "hosteler special" (60F). Reception M-F 11:30am-1:30pm and 6:30-8:30pm. 4- to 9-bed dorms 140F; singles 240F; doubles 350F; triples 465F.

Le Fourcy, 6, r. de Fourcy. M: St-Paul or Pont Marie. From M: St-Paul, walk opposite the traffic for a few meters down r. François-Miron and turn left on r. de Fourcy. Hostel surrounds a large courtyard ideal for meeting travelers or for open-air picnicking. Light sleepers should avoid rooms on the social courtyard. Elevator.

Le Fauconnier, 11, r. du Fauconnier. M: St-Paul or Pont Marie. From M: St-Paul, take r. du Prevôt, turn left on r. Charlemagne, and turn right on r. du Fauconnier. Ivy-covered building steps away from the Seine and Île St-Louis. Spacious 4-bed rooms, some doubles, some singles.

Maubuisson, 12, r. des Barres. M: Hôtel-de-Ville or Pont Marie. From M: Pont Marie, walk opposite traffic on r. de l'Hôtel de Ville and turn right on r. des Barres. A half-timbered former girls' convent that looks out onto a silent street by the St-Gervais monastery. Smaller 2- to 7-bed rooms with nice views. Elevator.

the BIG $plurge

IN THE 4ÈME

Hôtel de la Place des Vosges, 12, r. de Birague (☎42 72 60 46; fax 42 72 02 64; hotel.place.des.vosges@ogfornet.com). M: Bastille. Take the 3rd right off r. St-Antoine. Only steps away from pl. des Vosges, and once a stable for royal horsies. Location can't be beat. An *accueillant* and accomodating staff and a decor of uncommon taste and simplicity (and you thought this budget living!). TVs in all rooms. Rooms on higher floors do get a bit hot in summer. Elevator. Breakfast 40F. Reserve by fax 2 months ahead with one night's deposit. MC, V. Singles 495; doubles 660-690; 1 small quad with bath 900F.

IN THE 6ÈME

Hôtel du Lys, 23, r. Serpente (☎43 26 97 57; fax 44 07 34 90). M: Odéon or St-Michel. From either subway stop, take r. Danton; r. Serpente is a side street. With a no-holds-barred floral decorating theme, sky lights, chintz drapes, and fluffy bedspreads, this hotel feels like a warm English country house, or at least something from *Better Homes and Gardens*. All rooms include bath or shower, TV, phone, and hair dryer. Reserve one month in advance in summer. Singles 430/520F; doubles 550F; triples 680F. MC,V.

FIFTH ARRONDISSEMENT

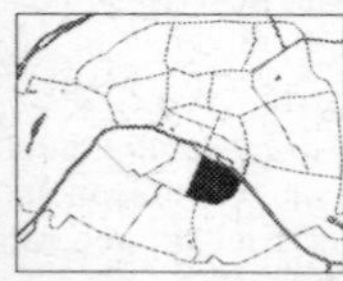

see map pp. 302–303

To stay in the *5ème*, **reserve well in advance**—from one week in winter to two months in summer. If foresight eludes you, don't despair: same-day vacancies occur at even the most popular hotels. In the fall, the return of students means more competition for *foyers*.

Hôtel St-Jacques, 35, r. des Ecoles (☎44 07 45 45; fax 43 25 65 50). M: Maubert-Mutualité. Turn left on r. des Carmes, then left on r. des Ecoles. Spacious, elegant rooms at reasonable rates, with balconies, large windows, and TVs. Chandeliers and walls decorated with *trompe l'oeil* designs give this great value a regal feel. English spoken. Elevator. Breakfast 35-45F. AmEx, MC, V. Singles 260F, with shower and toilet 480F; doubles 420-610; triples 680F.

Hôtel Marignan, 13, r. du Sommerard (☎43 54 63 81 or 43 25 31 03). M: Maubert-Mutualité. From the métro turn left on r. des Carmes, then right on r. du Sommerard. Spacious, bright, and quiet pastel rooms. Friendly owner welcomes everyone from backpackers and families to families in backpacks. Breakfast included. Free laundry. Kitchen. Reserve with check. Singles 210-260F; doubles 340-520F; triples 540-660F; quads 580-720F; quints 660-850F.

Hôtel du Progrès, 50, r. Gay-Lussac (☎43 54 53 18). M: Luxembourg. From the métro, walk away from Jardin du Luxembourg on r. Guy-Lussac. Clean, airy rooms with old decorative molding and hanging light fixtures. The best news is the view of the Panthéon from the balconies of the rooms on the top 2 floors; avoid the darker, cramped singles off the courtyard. Breakfast included. Reservation with deposit; call 2-3 weeks in advance. Cash or traveler's checks only. Singles 170-190F; doubles 260F, with shower 350F; triple 290-360F.

Hôtel le Central, 6, r. Descartes (☎46 33 57 93). M: Maubert-Mutualité. From the métro, walk up r. de la Montaigne Ste-Geneviève. Great location near r. Mouffetard and the Panthéon. Carpeted stairs lead to bright, newly painted rooms. Higher floors have views of the Right Bank. Rooms on pleasant pl. Contrescarpe somewhat noisy. All rooms have showers. Singles 163-188F; doubles and triples 236-266F. Cash only.

Hôtel Gay-Lussac, 29, r. Gay-Lussac (☎43 54 23 96; fax 40 51 79 49). M: Luxembourg. Stately old rooms, some with fireplaces. A bit worn, but with good beds. Elevator. Breakfast included. Singles 200F; doubles 400F; triples 500F; quads 600F.

Hôtel des Médicis, 214, r. St-Jacques (☎43 54 14 66). M: Luxembourg. From the métro, turn right on r. Gay-Lussac and then left on r. St-Jacques. Rickety old place that shuns right-angle geometry; perhaps that's why Jim Morrison slummed here (room #4) for 3 weeks in 1971. You get the feeling that no one has moved since he left. Has personality, which the owner happily preserves. Free showers. Reception 9am-11pm. No reservations in summer; arrive early in the morning and hope for a vacancy. Singles and doubles 180-200F.

Hôtel des Argonauts, 12, r. de la Huchette (☎43 54 09 82; fax 44 07 18 84). M: St-Michel. With your back to the Seine, take the first left off bd. St-Michel onto r. de la Huchette. Above a Greek restaurant of the same name. Clean, modern rooms with new linoleum floors and photographs of Greek islands. Courtyard rooms are quiet in comparison to those on the busy, tourist street. Breakfast 25F. Reserve 3-4 weeks in advance in high season. AmEx, MC, V. Singles with shower 285F; doubles with shower 410F, with bath and toilet 460F.

Hôtel d'Esmeralda, 4, r. St-Julien-le-Pauvre (☎43 54 19 20; fax 40 51 00 68). M: St-Michel. Walk along the Seine on quai St-Michel toward Nôtre-Dame, then turn right at Parc Viviani. Rooms have an ancient feel, with rickety, rustic chairs and desks that may qualify as "character." It might all be worth it, though, for the views of the park, the Seine, and Nôtre-Dame. Breakfast 40F. Singles 160F, with shower and toilet 350F; doubles 450-520F; triples 550F; quads 600F.

HOSTELS AND FOYERS

Young and Happy (Y&H) Hostel, 80, r. Mouffetard (☎45 35 09 53; fax 47 07 22 24; email smile@youngandhappy.fr). M: Monge. From the métro, cross r. Gracieuse and take r. Ortolan to r. Mouffetard. A lively hostel in the heart of the student quarter. Basic but cheerful. Clean rooms. Breakfast included. Sheets 15F. Towels 5F. Commission-free currency exchange. Laundry nearby. Lockout 11am-5pm. Curfew 2am. Dorms 127F, offseason 107F; doubles 127F.

Centre International de Paris (BVJ): Paris Quartier Latin, 44, r. des Bernardins (☎43 29 34 80; fax 53 00 90 91). M: Maubert-Mutualité. Walk with traffic on bd. St-Germain and turn right on r. des Bernardins. Immense, ultra-modern hostel with a shiny cafeteria. A boisterous crowd congregates in the huge common area. Breakfast included. Kitchen, TV, and message service. Showers in rooms. Lockers 10F. Reception 24hr. Check-in before 2:30pm. Check-out 9am. Reserve well in advance and confirm, or arrive at 9am to check for often available rooms. 138 beds. 5- and 6-person dorms 130F; singles 160F; doubles 140F per person.

SIXTH ARRONDISSEMENT

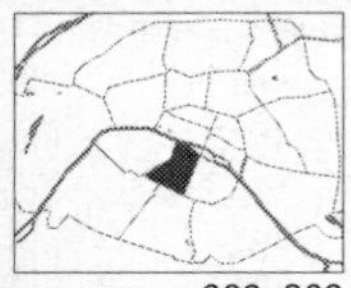

see map pp. 302–303

Hôtel de Neslé, 7, r. du Neslé (☎43 54 62 41; fax 43 54 31 88). M: Odéon. Walk up r. Mazarine, take a right onto r. Dauphine and then take a left on r. du Neslé. Fantastical and absolutely sparkling, the Neslé stands out in a sea of nondescript budget hotels. Every room is unique and recently renovated. For a treat, book the double room with Turkish *hammam* steam bath (600F). Garden with duck pond. No reservations accepted; come the morning you intend to stay around 10am. Singles 300-378F; doubles 400-600F; triples 478-675F. MC,V.

Dhely's Hotel, 22, r. de l'Hirondelle (☎43 26 58 25; fax 43 26 51 06). M: St-Michel. Just steps from pl. St-Michel and the Seine on a cobblestone way. The Dhely's wood paneling, flower boxes, modern facilities, and quiet location make for a pleasant stay. TV and phone in rooms. Breakfast included. Hall showers 25F. Each night must be paid in advance. Reserve well in advance with deposit. Singles 258-338F, with shower 428F; doubles 376F, 466F; triples 516F, 606F; extra bed 100F. AmEx, MC, V.

Hôtel St-André des Arts, 66, r. St-André-des-Arts (☎43 26 96 16; fax 43 29 73 34; email hsaintand@minitel.net). M: Odéon. From the métro, take r. de l'Ancienne Comédie, walk one block, and take the first right on r. St-André-des-Arts. The stone walls and exposed beams in each of the 31 rooms are not particularly elegant, but all the bathrooms are new. Rooms have showers, sinks, and toilets. Breakfast included. Singles 337-387F; doubles 484-524F; triples 591F; quads 658F. MC, V.

Hôtel de Chevreuse, 3, r. de Chevreuse (☎43 20 93 16; fax 43 21 43 72). M: Vavin. Walk up bd. du Montparnasse in the direction opposite the Tour and turn left on r. de Chevreuse. Now under new management, this hotel has gotten a major face-lift. Small, clean, quiet rooms with TV and Ikea furniture. Breakfast 35F. Reserve one week in advance and confirm by fax. Singles 235F; doubles 295F, with shower, TV, and toilet 375F, with full bath 415F; triples with full bath and TV 535F. MC, V.

Hotel Stella, 41, r. Monsieur-le-Prince (☎40 51 00 25; fax 43 54 97 28). M: Odéon. From the métro stop, walk against traffic on bd. St.-Germain and make a left on r. Monsieur-le-Prince. This hotel takes the exposed beam look to a whole new level, sporting some woodwork reportedly several centuries old. Spacious triples have pianos, for those who need one. All of the rooms have a shower and toilet. Reserve in advance with deposit. Singles 250F; doubles 300F; triples 450F; quads 500F. No credit cards.

HOSTELS AND FOYERS

Foyer International des Etudiantes, 93, bd. St-Michel (☎43 54 49 63). RER: Luxembourg. Across from the Jardin du Luxembourg. Marbled reception area, library, TV lounge, kitchenettes on the hallways, laundry facilities, and spacious rooms, all fitted with elegant wood paneling and some with balconies. Breakfast and shower included. July-Sept. hotel is coed, open 24hr.; Oct.-June women only. Reserve in writing two months in advance, and as early as January for the coed summer months. 200F deposit. Check-out 10am. Call ahead or arrive at 10am for no-shows. Two-bed dorms 120F, 2030F per month; singles 170F, 2990F. All prices 20F less Oct.-June.

Association des Etudiants Protestants de Paris, 46, r. de Vaugirard (☎43 54 31 49 or 53 10 21 00; fax 46 34 27 09; email aepp.resa@worldnet.fr; http://home.worldnet.fr/aepp). M: Odéon; RER: Luxembourg. From Odéon, go left up r. Condé and then right on Vaugirard. Overlooking the Jardin de Luxembourg, the Association lets its simple, tiered rooms to people aged 18-26. Part summer hostel, part university residence, the building includes a kitchen, lounge, and washing machines. Breakfast included. To stay for more than 7 days, make reservations 2 weeks in advance. No reservations for less than 7 days, but call ahead or show up at 10am the same day. 10F membership fee charged on arrival, plus 100F key deposit. Call, write, or email to request a long-term application (due before May 30). Dorms 82F; singles 100-120F; doubles 190-200F. Monthly 2100F. MC, V.

SEVENTH ARRONDISSEMENT

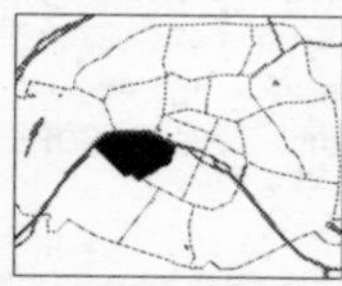

see map pp. 304–305

Hôtel du Champs de Mars, 7, r. du Champ de Mars (☎45 51 52 30; fax 45 51 64 36; email stg@club-internet.fr; www.adx.fr/hotel-du-champ-de-mars.com). M: Ecole-Militaire. Just off av. Bosquet. Only slightly more expensive, but worlds apart from its competitors in terms of quality, Hôtel du Champs de Mars offers budget travelers a welcoming and elegant option. Rooms have phone and satellite TV. Breakfast 35F; served 7-10am. Reserve 1 month ahead and confirm with 1 night's deposit by credit card. Small elevator. AmEx, MC, V. Singles with shower 390 F, with large bed and bath 425F; doubles with shower 430F, with bath 460F; triples with bath, 550F.

Grand Hôtel Lévêque, 29, r. Cler (☎47 05 49 15; fax 45 50 49 36; email info@hotelleveque.com; www.hotel-leveque.com). M: Ecole-Militaire. Take av. de la Motte-Picquet to cobbled and colorful r. Cler. 3-star quality: clean and cheery. Small lift, and baggage storage. Close to laundry, postoffice, banks, and market. English spoken. Satellite TV, safe (20F), private telephone line, ceiling fan and computer plug in all rooms. Breakfast 40F. Reserve 1 month ahead. AmEx, MC, V. Beds are slim. Singles 300F; doubles with shower and toilet 400-420F, with twin beds, shower, and toilet 420-470F; triples with shower and toilet 580F.

Hôtel Malar, 29, r. Malar (☎45 51 38 46; fax 45 55 20 19). M: Latou-Maubourg. From the métro, follow traffic on bd. de la Tour Maubourg, turn left on r. St-Dominique, and then right on r. Malar. Quiet rooms overlook a courtyard. Elegantly furnished. Each room has a matching, tiled bathroom. Twin beds can be made into doubles or triples with a system of latches. Friendly, multi-lingual staff. All rooms have satellite TV, telephones, showers, and hairdryers. Breakfast40F. AmEx, MC, V. Reserve in advance for Spring Break, or summer. Otherwise call 48hr. ahead. Singles 480F, with shower, 440F; Doubles 520F, with shower 480F. Extra Bed 100F.

Hôtel Eiffel Rive Gauche, 6, r. du Gros Caillou (☎45 51 24 56; fax 45 51 11 77; email eiffel@easynet.fr; www.france-hotel-guide.com/h75007/eifriv.htm). M: Ecole-Militaire. Walk up av. de la Bourdonnais, turn right on r. de la Grenelle, then left on Gros-Caillou. On a quiet street, this family-run hotel is a favorite of anglophone travelers. Rooms have cable TV, phone; upper floors see top of Eiffel. Multi-lingual receptionists. Dogs allowed; babysitting service available. Breakfast buffet served 8-11am 40F, in your room 47F. Hall showers 15F. AmEx, MC, V. Singles 240-435F; doubles 280-480F; triples 460-570F. Extra bed 90F.

Hôtel de la Paix, 19, r. du Gros-Caillou (☎45 51 86 17; fax 45 55 93 28). M: Ecole Militaire. Across from Hôtel Eiffel Rive Gauche (above), it's the cheapest of the bunch. Small, no frills, but clean. Breakfast 32F. Reserve one week ahead. Singles 180F, with shower 280F; doubles with shower 320F, and toilet 350-395F; triple 500F. Extra bed 100F. No credit cards, but accepts French traveler's checks.

Hotel Amelie, 5, r. Amelie (☎45 51 74 75; e-mail RESA@hotel-AMELIE.COM.) M: Latour-Maubourg or Invalides. On a charming back street, Hotel Amelie is a tiny and welcoming. Minibar in all rooms. Reserve 2 weeks in advance. Single with shower, 440F; double with shower 480F, with twin beds and shower 540F, with bath 540F.

Hôtel de France, 102 bd. de la Tour Maubourg (☎47 05 40 49; fax 45 56 96 78). M: Ecole Militaire. Directly across from the Hôtel des Invalides. Owners give advice on Paris in English, Spanish, or French. Beyond the purple-painted halls you'll find sparkling, clean rooms. Some rooms have spectacular views of the Eglise du Dôme and the Invalides. There are two wheelchair accessible rooms (500F). All rooms with phone and cable. Breakfast 35F. AmEx, MC, V. Singles 395F; doubles 500F; connecting rooms for 4-5 people 800-860F.

EIGHTH ARRONDISSEMENT

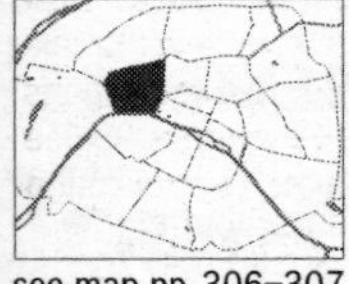

see map pp. 306–307

Hôtel Europe-Liège, 8, r. de Moscou (☎42 94 01 51; fax 43 87 42 18). M: Liège. From the métro, walk down r. d'Amsterdam and turn left on r. de Moscou. Very pleasant, quiet, and reasonably priced hotel with newly painted rooms. Many restaurants nearby. All rooms have TV, hair dryer, phone, shower, or bath. 2 wheelchair accessible rooms on the ground floor. Breakfast 37F. AmEx, MC, V. Singles 390F; doubles 500F.

Hôtel Madeleine Haussmann, 10, r. Pasquier (☎42 65 90 11; fax 42 68 07 93). M: Madeleine. From the métro walk up bd. Malesherbes and turn right on r. Pasquier. A bit expensive given the size of the rooms, but close to the Madeleine, pl. de la Concorde, and the Opéra. Tidy, comfortable and professional with a bathroom, hairdryer, TV with remote, safe box and minibar in every room. Two small rooms on the ground floor have handicapped access. Buffet breakfast 40F. Breakfast 40F. Reserve a month in advance. Singles 630F; doubles 680F; triples 790F.

Hôtel d'Artois, 94, r. La Boétie (☎43 59 84 12 or 42 25 76 65; fax 43 59 50 70). M: St-Philippe de Roule. From the métro, turn left and go down r. La Boétie. Near the Champs-Elysées. A bit worn and antiquey, but with spacious bathrooms and bedrooms. Plant-filled lobby and incense-scented breakfast room. Elevator. Breakfast 28F. Hall showers 22F. Reserve two weeks in advance Mar.-June. MC, V. Singles 265F, with bath 400F; doubles 310F, 450F.

HOSTELS AND FOYERS

Foyer de Chaillot, 28, av. George V (☎47 23 35 32; fax 47 23 77 16). M: George V. From the métro, make a right down av. George V and walk about 3 blocks (on the opposite side of the street) until you see a high-rise silver office building called Centre Chaillot Galliera. *Take the elevator to* the foyer on the 3rd floor. Cheerful, well equipped, modern rooms, in an upscale dorm-like environment for **women only.** Residents must be students, working, or hold an internship and be between the ages of 18-25; min. one-month stay. Singles all have a sink, while doubles have shower and sink. Toilets and additional showers in each hall. Large common rooms equipped with stereo and TV. Fully equipped kitchens. "Salle Informatique" with Internet access. Small gym with exercise bikes. Guests permitted until 10pm, and female guests may stay for a weekend at 70F per night with advance notice. 2100F deposit required to reserve a room along with an application or fax that states your age, the duration of your stay and a description of your activities in Paris. Breakfast and dinner included M-F. Doubles 7100F per month; after a stay of two months, you can request a single for 3550F per month.

UCJF (Union Chrétienne de Jeunes Filles, YWCA), 22, r. Naples (☎53 04 37 47; fax 53 04 37 54). M: Europe. From the métro, take r. de Constantinople and turn left onto r. de Naples. **Also at 168, r. Blomet, 15*ème*** (☎56 56 63 00; fax 56 56 63 12); M: Convention. Men should contact the YMCA Foyer Union Chrétienne de Jeunes Gens, 14, r. de Trévise, 9*ème* (☎47 70 90 94). Founded and funded by protestants, the Union houses women of all religious denominations. Well-kept environment **for women only.** Spacious, worn, quiet rooms with hardwood floors, sinks, and large desks. Large oak-paneled common room with fireplace, TV, VCR, books, theater space, and family-style dining room. June-Aug. 3-day min. stay; Sept.-May longer stays for women ages 18-26 (age flexible; June-Sept. they make exceptions, but the rest of the year priority is given to younger women). All guests pay 30F YWCA membership fee, as well as 50F (for 1-week stays) or 100F (for stays of 1 month or more) processing fee. Reception M-F 8am-12:30am, Sa-Su 9am-12:30pm and 1:30pm-12:30am. Guests permitted until 10pm; men not allowed in bedrooms. Curfew 12:30am (ask for key, 200F deposit). Kitchen, laundry. Breakfast and dinner included; monthly rates include demi-pension. Singles 165F, weekly 1000F, monthly 3260F; doubles 290F, 1600F, 5370-5760F; triples 435F, monthy 7710F.

on the cheap

The 10ème

Hôtel Moderne du Temple, 3, r. d'Aix (☎42 08 09 04; fax 42 41 72 17). M: Goncourt. Walk with the traffic on r. du Faubourg du Temple then turn right on r. d'Aix; the hotel is on the left. Located on a quiet street, and close to the beautiful Canal St-Martin, this Czech-owned hotel has immaculate and tastefully decorated rooms, some overlooking a courtyard. Breakfast 23F. Singles 130-150F, with shower 180F, with shower and WC 230F; doubles 170F, 210F, 250F. V, MC, AmEx.

Hôtel Lafayette, 198, r. Lafayette (☎40 35 76 07; fax 42 09 69 05). M: Louis Blanc. Walk opposite the traffic lane closest to you on r. Lafayette; hotel is on the left. Small, clean, no-frills rooms near the Canal St-Martin. Two wheelchair accessible rooms. Breakfast 20F. Hall showers 20F. Singles 120F; doubles 160-195F, with shower 240F. AmEx, MC, V.

NINTH ARRONDISSEMENT

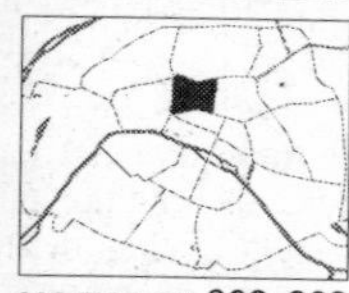

see map pp. 308–309

Hôtel Chopin, 10, bd. Montmartre, or 46, passage Jouffroy (☎47 70 58 10; fax 42 47 00 70). M: Grands Boulevards. Walk west on bd. Montmartre and make a right into Passage Jouffroy. Inside a spectacular old passage lined with shops. Very clean, very new rooms, decorated in a tasteful style a cut above most buget hotels. Some rooms have views of the Musée Grevin's wax studio (see p. 133). All rooms have TV, phone, and fans. Elevator. Breakfast 40F. Singles with shower 355F, with shower and WC 405-455F; doubles with shower and WC 450-520F; triples with shower and WC 595F. AmEx, MC, V.

Hôtel Beauharnais, 51, r. de la Victoire (☎48 74 71 13; fax 44 53 98 80). M: Le Peletier. Follow traffic on r. de la Victoire and look for flower boxes, since there is no Hôtel sign and the lobby looks like someone's sitting room. This small hotel exudes warmth: a welcoming staff speak English and are especially kind to young travelers. Elevator. Breakfast 30F. All rooms have shower. Special *Let's Go* rates. Doubles 320F; triples 490F; quads 550F; quints 640F.

Perfect Hôtel, 39, r. Rodier (☎42 81 18 86; fax 42 85 01 38; email perfecthotel@hotmail.com). Across from the Woodstock Hostel, see directions below. While "perfect" might be an overstatement, the hotel comes close with recent renovations. Some rooms have balconies, and the upper floors have a wonderful view. Phones, communal refrigerator, and beer vending machine. Elevator. Breakfast free for *Let's Go* readers. English-speaking receptionist. Singles and doubles 185-210F, with shower 285F; triples with bath 370F. MC, V.

Hôtel des Arts, 7, Cité Bergère (☎42 46 73 30; fax 48 00 94 42). M: r. Montmartre. Walk uphill on r. du Faubourg-Montmartre, turn right on Cité Bergère (there is a large sign outside the alleyway). A family hotel with small, but clean and comfortable, rooms on a very quiet pedestrian street lined with other hotels. All rooms have shower, TV, and hair dryers. Elevator. Breakfast 35F. Singles 360-390F; doubles 390-410F; triples 530F. AmEx, MC, V.

HOSTELS AND FOYERS

Woodstock Hostel, 48, r. Rodier (☎48 78 87 76; fax 48 78 01 63) www.woodstock.fr; flowers@woodstock.fr. M: Anvers or Gare du Nord. From M: Anvers, walk against traffic on pl. Anvers, turn right on av. Trudaine, and then left on r. de Rodier. From M: Gare du Nord, turn right on r. Dunkerque (with the station at your back); at pl. de Roubaix, veer left on r. de Maubeuge, veer right on r. Condorcet, and turn left on r. Rodier (15min.). A fun hostel with a lot of character and a great, friendly international staff. Located near Gare du Nord, Gare de l'Est, and Sacré Coeur. Cleaner than Yasgur's farm ever was, with quiet, affordable rooms, the nicest off their courtyard. Communal kitchen, safe deposit box, Internet access, and fax. Showers free (and clean). Call ahead to reserve a room. 4-person dorms Apr.-Oct. 117F, Sept.-May 77F; doubles 137F, 87F.

TENTH ARRONDISSEMENT

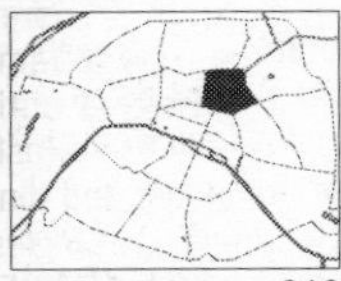

see map p. 310

Cambrai Hôtel, 129bis, bd. de Magenta (☎48 78 32 13; fax 48 78 43 55). M: Gare du Nord. Follow traffic on r. de Dunkerque to pl. de Roubaix and turn right on bd. de Magenta. The hotel is on the left. A family-owned hotel close to the *gare.* Clean, airy rooms with natural light, high ceilings, and TVs. Breakfast 45F. Showers 20F. MC, V. Singles 170-210F, with shower 270F, with shower and WC 300F; doubles 340F; triples 500F; family suite 550F is wheelchair accessible.

Hôtel Palace, 9, r. Bouchardon (☎40 40 09 46 or 42 06 59 32; fax 42 06 16 90). M: Strasbourg/St-Denis. Walk against traffic on bd. St-Denis until the small arch; follow r. René Boulanger on the left, then turn left on r. Bouchardon. The privacy of a hotel with the rates of a hostel. Undergoing major renovations for summer 2001. Breakfast 20F. Shower 20F. Reserve 2 weeks ahead. Singles 136F; doubles 146-236F; triples 362F; quad 362F; quint 400. MC, V.

Hôtel de Milan, 17, r. de St-Quentin (☎40 37 88 50; fax 46 07 89 48). M: Gare du Nord. Follow r. de St-Quentin from Gare du Nord; the hotel is on the right-hand corner of the 3rd block. Slightly more expensive, but the location right next to the Gare du Nord is very convenient. Breakfast 22F. Hall showers 18F. MC, V. Singles 160-280F; doubles 200-370F; triples 430F; extra person 103F.

ELEVENTH ARRONDISSEMENT

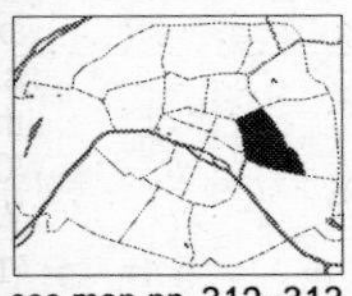

see map pp. 312–313

Hotel Moderne, 121, r. de Chemin-Vert (☎47 00 54 05; fax 47 00 08 31; email modern.hotel@wanadoo.fr; www.modern-hotel.fr). M: Père Lachaise. A few blocks from the métro on r. de Chemin-Vert, on the right. Newly renovated, with modern furnishings, pastel color scheme, and spanking clean bathrooms. Rooms are on the sixth floor; no elevator. Breakfast 25F. Reserve with credit card. MC, V. Singles 250-290F; doubles 290-350F; quads 510F; extra bed 80F.

Hôtel Rhetia, 3, r. du Général Blaise (☎47 00 47 18; fax 48 06 01 73). M: Voltaire or Saint-Ambroise. From the Voltaire métro, take av. Parmentier and turn right on r. Rochebrune, then left on r. du Général Blaise. In a calm, out-of-the-way neighborhood. Clean, with simple, aging furnishings and narrow single beds. Breakfast 15F. Hall showers 10F. Reception 7:30am-10pm. Singles 180F, with shower 290F; doubles 190F, 240F; triples 240F, 290F; extra bed 50F.

Hôtel Beaumarchais, 3, r. Oberkampf (☎53 36 86 86; fax 43 38 32 86). M: Oberkampf. Exit on r. de Malte and turn right on r. Oberkampf. More expensive, but a great price for what you get. Newly renovated with bright, trendy furniture, whitewashed walls, clean baths, and TVs. Suites include TV room with desk and breakfast table. Small elevator. A/C. Breakfast 40F. AmEx, MC, V. Singles 390-450F; doubles 550-600F; suites 750F.

Plessis Hôtel, 25, r. du Grand Prieuré (☎47 00 13 38; fax 43 57 97 87). M: Oberkampf. From the métro, walk north on r. du Grand Prieuré. 5 floors of clean, bright rooms. Rooms with showers have hair dryers, fans, TVs, and balconies. Lounge with TV and vending machines. "American" breakfast 38F. Open Sept-July. AmEx, MC, V. Singles 195F, with shower and toilet 285F, with bath 295F; doubles 215F, 325F, 350F; twin with shower 420F. 10% discount after 3rd night.

Hôtel Notre-Dame, 51, r. de Malte (☎47 00 78 76; fax 43 55 32 31; email hotelnotre-dame@wanadoo.fr). M: République. Walk down av. de la République and go right on r. de Malte. Eclectic decor, cheerful lounge, and elevator. Showers 20F. Breakfast 35F. Reserve 1 month ahead. MC, V. Single or double 200F, with shower 245-310F, with shower and toilet 340-390F.

Hôtel de Nevers, 53, r. de Malte (☎47 00 56 18; fax 43 57 77 39). M: Oberkampf or République. Next to Nôtre-Dame, above. Spacious rooms with high ceilings; some lovely, others a little worn down. Ask for a room on a high floor, away from the noise of the street. Refrigerator. Elevator. Pets welcome. Breakfast 25F. Hall showers 20F. Reception 24hr. Reserve 2 weeks ahead by credit card. MC, V. Singles and doubles 180F, with shower 235F, with shower and toilet 260-275F; triples with shower and toilet 330F; quads with shower and toilet 410F; extra bed 50F.

Hôtel de Belfort, 37, r. Servan (☎47 00 67 33; fax 43 57 97 98). M: Père-Lachaise, St-Maur, or Voltaire. From M: Père-Lachaise, take r. de Chemin-Vert and turn left on r. Servan. 15min. from Bastille. Dim corridors and clean, functional rooms. Popular with schools and tour groups. All rooms with shower, toilet, TV, and phone. Elevator. Breakfast (served 7:30-9:30am) 20F. MC, V. Call in advance and get a *Let's Go* special: 120F per person per night.

HOSTELS AND FOYERS

Auberge de Jeunesse "Jules Ferry" (HI), 8, bd. Jules Ferry (☎43 57 55 60; fax 43 14 82 09). M: République. Walk east on r. du Faubourg du Temple and turn right on the far side of bd. Jules Ferry. Wonderfully located in front of park and next to pl. de la République. Clean rooms with 100 bunk beds and sinks; mirrors and tiled floors. Doubles with big beds. Party atmosphere. Breakfast and rudimentary showers included. Lockers 10F. Sheets 5F. Laundry 20F wash, 10F dry. Week-long max. stay. Airport shuttle 89F. Internet access in lobby 1F per min. Lockout 10am-2pm. Reception and dining room 24hr. No reservations; arrive by 8am. If there are no vacancies, the hostel can book you in another nearby hostel. MC, V. 4- to 6-bed dorms 120F; doubles 250F.

Résidence Bastille, 151, av. Ledru Rollin (☎43 79 53 86; fax 43 79 35 63). M: Voltaire. Walk across pl. Léon Blum and head south onto av. Ledru Rollin. Less crowded and rowdy than most hostels. Modern building. Some recently renovated triples and quads have their own bathrooms. 2-4 wooden bunks per room. 150 beds. Couples accommodated in doubles. Breakfast, showers, and sheets included. Lockers 9am-6pm; 20F. Internet 1F per min. Wheelchair accessible. Ages 18-30. 5-night max stay. Lockout noon-4pm. Flexible 1am curfew. Reception 7am-10pm. Reservations by fax 10-15 days in advance. MC, V over 200F. Dorms Mar.-Oct. 150F, Nov.-Feb. 110F; singles 175F; deluxe, deliteful, delovely rooms for 4 with cable, chandeliers, and bath 200F per person. 10% reduction with ISIC or GO25.

TWELFTH ARRONDISSEMENT

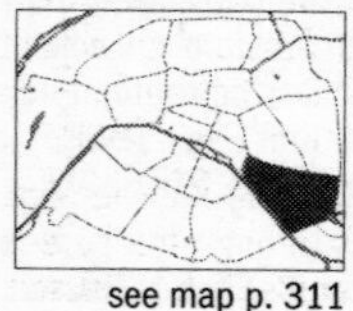

see map p. 311

Mistral Hôtel, 3, r. Chaligny (☎46 28 10 20; fax 46 28 69 66). M: Reuilly-Diderot. Walk west on bd. Diderot and take a left onto r. Chaligny. One of the best deals in Paris. A spectacularly clean, mostly renovated hotel. Each room is unique, with quality furniture from chandeliers to wicker headboards. All rooms have TV and phone. 24hr. parking 80F. 19 rooms. Breakfast 35F. Hall showers 15F. Quiet hours after 10pm. Call 7am-midnight to reserve 2 weeks in advance and confirm in writing or by fax; deposit required. MC, V. Singles 208F, with shower 253F; 1-bed doubles 216F, with shower 266F; 2-bed doubles with shower 296F; triples with shower and toilet 349F; quads with shower and toilet 412F.

Hôtel de Reims, 26, r. Hector Malot (☎43 07 46 18; fax 43 07 56 62). M: Gare de Lyon. Take bd. Diderot away from the tall buildings and make a left onto r. Hector Malot. Ignore the odd day-glo bedspreads; stay at this hotel for its central location, just off av. Daumesnil near Opéra Bastille and the Gare de Lyon. 27 rooms. Breakfast 30F. Reserve by phone 1 week in advance and confirm in writing or by fax. AmEx, MC, V. Singles 180F, with shower 250F; doubles 220F, with shower 260F, with shower and toilet 280F; triples with shower 300F. Tax 3F.

Nièvre-Hôtel, 18, r. d'Austerlitz (☎43 43 81 51). M: Gare de Lyon or Quai de la Rapée. From Gare de Lyon, walk away from the train station on r. de Bercy and take a right on r. d'Austerlitz. The sterile entry of the recently redone hotel leads to cheerful rooms. High-ceilings and spotless bathrooms. 27 rooms. Breakfast 25F. Hall showers free for *Let's Go* readers. Call for reservations and confirm in writing. MC, V. Singles 180F; doubles 220F, with shower 280F, with toilet 320F.

Hôtel Printania, 91, av. du Dr. Netter (☎43 07 65 13; fax 43 43 56 54). M: Porte de Vincennes. Walk west on the cours de Vincennes and turn left on av. du Dr. Netter. 25 spotless rooms with office-like carpets and formica headboards. 9 renovated rooms have TV, toilet, and shower. Breakfast 30F. Reserve by phone or fax with credit card number or check deposit. AmEx, MC, V. Doubles 180F, with shower and toilet 240F, with TV 260F, renovated 280F; triples 360F.

Hôtel de l'Aveyron, 5, r. d'Austerlitz (☎43 07 86 86; fax 43 07 85 20). M: Gare de Lyon. Walk away from the train station on r. de Bercy and take a right on r. d'Austerlitz. On a quiet street. Clean, unpretentious rooms with aged wallpaper and posters of the city. Downstairs lounge with TV. Fridge. English-speaking staff is eager to make suggestions. 26 rooms. Breakfast 25F. Reserve early. MC, V. Singles and doubles 190F, with shower 225F, with shower and toilet 260F; triples 250F, with shower and toilet 315F; quads with shower and toilet 360F.

FOYERS

Centre International du Séjour de Paris: CISP "Ravel," 6, av. Maurice Ravel (☎44 75 60 00; fax 43 44 45 30). M: Porte de Vincennes. Walk east on cours de Vincennes then take the first right on bd. Soult, left on r. Jules Lemaître, and right on av. Maurice Ravel (15min.). Associated with CISP "Kellerman" in the 13*ème* and just as cool. Large rooms (most with less than 4 beds), art exhibits, auditorium, and outdoor pool (25F). Cafeteria open daily 7:30-9:30am, noon-1:30pm, and 7-8:30pm. Restaurant open noon-1:30pm. Internet 10F per 10min. Breakfast, sheets, and towels included. 1-month max. stay. Reception daily 6:30am-1:30am. Curfew 1:30am. Reserve a few days ahead by phone. MC, V. Dorms with shower 143F; singles with shower, toilet, and phone 196F; doubles with shower, toilet, and phone 312F.

Centre Parisien de Zen, 35, r. de Lyon (☎44 87 08 13). M: Bastille. From the Opéra, walk down r. de Lyon; the hotel will be on your left. For a different scene, check out Dharma-master Grazyna Perl's week-long apartment rentals. 6 spotless rooms with private bath and kitchenette and views of the garden/courtyard. No shoes or smoking, and no TVs or phones in the rooms, but the center makes you forget those modern-day hang-ups with a soothing meditation room. One week for one person 1750F; for 2 people sharing a studio 2450F.

THIRTEENTH ARRONDISSEMENT

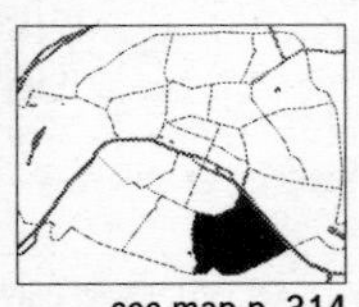

see map p. 314

HOSTELS AND FOYERS

CISP "Kellerman," 17, bd. Kellerman (☎44 16 37 38; fax 44 16 37 39; email 100616.2215@compuserve.com; www.cisp.asso.fr). M: Porte d'Italie. Cross the street and turn right on bd. Kellerman. This 392-bed hostel resembles a spaceship on stilts. In a drab area close to Cité Universitaire and the métro. Impeccably clean with TV room, laundry, and cafeteria (open daily noon-1:30pm and 6:30-9:30pm). Bunk beds. Breakfast included. Lockout 1:30-6:30pm. Wheelchair accessible. Good for last-minute reservations. MC, V. 8-bed dorms 101F; 2- to 4-bed dorms 126F; singles 146F, with shower and toilet 196F.

Maison des Clubs UNESCO, 43, r. de Glacière (☎43 36 00 63; fax 45 35 05 96). M: Glacière. Walk east on bd. Auguste Blanqui and take a left on r. de la Glacière. Enter through the garden on the right. Near the 5*ème,* this hostel offers 90 small, clean rooms. Common space is limited. Helpful management. Showers and breakfast included (7:45-9am). Reception 7am-2am. Check-out 10am, but the front desk can hold your bags for the day. Curfew 2am. Hosts many groups, so reservations recommended. Singles 170F; doubles 290F; triples 375F.

Association des Foyers de Jeunes: Foyer des Jeunes Filles, 234, r. de Tolbiac (☎44 16 22 22; fax 45 88 61 84; www.foyer-tolbiac.com). M: Glacière. Walk east on bd. Auguste Blanqui, turn right on r. de Glacière, then left on r. de Tolbiac. Large, modern foyer for women (ages 18-30). Excellent facilities include kitchen, TV, laundry, gym, library, and cafeteria. Helpful staff. 242 rooms. Showers, sheets, and breakfast included. Vacancies in summer. For short-term reserva-

on the cheap

The 14ème

Ouest Hôtel, 27, r. de Gergovie (☎45 42 64 99; fax 45 42 46 65). M: Pernety. Walk against traffic on r. Raymond Losserand and turn right on r. de Gergovie. A clean hotel with modest furnishings, but excellent rates and friendly staff. Breakfast 20F. Hall shower 20F (sometimes long waits). MC, V. Singles with small bed 120F; singles with larger bed and doubles 160F, with shower 220F; 2-bed doubles 200F, with shower 230F.

tions fax or call a few days ahead; for long-term, 3-4 months ahead. MC, V. 30F registration fee (good for 1 year). Sunny singles 120F, 2480F per month.

FOURTEENTH ARRONDISSEMENT

see map pp. 315–317

Hôtel de Blois, 5, r. des Plantes (☎45 40 99 48; fax 45 40 45 62). M: Mouton-Duvernet. From the métro, turn left on r. Mouton Duvernet then left on r. des Plantes. One of the better deals in Paris. Glossy wallpaper, ornate ceiling carvings, and velvet chairs. TVs, phones, hair dryers, and big, clean bathrooms. Laundromat across the street, pool next door. 25 rooms. Breakfast 30F. Reserve 10 days ahead. AmEx, MC, V. Singles 250F, with shower and toilet 280F; doubles 260F, with shower and toilet 300F, with bath and toilet 320F; triples 300-370F; extra bed 50F.

Hôtel du Midi, 4, av. René-Coty (☎43 27 23 25; fax 43 21 24 58). M: Denfert-Rochereau. From the métro, take av. Général Leclerc to pl. de l'Abbé Migne, by the catacombs, then turn right on av. René-Coty. Popular with business travelers, but serves many students over the summer. Marble bathrooms, hair dryers, TVs, fridges, and jacuzzis in some rooms. All have shower and toilet. Renovated rooms feature steam showers. Breakfast 38F. Parking 58F per day. Reserve 10-15 days in advance. AmEx, MC, V. Singles with shower 298F; doubles with shower and toilet 328-450F, with bath 498-600F; 3- to 4-person room 498-600F; large suite 800F. Tax 5F per night.

Hôtel du Parc, 6, r. Jolivet (☎43 20 95 54; fax 42 79 82 62; www.hotelduparc.com). M: Edgar-Quinet. Facing the Tour Montparnasse, turn left on r. de la Gaîté, right on r. du Maine, then right on r. Jolivet. Creative color schemes and floral wallpaper. Windows open onto the courtyard or a park. Well-lit rooms with TVs, phones, hair dryers. Does not accept big groups. 32 rooms. Breakfast 30F. Shower 20F. AmEx, MC, V. Singles 280F; doubles 390-420F; triples with shower 480F.

HOSTELS AND FOYERS

FIAP Jean-Monnet, 30, r. Cabanis (☎43 13 17 00; fax 45 81 63 91; www.fiap.asso.fr). M: Glacière. From the métro, take bd. Auguste-Blanqui, turn left on r. de la Santé and then right on r. Cabanis. With a high-end, pre-fab feel, as if IKEA had gotten into the hosteling game, this 500-bed international student center offers spotless rooms with phone, toilet, and shower. The fabulous concrete complex has a game room, TV rooms, laundry, sunlit piano bar, restaurant, outdoor terrace, and disco. Breakfast included, but add 10.50F for buffet. Curfew 2am. Reserve 2-4 weeks in advance. Be sure to specify if you want a dorm bed, or you will be booked for a single. 50F deposit per person per night in check or credit card. MC, V. Wheelchair accessible. 8-bed dorms 139-194F; singles 300-330F; doubles 394-490F; triples 516-690F; quads 688-860F.

FIFTEENTH ARRONDISSEMENT

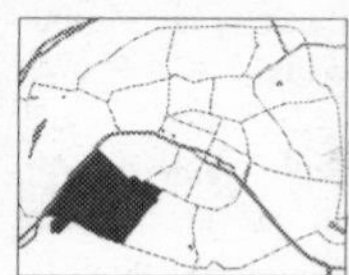

see map p. 315

Hôtel Printemps, 31, r. du Commerce (☎45 79 83 36; fax 45 79 84 88). M: La Motte-Picquet-Grenelle. In the middle of a busy, down-to-earth neighborhood and surrounded by practical shops (including Monoprix) and budget restaurants, this hotel is pleasant, clean, and cheap. Breakfast 20F. Hall showers 15F. Reserve 3-4 weeks ahead. MC, V. Singles and doubles with toilet 170F with shower 210F, with shower and toilet 230F; twin with shower 250F.

Pacific Hôtel, 11, r. Fondary (☎45 75 20 49; fax 45 77 70 73). M: Dupleix or Av. Emile Zola. Easily the most elegant of the bunch, but *way* out of the way. On a very quiet street. Spacious rooms with large desks. Renovations Jan.-July will cause reduced capacity; call well in advance. Breakfast 35F. MC, V. Singles and doubles with shower 325F, with bath 385F.

Hôtel Camélia, 24, bd. Pasteur (☎47 83 76 35 or 47 83 69 91; fax 40 65 94 98). M: Pasteur. On a main boulevard next to the métro and surrounded by shops and cafés, this simple hotel is convenient but can be noisy. Nice big baths. Closed for renovation in Aug. No elevator. Breakfast 30F. MC, V. Singles or doubles 210-380F, with shower and TV 220-400F; extra bed 50F.

Practic Hôtel, 20, r. de l'Ingénieur Keller (☎45 77 70 58; fax 40 59 43 75). M: Charles-Michels. From pl. Charles Michels, walk up r. Linois, turn left on r. des 4-Frères Peignot, then go right on r. de l'Ingénieur Keller. Small hotel run by a vigorous lady. Obsessively clean, perfectly preserved. AmEx, MC, V. Single or double with toilet 295F, shower or bath 370F; triple or quad 550F.

Hotel du Square, 80 r. du Commerce (☎53 68 16 60; fax 56 13 32). M: Commerce. On r. du Commerce, a street packed with delectable pastries, cheap eats, and bargain clothes shopping, this hotel is as central as you get in a spacious, residential district. Simple, cozy doubles. Welcomes young travelers. Single with shower 360F, with bath 400F; doubles 420F; triple 530F.

HOSTELS AND FOYERS

Three Ducks Hostel, 6, pl. Etienne Pernet (☎48 42 04 05; fax 48 42 99 99). M: Félix Faure. Walk against traffic on the left side of the church; the hostel is on the left. With palm trees in the courtyard, lavish use of blue paint, and beach-style shower shacks, this hostel is aimed at Anglo fun-seekers. The Three Ducks wants you to rock with them at the in-house bar until the 2am curfew (residents only)—probably the best late-night option in the 15*ème*. 15min. from the Eiffel Tower. Kitchen, lockers, and small 2- to 8-bed dorm rooms. Laundry and groceries nearby. Shower and breakfast included. Sheets 15F; towels 5F. Reserve with credit card a week to several days ahead. MC, V. Singles Mar.-Oct. 127F, Nov.-Feb. 117F; doubles 147F, 137F.

La Maison Hostel, 67b, r. Dutot (☎42 73 10 10). M: Volontaires. Cross r. de Vaugirard on r. des Volontaires, take the second right, and go 2 blocks. Excellent doubles and clean 2- or 3-bed dorms in a quiet neighborhood. All rooms have shower and toilet. Breakfast included. The doubles come with sheets; otherwise, sheets 15F to rent, with towels 5F. Jolly reception 8am-2am, has seated area, hot drinks, snack machines, Internet happy hour 2-3pm. Lockout 11am-5pm. Curfew 2am. Kitchen. Reserve 1 month in advance. MC, V. In summer 2- and 3-bed dorms 127F, doubles 147F; off season (starts Nov. 1) dorms 117F, doubles 137F.

Aloha Hostel, 1, r. Borromée (☎42 73 03 03; fax 42 73 14 14). M: Volontaires. Walk against traffic on r. de Vaugirard; turn right on r. Borromée. More tranquil and private than the 3 Ducks. International backpacking clientele. Music and drinks in the café. Thin mattresses. No alcohol on premises. Breakfast included. Safety deposit boxes. Sheets 15F, towels 10F. Reception 8am-2am. Lockout 11am-5pm. Curfew 2am. Reserve a week ahead in peak season with credit card deposit. MC, V. Dorms Nov.-Mar. 107F, July-Sept. 127F; doubles 127F (per person) 127F, 147F.

SIXTEENTH ARRONDISSEMENT

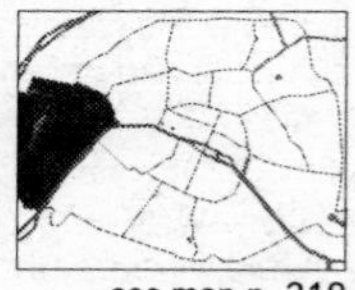

see map p. 318

Villa d'Auteuil, 28, r. Poussin (☎42 88 30 37; fax 45 20 74 70). M: Michel-Ange-Auteuil. Walk up r. Girodet and turn left on r. Poussin. At the edge of the Bois de Boulogne, on a peaceful street. High-ceilinged rooms have wood-frame beds, shower, toilet, phone, and TV. High rooms have good views, and help you work off those croissants—there's no elevator. Breakfast 30F. 10% discount for *Let's Go* travelers. MC, V. Singles 295-320F; doubles 340-370F; triples 425F.

Hôtel Keppler, 12, r. Keppler (☎47 20 65 05; fax 47 23 02 29). M: George V or Kléber. From George V, turn left on rue. Bassano and take the fourth right onto r. Keppler. Pleasant, clean hotel five minutes from the Champs-Elysées. Tan and blue rooms with high ceilings. Large, blue breakfast room and comfortable lobby with bar. Breakfast 30F. AmEx, MC, V. Twin bed with shower 430F; 2 single beds with bath 480F; 3 single beds 550F.

Hôtel Ribera, 66, r. La Fontaine (☎42 88 29 50; fax 42 24 91 33). M: Jasmin. Walk down r. Ribera to its intersection with r. La Fontaine. Pink and blue rooms, some with faux sculpture or marble fireplaces. Gender politics aside, the blue rooms are nicer. Rooms with shower have TV. Pull-out beds in doubles perfect for a small child. Breakfast 28F. 10% discount July 15-Aug. 31. AmEx, MC, V. Singles 230F, with shower, 300F; doubles 250F, 310-360.

SEVENTEENTH ARRONDISSEMENT

see map p. 319

Hôtel Riviera, 55, r. des Acacias (☎43 80 45 31; fax 40 54 84 08). M: Charles-de-Gaulle-Etoile. Walk north on av. MacMahon, then turn left on r. des Acacias. Close to the Arc de Triomphe, this hotel wins on location. Modern, quiet rooms have comfortable beds, TVs, and hairdryers. Elevator. Breakfast 30F. Reservations encouraged, by phone or fax. AmEx, MC, V. Singles with shower 255-425F; doubles with shower or bath and toilet 410-460F; triples with shower and toilet 535F.

Hôtel Belidor, 5, r. Belidor (☎45 74 49 91; fax 45 72 54 22). M: Porte Maillot. Go north on bd. Gouvion St-Cyr and turn right on r. Belidor. Dim halls give way to quiet rooms with floral wallpaper and Mondrian carpets. Most rooms face a quiet, tiled courtyard. Breakfast included. Open Sept.-July. MC, V. Singles 230F, with shower and toilet 340F; doubles with sink 260F, with bath and toilet 370F; 2-bed doubles with toilet 360F, with shower and toilet 450F; triples 390F.

Hôtel Jouffrey, 28, passage Cardinet (☎47 54 06 00; fax 47 63 83 12). M: Malesherbes. Follow r. Cardinet across bd. Malesherbes and r. de Tocqueville and turn left into passage Cardinet. In a quiet neighborhood far from the métro (10min.). Simple, clean, brown rooms. TVs and direct-line phones in every room. One room is wheelchair accessible. Dogs welcome. All rooms with shower and toilet. Breakfast 30F, in room 35F. MC, V. Singles 310F; doubles 340-400F.

Hôtel Champerret Héliopolis, 13, r. d'Héliopolis (☎47 64 92 56; fax 47 64 50 44). M: Porte de Champerret. Turn left off av. de Villiers. Clean and bright rooms, some of which open onto a terrace or balcony. TVs, phones, hairdryers. Close to the métro, with many eateries nearby. One wheelchair accessible room. Breakfast 38F. Singles 385F; doubles 450-495F; triples 580F.

EIGHTEENTH ARRONDISSEMENT

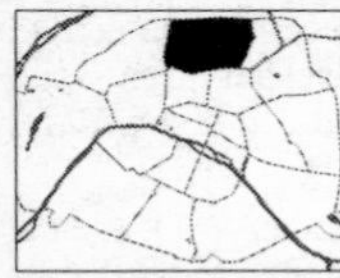

see map pp. 308–309

Hôtel Caulaincourt, 2, pl. Caulaincourt (☎46 06 42 99; fax 46 06 48 67). M: Lamarck-Caulaincourt. Walk up the stairs to r. Caulaincourt and proceed to your right, between no. 63 and 65. Formerly artists' studios, these large, simple rooms have great light and wonderful views. One of the best values around. Reserve up to one month in advance. MC, V. Singles with shower 190F, with shower and toilet 240F, with bath and toilet 270F; doubles 40F more; triples 80-100F more. 5 rooms with sink 145F for one person, 180F for two.

Hôtel André Gill, 4, r. André Gill (☎42 62 48 48; fax 42 62 77 92). M: Abbesses. Walk downhill on r. des Abbesses and turn right on r. des Martyrs and left on r. André Gill. A refuge from the noise and seediness of bd. de Clichy. TV in most rooms. Elevator. Breakfast 25F. Hall showers 25F. AmEx, MC, V. Singles 180F; singles or doubles with breakfast 240F, with shower 390F, with bath 390F; triples with bath and breakfast 530F.

Grand Hôtel de Clermont, 18, r. Veron (☎46 06 40 99). M: Abbesses. From the métro, walk west on r. Abbesses, go left on Germain Pilon and right on r. Veron. Clean and very basic rooms, not much beyond a thick-mattressed bed. The bar downstairs has bohemian character and offers guests a 48F *menu*. Be a little wary around here at night. Reserve two weeks ahead. MC, V. Singles with sink and toilet 120F; doubles with sink 160F.

Style Hôtel, 8, r. Ganneron (☎45 22 37 59; fax 45 22 81 03). M: Place de Clichy. Walk up av. de Clichy and go right onto Ganneron. Next to the cemetery. Two buildings: the newer recently renovated in Art Deco style, with larger rooms, nice wood floors, and armoires. Older building is quieter, slightly worn, with phones that only receive calls. All rooms with shower and toilet. MC, V. Singles 270F; doubles 295F; triples or quads 340F; extra bed 30F.

HOSTELS AND FOYERS

Village Hostel, 20, r. d'Orsel (☎42 64 22 02; fax 42 64 22 04; email bonjour@villagehostel.fr; www.villiagehostel.fr). M: Anvers. Go uphill on r. Steinkerque and turn right on r. d'Orsel. Right in the midst of the heavy Sacré-Coeur tourist traffic, but clean and cheap. Doubles and 3- to 5-bed dorms, some with a view of Sacré-Coeur, some off a spacious patio, and some facing the noisy street (make sure to specify). Fitness room. TV, stereo, and Internet access in the lounge. Every room has toilet and shower. Breakfast included. Sheets 15F. Towel 5F. Curfew 2am. Lockout 11am-4pm. 10-day max. stay. Reservations by fax with MC or V number. Same-day telephone reservations accepted—call at 7:30am when reception opens. Dorms 137F; 1-bed or 2-bed double 314F with sheets.

NINETEENTH ARRONDISSEMENT

see map p. 320

Rhin et Danube, 3, pl. Rhin et Danube (☎42 45 10 13; fax 42 06 88 82). M: Danube; or, bus #75 from M: Châtelet. Just steps from the métro, the R&D is a real deal for the budget traveler. Spacious, well-maintained rooms, most of which look onto a picture-perfect little *place*. All rooms have kitchens with fridges, dishes, and coffeemakers. Hairdryers, shower, WC, and color TVs with satellite. MC, V. Singles 270-290F; doubles 350-380F; triples 460F; quads 520F.

Crimée Hôtel, 188, r. de Crimée (☎40 36 75 29 or 01 40 35 19 57; fax 40 36 29 57). M: Crimée. By the métro at the corner of r. de Flandre. In the northern, commercial 19ème, relatively close to La Villette. Sparkling. Slightly less character than other 19*ème* options. Smallish rooms with hairdryers, TVs, radios, A/C, toilets, and showers. Elevator. Breakfast 32F. AmEx, MC, V. Singles 285F; doubles 330F; triples 365F; quads 440F. 10% off in July and August.

La Perdrix Rouge, 5, r. Lassus (☎42 06 09 53; fax 42 06 88 70). M: Jourdain. To your left if you are facing the church at the métro exit. No-nonsense staff welcomes you to a no-nonsense hostel. Spartan rooms with TV, toilet, and bath or shower. Breakfast 30F. Reserve by fax. AmEx, MC, V. Singles 285F; doubles 320F; triples 500F. Tax 5F per person per night.

TWENTIETH ARRONDISSEMENT

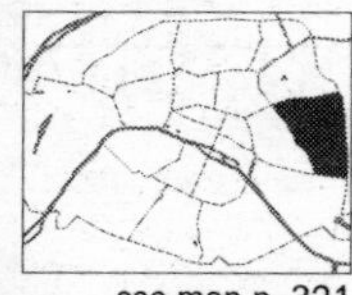

see map p. 321

Eden Hotel, 7, r. Jean-Baptiste Dumay (☎46 36 64 22; fax 46 36 01 11). M: Pyrénées. Off r. de Belleville; turn right from the métro. Eden is an oasis of hospitality, with good value for its two stars. Clean rooms with TVs and toilets. Elevator. Breakfast 28F. Bath or shower 25F. Hotel tends to be busier during the week; reserve rooms by fax 1 week in advance. MC, V. Singles 200-245F, with shower 275F; doubles with shower 285F, with bath 300F. Extra bed 60F. Dogs 30F.

L'Ermitage, 42bis r. de l'Ermitage (☎46 36 23 44). M: Jourdain. The lobby looks a bit like a garage sale, but a warm welcome at this family-run establishment and a clean, simple room make it all better. MC, V. Singles 170F, with TV and shower 210F; doubles 210F, 240F.

HOSTELS AND FOYERS

Auberge de Jeunesse "Le D'Artagnan" (HI), 80, r. Vitruve (☎40 32 34 56; fax 40 32 34 55; email paris.le-dartagnan@fuaj.org). M: Porte de Bagnolet or Porte de Montreuil. From Porte de Bagnolet, walk south on bd. Davout and make a right on r. Vitruve. A massive Martian outpost standing watch over the remote 20*ème*. Neon lights and funky decorations in every color imaginable welcome legions of boisterous backpackers. 439 beds. Restaurant (open 6-10:30pm), bar (open 8pm-2am; happy hour 8:30-9:30pm; occasional live music), Internet station 10F per 10min., and a small cinema (free films nightly). Breakfast and sheets included. Large lockers (10-30F per day). Laundry 15F per wash, 5F per dry. Reception 24hr. Lockout noon-3pm. Reservations by fax or email a must; hostel is packed Feb.-Oct. 2- to 8-bed dorms 115F.

JIM
CARREY
RENÉE ZELLWEGER
Fous
d'Iréne

INSIDE

Living in Paris

Good Americans when they die go to Paris.
-Oliver Wendell Holmes

STUDY AND WORK PERMITS

Only EU citizens have the right to work and study in France without a visa. Others wishing to study in France must apply for a special student visa, for which you will need proof of admission to a French university, proof of financial independence, proof of residence (a gas or electric bill in your name or a letter from your landlord), a medical certificate issued by a doctor approved by the French consulate, and proof of medical insurance. Foreigners studying in France must apply for a residence permit within two months of their arrival. Non-EU citizens wishing to work in France must have a firm offer of employment before applying for a visa; the employer should arrange for an official work contract to be sent to you, which must be presented upon arrival in France. You must also apply for a residence permit within eight days of your arrival. For **au pairs, scientific researchers,** and **teaching assistants,** special rules apply; check with your local consulate. In all cases, you must have a firm offer of employment before applying for a visa. For more information, see **Finding Work** and **Studying in Paris,** below.

FINDING WORK

Anyone hoping to come to France and slip easily into a job will face a tough reality on arrival: French unemployment remains stubbornly at 11%, and unqualified foreigners are unlikely to meet with much sympathy from French employers. In general, the French are more conservative about their job choices, so expect to see a much slower turn-over in terms of job openings. If you do find work, take comfort in government regulations that limit the work-week to a rocking 35-39 hours, a measure intended to encourage hiring.

OPTIONS FOR WORK

Non-EU citizens will find it well-nigh impossible to get a work permit without a firm offer of a job. In order to hire a non-EU foreigner legally in France, your employer must prove that you can perform a task which cannot be performed by a French person. Networking will prove your best bet for (illegal) employment.

STUDENTS. Students have two special options: *Au pair* employment (see below), and part-time work during the school year or summer. Foreign students attending a French university should take heart, as a temporary work permit (*autorisation provisoire de travail*) will permit you to hold a job. Such permits are not usually issued to students who have other means of supporting themselves, such as a scholarship or a grant. Check the French embassy's *Employment in France for Students* (see **French Government Information Offices,** p. 217). Full-time students at US universities can apply to work permit programs run by **Council on International Educational Exchange.** (1, pl. de l'Odéon, *6ème*. M: Odéon. ☎44 41 74 99; fax 43 26 97 45; email infofrance@ciee.org. Open M-F 9am-6pm.) For a US$225 application fee, Council can procure three- to six-month work permits and a handbook to help you find work and housing. It is difficult to land a job teaching English in France (see **Teaching English,** below) without a **TEFL** (Teaching of English as a Foreign Language) certificate and previous experience. If you are an experienced English teacher, you can try for an official position as a **Teaching Assistant** in a French school: contact your national French embassy for details. Students can also check with their university's French language department for connections to jobs abroad. For information on visas, see **Study and Work Permits,** p. 218.

EU CITIZENS. EU citizens can work in France without a visa or work permit, though they will need a **residency permit** (see p. 218). Those without an offer of employment have a grace period of three months in which to seek work; during this time they are eligible for social security benefits. To receive benefits, you must arrange it in advance with your local social security office before leaving for France; beware that French bureaucracy often takes three months just to process the paperwork. If you do not succeed in finding work in that time, you must return home unless you can prove your financial independence. By law, all EU citizens must be given equality of opportunity when applying to jobs not directly related to national security, so theoretically, if you speak French you have as much chance of finding a job as an equivalently qualified French person.

AU PAIR

Open to men and women 18-30 years old with some knowledge of French, the *au pair* position involves child care and light housework for a French family while enrolled at a French school or university. Talking with children can be a great way to improve your French, but looking after them can be strenuous. Know in advance what the family expects of you. Expect to receive room, board, and a small stipend. *Au pair* jobs (usually 6-18 months) can be arranged through individual connections, but make sure you have a contract detailing hours per week, salary, and accommodations. Check with the French embassy (see p. 217) and the following organizations for more info.

L'Accueil Familial des Jeunes Etrangers, 23, r. du Cherche-Midi, *6ème* (☎42 22 50 34; fax 45 44 60 48). M: Sèvres-Babylone. Arranges summer and 18-month *au pair* jobs (placement fee 650F for EU, 800F for non-EU). Will help switch families if your situation is unlivable. They can find you a room in exchange for 12hr. of work per week, or room-and-board for 18hr. of work (you must have a student visa). Also arranges similar jobs for non-students, which require 30hr. of work per week in exchange for room, board, employment benefits, as well as a métro pass.

Childcare International, Ltd., Trafalgar House, Grenville Place, London NW7 3SA (☎020 8906 3116; fax (0) 8906 3461; email office@childint.co.uk; www.childint.co.uk). Offers *au pair* positions in France. Provides information on qualifications required and local language schools. The organization prefers a long placement but does arrange summer work. UK£80 application fee.

TEACHING ENGLISH

Post a sign in markets and schools stating that you are a native speaker, and scan the classified ads of local newspapers. Securing a position will require patience and legwork. Because the job market is more accessible to British teachers, Americans will find the job search particularly difficult.

International Schools Services, Educational Staffing Program, P.O. Box 5910, Princeton, NJ 08543 (☎609 452 0990; fax 609 452 2690; email edustaffing@iss.edu; www.iss.edu). Recruits teachers and administrators for American and English schools in France. All instruction in English. Applicants must have a bachelor's degree and two years of relevant experience. Non-refundable US$100 application fee. Publishes *The ISS Directory of Overseas Schools* (US$35).

Office of Overseas Schools, A/OS Room 245, SA-29, Dept. of State, Washington, D.C. 20522 2902 (☎703 875 7800; fax 703 875 7979; email overseas.school@state.gov; http://state.gov/www/about_state/schools/). Keeps a list of schools abroad and agencies that arrange placement for Americans to teach abroad.

VOLUNTEER

REMPART, 1, r. des Guillemites, *4ème* (☎42 71 96 55; fax 42 71 73 00). Offers summer and year-long programs geared toward protecting French heritage. Restoration projects. Anyone 15 or over is eligible. Programs cost 40-50F per day, plus a 220F insurance fee.

Club du Vieux Manoir, 10, r. de la Cossonnerie, *1er* (☎45 08 80 40 or 03 44 72 33 18). Offers year-long and summer programs (as short as 15 days) restoring castles and churches throughout France. Anyone 15 or over is eligible. Programs cost 80F per day, plus 90F application fee.

United Nations Educational, Scientific, and Cultural Organization (UNESCO), (www.unesco.org). If your visit to UNESCO (see **Sights,** p. 82) leaves you ready to serve a greater cause, the organization offers unpaid internships of 3-6 months for university graduates. You must speak either French or English and be a citizen of a member country; if you aren't, try through a university. For more information check the website above or write, to the attention of your country's delegation, to UNESCO PER-Staff Training Section, 1, r. Miollis, 75732 Paris.

SCI International Voluntary Service (SCI-VS), 814 NE 40th St., Seattle, WA 98105 (☎/fax 206 545-6585; email sciivsusa@igc.apc.org). Arranges placement in work camps in Europe for those age 18 and over. Local organizations sponsor groups for physical or social work. Registration fees US$50-250, depending on camp location.

FINDING WORK ONCE THERE

TIPS

Check help-wanted columns in French newspapers, especially *Le Monde*, *Le Figaro*, and the English-language *International Herald Tribune*, as well as *France-USA Contacts*, a free weekly circular filled with classified ads, which can be picked up in Yankee hangouts. Many of these jobs are "unofficial" and therefore illegal (one risks deportation), but many people find them convenient because they often don't ask for presentation of a work permit. However, the best tips on jobs for foreigners come from other travelers. Be aware of your rights as an employee, and always get written confirmation of your agreements. Youth hostels frequently provide room and board to travelers willing to help run the place. Those seeking more permanent employment should have a **résumé** in both English and French. Type up your résumé for a prospective employer, but write the cover letter by hand. Handwriting is considered an important indicator of your character to French employers. Also, expect to be asked interview questions that might be considered inappropriate in another culture, such as your stance on ethical or political issues. The French workplace tends to be more conservative than Anglo offices, so your morals must (as far as your employer knows) mesh. Finally, an official job offer should be put in writing.

RESOURCES

American Church, 65 quai d'Orsay, *7ème* (☎40 62 05 00). M: Invalides. Posts a bulletin board (view M-Sa 9am-10:30pm and Su 2-7:30pm) full of job and housing opportunities targeting Americans and anglophones. Open M-Sa 9am-10pm.

American Chamber of Commerce in France, 156 bd. Haussmann, *8ème* (☎40 73 89 90; fax 47 20 18 62). M: Miromesnil. An association of American businesses in France, for those with ambition and an up-to-date résumé in both French and English. Your résumé will be kept on file for two months and placed at the disposal of French and American companies. Chamber of Commerce membership directories can be browsed in the Paris office. Open M-F 9am-5pm. Library open Tu and Th 10am-12:30pm; admission 50F.

Agence Nationale Pour l'Emploi (ANPE), 4, impasse d'Antin, 8*ème* (☎43 59 62 63; fax 53 40 48 99; www.enpe.fr). M: Franklin D. Roosevelt. Has specific info on employment. Remember to bring your work permit and your *carte de séjour.* (Open M-W and F 9am-5pm, Th 9am-noon.)

Centre d'Information et de Documentation Jeunesse (CIDJ), 101, quai Branly, 15*ème* (☎44 49 12 00; fax 40 65 02 61). M: Champs de Mars-Tour Eiffel. An invaluable state-run youth center provides info on education, résumés, employment, and careers. English spoken. Jobs are posted at 9am on the bulletin boards outside. Open M-F 9am-6pm, Sa 9:30am-1pm.

STUDYING IN PARIS

Every year, thousands of people from all over the world descend on France to study, whether for a few weeks of French language immersion or to enroll in an advanced degree program. In response to this demand, hundreds of institutions have mushroomed, offering courses that cater to every taste. You don't even need to speak French to get a degree; in 1999, in a bid to bolster the long-term standing of France (and earn a little foreign currency on the side), the French government announced a program to offer certain degree courses in English to overseas students.

All non-EU citizens need a **study visa** if they intend to spend more than three months studying in France; everyone will need a residency permit. If you have been accepted into a course and can show proof of financial independence, you should have no trouble getting a study visa. For more information, see **Visas and Work Permits,** p. 217.

FRENCH UNIVERSITIES

French universities (except for the Grandes Ecoles; see below) must admit anyone holding a *baccalaureat* (French school-leaving diploma) or a recognized equivalent to their first year of courses (British A-levels or 2 years of college in the US). Non-native French speakers must also pass a written and oral language test. At the end of the first year, exams separate the wheat from the chaff. The cream of the academic crop go to the elite **Grandes Ecoles** after passing notoriously difficult entrance exams that require a year of preparatory schooling in themselves.

French universities are far, far cheaper than American equivalents, including programs offered by US universities in France; however, expect to pay at least 2500F per month in living expenses. EU citizens studying in France can take advantage of the **SOCRATES** program, which offers grants to support inter-European educational exchanges. Most UK and Irish universities will have details on the grants and the application procedure. The listings below can supply further information and help organize an academic program in France.

If you are already fluent in French, direct enrollment in a French university can be more rewarding than a class filled with Americans. It can also be up to four times cheaper, although you may not receive academic credit at home. After 1968, the **Université de Paris** split into 10 independent universities, each at a different site and offering a different program. The Sorbonne, now the Université de Paris IV, devotes itself to the humanities. Contact the cultural services office at the nearest French consulate. As a student at a French university, you will receive a student card *(carte d'étudiant)* upon presentation of your residency permit and a receipt for your university fees. In addition to standard student benefits, many additional benefits are administered by the **Centre Régional des Oeuvres Universitaires et Scolaires (CROUS).** Founded in 1955 to improve the living and working conditions of students, CROUS welcomes foreign students. The brochure *Le CROUS et Moi* lists addresses and info on student life. Pick up their guidebook *Je Vais en France* (free), in French or English, from any French embassy.

The British Council, 11 Portland Place, London W1N 4EJ (☎020 7930 8466; fax 020 7389 3199; www.britishcouncil.org) has information on educational exchanges between the UK and France, and also administers the SOCRATES program in Britain.

Université Paris-Sorbonne, 1, r. Victor Cousin, 75230 Paris Cedex 05 (☎40 46 22 11; fax 40 46 25 88; www.paris4sorbonne.fr), the grand-daddy of French universities, was founded in 1253 and is still going strong. Enrollment in degree courses cost about 2500F per year. Also offers programs for US students lasting 3-9 months.

American University of Paris, 31 av. Bosquet, *7ème* (☎40 62 06 00; www.aup.fr) offers US-accredited degrees and summer programs taught in English at its Paris campus. Tuition and living expenses total about US$28,000 per year.

LANGUAGE SCHOOLS

Alliance Française, Ecole Internationale de Langue et de Civilisation Françaises, 101, bd. Raspail, *6ème,* Paris or 75270 Paris Cedex 06 (☎45 44 38 28; fax 45 44 89 42; email afparis_ecole@compuserve; http://www.paris.alliancefrancaise.fr). M: Nôtre-Dame-des-Champs. Instruction all levels, with specialized courses in legal, hotel/tourism and business French. From 1400F per month for evening classes (2hr. per day, 3 days a week); 4200F per month for an intensive course (4hr. per day). Oct.-June M-W two hours per day. During the summer the only class offered is intensive business French for beginners. MC, V.

Cours de Civilisation Française de la Sorbonne, 47, r. des Ecoles, *5ème* (☎40 46 22 11, 9am–5pm; fax 40 46 32 29; www.fle.fr/sorbonne/). Offers instruction at all levels in the French language, together with a comprehensive lecture program of French cultural studies taught by professors of the Sorbonne. Must be at least 18 and have completed high school. Semester- and year-long courses during the academic year, and 4-, 6-, 8-, and 11-week summer programs.

Institut de Langue Française, 3, av. Bertie Albrecht, *8ème* (☎45 63 24 00; fax 45 63 07 09; http://www.instlanguefr.com). M: Charles de Gaulle-Etoile. Language, civilization, and literature courses. 2 weeks, 20hr. per week, 3000F.

Institut Parisien de Langue et de Civilisation Française, 87, bd. de Grenelle, *15ème* (☎40 56 09 53; fax 43 06 46 30; email institut.parisien@dial.oleane.com). M: LaMotte-Picquet-Grenelle. French language, fashion, culinary arts, and cinema courses. Intensive language courses for 10, 15 (1050F per week), or 25 (1750F per week) hours per week.

LONG-TERM ACCOMMODATIONS

Almost every *arrondissement* in Paris contains some form of affordable housing and is well connected to the city by public transportation (except for the *16ème*, but it's full of mansions anyway). You will probably find the cheapest housing in peripheral *arrondissements*. Try the *12ème*, *13ème*, the northern half of the *17ème* (near La Fourche), *18ème*, *19ème*, or *20ème*. If you are set on a central location, the more commercial parts of the *2ème* may have something within your price range. During August, even ritzier locales can provide affordable housing, as the entire city empties for a month during the greatest Parisian vacation of them all, the *grandes vacances*. For more information on specific neighborhoods, see **Once in Paris,** p. 11.

STUDENTS

For travelers planning a summer, semester, or academic year visit to Paris, student housing is available in the dormitories of most French universities. Contact the **Centre Régional des Oeuvres Universitaires (CROUS)** for more information. Additional lodging is available on a month-to-month basis at the **Cité Universitaire,** 15, bd. Jourdan, *14ème;* (☎44 16 64 00), M: Cité Universitaire. For information, write to M. le Délégué Général de Cité Universitaire de Paris, 19, bd. Jourdan, 75690 Paris Cedex 14. Over 30 different nations maintain dormitories at the Cité Universitaire, where they board their citizens studying in Paris. In summer, dorms lodge anyone on a first-come, first-served basis. Reserve a bed months in advance. Some kitchens are available. (Singles 2000-3000F per month.) To stay in the **American House,** write to Fondation des Etats-Unis, 15, bd. Jourdan, 75690 Paris Cedex 14 (☎53 80 68 82. Rates vary according to demand: in summer 2900F per month; cheaper off season; office open M-F 9-5pm.)

PHARMACIES

Perhaps the easiest thing to do if you are a foreigner and get sick in Paris is to head for the pharmacy. Each arrondissement has a rotating system of 24-hour pharmacies *(pharmacies de garde)*. The police will be able to tell you which one is open on any given night, and at night and on Sundays pharmacies post a list on their door of those on duty. Like in England, French pharmacies have a monopoly on dispensing medication (often stronger in France than in other countries), and are staffed by highly trained individuals who assist you in dealing with your symptoms, whatever they might be. You can often avoid the time and money spent in going to a doctor by dealing with a pharmacist, as they can also provide basic services, like bandaging a wound or transplanting a kidney, for a small fee. In the event that you require a doctor's care, the pharmacist can provide you with a list of doctors in the arrondissement ranging from gynecologists to general-care practitioners.

RENTING AN APARTMENT

If you plan to stay in Paris for a longer period of time, consider renting an apartment. Although rent is high and utilities are expensive, apartments offer convenience, privacy, and a kitchen. Call, fax, write, or visit **Allô Logement Temporaire,** 4, pl. de Chapelle, 18*ème*. (☎42 09 00 07; email alt@claranet.fr. Open M-F noon-8pm.) This helpful, English-speaking association charges a membership fee of 300F if they succeed in finding an apartment for you, which is followed by an additional charge of 200F per month. The company suggests writing or calling before you leave for France. Be sure to leave a phone or fax number where you can be reached easily as vacancies come and go very quickly.

Alternatively, consult the French Department at your local university; it may be able to connect you with students abroad who want to sublet their apartments. Remember that short-term rentals, usually more expensive per month than longer rentals, can be difficult to procure, especially in winter months. The **Internet** can provide listings on Paris apartments, but these often tend to be more expensive places advertised by wealthy Parisians with computers and Internet access. Surf the web simply to get a sense of the market before you go.

If possible, stay in a hotel or hostel your first week in Paris and find an apartment while you're there. This will allow you to see what you're getting. Among the best places to look are the bulletin boards in the **American Church** (see p. 277). Those upstairs tend to advertise long-term rentals, while those downstairs list short-term, cheaper arrangements. A smaller list of apartments to rent or share can be found at the bookstore **Shakespeare and Co.** (see **Books and Magazines,** p. 145). Check listings in any of the English-French newsletters like **Paris Free Voice** or **France-USA Contacts (FUSAC),** a free publication found in English bookstores and restaurants throughout Paris. FUSAC is also distributed in the US (FUSAC, P.O. Box 115, Cooper Station, New York, NY 10276; ☎212-929-2929; fax 255-5555; email fusac@club-internet.fr). It includes an extensive section of classified ads, in which anglophones offer apartments for rent or sublet. FUSAC also has a bulletin board with listings at 26, r. Bénard, 14*ème*. (☎56 53 54 55. M: Pernety. Open M-Sa 10am-7pm). **De Particulier à Particulier** is a French publication that comes out on Thursdays with listings, as does the Tuesday **Le Figaro.**

Subletting is technically illegal, but many choose to do so anyway. Those who do sublet should work out a written agreement with the landlord, defining all of their mutual expectations regarding security deposits, utilities, maintenance, and rent. This document will help to avoid any misunderstandings. The original renter may require cash payments to avoid paying heavy taxes, and utilities and mailbox are likely to remain under the renter's name. The subletter may need to tell the building superintendent or *concierge* that he or she is a guest of the renter.

St. Germain-des-Pres

BANKING

If you are planning a long-term stay in Paris and have a permanent address and a letter of support from your bank at home, you can open an account at any convenient financial institution and obtain an ATM card drawn on your French account. Most foreign banks can wire money to French accounts (for US$30-40 per transfer). Required minimum balances vary but are usually not steep for residents. Non-resident bank accounts require a hefty opening deposit and a high minimum balance (50,000F). Banks' main offices (often located near the Opéra) have foreign affairs departments that deal with such issues. Note that *compte courant* means current account, *compte d'épargne* means savings account, *compte sur livret* means deposit account, and *relève de compte* means account statement.

Fruits and Legumes

MEDICAL CARE

Should you require a house call for a condition not requiring hospitalization, you can call any of the S.O.S. numbers listed in the **Service Directory,** p. 275. Request documentation (including diagnoses) and receipts to submit to your home insurance company for reimbursement. Any of these S.O.S. services can make referrals for internists, dentists, optometrists, and ophthalmologists in your arrondissement.

EU citizens can get reciprocal health benefits, entitling them to a practitioner registered with the state system, by filling out a **E111** or **E112** form before departure; this is available at most major post offices. They will generally treat you whether or not you can pay in advance. EU citizens studying in France also qualify for long-term care. Other travelers should ensure they have adequate medical insurance before leaving; if your regular **insurance** policy does not cover travel abroad, you may wish to purchase additional coverage. With the exception of Medicare, most health insurance plans cover members' medical emergencies during trips abroad; check with your insurance carrier to be sure.

If you need a **doctor (un médecin),** call the local hospital for a list of local practitioners. If you are receiving reciprocal health care, make sure you call a **honoraires opposables** doctor, who will be linked to the state health care system. They may not charge more than 110F for a consultation at their surgery office; this amount is reimbursable. Doctors described as **honoraires libres** are free to charge whatever they like, and their fees will not be reimbursed under reciprocal health care agreements. If they find something wrong, you may find yourself paying a lot for prescription drugs. Note that the same medicines may have different names in France than in your home country; check with your doctor before you leave. For lists of dentists, doctors, emergency numbers, hotlines, hospitals, pharmacies, and women's health resources, see **Service Directory,** p. 274.

Quai d'Anjou

Service Directory

A nightmare? But it was so real, so vivid. Two voluptuous women, grinding, heaving. How to describe it. Have you ever been to Paris?

-Brady Dewar

ACCOMMODATION AGENCIES

Allô Logement Temporaire, 64, r. du Temple, 3*ème* (☎42 72 00 06; fax 42 72 03 11; email alt@claranet.fr). M: Hôtel-de-Ville. Open M-F noon-8pm.

La Centrale de Réservations (FUAJ-HI), 60, r. Vitruve, 20*ème*. (☎55 25 35 20; fax 43 56 36 32). M: Port de Bagnolet or Maraichers. Open 9:30am-5:30pm.

Centre Régional des Oeuvres Universitaires (CROUS), 39, av. Georges Bernanos, 5*ème* (☎40 51 36 00; lodging ☎40 51 37 17 or 40 51 36 99). RER: Port-Royal. Open M-F 1-5pm.

Cité Universitaire, 19, bd. Jourdan, 14*ème* (☎44 16 64 00). M: Cité Universitaire. For info, write to M. le Délégué Général de Cité Universitaire de Paris, 19, bd. Jourdan, 75690 Paris Cedex 14.

OTU-Voyage (Office du Tourisme Universitaire), 119, r. St-Martin, 4*ème* (☎40 29 12 12). 10F service charge. Open M-F 9:30am-7pm. Sa 10am-noon and 1:30pm-5pm. Also at 2, r. Malus, 5*ème* (☎44 41 74 74). M: Place Monge. Open M-Sa 9-6pm.

BIKE RENTAL

Active Bike, 20, r. Acacias, 17*ème* (☎40 55 02 02; fax 48 25 30 88). M: Charles de Gaulle-Étoile. Rents scooters starting at 200F per day, 950F per week with 6000F deposit.

La Maison du Vélo, 11, r. Fénelon, 10*ème* (☎42 81 24 72). M: Poissonière. Rent mountain or hybrid bikes at 90F per day. 2000F deposit. Open Tu-Sa 10am-7pm.

Paris à velo, c'est sympa! 37, bd. Bourdon, 4*ème* (☎48 87 60 01). M: Bastille. Rentals available with a 2500F (or credit card) deposit. 24hr. rental 150F; 9am-7pm 80F. half-day (9am-2pm or 2-7pm) 60F.

Paris-Vélo, 2, r. de Fer-à-Moulin, 5*ème* (☎43 37 59 22). M: Censier Daubenton. Bike rental 90F per day with 2000F deposit includes accident insurance. Open M-Sa 10am-12:30pm and 2-7pm.

BUDGET TRAVEL AGENCIES

Council Travel, 1, pl. Odéon, 6*ème* (☎44 41 89 80; fax 01 40 51 89 12; email CouncilTravelFrance@ciee.org). M: Odéon. Open M-F 9:30am-6:30pm and Sa 10am-5pm.

Office de Tourisme Universitaire (OTU), 2, r. Malus, 5*ème* (☎44 41 74 74). M: Place Monge. Also at 119, r. St-Martin, 4*ème* (☎40 29 12 12). Open M-F 10am-6:30pm; St-Martin branch open Sa 10am-5pm.

CAR RENTAL

Inter Touring Service, 117, bd. Auguste Blanqui, 13*ème* (☎45 88 52 37; fax 01 45 80 89 30). M: Glacière.

Rent-a-Car, 79, r. de Bercy, 12*ème* (☎43 45 98 99; fax 43 45 65 00). Open M-Sa 8:30am-7pm. Amex, MC, V.

Autorent, 98, r. de la Convention, 15*ème* (☎45 54 22 45; fax 45 54 39 69). M: Boucicaut. Also at 36, r. Fabert, 7*ème* (☎45 55 12 54). M: Invalides. Open M-F 8:30am-7pm, Sa 8am-noon. AmEx, MC, V.

CHUNNEL RESERVATIONS

Eurostar, reservation ☎49 70 01 75; www.eurostar.co.uk.

Le Shuttle, ☎03 21 00 61 00; www.eurotunnel.co.uk.

CONSULATES & EMBASSIES IN PARIS

Australian Embassy and Consulate, 4 r. Jean Rey, 15*ème* (☎40 59 33 00; www.austgov.fr). M: Bir Hakeem. Open M-F 9:15am-noon and 2-4:30pm.

British Embassy, 35, r. du Faubourg-St-Honoré, 8*ème* (☎44 51 31 00; fax 44 51 31 27; www.amb-grandebretagne.fr). M: Concorde or Madeleine. **Visa Bureau Consulate,** 16, r. d'Anjou. M: Concorde. Open M-F 9:30am-12:30pm. **Consulate,** 18bis, r. d'Anjou. Open M-F 9:30am-12:30pm and 2:30-5pm.

Canadian Embassy and Consulate, 35 Ave. Montaigne, 8*ème* (☎44 43 29 00). M: Franklin-Roosevelt or Alma-Marceau. Open 9am-noon and 2-5pm. Consular services by appointment. Open M-F 2-4:30pm. **General Delegation of Quebec,** 66 r. Pergolèse, 16*ème* (☎40 67 85 00). Open 9am-5:30pm. **Delegation of Quebec for Immigration,** 87-89, r. de la Boetie (☎53 93 45 45). Open 9am-noon and 2-5pm.

Irish Embassy and Consulate, 12 av. Foch, 16*ème* (☎44 17 67 48; fax 44 17 67 50). M: Argentine or Charles-de-Gaule-Etoile. Open 9:30am-noon; phones open 9:30am-5:30pm. Consular services at 4, r. Rude. Open M-F 9:30am-noon.

New Zealand Embassy and Consulate, 7ter, r. Leonardo da Vinci, 16*ème* (☎45 00 24 11; fax 45 01 26 39). M: Victor-Hugo. Open M-F 9am-1pm and 2-5:30pm.

South African Embassy, 59, quai d'Orsay, 7*ème* (☎53 59 23 23; fax 47 53 99 70). M: Invalides. Open M-F 9am-noon.

United States Embassy, 2, av. Gabriel, 8*ème* (☎43 12 22 22; fax 42 66 97 83). M: Concorde. Open M-F 9am-6pm. Consulate, 2, r. St-Florentin, 1*er* (☎43 12 48 76 or 01 43 12 23 47 for automated information; passport division). Open M-F 9am-3pm.

CURRENCY EXCHANGE

American Express, 11, r. Scribe, 9*ème* (☎47 77 77 07; fax 47 77 74 57). M: Opéra or Auber. Open M-F 9am-6:30pm, Sa 10am-5:30pm; exchange counters open also Su 10am-5pm.

Thomas Cook, 73, av. des Champs-Elysées, 8*ème* (☎45 62 89 55; fax 45 62 89 55). M: Franklin D. Roosevelt. Open daily 8:30am-10pm.

DENTISTS & DOCTORS

Centre Médicale Europe, 44 r. d'Amsterdam, 9*ème* (☎42 81 93 33). M: St-Lazare. Open M-F 8am-7pm, Sa 8am-6pm.

SOS Dentaire, 87 bd. Port-Royal (☎43 37 51 00). RER: Port-Royal. Open daily 8am-11:45pm.

SOS Médecins, ☎47 07 77 77. Makes house calls.

SOS Oeil, ☎40 92 93 94. Open 24hr.

SOS Optique Lunettes, ☎48 07 22 00. Open 24hr.

Urgences Médicales de Paris, ☎48 28 40 04. Makes house calls.

DISABILITY RESOURCES

L'Association des Paralysées de France, Délégation de Paris, 22, r. de Père Guérion, 13*ème* (☎40 78 69 00). M: Place d'Italie. Open M-F 9am-12:30pm and 2-5:30pm.

Audio-Vision guides, at Parisian theaters such as the Théâtre National de Chaillot, 1, pl. Trocadéro, 11 Novembre, 16*ème* (☎53 65 31 00); the Comédie Française, 2, r. de Richelieu, 1*er* (☎44 58 15 15); and the Théâtre National de la Colline, 15, r. Malte-Brun, 20*ème* (☎44 62 52 00). design.

Comité National Français de Liaison pour la Réadaption des Handicapés (CNFLRH), 236bis, r. de Tolbiac, 13*ème* (☎53 80 66 66; fax 53 80 66 67; www.handitel.org).

DRY CLEANING

Buci Pressing, 7, r. Ancienne Comédie, 6*ème* (☎43 29 49 92). M: Odéon. Open M-Sa 8am-7:30pm; tailoring on Tu and F.

Pressing de Seine, 67, r. de Seine, 6ème (☎43 25 74 94). M: Odéon. Open M-Sa 8am-7:15pm. MC,V.

Pressing Villiers, 93, r. Rocher, 8ème (☎45 22 75 48. M: Villiers. Open M-Sa 8am-7:30pm.

EMERGENCY

Ambulance (SAMU), ☎15.

Fire, ☎18.

Poison, ☎40 05 48 48. In French, but some English assistance is available.

Police, ☎17. **For emergencies only.**

Rape: SOS Viol, ☎0 800 05 95 95. Open M-F 10am-7pm.

S.O.S Help! (☎47 23 80 80) An anonymous, confidential hotline for English speakers in crisis. Open daily (including holidays) 3-11pm.

ENTERTAINMENT INFO

Info-Loisirs, ☎08 36 68 31 12; 2.23F/min.

GAY/LESBIAN RESOURCES

ACT-UP PARIS, 45, r. de Sedene, 11*ème* (☎48 06 13 89). M: Bréguet-Sabin.

Centre du Christ Libérateur (métropolitan Community Church), 5, r. Crussol, 11*ème* (☎48 05 24 48 or 39 83 13 44). M: Oberkampf.

Centre Gai et Lesbien, 3, r. Keller, 11*ème* (☎43 57 21 47; fax 43 57 27 93). M: Ledru Rollin or Bastille. Open M-Sa 2-8pm, Sa 2-7pm.

Ecoute Gaie, ☎44 93 01 02. Crisis hotline. Open M 8-10pm, Tu and F 6-10pm.

Fréquence Gaie, 98.2FM (☎40 13 88 00). 24hr. radio station.

Maison des Femmes, 163, r. de Charenton, 12*ème* (☎43 43 41 13). Open W and F 3-6pm, Sa 5-8pm; café F 8pm-midnight.

SOS Homophobie, ☎48 06 42 41. Takes calls Sept.-June M-F 8-10pm; July-Aug. Tu-F 8-10pm.

GROOMING SERVICES

Space Hair, 10, r. Rambuteau, 3*ème* (☎48 87 28 51). M: Rambuteau. Cut and style women 205F, men 145F; 15% discount for students and between 9-11am. Open M noon-10pm, Tu-F 9am-11pm, Sa 9am-10pm.

Planet Hair, ☎48 87 38 86. M: Rambuteau. Women cut and style 250F, men 150F; student discount 20% Open Tu-W and F-Sa 10am-8pm, Th noon-9pm.

HOSPITALS

Hôpital Américain de Paris, 63, bd. Victor Hugo, Neuilly (☎46 41 25 25). M: Port Maillot, then bus #82 to the end of the line.

Hôpital Franco-Britannique de Paris, 3, r. Barbès, in the Parisian suburb of Levallois-Perret (☎46 39 22 22). M: Anatole-France. Considered a French hospital. Has some English-speakers, but don't count on it.

Hôpital Marmottan, 17-19, r. d'Armaillé, 17*ème* (☎45 74 00 04). M: Charles de Gaulle Étoile or Argentine. Not an emergency service. Open Sept.-July M and W-Th noon-7pm, F 10am-7pm, Sa noon-6pm; Aug. M-F only.

HOTLINES & SUPPORT CENTERS

AIDES, 247, r. de Belleville, 20*ème* (☎44 52 00 00). M: Télégraphe. Office open M-Sa 9am-6pm and Su 2-6pm. 24hr. hotline ☎0 800 84 08 00.

Alcoholics Anonymous, 3, r. Frédéric Sauton, 5*ème* (☎46 34 59 65). M: Maubert-Mutualité.

Free Anglo-American Counseling Treatment and Support (FACTS), ☎44 93 16 69. Open M, W, and F 6-10pm.

HIV, 43, r. de Valois, 1*ème* (☎42 61 30 04). M: Palais-Royal or Bourse. Open M-F 9am-7pm. HIV testing at 218, r. de Belleville, 20*ème* (☎47 97 40 49), M: Télégraphe. 3, r. de Ridder, 14*ème* (☎45 43 83 78), M: Plaisance. Testing M-F noon-6:30pm, Sa 9:30am-noon.

International Counseling Service (ICS), ☎45 50 26 49. Open M-F 9:30am-6pm, Sa 9:30am-1pm.

SOS Crisis Help Line Friendship, ☎47 23 80 80. English-speaking. Open daily 3-11pm.

INTERNET ACCESS

AMAC, 141, bd. du Montparnasse, *6ème* (☎55 42 10 60). M: Vavin. Also in the *5ème* at 4, r. de la Sorbonne (☎55 42 10 60). M: St-Michel. 5F for 5min., 50F for 1hr. Student cards 200F for 5hr., 350F for 10hr., 600F for 20hr. *6ème* open M-Sa 9am-7:30pm; *5ème* M-F 9am-7pm, Sa 1-7pm.

Café Orbital, 13, r. du Médicis, *6ème* (☎43 25 76 77). M: Odéon; bus #21, 38, or 84-86. 1F per min.; beware 30min. minimum. 55F per hr. Students 200F for 5hr., 300F for 10hr. Open M-Sa 9am-10pm, Su noon-10pm.

Cyber Cube, 5, r. Mignon, *6ème* (☎53 10 30 50). M: St-Michel or Odéon. 1F per min. Students 200F for 5hr. or 300F for 10hr. Open M-Sa 10am-10pm. Also in the *11ème* at 12, r. Daval (☎49 29 67 67). M: Bastille.

Hammam Café, 4, r. des Rosiers, *3ème* (☎42 78 04 45). M: St-Paul. 1F per min. Open Su-Th noon-midnight, F noon-4pm, Sa sundown-2am.

Le Jardin de l'Internet, 79, bd. St-Michel, *5ème* (☎44 07 22 20). RER: Luxembourg. 1F per min., 25F for 30min., 48F for 1hr., 190F for 5hr. Open daily 9am-11pm.

Luxembourg Micro, 83, bd. St-Michel, *5ème* (☎46 33 27 98). RER: Luxembourg. 0.75F per min., 23F for 30min., 45F for 1hr. Membership 100F for 2½hr., 180F for 5hr., and 275F for 10hr. Open daily 9am-9pm.

WebBar, 32, r. de Picardie, *3ème* (☎42 72 66 55). M: République. 40F per hr., 300F for 10hr. Open daily 8:30am-2am.

LIBRARIES

The American Library, 10, r. Général Camou, *7ème* (☎53 59 12 60; email 100142.1066@compuserve.com). M: Ecole Militaire. Membership 570F per year, student 460F, summer 240F, day entry 70F. Open Tu-Sa 10am-7pm.

Bibliothèque Marguerite Durand, 79, r. Nationale, *13ème* (☎45 70 80 30). M: Nationale. Open M-Sa 2-6pm.

Bibliothèque National de France includes the monstrous Mitterrand branch at 11, quai François Mauriac, *13ème* (☎53 79 59 59). M: Quai de la Gare or Bibliothèque. Reading rooms open Tu-Sa 10am-8pm, Su noon-7pm. Branches at 66-68, r. de Richelieu, *2ème*; Bibliothèque de l'Opéra, in the Opéra, 8, r. Scribe, *9ème* (☎47 42 07 02), M: Opéra. Readers card 20F per day, 200F per year.

Bibliothèque Publique, in the Centre Pompidou, *4ème* (☎44 78 12 33). M: Rambuteau. Open M and W-F noon-10pm, Sa-Su 10am-10pm.

The British Council Library, 9-11, r. Constantine, *7ème* (☎49 55 73 23; fax 49 55 73 02). M: Invalides. Membership 250F per year, 130F for 6 months; student rate 200F per year, 110F for 6 months; day entry 30F. Open M-Tu and Th-F 11am-6pm, W 11am-7pm. Closed Aug.

MAIL

Federal Express, ☎0 800 12 38 00. Call M-F before 5pm for pick up. Or, drop off at 2, r. du 29 Juillet, between Concorde and r. du Rivoli, *1er*. Open M-Sa 9am-7pm; drop off by 4:45pm. Also at 63, bd. Haussmann, *8ème*.

Poste du Louvre, 52, r. du Louvre, *1er* (postal info ☎40 28 20 40; telegrams ☎40 28 20 00). M: Louvre. Open daily 7am-6:20am.

MINORITY RESOURCES

Agence pour le développement des relations interculturelles, 4, r. Réne-Villermé, *11ème* (☎40 09 69 19). M: Père-Lachaise. Open M and W-Th 9:30am-1pm and 2-6pm, F 9:30am-1pm and 2-5pm.

Association des Trois Mondes, 63bis, r. du Cardinal Lemoine, *5ème* (☎42 34 99 09). M: Cardinal-Lemoine. Open M-F 9am-1pm and 2-6pm.

Centre Culturel Algérien, 171, r. de la Croix-Nivert, *15ème* (☎45 54 95 31). M: Boucicault. Open M-F 9am-5pm. Closed Aug.

Centre Culturel Coréen, 2, av. d'léna, *16ème* (☎47 20 84 15). M: léna. Open M-F 9:30am-12:30pm and 2:30-6pm.

Centre Culturel Égyptien, 111, bd. St Michel, *5ème* (☎46 33 75 67). M: Luxembourg. Open M-F 10am-7pm, Sa 3-7pm. Closed Aug.

Maison de l'Asie, 22, av. du Président Wilson, *16ème* (☎53 70 18 46). M: léna or Trocadéro. Open M-F 9am-6pm.

MRAP (Mouvement contre le racisme et pour l'amitié entre les peuples), 43, bd. Magenta, *10ème* (☎53 38 99 99).

SOS Racisme, 28, r. des Petites Ecuries, *10ème* (☎53 24 67 67).

PHARMACIES

Grande Pharmacie Daumesnil, 6, pl. Félix-Eboué, *12ème* (☎43 43 19 03). M: Daumesnil. Open 24hr.

Pharmacie Dhéry, in the Galerie des Champs, 84, av. des Champs-Elysées, *8ème* (☎45 62 02 41). M: George V. Open 24hr. Provides the **Pharma Presto** service, which delivers prescription medicines for 120F daily 8am-6pm, 180F 6pm-8am.

Pharmacie des Halles, 10, bd. de Sébastopol, 1*er* (☎42 72 03 23). M: Châtelet-Les-Halles. Open M-Sa 9am-midnight, Su noon-midnight.

Pharmacie Européenne, 6, pl. de Clichy, 9*ème* (☎48 74 65 18). M: Place de Clichy. Open 24hr.

Pharmacie Opéra Capucines, 6, bd. des Capucines, 9*ème* (☎42 65 88 29). M: Opéra. Open M-Sa 8am-12:30am, Su 10pm-12:30am. AmEx, MC, V.

RELIGIOUS SERVICES

American Cathedral (Anglican and Episcopalian), 23, av. George V, 8*ème* (☎53 23 84 00). M: George V. English services daily 9am. Open M-F 9am-5pm.

American Church in Paris, 65, quai d'Orsay, 7*ème* (☎40 62 05 00). M: Invalides or Alma-Marceau.

Buddhist Temple, Centre de Kazyn Dzong, route de la ceinture du Lac Daumesnil, 12*éme* (☎40 04 98 06). M: Porte Dorée. A Buddhist temple and meditation center. Meditations Tu-F 9:30-10:30am, 6 and 7:30pm; Sa-Su 10am-noon and 2:30-5:30pm.

Eglise Russe (Russian Eastern Orthodox), also known as **Cathédrale Alexandre-Nevski,** 12, r. Daru, 8*ème* (☎42 27 37 34). M: Ternes. Open Tu, F and Su 3-5pm. Services (in French and Russian) Su 10am.

Mosque de Paris, Institut Musulman, pl. de l'Ermite, 5*ème* (☎45 35 97 33). M: Place Monge. Open Sa-Th 9am-noon and 2-6pm.

St. Joseph's Church (Catholic), 50, av. Hoche, 8*ème* (☎42 27 28 56). M: Charles de Gaulle-Etoile. English mass M-F 8:30am, Sa 11:30am and 6:30pm, Su 9:45, 11am, 12:15, and 6:30pm; July-Aug. Su mass at 10am, 12:15, and 6:30pm. Open M-Sa 10am-6pm.

St. Michael's Church (Anglican and Episcopalian), 5, r. d'Aguesseau, 8*ème* (☎47 42 70 88). M: Concorde. Services in English Su 10:30am and 6:30pm. Open M-Tu and Th-F 10am-1pm and 2-5:30pm.

Union Libéral Israélite de France (Jewish), 24, r. Copernic, 16*ème* (☎47 04 37 27). M: Victor-Hugo. Services F 6pm and Sa 10:30am, mostly in Hebrew with a little French. Services in the evenings and mornings of High Holy Days; call for info. Open M-Th 9am-noon and 2-6pm, F-Sa 9am-noon.

SHOE REPAIR

Oziel Emile, 4, r. Lobineau, Marché St-Germain (☎46 34 58 05). M: St-Germain-des-Prés. Open Tu-F 8:30am-1pm and 4-7:15pm, Sa 8:30am-1pm.

TAXIS

Alpha Taxis, ☎45 85 85 85.

Service des Taxis de la Préfecture de Police, 36, r. des Morillons, 75015 (☎55 76 20 00). M: Convention.

Taxis 7000, ☎42 70 00 42.

Taxis Bleus, ☎49 36 10 10.

Taxis G7, ☎47 39 47 39.

Taxis Radio Etoile, ☎41 27 27 27.

TICKET SERVICES

Kiosque-Théâtre, 15, pl. de la Madeleine, 8*ème*. M: Madeleine. Open Tu-Sa 12:30-7:45pm, Su 12:30-3:45pm. No credit cards.

Kiosque Info Jeune, 25, bd. Bourdon, 4*ème* (☎42 76 22 60). M: Bastille. Also at 101, quai Branly, 5*ème* (☎43 06 15 28). M: Bir Hakeim. Bastille branch open M-F 10am-7pm; quai Branly branch open M-F 9:30-6pm.

Alpha FNAC: Spectacles, 136, r. de Rennes, 6*ème* (☎49 54 30 00). M: Montparnasse-Bienvenüe. Also at Forum des Halles, 1-7, r. Pierre Lescot, 1*er* (☎40 41 40 00), M: Châtelet-Les-Halles; 26, av. des Ternes, 17*ème* (☎44 09 18 00), M: Ternes; and 71, bd. St-Germain, 5*ème* (automated ☎44 41 31 50). Open M-Sa 10am-7:30pm. AmEx, MC, V.

TOURIST OFFICES

Bureau d'Accueil Central: 127, av. des Champs-Elysées, 8*ème* (☎08 36 68 31 12; www.paris-touristoffice.com). M: Georges V. Open in summer daily 9am-8pm; off season Su 11am-6pm.

Bureau Gare de Lyon, 12*ème* (☎43 43 33 24). M: Gare de Lyon. Open M-Sa 8am-8pm.

Bureau Tour Eiffel, Champs de Mars, 7*ème* (☎45 51 22 15). M: Champs de Mars. Open May-Sept. daily 11am-6pm.

Bureau de Tourisme RATP, pl. de la Madeleine, 8*ème* (☎40 06 71 44). M: Madeleine. Open M-Sa 8:30am-6:45pm, Su 6:30am-1pm.

Orly: Sud, Gate H (☎49 75 00 90). **Ouest,** Gate F (☎49 75 01 39). Both open daily 6am-11:30pm.

Roissy-Charles de Gaulle, Gate 36, arrival level (☎48 62 27 29). Open daily 7am-10pm.

TOURS

Bateaux-Mouches (☎42 25 96 10; info ☎40 76 99 99). M: Alma-Marceau. 1½hr. tours in English. Departures every 30min. 10am-11pm from the Right Bank pier near Pont d'Alma. 40F, ages 4-14 20F, under 4 free.

Bullfrog Bike Tours, (☎06 09 98 08 60; email BullfrogBikes@hotmail.com; www.bullfrogbikes.com). Tours meet on the Champ de Mars in front of the Eiffel Tower (look for the flag). May 10-Sept. 15, rain or shine, daily 11am and 3:30pm. Night tours Su-Th 8pm; reservations required. Tickets 130F or $20US.

Canauxrama, 13, quai de la Loire, 19*ème* (☎42 39 15 00; fax 42 39 11 24). Reservations required. Departures either from Port de l'Arsenal (M: Gaures) or La Villette (M: Bastille) at 9:45am and 2:45pm. Call ahead to book and find out departure point.

Paris à velo, c'est sympa!, 37, bd. Bourdon, 4*ème* (☎48 87 60 01). M: Bastille. 3hr. tours 10am, 3pm. 170F, under 26 150F. Rentals available with a 2000F (or credit card) deposit. 24hr. rental 150F; 9am-7pm 80F. ½day (9am-2pm or 2pm-7pm) 60F.

Paristoric, 11bis, r. Scribe, 9*éme*(☎42 66 62 06; www.paris-story.com), M: Opéra. Shows daily on the hour Nov.-Mar. 9am-8pm; Apr.-Oct. 10am-6pm. 50F, students and children 30F, under 6 and 2nd child in a family free.

Paris-Vélo, 24, r. de Fer-à-Moulin, 5*ème* (☎43 37 59 22). M: Censier Daubenton. 150F per person, 26 and under 120F. Open M-Sa 10am-12:30pm and 2-7pm.

Vedette Pont-Neuf Boats (☎46 33 98 38). M: Pont-Neuf or Louvre. Departures daily 10:30, 11:15am, noon, and every 30min. between 1:30 and 6:30pm. Leave from the Pont Neuf landing. 50F, under 12 25F.

TRANSPORTATION

Aéroport d'Orly, English info ☎49 75 15 15. Open 6am-11:45pm.

Air France/Charles de Gaulle Airport, ☎48 62 22 80. 24hr. English hotline.

Air France/Charles de Gaulle Airport Buses, ☎41 56 89 00.

Airport Shuttle to Charles de Gaulle, ☎45 38 55 72.

Eurolines, ☎08 36 69 52 52.

Orlyval, ☎43 46 14 14.

Paris Airports Service, ☎49 62 78 78.

Paris Shuttle, ☎43 90 91 91.

RATP, ☎08 36 68 77 14 (French), ☎08 36 68 41 14 (English).

Roissybus, ☎48 04 18 24.

SNCF, ☎08 36 35 35 (3F per min.).

WOMEN'S RESOURCES

Bibliothèque Marguerite Duras, 79, r. Nationale, 13*ème* (☎45 70 80 30). M: Nationale. Open M-Sa 2-6pm.

Centre de Planification et d'Education familiale, 27, r. Curnonsky, 17*ème* (☎48 88 07 28). M: Porte de Champerret. Open M-F 9am-5pm.

Maison des Femmes, 163, r. de Charenton, 12*ème* (☎43 43 41 13; fax 43 43 42 13). M: Gare de Lyon. Open M-Tu and Th 9am-1pm, W and F 3-7pm; library open W 6-8pm.

Mouvement Français pour le Planning Familial (MFPF), 10, r. Vivienne, 2*ème* (☎42 60 93 20). M: Bourse. Open M-F 9:30am-5:30pm. On F, the clinic is held at 94, bd. Massanna, on the 1st fl. of the Tour Mantoue, door code 38145, *13ème* (☎45 84 28 25). M: Porte Ivry.

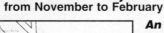

Index

a

d

e

f

g

h

i

j

k

l

m

n

t

V

W

XYZ

Maps

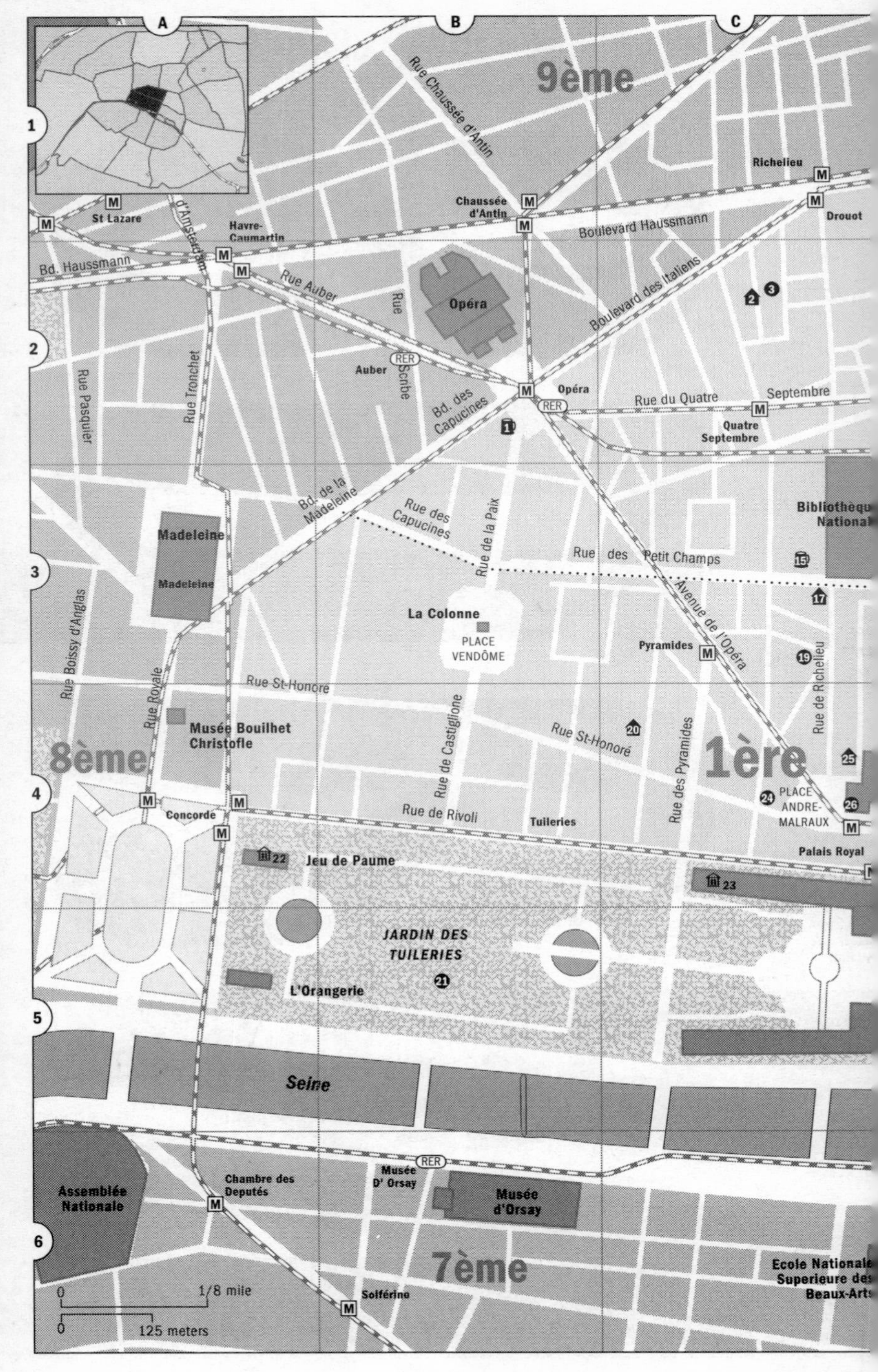

A
B
C
1
2
3
4
5
6
9ème
8ème
1ère
7ème
Rue Chaussée d'Antin
Richelieu
St Lazare
Chaussée d'Antin
Drouot
Havre-Caumartin
d'Amsterdam
Boulevard Haussmann
Bd. Haussmann
Rue Auber
Rue Scribe
Opéra
Boulevard des Italiens
Auber
RER
Rue Tronchet
Rue Pasquier
Bd. des Capucines
Rue du Quatre Septembre
Quatre Septembre
Bd. de la Madeleine
Rue des Capucines
Rue de la Paix
Bibliothèque National
Madeleine
Rue des Petit Champs
Avenue de l'Opéra
La Colonne
PLACE VENDÔME
Pyramides
Rue Boissy d'Anglas
Rue Royale
Rue St-Honore
Rue St-Honoré
Rue de Castiglione
Rue des Pyramides
Rue de Richelieu
Musée Bouilhet Christofle
Concorde
Rue de Rivoli
Tuileries
PLACE ANDRE-MALRAUX
Palais Royal
Jeu de Paume
JARDIN DES TUILERIES
L'Orangerie
Seine
Musée D' Orsay
Chambre des Deputés
Assemblée Nationale
Musée d'Orsay
Ecole Nationale Superieure des Beaux-Arts
Solférino
0
1/8 mile
125 meters

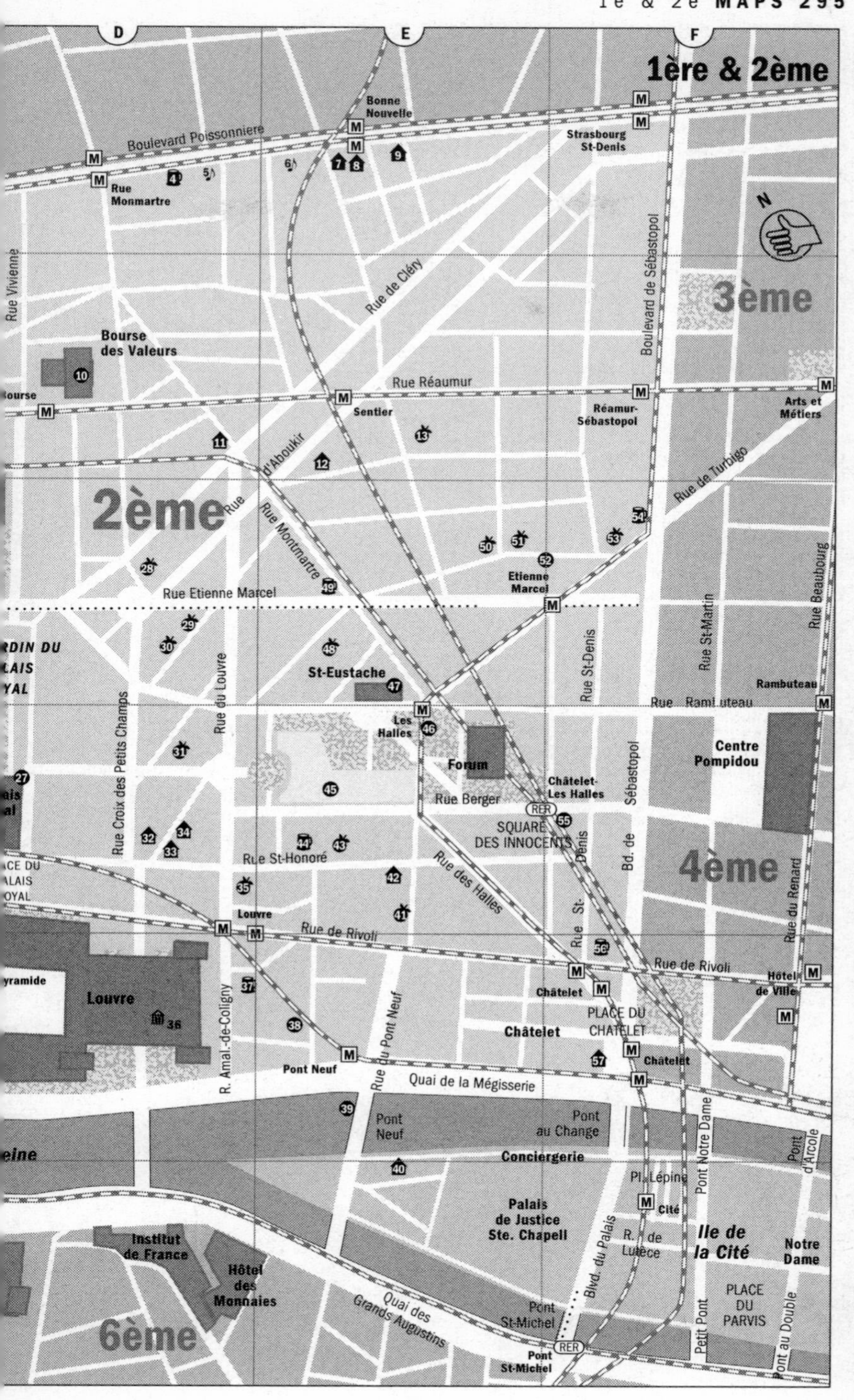

1ère & 2ème
Bonne Nouvelle
Boulevard Poissonniere
Strasbourg St-Denis
Rue Monmartre
Rue Vivienne
Rue de Cléry
Boulevard de Sébastopol
3ème
Bourse des Valeurs
Rue Réaumur
Sentier
Réaumur-Sébastopol
Arts et Métiers
Rue d'Aboukir
Rue de Turbigo
2ème
Rue Montmartre
Etienne Marcel
Rue Etienne Marcel
Rue Beaubourg
Rue St-Martin
Rue St-Denis
Rue du Louvre
St-Eustache
Rambuteau
Rue Rambuteau
Les Halles
Forum
Centre Pompidou
Rue Croix des Petits Champs
Châtelet-Les Halles
Rue Berger
RER
SQUARE DES INNOCENTS
Bd. de Sébastopol
4ème
Rue St-Honoré
Rue des Halles
Rue du Renard
Louvre
Rue de Rivoli
Hôtel de Ville
Louvre
Châtelet
PLACE DU CHATELET
R. Amal.-de-Coligny
Rue du Pont Neuf
Pont Neuf
Quai de la Mégisserie
Pont Neuf
Pont au Change
Conciergerie
Pont Notre Dame
Pont d'Arcole
Pl. Lépine
Cité
Palais de Justice Ste. Chapell
Institut de France
Hôtel des Monnaies
Blvd. du Palais
R. de Lutèce
Ile de la Cité
Notre Dame
PLACE DU PARVIS
Quai des Grands Augustins
Pont St-Michel
Petit Pont
Pont au Double
6ème

1ère & 2ème

ACCOMMODATIONS

Name	Grid
Centre International de Paris, 34	D4
Henri IV, 40	E6
Hôtel Bonne Nouvelle, 9	E1
Hôtel des Boulevards, 8	E1
Hôtel du Palais, 57	F5
Hôtel Favart, 2	C2
Hôtel La Marmotte, 12	E2
Hôtel Lion d'Or, 20	C4
Hôtel Louvre-Richelieu, 17	C3
Hôtel Montpensier, 25	C4
Hôtel Saint-Honoré, 42	E4
Hôtel Ste-Marie, 14	E1
Hôtel Vivienne, 11	D1
Maison des Jeunes de Rufz de Lavision, 33	D4
Timhotel Le Louvre, 32	D4

SIGHTS

Name	Grid
Arc de Triomphe du Carrousel, 24	C4
Bibliothèque Nationale Site Richelieu, 14	D3
Bourse des Valeurs, 10	D4
Bourse du Commerce, 45	E4
Comédie Francaise, 26	C4
Eglise de St-Eustache, 47	E3
Eglise St-Germain l'Auxerrois, 38	E5
Fontaine des Innocents, 55	F4
Fontaine Molière, 19	C3
Jardin des Tuileries, 21	B5
Les Halles, 46	E4
Opéra Comique, 3	C2
Palais Royal, 27	D4
Pont Neuf, 39	E5
Tour de Jean Sans Peur, 52	E3

FOOD

Name	Grid
Au Vide Gousset, 28	D3
Babylone Bis, 51	E3
Café de l'Epoque, 31	D4
Japanese Barbecue, 13	E2
Jules, 48	E3
La Victoire Suprême du Coeur, 41	E4
Le Dénicheur, 53	F3
Le Fumoir, 35	D4
Le Loup Blanc, 50	E3
L'Epi d'Or, 30	D3
Papou Lounge, 29	D3
Pizza Sicilia, 18	D3
Signorelli, 43	E4

CLUBS

Name	Grid
Rex Club, 6	D2
Pulp!, 5	D1

MUSEUMS

Name	Grid
Galerie National du Jeu de Paume, 22	A4
Le Louvre, 36	D5
Musée de la Mode et du Textile, 23	C4

PUBS

Name	Grid
Banana Café, 44	E4
Café Oz, 56	F5
Flann O'Brien's, 37	D4
Frog & Rosbif, 54	F3
Harry's Bar, 1	B2
Le Café Noir, 49	E3
Le Champmeslé, 15	C3
Le Fumoir, 35	D4
Le Scorp, 4	D1

3ème & 4ème

ACCOMMODATIONS

Castex Hôtel, 73	E5
Grand Hôtel Jean d'Arc, 65	D4
Hôtel Andrea, 86	A4
Hôtel Bellevue et du Chariot d'Or, 8	A2
Hôtel de Bretagne, 5	C2
Hôtel de la Place des Vosges, 71	E4
Hôtel de Nice, 48	C4
Hôtel de Roubaix, 9	A2
Hôtel de Sejour, 14	A3
Hôtel Paris France, 1	B2
Hôtel Picard, 4	C2
Hôtel Practic, 66	D4
Le Fauconnier, 78	D5
Le Fourcy, 77	D5
Maubuisson, 84	C5

PUBS

Au Petit Fer a Cheval, 51	C4
Chez Richard, 38	C4
Cox, 44	B4
La Belle Hortense, 50	C4
L'Apparement Café, 18	D3
L'Attiral, 7	B2
Le Détour, 59	D4
Le Piano Zinc, 36	B4
Le Quetzal, 45	C4
Les Scandaleuses, 55	C4
Lizard Lounge, 47	C4
L'Unity, 30	A3
Open Café, 43	B4
Utopia, 16	B3
WebBar, 3	D2

SIGHTS

Archives Nationales, 23	C3
Carreau du Temple, 2	C2
Centre Pompidou, 32	A4
Eglise St-Gervais-St-Protais, 84	C5
Eglise St-Paul-St-Louis, 75	D5
Fontaine Stravinsky, 34	B4
Hôtel Carnavalet, 62	D4
Hôtel de Beauvais, 81	C5
Hôtel de Lamoignon, 64	D4
Hôtel de Sens, 78	D5
Hôtel de Sully, 68	E4
Hôtel de Ville, 85	B5
Hôtel Libéral-Bruant, 21	D3
Hôtel Salé, 20	D3
La Maison Européen de la Photographie, 79	D5
Mémorial du Martyr Juif Inconnu, 82	C5
pl. des Vosges, 67	E4
Tour St-Jacques, 88	A4

FOOD

Amnésia Café, 49	C4
Aquarius, 35	B4
Au Gamin de Paris, 39	C4
Au Petit Fer à Cheval, 42	C4
Café Beaubourg, 31	A4
Chez Marianne, 41	C4
Chez Omar, 6	C2
En Attendant Pablo, 22	C3
Equinox, 54	C4
La Baromètre, 10	C3
La Belle Hortense, 40	C4
La Théière Dans Les Nuages, 80	C4
L'Apparemment Café, 18	D3
L'As du Falafel, 53	D4
Le Divin, 37	B4
Le Grizzli, 87	A4
Le Hangar, 28	B3
Le Marais Plus, 61	D4
Le Petit Bofinger, 72	F4
Le Petit Gavroche, 46	C4
Le Réconfort, 11	C3
Le Tapis Franc, 25	B3
Le Vieux Comptoir, 69	E4
Les Enfants Gâtés, 57	D4
L'Excuse, 74	E5
Okhawa Café, 54	C4
Piccolo Teatro, 56	C4
Restaurant Pachamama, 29	B3
Taxi Jaune, 12	B3

CLUBS

Les Bains, 13	A3
Le Café du Trésor, 52	C4
Le Duplex, 15	B3

MUSEUMS

Maison de J. Hérouet, 58	C4
Maison de Victor Hugo, 70	E4
Musée Adam Mickiewicz, 89	C6
Musée Carnavalet, 63	D4
Musée Cognacq-Jay, 60	D4
Musée de la Chasse, 17	C3
Musée de la Poupée, 27	B3
Musée de l'Art et d'Histoire de Judaism, 26	B3
Musée de l'Histoire de France, 24	C3
Musée Natioonal d'Art Moderne, 33	B4
Musée Picasso, 19	D3

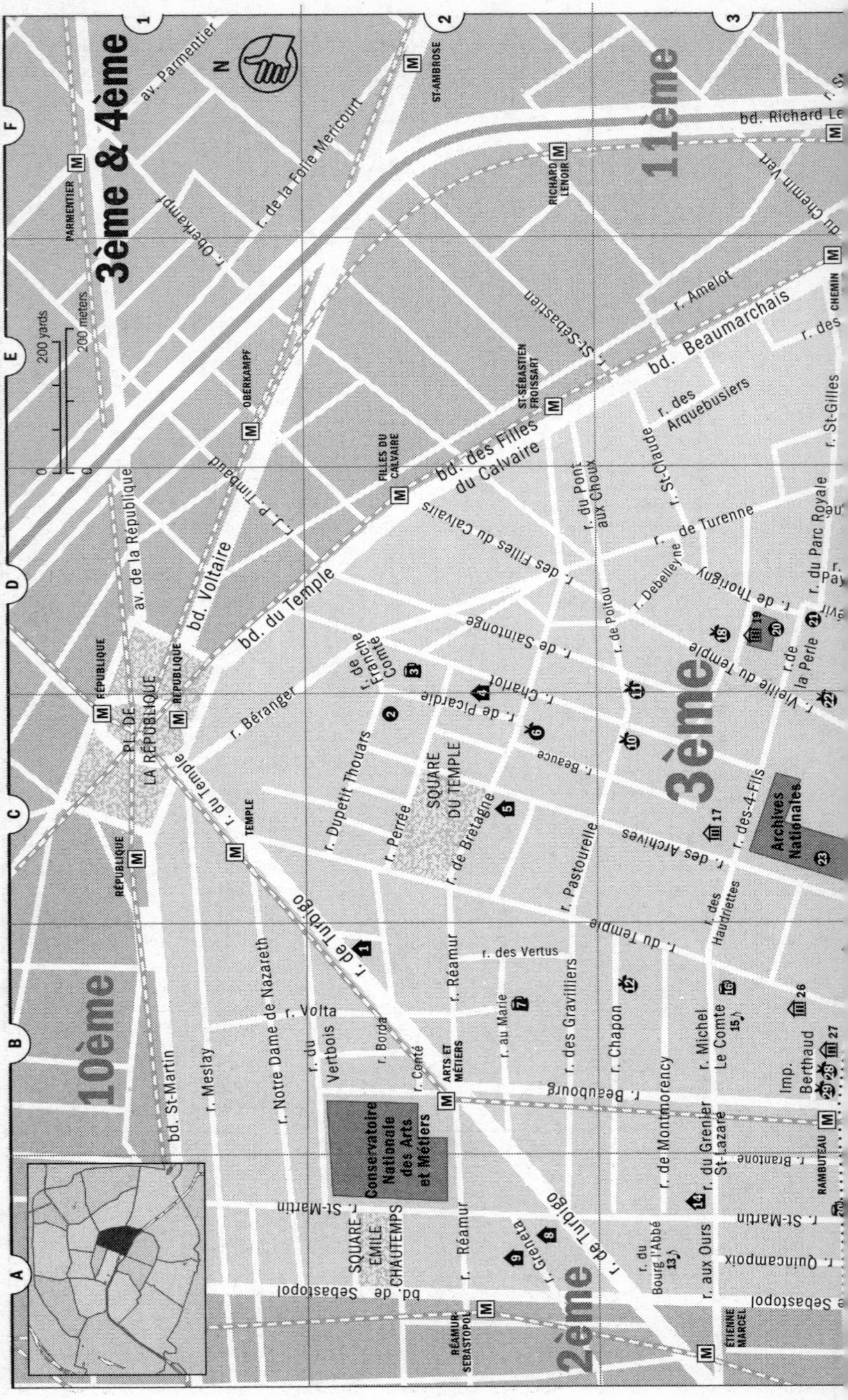

3ème & 4ème

N

0 200 yards
0 200 meters

10ème
11ème
3ème
2ème

PL. DE LA RÉPUBLIQUE
SQUARE DU TEMPLE
SQUARE EMILE CHAUTEMPS
Conservatoire Nationale des Arts et Métiers
Archives Nationales

PARMENTIER
RÉPUBLIQUE
TEMPLE
OBERKAMPF
FILLES DU CALVAIRE
ST-AMBROSE
RICHARD LENOIR
ST-SÉBASTIEN FROISSART
CHEMIN
ARTS ET MÉTIERS
RÉAUMUR-SEBASTOPOL
RAMBUTEAU
ETIENNE MARCEL

av. Parmentier
r. de la Folie Mericourt
r. Oberkampf
bd. Richard Le
r. du Chemin Vert
r. Amelot
r. St-Sébastien
bd. Beaumarchais
r. des Arquebusiers
r. St-Claude
r. St-Gilles
bd. des Filles du Calvaire
r. J. P. Timbaud
av. de la République
bd. Voltaire
bd. du Temple
r. du Pont aux Choux
r. de Turenne
r. des Filles du Calvaire
r. du Parc Royale
r. Debelleyne
r. de Poitou
r. de Thorigny
r. de Santonge
r. de Franche Comté
r. Béranger
r. Charlot
r. de Picardie
r. Dupetit Thouars
r. Perrée
r. de Bretagne
r. Beauce
r. du Temple
r. Vieille du Temple
r. de la Perle
r. des Archives
r. des-4-Fils
r. Pastourelle
r. des Haudriettes
r. de Turbigo
r. des Vertus
r. Réaumur
r. au Marie
r. des Gravilliers
r. Chapon
r. Michel Le Comte
Imp. Berthaud
r. Volta
r. Notre Dame de Nazareth
r. du Vertbois
r. Borda
r. Conté
r. Meslay
bd. St-Martin
r. Beaubourg
r. de Montmorency
r. du Grenier St-Lazare
r. Brantone
r. St-Martin
r. aux Ours
r. du Bourg l'Abbé
r. Quincampoix
r. Greneta
bd. de Sebastopol
r. Payenne

1 2 3 4 5 6 7 8 9 10 11 12 13 14 15 16 17 18 19 20 21 22 23 26 27 28 29

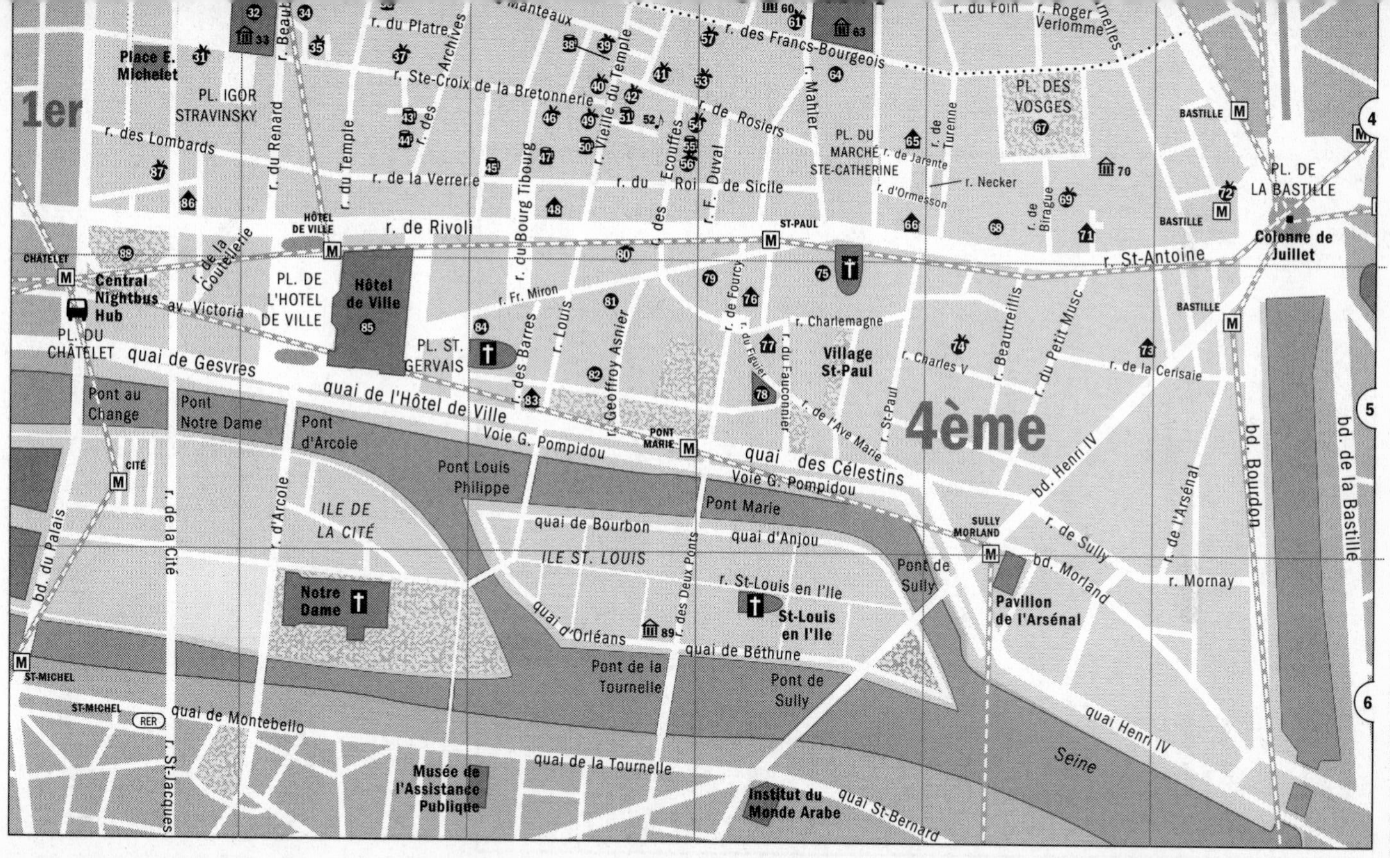
1er
4ème
Place E. Michelet
PL. IGOR STRAVINSKY
r. du Platre
r. des Archives
r. Ste-Croix de la Bretonnerie
r. Vieille du Temple
r. des Francs-Bourgeois
r. du Foin
r. Roger Verlomme
PL. DES VOSGES
r. des Lombards
r. du Renard
r. du Temple
r. des Ecouffes
r. de Rosiers
r. Mahler
PL. DU MARCHÉ STE-CATHERINE
r. de Jarente
r. de Turenne
r. Necker
r. d'Ormesson
r. de Birague
PL. DE LA BASTILLE
Colonne de Juillet
BASTILLE
r. de la Verrerie
r. du Bourg Tibourg
r. du Roi de Sicile
r. F. Duval
ST-PAUL
HÔTEL DE VILLE
r. de Rivoli
r. St-Antoine
CHATELET
r. de la Coutellerie
Central Nightbus Hub
av. Victoria
PL. DE L'HOTEL DE VILLE
Hôtel de Ville
r. Fr. Miron
r. Louis
r. des Barres
r. Geoffroy Asnier
r. de Fourcy
r. du Figuier
r. du Fauconnier
r. Charlemagne
Village St-Paul
r. Charles V
r. Beautreillis
r. du Petit Musc
r. de la Cerisaie
PL. DU CHÂTELET
quai de Gesvres
PL. ST. GERVAIS
quai de l'Hôtel de Ville
r. de l'Ave Marie
r. St-Paul
bd. Henri IV
bd. Bourdon
bd. de la Bastille
Pont au Change
Pont Notre Dame
Pont d'Arcole
Voie G. Pompidou
PONT MARIE
quai des Célestins
CITÉ
Pont Louis Philippe
Pont Marie
r. de la Cité
r. d'Arcole
ILE DE LA CITÉ
quai de Bourbon
quai d'Anjou
ILE ST. LOUIS
SULLY MORLAND
r. de Sully
r. de l'Arsénal
bd. du Palais
Notre Dame
r. des Deux Ponts
r. St-Louis en l'Ile
St-Louis en l'Ile
Pont de Sully
bd. Morland
r. Mornay
Pavillon de l'Arsénal
quai d'Orléans
quai de Béthune
ST-MICHEL
Pont de la Tournelle
RER
quai de Montebello
quai Henri IV
Seine
quai de la Tournelle
r. St-Jacques
Musée de l'Assistance Publique
Institut du Monde Arabe
quai St-Bernard

5ème & 6ème

ACCOMMODATIONS

Association des Etudiants Protestants de Paris, 28	B4
Dhely's Hôtel, 41	C2
Foyer International des Etudiantes, 35	C4
Hôtel de Chevreuse, 32	C4
Hôtel de Neslé, 5	B2
Hôtel des Medicis, 38	C4
Hôtel du Lys, 42	C2
Hôtel du Progrès, 40	C5
Hôtel Gay Lussac, 39	D4
Hôtel le Central, 56	D3
Hôtel Marignan, 42	C2
Hôtel St-André des Arts, 15	B2
Hôtel Stella, 34	C4
Hôtel St-Jacques, 53	D3

SIGHTS

Collège de France, 52	C3
Ecole Nationale Supérieur des Beaux Arts, 1	A2
Eglise de St-Germain-des-Prés, 10	A2
Eglise St-Julien-le-Pauvre, 49	C2
Eglise St-Sulpice, 26	B3
Hôtel Cluny, 43	C3
Jardin des Plantes, 68	E3
Jardin des Sculptures en Plein Air, 70	F3
Jardin du Luxembourg, 30	B4
La Sorbonne, 46	C3
Ménagerie, 71	F3
Mosquée de Paris, 67	E4
Palais de l'Institut de France, 2	A1
Palais du Luxembourg, 27	B4
The Pantheon, 58	D4
Théâtre de l'Odeon, 25	B3

MUSEUMS

Grande Galerie d'Evolution, 69	F4
Institut du Monde Arabe, 64	E3
Musée de Cluny, 45	C3
Musée de la Monnaie, 3	B2
Musée de Minéralogie, 63	E3
Musée Delacroix, 9	A2
Musée d'Histoire Naturelle, 69	F4
Musée Zakadine, 33	B5

FOOD

Au Jardin des Patés, 65	E4
Aux Deux Magots, 11	A2
Bistro Mazarin, 6	B2
Café de Flore, 14	A3
Café de la Mosquée, 66	E4
Café Mabillon, 13	A2
Coffee Parisien, 18	A3
Comptoir Méditerrainée, 59	D3
Cosi, 7	B2
Crêperie St-Germain, 16	B2
Guen Mai, 8	A2
La Cambuse, 24	B3
La Truffière, 61	D4
L'Apostrophe, 55	D3
Le Crêpe Rit du Clown, 19	A3
Le Grenier de Notre-Dame, 50	D2
Le Machon d'Henri, 21	A3
Le Petit Vatel, 22	B3
Le Procope, 17	B2
Le Séléct, 31	A6
Mexi and Co., 48	C2
Restaurant Perraudin, 37	C4
Sans Frontières, 29	A4
Savanah Café, 57	D3

PUBS

Café Mabillon, 12	A2
Chez Georges, 20	A3
Finnegan's Wake, 62	E3
Greuze, 36	C4
L'Assignat, 4	B2
Le Bar Dix, 23	B3
Le Piano Vache, 54	D3
Le Reflet, 44	C3
Sarl le Salon Egyptien, 60	D3

CLUBS

Le Saint, 47	C2

9ème & 18ème

ACCOMMODATIONS

Grand Hôtel de Clermont, 9	*C2*
Hôtel André Gill, 17	*D3*
Hôtel Beauharnais, 27	*C5*
Hôtel Caulaincourt, 2	*C1*
Hôtel Chopin, 32	*D6*
Hôtel des Arts, 29	*E6*
Perfect Hôtel, 25	*D4*
Style Hôtel, 5	*A2*
Village Hostel, 13	*E2*
Woodstock Hostel, 26	*E4*

CLUBS

Bus Palladium, 22	*C3*
Divan du Monde, 19	*D3*
Elysée Montmartre, 20	*D3*
Folies Pigalle, 21	*C3*
La Cigale, 16	*D3*

PUBS

Chez Camille, 6	*C2*
Le Fourmi, 18	*D3*

FOOD

Au Grain de Folie, 11	*D2*
Café de la Paix, 33	*B6*
Chez Ginette, 3	*D1*
Deli's Café, 30	*D6*
Halle St-Pierre, 14	*E2*
Haynes Bar, 24	*D4*
La Petite Charlotte, 8	*C2*
Le Café Zephyr, 31	*D6*
Le Sancerre, 10	*C2*
Le Soleil Gourmand, 7	*C2*
Pizzéria King Solomon, 28	*D5*
Rayons de Santé, 15	*D3*
Refuge des Fondues, 12	*D2*
Rendez-vous des Chauffeurs, 4	*F1*
Sarangui, Anarkali, 23	*C4*
Wassana, 1	*B1*

7ème

ACCOMMODATIONS

Grand Hôtel Lévêque, 9	*C3*
Hôtel Amelie, 7	*C3*
Hôtel de France, 16	*C4*
Hôtel de la Paix, 6	*B3*
Hôtel du Champs de Mars, 11	*C4*
Hôtel Eiffel Rive Gauche, 15	*C4*
Hôtel Malar, 5	*B3*
Royal Phare Hôtel, 13	*C4*

FOOD

Au Pied de Fouet, 23	*E5*
Café des Lettres, 26	*F3*
Café du Marché, 10	*C3*
Chez Lucie, 3	*B3*
Grannie, 24	*E5*
La Varangue, 4	*B3*
Le Club des Poètes, 22	*D3*
Le Comptoir du 7ème, 14	*C4*
Le Lotus Blanc, 21	*D3*

MUSEUMS

Musée de l'Armée, 18	*D3*
Musée de l'Ordre de la Libération, 17	*D4*
Musée des Egouts de Paris, 1	*B2*
Musée des Plans-Reliefs, 19	*D4*
Musée d'Histoire Contemporaine, 19	*D4*
Musée d'Orsay, 25	*F3*
Musée Rodin, 20	*D4*
Musée-Galerie de la SEITA, 2	*C2*

PUBS

Master's Bar, 12	*C4*
O'Brien's, 8	*C3*

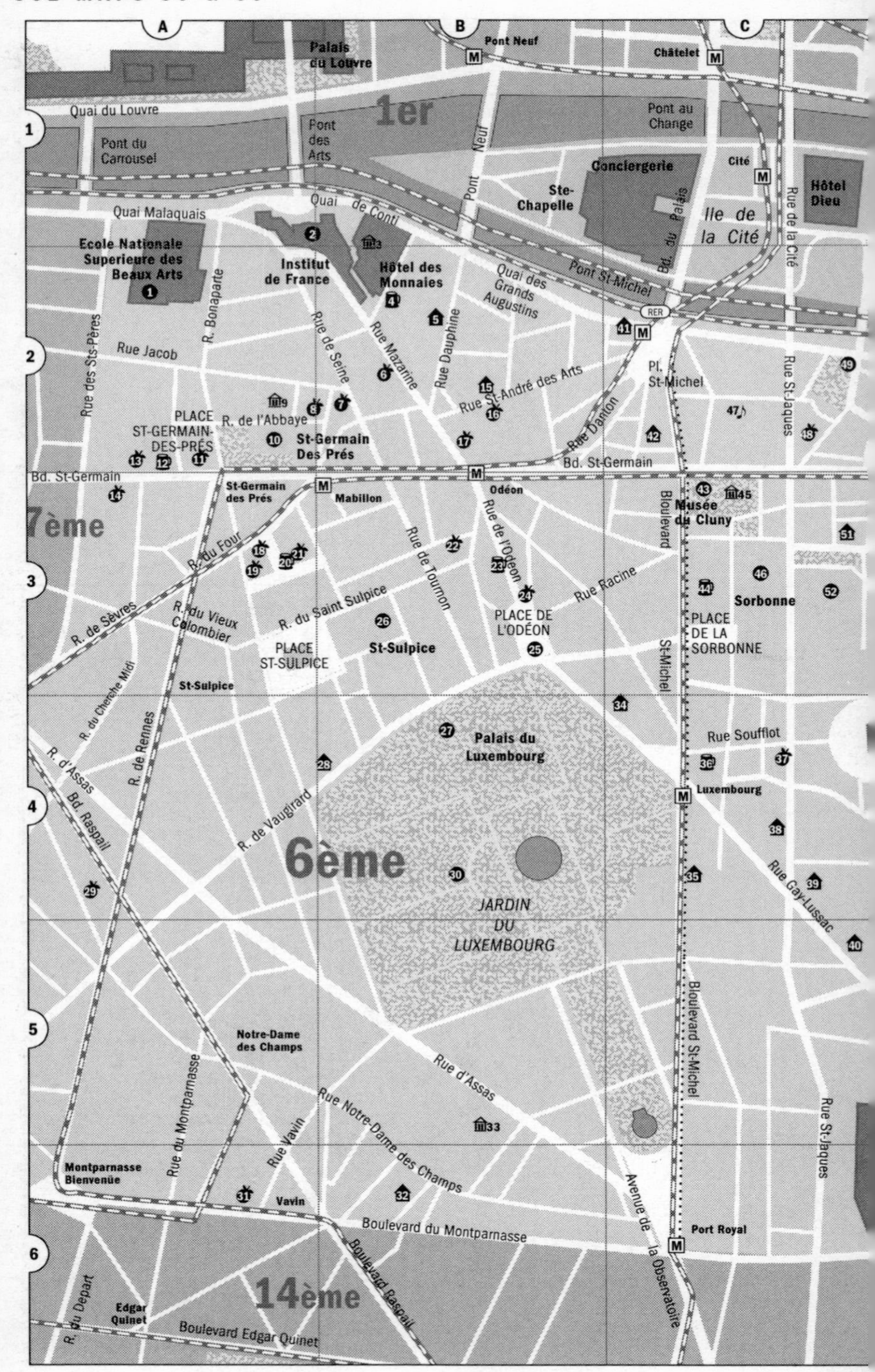

Palais du Louvre
Pont Neuf
Châtelet
1er
Quai du Louvre
Pont du Carrousel
Pont des Arts
Pont au Change
Cité
Conciergerie
Ste-Chapelle
Hôtel Dieu
Ile de la Cité
Quai de Conti
Quai Malaquais
Ecole Nationale Superieure des Beaux Arts
Institut de France
Hôtel des Monnaies
Quai des Grands Augustins
Pont St-Michel
Bd. du Palais
Rue de la Cité
R. Bonaparte
Rue de Seine
Rue Mazarine
Rue Dauphine
RER
Rue des Sts-Pères
Rue Jacob
Rue St-André des Arts
Pl. St-Michel
Rue St-Jacques
PLACE ST-GERMAIN-DES-PRÉS
R. de l'Abbaye
St-Germain Des Prés
Rue Danton
Bd. St-Germain
St-Germain des Prés
Mabillon
Odéon
Boulevard St-Michel
Musée du Cluny
7ème
R. du Four
Rue de Tournon
Rue de l'Odéon
Rue Racine
Sorbonne
R. du Vieux Colombier
R. du Saint Sulpice
PLACE DE L'ODÉON
PLACE DE LA SORBONNE
R. de Sèvres
PLACE ST-SULPICE
St-Sulpice
R. du Cherche Midi
R. de Rennes
Palais du Luxembourg
Rue Soufflot
R. d'Assas
Bd. Raspail
R. de Vaugirard
Luxembourg
6ème
Rue Gay-Lussac
JARDIN DU LUXEMBOURG
Notre-Dame des Champs
Rue d'Assas
Rue du Montparnasse
Rue Notre-Dame des Champs
Rue Vavin
Montparnasse Bienvenüe
Vavin
Avenue de la Observatoire
Port Royal
Boulevard du Montparnasse
Boulevard Raspail
14ème
R. du Depart
Edgar Quinet
Boulevard Edgar Quinet
A
B
C
1
2
3
4
5
6

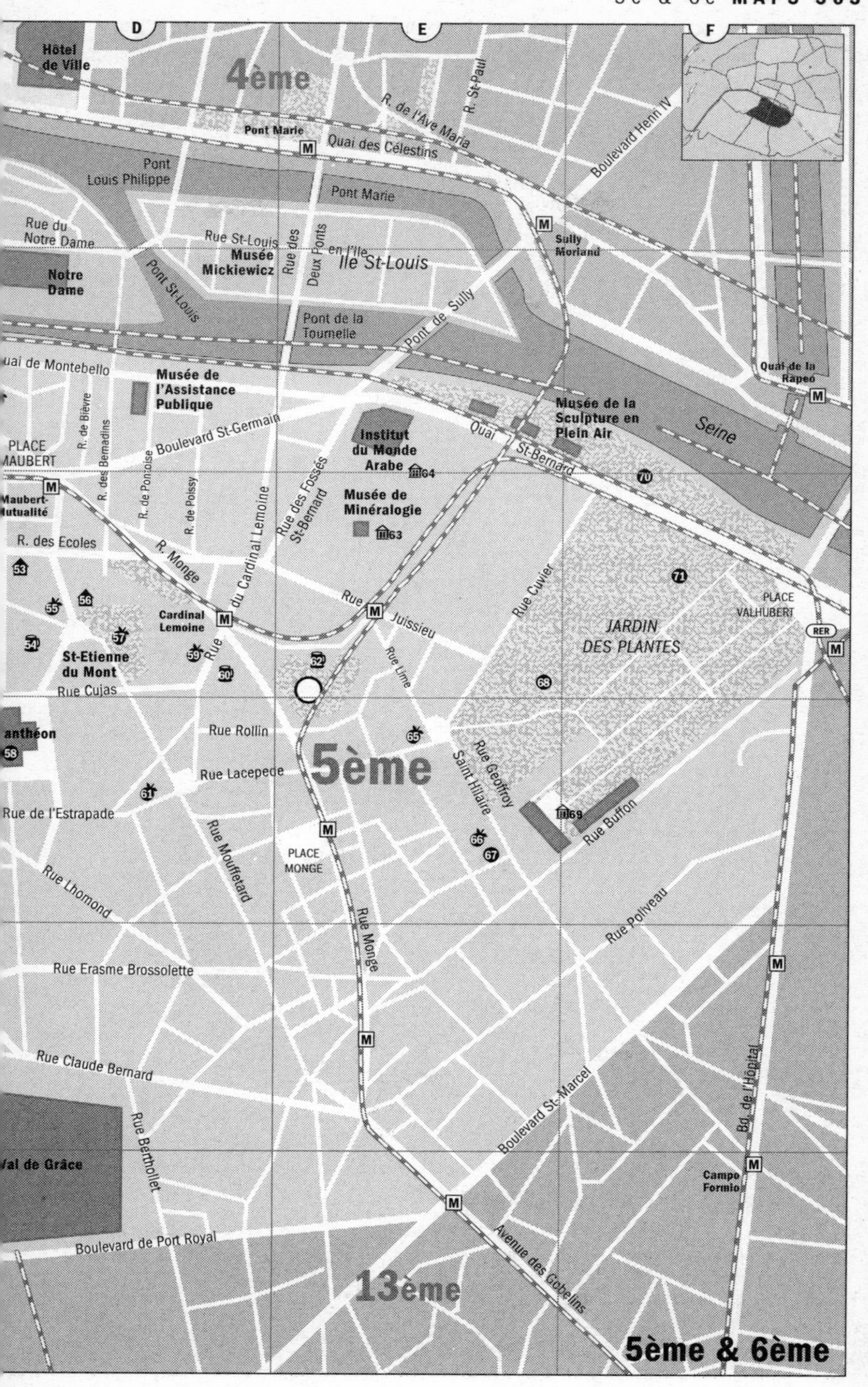
D
E
F
Hôtel de Ville
4ème
R. St-Paul
R. de l'Ave Maria
Pont Marie
Quai des Célestins
Boulevard Henri IV
Pont Louis Philippe
Pont Marie
Rue du Notre Dame
Rue St-Louis en l'Ile
Musée Mickiewicz
Rue des Deux Ponts
Ile St-Louis
Sully Morland
Notre Dame
Pont St-Louis
Pont de Sully
Pont de la Tournelle
Quai de Montebello
Musée de l'Assistance Publique
Quai de la Rapée
Musée de la Sculpture en Plein Air
Seine
R. de Bièvre
R. des Bernadins
PLACE MAUBERT
Boulevard St-Germain
Institut du Monde Arabe
64
Quai St-Bernard
70
Maubert-Mutualité
R. de Pontoise
R. de Poissy
Rue du Cardinal Lemoine
Rue des Fossés St-Bernard
Musée de Minéralogie
63
R. des Ecoles
R. Monge
53
Rue Cuvier
71
Rue Juissieu
PLACE VALHUBERT
55
56
Cardinal Lemoine
JARDIN DES PLANTES
RER
54
57
St-Etienne du Mont
59
62
Rue Lime
60
Rue Cujas
68
Panthéon
Rue Rollin
65
58
Rue Geoffroy Saint Hilaire
5ème
Rue Lacepede
61
69
Rue de l'Estrapade
Rue Buffon
Rue Mouffetard
66
67
PLACE MONGE
Rue Lhomond
Rue Poliveau
Rue Monge
Rue Erasme Brossolette
Rue Claude Bernard
Boulevard St-Marcel
Bd. de l'Hôpital
Rue Berthollet
Val de Grâce
Campo Formio
Avenue des Gobelins
Boulevard de Port Royal
13ème
5ème & 6ème

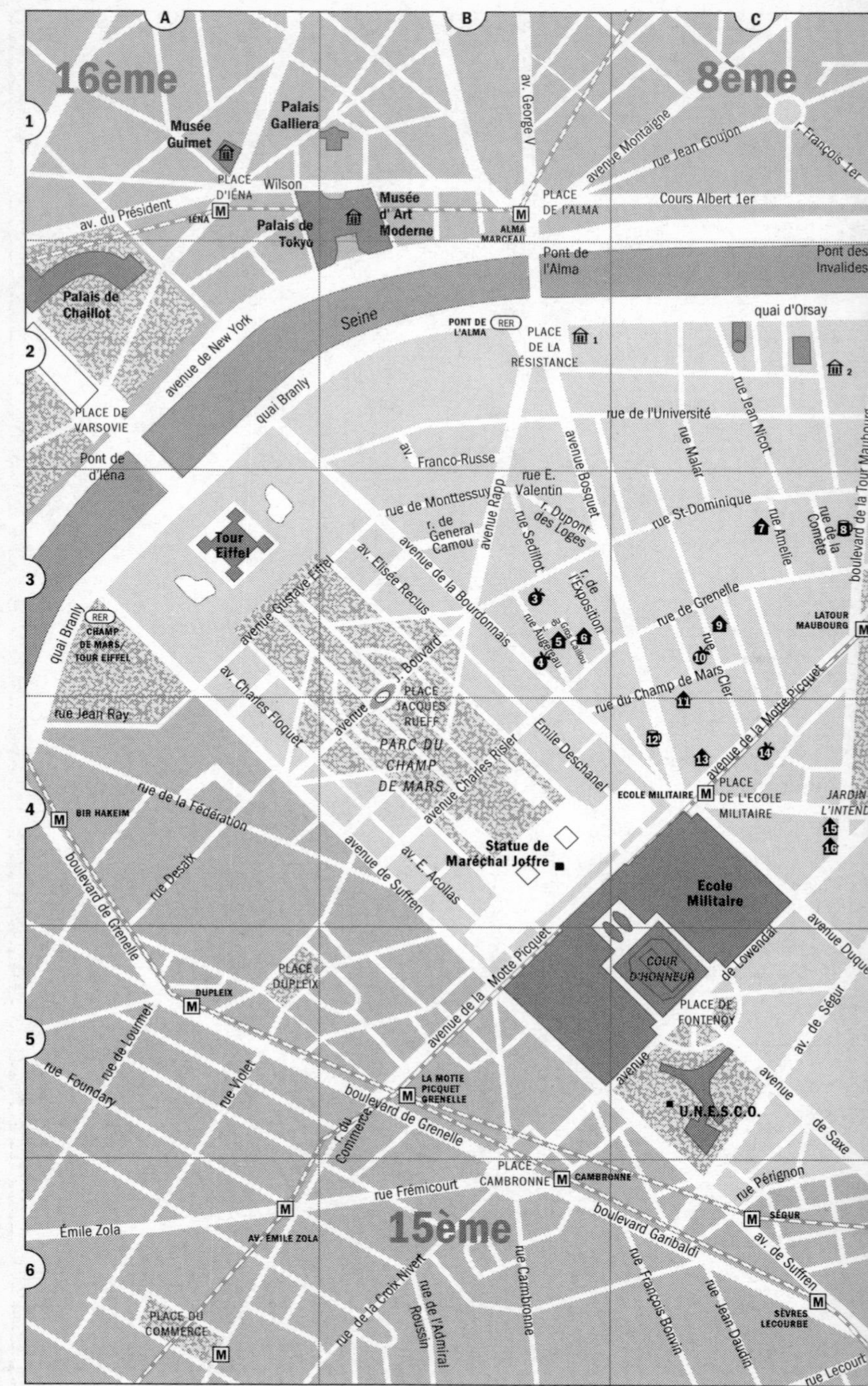
16ème
8ème
15ème
Musée Guimet
Palais Galliera
Musée d'Art Moderne
Palais de Tokyo
Palais de Chaillot
PLACE D'IÉNA
IÉNA
ALMA MARCEAU
PLACE DE L'ALMA
Pont de l'Alma
Pont des Invalides
Seine
PONT DE L'ALMA
RER
PLACE DE LA RÉSISTANCE
PLACE DE VARSOVIE
Pont de d'Iéna
Tour Eiffel
CHAMP DE MARS/ TOUR EIFFEL
PLACE JACQUES RUEFF
PARC DU CHAMP DE MARS
Statue de Maréchal Joffre
Ecole Militaire
COUR D'HONNEUR
ECOLE MILITAIRE
PLACE DE L'ECOLE MILITAIRE
LATOUR MAUBOURG
JARDIN L'INTEND
PLACE DE FONTENOY
U.N.E.S.C.O.
BIR HAKEIM
DUPLEIX
PLACE DUPLEIX
LA MOTTE PICQUET GRENELLE
PLACE CAMBRONNE
CAMBRONNE
SÉGUR
AV. ÉMILE ZOLA
PLACE DU COMMERCE
SÈVRES LECOURBE
av. du Président Wilson
av. George V
avenue Montaigne
rue Jean Goujon
r. François 1er
Cours Albert 1er
quai d'Orsay
avenue de New York
quai Branly
rue de l'Université
rue Jean Nicot
rue Malar
boulevard de la Tour Maubourg
av. Franco-Russe
avenue Bosquet
rue E. Valentin
rue de Monttessuy
r. de General Camou
avenue Rapp
rue Sédillot
r. Dupont des Loges
rue St-Dominique
rue Amélie
rue de la Comète
av. Elisée Reclus
avenue de la Bourdonnais
avenue Gustave Eiffel
r. de l'Exposition
rue Augereau
r. du Gros Caillou
rue de Grenelle
rue Cler
rue du Champ de Mars
avenue de la Motte-Picquet
av. Charles Floquet
avenue J. Bouvard
Emile Deschanel
avenue Charles Risler
rue Jean Ray
rue de la Fédération
avenue de Suffren
av. E. Acollas
rue Desaix
boulevard de Grenelle
avenue de la Motte Picquet
de Lowendal
avenue Duquesne
av. de Ségur
avenue de Saxe
rue de Lourmel
rue Foundary
rue Violet
r. du Commerce
rue Frémicourt
rue Pérignon
Émile Zola
boulevard Garibaldi
av. de Suffren
rue de la Croix Nivert
rue de l'Admiral Roussin
rue Cambronne
rue François Bonvin
rue Jean Daudin
rue Lecourbe
A
B
C
1
2
3
4
5
6

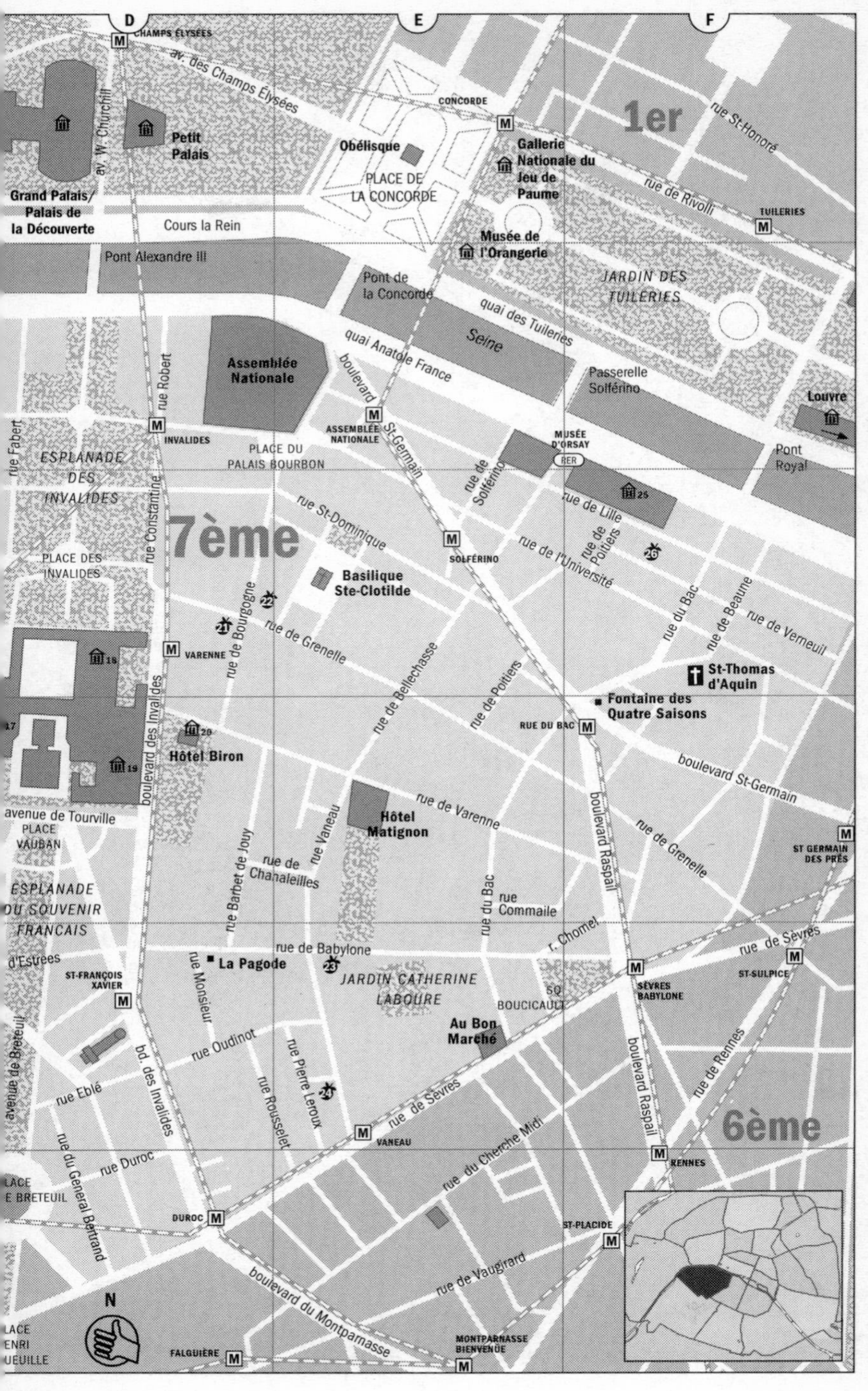
D
E
F
CHAMPS ÉLYSÉES
av. des Champs Élysées
CONCORDE
1er
rue St-Honoré
av. W. Churchill
Petit Palais
Obélisque
Gallerie Nationale du Jeu de Paume
PLACE DE LA CONCORDE
rue de Rivoli
Grand Palais/ Palais de la Découverte
TUILERIES
Cours la Rein
Musée de l'Orangerie
Pont Alexandre III
Pont de la Concorde
JARDIN DES TUILERIES
quai des Tuileries
Seine
quai Anatole France
Assemblée Nationale
boulevard St-Germain
rue Robert
Passerelle Solférino
Louvre
INVALIDES
ASSEMBLÉE NATIONALE
MUSÉE D'ORSAY
RER
rue Fabert
ESPLANADE DES INVALIDES
PLACE DU PALAIS BOURBON
Pont Royal
rue de Solférino
25
rue de Lille
rue St-Dominique
7ème
rue Constantine
rue de Poitiers
26
rue de l'Université
SOLFÉRINO
PLACE DES INVALIDES
Basilique Ste-Clotilde
22
rue du Bac
rue de Beaune
rue de Verneuil
21
rue de Bourgogne
rue de Grenelle
VARENNE
18
rue de Bellechasse
rue de Poitiers
St-Thomas d'Aquin
Fontaine des Quatre Saisons
17
20
RUE DU BAC
Hôtel Biron
19
boulevard des Invalides
boulevard St-Germain
avenue de Tourville
PLACE VAUBAN
rue Vaneau
Hôtel Matignon
rue de Varenne
boulevard Raspail
rue de Grenelle
rue Barbet de Jouy
rue de Chanaleilles
ST GERMAIN DES PRES
ESPLANADE DU SOUVENIR FRANCAIS
rue du Bac
rue Commaile
r. Chomel
rue de Babylone
rue de Sèvres
d'Estrees
La Pagode
23
ST-FRANÇOIS XAVIER
JARDIN CATHERINE LABOURE
SÈVRES BABYLONE
ST-SULPICE
rue Monsieur
SQ BOUCICAULT
Au Bon Marché
avenue de Breteuil
rue Oudinot
rue de Rennes
bd. des Invalides
rue Pierre Leroux
rue Rousselet
boulevard Raspail
rue Eblé
24
rue de Sèvres
6ème
VANEAU
rue du Cherche Midi
rue Duroc
RENNES
rue du General Bertrand
LACE E BRETEUIL
DUROC
ST-PLACIDE
rue de Vaugirard
N
boulevard du Montparnasse
LACE ENRI UEUILLE
FALGUIÈRE
MONTPARNASSE BIENVENÜE

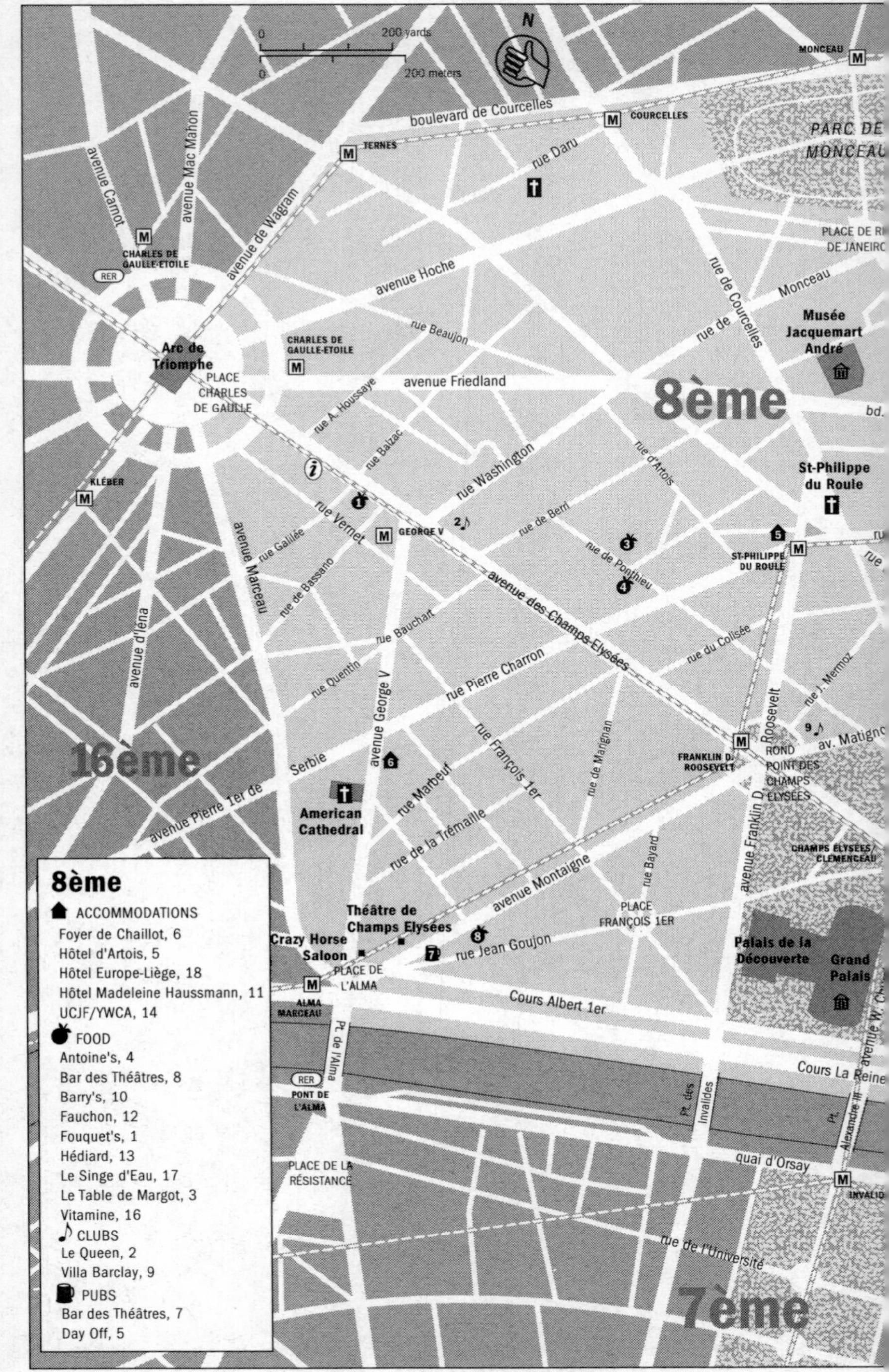

8ème
ACCOMMODATIONS
Foyer de Chaillot, 6
Hôtel d'Artois, 5
Hôtel Europe-Liège, 18
Hôtel Madeleine Haussmann, 11
UCJF/YWCA, 14
FOOD
Antoine's, 4
Bar des Théâtres, 8
Barry's, 10
Fauchon, 12
Fouquet's, 1
Hédiard, 13
Le Singe d'Eau, 17
Le Table de Margot, 3
Vitamine, 16
CLUBS
Le Queen, 2
Villa Barclay, 9
PUBS
Bar des Théâtres, 7
Day Off, 5
boulevard de Courcelles
avenue Hoche
avenue Friedland
avenue de Wagram
avenue Marceau
avenue des Champs-Elysées
avenue George V
avenue Montaigne
Cours Albert 1er
Cours La Reine
quai d'Orsay
rue de l'Université
Arc de Triomphe
PLACE CHARLES DE GAULLE
American Cathedral
Théâtre de Champs Elysées
Crazy Horse Saloon
Palais de la Découverte
Grand Palais
Musée Jacquemart André
St-Philippe du Roule
PARC DE MONCEAU
8ème
16ème
7ème

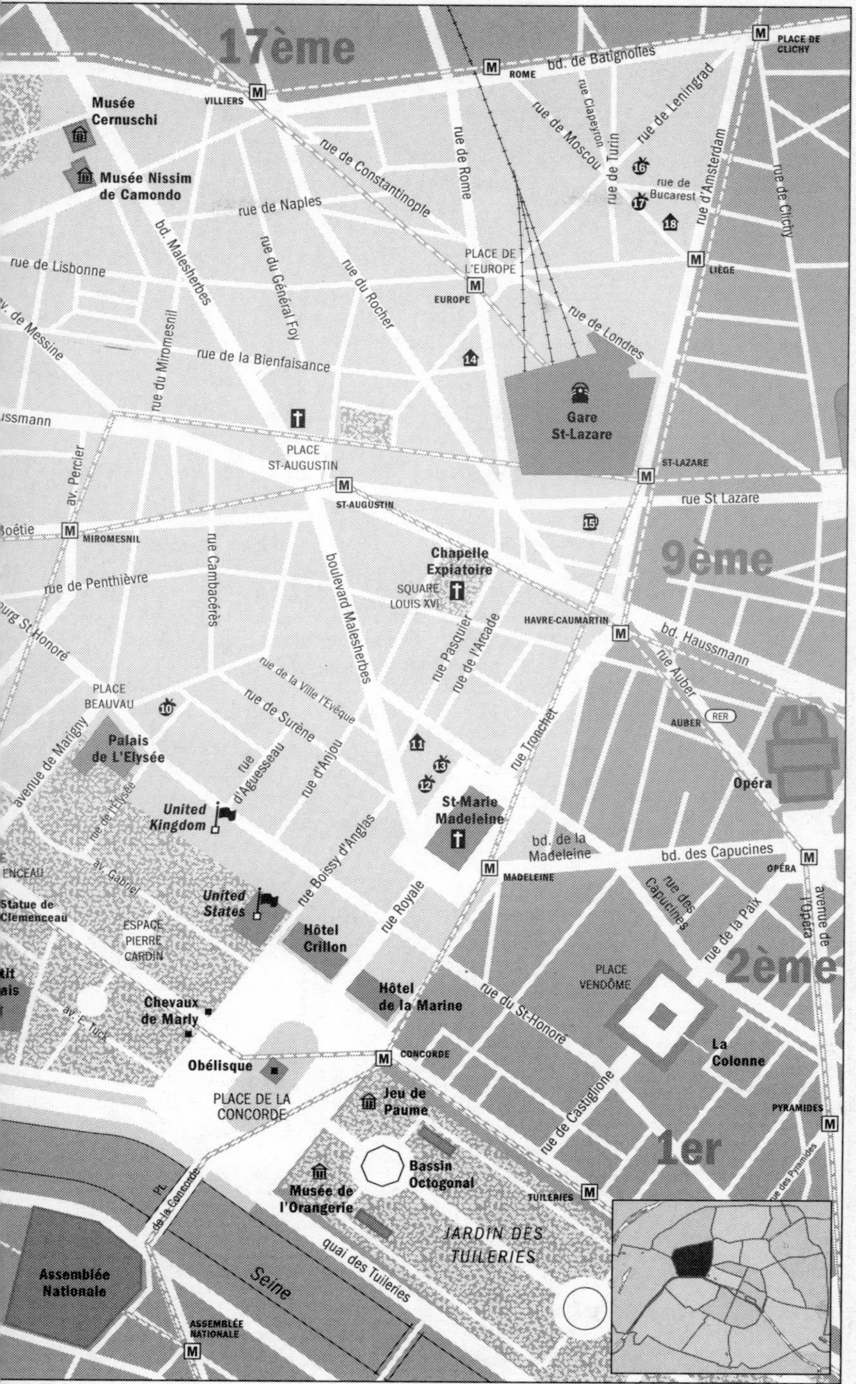

17ème
9ème
2ème
1er
bd. de Batignolles
PLACE DE CLICHY
ROME
VILLIERS
Musée Cernuschi
Musée Nissim de Camondo
rue de Constantinople
rue de Rome
rue de Moscou
rue Clapeyron
rue de Turin
rue de Leningrad
rue d'Amsterdam
rue de Clichy
rue de Bucarest
rue de Naples
bd. Malesherbes
rue du Général Foy
rue du Rocher
PLACE DE L'EUROPE
EUROPE
LIÈGE
rue de Lisbonne
av. de Messine
rue du Miromesnil
rue de la Bienfaisance
rue de Londres
Gare St-Lazare
PLACE ST-AUGUSTIN
ST-AUGUSTIN
ST-LAZARE
rue St Lazare
av. Percier
MIROMESNIL
rue Cambacérès
boulevard Malesherbes
Chapelle Expiatoire
SQUARE LOUIS XVI
rue de Penthièvre
HAVRE-CAUMARTIN
bd. Haussmann
rue Auber
AUBER
RER
rue Pasquier
rue de l'Arcade
rue Tronchet
rue de la Ville l'Evêque
rue de Surène
rue d'Anjou
rue d'Aguesseau
PLACE BEAUVAU
Palais de L'Elysée
avenue de Marigny
Opéra
St-Marie Madeleine
United Kingdom
rue Boissy d'Anglas
bd. de la Madeleine
bd. des Capucines
MADELEINE
OPÉRA
rue des Capucines
rue de la Paix
avenue de l'Opéra
av. Gabriel
Statue de Clemenceau
United States
ESPACE PIERRE CARDIN
Hôtel Crillon
rue Royale
PLACE VENDÔME
Hôtel de la Marine
rue du St-Honoré
Chevaux de Marly
av. E. Tuck
La Colonne
CONCORDE
Obélisque
PLACE DE LA CONCORDE
Jeu de Paume
rue de Castiglione
PYRAMIDES
Bassin Octogonal
Musée de l'Orangerie
TUILERIES
rue des Pyramides
Pt. de la Concorde
JARDIN DES TUILERIES
quai des Tuileries
Seine
Assemblée Nationale
ASSEMBLÉE NATIONALE

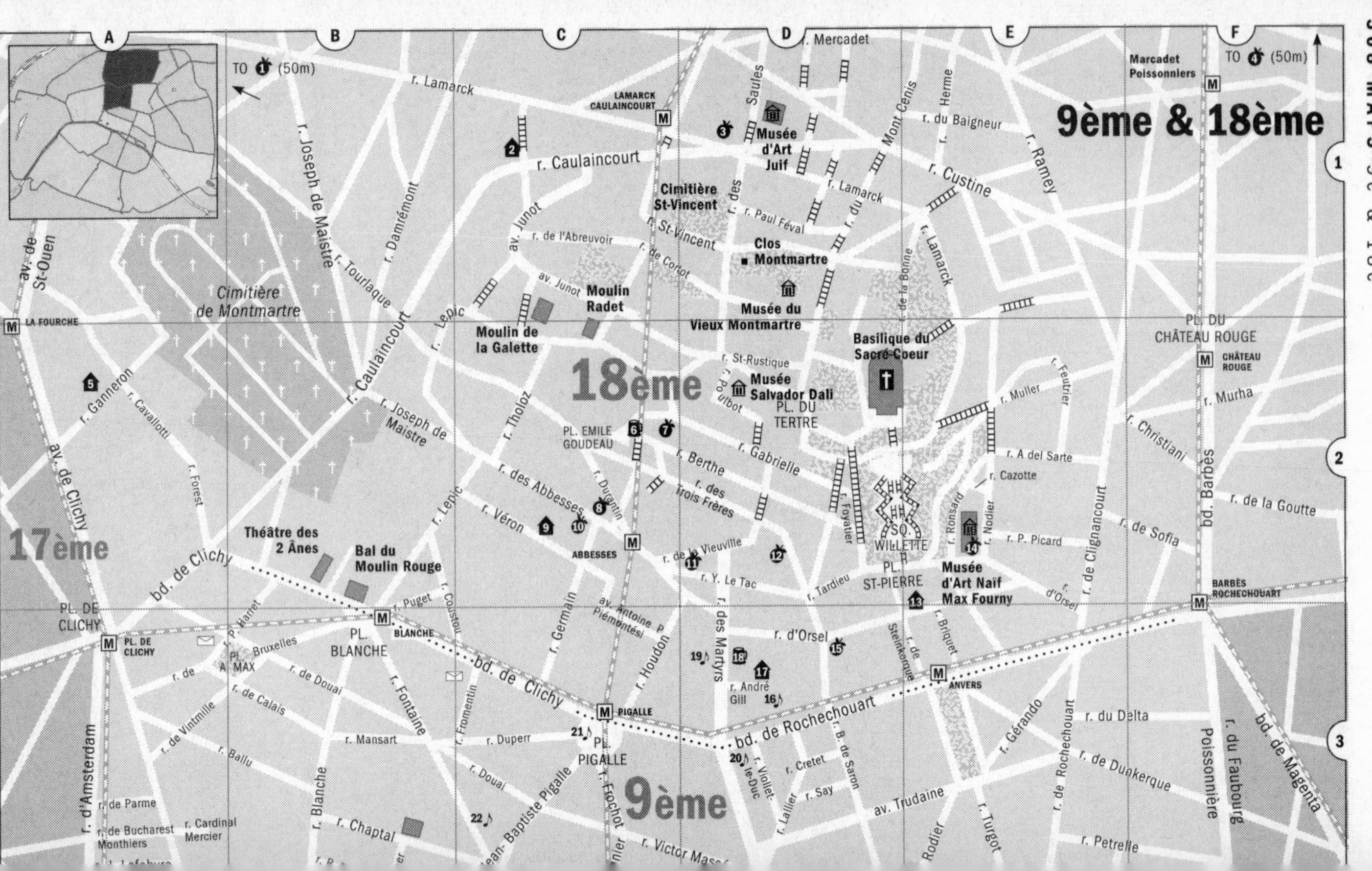
9ème & 18ème
18ème
9ème
17ème
TO (50m)
Marcadet Poissonniers
LAMARCK CAULAINCOURT
LA FOURCHE
ABBESSES
PL. DU CHÂTEAU ROUGE
CHÂTEAU ROUGE
BARBÈS ROCHECHOUART
ANVERS
PIGALLE
BLANCHE
PL. DE CLICHY
r. Mercadet
r. Lamarck
r. Caulaincourt
Cimitière St-Vincent
Musée d'Art Juif
r. du Mont Cenis
r. Hermel
r. du Baigneur
r. Custine
r. Ramey
r. des Saules
r. Paul Féval
r. St-Vincent
r. de Cortot
r. de l'Abreuvoir
av. Junot
Clos Montmartre
Musée du Vieux Montmartre
Moulin Radet
Moulin de la Galette
r. Lepic
r. Joseph de Maistre
r. Damrémont
r. Tourlaque
av. de St-Ouen
Cimitière de Montmartre
r. Ganneron
r. Cavallotti
r. Forest
av. de Clichy
r. Tholoz
r. de la Bonne
Basilique du Sacré-Coeur
r. St-Rustique
r. Poulbot
Musée Salvador Dali
PL. DU TERTRE
PL. EMILE GOUDEAU
r. Berthe
r. Gabrielle
r. des Trois Frères
r. des Abbesses
r. Durantin
r. Véron
r. Foyatier
SQ. WILLETTE
PL. ST-PIERRE
r. Muller
r. Feutrier
r. A del Sarte
r. Cazotte
r. Ronsard
r. Nodier
r. P. Picard
Musée d'Art Naif Max Fourny
r. d'Orsel
r. de Clignancourt
r. Christiani
r. Murha
bd. Barbès
r. de la Goutte
r. de Sofia
Théatre des 2 Ânes
Bal du Moulin Rouge
bd. de Clichy
r. Puget
r. Coustou
r. Germain
av. Antoine. P. Piémontési
r. de la Vieuville
r. Y. Le Tac
r. Tardieu
r. des Martyrs
r. Houdon
r. d'Orsel
r. de Steinkerque
r. Briquet
r. Hamet
PL. A. MAX
r. Bruxelles
PL. BLANCHE
r. de Douai
r. de Calais
r. de Vintimille
r. Ballu
r. Fontaine
r. Fromentin
r. Mansart
r. Duperr
r. André Gill
PL. PIGALLE
bd. de Rochechouart
r. B. de Saron
r. Cretet
r. Say
r. Lallier
r. Viollet-le-Duc
r. Gérando
r. de Rochechouart
r. du Delta
r. de Dunkerque
r. du Faubourg Poissonnière
bd. de Magenta
r. d'Amsterdam
r. de Parme
r. de Bucharest
Monthiers
r. Cardinal Mercier
r. Blanche
r. Chaptal
r. Douai
r. Jean-Baptiste Pigalle
r. Frochot
r. Victor Massé
av. Trudaine
r. Rodier
r. Turgot
r. Petrelle

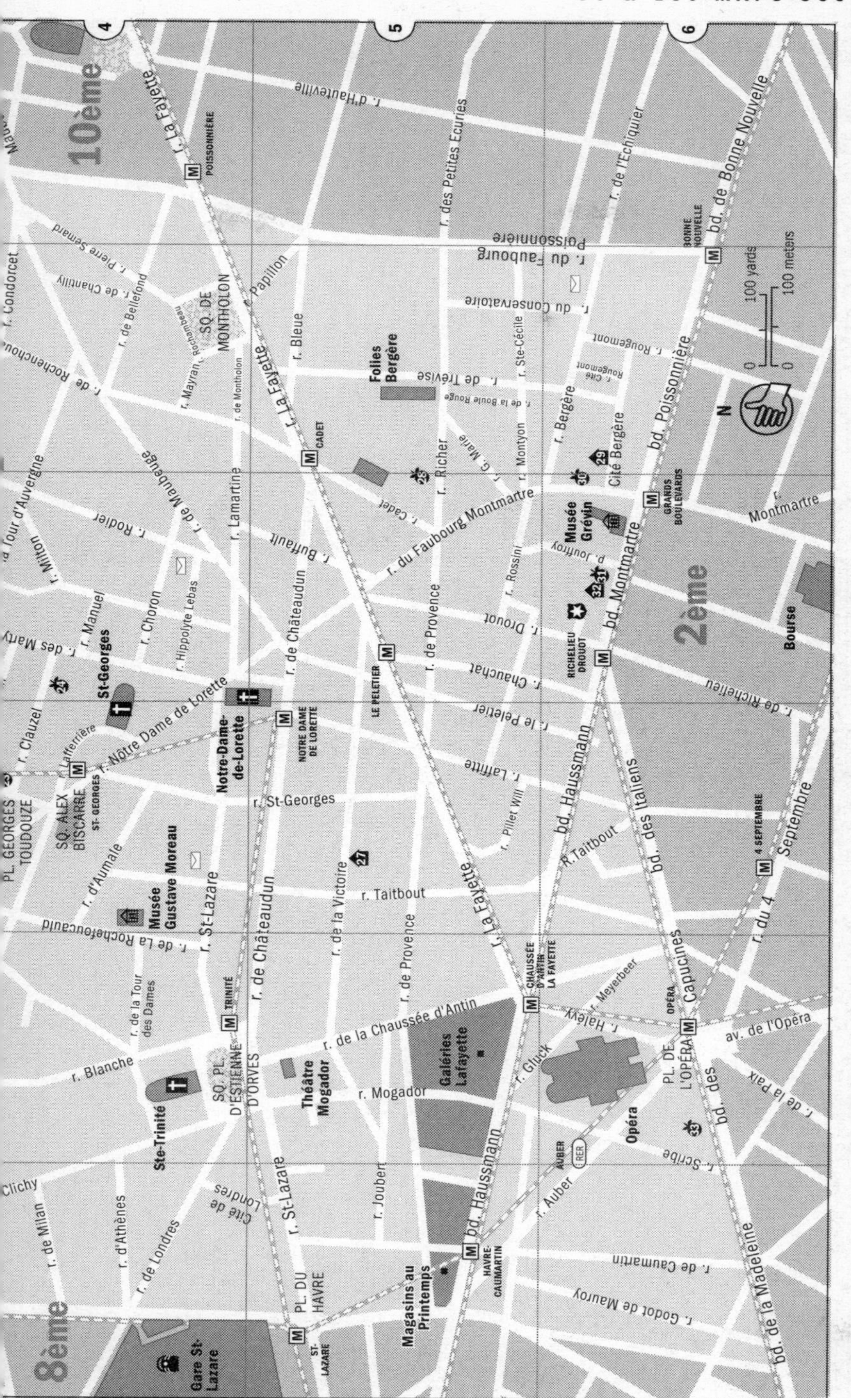
10ème
2ème
8ème
4
5
6
r. La Fayette
r. d'Hauteville
POISSONNIÈRE
r. des Petites Ecuries
r. de l'Echiquier
bd. de Bonne Nouvelle
BONNE NOUVELLE
r. du Faubourg Poissonnière
r. du Conservatoire
r. Rougemont
r. Cité Rougemont
r. Pierre Semard
r. de Chantilly
r. de Bellefond
r. Condorcet
SQ. DE MONTHOLON
r. Rochambeau
r. Mayran
r. de Montholon
r. Papillon
r. Bleue
Folies Bergère
r. de Trévise
r. de la Boule Rouge
r. Ste-Cécile
r. Bergère
Cité Bergère
bd. Poissonnière
100 yards
100 meters
N
r. de Rochechouart
r. Tour d'Auvergne
r. de Maubeuge
r. Lamartine
CADET
r. Richer
r. G. Marie
r. Montyon
r. Cadet
r. Rodier
r. Milton
r. Buffault
r. du Faubourg Montmartre
Musée Grévin
p. Jouffroy
GRANDS BOULEVARDS
r. Montmartre
r. des Martyrs
r. Manuel
r. Choron
r. Hippolyte Lebas
r. de Châteaudun
r. de Provence
r. Rossini
r. Drouot
RICHELIEU DROUOT
bd. Montmartre
Bourse
r. Clauzel
St-Georges
r. Notre Dame de Lorette
Notre-Dame-de-Lorette
NOTRE DAME DE LORETTE
LE PELETIER
r. Chauchat
r. de Richelieu
r. Laferrière
PL. GEORGES TOUDOUZE
SQ. ALEX BISCARRE
ST-GEORGES
r. St-Georges
r. Le Peletier
r. Laffitte
r. Pillet Will
bd. Haussmann
r. d'Aumale
Musée Gustave Moreau
r. St-Lazare
r. de la Victoire
r. Taitbout
R.Taitbout
bd. des Italiens
4 SEPTEMBRE
r. du 4 Septembre
r. de La Rochefoucauld
r. de la Tour des Dames
TRINITÉ
r. de Châteaudun
r. de Provence
r. La Fayette
CHAUSSÉE D'ANTIN LA FAYETTE
r. Meyerbeer
r. de la Chaussée d'Antin
r. Halévy
OPÉRA
Capucines
r. Blanche
Ste-Trinité
SQ. PL. D'ESTIENNE D'ORVES
Théâtre Mogador
Galéries Lafayette
r. Mogador
r. Gluck
PL. DE L'OPÉRA
av. de l'Opéra
r. de la Paix
Opéra
AUBER
RER
r. Scribe
bd. des
Clichy
r. de Milan
r. d'Athènes
r. de Londres
Cité de Londres
r. St-Lazare
r. Joubert
bd. Haussmann
r. Auber
r. de Caumartin
HAVRE CAUMARTIN
Magasins au Printemps
PL. DU HAVRE
ST-LAZARE
Gare St-Lazare
r. Godot de Mauroy
bd. de la Madeleine

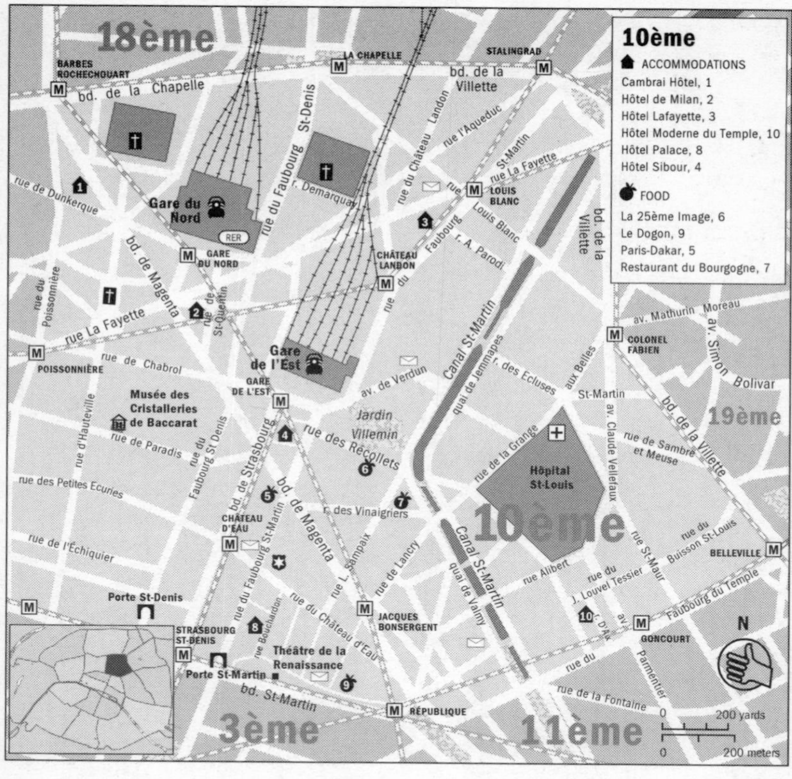
10ème
ACCOMMODATIONS
Cambrai Hôtel, 1
Hôtel de Milan, 2
Hôtel Lafayette, 3
Hôtel Moderne du Temple, 10
Hôtel Palace, 8
Hôtel Sibour, 4
FOOD
La 25ème Image, 6
Le Dogon, 9
Paris-Dakar, 5
Restaurant du Bourgogne, 7
18ème
19ème
10ème
3ème
11ème
BARBES ROCHECHOUART
LA CHAPELLE
STALINGRAD
bd. de la Chapelle
bd. de la Villette
Gare du Nord
RER
GARE DU NORD
Gare de l'Est
GARE DE L'EST
CHÂTEAU LANDON
LOUIS BLANC
COLONEL FABIEN
POISSONNIÈRE
Musée des Cristalleries de Baccarat
CHÂTEAU D'EAU
STRASBOURG ST-DENIS
Porte St-Denis
Porte St-Martin
Théâtre de la Renaissance
JACQUES BONSERGENT
RÉPUBLIQUE
GONCOURT
BELLEVILLE
Hôpital St-Louis
Jardin Villemin
Canal St-Martin
rue de Dunkerque
rue La Fayette
rue de Chabrol
rue de Paradis
rue des Petites Ecuries
rue de l'Échiquier
bd. de Magenta
bd. de Strasbourg
rue du Faubourg St-Denis
rue du Faubourg St-Martin
rue des Récollets
r. des Vinaigriers
av. de Verdun
quai de Jemmapes
quai de Valmy
r. des Ecluses
rue de la Grange aux Belles
av. Claude Vellefaux
rue de Sambre et Meuse
av. Simon Bolivar
av. Mathurin Moreau
bd. de la Villette
rue du Faubourg du Temple
rue de la Fontaine
av. Parmentier
rue Alibert
rue St-Maur
rue du Buisson St-Louis
rue de Lancry
rue L. Sampaix
rue du Château d'Eau
rue Bouchardon
bd. St-Martin
rue d'Hauteville
rue du Poissonnière
rue du Château Landon
rue l'Aqueduc
Louis Blanc
r. A. Parodi
r. Demarquay
rue de St-Quentin
0 200 yards
0 200 meters
N

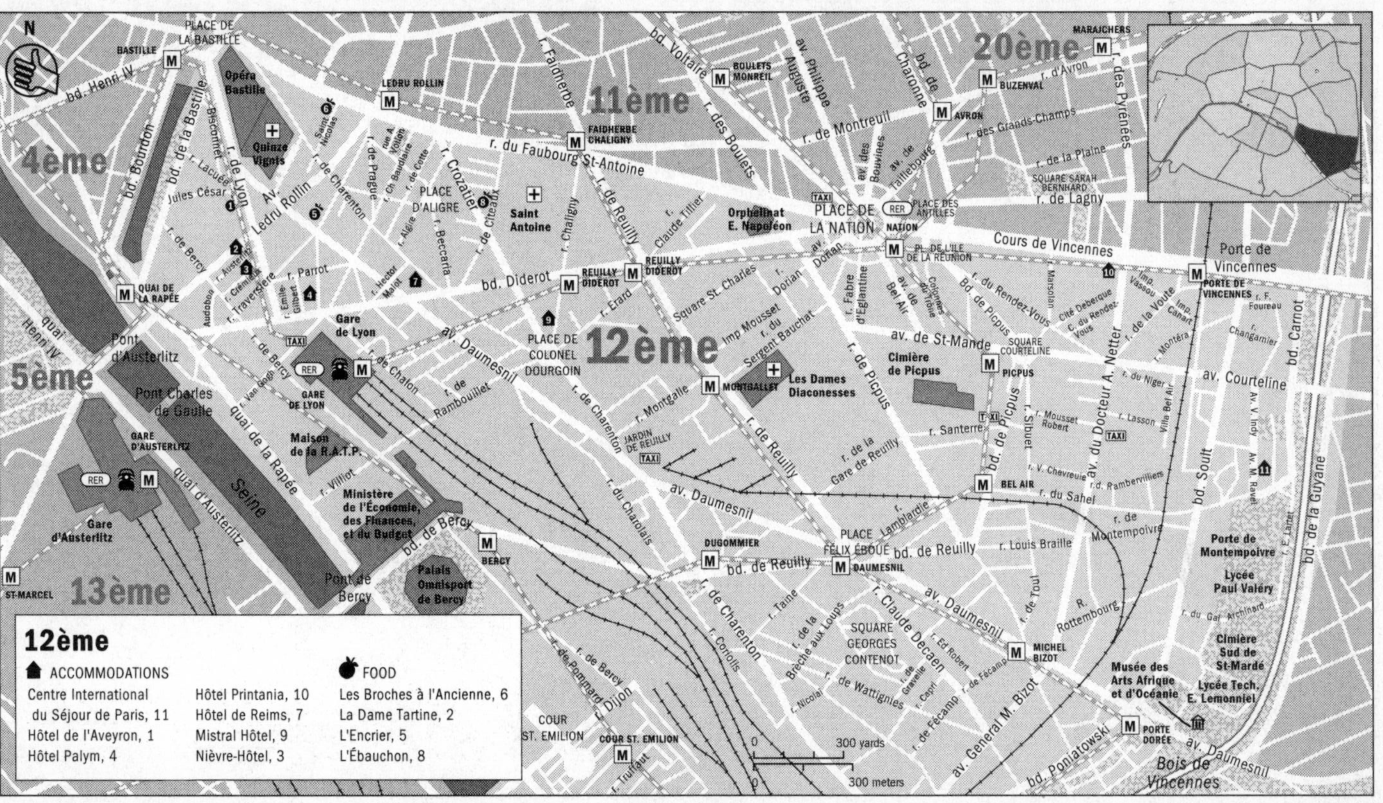

12ème
ACCOMMODATIONS
Centre International du Séjour de Paris, 11
Hôtel de l'Aveyron, 1
Hôtel Palym, 4
Hôtel Printania, 10
Hôtel de Reims, 7
Mistral Hôtel, 9
Nièvre-Hôtel, 3
FOOD
Les Broches à l'Ancienne, 6
La Dame Tartine, 2
L'Encrier, 5
L'Ébauchon, 8
N
4ème
5ème
11ème
12ème
13ème
20ème
PLACE DE LA BASTILLE
BASTILLE
Opéra Bastille
Quinze Vignts
LEDRU ROLLIN
FAIDHERBE CHALIGNY
BOULETS MONREIL
MARAICHERS
BUZENVAL
AVRON
QUAI DE LA RAPÉE
Gare de Lyon
GARE DE LYON
GARE D'AUSTERLITZ
Gare d'Austerlitz
Maison de la R.A.T.P.
Ministère de l'Économie, des Finances, et du Budget
Palais Omnisport de Bercy
BERCY
ST-MARCEL
COUR ST. EMILION
Seine
Pont d'Austerlitz
Pont Charles de Gaulle
Pont de Bercy
quai de la Rapée
quai d'Austerlitz
quai Henri IV
bd. Henri IV
bd. Bourdon
bd. de la Bastille
r. de Lyon
Av. Ledru Rollin
r. du Faubourg St-Antoine
Saint Antoine
PLACE D'ALIGRE
r. Crozatier
bd. Diderot
REUILLY DIDEROT
PLACE DE COLONEL DOURGOIN
av. Daumesnil
r. de Charenton
r. de Reuilly
Orphelinat E. Napoléon
PLACE DE LA NATION
NATION
PLACE DES ANTILLES
PL. DE L'ILE DE LA REUNION
Cours de Vincennes
Porte de Vincennes
PORTE DE VINCENNES
MONTGALLET
Les Dames Diaconesses
r. de Picpus
av. de St-Mandé
Cimière de Picpus
PICPUS
SQUARE COURTELINE
bd. de Picpus
BEL AIR
av. du Docteur A. Netter
bd. Soult
av. Courteline
bd. Carnot
bd. de la Guyane
JARDIN DE REUILLY
DUGOMMIER
PLACE FÉLIX ÉBOUÉ
DAUMESNIL
bd. de Reuilly
r. Claude Decaen
SQUARE GEORGES CONTENOT
MICHEL BIZOT
av. General M. Bizot
PORTE DORÉE
bd. Poniatowski
Musée des Arts Afrique et d'Océanie
Lycée Tech. E. Lemonniel
Cimière Sud de St-Mardé
Lycée Paul Valéry
Porte de Montempoivre
Bois de Vincennes
0 300 yards
0 300 meters

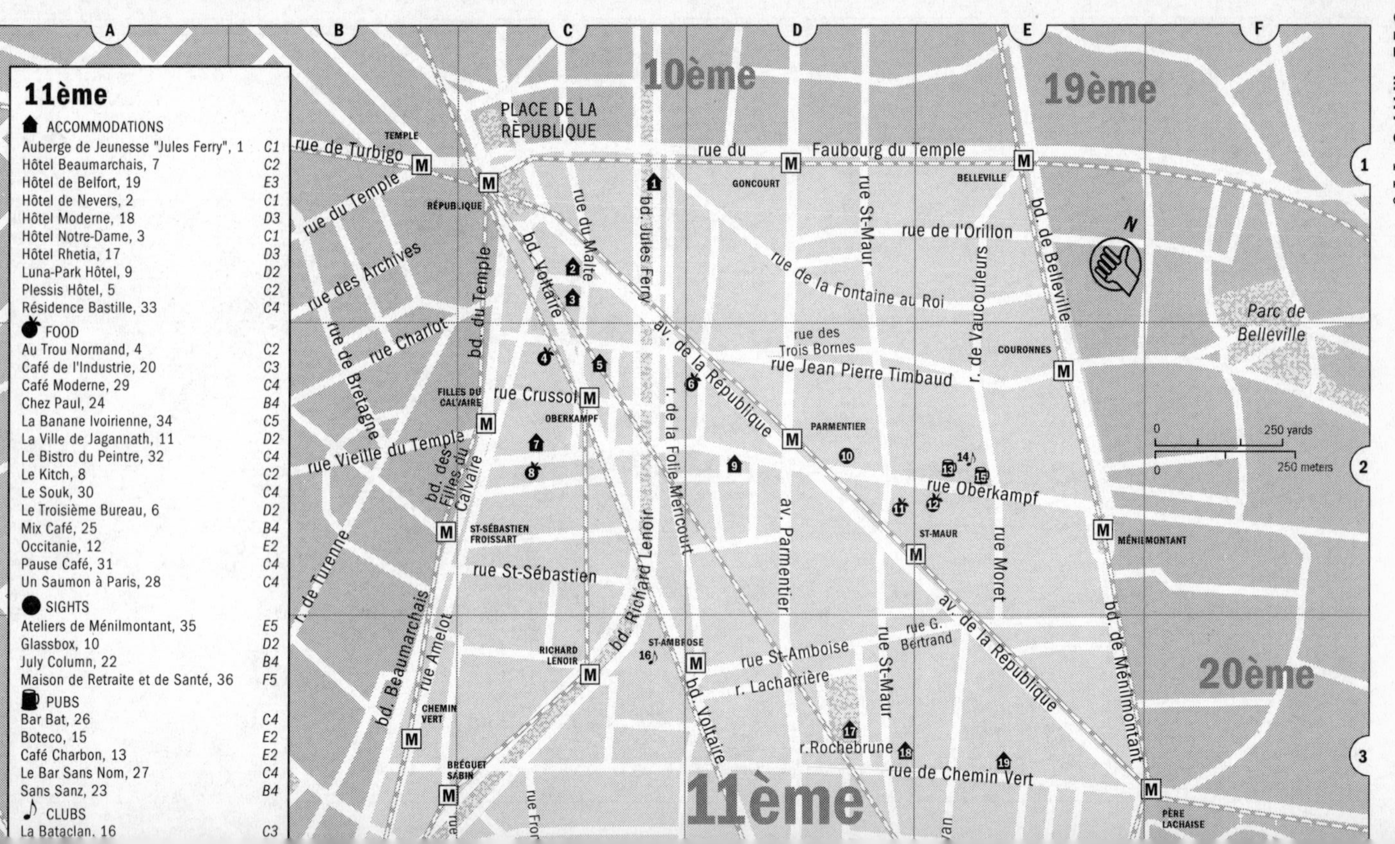
11ème
ACCOMMODATIONS
Auberge de Jeunesse "Jules Ferry", 1 C1
Hôtel Beaumarchais, 7 C2
Hôtel de Belfort, 19 E3
Hôtel de Nevers, 2 C1
Hôtel Moderne, 18 D3
Hôtel Notre-Dame, 3 C1
Hôtel Rhetia, 17 D3
Luna-Park Hôtel, 9 D2
Plessis Hôtel, 5 C2
Résidence Bastille, 33 C4
FOOD
Au Trou Normand, 4 C2
Café de l'Industrie, 20 C3
Café Moderne, 29 C4
Chez Paul, 24 B4
La Banane Ivoirienne, 34 C5
La Ville de Jagannath, 11 D2
Le Bistro du Peintre, 32 C4
Le Kitch, 8 C2
Le Souk, 30 C4
Le Troisième Bureau, 6 D2
Mix Café, 25 B4
Occitanie, 12 E2
Pause Café, 31 C4
Un Saumon à Paris, 28 C4
SIGHTS
Ateliers de Ménilmontant, 35 E5
Glassbox, 10 D2
July Column, 22 B4
Maison de Retraite et de Santé, 36 F5
PUBS
Bar Bat, 26 C4
Boteco, 15 E2
Café Charbon, 13 E2
Le Bar Sans Nom, 27 C4
Sans Sanz, 23 B4
CLUBS
La Bataclan, 16 C3
10ème
19ème
20ème
11ème
PLACE DE LA RÈPUBLIQUE
Parc de Belleville
N
0 250 yards
0 250 meters
TEMPLE
RÉPUBLIQUE
GONCOURT
BELLEVILLE
COURONNES
PARMENTIER
OBERKAMPF
FILLES DU CALVAIRE
ST-SÉBASTIEN FROISSART
ST-MAUR
MÉNILMONTANT
RICHARD LENOIR
ST-AMBROSE
CHEMIN VERT
BRÉGUET SABIN
PÈRE LACHAISE
rue de Turbigo
rue du Faubourg du Temple
rue du Temple
rue des Archives
rue Charlot
rue de Bretagne
rue Vieille du Temple
r. de Turenne
bd. Beaumarchais
rue Amelot
bd. des Filles du Calvaire
bd. du Temple
bd. Voltaire
rue du Malte
bd. Jules Ferry
rue Crussol
rue St-Sébastien
bd. Richard Lenoir
r. de la Folie Mericourt
av. de la République
rue de la Fontaine au Roi
rue St-Maur
rue de l'Orillon
rue des Trois Bornes
rue Jean Pierre Timbaud
av. Parmentier
r. de Vaucouleurs
bd. de Belleville
rue Oberkampf
rue Moret
bd. de Ménilmontant
rue St-Amboise
r. Lacharrière
rue G. Bertrand
r.Rochebrune
rue de Chemin Vert

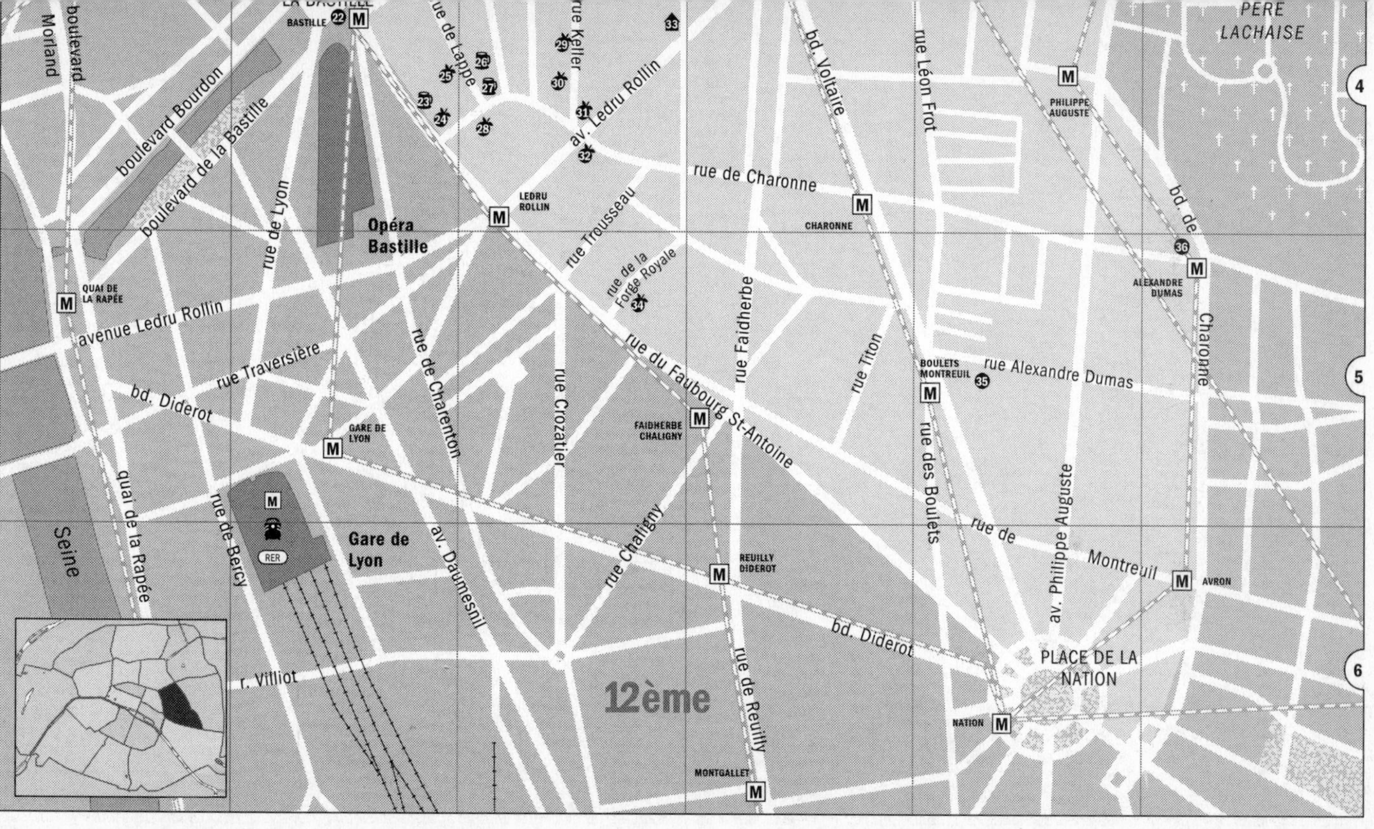

BASTILLE
boulevard Morland
boulevard Bourdon
boulevard de la Bastille
rue de Lappe
rue Keller
av. Ledru Rollin
PERE LACHAISE
PHILIPPE AUGUSTE
bd. Voltaire
rue Léon Frot
rue de Charonne
CHARONNE
LEDRU ROLLIN
Opéra Bastille
rue de Lyon
QUAI DE LA RAPÉE
avenue Ledru Rollin
rue Trousseau
rue de la Forge Royale
bd. de Charonne
ALEXANDRE DUMAS
rue Faidherbe
rue Titon
BOULETS MONTREUIL
rue Alexandre Dumas
rue Traversière
bd. Diderot
rue de Charenton
rue Crozatier
rue du Faubourg St-Antoine
FAIDHERBE CHALIGNY
GARE DE LYON
rue des Boulets
av. Philippe Auguste
rue de Montreuil
AVRON
Seine
quai de la Rapée
rue de Bercy
RER
Gare de Lyon
av. Daumesnil
rue Chaligny
REUILLY DIDEROT
bd. Diderot
PLACE DE LA NATION
NATION
r. Villiot
12ème
rue de Reuilly
MONTGALLET

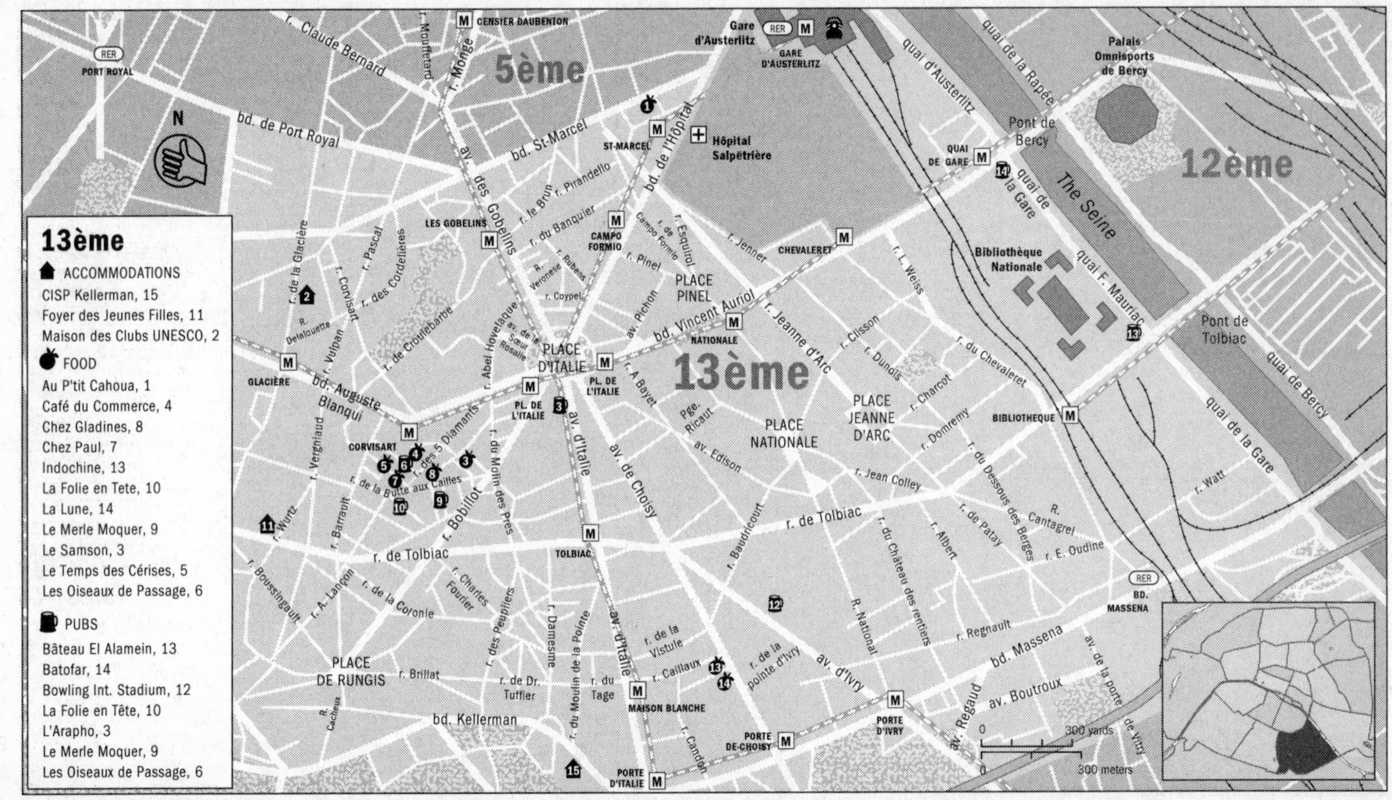
13ème
ACCOMMODATIONS
CISP Kellerman, 15
Foyer des Jeunes Filles, 11
Maison des Clubs UNESCO, 2
FOOD
Au P'tit Cahoua, 1
Café du Commerce, 4
Chez Gladines, 8
Chez Paul, 7
Indochine, 13
La Folie en Tete, 10
La Lune, 14
Le Merle Moquer, 9
Le Samson, 3
Le Temps des Cérises, 5
Les Oiseaux de Passage, 6
PUBS
Bâteau El Alamein, 13
Batofar, 14
Bowling Int. Stadium, 12
La Folie en Tête, 10
L'Arapho, 3
Le Merle Moquer, 9
Les Oiseaux de Passage, 6
N
5ème
12ème
13ème
The Seine
Palais Omnisports de Bercy
Gare d'Austerlitz
Hôpital Salpêtrière
Bibliothèque Nationale
PLACE D'ITALIE
PLACE PINEL
PLACE JEANNE D'ARC
PLACE NATIONALE
PLACE DE RUNGIS
quai d'Austerlitz
quai de la Rapée
quai de Bercy
quai de la Gare
quai F. Mauriac
Pont de Bercy
Pont de Tolbiac
bd. de l'Hôpital
bd. St-Marcel
bd. de Port Royal
bd. Vincent Auriol
bd. Auguste Blanqui
bd. Kellerman
bd. Massena
av. des Gobelins
av. d'Italie
av. de Choisy
av. d'Ivry
av. de la porte de Vitry
av. Boutroux
av. Edison
r. de Tolbiac
r. Jeanne d'Arc
r. Claude Bernard
r. Mouffetard
r. Monge
r. Watt
R. National
r. du Chevaleret
r. Corvisart
r. de la Glacière
r. Pascal
r. Bobillot
r. du Molin des Pres
r. de la Butte aux Cailles
r. des 5 Diamants
r. Damesme
r. de la Colonie
PORT ROYAL
CENSIER DAUBENTON
LES GOBELINS
ST-MARCEL
CAMPO FORMIO
CHEVALERET
NATIONALE
BIBLIOTHEQUE
QUAI DE GARE
GARE D'AUSTERLITZ
PL. DE L'ITALIE
TOLBIAC
CORVISART
GLACIÈRE
MAISON BLANCHE
PORTE D'ITALIE
PORTE DE-CHOISY
PORTE D'IVRY
BD. MASSENA
0
300 yards
300 meters

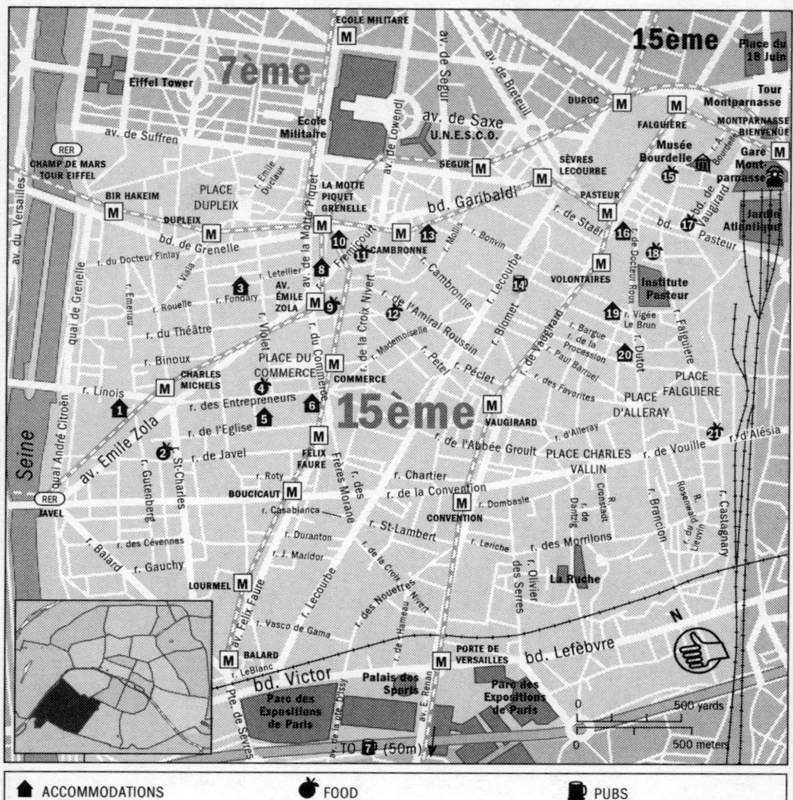

ACCOMMODATIONS
- Aloha Hostel, 19
- Hôtel Camélia, 16
- Hôtel de la Paix, 13
- Hôtel Printemps, 8
- La Maison Hostel, 20
- Mondial Hôtel, 10
- Nainville Hôtel, 5
- Pacific Hôtel, 3
- Practic Hôtel, 1
- Three Ducks Hostel, 6

FOOD
- Aux Artistes, 17
- Café du Commerce, 9
- Chez Foong, 11
- Chez Francois, 2
- L'Armoise, 4
- Piccola Italia, 21
- Restaurant Le Listines, 15
- Sampieru Corsu, 13
- Ty Breiz, 18

PUBS
- Aquaboulevard, 7
- Saint-Louis Blues, 14

14ème

ACCOMMODATIONS

FIAP Jean-Monnet, 14	F3
Hôtel Broussais, 22	B5
Hôtel de Blois, 15	C3
Hôtel du Midi, 10	D2
Hôtel du Parc, 7	B1
Ouest Hôtel, 20	B4
FOOD	
Aquarius Café, 19	B4
Au Produits du Sud-Ouest, 5	B1
Au Rendez-Vous Des Camionneurs, 21	C4
Chez Papa, 8	C2
Creperie de Josselin, 1	B1
La Coupole, 2	C1
La Dome, 3	C1
La Route du Château, 12	B3
Le Colvert, 11	B3
Les Petites Sorcières, 9	C3
N'Zadette-M'foua, 14	C3
Phinéas, 18	B4
CLUBS	
L'Enfer, 6	B1
PUBS	
L'Entrepot, 16	B3
Le Troupeau, 15	B3
Smoke Bar, 4	B1

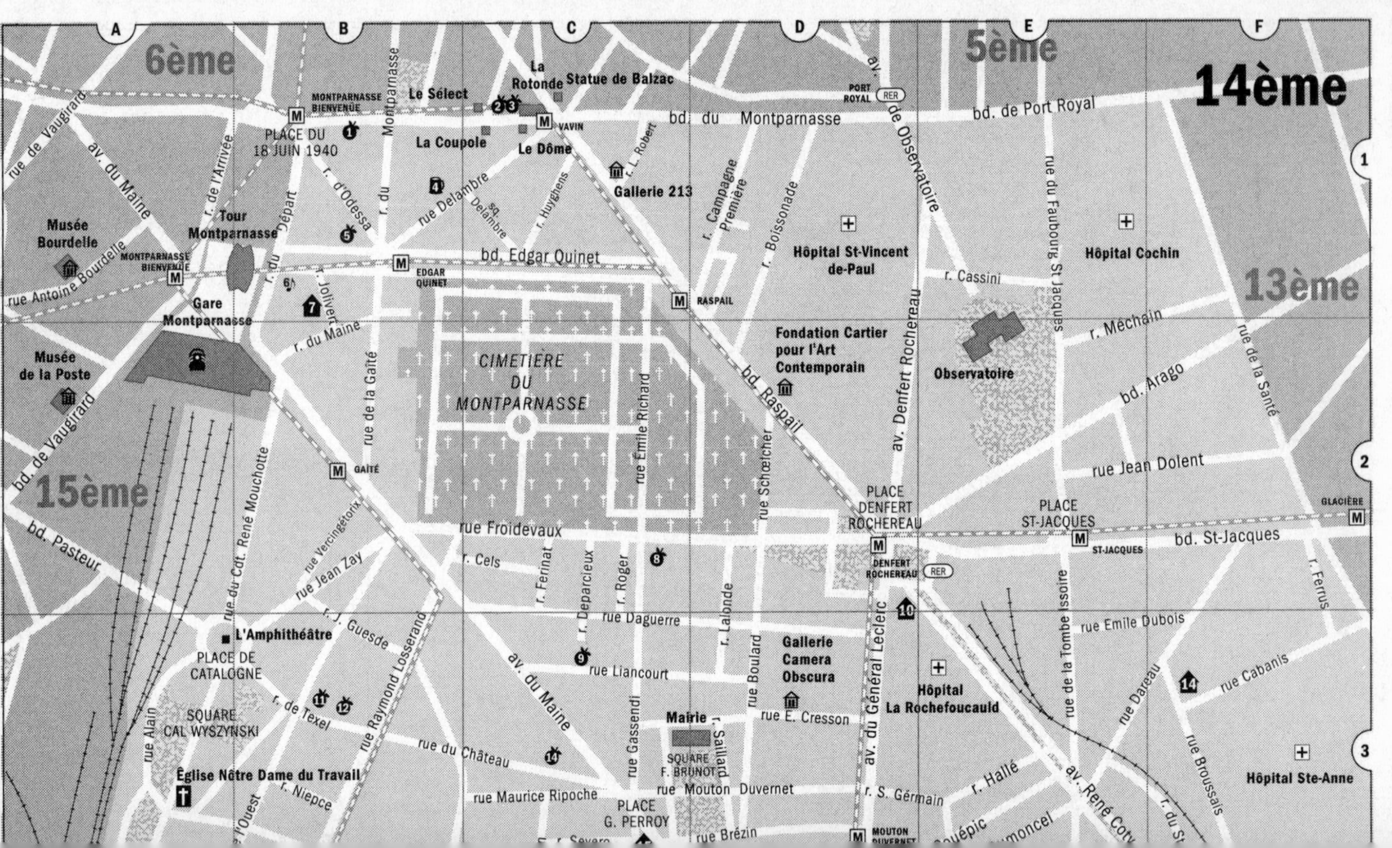
14ème
13ème
5ème
6ème
15ème
Hôpital Cochin
Hôpital St-Vincent de-Paul
Fondation Cartier pour l'Art Contemporain
Observatoire
Hôpital Ste-Anne
Hôpital La Rochefoucauld
Gallerie Camera Obscura
Mairie
CIMETIÈRE DU MONTPARNASSE
La Rotonde
Statue de Balzac
Le Dôme
Le Sélect
La Coupole
Gallerie 213
Tour Montparnasse
Gare Montparnasse
Musée Bourdelle
Musée de la Poste
L'Amphithéâtre
Église Nôtre Dame du Travail
PLACE DU 18 JUIN 1940
PLACE DENFERT ROCHEREAU
PLACE ST-JACQUES
PLACE DE CATALOGNE
PLACE G. PERROY
SQUARE CAL WYSZYNSKI
SQUARE F. BRUNOT
bd. de Port Royal
bd. du Montparnasse
bd. Raspail
bd. Edgar Quinet
bd. Arago
bd. St-Jacques
bd. Pasteur
bd. de Vaugirard
av. de Observatoire
av. Denfert Rochereau
av. du Général Leclerc
av. René Coty
av. du Maine
rue de la Santé
rue du Faubourg St Jacques
rue de la Tombe Issoire
rue Froidevaux
rue Daguerre
rue de la Gaîté
rue du Cdt. René Mouchotte
rue Raymond Losserand
rue Emile Richard
rue Schœlcher
rue Boulard
rue Gassendi
rue Liancourt
rue Jean Dolent
rue Emile Dubois
rue Broussais
rue Cabanis
rue Dareau
rue du Château
rue Maurice Ripoche
rue Mouton Duvernet
rue Brézin
rue Jean Zay
rue Vercingétorix
rue Alain
rue de l'Arrivée
rue Antoine Bourdelle
rue de Vaugirard
rue Delambre
r. Ferrus
r. Méchain
r. Cassini
r. Boissonade
r. Campagne Première
r. Huyghens
sq. Delambre
r. L. Robert
r. du Montparnasse
r. d'Odessa
r. Jolivet
r. du Départ
r. du Maine
r. Lalande
rue E. Cresson
r. Saillard
r. Roger
r. Deparcieux
r. Ferinat
r. Cels
r. S. Germain
r. Hallé
r. J. Guesde
r. de Texel
r. Niepce
r. de l'Ouest
PORT ROYAL
RASPAIL
VAVIN
EDGAR QUINET
GAÎTÉ
MONTPARNASSE BIENVENUE
DENFERT ROCHEREAU
ST-JACQUES
GLACIÈRE
MOUTON DUVERNET
RER
A
B
C
D
E
F
1
2
3

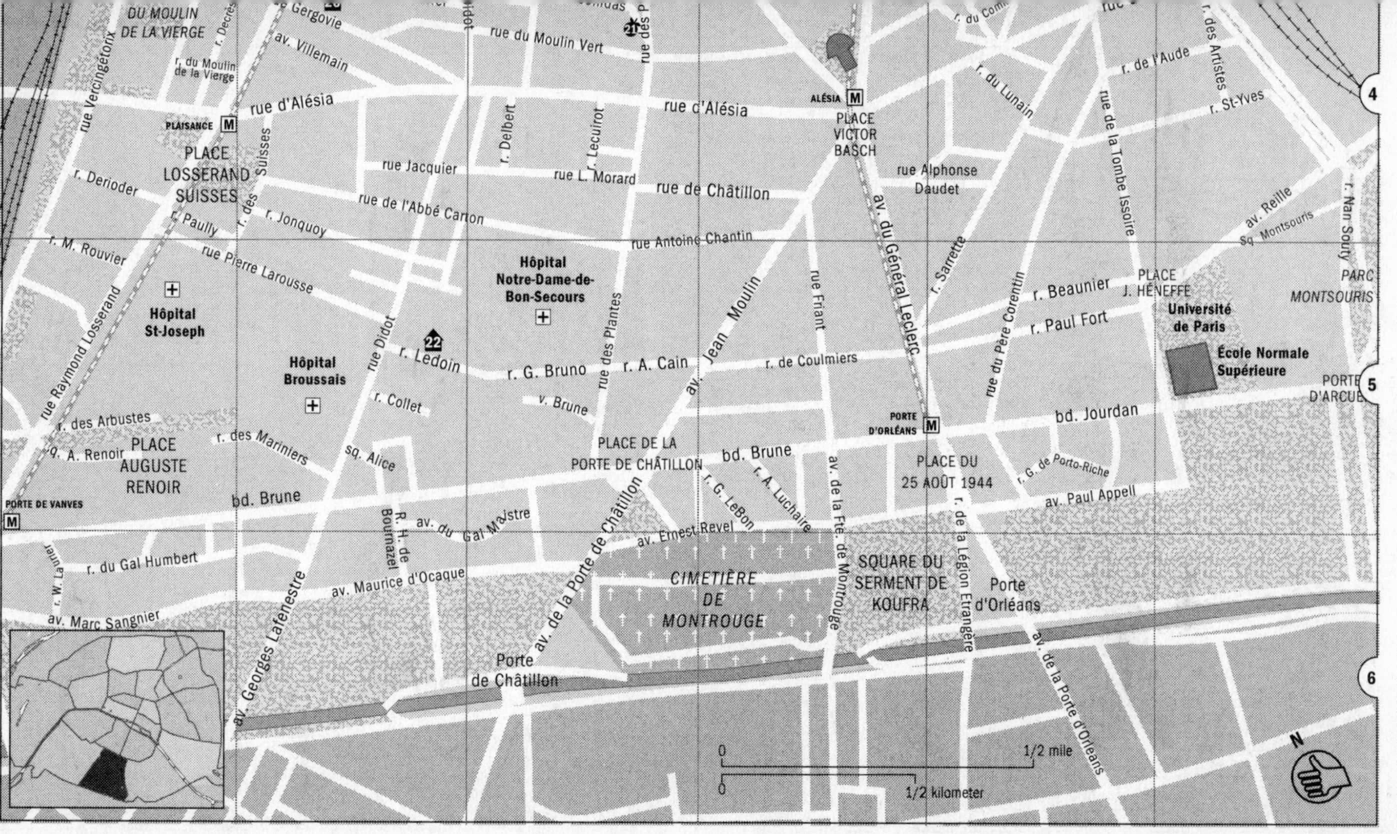

DU MOULIN DE LA VIERGE
av. Villemain
rue du Moulin Vert
r. du Moulin de la Vierge
rue Vercingétorix
rue d'Alésia
PLAISANCE
PLACE LOSSERAND SUISSES
r. Derioder
r. des Suisses
r. Paully
r. Jonquoy
rue Jacquier
rue de l'Abbé Carton
r. Delbet
r. Lecuirot
rue L. Morard
rue de Châtillon
rue Antoine Chantin
ALÉSIA
PLACE VICTOR BASCH
r. du Lunain
r. de l'Aude
r. des Artistes
r. St-Yves
rue de la Tombe Issoire
rue Alphonse Daudet
av. du Général Leclerc
av. Reille
Sq. Montsouris
r. Nan Souty
PARC MONTSOURIS
r. M. Rouvier
rue Pierre Larousse
Hôpital St-Joseph
rue Raymond Losserand
Hôpital Notre-Dame-de-Bon-Secours
r. Sarrette
rue du Père Corentin
r. Beaunier
PLACE J. HÉNEFFE
Université de Paris
École Normale Supérieure
r. Paul Fort
rue Didot
r. Ledoin
Hôpital Broussais
r. G. Bruno
rue des Plantes
r. A. Cain
av. Jean Moulin
rue Friant
r. de Coulmiers
PORTE D'ARCUEIL
r. Collet
v. Brune
r. des Arbustes
r. des Mariniers
sq. Alice
PLACE DE LA PORTE DE CHÂTILLON
bd. Brune
PORTE D'ORLÉANS
bd. Jourdan
sq. A. Renoir
PLACE AUGUSTE RENOIR
PLACE DU 25 AOÛT 1944
r. G. de Porto-Riche
r. G. LeBon
r. A. Luchaire
PORTE DE VANVES
av. du Gal Maistre
R. H. de Bournazel
av. Paul Appell
av. de la Porte de Châtillon
av. Ernest Revel
av. de la Fte. de Montrouge
r. de la Légion Etrangère
r. du Gal Humbert
r. W. Launer
CIMETIÈRE DE MONTROUGE
SQUARE DU SERMENT DE KOUFRA
Porte d'Orléans
av. Maurice d'Ocagne
av. Marc Sangnier
av. Georges Lafenestre
Porte de Châtillon
av. de la Porte d'Orleans
0
1/2 mile
1/2 kilometer
N
4
5
6
21
22

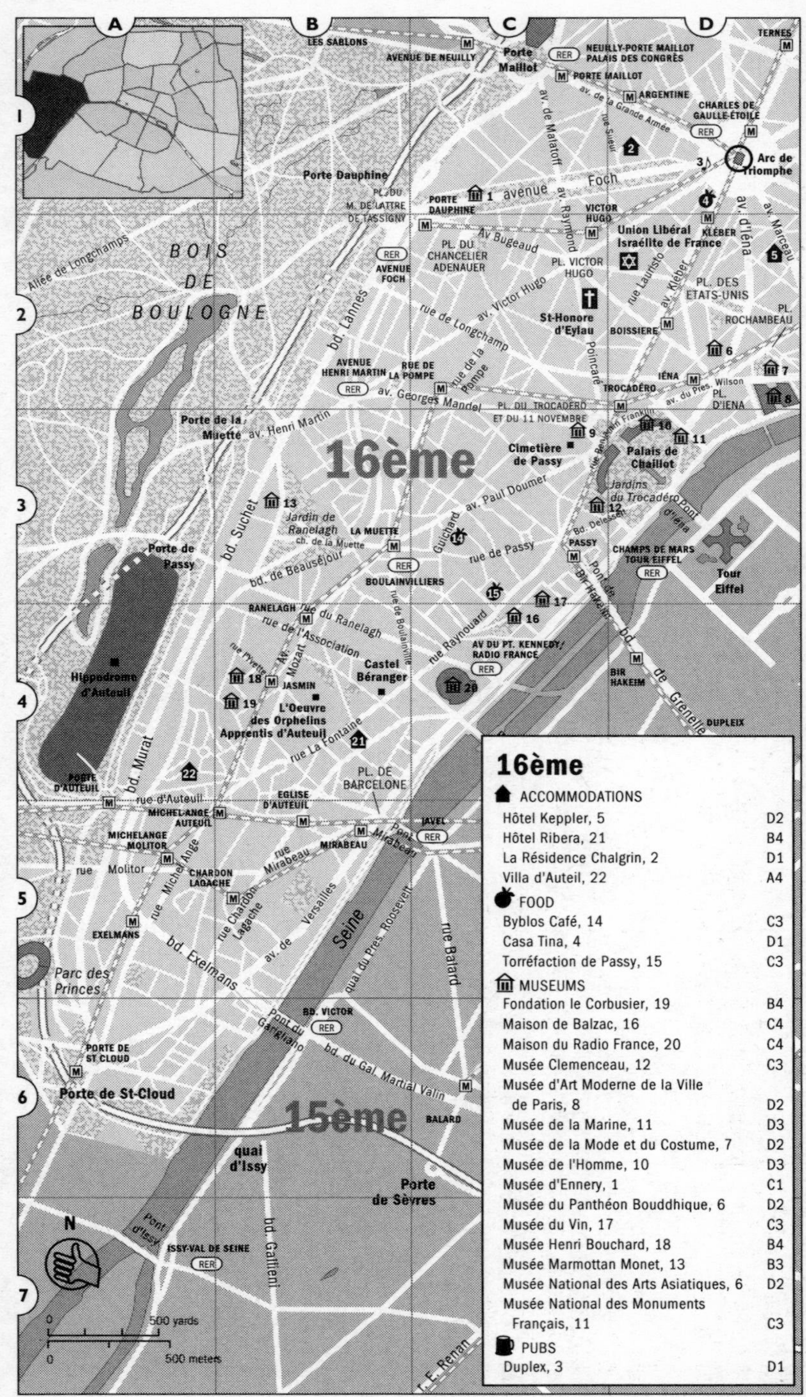
A
B
C
D
1
2
3
4
5
6
7
LES SABLONS
AVENUE DE NEUILLY
Porte Maillot
NEUILLY-PORTE MAILLOT PALAIS DES CONGRÈS
PORTE MAILLOT
ARGENTINE
TERNES
CHARLES DE GAULLE-ÉTOILE
Arc de Triomphe
av. de la Grande Armée
av. de Malakoff
rue Sueur
Porte Dauphine
PL. DU M. DE LATTRE DE TASSIGNY
PORTE DAUPHINE
avenue Foch
VICTOR HUGO
KLÉBER
av. d'Iéna
av. Marceau
Union Libéral Israélite de France
BOIS DE BOULOGNE
Allée de Longchamps
av. Bugeaud
PL. DU CHANCELIER ADENAUER
AVENUE FOCH
PL. VICTOR HUGO
av. Victor Hugo
rue de Longchamp
rue Lauriston
av. Kléber
PL. DES ETATS-UNIS
PL. ROCHAMBEAU
St-Honore d'Eylau
BOISSIERE
bd. Lannes
AVENUE HENRI MARTIN
RUE DE LA POMPE
rue de la Pompe
av. Georges Mandel
Poincaré
IÉNA
TROCADÉRO
av. du Pres. Wilson
PL. D'IENA
PL. DU TROCADÉRO ET DU 11 NOVEMBRE
Porte de la Muette
av. Henri Martin
16ème
Cimetière de Passy
Palais de Chaillot
Jardins du Trocadéro
av. Paul Doumer
bd. Suchet
Jardin de Ranelagh
ch. de la Muette
LA MUETTE
Guichard
rue de Passy
Bd. Delessert
PASSY
Pont d'Iéna
CHAMPS DE MARS TOUR EIFFEL
Tour Eiffel
Porte de Passy
bd. de Beauséjour
BOULAINVILLIERS
Pont de Bir Hakeim
RANELAGH
rue du Ranelagh
rue de l'Association
rue de Boulainvilliers
rue Raynouard
AV DU PT. KENNEDY/ RADIO FRANCE
rue Pyvette
Av. Mozart
Castel Béranger
Hippodrome d'Auteuil
JASMIN
L'Oeuvre des Orphelins Apprentis d'Auteuil
BIR HAKEIM
bd. de Grenelle
DUPLEIX
rue La Fontaine
bd. Murat
PL. DE BARCELONE
PORTE D'AUTEUIL
rue d'Auteuil
EGLISE D'AUTEUIL
MICHEL-ANGE AUTEUIL
JAVEL
MICHELANGE MOLITOR
MIRABEAU
rue Mirabeau
Pont Mirabeau
rue Molitor
rue Michel Ange
CHARDON LAGACHE
rue Chardon Lagache
av. de Versailles
Seine
quai du Pres. Roosevelt
rue Balard
EXELMANS
bd. Exelmans
Parc des Princes
BD. VICTOR
Pont du Garigliano
bd. du Gal. Martial Valin
PORTE DE ST CLOUD
Porte de St-Cloud
15ème
BALARD
quai d'Issy
Porte de Sèvres
N
Pont d'Issy
ISSY-VAL DE SEINE
bd. Galliéni
0 500 yards
0 500 meters
r. E. Renan
16ème
ACCOMMODATIONS
Hôtel Keppler, 5 D2
Hôtel Ribera, 21 B4
La Résidence Chalgrin, 2 D1
Villa d'Auteuil, 22 A4
FOOD
Byblos Café, 14 C3
Casa Tina, 4 D1
Torréfaction de Passy, 15 C3
MUSEUMS
Fondation le Corbusier, 19 B4
Maison de Balzac, 16 C4
Maison du Radio France, 20 C4
Musée Clemenceau, 12 C3
Musée d'Art Moderne de la Ville de Paris, 8 D2
Musée de la Marine, 11 D3
Musée de la Mode et du Costume, 7 D2
Musée de l'Homme, 10 D3
Musée d'Ennery, 1 C1
Musée du Panthéon Bouddhique, 6 D2
Musée du Vin, 17 C3
Musée Henri Bouchard, 18 B4
Musée Marmottan Monet, 13 B3
Musée National des Arts Asiatiques, 6 D2
Musée National des Monuments Français, 11 C3
PUBS
Duplex, 3 D1

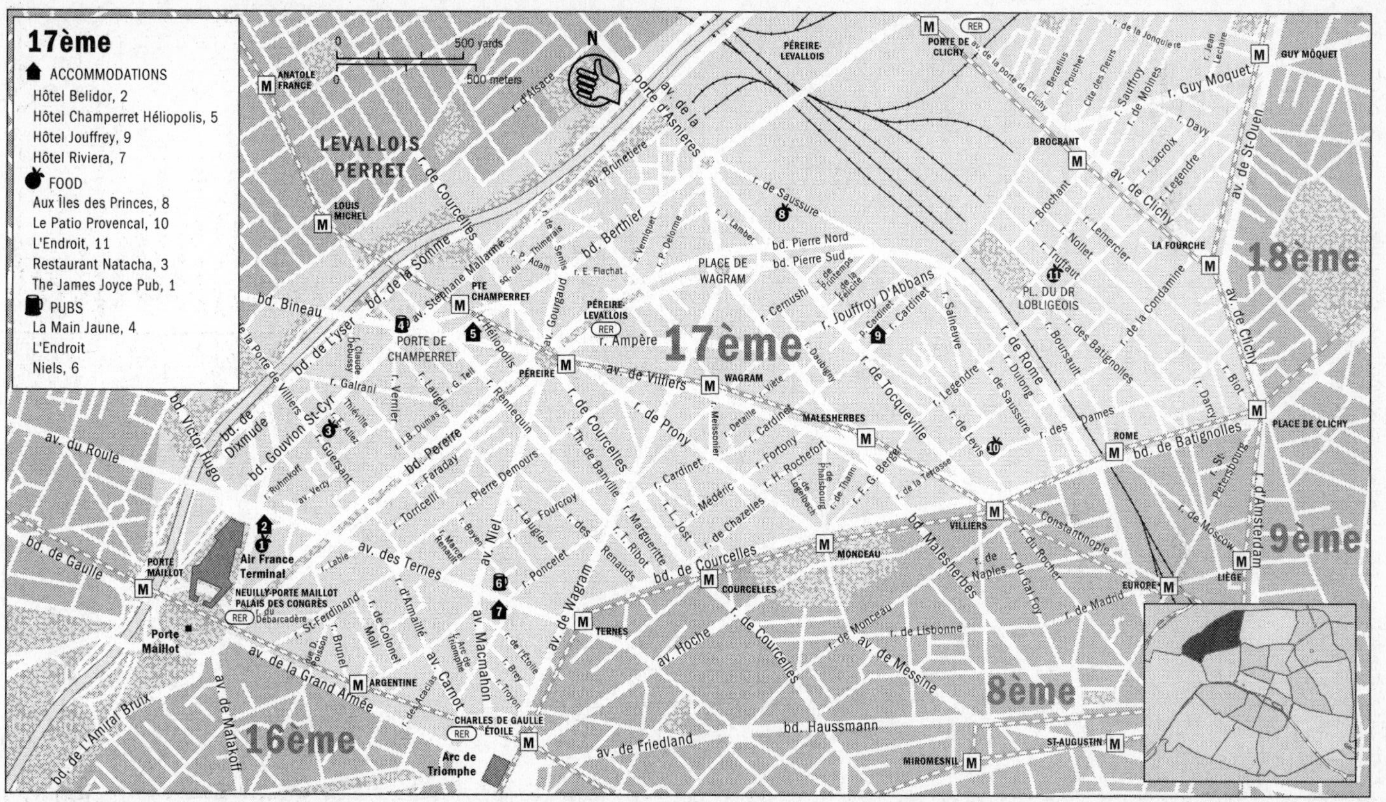
17ème
ACCOMMODATIONS
Hôtel Belidor, 2
Hôtel Champerret Héliopolis, 5
Hôtel Jouffrey, 9
Hôtel Riviera, 7
FOOD
Aux Îles des Princes, 8
Le Patio Provencal, 10
L'Endroit, 11
Restaurant Natacha, 3
The James Joyce Pub, 1
PUBS
La Main Jaune, 4
L'Endroit
Niels, 6
0
500 yards
500 meters
N
LEVALLOIS PERRET
17ème
18ème
9ème
8ème
16ème
PLACE DE WAGRAM
PL. DU DR LOBLIGEOIS
PORTE DE CHAMPERRET
Air France Terminal
Porte Maillot
Arc de Triomphe

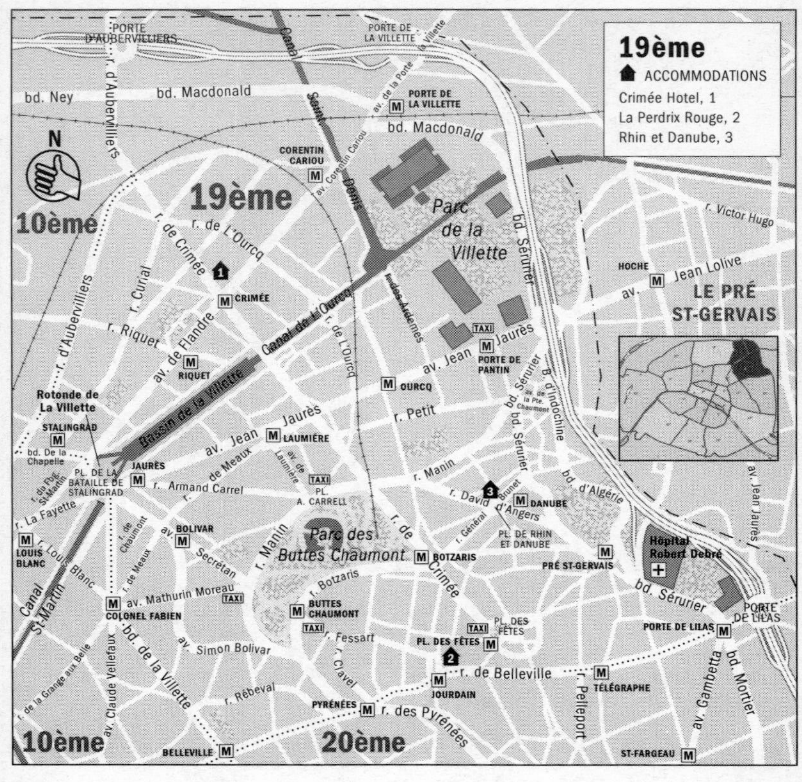
19ème
ACCOMMODATIONS
Crimée Hotel, 1
La Perdrix Rouge, 2
Rhin et Danube, 3
19ème
10ème
20ème
10ème
LE PRÉ ST-GERVAIS
Parc de la Villette
Parc des Buttes Chaumont
Rotonde de La Villette
Hôpital Robert Debré
PORTE D'AUBERVILLIERS
PORTE DE LA VILLETTE
PORTE DE LILAS
bd. Ney
bd. Macdonald
bd. Sérurier
r. Victor Hugo
av. Jean Lolive
av. Jean Jaurès
r. de Crimée
r. de L'Ourcq
Canal de L'Ourcq
Bassin de la Villette
Canal St-Martin
Canal Saint Denis
r. Curial
r. Riquet
av. de Flandre
r. d'Aubervilliers
r. Petit
r. Manin
r. de Meaux
r. Armand Carrel
r. La Fayette
r. Louis Blanc
av. Secrétan
av. Mathurin Moreau
av. Simon Bolivar
bd. de la Villette
av. Claude Vellefaux
r. Rébeval
r. Botzaris
r. Fessart
r. Clavel
r. de Belleville
r. des Pyrénées
r. Pelleport
av. Gambetta
bd. Mortier
bd. d'Algérie
B. d'Indochine
r. David d'Angers
r. Général Brunet
r. des Ardennes
PL. DE RHIN ET DANUBE
PL. DE LA BATAILLE DE STALINGRAD
PL. A. CARRELL
PL. DES FÊTES
CORENTIN CARIOU
PORTE DE LA VILLETTE
CRIMÉE
RIQUET
STALINGRAD
JAURÈS
LAUMIÈRE
OURCQ
PORTE DE PANTIN
HOCHE
DANUBE
BOTZARIS
PRÉ ST-GERVAIS
BOLIVAR
LOUIS BLANC
COLONEL FABIEN
BUTTES CHAUMONT
PL. DES FÊTES
JOURDAIN
PYRÉNÉES
BELLEVILLE
TÉLÉGRAPHE
PORTE DE LILAS
ST-FARGEAU
TAXI

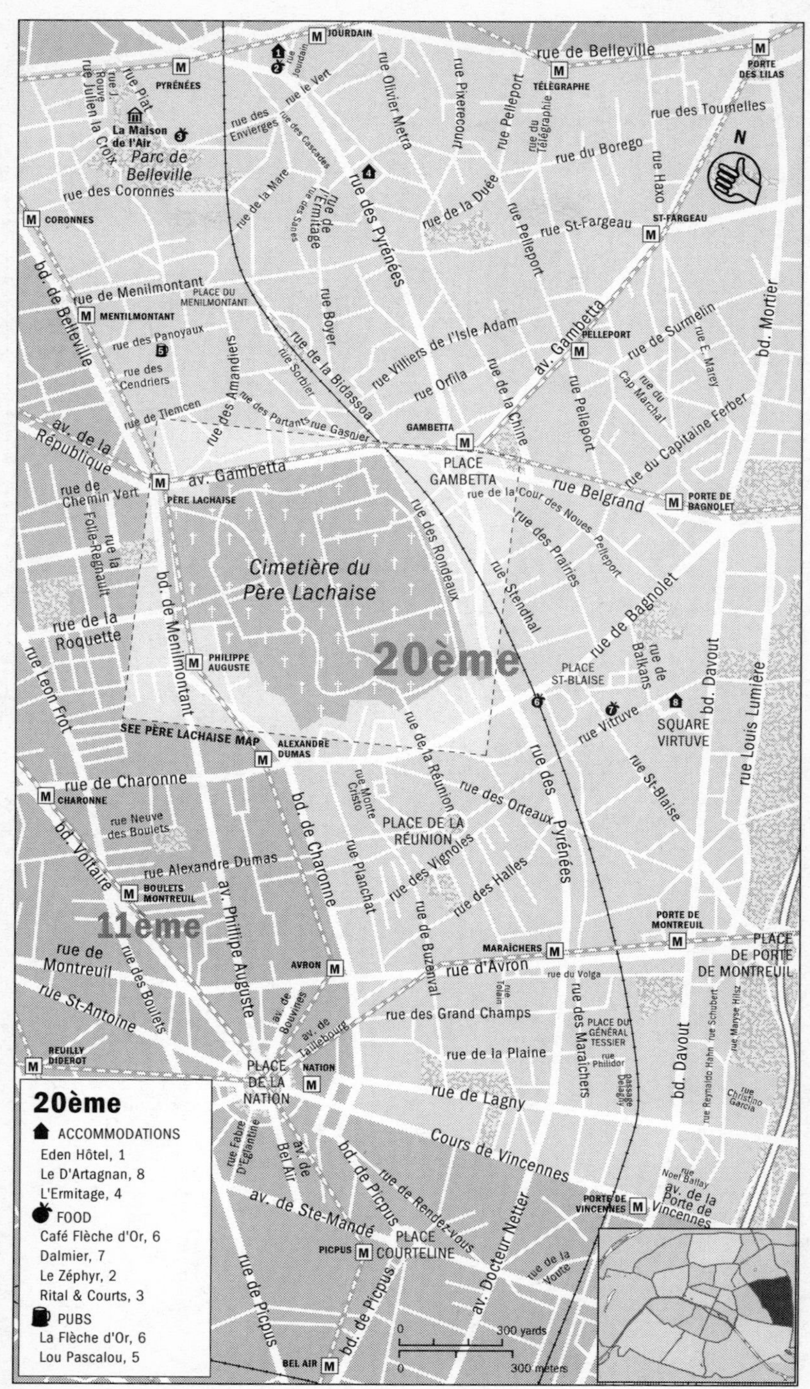

JOURDAIN
rue de Belleville
PORTE DES LILAS
TÉLÉGRAPHE
PYRÉNÉES
rue Piat
rue J. Rouvet
rue Julien la Croix
La Maison de l'Air
Parc de Belleville
rue des Envierges
rue le Vert
rue Jourdain
rue des Cascades
rue Olivier Metra
rue Pixerecourt
rue Pelleport
rue du Télégraphe
rue des Tournelles
rue du Borego
rue Haxo
rue des Coronnes
CORONNES
rue de la Mare
rue des Saules
rue de l'Ermitage
rue des Pyrénées
rue de la Duée
rue St-Fargeau
ST-FARGEAU
bd. de Belleville
rue de Menilmontant
PLACE DU MENILMONTANT
MENTILMONTANT
rue Boyer
av. Gambetta
PELLEPORT
rue de Surmelin
rue E. Marey
bd. Mortier
rue des Panoyaux
rue des Cendriers
rue des Amandiers
rue Sorbier
rue de la Bidassoa
rue Villiers de l'Isle Adam
rue Orfila
rue de la Chine
rue du Cap Marchal
rue du Capitaine Ferber
rue de Tlemcen
rue des Partants
rue Gasnier
GAMBETTA
av. de la République
PÈRE LACHAISE
PLACE GAMBETTA
rue de la Cour des Noues
rue Belgrand
PORTE DE BAGNOLET
rue de Chemin Vert
rue la Folie-Regnault
rue des Rondeaux
rue des Prairies
rue Pelleport
rue Stendhal
Cimetière du Père Lachaise
bd. de Menilmontant
rue de la Roquette
rue de Bagnolet
rue de Balkans
rue Leon Frot
PHILIPPE AUGUSTE
20ème
PLACE ST-BLAISE
bd. Davout
rue Louis Lumière
rue Vitruve
SQUARE VIRTUVE
SEE PÈRE LACHAISE MAP
ALEXANDRE DUMAS
rue de la Réunion
rue des Pyrénées
rue St-Blaise
rue de Charonne
CHARONNE
rue Monte Cristo
rue des Orteaux
rue Neuve des Boulets
PLACE DE LA RÉUNION
bd. Voltaire
rue Alexandre Dumas
bd. de Charonne
rue Planchat
rue des Vignoles
rue des Halles
BOULETS MONTREUIL
11ème
av. Philippe Auguste
rue de Buzenval
PORTE DE MONTREUIL
PLACE DE PORTE DE MONTREUIL
MARAÎCHERS
rue de Montreuil
rue des Boulets
AVRON
rue d'Avron
rue du Volga
rue Tolain
rue St-Antoine
av. de Bouvines
av. de Taillebourg
rue des Grand Champs
rue des Maraichers
PLACE DU GÉNÉRAL TESSIER
rue Philidor
passage Delagny
rue Schubert
rue Maryse Hilsz
REUILLY DIDEROT
rue de la Plaine
PLACE DE LA NATION
NATION
rue de Lagny
rue Reynaldo Hahn
rue Christino Garcia
rue Fabre d'Eglantine
av. de Bel Air
bd. de Picpus
Cours de Vincennes
rue de Rendez-vous
rue Noel Ballay
av. de la Porte de Vincennes
av. de Ste-Mandé
PORTE DE VINCENNES
PLACE COURTELINE
PICPUS
av. Docteur Netter
rue de la Voute
rue de Picpus
bd. de Picpus
0 300 yards
0 300 meters
BEL AIR
N
20ème
ACCOMMODATIONS
Eden Hôtel, 1
Le D'Artagnan, 8
L'Ermitage, 4
FOOD
Café Flèche d'Or, 6
Dalmier, 7
Le Zéphyr, 2
Rital & Courts, 3
PUBS
La Flèche d'Or, 6
Lou Pascalou, 5

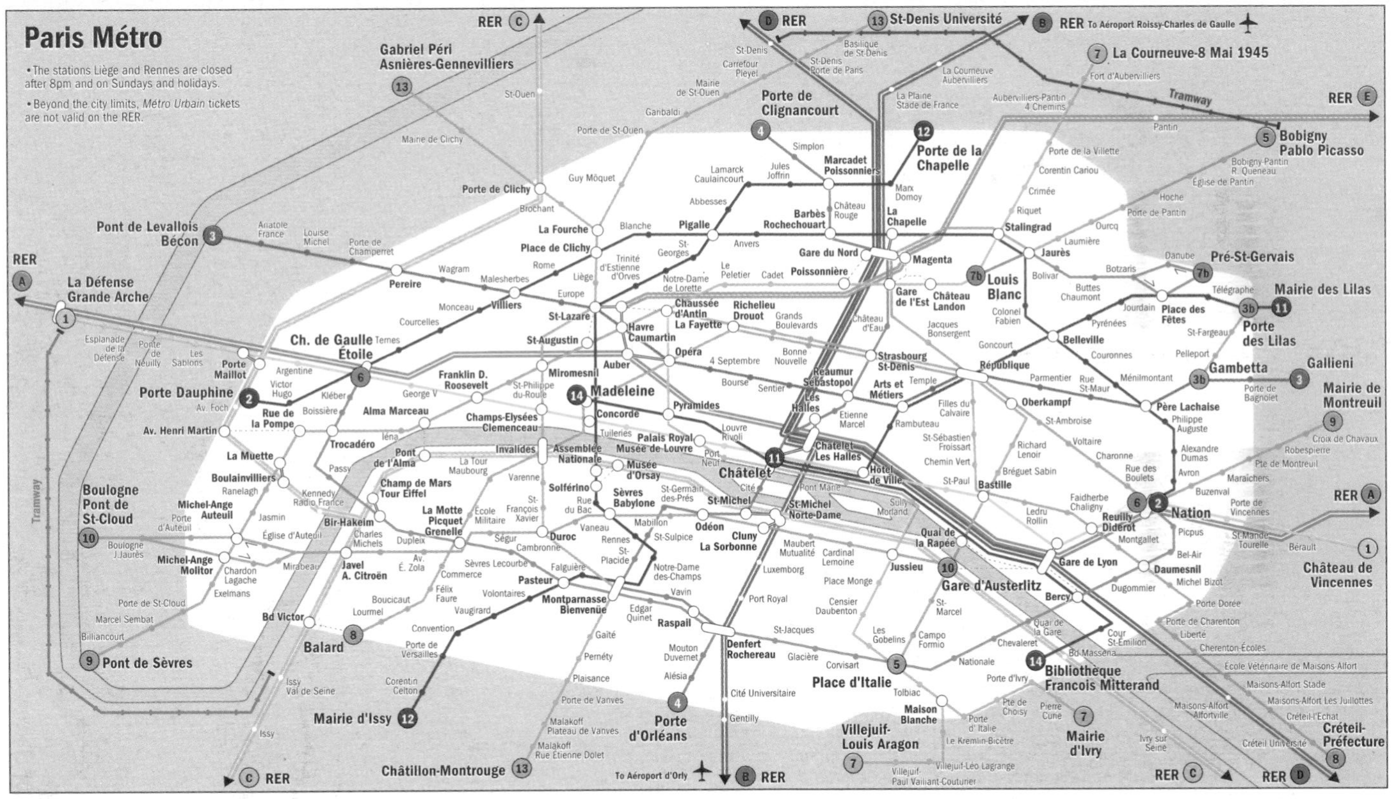
Paris Métro
• The stations Liège and Rennes are closed after 8pm and on Sundays and holidays.
• Beyond the city limits, Métro Urbain tickets are not valid on the RER.
RER A
La Défense Grande Arche
Pont de Levallois Bécon
Gabriel Péri Asnières-Gennevilliers
RER C
Porte de Clignancourt
RER D
St-Denis Université
RER B To Aéroport Roissy-Charles de Gaulle
La Courneuve-8 Mai 1945
Tramway
RER E
Bobigny Pablo Picasso
Porte de la Chapelle
Pré-St-Gervais
Mairie des Lilas
Porte des Lilas
Gallieni
Mairie de Montreuil
Nation
Château de Vincennes
Créteil-Préfecture
Bibliothèque Francois Mitterand
Mairie d'Ivry
Villejuif-Louis Aragon
Place d'Italie
Porte d'Orléans
To Aéroport d'Orly
Châtillon-Montrouge
Mairie d'Issy
Balard
Pont de Sèvres
Boulogne Pont de St-Cloud
Porte Dauphine
Ch. de Gaulle Étoile
Madeleine
Châtelet
Gare d'Austerlitz
Gare de Lyon
Gare du Nord
Louis Blanc
Gambetta
République
Montparnasse Bienvenüe

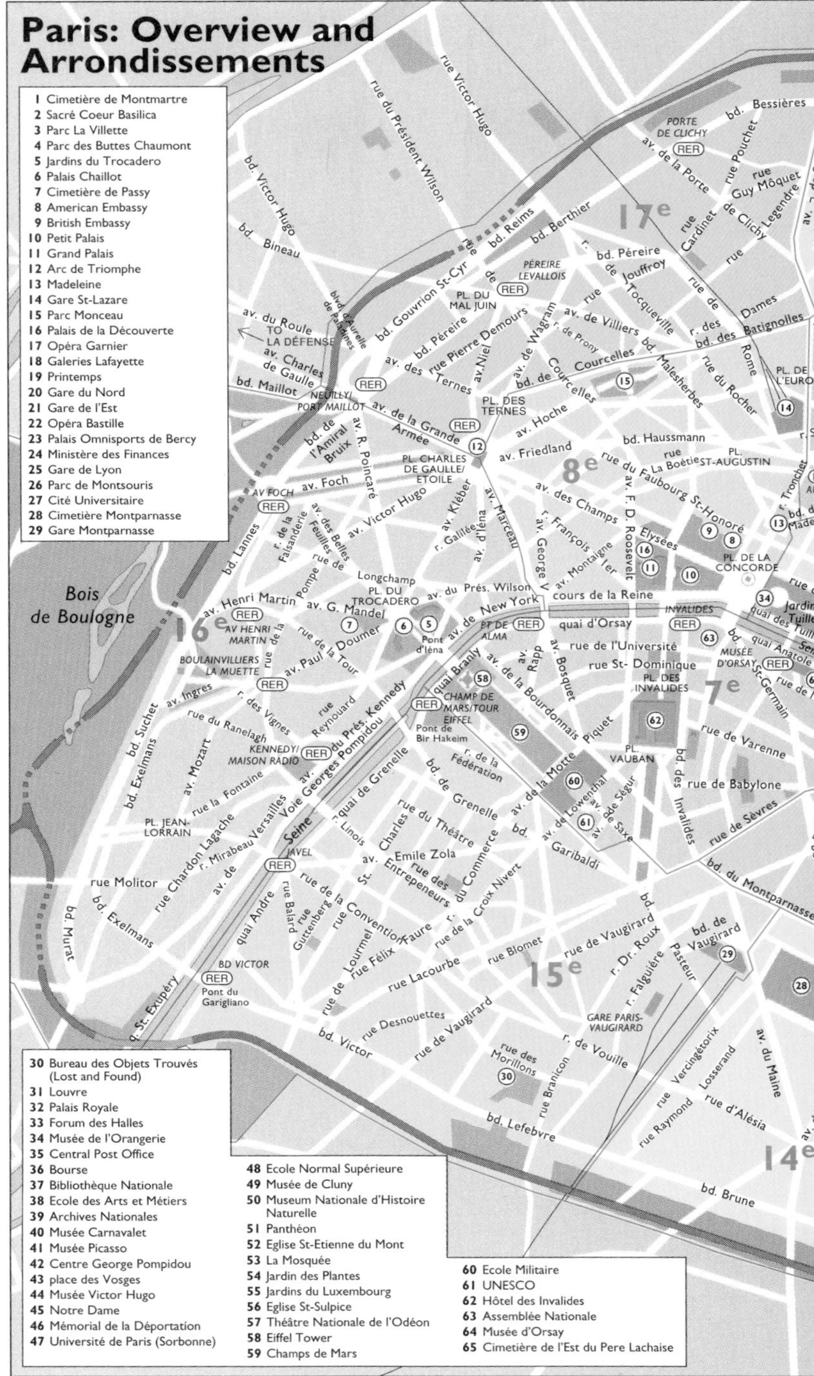
Paris: Overview and Arrondissements
1 Cimetière de Montmartre
2 Sacré Coeur Basilica
3 Parc La Villette
4 Parc des Buttes Chaumont
5 Jardins du Trocadero
6 Palais Chaillot
7 Cimetière de Passy
8 American Embassy
9 British Embassy
10 Petit Palais
11 Grand Palais
12 Arc de Triomphe
13 Madeleine
14 Gare St-Lazare
15 Parc Monceau
16 Palais de la Découverte
17 Opéra Garnier
18 Galeries Lafayette
19 Printemps
20 Gare du Nord
21 Gare de l'Est
22 Opéra Bastille
23 Palais Omnisports de Bercy
24 Ministère des Finances
25 Gare de Lyon
26 Parc de Montsouris
27 Cité Universitaire
28 Cimetière Montparnasse
29 Gare Montparnasse
30 Bureau des Objets Trouvés (Lost and Found)
31 Louvre
32 Palais Royale
33 Forum des Halles
34 Musée de l'Orangerie
35 Central Post Office
36 Bourse
37 Bibliothèque Nationale
38 Ecole des Arts et Métiers
39 Archives Nationales
40 Musée Carnavalet
41 Musée Picasso
42 Centre George Pompidou
43 place des Vosges
44 Musée Victor Hugo
45 Notre Dame
46 Mémorial de la Déportation
47 Université de Paris (Sorbonne)
48 Ecole Normal Supérieure
49 Musée de Cluny
50 Museum Nationale d'Histoire Naturelle
51 Panthéon
52 Eglise St-Etienne du Mont
53 La Mosquée
54 Jardin des Plantes
55 Jardins du Luxembourg
56 Eglise St-Sulpice
57 Théâtre Nationale de l'Odéon
58 Eiffel Tower
59 Champs de Mars
60 Ecole Militaire
61 UNESCO
62 Hôtel des Invalides
63 Assemblée Nationale
64 Musée d'Orsay
65 Cimetière de l'Est du Pere Lachaise
Bois de Boulogne
16e
17e
8e
7e
15e
14e
PORTE DE CLICHY
PÉREIRE LEVALLOIS
PL. DU MAL JUIN
NEUILLY/PORT MAILLOT
PL. DES TERNES
PL. CHARLES DE GAULLE/ETOILE
AV FOCH
PL. DU TROCADERO
AV HENRI MARTIN
BOULAINVILLIERS LA MUETTE
KENNEDY/MAISON RADIO
PT DE L'ALMA
INVALIDES
MUSÉE D'ORSAY
PL. DE LA CONCORDE
PL. ST-AUGUSTIN
PL. DE L'EUROPE
PL. DES INVALIDES
PL. VAUBAN
CHAMP DE MARS/TOUR EIFFEL
JAVEL
BD VICTOR
GARE PARIS-VAUGIRARD
Pont d'Iéna
Pont de Bir Hakeim
Pont du Garigliano
TO LA DÉFENSE
Seine
av. des Champs Elysées
av. de la Grande Armée
av. Foch
av. Victor Hugo
av. Kléber
av. d'Iéna
av. Marceau
av. George V
av. Montaigne
av. F. D. Roosevelt
av. Friedland
av. Hoche
av. de Wagram
bd. Haussmann
rue du Faubourg St-Honoré
bd. Malesherbes
bd. de Courcelles
bd. des Batignolles
bd. Berthier
bd. Pereire
av. de New York
av. du Prés. Wilson
av. Henri Martin
av. Paul Doumer
av. de la Bourdonnais
av. Bosquet
av. Rapp
quai d'Orsay
rue de l'Université
rue St- Dominique
rue de Varenne
rue de Babylone
rue de Sèvres
bd. des Invalides
bd. du Montparnasse
bd. de Grenelle
bd. Garibaldi
rue de Vaugirard
bd. Pasteur
bd. Lefebvre
bd. Brune
bd. Victor
av. du Maine
rue d'Alésia
rue de la Convention
rue Lecourbe
av. Emile Zola
av. de Suffren
av. de la Motte Picquet
bd. Exelmans
bd. Suchet
bd. Murat
av. de Versailles
rue Molitor
av. Mozart
rue du Ranelagh
bd. Lannes
bd. Victor Hugo
bd. Bineau
rue Victor Hugo
rue du Président Wilson
av. Charles de Gaulle
bd. Maillot
av. du Roule
av. des Ternes
cours de la Reine
quai Anatole France
bd. St-Germain
bd. Raspail